A Biographical Dictionary of Women's Movements and Feminisms

Central, Eastern, and South Eastern Europe, 19th and 20th Centuries

A Biographical Dictionary of Women's Movements and Feminisms

Central, Eastern, and South Eastern Europe, 19th and 20th Centuries

Edited and with an Introduction by

FRANCISCA DE HAAN, KRASSIMIRA DASKALOVA
AND ANNA LOUTFI

Central European University Press
Budapest • New York

Published in 2006 by
Central European University Press

An imprint of the
Central European University Share Company
Nádor utca 11, H-1051 Budapest, Hungary
Tel: +36-1-327-3138 or 327-3000
Fax: +36-1-327-3183
E-mail: ceupress@ceu.hu
Website: www.ceupress.com

400 West 59th Street, New York NY 10019, USA
Tel: +1-212-547-6932
Fax: +1-646-557-2416
E-mail: mgreenwald@sorosny.org

Research for this book was supported in part by the Central European University (CEU). The opinions expressed herein are the authors' own and do not necessarily express the views of CEU.

Every effort has been made to establish picture credits. However, if there are any questions regarding picture credits, please contact the editors.

ISBN 963 7326 39 1 cloth
978-963-7326-39-4

Library of Congress Cataloging-in-Publication Data

A biographical dictionary of women's movements and feminisms. Central, Eastern, and South Eastern Europe ; 19th and 20th centuries / edited and with an Introduction by Francisca de Haan, Krassimira Daskalova and Anna Loutfi.- 1st ed.
p. cm.
Includes index.
ISBN 9637326391 (hb) - ISBN 9637326405 (pb)
1. Feminists–Europe, Eastern–Biography–Dictionaries. 2. Feminists–Europe, Central–Biography-Dictionaries. 3. Feminists-Europe, South Eastern-Biography-Dictionaries. I. Haan, Francisca de, 1957- II. Daskalova, Krasimira. III. Loutfi, Anna. IV. Title.

HQ1590.7.Z75A336 2005
305.42092'24–dc22

2005028309

Prepress Vetula Visual Bt. Hungary
Printed in the USA

Table of Contents

Acknowledgments

Making this *Biographical Dictionary* was a complex but also highly rewarding task. Now that the book is in its final stage, it is a pleasure to thank all those who have helped us with it. First Susan Zimmermann, who suggested to one of us a project in which students might cooperate: a calendar containing biographical portraits of feminists from Central, Eastern and South Eastern Europe. This idea was the seed that developed into this *Biographical Dictionary*.

The book would not exist without the dedicated work of the Advisory Board members/Country Coordinators: *Albania:* Zenepe Dibra, *Austria:* Edith Saurer, *Belarussia:* Elena Gapova, *Bosnia and Herzegovina:* Jelica Zdero, *Bulgaria:* Krassimira Daskalova, *Croatia:* Sandra Prlenda, *Czech Republic:* Jirina Smejkalova, *Estonia:* Sirje Tamul, *Greece:* Eleni Fournaraki, *Hungary:* Susan Zimmermann, *Latvia:* Irina Novikova, *Lithuania:* Rima Praspaliauskiene, *Macedonia:* Jasna Koteska and Vera Veskovic Vangeli, *Moldova:* Maria Bucur, *Poland:* Anna Zarnowska and Magda Gawin, *Romania:* Maria Bucur, *Russian Federation:* Natalia Pushkareva, *Serbia and Montenegro:* Dubravka Stojanovic and Ivana Pantelic, *Slovakia:* Etela Farkasova, *Slovenia:* Milica Antic, *Turkey:* Serpil Çakir, *Ukraine:* Teresa Polowy. The Country Coordinators proposed the names of the subjects to be included, suggested authors and continued to give advice, practical information and moral support. Most of them also wrote one or more entries themselves. We are also deeply grateful to the eighty authors for their invaluable work. Most carried out primary research for this book and all were willing to answer what sometimes must have seemed endless requests from the editors for further information or clarification. Their combined efforts have led to this unique reference work.

Most of the data in the entry on Mrs Artur Meller, born Eugénia Miskolczy, was taken from László Strasser's Minibiography of Mrs Meller (MS Manuscript). We would like to express our gratitude to Mr Strasser and his wife Pauline Strasser for sharing this information with us. We would also like to thank the director of the *Politikatörténeti Intézet Levéltára* (Archive of the Institute of Political History), Katalin Zalai, and her colleagues at the archive for the photographs of Mariska Gárdos and Szeréna Stern, as well as for their indispensable and continual support concerning research for this book.

Heartfelt thanks too, must go to Annette Mevis, archivist at the International Information Center and Archives for the Women's Movement (IIAV) in Amsterdam, and Els Flour, archivist of the *Archiefcentrum voor Vrouwengeschiedenis* (Archive Centr for Women's History) in Brussels (where the archive of the International Council of Women is kept), who very kindly checked information for us.

Most of the entries were sent to us in English. We would like to express our appreciation to all those–Country Coordinators, students at the Central European University and other colleagues–who, at different stages of the project, translated entries into English. We would like to thank the many individuals who have provided various forms of support and information for this project: Meltem Ahiska, Nitza Berkovitch, Gisela Bock, Maria Bucur, Roxana Cheschebec (especially for the information about the Little Entente of Women), Rasa Erentaite, Eva Fodor, Dominika Gruziel, Elissa Helms, Hasmik Khalapyan, Jasmina Lukić, Mihaela Mudure, Nil Mutluer, Karen Offen, Raluca Popa, Maria Rentetzi, Leila Rupp, Irena Selisnik, Michael Szporluk, Sirin Tekeli, Antonia Young and Angelina Zueva. Towards the end of the project, Francisca de Haan participated in the international seminar "Who's Afraid of Feminism? [!] Teaching and Researching Gender in the CEE Region" (University of the West, Timisoara, 5–8 May 2005). She would like to express her gratitude to the organizers for the hospitality and practical assistance regarding the *Biographical Dictionary*. We also thank the office staff at the Department of Gender Studies at the Central European University, especially Maria Szecsenyi and Judit Zotter, for their kind help, as well as various members of the ITSU at the CEU.

We express our gratitude to the Central European University Research Board for financial support for the Biographical Dictionary research project, which enabled us to have a research assistant, and to pay for some translations and pictures. We greatly appreciate the encouragement and support of the CEU Press; it was particularly a pleasure to work with their assistant editor, Linda Kunos. Finally, we thank our students, colleagues, family and friends for support, the willingness to listen to endless stories about the *Biographical Dictionary*, and for allowing it to temporarily take over our lives.

This book represents the first attempt on this scale to bring together information on women's movements and feminisms in Central, Eastern and South Eastern Europe. We have not aimed to be 'comprehensive'–that would by definition be impossible. We do think that a second edition of the *Dictionary* would have to pay greater attention to significant minority groups within the geographical territory covered here, and possibly even beyond (after all, where does 'Europe' end?). Inevitably, there will be some inaccuracies; hopefully, new materials will come to light; ideally, discussion will be provoked. The editors would therefore wholeheartedly welcome any feedback and/or contributions to the debates surrounding women's activism in the region of Central, Eastern and South Eastern Erope, possibly for a second, revised edition of the *Biographical Dictionary*.

Francisca de Haan, Krassimira Daskalova and Anna Loutfi
Budapest and Sofia, May 2005

Advisory Board Members (Country Coordinators)

Often Used Abbreviations

CESEE	Central, Eastern, and South Eastern Europe
IAW	International Alliance of Women
IAWSEC	International Alliance of Women for Suffrage and Equal Citizenship
ICW	International Council of Women
IFUW	International Federation of University Women
IIAV	International Information Center and Archives for the Women's Movement
IWSA	International Woman Suffrage Alliance
LEW	Little Entente of Women
WILPF	Women's International League for Peace and Freedom
WWI	World War I
WWII	World War II

Symbols Used in the Lists of Sources

(A) Archival material
(B) Printed primary sources
(C) Work(s) BY the subject (in chronological order)
(D) Work(s) ABOUT the subject (in chronological order)
(E) Other works used while preparing this piece
(F) Internet sources

Maps

Map 1
"Emergence of Modern Balkan States, 1804–1862."

Source: Map 25 in Dennis P. Hupchick and Harold E. Cox. *The Palgrave Concise Historical Atlas of the Balkans.* New York: Palgrave, 2001.

Map 2
"The Austro-Hungarian Ausgleich, 1867."

Source: Map 34 in Dennis P. Hupchick and Harold E. Cox. *The Palgrave Concise Historical Atlas of Eastern Europe.* New York: Palgrave, 2001.

Map 3
"Balkan State Territorial Expansion, 1881–1886."

Source: Map 29 in Dennis P. Hupchick and Harold E. Cox. *The Palgrave Concise Historical Atlas of the Balkans.* New York: Palgrave, 2001.

Map 4
"June 1914: Map of Europe"

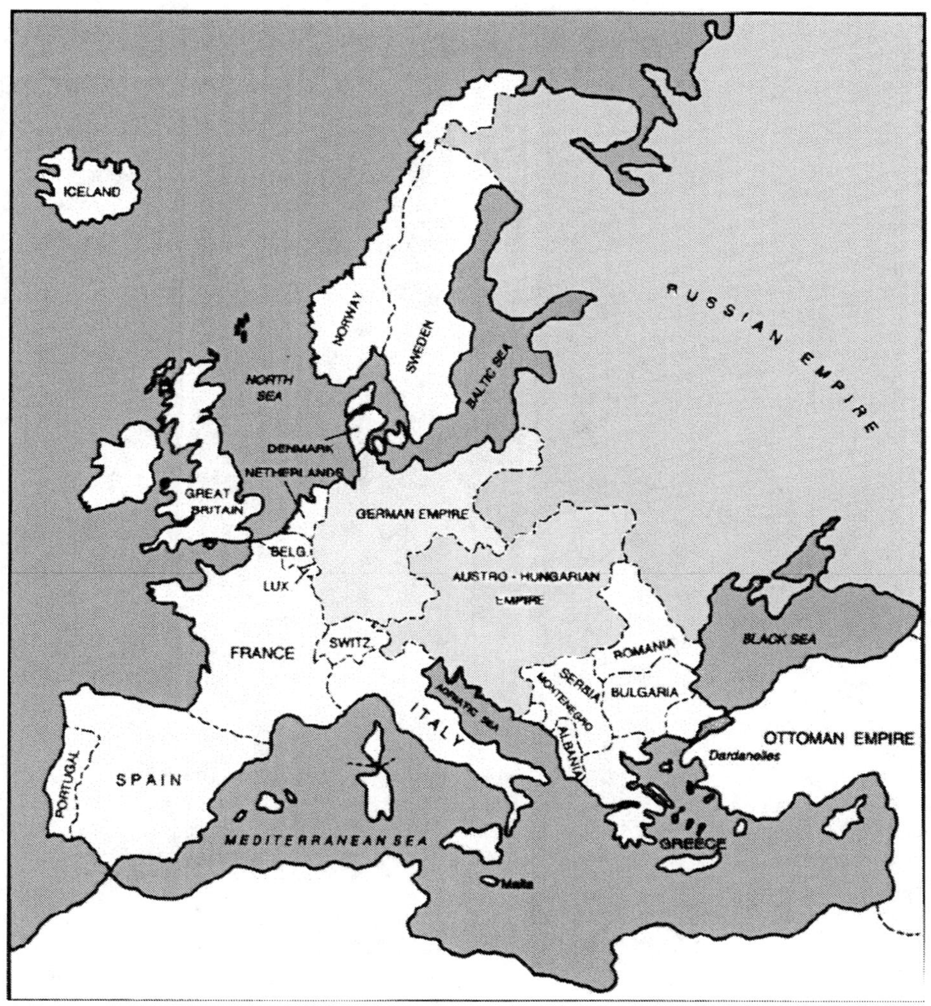

Source: http://www.westernfront.co.uk/thegreatwar/articles/timeline/images/Europe14.jpg

Map 5
"The Countries of Europe, 1919"

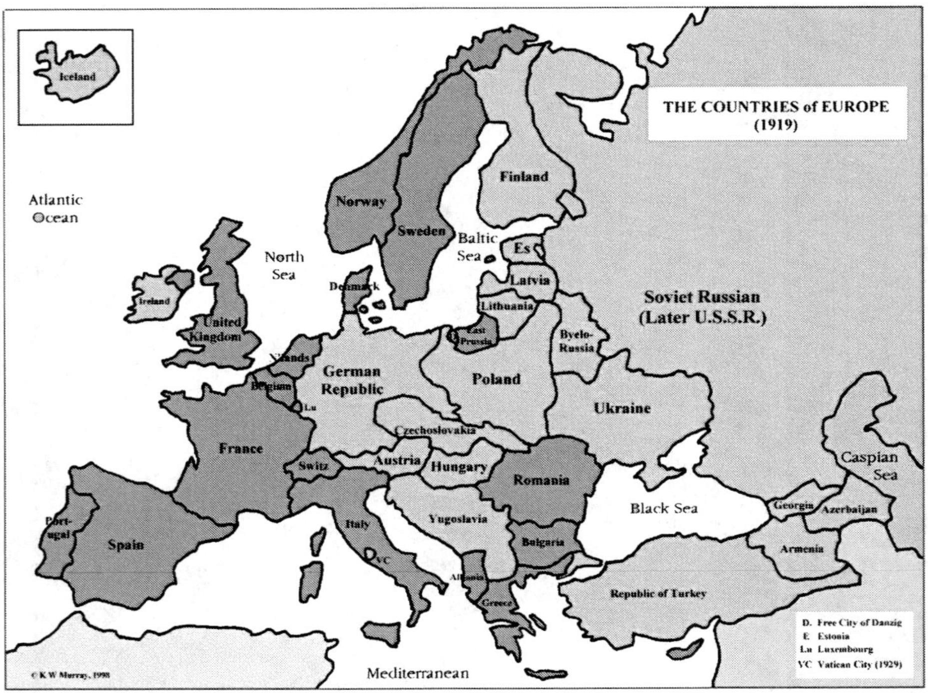

Source: http://users.tibus.com/the-great-war/states19.htm

In Europe, after World War I ended, some new countries were created and others had their former existing borders redrawn (both types colored light grey in the above map). During the early 1920s a number lost their independence (for example; the Ukraine, and Belarus) and were incorporated into the, then, new USSR. Their sovereignty was only regained during the 1990s.

Map 6
"Europe in 2005"

Source: http://en.wikipedia.org/wiki/Image:Europe-large.png

Introduction

I. Why this book?

This book describes the lives, works and aspirations of more than 150 women and men who were active in, or part of, women's movements and feminisms in 22 countries in Central, Eastern and South Eastern Europe. In doing so, it challenges the widely held belief that there was no feminism in this part of Europe. Taken together, the biographical portraits not only show that feminists (we will come back to this term) existed here, but also that they were widespread and diverse, and included Romanian princesses, Serbian philosophers and peasants, Latvian and Slovakian novelists, Albanian teachers, Hungarian Christian social workers and activists of the Catholic women's movement, Austrian factory workers, Bulgarian feminist scientists and socialist feminists, Russian radicals, philanthropists, militant suffragists and Bolshevik activists, prominent writers and philosophers of the Ottoman era, as well as Turkish republican leftist political activists and nationalists, internationally recognized Greek feminist leaders, an Estonian pharmacologist and science historian, a Slovenian 'literary feminist,' a Czech avant-garde painter, a Ukrainian feminist scholar and Polish and Czech Senate Members. There were feminists of liberal persuasion, Social Democrats, communists, partisans, Catholics, Jews, Protestants, members of the Orthodox Church and atheists; in sum women, and some men, from all walks of life. Their stories together constitute a rich tapestry of feminist activity.

The belief that there was no feminism in this part of Europe (probably with the exception of Russia, where the history of women's movements has been well documented)[1] is not limited to 'ordinary people,' but is shared by academics as well. Such a fine historian as Eric Hobsbawm wrote only a few years ago with respect to the period around 1900 that "In the condition of the great majority of the world's women, those who lived in Asia, Africa, Latin America and the peasant societies of southern and eastern Europe, or indeed in most agrarian societies, there was as yet no change whatever."[2] It is true that supporters of women's movements and feminist causes in those regions formed a relatively small part of the population in the nineteenth and early twentieth centuries–perhaps smaller than in some of the (more industrialized) countries of Western Europe in the same period. Yet, rather than *a priori* assuming that there was no change, it may be more constructive for historians to pay close attention to the undoubted presence and influence of women's activities and protests, trying to understand in which contexts they developed and how. Women's activities in Central, Eastern and South Eastern Europe (CESEE) produced (as in 'the West') "a small but unprecedented number of women who were active" and "distinguished, in fields previously confined entirely to men"[3]: dynamic personalities such as Callirhoe Parren (Greece), Elena Ghica/Dora d'Istria (a Romanian of Albanian descent), Fatma Aliye and Halide Edib Adıvar (Turkey), Milica Ninković (Serbia), Vela Blagoeva and Anna Karima (Bulgaria), the Croatian Dragojla Jarnević, Bosnians Stoja Kašiković and Staka Skenderova, and many, many others.

Western feminist historians may not have been so blunt as Hobsbawm, but until recently their work has been generally limited to the Western European continent (or even to a limited number of countries there: namely England, Germany and France). Karen Offen, in her important book *European Feminisms 1700–1950* (2000), has clearly made all possible efforts to include data about Central, Eastern and South Eastern Europe, but was restricted by the piecemeal and limited information available for most countries of these regions.[4] The history of women's movements in this part of Europe by and large has either not been researched or published only in local languages (the books in Romanian by Ştefania Mihăilescu and Ghizela Cosma are good examples of the latter),[5] without a bridge to the mainly Anglophone world of international scholarship. Of course there are differences in this respect between the various countries, and projects are underway, but it is safe to say that the history of women's movements and feminisms is largely unwritten and that most recent publications deal with the contemporary history of women's movements/feminisms after 1989.[6] The recent (2004) volume *Women's Emancipation Movements in the Nineteenth Century: A European Perspective*, edited by Sylvia Paletschek and Bianka Pietrow-Ennker, does include some countries from the Eastern half of the European continent, but only a handful (the Czech Republic, Hungary, Poland, Russia, and Greece);[7] our book, with its focus on 22 countries, aims (through biographical accounts) to give a broader overview of the social-economic-cultural-political factors shaping women's movements and feminisms across the diverse countries of this part of Europe.[8] Therefore the first goal of this *Biographical Dictionary* is to provide reliable information–in principle based on primary research–about women and men who were involved in women's movements and feminisms in Central, Eastern and South Eastern Europe. We hope to initiate cross national discussions of the history and meaning of feminism(s) in CESEE, and thus to contribute to the expanding field of international and comparative historical research of women's movements and feminisms, as well as contributing in a more general sense to building women's and gender history as an academic field of teaching and research in CESEE.

By uncovering and making accessible this wealth of information, we also hope to challenge the above-mentioned view that there was no feminism in CESEE, as well as the commonly accepted notion that feminism in the region was 'imported' from 'the West' and alien to 'local traditions.' These two (related) assertions are clearly not innocent. They have been and still are used in many countries around the world to discredit local women's movements and feminisms. Yet "in every society, in every generation, women protest gender injustice,"[9] and any suggestion to the contrary is a denial of the intelligence and human agency of countless women and men, including those featured in this *Biographical Dictionary*. As Judit Ascady has recently put it with respect to Hungary, "If attention is not drawn to this historical background of ... feminism, all the efforts of those who once devoted their energies to this cause will be wasted, and modern-day feminism will be seen as alien and unconnected."[10] The biographies here not only provide a window onto that historical background (thus giving present-day women's movements the 'historical support' that they need and are entitled to), in some cases they demonstrate explicitly the historical continuities between feminisms past and present (as in the case of Veselinka Malinska from Macedonia).

Finally, writing the histories of women's movements and feminisms in CESEE will hopefully increase tolerance and understanding of women's movements and feminisms today, if only by showing the many historical connections between them—particularly before 1940.

II. Choices and Methodology

Biographies

We have chosen to reconstruct the history of women's movements and feminisms in CESEE in the form of biographical portraits. One of the main reasons for doing so is our belief that—within all the structural limitations that have existed and continue to exist—human history is made by human beings. In the context of fundamental social changes taking place everywhere in Europe in the nineteenth century (urbanization, industrialization, literacy and education programs, technological changes, 'modernization'), women and men were moved and inspired—by religious beliefs, the struggle for national liberation, socialism and/or feminism—to reject women's secondary status, their poverty and/or illiteracy, discriminating laws, women's exclusion from the realms of culture, higher education, science and politics, age-old traditions presented as unchangeable as well as, for that matter, modern forms of patriarchy promoted by the new 'inclusive' social and political movements such as nationalism and socialism. In order to understand why some women and men opted for change, or even devoted their lives to the struggle for social justice (including gender equality), we have to situate their personalities and personal histories in the broader social-economic-cultural-political context, which is what the entries generally do.

Moreover, the biographical perspective not only clarifies why some individuals opted for change, but also explains the fields in which they became active, usually (as many entries show) connected to their own specific aspirations and the problems and barriers they encountered—yet another example of the feminist insight that the so-called 'public' and 'private' spheres are intimately connected. A focus on individual life stories in the context of wider social-economic-cultural-political structures brings out these connections: women such as Hermin Beniczky (1815–1895), Eliška Krásnohorská (1847–1926), and Terézia Vansová (1857–1942), who personally suffered from not having had a thorough and structured education and then went on to become pioneers of women's education; Bulgarian women lawyers prevented from practicing their profession such as Dimitrana Ivanova (1881–1960) and Vera Zlatareva (1905–1977), whose life stories merged with the interwar Bulgarian feminist movement to form a personal and political history of struggle with the male legal (and other) professions; or women such as the Turkish Nurser Öztunalı (1947–1999) who, on the basis of her own experience with marital violence, initiated a huge campaign against violence against women as a social/structural rather than individual phenomenon. The biographical/individual level also enables readers to trace which persons (e.g. family members or others) and literature most influenced the ways our subjects/protagonists thought and acted, and in which formal and informal networks they operated—locally, nationally and internationally.

A third reason for choosing the form of biographical entries is the sheer pleasure or inspiration that we derive from reading about other people's lives, a pleasure we hope our readers will share.

Women's Movements and Feminisms

One of the reasons why feminism is often seen as a 'Western' phenomenon is that (Western) feminists themselves have conveyed that perspective—often with the concomitant notion of superiority and the belief in having *the* right perspective, if not the duty to impose that on others. Indeed historically, as has been documented extensively over the last ten to fifteen years, many Western feminists have shared the imperialist perspective of their governments and co-nationals[11] (and with respect to CESEE, some would argue, similar missionary/imperialist tendencies have become prevalent after 1989 as well).[12]

In order to avoid reproducing such tendencies, and in line with our belief that 1) women's movements and feminisms always have to be contextualized and 2) historically have taken many forms, we have not pre-defined what we understand by 'women's movements and feminisms.' Instead we have asked local experts—the Advisory Board members or Country Coordinators (see page xiii)—to put together lists of names of those subjects they felt should be included in this *Dictionary*. Similarly, in drawing a distinction between 'women's movements' and 'feminisms,' we sought to keep an open mind in order not to exclude *a priori* writings and activities that aimed to improve women's status and position (as part of a 'women's movement'), yet did not necessarily aim for women's equality with men and/or to challenge patriarchal structures (as 'feminism' is generally defined as doing).[13]

Indeed, we provided only two 'hard' criteria regarding the inclusion of subjects: that they were active in the nineteenth or twentieth century, and that the subject no longer be alive (which is the reason why the *Biographical Dictionary* contains very few entries about contemporary activists/feminists). We informed the Country Coordinators that, considering the state of the research, we were interested in women and men who had established women's organizations and journals, as well as in all kinds of international connections. Of course, the choices that the Country Coordinators made were shaped not only by the state of women's history in their respective countries (which varies widely), but also by their own disciplinary backgrounds and interests. That is why for some countries we have more 'literary feminists' than 'feminist activists' affiliated to women's organizations.

The Countries

The question of which countries to include in a biographical dictionary of this nature is a difficult one. There is no such thing as a simple definition of 'Europe' nor any simple division of Europe into 'East' and 'West,' as many authors have shown. The labels 'East' and 'West' are relative, historically changing, mutually constitutive and politically laden. In addition, these labels suggest homogenous entities that do not exist.[14] We have decided to include countries in the Eastern half of the European continent generally perceived to be 'outside' the 'core,' yet nevertheless part of Europe. Most of them have shared histories as parts of the Russian, Prussian, Habsburg and Ottoman empires. This includes Turkey which, through the Ottoman Empire, has a shared history with the South Eastern European peninsula–'European Turkey' seen by some as part of the Balkans. Of course many of these countries also share a history of state socialism.

On the basis of the current map of this part of Europe, the countries included in the *Biographical Dictionary* therefore are: Albania, Austria, Bosnia and Herzegovina, Belarus, Bulgaria, Croatia, the Czech Republic, Estonia, Greece, Hungary, Latvia, Lithuania, Macedonia, Moldova, Poland, Romania, Russia, Serbia and Montenegro, Slovakia, Slovenia, Turkey and Ukraine.

III. What have we found?

Altogether, if we consider the differences between all these 22 countries (of which there are many–too complex and varied to address here), the similarities from a gender perspective are overriding. All countries reveal male domination at both the symbolic and the material level, which is to say that despite the differences, common oppressive gender principles and hierarchies were at work in the historical period covered by the *Dictionary*. Women were subordinated to the 'first sex' and this was reflected in the many common features of their status–devalued motherhood, moral (but not legal or financial) responsibility for family life, vulnerability to violence, high levels of illiteracy and high mortality rates (e.g. in childbirth) etc.–that were a consequence of their being regarded as the 'second sex.' All the same, gender is not the only category of social organization that affects women's lives. The similarities and differences between women's conditions are not only a question of the degree to which 'the masculine principle' is dominant, but also of how this principle intersects with other social demarcations.

What we have found striking is that there does not seem to have been an ideological position or party line, faith, political modernization program or cultural/religious national movement that was exempt from the burning issues of the day raised by what was known across all spectrums of intellectual endeavor as 'the woman question.' All the same, two ideologies stand out in their involvement with 'the woman question': nationalism and socialism. These two ideologies in particular brought men and women together to fight for what many perceived as a 'common cause.' 'The woman question' was set within a wider 'national question' or a wider 'social question' and thus the issues and problems raised–touching among other things on increased opportunities and rights for women in the fields of education, employment and the civil law–were seen to be of relevance to the whole of society. Socialist and nationalist organizations, often in alliance with one another, produced intellectuals and ideologues of both sexes who criticized the subordinated position of women under imperial despotism, capitalism and/or patriarchy as a sign of a 'deeper' problem (that it would later be the job of state-socialist or republican models of government to address). In these contexts, individual women, feminists and organized women's movements often (but by no means always) saw alliance and even compliance with male-dominated organizations, parties and structures as necessary to the realization of their own goals. This kind of approach to women's and feminist issues and causes may be seen in (Romanian) Eugenia de Reuss Ianculescu's philosophy that "both men and women were engaged in a common struggle for the country's social and economic progress,"[15] or the decision, in the 1920s, of the Greek *Syndesmos gia ta Dikaiomata tis Gynaikas* (League for Woman's Rights) to work with men "for strategic reasons."[16]

While this close relation between nationalism and socialism and 'the woman question' is not a new finding in itself, the entries show that women's involvement in nationalism and socialism not only allowed them to articulate certain demands (mostly for women's education, sometimes for the vote), but also to challenge the limits of those ideologies or to criticize them from within. These findings support an alternative feminist reading that does not reduce the histories of nationalism or socialism to male-dominated rhetorical exercises in gender equality. Instead, the attention of readers is drawn to the manifest ways in which women saw nationalist and socialist projects as necessary to their own emancipation as women,[17] while many at the same time recognized gendered exclusionary practices as problematic features of those projects. The Polish Narcyza Żmichowska and Hungarian Mária Gárdos are examples. In 1895 the Ukrainian Natalia Kobrynska wrote: "It would be more realistic for women workers, while admitting that the victory of the workers will also be their victory, to ensure their own rights and not become dependent upon the grace of men." Similarly, the well-known Russian Bolshevik Alexandra Kollontai was by the 1920s already expressing doubts that economic conditions under communism would lead "automatically to harmonious relations between the sexes."[18] In this respect, the lives and work of women such as Żmichowska, Gárdos, Kobrynska and Kollontai reflect debates and questions regarding gender policies that have been present throughout the history of modern nationalism and socialism in CESEE [for the postwar period see for example the work of critical intellectuals such as Croatian philosopher Blaženka Despot (1930–2001)].[19]

Another important finding is that, although women's organizations in CESEE were urban phenomena, women's movements and feminisms here often addressed a wide, agrarian social base in ways that would seem to contradict Hobsbawm's assumption (previously mentioned) that social change was not a factor in "the peasant societies of southern and eastern Europe." Liberal newspapers in Lithuania edited by women in the early twentieth century targeted a large Lithuanian population (85 percent) living in the countryside, as well as providing women's supplements addressed to women of both the towns and the countryside. In late nineteenth-century Ukraine, women activists competed with national 'populist' or socialist women's organizations that appealed to a primarily agrarian base, Belarussian nationalist feminists wrote poems "to peasant women," Romanian feminists opened schools for peasant girls and Russian feminists protested land reforms (1906) that they feared would threaten the existing rights of peasant women. Feminist and women's activities were thus part of radical changes in the lives of both urban and rural populations, and raise questions about dichotomies such as native/foreign, urban/peasant and traditional/modern.

Three other similarities between the 22 countries are also worth mentioning here. Firstly, there is the importance of education in the history of European women's movements and feminisms. In almost all cases, this is what the first initiatives to improve women's lives focused on. Suffrage, as in most Western countries, only became an issue later. To a certain extent, this finding is evidence of the dramatic impact Enlightenment and liberal thought had on the subjects from all 22 countries, many of whom were influenced by core Enlightenment theories of citizenship and education by men such as Jean-Jacques Rousseau and Johann Heinrich Pestalozzi, and many of whom reacted negatively to the lack of attention paid to women's education and their accompanying lack of civil and civic status. The overwhelmingly positive reception across the region of John Stuart Mill's *The Subjection of Women* (1869) suggests that in Eastern as well as Western Europe, women and men had been growing increasingly frustrated with male-centered views on the functions of education, politics and social roles. It also demonstrates the relevance of Mill's (and other key feminist thinkers') works for CESEE—works that were often translated into local languages. Secondly, it is remarkable how many of our biographical subjects expressed an interest in women's history and the history of women's movements in their own countries and beyond.[20] This is true of Fatma Aliye (Turkey), Callirhoe Parren (Greece), Zinaida Mirovich, Inessa Armand and Ekaterina Nikolaevna Shchepkina (Russia), Lydia Sklevicky (Croatia), Eliza Orzeszkowa (Poland) and Milica Ninković (Serbia) to name but a few. Thirdly, many of our subjects were activists who expressed a powerful belief in the force of internationalism. This belief often (but not always) remained unshaken even in the aftermath of the devastation caused by the two World Wars. Perhaps (as the Hungarian Ilona Stetina seemed to suggest) the extent of the devastation wreaked upon Europe in the first half of the twentieth century strengthened the commitment of activists to the international women's movement, seeing international connections and contacts as vital to the success of their own particular, local struggles.

In addition to these specific results, the entries taken together raise questions about the categories that we use in writing the history of women's movements and feminisms. Thus, we have noticed a certain hesitancy among scholars about including socialist or communist feminists, indeed, some would argue that a 'communist feminist' is in itself a *contradictio in terminis*, "no matter how many specific examples of [communist] policies in favor of women we may find."[21] Arguments against 'communist feminists' have pointed to the fact that first socialists and later communists have denounced and attacked the women's movement as 'bourgeois,' and made explicit their aversion to 'feminism.' This approach has seen gender policies, especially for the communist era in Eastern Europe, as 'state directed' (i.e. motivated by the economic interests of the party or state), rather than reflecting women's 'own aspirations.'

However, for many socialist and communist women at the time, socialism was not just the only political stream that advocated women's equality (and therefore attractive), but they themselves were deeply convinced that the only way to social justice, including gender equality, was through socialism (as for instance the Macedonian entries demonstrate). Secondly, some women, such as the Austrian Social Democrat Käthe Leichter, did not consider themselves part of the women's movement, yet through their writings and activities they contributed significantly to knowledge about women's, especially working women's situation. In the case of Leichter it is clear that no matter how we categorize her, neither this categorization nor Leichter's own self-identification (*Selbstzuordnung*) encompass all aspects of her individual and political biography.[22] Thirdly, there were women, probably quite a few, who identified with, and remained active within the socialist movement, even though they disagreed with its patriarchal practices and sidelining of 'women's issues' in the name of socialism (as discussed above). Fourthly, and conversely, there were many women—as the Bulgarian and Polish entries in particular show—who seemingly identified as *both* feminists and socialists without much effort. Lastly, and specifically relating to the period of state socialism, there were women such as the Slovenian Vida Tomšič (1913-1998), with a high-ranking position in the communist state hierarchy, who contributed significantly to improving women's status and situation. Tomšič truly believed that private property had to be dismantled in order for patriarchal relations to 'wither away.' She participated in the twentieth Triennial Plenary Conference of the International Council of Women (Vienna, 1973) and in three of the major UN Women's Conferences (1975, 1980, 1985), at which she, as the author writes, "represented the 'official' Yugoslav position ... [Vida Tomšič] contributed a great deal to the new legislation issued during the socialist period of 1945 to 1990 as a specialist on gender questions, and it seems reasonable to suppose that the policies she advocated [such as freedom of reproductive choice] combined both official ideology and [her] own ideas." At the same time, she was part of a government that had declared feminism "an unnecessary, even harmful, 'bourgeois' phenomenon" and which had abolished "all women's civil organizations from 'pre-communist' times—the *Jugoslovanska ženska zveza* (Yugoslav Women's Union), the *Splošno slovensko žensko društvo* (General Slovene Women's Association) and the *Krščanska ženska zveza* (Christian Women's Union)."[23] So, how is one to categorize someone like Tomšič? Was she a communist feminist? Karmen Klavžar, the author of one of our entries on Slovenian feminist Angela Vode, explicitly refers to Tomšič as "feminist."[24] Clearly, the last word about this complex issue has not yet been said, and we hope that the material offered here will initiate further debate.

Secondly, similar questions can be asked about philanthropic and/or religious organizations with a focus on women (and children): were these charity organizations—which sought to provide material relief/assistance, to give girls and women opportunities in a modern environment that seemed by and large hostile to their needs [such as the *Pesti Izraelita Nőegylet* (Pest Israelite Women's Association), Hungary's largest Jewish women's association], and which often emphasized 'conservative' family values and shied away from the political voice of feminism—were these organizations part of the women's movement?[25] Taking a broad definition of women's movements to include those initiatives that aimed at improving women's lives, we believe that they were. Moreover, contextualization is again crucial. Under tsarist law in late nineteenth- and early twentieth-century Russia, explicitly political organization/agitation was dangerous for women as well as for men. 'Conservative' Shabanova (1848-1932), the founder and Chairwoman of the *Russkoe Zhenskoe Vzaimno-Blagotvoritel'noe Obshchestvo* (Russian Women's Mutual Philanthropic Society) was imprisoned in her early career for anti-tsarist/revolutionary activities; Filosofova (1837-1912), her colleague, was exiled for the same. These women did not refrain from voicing opposition to existing structures because of religious, pious or other kinds of conservatism. Similarly, women in Republican, interwar Turkey worked within the 'harmless' framework of philanthropy—often refusing to compromise their political agendas. As Serpil Çakır writes: "Official authorization of the *Kadınlar Halk Fırkası* [Women's People's Party] was refused on the grounds that women did not yet have political rights and members were advised to set up a women's association, suggesting the extent to which the perimeters for the granting of social and political rights for women were largely set by men as founders of Republican Turkey. The *Kadınlar Halk Fırkası* became an association: the *Türk Kadınlar Birliği* (Turkish Women's Association), but its founding principles were in fact similar to the proposed program of the political party."[26] In our view, the question therefore is not "what were these women?" but "what forums did they have and what did they do with them?"

Lastly, some of the entries here also challenge the way in which we think about the history of the international women's movement. There is consensus that the three major international organizations, the International Council of Women (ICW), the International Woman Suffrage Alliance, later International Alliance of Women for Suffrage and Equal Citizenship (IWSA/IAWSEC) and the Women's International League for Peace and Freedom (WILPF) occupied a political 'scale'—from moderate/conservative (ICW) to (liberal) feminist to leftish/progressive feminist.[27] Yet interestingly, many Polish socialist feminists who were involved in the IAWSEC and the Polish *Związek Pracy Obywatelskiej Kobiet* (Women's Association for Civil Labor), affiliated to the IAWSEC from 1929, challenge this scheme. So does someone like Angela Vode, co-founder in 1920 of the Communist Party in Slovenia, a member of that party until 1939, and simultaneously involved in the ICW and IAWSEC.[28] It is worth bearing in mind that if our biographical subjects were able to bridge the contradictions between feminism, nationalism, socialism, communism, philanthropy and revolution in their own lives—then surely historians, including women's historians, must adopt similarly open approaches to their own research and methodologies, rather than creating forms of closure through the use of predefined and potentially limited categories.

IV. Further research and wishes

While the process of compiling this book has brought together a wealth of information, it also highlights areas for further research of women's movements and feminisms in Central, Eastern and South Eastern Europe. Many authors of entries included in this *Biographical Dictionary* note that in their respective countries, there continues to be little academic interest in the "rich and colorful" and "fully-fledged" feminist movements that may have existed and have been subjected to "collective amnesia" in the historiography of the twentieth century.[29] Potential areas of further research include more full-scale biographies of women's leaders and activists; the complex interrelation between religion and women's movements; different forms of women's organizing across the CESEE countries, with a focus on various class, ethnic and minority groups; the connections between liberal feminism and socialism (both before and after 1945) and interregional, international and transnational connections based on joint research projects of scholars from different parts of Europe.

Several of the research areas mentioned here will undoubtedly help shed light on life 'under communism,' including personal experiences of confronting, contesting and interpreting official Party narratives, and raising questions about the meaning of 'socialist emancipation' (i.e. of women) and 'state feminism.' It is also hoped that further attention to these research areas will contribute to the creation of more comparative and integrative perspectives on the history of CESEE, possibly by those involved in the network formed through the making of this *Dictionary*.

V. Practical and Technical Issues

Women's names

As a rule, this book has taken to using the family (i.e. surname) of each individual subject in order to convey that person's *adult* status–be it a woman or a man. (This rule may be waived when describing the subject's childhood or early years). However the business of naming, especially women, is particularly complex. For feminists, the issue of a woman's family name, generally that of her father's and changing upon marriage (in some women's lives this means several changes of name), may be troubling in and of itself as a patriarchal practice. Even though it is historically accurate to refer to a Hungarian woman by her husband's full name, as "Mrs Artur Meller" (possibly then followed by her full maiden name), it may not always 'feel right' to do so. The problem is practical as well as ideological, at least in so far as writing women's history is concerned. For the case of Turkey, Fatmagül Berktay has pointed out to us that in the Ottoman era there were no surnames or official birth records. Sometimes the 'pater familias' would record names of newborns on the family Quoran, but not always and not usually of the females. Likewise, former slave girls bought or given to the Palace and often married off to 'pashas' were 'given' names, with the result that accurate information about women's 'real names' is obscured. Across the 22 countries (as elsewhere in Europe), a woman, whether married or single, may have chosen a pseudonym for herself–as many of our *Dictionary* subjects did–to avoid political persecution for her beliefs or (especially in the case of writers) to avoid the bias of male critics towards her as a 'woman writer.' In such cases, it 'feels right' to name the subject at times as she named herself. Many women adopted several pen-names and pseudonyms over the course of their lives, not only in their literary activities, but also in public and political life. The Latvian writer and politician Ivande Kaija (1876–1941), whose name (meaning 'Seagull' in Latvian) she chose for herself, is a case in point. These examples draw attention not only to the patriarchal practice of denying women their own names and the historical dilemmas of reproducing those practices, but also to the alternative naming practices that women devised for themselves.

The names that appear italized and in bold refer to the names of subjects included in this *Biographical Dictionary*, in order to highlight the connections between some of the subjects.

Names of organizations

Where possible, we have used the original names of organizations followed by the English translation the first time the organization appears in the text, rather than using translated names of organizations. There are three reasons for this approach: one, to avoid linguistic insensitivity; two, to convey a sense of the worlds in which these organizations operated and three, to facilitate the further research of scholars interested in the histories of organizations and/or their members.

Sources

Each entry ends with an overview of the sources used for that piece. For the system employed in the organization of sources, see page xiv with Often Used Abbreviations and Symbols Used in the Lists of Sources.

The *Biographical Dictionary* does not give, or aim to give complete bibliographies of subjects at the end of each entry. The bibliographies provided are lists of sources from which the information contained in each entry has been drawn, and may be treated as preliminary bibliographies for those interested in carrying out further research.

Notes to the Introduction

1 See among other publications, Richard Stites, *The Women's Liberation Movement in Russia: Feminism, Bolshevism and Nihilism, 1860-1930*, Princeton: Princeton University Press, 1978; reprint 1991; Linda Harriet Edmondson, *Feminism in Russia, 1900-17*, Stanford, Calif.: Stanford University Press, 1984; Marina Ledkovsky, Charlotte Rosenthal and Mary Zirin, eds., *Dictionary of Russian Women Writers*, Westport, Conn.: Greenwood Press, 1994; Norma Corigliano Noonan and Carol Nechemias, eds., *Encyclopedia of Russian Women's Movements*, Westport, Conn.: Greenwood Press, 2001; *Adam i Eva: Al'manakh gender'noi istorii* (Adam and Eve. An almanac of gender history), Moscow: Rossiiskaia akademiia nauk, Institut vseobshchei istorii, 2002.

2 E. J. Hobsbawn, *The Age of Empire 1875-1914*, New York: Vintage Books, 1989, 193.

3 *Ibid.,* 192.

4 Important exceptions are Russia (see note 1) and Ukraine. See M. Bohachevsky-Chomiak, *Feminists Despite Themselves. Women in Ukrainian Community Life: 1884-1939*, University of Alberta: CIUS Press, 1988. Susan Zimmermann's monograph about the Hungarian women's movement only appeared in 1999. See Susan Zimmermann, *Die bessere Hälfte? Frauenbewegungen und Frauenbestrebungen im Ungarn der Habsburgermonarchie 1848 bis 1918* (The better half? Women's movements and women's aspirations in Hungary in the Habsburg Monarchy 1848 to 1918), Vienna/Budapest: Promedia Verlag/Napvilág Kiadó, 1999.

5 Ştefania Mihăilescu, *Emanciparea femeii române: Antologie de texte. Vol. I 1815-1918* (The emancipation of Romanian women: an anthology of texts. Vol. 1 1815-1918), Bucharest: Editura Ecumenica, 2001; Ghizela Cosma, *Femeile şi politica în România. Evoluţia dreptului de vot în perioada interbelică* (Women and politics in Romania. The evolution of suffrage rights in the interwar period), Cluj: Presa Universitară Clujeană, 2002.

6 See e.g. Sabine Lang, "Women's Movements in Eastern and Central Europe," Eva Maleck-Lewy, "The East German Women's Movement After Unification," Malgozata Fuszara, "Women's Movements in Poland" and Krassimira Daskalova, "The Women's Movements in Bulgaria After Communism," all in the book *Transitions, Environments, Translations: Feminisms in International Politics*, Joan W. Scott, Cora Kaplan and Debra Keates, eds., New York: Routledge, 1997; Laura Grunberg, "Women's NGOs in Romania," in Susan Gal and Gail Kligman, eds., *Reproducing Gender. Politics, Publics, and Everyday Life after Socialism*, Princeton: Princeton University Press, 2000, 307-335; various pieces in Gabriele Jaehnert, Jana Gohrisch et. al., eds., *Gender in Transition in Eastern and Central Europe. Proceedings*, Berlin: Trafo Verlag, 2001.

7 Sylvia Paletschek and Bianka Pietrow-Ennker eds., *Women's Emancipation Movements in the Nineteenth Century: a European Perspective*, Stanford CA.: Stanford University Press, 2004.

8 Other English-language anthologies with some articles about the historical women's movement in CESEE include Tanya Renne, ed., *Ana's Land. Sisterhood in Eastern Europe,* Boulder and Oxford: Westview Press, 1997, and Gabriela Griffin and Rosi Braidotti (ATHENA), eds., *Thinking Differently. A Reader in European Women's Studies*, London and New York: Zed Books, 2002.

9 Shawn Megan Burn, *Women Across Cultures. A Global Perspective*, London and Toronto: Mountain View 2000, 220.

10 Judit Ascady, "The Construction of Women's Case. Turn-of-the Century Hungarian Feminism," in Tanya Renne, ed., *Ana's Land. Sisterhood in Eastern Europe*, Boulder and Oxford: Westview Press, 1997, 106. It may also be worthwhile to repeat the observation made before that 'feminism' is no more or less 'foreign to the region' than socialism, about which no such accusations are made. Finally, women in Western countries, such as the Dutch feminist Anna Maria Storm-Van der Chijs in the 1860s, were *also* inspired by what happened elsewhere and consciously brought that to bear upon their activities at home. For connections between feminists in mostly Western countries, see M. McFadden, *Golden Cables of Sympathy: the Transatlantic Sources of Nineteenth-century Feminism*. Lexington, Ky.: University Press of Kentucy, 1999.

11 See among many others, Antoinette Burton, *Burdens of History: British Feminists, Indian*

Women, and Imperial Culture, 1865-1915, Chapel Hill: University of North Carolina Press, 1994; Mineke Bosch, "Colonial Dimensions of Dutch Women's Suffrage: Aletta Jacob's Travel Letters from Africa and Asia, 1911-1912," *Journal of Women's History* 11, no. 2 (1999): 8-34.

12 See e.g. various pieces in Tanya Renne, ed., *Ana's Land. Sisterhood in Eastern Europe*, Boulder and Oxford: Westview Press, 1997, and Barbara Einhorn and Charlotte Sever, "Gender and Civil Society in Central and Eastern Europe," *International Feminist Journal of Politics* 5, no. 2 (2003): 163-190.

13 For this distinction see e.g. A. van Drenth and F. de Haan, *The Rise of Caring Power. Elizabeth Fry and Josephine Butler in Britain and the Netherlands*, Amsterdam: Amsterdam University Press, 1999, 46. A useful definition of feminism is given by Kumari Jayawardena in her *The White Woman's Other Burden. Western Women and South Asia During British Rule*, New York and London: Routledge, 1995, 9: "Feminism can be defined as a consciousness of injustices based on gender hierarchy, and a commitment to change."

14 Edward W. Said, *Orientalism*, London etc.: Penguin Books, 1995; first published by Routledge & Kegan Paul, 1978. For Europe see Larry Wolff, *Inventing Eastern Europe. The Map of Civilization on the Mind of the Enlightenment*, Stanford: Stanford University Press, 1994; for South Eastern Europe/the Balkans see Maria Todorova, *Imagining the Balkans*, Oxford: Oxford University Press, 1997.

15 See the entry by Raluca Maria Popa about Eugenia de Reuss Ianculescu.

16 See the entry by Aleka Boutzouvi about Avra Theodoropoulou.

17 As Katherine David has pointed out with respect to Czech feminism: "The national cause and the feminist cause seemed to them to be complementary and indeed interrelated aspects of a common challenge ...." See her "Czech Feminists and Nationalism in the Late Habsburg Monarchy: 'The First in Austria'," *Journal of Women's History* 3 no.2 (1991): 26-45; here 26. For socialism see also Richard Stites, "The Socialist Women's Movement" in *The Women's Liberation Movement in Russia. Feminism, Nihilism, and Bolshevism 1860-1930*, Princeton: Princeton University Press, 1978; reprint 1991, 233-277.

18 See the entries about Żmichowska by Grażyna Borkowska, about Gárdos by Susan Zimmermann, about Kobrynska by Martha Bohachevsky-Chomiak, and about Kollontai by Natalia Gafizova.

19 See the entry about Despot by Gordana Bosanac.

20 See on this point also Francisca de Haan, "A 'Truly International' Archive for the Women's Movement (IAV, now IIAV): From its Foundation in Amsterdam in 1935 to the Return of its Looted Archives in 2003," *Journal of Women's History* 16 no.4 (2004): 148-172; here 149.

21 This argument is made by Mihaela Miroiu in her *Drumul Către Autonomie. Teorii politice feministe* (The road to autonomy. Political feminist theories), Iaşi: Polirom, 2004, 185, where she asks, "Există un feminism comunist?"

22 Edith Saurer in an e-mail, 3 July 2004.

23 See the entry by Mateja Jeraj about Vida Tomšič.

24 See the entry by Karmen Klavžar about Angela Vode.

25 The same question might be asked about one particular entry, Sarolta Geőcze from Hungary, who, while dedicating her life to women's causes, combined an overt right-wing nationalism with an explicit anti-feminist stance.

26 See the entry by Serpil Çakır about Nezihe Muhittin.

27 See in particular the important book by Leila Rupp, *Worlds of Women: the Making of an International Women's Movement*, Princeton, N.J.: Princeton University Press, 1997.

28 For a similar comment, see Sylvia Paletschek and Bianka Pietrow-Ennker, eds, *Women's Emancipation Movements in the Nineteenth Century: a European Perspective*, Stanford CA.: Stanford University Press, 2004, 326.

29 See Judith Szapor, "Sisters or Foes: The Shifting Front Lines of the Hungarian Women's Movement, 1896-1918," in Sylvia Paletschek and Bianka Pietrow-Ennker, eds, *Women's Emancipation Movements in the Nineteenth Century: a European Perspective*, Stanford CA.: Stanford University Press, 2004, 189-205; here 190.

Subjects per Country*

Albania:	Shaqe Çoba (1875–1954)
	Elena Gjika (Dora d'Istria) (1828?–1888?)
	Sevasti (1870–1949) and Parashqevi (1880–1970) Qiriazi
	Urani Rumbo (1895–1936)
Austria:	Ingeborg Bachmann (1926–1973)
	Auguste Fickert (1855–1910)
	Marianne Hainisch (1839–1936)
	Käthe Leichter (1895–1942)
	Rosa Mayreder (1858–1938)
	Karoline von Perin-Gradenstein (1806–1888)
	Adelheid Popp (1869–1939)
	Therese Schlesinger (1863–1940)
Belarus:	Esther Frumkin (1880–1943)
	Vera Matejczuk (1896–1981)
	Alaiza Pashkevich ('Tsiotka') (1876–1916)
	Nadzeja Sznarkiewicz (1897–1974)
Bosnia and Herzegovina:	Jelica Belović-Bernadzikowska (1870–1946)
	Stoja Kašiković (c. 1865–?)
	Staka Skenderova (1831–1891)
Bulgaria:	Vela Blagoeva (1858–1921)
	Dimitrana Ivanova (1881–1960)
	Elissaveta Karamichailova (1897–1968)
	Lyuben Karavelov (1834–1879)

* This list is only intended to provide a guideline to readers wishing to locate the current nation states where the subjects listed above were active, or to identify the nationalizing/nationalist contexts in which their feminist and women's organizations operated.

	Ekaterina Karavelova (1860-1947) Anna Karima (1871-1949) Kina Konova (1872-1952) Julia Malinova (1869-1953) Vera Zlatareva (1905-1977) Ekaterina Zlatoustova (1881-1952)
Croatia:	Blaženka Despot (1930-2001) Dragojla Jarnević (1812-1875) Marija Jurić (1873-1957) Adela Milčinović (1878-1968) Kata Pejnović (1899-1966) Lydia Sklevicky (1952-1990)
Czech Republic:	Milada Horáková (1901-1950) Milena Jesenská (1896-1944) Eliška Krásnohorská (1847-1926) Charlotta Garrigue Masaryková (1850-1923) Božena Němcová (1820?-1862) Teréza Nováková (1853-1912) Františka Plamínková (1875-1942) Karolína Světlá (1830-1899) Toyen (Marie Čermínová) (1902-1980) Božena Viková-Kunětická (1862-1934)
Estonia:	Elise Käer-Kingisepp (1901-1989) Vera Poska-Grünthal (1898-1986) Lilli (Caroline) Suburg (1841-1923)
Greece:	Callirhoe Parren (1859-1940) Maria Svolou (1892?-1976) Avra Theodoropoulou (1880-1963)
Hungary:	Countess Apponyi (1867-1942) Hermin Beniczky (Mrs Pál Veres) (1815-1895) Johanna Bischitz (1827-1898) Mariska Gárdos (1885-1973) Sarolta Geőcze (1862-1928) Vilma Glücklich (1872-1927) Emilia Kánya (1830-1905) Teréz Karacs (1808-1892)

Eugénia Miskolczy Meller (Mrs Artur Meller) (1872-1944)
Róza Schwimmer (1877-1948)
Margit Slachta (1884-1974)
Szeréna Stern (Mrs Pollák) (1894-1966)
Ilona Stetina (1855-1932)

Latvia:

Aspazija (1865-1943)
Regina Ezera (1930-2002)
Ivande Kaija (1876-1941)
Klāra Kalniņa (1874-1964)
Karolīne Kronvalde (1836-1913)
Berta Pīpiņa (1883-1942)

Lithuania:

Felicija Bortkevičienė (1873-1945)
Magdalena Galdikienė (1891-1979)
Ona Mašiotienė (1883-1949)
Gabrielė Petkevičaitė (1861-1943)

Macedonia:

Kostadina Bojadjieva Nasteva-Rusinska (1880-1932)
Veselinka Malinska (1917-1988)
Estreya Haim Ovadya (1922-1944)
Rosa Plaveva (1878-1970)
Kočo Racin (1908-1943)

Moldova:

Elena Djionat (1888-?)

Poland:

Justyna Budzińska-Tylicka (1867-1936)
Kazimiera Bujwidowa (1867-1932)
Zofia Daszyńska-Golińska (1866-1934)
Paulina Kuczalska-Reinschmit (1859-1921)
Teodora Męczkowska (1870-1954)
Zofia Moraczewska (1873-1958)
Iza Moszczeńska (1864-1941)
Eliza Orzeszkowa (1841-1910)
Anna Szelągowska (1880-1962)
Maria Szeliga (1854-1927)
Tadeusz Żeleński (Boy) (1874-1941)
Narcyza Żmichowska (1819-1876)

Romania:

Maria Baiulescu (1860-1941)
Calypso Botez (1880-?)
Princess Alexandrina Cantacuzino (1876-1944)

Elena Meissner (1867-1940)
Sofia Nădejde (1856-1946)
Ella Negruzzi (1876-1948)
Eugenia de Reuss Ianculescu (1866-1938)
Alice Voinescu (1885-1961)
Adela Xenopol (1861-1939)

Russia:

Praskov'ia Arian (1864/5-1949)
Inessa Armand (1874-1920)
Mariia Chekhova (1866-1934)
Anna Engelgardt (1838-1903)
Anna Filosofova (1837-1912)
Liubov' Gurevich (1866-1940)
Anna Kal'manovich (?-?)
Alexandra Kollontai (1872-1952)
Nadezhda Krupskaia (1869-1939)
Ekaterina Kuskova (1869-1958)
Zinaida Mirovich (1865-1913)
Serafima Panteleeva (1846-1918)
Anna Shabanova (1848-1932)
Ol'ga Shapir (1850-1916)
Ekaterina Shchepkina (1854-1938)
Poliksena Shishkina-Iavein (1875-1947)
Nadezhda Stasova (1822-1895)
Mariia Trubnikova (1835-1897)
Ariadna Tyrkova-Williams (1869-1962)

Serbia:

Ksenija Atanasijević (1894-1981)
Draga Dejanović (Dejanovich) (1840-1871)
Biljana Jovanović (1953-1996)
Draga Ljočić (Ljotchich)-Milošević (1855-1926)
Milica Ninković (Ninkovich) (1854-1881)
Žarana Papić (1949-2002)
Isidora Sekulić (1877-1958)

Slovakia:

Hana Gregorová (1885-1958)
Elena Maróthy-Šoltésová (1855-1939)
L'udmila Podjavorinská (1872-1951)
Barbora Rezlerová-Švarcová (1890-1941)
Terézia Vansová (1857-1942)

Slovenia:	Zofka Kveder (1878-1926) Pavlina Pajk (1854-1901) Alojzija Štebi (1883-1956) Vida Tomšič (1913-1998) Angela Vode (1892-1985)
Turkey:	Fatma Aliye (1862-1936) Suat Derviş (1905-1972) Halide Edib Adıvar (1884-1964) Ulviye Mevlan Civelek (1893-1964) Nezihe Muhittin (1889-1958) Nurser Öztunalı (1947-1999) Sabiha Sertel (1895-1968)
Ukraine:	Natalia Kobrynska (1851-1920) Olha Kobylianska (1863-1942) Solom'iya Pavlychko (1958-1999) Olena Pchilka (1849-1930) Milena Rudnytska (1892-1979) Lesia Ukrainka (1871-1913)

ALİYE, Fatma (1862–1936)

Prominent Turkish woman writer and philosopher of the Ottoman era; advocate of (Muslim) women's rights; founder of the *Cemiyet-i İmdadiye* (Charity Society, 1897–?).

Fatma Aliye was born on 26 October 1862 into a mansion in Istanbul. Her father, Ahmet Cevdet Pasha (1822–1895), was an influential bureaucrat of the Ottoman State, a lawyer and a historian. Her mother was Adviye Rabia Hanım. Fatma had a brother, Ali Sedat, and a sister, Emine Semiye (1864–1944), also a prominent figure in her time, though less so than Fatma.

A Member of the Ottoman Parliament, Fatma Aliye's father was appointed Governor of Egypt when Fatma was three years old and the family spent the years 1866 to 1868 in Aleppo. When she was thirteen, her father was appointed to another governorship and for six months the family resided in Janina (in the western Ottoman Empire; today Ioannina, Greece). Fatma Aliye's early years as the daughter of a traditional Ottoman bureaucrat in the post-*Tanzimat* period were a mixture of mansion life and the new cultural milieu that accompanied 'Westernization' (i.e. political reconstruction through the adoption of 'Western' public and legal institutions). Fatma received no formal schooling, since at that time there were no high schools or colleges open to women, but was privately tutored at home until the age of thirteen; her father taught her Arabic, history and philosophy and she also took other private lessons. In 1875, her father became the Minister of Education. Fatma Aliye, who had now come of age, was not permitted to take lessons with male teachers and ordered to stay away from the *selamlık* (traditionally the part of the house reserved for men) and move into the *harem* (the part reserved for women). In 1878, the family spent nine months in Damascus due to her father's new position. The following year, at the age of seventeen, Fatma Aliye was married upon her father's wishes to Captain Mehmet Faik Bey (died 1928), one of the *aide-de-camps* of Sultan Abdülhamid. It was not a marriage based on love; Aliye's husband was intellectually far less qualified than she and tried to keep her away from intellectual pursuits–at least for a while. Fatma Aliye gave birth to four girls: Hatice Faik Topuz Muhtar (born 1880); Ayşe Faik

Topuz (1884–1967); Nimet Faik Topuz Selen (1900–1972) and Zübeyde İsmet Faik Topuz (born 1901). In 1885, her husband was posted to the central Anatolian province of Konya for a period of eleven months and Fatma Aliye, who had remained in Istanbul with her children, had the opportunity to return to intellectual pursuits, particularly writing. Later, her husband's negative attitude to her intellectual life would change and he would even encourage her to publish.

The fact that the Ottoman Empire was ruled by the *Shari'a* (Islamic law) had an impact not only on religious, but also cultural life. The dominant ideology of the period aimed at a synthesis between Islam and 'the West' and the resulting 'civilizationalism' found its way into Fatma Aliye's views on women and women's rights. She placed primary importance on the family and regarded women as the driving force of 'civilization' via their roles as mothers, emphasizing the need for women's education, raising the problem of women's freedom and responsibilities in 'the family' and in 'society,' and demanding rights for women within these prescribed boundaries. Some of her arguments, calling for sexual equality as well as the preservation of gender differences, reflected widespread currents of nineteenth-century European feminist thought.

Her first translation from French, of George Ohnet's novel *Volonté* (*Meram* in Turkish), was published in 1889. She did not use her own name for the reason that it was then considered inappropriate for a woman to publish and write. In *Meram*, the translator's name appeared as "a Lady," but among intellectual circles it was considered improbable that a woman could have really completed such an impressive translation. For a long time after, Fatma Aliye employed the pseudonym *Mütercime-i Meram* (the [female] translator of *Volonté*), but she published her novel *Muhazarat* (Useful information, 1892) under her real name. *Muhazarat*, which came out in a second edition in 1908, was the first novel by a woman in the Ottoman Empire. After its publication, Fatma Aliye's name began appearing in newspapers and magazines.

For thirteen years (1895–1908), Fatma Aliye wrote the editorial column for the *Hanımlara Mahsus Gazete* (Newspaper for women). The publication, which came out twice a week, debated women's issues and provided Turkish women intellectuals (such as Emine Semiye, Fatma Fahrünnisa, Gülistan İsmet, Nigar Osman and Leyla Saz) with a public forum. Aliye's novels *Ra'fet* and *Udi* (The lute player), published in 1898 and 1899 respectively, also dealt with the kinds of subjects discussed in the pages of the *Hanımlara Mahsus Gazete*, such as women's entrapment in arranged marriages. Aliye saw economic independence for women as a solution to this, and many other problems faced by women. *Ra'fet* and *Udi* were later translated into French, as was Fatma Aliye's 1895 book about Muslim women, called *Les femmes musulmanes*. In a letter (dated 2 April 1895) sent by Nicolas Nicolaides, an editor of 'L'agence Ottomane' (a well-known contemporary publisher of works on 'the Orient'), Aliye was informed that *Les femmes musulmanes* was being published at the same time by another publisher under another title and writer's name!

Fatma Aliye's biography, covering her life until the age of 33, was written by Ahmet Mithat Efendi (a prominent intellectual of the period) and published in 1911 under the title of *Fatma Aliye: Bir Osmanlı Kadın Yazarının Doğuşu* (Fatma Aliye: the birth of an Ottoman woman writer). Aliye herself co-authored *Hayal ve Hakikat* (Dream and truth) with Ahmet Mithat Efendi in 1894. Following her interest in philosophy, Aliye wrote *Teracim-i Ahval-i Felasife* (Biographies of philosophers, 1900), in which she criticized 'Western' writers for their lack of knowledge regarding 'Eastern' societies, Muslim women and Islam. In a similar vein, she contributed to written debates with orientalists (such as the writer Emile Julyar) in articles published in French newspapers and wrote *Nisvan-ı Islam* (Women of Islam, 1896; translated into French and Arabic) and *Taaddüd-i Zevcat'a Zeyl* (Polygamy–an appendix, 1899).

Further research by Aliye, published under the title "Ünlü İslam Kadınları" (Famous Muslim women, 1895), aimed to provide readers with examples of publicly active and intellectual 'Eastern' women performing socially valued roles. She demanded to know how women could remain so unaware of their own history (a critical issue for women abroad, as well as in Turkey). As a distinguished writer, she won international prestige, appearing in biographies of women writers, having her work exhibited at the library of the World's Columbian Exposition (Chicago, August 1893) and cited in the catalogue of the Women's Library at the same World Fair. Seven years later, she was invited to another exhibition in Paris, but could not accept.

Fatma Aliye is also known as the founder of the first women's association in the Ottoman Empire, the *Cemiyet-i İmdadiye* (Charity Society), established after the Greek war of 1897, in order to provide bereaved wives and children, as well as war veterans with material assistance. In recognition of her efforts she received a medal from Sultan Abdülhamid in 1899. She also worked for other charity societies: the *Osmanlı Hilal-i Ahmer* (Ottoman Red Crescent) and the *Müdafaa-i Milliye Osmanlı Kadınlar Heyeti* (National Defence Women's Committee), founded by women following the Tripoli and Balkan Wars of 1911 and 1912.

In order to defend her father and teacher, Ahmet Cevdet Pasha, against political attacks, Fatma Aliye wrote the book *Cevdet Paşa ve Zamanı* (Cevdet Pasha and his time), published in 1911. Between 1921 and 1929, she traveled to France several times for health reasons and to search for her daughter, Zübeyde İsmet, who had converted to Christianity and left Turkey. In the final years of her life, Aliye's work did not receive much attention and she suffered increasingly from financial difficulties and poor health. She died on 14 July 1936 in Istanbul.

General neglect of the Ottoman era in Turkish scholarship can be attributed in part to the ideological preferences of the Republican regime, through the decades from the 1920s up until the 1980s. In this latter decade, the number of studies on Ottoman society and Ottoman women began to increase in number and ideological paradigms have since shifted. Fatma Aliye is remembered in Turkish historiography today as a pioneering woman-writer and intellectual.

Serpil Çakır
University of Istanbul

SOURCES

(A) Fatma Aliye's personal archival collection at the Library of Istanbul Municipality. Contains manuscripts, letters, documents and photographs. For further information see Mübeccel Kızıltan and Tülay Gençtürk, eds. *İstanbul Belediye Kitaplığı Fatma Aliye Hanım Evrakı Katoloğu* (Istanbul Municipal Library: the catalogued documents of Fatma Aliye Hanım). Istanbul: Istanbul Municipality Publishing, 1993.
(B) *Hanımlara Mahsus Gazete* (Newspaper for women) (1895-1908).
(C) Fatma Aliye, "Ünlü İslam Kadınları" (Famous Muslim women), *Hanımlara Mahsus Gazete* (Newspaper for Women), no. 8 (14 September 1895): 3-4 and no. 9 (18 September 1895): 2-3.
(D) Aşa, Emel. *Fatma Aliye Hanım*. PhD thesis. University of Istanbul, 1993.
(D) Mithat Efendi, Ahmet. *Bir Osmanlı Kadın Yazarının Doğuşu* (Fatma Aliye: the birth of an Ottoman woman writer) (1911). Istanbul: Kırkambar Publishing, 1994.

APPONYI, Countess, Mrs Count Albert Apponyi, born Countess Clotilde, Klotild Dietrichstein-Mensdorff-Pouilly (1867–1942)

Mrs Apponyi with her famous husband and three children in the 1920s or early 1930s

Long-standing President (from 1910) of the *Magyarországi Nőegyesületek Szövetsége* (*MNSz*, Alliance of Women's Associations in Hungary); Hungarian representative to the International Council of Women (ICW); holder of various positions in the League of Nations throughout the interwar period.

Countess Dietrichstein-Mensdorff-Pouilly was born on 23 December 1867 in Vienna, the daughter of Catholic parents: Count Alexander Mensdorff-Pouilly, later also Prince of Dietrichstein zu Nikolsburg, high-ranking member of the Austrian military and statesman (1813-1871), and Countess Alexandrine (Den Priskau) Dietrichstein zu Nikolsburg. Countess Clotilde had two older brothers: Hugo (1858-1920) and Albert (1861-?). As a young woman, she was awarded the title of Dame of the Star-Cross Order to the imperial court in Vienna. In 1897, she married the politician Count Albert Apponyi (1846-1933), who was more than twenty years her senior and then (later even more so) a leading figure among those nationalist-liberal elements of the Hungarian political elite who sought greater autonomy from Austria. "Hardly ... more divergent milieus" and political backgrounds "could be imagined" than those of the newly married couple. Yet Countess Klotild–knowing that the "woman" of Count Albert Apponyi "could be nothing else but Hungarian with heart and soul [–] took the big step and did so completely" (Apponyi *sine anno*, 238). The newly married Countess moved to Budapest, learned Hungarian perfectly and entered 'high society' in the Hungarian capital, soon coming to identify entirely with the Hungarian nation. Her first child was a son, Count György Apponyi (Eberhard, 1898-1970), followed by two girls; one of them named Mária.

Soon after moving to Budapest, Countess Apponyi became involved in a broad spectrum of welfare and women's associations. From at least 1908, she was (and is very likely to have remained for decades) the President of the *Női Munkát Értékesítő*

Klotild Nőegyesület (Klotild Women's Association for the Sale of Work by Women); in 1913, she became a member of the Executive Board of the *Országos Katholikus Nővédő-Egyesület* (National Catholic Association for the Protection of Women) and in 1930, she became the President of the highly respected association of female teachers, the *Mária Dorothea Egyesület* (Mária Dorothea Association). Among her long-standing interests was the protection of children–e.g. from harm inflicted through unrestricted access to cinema–and she was stoutly devoted to the ideals of temperance and other, related movements.

In 1910, Countess Apponyi became the President of the *Magyarországi Nőegyesületek Szövetsége* (*MNSz*, Alliance of Women's Associations in Hungary), an umbrella organization for women's associations of all kinds (excluding socialist ones) and a huge number of welfare organizations, mostly focusing on women and children. The *MNSz* had been founded in 1904 upon the initiative of the *Országos Nőképző Egyesület* (National Association for Women's Education) and of Auguszta Rosenberg (long-standing Acting President who in 1946, at the age of 88, held the title of Permanent Acting President). Immediately upon its foundation, the *MNSz* became a member of the International Council of Women (ICW); the impetus to found the *MNSz* was bound up with the organizational aspirations of the ICW in Central-Eastern Europe and (in tension) with the emerging organizational endeavors of progressive and leftist women.

Countess Apponyi was President of the *MNSz* for about three decades. In 1912, in her capacity as President of the *MNSz* and against the background of ongoing suffrage reform, she addressed the House of Representatives of the Hungarian Parliament with a request for the enfranchisement of a small group of women of distinguished intellectual, economic or social status. From this time on, Countess Apponyi publicly advocated women's suffrage. In 1917, utilizing her social position and connections, she negotiated at the highest political level for the inclusion of women's suffrage into planned new suffrage legislation–without immediate success. In 1918, she publicly supported the campaign for women's suffrage, organized mainly by the progressive *Feministák Egyesülete* (*FE*, Feminist Association).

In the interwar period, the *MNSz* acquired a somewhat marginalized position on the political landscape. Many of the moderate and conservative associations, particularly those related to various Christian denominations, were now united under the banner of the right-wing nationalist and revisionist *Magyar Asszonyok Nemzeti Szövetsége* (*MANSz*, Hungarian National Women's Union), presided over by the well-known writer Cecile Tormay (1876–1937) from the foundation of the organization in 1918 until Tormay's death. Countess Apponyi was open to cooperation with both the *MANSz* and with the *Keresztény Női Tábor* (Christian Women's League). On the opposite end of the spectrum of non-socialist women's organizations stood the *Feministák Egyesülete*, with ***Eugénia (Miskolczy) Meller*** and ***Vilma Glücklich*** as its leading representatives; on several occasions the *FE* aimed (successfully) to strengthen its position by aligning itself publicly with the *MNSz* and its President, Countess Apponyi. A key event in this regard was a large meeting of women's associations from across the political landscape held in 1929. Countess Apponyi of the *MNSz*, encouraged by the *FE*, called the meeting to protest the planned (and eventually partially realized) abolition of women's eligibility for election to village, town, city and county parliaments or councils. As a follow-up to the meeting, the Countess herself published a much discussed leading article in the conservative daily *Új Nemzedék* (New generation, 10 April 1929), underlining the importance of this issue for Hungarian women's associations. Ten years later, when the Hungarian Parliament debated a law in favor of dismissing married women from the civil service, the Countess again assumed leadership of a delegation representing the *MNSz*, the *MANSz*, the *FE* and other important associations, handing over a memorandum to the Minister of Finance.

After her first election as President of the *MNSz*, Countess Apponyi began to increasingly emphasize international engagement. Having already represented the *MNSz* at the Rome Quinquennial of the ICW in 1914, her international activities broadened during World War I, when she worked in Switzerland on matters relating to Hungarian international affairs. By the end of the 1920s, Apponyi was developing a particularly strong international profile. The Countess represented Hungary as a substitute delegate (1928–1934), later delegate (1935 to at least 1937) to the annual Assembly of the League of Nations and participated repeatedly (as an official delegate of her government in Geneva) in the activities of, or formally related to the League of Nations. Initially, these developments were closely linked to the fact that Apponyi's husband had also been regularly representing his country at the League Assembly. But after the death of Count Apponyi (in 1933), Countess Apponyi continued, independently, to build on her reputation as an individual international representative of her country (although her involvement in women's activities in Geneva is unresearched to date). In 1930, she was elected to the prestigious position of President of the Committee on "Social and General Questions"–the fifth of the six principle committees of the Assembly of the League of Nations. She was re-elected for this position in 1935 and 1937 (but not in 1936).

Countess Apponyi died on 1 September 1942. The long-standing President of the *MNSz* had begun her career as a "celebrated female member of the Viennese aristocracy" (Apponyi *sine anno*, 238). At the end of World War I, a respected, politically influential and leading representative of the non-socialist women's movement in Hungary, she witnessed the declaration of Hungarian independence, a development completely in compliance with the world-view she had always so whole-heartedly advocated alongside her husband. In the interwar period, due to the dominance of conservative and in part anti-Semitic women's organizations, she became less influential at home, in spite of her leanings towards territorial revision of the Paris Peace Treaty in favor of Hungary. Nevertheless, she continued to play her centrist role in the Hungarian women's movement, as well as abroad. In the years leading up to her death, she experienced the dramatic growth of undemocratic elements in Hungarian political life and legislation, a tendency that very much went against the grain of the national liberalism she had adopted as a young woman and kept at the core of her identity ever since. Her son György (a Member of Parliament from 1931 to 1944) actively opposed anti-Jewish legislation and German-friendly politics in the late 1930s. Upon German occupation in March 1944, he was arrested by the Gestapo and taken to the concentration camp in Mauthausen, Austria. Although he survived, he never returned to Hungary.

Susan Zimmermann
Department of Gender Studies, Department of History,
Central European University, Budapest

Claudia Papp, Ph.D.
Municipal Museum and Archive
of Sachsenheim/Baden-Württemberg, Germany

SOURCES

(A) New York Public Library, MSS. & Archives Section, Schwimmer-Lloyd Collection, I Series.

(B) *Egyesült Erővel* (With united strength). The official journal of the *Magyarországi Nőegyesületek Szövetsége* (Alliance of Women's Associations in Hungary) (1909–1914).

(B) *Magyar Asszony. A Magyar Asszonyok Nemzeti Szövetségének Értesitője* (Hungarian woman. The bulletin of the Hungarian National Women's Union) (1921–1942).

(B) Bozzay, Margit. *Magyar Asszonyok Lexikona* (Encyclopedia of Hungarian women). Budapest, 1931.

(B) *Annuaire de La Sociéte des Nations* (Yearbook of the League of Nations) (1920–1931; 1936–1938).

(B) *Essential Facts about the League of Nations.* Fourth revised edition. Geneva: League of Nations, 1935.

(B) Gyulás, Pál. *Magyar írók élete és munkái* (Hungarian writers and their lives and works). Vol. 5. Budapest, 1943.

(B) Count Apponyi, Albert. *Emlékirataim. Ötven év. Ifjúkorom. Huszonöt év az ellenzéken* (My memoirs. Fifty years. My youth. Twenty five years in opposition). Budapest: second edition, *sine anno.*

(C) Apponyi, Countess / Mrs Albert. "Az alkohol" (Alcohol). In Countess / Mrs Albert Apponyi, et. al. *Asszonyokról asszonyoknak* (On women for women). Budapest, 1913, 40–45.

(E) *A Pallas Nagy Lexikona* (The big Pallas encyclopedia), various volumes.

(E) *A Révai Nagy Lexikona* (The big Révai encyclopedia), various volumes.

(E) *Magyar életrajzi lexikon* (Hungarian biographical dictionary) (1000–1990). CD-Rom edition.

(E) Zimmermann, Susan. *Die bessere Hälfte? Frauenbewegungen und Frauenbestrebungen im Ungarn der Habsburgermonarchie 1848 bis 1918* (The better half? Women's movements and women's aspirations in Hungary in the Habsburg Monarchy, 1848 to 1918). Vienna/Budapest: Promedia Verlag/Napvilág Kiadó, 1999.

(E) Papp, Claudia. *'Die Kraft der weiblichen Seele.' Feminismus in Ungarn 1918-1941* ('The strength of women's soul.' Feminism in Hungary 1918-1941). Münster: LIT-Verlag, 2004.

(E) Zimmermann, Susan. "Reich, Nation, und Internationalismus. Konflikte und Kooperationen der Frauenbewegungen der Habsburgermonarchie" (Empire, Nation and Internationalism. Conflict and cooperation among the women's movements of the Habsburg Monarchy). In Waltraud Heindl, Edit Király and Alexandra Millner (eds), *Frauenbilder, feministische Praxis und nationales Bewusstsein in Österreich-Ungarn 1867-1918* (Envisioning women, feminist practice, and national consciousness in Austria-Hungary 1867-1918). Tübingen 2005 (forthcoming).

ARIAN, Praskov'ia Naumovna Belenkaia (1864/5-1949)

Russian feminist. Founder, editor and publisher of the *Pervyi Zhenskii Kalendar'* (First Women's Calendar) (1899–1915). Founder of the *Pervyi Zhenskii Politekhnicheskii Institut* (First Women's Technical Institute) (in existence from 1906 to 1924).

Praskov'ia Naumovna Belenkaia was born on 12 April 1864 or 1865 (her Moscow archive lists her date of birth as 1865 but the autobiographical statement in her St Petersburg archive lists it as 1864), to a Jewish family in St Petersburg, probably of the merchant class since Jewish residence in the Imperial capital was strictly limited.

Admitted to the physics and mathematics section of the St Petersburg *Vysshie Zhenskie (Bestuzhevskie) Kursy* (Bestuzhev Higher Women's Courses), Belenkaia completed the third graduating class of the Courses in 1884. She never took her final exam–perhaps due to her political activities; the Courses were a hotbed of radicalism and, like a number of other feminist activists, Belenkaia was a student radical. The date of Belenkaia's marriage is not known, but upon marriage she adopted the family name of her husband, Miron Isaevich Arian.

Praskov'ia Arian supported herself as a translator and journalist–forms of employment available to educated Russian women–while seeking to combine her work with her ideals. She wrote for a range of publications, including the *Birzhevye Vedomosti* (Stock market gazette), the *Sputnik Zdorov'ia* (Health guide), the *Vestnik Blagotvoritel'nosti* (Philanthropy bulletin) and *Iskusstvo i Zhizn'* (Art and life). In 1884, she founded a daycare center, *Detskaia Pomoshch'* (Children's Aid), for children of workers in St Petersburg, where she worked for ten years alongside the center's first President (and feminist pioneer), ***Nadezhda Vasil'evna Stasova***.

In 1899, Arian founded the *Pervyi Zhenskii Kalendar'* (First Women's Calendar), single-handedly compiling, editing and publishing this compendium of information for women (each year from 1899 to 1915). The *Kalendar'* contained articles on religion, health, employment and education, as well as biographical sketches of Russian feminists, radical activists and literary figures, with accompanying photos. It chronicled the activities of the major feminist organizations, such as the *Russkoe Zhenskoe Vzaimno-Blagotvoritel'noe Obshchestvo* (Russian Women's Mutual Philanthropic Society)–including photos of the society's facilities–and the *Liga Ravnopraviia Zhenshchin* (League for Women's Equal Rights). Feminist congresses also received detailed coverage: in particular the 1908 *Pervyi Vserossiiskii Zhenskii S'ezd* (First All-Russian Congress of Women) and the *Pervyi Vserossiiskii S'ezd po Obrazovaniiu Zhenshchin* (First All-Russian Congress on Women's Education; held from 26 December 1912 to 4 January 1913). Arian recruited a wide range of contributors to the *Kalendar'*, including the writer Maxim Gorky, the radical activist Vera Figner, the artist Il'ia Repin and the psychologist Vladimir Bekhterev.

Arian traveled widely. Working in the archives of Swiss universities, she gathered data on Russian women studying abroad for the *Kalendar'* issues of 1899 and 1912 and, after a trip to Japan, published articles on the Women's University in Tokyo and the status of Japanese women (see the *Kalendar'* issues of 1904 and 1905). News about the international women's movement was a regular feature of the *Kalendar'*.

The *Kalendar'* dwelled on a range of issues affecting women. Prominent among them was health, both physical and mental. Each issue contained nutritional advice and pointers on personal hygiene and behavior. The 1912 *Kalendar'*, for example, included the article "Nervnost' i mery dlia bor'by s nei" (Anxiety and ways to fight it).

Arian is perhaps best known as the driving force behind the establishment of the First Women's Technical Institute. It was Arian who lobbied the government tirelessly for permission to open what were originally called the *Vysshie Zhenskie Politekhnicheskie Kursy* (Women's Higher Polytechnical Courses); she also carried out the fundraising necessary to sustain the new venture, hired the staff and rented the initial space (an apartment) in her own name. When the Courses opened on 15 January 1906, they were the first in the world to train women engineers. Arian remained committed to providing educational opportunities for workers of both sexes. In the year that the *Vysshie Zhenskie Politekhnicheskie kursy* opened (1906), she was granted permission to open an evening school for workers in the Narva Gate section of St Petersburg. Despite government harassment, closings and arrests of students, the school survived for ten years.

Never once imprisoned for her activities, Arian maintained ties with those who had been incarcerated for their opposition to the tsarist regime. From 1907–1917, she was an active member of the support group for prisoners in the notorious Schlusselburg Fortress.

Arian was among a number of women activists in this period to maintain ties with political radicals and with legal feminist groups. The pattern of her activism challenges the notion that women of her generation went 'from feminism to radicalism' and that feminism and radicalism were separate, mutually exclusive spheres. Arian was active in the *Russkoe Zhenskoe Vzaimno-Blagotvoritel'noe Obshchestvo* (Russian Women's Mutual Philanthropic Society), speaking and writing for the society, working in its library and chairing the committee researching conditions of women's work in Russia.

After the October Revolution of 1917, Arian complained privately to friends about the mere lip service paid by the Bolsheviks to women's rights. In the 1930s, she conducted courses for workers at the Kirov factory in Leningrad (today St Petersburg), lecturing on Pushkin. In 1942, during the siege of Leningrad, she was evacuated to Piatigorsk and then to Tashkent. She died in Moscow (?) on 28 March 1949.

Rochelle Goldberg Ruthchild
The Union Institute and University
and the Davis Center for Russian and Eurasian Studies,
Harvard University

SOURCES

(A) Arian's personal archives are located at the *Institut russkoi literatury* (*IRLI*, Institute for Russian Literature) or *Pushkinskii Dom* (Pushkin House) in St Petersburg (Fond 117), and at the *Rossiiskii gosudarstvennyi arkhiv literatury i iskusstva* (*RGALI*, Russian State Archive of Literature and Art) in Moscow (Fond 1018).

(C) Arian, Praskov'ia N., ed. *Pervyi zhenskii kalendar*' (First Women's Calendar) (1899-1915).

(D) Ruthchild, Rochelle Goldberg. "Ariian, Praskov'ia Naumovna Belenkaia." In Norma Corigliano Noonan and Carol Nechemias, eds. *Encyclopedia of Russian Women's Movements*. Westport, Connecticut: Greenwood Press, 2001, 4-6.

(E) Goldberg, Rochelle. *The Russian Women's Movement 1859-1917*. Doctoral Dissertation. University of Rochester, 1976.

(E) Stites, Richard. *The Women's Liberation Movement in Russia. Feminism, Nihilism, and Bolshevism*. Princeton: Princeton University Press, 1978; 1991.

ARMAND, Inessa-Elizaveta Fiodorovna (1874–1920)

Activist of the Russian and international workers' and feminist movements. Pseudonym: Elena Blonina.

Inessa Armand was born Inessa Steffen in Paris on 26 April 1874, the illegitimate child of Theodore Steffen, a British opera singer, and Nathalie Vil'd, a French actress. She grew up speaking French and English and later learned Russian, German and Polish. After her father died in 1889, she moved to Russia to stay with relatives. In 1893, she married Alexander Evgen'evich Armand (died 1943), whose family were wealthy manufacturers of French origin. By 1903, Inessa Armand had given birth to four children (Alexander, Varvara, Inna and Vladimir). In 1902, she left her husband; in 1903, she married his younger brother Vladimir, who shared her radical political views and bore him her last child, Andrei.

In the summer of 1903, Vladimir and Inessa Armand went to Moscow to become professional revolutionaries. Under the influence of Marxism, Inessa regarded the women's movement as merely the 'female equivalent' of the male workers' struggle for liberation. She believed the 'class criterion' most always be taken into account when defining a revolutionary attitude to the struggle for women's rights, since participants in that struggle from different social strata would have different social concerns.

Under the threat of arrest, the Armand family emigrated for Paris. After her husband's death from tuberculosis, Inessa Armand remained politically active, in spite of the everyday hardships she faced bringing up five children alone. In 1904, Armand joined the *Parti Socialiste Français* (French Socialist Party). In the same year, she returned to Russia (Moscow) and became a member of the *Rossiiskaia Social-Demokraticheskaia Rabochaia Partiia* (Russian Social Democratic Labor Party). It was also in 1904 that the *Moskovskoe Obshchestvo Uluchsheniia Uchasti Zhenshchin* (Moscow Society for the Improvement of the Situation of Women), established in 1899, elected Armand Chair of its Commission on Education.

With the outbreak of the 1905–1907 Russian Revolution, Armand began organizing Sunday schools for craftswomen, female workers, maids and housewives. The aim was to turn these units into centers for revolutionary propaganda, where women might be encouraged to discard their traditional views on the family. On 7 February 1905, Armand was arrested in St Petersburg but released three months later. She immediately resumed revolutionary agitation among women workers and also made efforts to establish contacts between Russian and foreign socialist feminists, as part of efforts to unify the international women's labor movement.

The failed Revolution of 1905–1907 was followed by a wave of political reaction and Armand's activities were noted by the authorities. In the fall of 1907, Armand managed to emigrate, again to France where she joined the most vigorous activists of the Presidium of the emigrant Bolshevik organization: "The Group for Assistance to the Party." In 1908, she traveled illegally to St Petersburg in order to participate in the First All-Russian Women's Congress but did not play any active role in organizing the Congress or its sessions. (Her own views did not correspond with those of the liberal wing of the Russian women's movement, which had initiated the Congress.)

At the end of December 1909, in Paris, Armand met the leader of the Russian Social Democratic Party, Vladimir Ul'ianov (Lenin) (1870–1924). The beginning of their friendship dates from the spring of 1911, when the socialists succeeded in opening a party school in Longumeaux (near Paris) where Armand worked as a lecturer. Lenin found himself among one of the many unable to resist the beauty and charm of this remarkable feminist.

In the spring of 1912, socialist emigrants sent Armand to Russia to organize underground party activities. By this point Armand, along with other Russian and foreign colleagues, had become actively involved in setting up a foreign version (i.e. to be published abroad) of the new women's magazine *Rabotnitsa* (Female worker)–initially intended for a Russian proletarian female readership. The first issue of this magazine came out on 8 March 1914 (International Women's Day).

Armand grew increasingly fascinated by socialist feminism. In January 1915, she composed a brief draft of an article on feminism and sent a draft version of a pamphlet on women's rights to Lenin. He sharply criticized Armand's program for women's liberation and recommended that she remove her demand for free love, since it seemed a bourgeois demand to him–an appeal to "freedom of adultery" and a threat to the emergent new communist society (Stites 1978, 260–261). It was always necessary, declared Lenin, "to take into account the objective logic of class relations in matters of love" (Margar'an 1962, 213–215). Armand chose not to agree.

Armand represented Russian Social Democrats at several key international events: the International Socialist Women's conference (1915), the International Conference of Youth (1916) and the Zimmerwald (1915) and Kintal (1916) conferences of the social democratic internationalists. From 1916, she lived in Paris. Sharing some of Lenin's ideas–in particular the importance he placed on the role of women workers in preparing for socialist revolution–she translated many of his works into French.

After the fall of the Russian Monarchy in February 1917, Armand returned to Russia via Germany. In April 1917, she was an elected delegate to the *Sed'maia Vserossi-*

iskaia Konferenciia Rossiiskoi Social-Demokraticheskoi Rabochei Partii (Seventh All-Russian Conference of the *RSDRP*, Russian Social Democratic Party of Workers). After that she moved to Moscow to be with her children (her youngest son Andrej had become sick and there was a chance that he had tuberculosis). In Moscow, Armand set up courses for the education of agitators and propagandists; she wrote speeches for workers and participated in the work of the *Moskovskogo Soveta Rabochih Deputatov* (Moscow Deputies' Council). In the summer of 1917, she took her children to the south of Russia, returning to Moscow in the midst of the Revolution. After Soviet rule had been established, she took part in new Party activities. She had an incredible capacity for hard work, often working up to fourteen hours a day. She found herself among the most prominent party leaders and was an elected member of the *Moskovskii Gubernskii Komitet Partii* (Party Committee for the Province of Moscow); later, she became Chair of the *Moskovskii Gubernskii Economicheskii Komitet* (Moscow Economic Council).

'The woman question' continued to be regarded as an important aspect of social change. Even Vladimir Lenin, Armand's idol, finally agreed (not without her influence) that now was the time to recognize that women had their special demands and needs, and that it was necessary to devise new working methods to improve women's situation. In the spring of 1918, Armand began organizing the "School of Soviet Work," which was to have, for the first time, a special *Zhenotdel* (Women's Bureau). It was at this time that Armand's interest in the history and theory of 'the woman question' intensified and she became editor of a new magazine, *Zhizn' Rabotnitsy*" (The life of a woman worker).

From 1918 to 1919, Armand was the head of the *Zhenotdel* at the Central Committee of the Russian Social Democratic Bolshevik Party, which held executive power. Back then she also worked–under the pseudonym Yelena Blonina–for another magazine, *Kommunistka* (Woman-communist).

In 1919, Armand began working for the Second Communist International Congress, where she defended ideas of social equality between men and women. She was concerned about the ways in which everyday life and family relations in Russia were to be practically restructured; in her view, the new Russia lacked the necessary resources to liberate women. In a society struggling for survival, the creation of facilities that could have freed women from daily chores (something often cited by male discussants of 'the woman question') seemed an impossible dream. One had to search for other ways of liberating women. Armand saw all the hardships her contemporaries endured and treated them as her own, prompting her to organize and lead the *Pervaia Mezhdunarodnaia Konferenciia Zhenshchin-Kommunistok* (First International Conference of Women Communists).

Years of overwork (including care for her children), fatigue and hunger all took their toll on Armand's energy and strength. In the fall of 1920, she contracted cholera and died on 24 September 1920. The urn containing her ashes was buried in Moscow in the Kremlin wall. Soviet historiography has mostly paid attention to her Party activities and her work during the first years of the Soviet regime. The work of western historians has often dwelled on the relationship between Lenin and Armand. No publications have yet addressed her impact on the Russian feminist movement.

Natalia Pushkareva
Institute of ethnology and anthropology (Moscow),
Russian Academy of Sciences

SOURCES

(B) Voitinskaia, O. "Leninskie pis'ma k Inesse Armand" (Lenin's letters to Inessa Armand). *Pod znamenem marxizma* (Under the banner of Marxism), no. 11 (1939): 72-85.
(C) Blonina, Yelena. [Armand I. F.] *K istorii dvizheniia rabotnits v Rossii* (On the history of the working women's movement in Russia). Kharkov, 1920.
(C) Blonina, Yelena. [Armand I. F.] *Stat'i, rechi, pis'ma* (Articles, speeches, letters). Moscow 1975.
(D) Freville J. *Une grande figure de la Revolution russe. Inesse Armand* (A key figure of the Russian Revolution. Inessa Armand). O., 1957.
(D) Margar'an, A. E. "Novoe ob Inesse Armand" (New findings on Inessa Armand). *Voprosy istorii* (Historical questions) no. 3 (1962): 213-215.
(D) Stites, R. "Kollontai, Inessa, Krupskaia." *Canadian-American Slavic Studies* 9, no. 1 (Spring 1975): 84-92.
(D) Vitalii, Vul'f. "Ideia zhenschiny. Inessa Armand" (The idea of woman. Inessa Armand). *L'Officièl* (The Russian edition), no. 46 (April 2003).
(E) Stites, R. *The Women's Liberation Movement in Russia: Feminism, Nihilism, and Bolshevism 1860-1930*. Princeton: Princeton University Press, 1978.

ASPAZIJA (Elza Rozenberga, in marriage Pliekšāne) (1865–1943)

Latvian poetess, public figure, feminist. Pen-names 'Aspazija' and 'Kalna.'

Elza Rozenberga was born on 16 March 1865 at the farmstead Zaļenieku Daukšas. Her parents were the landowner Dāvis Rozenbergs-Rozenvalds and his wife Grieta. Elza had two brothers, Kristaps and Zamuēls, and one sister, Dora. The pen-name 'Aspazija' came from Elza's fascination with the Austrian writer Robert Hammerling's cultural-historical novel *Aspasia* (1876) about the great Aspasia of Miletus. The young Elza Rozenberga was attracted to Aspasia's exceptional life and accomplishments, as well as to her knowledge, which had influenced great thinkers such as Plato, Pericles and Socrates. Ironically for the future life of Elza Rozenberga, Aspasia's work survived only through the voices of the men she had inspired. In a similar vein, even nowadays, Aspazija is valued not so much for her own works, as for her influence on and assistance to the poet Rainis, her life-long partner.

For ten years, Elza Rozenberga studied at Doroteja's school for girls in the city of Jelgava. Under the pen-name of 'Kalna' (literal translation: 'She-Mountain'), Rozenberga published her first article in the newspaper *Baltijas Vēstnesis* (Baltic herald). In 1886, she married Vilhelms Maksis Valters who, in accordance with contemporary marriage law, became the legal owner of her homestead property, subsequently lost it and later disappeared after leaving for America. Together with her relatives, Rozenberga moved to the city of Jelgava, where she held several jobs to support her family. Her first poem, published under the new pen-name of 'Aspazija,' appeared in 1887 in the newspaper *Dienas Lapa* (Daily paper). In 1888, she took part in a contest arranged by the Rīga Latvian Society (which was at the helm of the Latvian national awakening movement in the second half of the nineteenth century). Her play *Atriebēja* (She–the avenger) won first prize but was never staged due to stringent criticisms by members of the contest commission, who wanted to see a happy ending. Even reworked, the play was not staged because of its critical representation of the economic and social colonization of Latvian peasants by despotic Baltic German oppressors.

In 1891–93, Aspazija, while working as a private teacher, wrote the social drama *Vaidelote* and the poem "Saules meita" (The daughter of the sun) about women's experiences and values. In 1893, she began working at the Latvian Theater in Riga as a playright, and was introduced to the cultural, poetic and artistic milieu of Riga. She also tried to launch an acting career, but soon gave up. The following year, this theater staged Aspazija's *Zaudētas tiesības* (Lost rights), which explored a young working woman's insecurities, the social and sexual pressures restricting her choices in life, and society's double standards. In the same year, The Latvian Theatre in Riga staged Aspazija's earlier work, *Vaidelote,* in which she employed mythology to represent a woman's struggle against prejudice and dogma, her right to live and feel on her own terms. Aspazija's plays caused controversy in a society that was coming to grips with modern ideas of women's emancipation and rights.

In the 1890s, Aspazija not only became a well-known journalist and literary critic, but also an outstanding figure in women's groups connected with the organization *Jaunā Strāva* (The new current), which she joined in 1894. *Jaunā Strāva* fought against the Russian imperial power on the one hand, and local Baltic German rule on the other, but also openly supported women's emancipation. This movement attracted a number of young women, still school students, from the educated circles of Latvian society, who linked the emancipation of women with the political and economic emancipation of the nation. Of all the social issues of her time, 'the woman question' and the debates it generated in Europe and in the Russian Empire interested Aspazija the most. She was particularly influenced by August Bebel's *Die Frau und der Sozialismus* (Woman and socialism, 1879; published in Latvian in 1912). For Aspazija, the idea of a free Latvian nation was directly related to the overall emancipation of Latvian women. Together with other women from *Jaunā Strāva,* she became an active supporter of women's rights and emancipation, contributing to debates in Latvian literature and the press.

Latvian women of the late nineteenth century could not organize political movements similar to the suffrage campaigns of the USA and Great Britain because they did not have the political and economic sovereignty that would have provided the specific spaces in which experiences, traditions and institutions of statehood could have been established and developed. Women's emancipation in Latvia, within the confines of the Russian Empire and under the local rule of the Baltic German elite, occupied those spaces that appeared most 'friendly' to the participation of women: namely culture, art, literature and voluntary public organizations (e.g. charity and temperance). Aspazija was deeply impressed by Henrik Ibsen's drama *A Doll's House* (1880, first staged in Latvia in 1897), whose protagonist, Nora, struggles to emancipate herself from the burden of old traditions. Aspazija considered theater to be a medium that could facilitate engagement with social issues and change values, attitudes and traditions. In her plays from the turn of the century, in which she defended women's right to individuality and self-esteem and protested women's socially constructed inferiority, her central characters are consistently women. Aspazija's collections of poems were dedicated 'to woman' and her value as a human being.

While active in *Jaunā Strāva*, Aspazija had become acquainted with Jānis Pliekšāns (1865-1929), pen-name 'Jānis Rainis,' the editor-in-chief of the progressive newspaper *Dienas Lapa* (Daily paper). He became Aspazija's partner in life and work and in 1897, Aspazija and Rainis got married, after which "Aspazija was still recognized as an outstanding literary figure in Latvian culture. However, she was increasingly perceived as *the second half*–the *Muse* of Rainis" (Cimdiņa http://www.women.it). They did not have children but recently published documents indicate that Rainis had a son from his secretary and, when Aspazija discovered this, she insisted the child be sent to an ophanage.

Having become Rainis's 'other half' and 'supporter,' Aspazija nevertheless continued to write. The romantic drama *Sidraba šķidrauts* (Silver veil, 1905) displayed a shift in Aspazija's writing from women's social issues to romantic dramas and poetry–a shift that reflected changes in early twentieth-century Latvia. In the tragic aftermath of the Russian Revolution of 1905, Rainis and Aspazija emigrated to Switzerland. In 1920, both returned to the newly proclaimed independent Republic of Latvia. Aspazija became very active in the public and political activities of the Republic of Latvia and was elected to the Constitutional Assembly, a special representative body set up to write and oversee the implementation of the *Satversme* (the Latvian Constitution, adopted in 1922, after which the Assembly was officially dissolved).

After the proclamation of Latvian independence, women were granted equal political rights with men. However, the interwar gender regime in Latvia exposed a certain contradiction between modern discourses of emancipated womanhood and traditionalist discourses of female roles; individualism and modernism against community and traditionalism. As in other European countries, the modernization of women's roles in the family and the labor market was combined with women's exclusion from the political sphere and social and economic marginalization. Like ***Klāra Kalniņa*** and other women activists of the pre-independence period, Aspazija kept writing about the significance of women's participation in public and political activities, but was gradually marginalized in public life.

The death of Rainis in 1929 came as a serious shock to Aspazija, though she continued with her literary work. From 1933 until her death in 1943, she lived in Dubulti, a small part of the sea-resort Jūrmala, beside Riga. She wrote collections of poems and dramas, noted for their mysticism, published the last autobiographical volumes of *Mana dzīve un darbi* (My life and works, 1931-1940) and worked on the literary legacy of Rainis. In the mid-1930s, she was offered the post of honorary director at the "Daile" Theater and in 1939, received the *Tēvzemes balva* (Fatherland Award).

Aspazija witnessed further crucial changes in the political situation of her nation: the authoritarian regime (1934), the annexation of Latvia by the USSR (1940) and the

Nazi occupation (1941). She faced serious financial problems, illness and loneliness in Dubulti, though supported by close friends and relatives–among them V. Strēlerte, K. Skalbe and Z. Mauriņa. She published little in the last years of her life. During the Nazi occupation, she was invited to write poetry and film scripts for her plays in German as an outstanding figure of Latvian culture and literature but declined, seeing the offers as ideological cooptation. When her 75th anniversary was celebrated in 1943 in the form of a public event held at the National Theater, she did not attend, reportedly saying: "it would make me shiver to shake hands with all these *Zonderführers*, or whatever one should call them" (cited in Viese 1975, 225). In the last, lonely years of her life, Aspazija received care and support from the students and teachers of a local school. She died on 5 November 1943.

Irina Novikova
University of Latvia

SOURCES

(A) A large number of archival documents related to Aspazija's life as well as her manuscripts are in the fonds of the Rainis Museum of Literature and Art.

(C) Aspazija. *Atriebēja* (The avenger). Written in 1888. Pub. St Petersburg, 1904.

(C) Aspazija. *Vaidelote*. Jelgava, 1894.

(C) Aspazija. *Zaudētas tiesības* (Lost rights). 1894.

(C) Aspazija. *Saules meita* (The daughter of the sun). Jelgava, 1894.

(C) Aspazija. *Neaizsniegts mērķis* (An unattained goal). Riga, 1895.

(C) Aspazija. *Sarkanās puķes* (Red flowers). Jelgava, 1897.

(C) Aspazija. *Sidraba šķidrauts* (Silver veil). Cēsis, 1905.

(C) Aspazija. *Mana dzīve un darbi. Autobiogrāfija un kopoti raksti* (My life and works). 6 Vols. Riga, 1931-1940.

(C) Aspazija. *Rudens lakstīgala* (The autumn nightingale). *Atpūta* (1933): 430–460.

(D) Brant, Līlija. *Latviešu sieviete*. Riga: A/S Valters un Rapa Ģenerālkommisijā, 1931.

(D) Viese, Saulcerīte. *Aspazija*. Riga: Liesma, 1975.

(D) Stahnke, Astrida B. *Aspazija, her life and her drama*. Lanham, MD: University Press of America, 1984.

(D) Amoliņa, Brigita. *Aspazija*. Riga: Avots, 1990.

(D) Viese, Saulcerīte. *Gājēji uz Mēnessdārzu*. Riga: Liesma, 1990.

(D) Grīnuma, Gundega, ed. *Aspazija un Rainis šodienas skatījumā: literatūrzinātnisku rakstu krājums*. Riga: Zinātne. LU Literatūras, folkloras un mākslas institūts, 2004.

(D) Viese, Saulcerīte. *Mūžīgie Spārni*. Riga: Jaunā Daugava, 2004.

(F) Cimdiņa, Ausma. *The Origins of Feminism in Latvian Literature and Criticism*, at http://www.women.it/4thfemconf/workshops/refusing8/acimdina.htm.

ATANASIJEVIĆ, Ksenija (1894–1981)

Serbian philosopher, thinker, professor; leading feminist in Yugoslavia in the first half of the twentieth century; member of the presidium of the *Skupštine Lige žena za mir i slobodu* (Serbian Women's League for Peace and Freedom) and editor of the first feminist journal in the country, *Ženski pokret* (The Women's Movement, published from 1920 to 1938).

Ksenija Atanasijević was born on 5 February 1894 in Belgrade. Her mother died during childbirth, a tragedy affecting Ksenija's life in later years. Her father, from a well-off family, was the director of the State Hospital in Belgrade. He passed away when she was just twelve, an event swiftly followed by the death of her brother in World War I. Ksenija Atanasijević was then brought up by her stepmother, Sofija Kondić, an educated woman who taught at the *Viša ženska škola* (Women's College) in Belgrade.

During her high school years, Atanasijević was influenced by a philosophy professor, Nada Stoiljković; it was probably Stoiljković who encouraged her to study philosophy at Belgrade University. She graduated in July 1920 with the highest marks in her graduating class, obtaining a university diploma in "pure and applied philosophy and classics." An excellent student, Ksenija Atanasijević decided to pursue an academic career in philosophy and soon after the graduation, began working on a doctoral thesis on Giordano Bruno's *De triplici minimo.* She visited Geneva and Paris to discuss her thesis with specialists and, on 20 January 1922, defended her Ph.D. with honors in Belgrade. Her thesis was entitled *Brunovo učenje o najmanjem* (Bruno's teaching as given in his work 'De triplici minimo'); upon its completion and successful defense, Atanasijević became the first woman to hold a Ph.D. in Serbia. She was then 28 years old. Soon after, she became the first female university professor to be appointed to the Department of Philosophy at Belgrade University, where she taught classics, medieval and modern philosophy and aesthetics.

Ksenija Atanasijević left a substantial volume of work, including over four hundred texts, among them books and essays in philosophy, psychology, history and literature. Her interest in philosophy was broad and eclectic, covering ethics, metaphysics, logic, aesthetics and the history of philosophy. She is best known for her original interpretations of Giordano Bruno's work and for her 'philosophy of meaning' developed in *Filozofski fragmenti* (Philosophical fragments, 1928–1929), considered by many to be her most significant work. In this, as well as in *Aspekti i analize filozofije humanizma* (Aspects and analyses of a philosophy of humanism, 1969) and *Značenje i vrednost egzistencije* (The meaning and value of existence, 1968), Atanasijević developed an innovative ontological-axiological philosophy of the meaning of human existence across several fields. Some authors regard these works as a blend of different subjects and modes of thought; others insist on speaking of 'intuition' in her philosophical discourse. Her thinking on individuality and social meanings in the form of aphorism anticipated the existentialism of Kafka and J. P. Sartre. She perceived herself not as a 'discursive' but as an 'intuitive' philosopher, yearning to create a philosophy from elements of intuitive-imaginative consciousness. Indeed, Ksenija Atanasijević truly *lived* her philosophy as the praxis of a liberal and moral person. Among the first in Yugoslavia to plainly oppose German nationalism and anti-Semitism in an essay, "Oko za oko" (Eye for an eye), published in the newspaper *Pravda* (Truth) in 1933, she held several lectures on the Jewish contribution to world culture and was subsequently arrested by the Germans in 1942. After the war, the same liberal and moral praxis would lead to Atanasijević's arrest by members of the newly established communist regime.

Ksenija Atanasijević was a committed feminist both in theory and in practice. She was a member of the Presidium of the *Skupštine Lige žena za mir i slobodu* (Serbian Women's League for Peace and Freedom) and editor of the first feminist journal in the country, *Ženski pokret* (The Women's Movement, published from 1920 to 1938).

Atanasijević was also a prominent member of the *Alijansa ženskog pokreta* (Women's Movement Alliance). In this latter capacity, she wrote a number of articles and essays discussing feminist issues relevant to the Serbian society of the time–the place of women in Serbian public sphere, the leadership of the feminist movement and women's suffrage rights–thereby helping to define the main issues and future course of Yugoslav feminism in her time. Her philosophical treatments of the position of 'woman' in culture covered a wide range of themes, from female characters in Greek tragedies to women's emancipation in modern times. She saw the latter as a process, to be realized through the "enhancement of [women's] ethical awareness" and the "conscious determining of her spirituality" (Petrović 2003, 7). Atanasijević's important feminist works include *Etička podloga feminizma* (The ethical basis of feminism, 1927), *Položaj žene u našem javnom životu* (The position of woman in our public life, 1928) and *Feministički pokret i njegove vodje* (The feminist movement and its leaders, 1938).

In 1936, after twelve years of teaching practice, Atanasijević was removed from her university position, the result of a reaction to the liberal ideas she promoted and especially to her decision not to become part of any academic ideological clique. Ksenija Atanasijević's sense of intellectual autonomy meant that not only was she unwilling to accept conservative ideologies structuring her teaching and writing, she was also capable of criticizing the work of her professors and colleagues. At the time, women in Serbia rarely occupied such powerful positions as that of university professor and Atanasijević was perceived as a potential threat to male-dominated philosophy. Although a number of professionals within the academic community saw her dismissal as illegal, with public figures formally protesting the decision (among them the writer Sima Pandurović and other women's activists), Atanasijević's position at Belgrade University was never restored to her. She was later offered a position with the Ministry of Education, followed by a period working for the university and the National Library. She retired in 1946 as an employee of the National Library.

To this day, the bulk of Ksenija Atanasijević's work, which addresses a comprehensive set of important philosophical and cultural questions, continues to be kept out of the academic mainstream in contemporary Serbia.

Iva Nenić
Teaching assistant,
Belgrade Open School

SOURCES

(C) Atanasijević, Ksenija. *O emancipaciji žena kod Platona* (On women's emancipation in Plato). Belgrade: Ženski pokret (Women's movement), 1923.

(C) Atanasijević, Ksenija. *Etička podloga feminizma* (The ethical basis of feminism). Belgrade: Ženski pokret (Women's movement), 1927.

(C) Atanasijević, Ksenija. *Položaj žene u našem javnom životu* (The position of woman in our public life). Belgrade: Reč, 1928.

(C) Atanasijević, Ksenija. *Filozofski fragmenti I i II. Život i rad* (Philosophical fragments. Vols. 1/2. Life and work). Belgrade, 1929–1930.

(C) Atanasijević, Ksenija. *Feministički pokret i njegove vodje* (The feminist movement and its leaders). Belgrade: Život i rad, 1938.

(C) Atanasijević, Ksenija. *La doctrine metaphysique et geometrique de Bruno* (The metaphysical and geometric doctrine of Bruno). Paris/Belgrade, 1933; published in English under the title "The metaphysical and geometric doctrine of Bruno as given in his work 'De triplici minimo'." St. Louis, Mo: W. H. Green, 1972.

(D) Šešić, Bogdan. *Filozofija smisla Ksenije Atanasijević* (preštampano iz *Zbornika za društvene nauke* br. 65) [The philosophy of meaning of Ksenija Atanasijević (from: collection of essays in social sciences number 65)]. Belgrade: Matica Srpska, 1978.

(D) Petrović, Ružica. *Filozofska misao Ksenije Atanasijević* (The philosophical thought of Ksenija Atanasijević). Belgrade: Filozofski fakultet, 2003. Ph.D. thesis.

(E) Pantelić, Ivana. "Prepreke emancipaciji žena u kraljevini Jugoslaviji (1931–1933)" (The obstacles of the women's emancipation in the Kingdom of Yugoslavia, 1931–1933). In *Zbornik Beogradske otvorene škole* (Collection of essays of the Belgrade Open School, BOS). Belgrade: BOS, 2002.

BACHMANN, Ingeborg (1926–1973)

Austrian writer.

Ingeborg Bachmann was born in Klagenfurt in the Austrian state of Carinthia on 25 June 1926. Her mother, Olga Bachmann, born Haas (1901–1998), came originally from Heidenreichstein in Lower Austria, where her family owned a knitwear factory. Her father, Matthias Bachmann (data unknown), came from a Protestant farming family in Obervellach in Carinthia and trained as a primary school teacher in Klagenfurt. He was headmaster of a school in Klagenfurt for many years and served in both World Wars as an officer. Ingeborg Bachmann had two younger siblings: a sister Isolde, born in 1928, and a brother Heinz, born in 1939. From 1932 onwards, she attended primary and secondary school in Klagenfurt, sitting her Matura in 1944 and subsequently attending a teacher training institute until May 1945. Here, Bachmann's German teacher was the popular local writer of 'Heimat' literature and one-time Nazi sympathizer Josef Friedrich Perkonig, whose parochial influence would be significant in, among other works, her first publication, *Die Fähre* (The ferry, 1946).

Bachmann's perception of the dual nature and inheritance of her childhood environment had a lasting effect on her work. On the one hand, the area around Obervellach, situated at the intersection of the geographical and linguistic borders of Austria, Italy and Slovenia, is characterized as an idealized microcosm of the Habsburg Empire, where different peoples, cultures and languages mingled peacefully within one political unit. Following the writer Joseph Roth, Bachmann called this mythical, childhood place Galicien, but in later works its utopian strain is increasingly challenged by its darker, historical aspect. An awareness of the destruction brought about in history is certainly heightened in retrospect, but extracts from Bachmann's diary, written during the summers of 1944 and 1945, show a clear, contemporaneous rejection of Nazi ideology. It could be argued that both Bachmann's life and her life's work are wedged between, on the one hand, the dream of an impossible utopian state in private and public, fictional and historical forms, and on the other hand, between the individual and collective modes of behavior that beset that dream from the outset.

Leaving Klagenfurt in the autumn of 1945, Bachmann studied philosophy, German and psychology, first in Innsbruck, then Graz and finally (from 1946–1949) in Vienna, where she graduated in 1950 with a dissertation on Heidegger, *Die kritische Aufnahme der Existentialphilosophie Martin Heideggers* (Critical reception of the existentialist philosophy of Martin Heidegger, 1949). During this period as a student, she published a number of short stories as well as her first poems and also worked on a novel, *Stadt ohne Namen* (The town without a name), for which she was unable to find a publisher and which subsequently disappeared. But it was as a poet, exploring the nature of time, love and memory that Bachmann was to become famous. It was also during this period that she became part of the literary establishment of post-war Vienna. As a member of Hans Weigel's group in Café Raimund, Bachmann became acquainted with the most important literary figures of post-war Vienna, including Ilse Aichinger and many others. Her most significant contact here was Paul Celan, with whom Bachmann conducted an extraordinary literary dialogue through her work. They dedicated work to one another and, within their texts, wove a complex network of mutual quotations and references. Their close personal and intellectual relationship was to endure until Celan's death in 1971.

In April 1952, Hans Werner Richter, the established West-German writer and editor, invited Bachmann and Celan to attend a meeting of the *Gruppe '47* (Group '47) in Niendorf an der Ostsee. The following year, Bachmann was awarded the prestigious *Preis der Gruppe '47* (Group '47 Prize), an event that marked Bachmann's breakthrough as a writer and her branching out from the Viennese cultural milieu. She resigned from her job as a scriptwriter with the radio-broadcaster *Rot-Weiß-Rot* (Red-White-Red) in Vienna and shortly afterwards moved to Rome. From 1953 onwards, Bachmann collaborated with Hans Werner Henze, contributing poems and libretti for (among others) his *Nachtstücke und Arien* (Night-pieces and arias), *Der Prinz von Homburg* (The prince of Homburg), and *Der junge Lord* (The young lord). In 1953, her first collection of poetry, *Die gestundete Zeit* (Mortgaged time) was published to critical acclaim, followed in 1956 by a second collection, *Anrufung des Großen Bären* (Incantation of the great bear). Despite the fact that Bachmann had also by now published short stories and essays (on Wittgenstein, Musil and others) and had broadcast her first radio play, *Ein Geschäft mit Träumen* (The business of dreams, 1952), she was publicly cast in the role of a slightly helpless, faltering and feminine, if intellectually brilliant poet. This image was to dominate until she was re-read in the context of feminist and critical theory in the 1980s.

In July 1958, Bachmann met the Swiss writer Max Frisch in Paris and began a relationship that was to have a significant personal impact on her life and work. Between 1958 and 1962, they lived in Zurich and Rome. In 1959, Bachmann was awarded the *Hörspielpreis der Kriegsblinden* (Radio Play Prize of the War-blind) for her radio play *Der gute Gott von Manhattan* (The good God of Manhattan, 1958). In 1959/60, she was a guest lecturer at the Universität Frankfurt, where she met the Frankfurt School philosopher T. W. Adorno, and, through him, Gerschom Scholem. In June 1961, she published translations of the poetry of Giuseppe Ungaretti as well as *Das dreißigste*

Jahr (The thirtieth year), her first collection of short stories. It received a mixed reaction, but the dominant view was that articulated by the influential critic Marcel Reich-Ranicki, that it was the work of a fallen poet.

Following the end of her relationship with Frisch in autumn 1962, Bachmann suffered a nervous breakdown, delaying her move to Berlin to take up a Ford Foundation scholarship until the spring of 1963. During this period, she began work on what was to develop into the *Todesarten* Project (Ways of death)–a compendium of the means by which society murders women. By the time of her death in 1973, thousands of pages of *Todesarten* fragments existed; but only one completed novel, *Malina* (1971), described by the author as an overture to the cycle, and a loosely related collection of short stories, *Simultan* (Paths to the lake, 1972), had been published.

Thematically, it could be said that the *Todesarten* texts cohere around the redefinition of war. They look to the perpetuation of fascist modes of behavior in the acceptable practices of society and individuals, and in particular in the relationships between men and women. One of the dominant means of death suffered by the protagonists in the *Todesarten* is the attack on their ability to speak for and define themselves; they suffocate in gas chambers, they have their mouths attacked, their language stolen, they become the objects of someone else's study, they become trapped in the texts of others. This was a fate Bachmann herself suffered repeatedly. From Hans Weigel's book, *Unvollendete Symphonie* (Unfinished symphony, 1951), to Max Frisch's *Mein Name sei Gantenbein* (Gantenbein, 1965), and *Montauk* (Montauk, 1975), to Adolf Opel's *Ingeborg Bachmann in Ägypten* (Ingeborg Bachmann in Egypt, 1996), and *'Wo mir das Lachen zurückgekommen ist...' Auf Reisen mit Ingeborg Bachmann* ('Where I rediscovered laughter...' Travels with Ingeborg Bachmann, 2001), the writer's private life was repeatedly made into the fodder of others' publications, a fate referred to in the *Todesarten* fragment, *Fanny Goldmann* (1978) as "slaughter on 386 pages" (Koschel et al. 1978, 515). The project as a whole is thus a collection of lives, stories and histories that have been erased from public view; it makes visible the invisible murders in society and links them to the manner of exercising power that also underpinned the Holocaust. In Bachmann's work, where the women repeatedly fall victim to men yielding power in the manner of Bluebeards, fascists and colonizers, relations between the sexes offer a prototype for the destruction of one human life by another. It is this fundamental structuring principle and theme of her work that was only highlighted from the 1980s onwards, when feminist critics recognized that the seemingly vulnerable, low-voiced poet was engaged in an uncompromisingly critical exploration of patriarchy. While Bachmann did not identify herself as a feminist and was not associated with the feminist movement, her intellectual contribution to the analysis of the gender of power is unique. By allowing historical truths to emerge in the fates of fictional victims, Bachmann not only followed her own conviction that "the individual does not live in history, but history in the individual" (Koschel et al. 1978, 230), but also linked a specifically patriarchal history to the smothering of a female voice. That smothering, according to Bachmann, takes place in marriage as it does in murder, in grand narratives as in small.

From 1965 onwards, Bachmann was again based in Rome but continued to travel extensively. Among her most important trips were those to Athens and Egypt (1964) and to Poland (including Auschwitz) in 1973. She was now working primarily on the *Todesarten* texts, while also continuing her collaboration with Hans Werner Henze. She was awarded the *Georg Büchner Preis* (Georg Büchner Prize) in 1964 and the *Großer Österreichischer Staatspreis* (Austrian State Prize) in 1968.

Bachmann died in Rome on 17 October 1973 as a combined result of injuries sustained in a burning accident in her apartment on 26 September 1973 and complications caused by her addiction to prescription drugs. Bachmann herself dated this problem back to the break-up of her relationship with Max Frisch in 1962. She was buried in Annabichl Cemetery in Klagenfurt on 25 October 1973.

Since the first publication of her collected works (four volumes) in 1978, the characterization of Bachmann as a lost poet has been increasingly challenged by a more politically charged view of her social and literary concerns. During the 1980s, critical attention shifted steadily from her early work to a focus on the *Todesarten* Project. Since the publication of the *Todesarten* critical edition (four volumes) in 1995, two volumes of finished and unfinished poetry have been published, *Letzte, unveröffentlichte Gedichte. Entwürfe und Fassungen* (Final unpublished poems. Sketches and versions, 1998). *Ich weiß keine bessere Welt* (I know of no better world, 2000), and extracts of her 1945/46 diary have also been released. Her 8,000 page estate, of which some 300 pages have been locked away until 2025, is held at the National Library in Vienna.

Caitríona Leahy
Trinity College, Dublin

SOURCES

(B) Albrecht, Monika and Dirk Göttsche, eds. *Bachmann Handbuch. Leben–Werk–Wirkung* (Bachmann handbook. Life–work–legacy). Stuttgart, Weimar: Verlag J. B. Metzler, 2002.

(C) Koschel, Christine, Inge von Weidenbaum and Clemens Münster, eds. *Ingeborg Bachmann. Werke I-IV* (Ingeborg Bachmann. Works I-IV). Munich, Zurich: Piper Verlag, 1978.

(C) Albrecht, Monika and Dirk Göttsche, eds. *Ingeborg Bachmann. "Todesarten"-Projekt. Kritische Ausgabe* (Ingeborg Bachmann. Ways of death. Critical edition). Unter Leitung von Robert Pichl. Munich, Zurich: Piper Verlag, 1995.

(D) Höller, Hans. *Ingeborg Bachmann.* Reinbek bei Hamburg: Rowohlt Taschenbuch Verlag, 1999.

(D) Weigel, Sigrid. *Ingeborg Bachmann. Hinterlassenschaften unter Wahrung des Briefgeheimnisses* (Ingeborg Bachmann. Secret legacies). Vienna: Paul Zsolnay Verlag, 1999.

(D) Hoell, Joachim. *Ingeborg Bachmann.* Munich: Deutscher Taschenbuch Verlag, 2001.

BAIULESCU, Maria (1860–1941)

Accomplished author, civic organizer, Romanian nationalist and feminist leader.

Daughter of Orthodox Archpriest (Protopop) Bartolomeu (1831–1909) and Elena Baiulescu, Maria Baiulescu grew up in an intellectual family in the relatively prosperous region of Brasov and received an exceptionally good education for a Romanian woman at the time. After graduating from the Girls French Institute and the German Secondary School in Brasov, Baiulescu began her writing career as a translator. She published some early articles under the pseudonym of Sulfina. She later used her own name and published widely in Transylvanian newspapers and in the *Enciclopedia română* (Romanian Encyclopedia). Her topics included poetry, prose and commentaries on society and politics. Her correspondence indicates that she was well connected among Romanian leaders and intellectuals and generally admired for her views.

Baiulescu was notably active in Transylvanian civil associations. She translated and wrote plays for the popular *Societatea pentru crearea unui fond de teatru român* (Society for the Creation of a Romanian Theater Fund). She also served as a lecturer and an author for 'Astra,' or the *Asociațiunea transilvană pentru literatura și cultura poporului român* (Transylvanian Association for the Literature and Culture of the Romanian People)–the largest Romanian civil association in the Habsburg Empire–before leading the women's subsection of Astra's medical and biopolitical section from 1927 until 1935. A long-standing activist in the *Reuniunea Femeilor Române din Brașov* (Brasov's Romanian Women's Society), she served as the society's President from 1908 until 1935. In 1913, Baiulescu also initiated the *Uniunea Femeilor Române* (Union of Romanian Women), an association that brought together over one hundred women's organizations for the purpose of creating a center where women could meet one another, exchange ideas and work together for common goals. After World War I, she headed the *Uniunea Femeilor Române*, withdrawing from the leadership of the association in 1935 at the age of seventy five.

In her leadership roles and in her writings, Baiulescu emphasized three primary spheres in which women contributed to their communities: the social and philanthropic, the national and the political. Her own social and philanthropic work concentrated on children, the infirm and the elderly. She is often noted for supporting the boarding school for poor or orphaned girls funded by the *Reuniunea Femeilor Române*. Under her direction the school taught housekeeping and household industry, theoretical and practical instruction in subjects such as sewing, gardening and hygiene, in addition to academic disciplines such as foreign languages and history. Although the practical skills in housekeeping and household industry confined women to a distinctly 'feminine' sphere, they also enabled graduates to support themselves as dressmakers, teachers or governesses.

Baiulescu envisioned women at the forefront of the Romanian national movement. Priests and male school teachers had traditionally served as national leaders for village communities (where most Romanians lived), but Baiulescu believed that they had largely abandoned their national roles, for fear of losing their living stipends from what most Romanian nationalists viewed as a centralizing Hungarian state intent on assimilating non-Hungarians (i.e. before 1918). She argued that only women were capable of preserving the Romanian nation. By providing proper care and education for their children, women raised both health standards and national consciousness. Their work, in short, safeguarded the health of the nation. To realize her vision, Baiulescu strove to improve the basic care of children and reduce infant mortality through, for example, basic hygiene standards. She urged Romanian women to teach their children the Romanian language and national traditions and assigned to women the task of preserving Romanian folk costumes. These symbols of Romanian nationality ostensibly separated Romanians from Hungarians, Germans, Jews, Gypsies and all other 'non-Romanians' in Hungary, and Baiulescu counted on women to maintain the distinctions.

In many ways Baiulescu's feminism resembles what scholars such as Mary Beth Norton have called "republican motherhood," especially the ideal of the "mother-educator"; but, unlike many advocates of a domestic sphere for wives and mothers, Baiulescu also worked to have women accepted in society as equals to men. She was, for instance, a forceful voice for extending suffrage and civil rights to women. In 1918, Baiulescu was a founding member of the *Asociația pentru emanciparea civilă și politică a femeilor române* (*AECPFR*, Association for the Civil and Political Emancipation of Romanian Women), dedicated to preparing women for exercising political rights and taking on public duties. In the 1920s, Baiulescu was one of a handful of women in dialogue with the Romanian Minister of Justice on drafts of civil rights legislation (which remained in draft form). She was also well informed of events across Europe and in frequent contact with supporters of women's rights in France, Switzerland, Sweden, Belgium and Hungary. The Red Cross in Sweden (1929) and Belgium (1935) commemorated her work with medals. The *Országos Gyermekvédő Liga* (Hungarian League for the Protection of Children) also recognized her specific work with children.

Baiulescu's feminist views are best understood within the context of a larger Romanian national movement. Throughout Baiulescu's lifetime, Romanian leaders worked to build an autonomous national community. Baiulescu fully participated in this work, striving to create a significant place for women in the Romanian national community while it was being organized. Baiulescu often referred to Romanian women as "the mothers of our people," a telling expression indicating that her feminism was subordinated to her nationalism. This contextualization of women's roles within the nation follows the views of her parents who, as leaders of Romanian civil associations, promoted women as mothers with moral duties to their families and to their extended national family. (Elena Baiulescu, for example, served on the leadership committee of the Romanian Women's Society in Brasov during the 1890s.) After the creation of Greater Romania in 1918, the focus of Romanian nationalists changed; they no longer needed to defend the Romanian nation from a centralizing Hungarian state but aimed to strengthen and unify the fledging national community. In this very different context, Maria Baiulescu's views do not seem to have changed much. Although her correspondence offers little insight on her specific views of the burgeoning feminist movement in interwar Romania, her continued activism until her death on 24 June 1941 demonstrated that she supported women's emancipation because women made important philanthropic and educational contributions to the nation.

Tanya Dunlap
Rice University, Houston,
Texas, U.S.A.

SOURCES

(C) Nazare, Ruxandra Moaşa, ed. *Maria Baiulescu (1860-1941) Corespondenţă* (Maria Baiulescu, 1860-1941. Correspondence). Bucharest: Ars Docendi, 2001.

(E) Glodariu, Elena. "Unele consideraţii privind mişcarea feministă din Transilvania (a doua jumătate a sec. al XIX-lea - începutul sec. al XX-lea)" (Considerations on the feminist movement in Transylvania from the second half of the nineteenth century until the beginning of the twentieth century). *Acta Musei Napocensis* XX (1983): 231-40.

(E) Radu, Măriuca. "File din activitatea Reuniunii femeilor române din Braşov (1850-1918)" (Activities of the Romanian Women's Society in Brasov, 1850-1918). *Cumidava* XV-XIX (1990-94): 161-76.

(E) Mihăilescu, Ştefania. *Emanciparea femeii române: Antologie de texte. Vol. I 1815-1918* (The emancipation of Romanian women: an anthology of texts. Vol. 1 1815-1918). Bucharest: Editura Ecumenica, 2001.

BELOVIĆ-BERNADZIKOWSKA, Jelica (1870–1946)

Bosnian pedagogue, ethnographer and writer; editor-in-chief of *Srpkinja* (The Serbian woman, 1913); pseudonyms Ljube T. Daničić, Jelica, Jele, Jasna, Hele, teta Jelica and Mlada Ana gospoja.

Jelica Belović was born in Osijek, Croatia on 25 February 1870, into an ethnically mixed middle-class family of teachers. Josip, her Croatian-born father of Montenegrin descent, taught at the Osijek gymnasium. Her Croatian-born mother Katerina (born Fragner) was of German descent and tutored young children in order to make ends meet, following the untimely death of her husband in 1875. At home, Jelica and her younger siblings, Gabriela and Josip, spoke French, German, Italian and Serbo-Croatian. By her own admission she was a precocious, highly-strung child. According to Belović this often got her into trouble with her mother, who favored her son over her daughters. This early experience sensitized her to sexual inequality that she would later challenge. Despite having lost her father at the tender age of five, Belović later attributed her love of books and learning to him. She graduated from elementary school in Osijek, gymnasium in Djakovo, teacher's college in Zagreb and later went on to higher pedagogical studies in Vienna and Paris. She went on to teach in various locations including Zagreb and Osijek.

In 1895, Jelica Belović moved to Bosnia-Herzegovina to teach in girls' schools in Mostar and Sarajevo. The country had been an occupied territory of the Austro-Hungarian Empire since the Congress of Berlin in 1878. While working in Mostar, she met and fell in love with a handsome civil servant of the Austro-Hungarian Empire named Janko Bernadzikowski. They married in February 1896. She was thereafter known as Jelica Belović-Bernadzikowska. With Janko she had two children, Vladimir and Jasna. In 1898 she became the principal (*upraviteljica*) of the girls' gymnasium in Banja Luka in Bosnia, where she remained until the end of WWI.

Her passion for education led her to become among the most prolific contemporary female writers of the South Slavs. The two subjects that consumed her throughout her life were pedagogy and ethnography. She contributed articles to several periodicals on the subject of pedagogy, including *Školski Vjesnik* (The school courier),

Školski Odjek (The school echo) and *Školski List* (The school journal). She also translated studies on pedagogy and wrote books on the subject, including *Iz moga albuma* (From my album, 1900). Belović-Bernadzikowska also contributed to children's periodicals such as *Spomenak* (Forget-me-not) and wrote children's books including *Naša omladinska literature* (Our youth literature, 1897) and *Meanderi* (Meanderings, 1900).

Belović-Bernadzikowska's second great passion was ethnography, especially folk arts. Her contemporaries called her the female counterpart to Vuk Karadžic (1787–1864), ethnographer and the father of Serbian folk studies. Among some of her best known works were the *Gradja za Tehnološki Rječnik Ženskog Ručnog Rada* (Technical dictionary of women's handiwork, 1898), *Poljske cvijeće* (Polish blooms, 1899), *Hrvatska čitma* (Croatian lace, 1906) and *Srpski narodni vez I tekstilna ornamenti* (Serbian national embroidery and textile ornaments, 1907). Belović-Bernadzikowska also collaborated over a long time with the well-known ethnographer, sexologist and editor-in-chief of *Anthropophyteia* (1904–1913), Dr. Friedrich Salomo Krauss (1859–1938).

Keenly aware of her unusual position as a highly educated woman and sensitive to sexual inequality (having experienced it firsthand on more than one occasion), Belović-Bernadzikowska became involved in improving the social and cultural status of women. Over the years she published numerous articles on the changing roles of women in the public and private spheres. Some of these included "Žena Budućnosti" (Woman of the future) and "Moderne Žene" (Modern women), both of which appeared in a special women's issue of Herzegovina's literary-cultural journal *Zora* (Dawn) in 1899. Here, Belović-Bernadzikowska argued that the modern woman was not limited by her obligations as wife and mother; that the ideal modern woman understood that it was her duty to contribute to the social and cultural welfare of her people. She needed to be well-read and educated so that she could better serve both her community and her family. In this way she could become a completely developed individual, tender-hearted and enlightened, mother of her family and mother to her nation. In Krauss' *Anthropophyteia* and under the pseudonym Ljube T. Daničić, she also contributed a series of articles on the social and sexual lives of rural South Slavs.

A turning point in her career came in 1910, at a pan-Slav congress in Prague. The congress featured an exhibition of Serbian women's arts and crafts where Belović-Bernadzikowska displayed embroidery from Bosnia-Herzegovina. It was here that the idea of a Serbian women's almanac was conceived. In 1913, the first and only volume of *Srpkinja* (The Serbian woman) was produced in Sarajevo with Belović-Bernadzikowska as its editor-in-chief. It was the first Serbian magazine to be produced by women for women. Until then, Serbian women writers had been dependent on the patronage of their male counterparts. The almanac's purpose was two-fold: to introduce women's folk arts and to highlight the literary and cultural work of leading women. While putting together the almanac, she corresponded with over eighty women and in the process identified 150 Serbian women writers in the almanac.

Over the years, Belović-Bernadzikowska had acquired numerous professional contacts. Among them were established Serbian male intellectuals and publicists such as Jovan Jovanović Zmaj (1833–1904), Vid Vuletić Vukašović (1853–1939) and Tihomir Ostojić (1865–1921). She also corresponded with women writers and publicists such as Savka Subotić (b.1834), ***Stoja Kašiković*** (b.1865) and mentored others. By her own account she corresponded with over four hundred intellectuals across Europe.

Following WWI, Belović-Bernadzikowska continued to teach and write. She was a teacher at a co-ed school in Novi Sad, Serbia (1918–1936). Although her publishing career slowed down, it did not cease altogether. In 1918, she edited the Yugoslav journal *Naša snaga* (Our strength) and among her books was *Die Sitten der Südslawen* (The customs of the South Slavs), published in 1927. Belović-Bernadzikowska remained in Novi Sad until her death on 30 June 1946.

Belovic-Bernadzikowska's personal motto "U borni je život—u radu je spas!" can be roughly translated as "In the struggle of life, work brings salvation!" (Jelkić 1929, 66). She was indeed a prolific writer who published close to forty books and numerous articles. In this way, she contributed to the growth of women's cultural and social activism in Bosnia-Herzegovina.

Jelica Zdero
PhD Candidate,
The University of Western Ontario, Canada

SOURCES

(A) Historical Archive of Sarajevo, Family and Individual Archival Collection, Belović-Bernadzikowska, Jelica (1875–1909), Box 1. Jelica Belović-Bernadzikowska's personal archival collection includes official documents, letters written to her and by her, as well as a lengthy memoir that encompasses all major developments in her personal and professional life up to about 1909.

(A) Historical Archive of Bosnia-Herzegovina, Provincial Government of Sarajevo, Collection of Personnel Files, Belović-Bernadzikowska, Jelica. Jelica Belović-Bernadzikowska's professional archival collection includes mainly official letters between herself and the Provincial Government of Sarajevo which was the Austro-Hungarian Empire's official administrative institution in Bosnia-Herzegovina. Also included are official documents about the Banja Luka girls' school and other printed material about her.

(B) Journal *Škola* (School) (1898).

(B) Journal *Smilje* (Immortelle) (1898).

(B) Journal *Zora* (Dawn) (1899).

(B) Almanac *Srpkinja* (The Serbian woman) (1913).

(D) Jelkić, Dušan. *Četrdeset Godina Književnog Rada Jelice Belović-Bernadzikowske* (Forty years of the literary work of Jelica Belović-Bernadzikowska). Sarajevo: Štamparija Obod, 1925.

(D) Jelkić, Dušan. *Jelica Belović. Njezin Život i Rad.* (Jelica Belović. Her life and work). Novi Sad, 1929.

BENICZKY, Hermin (Mrs Pál Veres) (1815-1895)

Campaigner for women's education in Hungary; founder (1868) and President (1868–1895) of the Hungarian *Országos Nőképző Egyesület* (*ONKE*, National Association for Women's Education); co-founder (1869) of the first high school for girls in Hungary.

Statue of Mrs Pál Veres in Erzsébet Square, Budapest, surrounded by pupils from the schools of the *Országos Nőképző Egyesület* (ONKE), 1916. The statue, still there today, bears an inscription that reads: "Mrs Pál Veres, Hermin Beniczky. She fought so that women, with their education and their hearts, could advance the welfare of the nation."

On 13 December 1815, Hermin Beniczky was born in Losonc, Nógrád County (today Lučenec, central Slovakia) and baptized in the local Lutheran church. Hermin Beniczky's father, Pál Beniczky (died 1816), was a Nógrád landowner from a high ranking Protestant family. Her mother, Karolina Sturmann (died 1831), was from a wealthy entrepreneurial family; Hermin's maternal grandfather, Márton Sturmann, was well known for his philanthropy and dedication to national causes and to Protestantism.

Most sources agree that Hermin was the second of three girls. After the death of Pál Beniczky, she and her two sisters (Maria and Lotti), her mother and her mother's widowed sister–all German speaking–moved to a residence in Buda purchased for them by Márton Sturmann. When Hermin was sixteen, her mother died in a cholera epidemic. An erudite, literary woman who had undertaken philanthropic work in the field of education, Karolina Sturmann continued to be a role model for her daughter after her death.

Having lost both their parents, the three Beniczky sisters went to live with their grandfather at Tótgyörk in Pest County (today Galgagyörk). Throughout the 1830s, Hermin attempted to structure study periods for herself in geography and history, but an eye-infection made reading difficult. She began keeping diaries, in which she emphasized the values of discipline, application and self-development.

In 1839, Hermin Beniczky married Pál Veres (1815-1886), a Protestant public notary and executive county deputy from a wealthy landowning family in Nógrád County. The couple settled in Vanyarc (Nógrád County) and in 1842 a daughter, Szilárda, was born. In 1844, a son was also born but he died a few days later, bringing on a persistent state of ill health for Mrs Pál Veres Hermin Beniczky (hereafter Beniczky) and an intense attachment to Szilárda, whom she took wherever she went. Beniczky was an avid observer of the 1848 revolutions and savored the political language of autonomy for the individual and the nation in which they were embedded. Surrounded by a social circle of famous revolutionary figures, including Lajos Kossuth, and influenced by theories of education developed by Jean-Jacques Rousseau, Johann Heinrich Pestalozzi and Jean Paul Richter, Beniczky began to reflect on the lack of importance attached to girls' education and on ways to increase the 'social value' of young girls and provide them with a sense of self-worth. As Szilárda grew older, Beniczky employed university-trained teachers to give her daughter classes in Hungarian literature and history, in which Beniczky herself routinely participated. During the frequent absences of Pál Veres, Beniczky worked hard on her Hungarian language skills and read Hungarian literature. The relationship between a woman's self-esteem and her national identity was becoming increasingly central to Beniczky's personal views; later, it would also be a strong motivational element in her public initiatives to transform the young Hungarian woman into "a more valuable and useful member of Hungarian society" through "valuing herself more highly" (*ONKE Évkönyve* 1868/69, 1–2).

Szilárda married and moved away in 1861. By this time, Hermin Beniczky had made friends with the writer and poet Imre Madách. In 1864, Madách gave a public lecture in which he spoke of women's incapacities and fundamental weaknesses. Dismayed and angry, Beniczky wrote to Madách criticizing the contradictions of his position; that if, as Madách had asserted in his lecture, women were the basis of the family then this was an argument for, and not against the education of women. Madách apologized, but in Beniczky's mind the writer had inadvertantly drawn attention to a more pervasive problem in need of address. In 1865 she published an article, "Felhívás a nőkhöz" (Call to women), in the national newspaper *Hon* (Homeland), in which she argued that if women had a primary role in bringing up children and the future nation, their education was in the national interest. She urged her readers to promote girls' education and encourage their daughters in academic study, concluding with the suggestion that women of the larger towns hold a meeting to discuss the problem and collect ideas.

After the publication of "Felhívás a nőkhöz," Beniczky spent the next year eliciting support from prominent individuals and women's organizations across the country. On 24 May 1867, 22 of Beniczky's contacts–all of them women–gathered in Pest and debated the need for a national organization to develop women's intellectual and practical skills. In January 1868, the Hungarian Ministry of the Interior approved the *Országos Nőképző Egyesület* (*ONKE*, National Association for Women's Education) with Hermin Beniczky as President and Countess Josefin Teleki as Vice President. In that year, Beniczky published a pamphlet, *Nézetek a női ügy érdekében* (For the woman's cause), which denounced lack of access to education as a state of ignorance enforced upon women of all social classes.

The first years of *ONKE* were busy ones of networking, at home and abroad. In 1869, Beniczky was invited to Germany by the *Allgemeiner Deutscher Frauenverein* (General German Women's Association). At a speech delivered to an international philosophy congress in Frankfurt in the October of that year, she spoke on behalf of "we Hungarian women" in her native language, German (Rudnay Józsefné 1902, 254). For Beniczky and the women of *ONKE*, nothing less than a fully integrated system of public secondary education for girls was required. Hungarian legislation on national education, passed in 1868, had made primary education for girls compulsory but provided no "institutional support" for their secondary schooling, as it did for boys (*ONKE Évkönyve* 1868/69, 1). Beniczky supervised the collection of nine thousand women's signatures for a petition demanding that women's further education be brought to the attention of Parliament. On 17 October 1869, *ONKE* opened a private school for girls over thirteen in the two rooms of a Pest apartment. The two-year syllabus consisted of 24 classes weekly in the first year and 22 in the second. Particular emphasis was placed on the study of Hungarian language and culture. Other subjects included psychology, German, French, arithmetic, aesthetics, natural science, health education, housekeeping, logic and ethics. In 1881, in part thanks to Beniczky's fundraising activities, the school acquired larger premises in Budapest's Zöldfa Street (today Veres Pálné utca, Mrs Pál Veres Street).

At times, work at the new school could be especially demanding. Early in the 1870s, Beniczky gave in to Catholic parents' demands that teachers in the school should not be Protestant. Tensions escalated and almost resulted in her resignation as President of *ONKE*, but she was persuaded that such a step would be beneficial neither for the association nor the school. By 1893 (*ONKE*'s jubilee year), the school had grown to eight hundred students from an initial fourteen. The Mayor of Budapest attended the jubilee celebrations and tribute was paid to Beniczky's work. Back in 1879, Hermin Beniczky had become one of the first non-noble women to receive the *Koronás Arany Érdemkereszt* (Crown Golden Order of Merit) from the King of Hungary; now, the school itself received a Golden Cross from Ferenc József. In that same jubilee year (1893), Erzsébet (Elizabeth), Queen of Hungary, visited the school for the third time since its relocation to Zöldfa Street, where Beniczky met her in poor health.

Hermin Beniczky spent the last two years of her life organizing housekeeping courses on behalf of *ONKE* with the help of her daughter Szilárda. She also compiled accounts of her own and others' teaching experiences, showing the positive effects of women's education. These were published as a book, *Tapasztalati lélektan felnőttek számára* (Practical psychology for adults) in 1895, the year of Hermin Beniczky's death and the year women were first admitted to university courses in Hungary. In reaction to this latter development, the *ONKE* school became the first Hungarian *gimnázium* (high school) for girls on 2 October 1896. In 1906, a statute was erected in

Budapest in memory of Hermin Beniczky, bearing an inscription that reads (in part): "She fought so that women, with their education and their hearts, could advance the welfare of the nation."

Anna Loutfi
Doctoral Candidate, Department of History,
Central European University, Budapest

SOURCES

(B) *Országos Nőképző Egylet Évkönyvei, 1868-1894* (Yearbooks of the National Association for Women's Education, 1868-1894).

(B) Rudnay, József (Mrs) (Hermin Beniczky's daughter). *Emlékeim, 1847-1917* (My memoirs, 1847-1917). Budapest, 1922.

(C) Beniczky, Hermin. "Felhívás a nőkhöz" (Call to women) (1865). In Mrs József Rudnay and Mrs Gyula Szigethy. *Veres Pálné Beniczky Hermin élete es működése* (The life and works of Mrs Pál Veres, Hermin Beniczky). Budapest: Országos Nőképző Egylet, 1902, 136-139.

(C) Beniczky, Hermin. *Nézetek a női ügy érdekében* (For the woman's cause). Pest, 1868.

(C) Beniczky, Hermin. *Tapasztalati lélektan felnőttek számára* (Practical psychology for adults). Budapest, 1895.

(C/D) Rudnay, József (Mrs) and Mrs Gyula Szigethy. *Veres Pálné Beniczky Hermin élete és működése* (The life and works of Mrs Pál Veres, Hermin Beniczky). Budapest: Országos Nőképző Egylet, 1902. This volume, in addition to biographical information, includes assorted writings and personal correspondance.

(D) Szinnyei, József. "Veres Pálné." In *Magyar írók* (Hungarian writers). Budapest, 1914, XIV: 1112-1114.

(D) Béla Gonczy, ed. *Veres Pálné szül. Beniczky Hermin emlékezete. Az Országos Nőképző-Egyesület emlékünnepélyei* (In memory of Mrs Pál Veres, born Hermin Beniczky. The memorial celebrations of the National Association for Women's Education). Budapest: Országos Nőképző Egylet, 1915/16.

(D) Bagossy, Éva M. [Hermin Beniczky's great-great-granddaughter]. *Veres Pálné*. Budapest, 1996.

BISCHITZ, Johanna (born Hani Fischer, later Johanna Hevesi Bischitz) (1827–1898)

Founder and long-term President of the *Pesti Izraelita Nőegylet* (Pest Israelite Women's Association), Hungary's largest Jewish women's association; member and Honorary Member of numerous other women's associations in and outside of Hungary.

Johanna Bischitz was born Hani Fischer in the Hungarian town of Tata (Komárom County) in 1827, the third of ten children of Moritz (Mór) Fischer (1799–1880), director and owner of the world-famous 'Herend' porcelain factory, and Mária Salzer (1799–1886), of whom little is known. During the Hungarian Revolution of 1848/49, Hani (Johanna) cared for the wounded Hungarian soldiers her father had accommodated in his house. Due to his internationally renowned financial success, Fischer was ennobled in 1867 and added the Hungarian name 'Farkasházi' to his own family name. In October 1852, Johanna married the widower David Bischitz (1811–1897), a well-off merchant and landowner from Sárbogárd (Fejér County), and moved to Pest (one of the cities unified as Budapest in 1873). She became the stepmother of three children from her husband's previous marriage and gave birth to another four children.

Reacting to the pauperization of a large segment of the Jewish urban (particularly female) population, Johanna Bischitz set up a women's association to provide relief, together with eleven other women. After an initial refusal by the city of Pest to accept a Jewish women's association, on the grounds that the women should join non-Jewish associations, Bischitz, with the support of Chief Rabbi Wolf A. Meisel (1816–1867), finally succeeded in founding the *Pesti Izraelita Nőegylet* (*PIN*, Pest Israelite Women's Association) in the spring of 1866. Mária Gottesmann was elected President and Bischitz, Vice-President; later, from 1873 until her death in 1898, Bischitz presided over the *PIN*. Her tireless efforts helped make the association one of the best-known institutions in Budapest.

An important accomplishment of the *PIN* was the establishment of Hungary's first Jewish *leány árvaház* (girls' orphanage), which opened on 6 October 1867. Later, on 1 November 1875, a similar institution was set up, a *leány árvamenhely* (orphan girls' asylum) for girls who had lost one or both of their parents. Katalin Gerő (1853–1944) was the director of the girls' orphanage and asylum from 1898 until the end of her life. During this period–spanning two world wars–the orphanage took care of over 1300 Jewish girls. It ran one of the most progressive teacher-training schools in the country and worked closely with different vocational training programs for women in Budapest.

One particularly successful initiative launched by the *Pesti Izraelita Nőegylet* was its *népkonyha* (soup kitchen), opened on 15 November 1869. Working in close cooperation with the Pest authorities, the kitchen was not only open throughout the year, but became a model for other soup kitchens established after 1873. The activities of the *Pesti Izraelita Nőegylet* also fostered exchange between Jewish and non-Jewish communities; in the kosher soup kitchen, people of different religions could meet in a 'semi-public' space on a regular basis. In the 1870s, over 65,000 warm meals were served per year. At the outbreak of World War I, this number had risen to 280,000. For this project alone, the women of the *Pesti Izraelita Nőegylet* set up a large-scale network of donations. Johanna Bischitz made contact with Baron Moritz de Hirsch (1831–1896) in Paris, one of the great Jewish philanthropists of his time, whom she convinced in the 1870s to set up a foundation in Hungary and who annually donated an incredible 120,000 gulden.

Besides her highly professional charitable work, Bischitz believed in modern educational programs and solid vocational training for women and girls. As part of her efforts to improve the situation of women in Budapest, she entered into long-lasting forms of cooperation with other women's associations: the *Fővárosi Szegény Gyermekekért Egylet* (Capital's Kindergarten Association for Poor Children); the *Fröbel Frauenverein* (Fröbel Women's Association); the *Országos Nőképző Egyesület* (National Association for Women's Education), which led campaigns for the education and vocational training of women after its foundation in 1868, and the *Mária Dorothea Egyesület* (Mária Dorothea Association), which represented the interests of female teachers. In the early twentieth century, some members of the *Pesti Izraelita Nőegylet* also made contact with the *Feministák Egyesülete* (Feminist Association) (research is still in its initial stages).

Johanna Bischitz was one of the very few women in Hungary to become famous in her own lifetime. In 1871, as a representative of the *PIN*, Bischitz was visited by the Austrian Empress and Queen of Hungary, Elizabeth, in the Jewish girls' orphanage. In 1879, Bischitz received the *Koronás Arany Érdemkereszt* (Crown Golden Order of Merit), very likely the first non-noble woman of Hungary to be decorated in this way. She also gained international recognition, receiving the *Natalie medal* from the Serbian royal family and the medal of the *Société royale et centrale des sauveteurs de Belgique* (Royal and Central Society of Rescuers in Belgium) from King Leopold I of Belgium. In 1895, the Bischitz family was ennobled (probably because of Johanna Bischitz's achievements but in this period it was customary to use the name of the 'paterfamilias' only) and added the Hungarian name 'Hevesi' to its family name (indicating that the family originated from the area of Heves; later they shortened the entire family name to simply 'Hevesy'). The famous chemist George de Hevesy (1885–1966), awarded the Nobel Prize in his field in 1943, was a grandson of Johanna Bischitz.

Johanna Bischitz died on 28 March 1898 at the age of 71. When she was buried on 30 March, newspapers reported a funeral "like Kossuth's," referring to Lajos Kossuth, the Hungarian national hero of the 1848/49 revolution, [*Egyenlőség* (Equality), no. 14 (3 April 1898): 8]. Like Kossuth's, her coffin was accompanied by thousands of mourners.

Her tireless initiatives and hard-won accomplishments made her the most prominent representative of Jewish charitable work in Hungary in the second half of the nineteenth century. She was charismatic, intelligent and empathetic, an excellent networker and organizer. Her work combined bourgeois charitable work, a modernized form of religious *zedaka* (the Jewish obligation to help the poor) and a far-sighted awareness of the increasing need to create forms of support for women and girls, whom she saw as particularly vulnerable social groups in the evolution of the modern *condicio humana*.

Johanna Bischitz was one of the few women in Hungary to tackle women-specific issues long before there was a 'women's rights' or feminist movement in the country. She was not only respected during her lifetime, but remained well-known until the outbreak of World War II. However after 1945, her biography, along with the entire history of Jewish women's associations in Hungary, was almost completely forgotten. In the last few years, historians have recovered traces of the history and role of Jewish women as pioneers of modern charitable ventures and as activists in women's movements and feminist organizations.

Julia Richers
Assistant and Lecturer in East European History,
University of Basel, Switzerland

SOURCES

(A) *Magyar Országos Levéltár* (Hungarian State Archive), K 148 1879 I.B. 670: Johanna Bischitz's Order of Merit.

(B) Ervin Szabó City Library, Budapest, Budapest Collection: *Pesti Izraelita Nőegylet évi jelentései* (Annual reports of the Pest Israelite Women's Association) (1875–1943).

(B) *Budapesti Közlöny* (Budapest Gazette) (13 May 1879).

(B) *Egyenlőség* (Equality), no. 14 (3 April 1898).

(B) Gerő, Katalin. *A szeretet munkásai, a Pesti Izraelita Nőegylet története* (Workers of love, the history of the Pest Israelite Women's Association). Budapest, 1937.

(D) "Johanna Bischitz." In Ignatz Reich. *Beth-El, Ehrentempel verdienter ungarischer Israeliten* (Beth-El, Monument in Honor of Meritorious Hungarian Israelites). Budapest: Alois Bucsánsky, 1882, 3: 77-93.

(D) "Hevesi Bischitz Dávidné" (Mrs David Hevesi Bischitz). In Hermán Zichy. *Magyar zsidók a Millenniumon* (Hungarian Jews in the millennium). Budapest: D. Miljkovic, 1896, 113-114.

(E) Vincze, László. "Hová jutottak el ezek az emberek! Töredékek a Bischitz-család történetéből" (What those people achieved! Fragments of the Bischitz family history). In *Magyar Izraeliták Országos Képviselete (MIOK) évkönyv* (Yearbook of the National Agency of Hungarian Israelites), 1983/84, 489-509.

(E) Richers, Julia. *Der Pester israelitische Frauenverein von 1866 bis 1914. Ein Beitrag zur jüdischen Frauen- und Alltagsgeschichte aus kulturwissenschaftlicher Perspektive* (The Pest Israelite Women's Association from 1866 to 1914. A contribution to Jewish women's and everyday life history). M.A. Thesis. University of Basel, 2001.

(E) Richers, Julia. "'Jótékony rablás' csupán? A Pesti Izraelita Nőegylet tevékenységi körei, 1866-1943" (Merely 'charitable robbery'? The range of activities of the Pest Israelite Women's Association, 1866-1943). In Zsuzsanna Toronyi, ed. *A zsidó nő* (The Jewess). Budapest, 2002, 65-75.

BLAGOEVA, Vela (1858-1921)

Bulgarian teacher, journalist, writer, translator. Founder and one of the leaders of the socialist women's movement in Bulgaria.

On 29 September 1858, Vela Blagoeva was born Victoria Atanasova Zhivkova in Turnovo, an old town at the foot of the Balkan mountains, the last capital of the Bulgarian medieval kingdom, a prosperous economic and cultural center during the nineteenth-century Bulgarian national revival, and home to Vela's upper middle-class family. Her parents, the trader Atanas Zhivkov and housewife Neda Spiridonova, had two daughters and two sons. Her brothers, Georgi Zhivkov (1844-1899) and Nikola Zhivkov (1847-1901), were well-known public figures in the new Bulgarian state: Georgi was a politician; Nikola was a teacher and man of letters. In later life, Vela Blagoeva would note in her (unpublished) memoirs that she, the youngest, was her father's favorite, but that her mother did not like that she was a girl, her pride and joy being her two sons. After finishing the middle school for girls in Turnovo, and high school in Gabrovo, Vela Zhivkova taught in Berkovitsa, Varna, Constantinople and Turnovo. In 1877-1878, during the Russian-Turkish War of Liberation, she served as a nurse. Obtaining a fellowship from the Slavic Charity Committee in St Petersburg, she was able to graduate from the high school for girls there in 1881. Between 1881 and 1882, she returned to Bulgaria to teach: first in Edirne (today in Turkey), later in Bitolia (today in Macedonia). From 1882-1884, she continued her studies, attending the Higher Women's Courses (popularly known as 'the Bestuzhev Courses') in St Petersburg and training as a teacher. Student protests against the Russian autocracy, which continued unabated throughout these years, had a significant impact on Blagoeva's political development.

Vela Blagoeva was the life partner of Dimitur Blagoev (1856-1924), the founder, in 1883, of one of the first socialist groups in Russia and of the Bulgarian socialist party in 1891. He was the recognized leader of the 'narrow socialist' wing of the Bulgarian Socialist Party, which Bolshevized after 1919. The couple had four children: two daughters, Stela (1887-1954) and Natalia (1889-1943); and two sons, Dimitur (1895-1918) and Vladimir (1893-1925). Dimitur was killed in World War I and Vladimir 'disappeared' in 1925, during the government reprisals and political terror that followed the communist bombing of *Sveta Nedelia*, a church in Sofia.

Vela Blagoeva was imbibed with the free spirit of the Bulgarian National Revival; she had been brought up in Turnovo after all, a town with a tradition of women's activism (especially regarding education), and she had been educated under the influence of the Russian *narodnics* and revolutionary democrats. It was therefore almost inevitable that she became orientated towards socialism. In Russia, she had already immersed herself in radical politics. The late nineteenth century saw socialist ideas spread to Bulgaria as well. Upon returning to Bulgaria (1884), Blagoeva immediately began disseminating socialist propaganda. Together with Dimitur Blagoev, she edited the socialist journal *Suvremenen pokazatel* (Contemporary trend), in which she discussed, among other issues, women's education, equality and discrimination against women teachers. At the end of the nineteenth century, high schools for girls in Bulgaria (called gymnasiums as in Germany) offered six grades above the primary (four-grade) level, while high schools for boys offered seven grades. This difference would later serve as a pretext to deny women access to higher education at the University in Sofia, the first and for a long time the only university in Bulgaria (established in 1888). Blagoeva criticized this education system for not giving equal opportunities to girls and boys. "Currently, our high schools for girls can only prepare schoolgirls to become courtesans and cooks," she wrote, "but not to become educated teachers and certainly not to become citizens" (cited in Bogdanova 1969, 47). A teacher herself by profession, Blagoeva was constantly on the move; she was dismissed on more than one occasion by the Bulgarian government on account of her socialist ideas. She taught in Sofia (1884-1885, 1905-1907), Shumen (1886-1887), Vidin (1897-1890), Turnovo (1890-1892), Stara Zagora (1892-1893), Plovdiv (1893-1896, 1902-1903), Tulcha (today in Romania) (1901-1902) and Marashki Trustenik (1907-1912).

Vela Blagoeva was one of the first women socialists in Bulgaria. In 1901, she participated in the founding of the first national women's organization, the *Bulgarski Zhenski Sujuz* (*BZhS*, Bulgarian Women's Union). Within the *BZhS*, two basic political positions emerged: liberal ('bourgeois') feminist (embraced by ***Anna Karima, Julia Malinova,*** Sanda Iovceva and others), and socialist. Although the socialist women led by Blagoeva initially joined the *BZhS*, they later took up the socialist party line, accusing the liberal feminists of separatism. In 1903, the socialist women split from the *BZhS*, objecting to its attempts to 'transcend class.' In a sense, this split by the women socialists mirrored that which had taken place earlier in the year between the 'narrow' and 'broad' socialists. In her newly established journal *Zhenski trud* (Women's labor), Vela Blagoeva offered the following justification for leaving the *BZhS*: "The Women's Union has been transformed into a purely feminist organization that wanders without direction while the conscious women who have supported it are cheated, slandered and insulted by the arrogant feminists" [*Zhenski trud* 1, no. 2 (1904-1905)].

Vera Blagoeva founded the first educational social democratic group for women workers in Sofia at the beginning of 1905, and organized the first conference of socialist women in August 1905. These activities provoked heated debate in the socialist periodicals. Some influential male socialists were afraid that a separate women's organization would raise proletarian women's opposition to the united workers' movement. Led by Dimitur Blagoev (Vela Blagoeva's husband), the 'narrow' socialist wing (i.e. orthodox socialists and future Bolsheviks) were against the establishment of 'a neutral women's union,' whereas the 'broad' socialists (later named Social Democrats) favored an independent women's organization. No separate organization of women Social Democrats came into existence at the time, but the idea nevertheless challenged the so-called 'bourgeois' *BZhS* in its efforts to unite all the women activists in the country. Although in 1903, Vela Blagoeva seemed to have adopted a 'narrow' socialist perspective regarding women's social and political activism, in 1905 she published articles directed against her male comrades (in particular Georgi Bakalov), insisting that women socialists had the right to decide whether or not they wanted to stay in the *BZhS*. Nine years later, in late July–August 1914, Vela Blagoeva chaired the Founding Conference of the Women's Socialist Clubs in Bulgaria, following instructions from the Central Committee of the Bulgarian Workers' Social Democratic Party (the 'narrow' socialists).

Vela Blagoeva edited several journals, including *Delo* (Deed) and *Zhenski bjuletin* (Women's bulletin). She published articles in journals such as *Novo vreme* (New times), *Den* (Day), *Pravo delo* (Just deed), *Bulgarska sbirka* (Bulgarian collection), *Uchitel* (Teacher), *Democraticheski pregled* (Democratic review), *Uchilishten pregled* (School review), *Svetulka* (Firefly) and *Cherven smjah* (Red laughter). She left an extensive oeuvre of journalistic pieces, textbooks, translations, novels and short stories. These dealt with various aspects of women's emancipation: school and university education for girls and boys; the role of the family (especially of mothers); women's paid labor; women's access to various professions; women's personal independence; peace; the abolition of prostitution and women's political rights. She fiercely criticized her society, in which a woman was treated as "an irrational child," controlled, subordinated to and patronized by men (*Tsentralen Partien Archiv*, f. 197, op. 1, a. e. 27). She argued against widely held opinions that considered prostitution to be the result of women's sinful nature. Some of her stories about women activists, such as those dealing with 'the Macedonian question' (i.e. the question of which Balkan state Macedonia belonged to), combined socialist ideas of emancipation with nationalist and feminist approaches. Other writings dealt with various social groups such as domestic servants, widows and prostitutes.

Vela Blagoeva firmly believed in the triumph of socialism. Her unbending spirit and devotion was a constant source of energy. She toured workers' districts and roused women to action with her simple, clear, accessible and moving manner of speech. She sacrificed everything to the socialist cause: personal comfort, ambitions, labor and resources. She materially supported her entire family when her husband was unemployed because of his socialist activities and he later wrote of this moral and material support in his memoirs, adding that she had never once lost her spirit, not in any circumstances, not even during the most difficult moments of their life together. There were moments of conflict, due, as he put it, "to differences in character, but her energy, unbelievable spirit, courage and loyalty to the principles of revolutionary socialism kept me attached to her" (Blagoev 1977, 110). The writer Dimitur Poljanov likened the life "of our beloved Vela" to a "long, heroic poem." "In our backward conditions," he wrote, "she was a unique combination of a liberal mind, great enthusiasm, firm will, hard work and a loving hearth" (*Durzhaven Istoricheski Archiv*, f. 1337, op. 1, a. e. 16, l. 97). Vela Blagoeva died in Sofia on 21 July 1921.

Krassimira Daskalova
St. Kliment Ohridski, University of Sofia

SOURCES

(A) *Tsentralen Partien Archiv* (Central Party Archive), f. 197 (Vela Blagoeva).
(A) *Tsentralen Partien Archiv* (Central Party Achive), f. 140 (Dimitar Blagoev).
(A) *Tsentralen Partien Archiv* (Central Party Achive), f. 141 (Stela Blagoeva).
(A) *Durzhaven Istoricheski Archive* (State Historical Archive), f. 1337 (Koika Tineva), op. 1, a. e. 16, 71.
(B) *Zhenski trud* (Women's labor) 1 (1904–1905).
(C) Blagoeva, Vela. *Protses. Roman* (The trial. A novel). Plovdiv: Ivan Ignatov, 1898.
(C) Blagoeva, Vela. *Dve povesti iz narodnia zhivot na bulgarite* (Two stories from the everyday life of Bulgarians). Sofia, 1904.
(D) Bogdanova, Elena. *Vela Blagoeva. Biografichen ocherk* (Vela Blagoeva. A Biography). Sofia: BCP Publishing House, 1969.
(D) Bogdanova, Elena and Amalia Racheva. *Vela Blagoeva. Album.* Sofia: Septemvri, 1981.
(E) Blagoev, Dimitur. *Kratki belezhki iz moia zhivot* (Short notes on my life). Sofia: Partizdat, 1977.
(E) *Rechnik na Bulgarskata Literatura* (Dictionary of Bulgarian literature). Sofia, 1969, 1: 101–102.

BOJADJIEVA NASTEVA-RUSINSKA, Kostadina (1880–1932)

Macedonian intellectual and revolutionary, supporter of social democracy and its ideas regarding women's equality; pioneer of the Macedonian women's movement; leader of the women's society *Uspenie Bogorodichno* (Virgin Mary's Assumption).

Kostadina Bojadjieva was born in Ohrid in 1880, the only child of Eftim Nastev Bojadjiev, a wealthy Orthodox Christian merchant from Ohrid. Her mother probably died very young (no data on her exists). Kostadina completed her primary education in Ohrid and her secondary education in Bulgaria, teaching at a primary school for boys and girls in Ohrid from around the turn of the century.

In the late nineteenth century, an intellectual elite developed in Macedonia in which female teachers played an important role. Teaching was the most socially acceptable profession for women, especially if they were single. Many young female teachers adopted socialist ideas, including Kostadina Bojadjieva. The program of the Social Democrats was the only one to include the emancipation of women in its agenda, making their party—established on the territory of Macedonia in 1893—attractive to women. As members of the Socialist Party and the Macedonian intelligentsia (which also played a major role in the national liberation movement), women such as Kostadina Bojadjieva were able to establish international contacts.

Literature on the French Revolution, human rights and the European social democratic movement came to Macedonia via Thessaloniki and greatly influenced both the female intelligentsia and the women's emancipation movement. Numerous women's societies and organizations were established in the mid-nineteenth century, many of them led by female teachers–including the *Kostursko zensko drustvo* (Kostur Women's Association); the *Tajno zensko drustvo* (Secret Women's Association), founded in Struga; the *Zensko drustvo* (Women's Association), founded in Krusevo before the *Ilinden* uprising; the *Tajno zensko drustvo* (Secret Women's Association), founded in Bitola and the *Zensko biblisko drustvo* (Women's Biblical Association), founded in Bansko by the Protestant Mission of American missionary Helen Stone. Since Macedonians had the status of *raya* (Christian subjects with no rights) in the Ottoman Empire, the agenda of the Macedonia female intelligentsia focused on women's and national emancipation. Such women joined the *Tajna makedonsko-odrinska revolucionerna organizacija* (*TMORO*, Clandestine Macedonian-Odrin Revolutionary Organization), established in 1893, which adopted socialist ideas on the emancipation of women and organized the *Ilinden* uprising against the Ottoman Empire (2 August–November 1903).

Ohrid, Kostadina Bojadjieva's native town, is famous for its tradition in education. It was here that St. Kliment Ohridski (St. Clement of Ohrid, app. 830/840–27 July 916), disciple of the saints Cyril and Method, established the Ohrid Literary School (after 886), which played a key role in spreading literacy among the Slavs. In the spirit of this tradition, female teachers from Ohrid in 1885 established the women's society, the *Uspenie Bogorodichno* (Virgin Mary's Assumption), better known as the *Nedelno uchilishte* (Sunday School). The *Uspenie Bogorodichno* aimed to provide material assistance and education to the poor, especially women. It organized weekly literacy classes and lectures on emancipation, drawing upon the slogan "when we liberate Macedonia, women will enjoy the same rights" (Rusinski 1997, 194). In the fall of 1900, the *Uspenie Bogorodichno* joined the revolutionary national movement *TMORO*, then in the process of preparing for the uprising. Kostadina Bojadjieva led the *Uspenie Bogorodichno* from 1901 until the end of 1903. Vasilka Razmova, Klio Samardjieva, Atina Shahova, Poliksena Manasieva, Maria Parmakova and other female teachers from Ohrid were among the members of the *Uspenie Bogorodichno*.

In his *Spomeni* (Memoirs), Kostadina Bojadjieva's husband (Nikola Rusinski) recalled an anecdote from a conference of the *TMORO* in Ohrid on 14 November 1901, at which, while discussing current issues, "one of the participants jokingly asked 'And women; what rights shall we give them tomorrow, after Macedonia's liberation?' This friend had most probably read August Bebel's *Zenata: nejzinoto minato, segasnost i idnina* [Woman: her past, present and future] and wanted to make a joke, failing to understand the deeper meaning. I told him that women were an inseparable part of humanity, bearing all the difficulties of family life together with men. As a mother, an educator and a housewife, a woman carries a greater burden than a man in today's capitalist society, which has two dictums: rights for men and no rights for women. In our organization's fight for liberation, a woman is not treated unequally. She participates and sacrifices as we do and is entitled to the same rights. It is very naive and silly to believe that women do not sacrifice. ... The teacher Kostadina Nasteva strongly supported my views on the rights of women today and in the future, after the liberation of Macedonia ..." (Rusinski, 193–194).

During the *Ilinden* uprising and supported by the local *TMORO* Committee and local people, Kostadina Bojadjieva and other female teachers from Ohrid (Poliksena Mosinova, Kata Samardjieva, Fanche Chuleva, Hristina Miskarova, Careva Botushkova, Atina Shahova, Flora Georgieva, Despina Vasilcheva, Elena Kackova and Aspasya Misheva-Kanveche) opened a clandestine hospital. The hospital was situated in an old archbishopric building in Ohrid's *Varos* district, the house of Metodi Patchev (Chairman of the local *TMORO*; killed in a skirmish with Turkish forces in 1902, in the village of Kadino near Prilep). The Turkish authorities soon uncovered the hospital but found no evidence against the female teachers, releasing them after interrogation, brutal beatings and brief imprisonment for actions against the Ottoman Empire. For the next three months, until the English humanitarian mission took over, the teachers continued to work at the hospital with the agreement of the Mayor of Ohrid, Mejdi Bej, who provided the hospital with a daily ration of milk.

In November 1902, Kostadina Bojadjieva became engaged to Nikola Petrov-Rusinski (see above), a socialist, participant in the *Ilinden* uprising and an important influence on Bojadjieva's ideas. After the suppression of the *Ilinden* uprising in November 1903, the two of them emigrated to Bulgaria, where Bojadjieva received a teaching post in Skrvena (a village in the region of Orhanije). Kostadina and Nikola married in Sofia on 4 April 1904. They had three daughters, each of them named after a flower: Ruzha (wild rose), Roza (rose) and Karanfilka (carnation). Nikola Rusinski wrote proudly in his memoirs that his daughter Roza carried the name of the European revolutionary, Rosa Luxemburg.

The Rusinski family experienced the Balkan Wars (1912–1913) and World War I first hand. The Balkan Wars ended with the Bucharest Treaty (10 August 1913) and the division of Macedonia among Serbia, Bulgaria and Greece. During World War I, Nikola Rusinski became a volunteer fighting in the Malesevo region of eastern Macedonia; Bojadjieva, who accompanied him, worked as a teacher in Berovo (1915–1918). The two hoped that the outcome of the war would change the Bucharest Treaty but the Versailles Treaty (1919) sanctioned Macedonia's division and the Malesevo region once again became a Serbian protectorate. Subsequently, the Rusinskis and their three daughters left Rusinovo (Berovo region), Nikola Rusinski's native village where the family had been living. Their socialist ideas and cooperation with left political forces in the Kingdom of Serbs, Croats and Slovenes (SCS) made it difficult for the family to stay, particularly because Nikola Rusinski had carried out political agitation for the candidate list of the Communist Party of Yugoslavia (*KPJ*) in the municipal and parliamentary elections of August and September 1920, and also because the SCS government had outlawed the Communist Party of Yugoslavia with the *Obznana* (Notification) of 30 December 1920. On 27 February 1921, in mid-winter, the Rusinskis illegally crossed the Yugoslav–Bulgarian border on horseback and on foot, emigrating (for the second time) to Bulgaria and becoming refugees in Kustendil, where they lived in poor conditions.

The whole family fell sick because of the cold weather. Kostadina caught pneumonia from which she never recovered. Her fourth daughter, born while Kostadina was sick, died of bronchitis soon after her birth. Nikola worked as a carpenter in Gorna Djumaja (today's Blagoevograd) and financial difficulties forced Kostadina to take on work as a teacher in the village of Djumaja (1922–1923), even though she was not yet fully recovered. Her daughters Roza and Karanfilka lived with her and Ruzha lived in a boarding school, where she received a secondary education that she funded herself. In the meantime, Roza developed tuberculosis and Kostadina took up work as a factory worker in order to support her two sick children and husband. Family misfortunes took another turn when, in 1929, just seventeen, Roza died.

From this time on, the Rusinskis' conditions rapidly deteriorated; without a steady income, they could not afford medical treatment for Kostadina's illness, which persisted throughout the years 1930 to 1932. During this period, Nikola provided for the family and took over the housework. Literally starved and sick, Kosatadina died of pneumonia in 1932. In 1938, Karanfilka (the couple's second daughter) also died. Only Ruzha, the eldest daughter, and Nikola Rusinski survived–the latter impoverished, sick, exhausted and disappointed. In the fall of 1941, he returned to Rusinovo, his native village in Macedonia, where he died in the early spring of 1943.

Kostadina Bojadjieva-Rusinska, one of the pioneers of the Macedonian women's movement, absorbed contemporary European discourses on women's rights. Until the end of her life she remained faithful to the ideals of a liberated Macedonia and total emancipation for both men and women. Today she has an especially high standing among Macedonian women intellectuals and teachers.

Prof. Dr. Vera Veskovic-Vangeli
Senior Scientific Researcher,
Institute of National History, Skopje

Translated from the Macedonian by Nevenka Grceva, MA student, Department of Gender Studies, CEU, Budapest.

SOURCES

(B) Nasteva Bojadjieva, Kostadina. *Makedonski vesti* (Macedonian news), no. 38 (Sofia, 1935): 7.

(E) Veskovic-Vangeli, Vera. *Zenata vo osloboditelnite borbi na Makeodnija (1893-1945)* (Woman in the Macedonian liberation wars, 1893-1945). Skopje: Kultura, 1990.

(E) Petrov-Rusinski, Nikola. *Spomeni* (Memoirs). Darinka Pachemska-Petreska and Vojo Kushevski, eds. Skopje: Institut za nacionalna istorija Skopje, 1997.

BORTKEVIČIENĖ, Felicija (1873–1945)

Lithuanian journalist, public activist. Chairwoman in the 1920s of the liberal *Lietuvos moterų sąjunga* (Lithuanian Women's Union); member of the *Lietuvos moterų globos komitetas* (Lithuanian Women's Wardship Committee); Board Member of the *Lietuvos moterų, baigusių aukštąjį mokslą sąjunga* (Association of Lithuanian Women with University Education); Chairwoman of the association *Žiburėlis* (Light).

Felicija Bortkevičienė was born Felicija Povickaitė on 1 September 1873 on the Linkaučiai Estate in Panevėžys County (in the district of Krekenava), into a noble family. Her parents, evicted from the estate by the Russian government for their part in the rebellion of 1863, moved to Ukmergė city. Progressive Polish and Russian intellectuals would often gather in the Povickiai house. Felicija's mother, Antanina-Ona Liutkevičienė-Povickienė (1850–1922), and father, Povickis (personal data unknown), had two daughters and a son. Antanina-Ona Povickienė spoke Polish but passed her knowledge of the Lithuanian language not only to her own children, but also the children of estate workers.

From 1883 to 1889, Felicija Povickaitė studied at Kaunas Girls' Gymnasium, from which she was expelled during her sixth grade for anti-Russian ideas. Later, she graduated from Vilnius Girls' Gymnasium and in 1890, attended illegal courses in history and French at the *Skrajojantis arba Bobiškasis Universitetas* (Flying University) in Warsaw. When the courses were closed in 1891, Felicija Povickaitė returned to her parents in Lithuania (to Ukmergė). She worked as a schoolteacher and later in a bank while studying Lithuanian.

In 1899, Felicija Povickaitė married Jonas Bortkevičius (1871–1906), an engineer. She assumed his family name, becoming Bortkevičienė (the Lithuanian ending -ienė indicates marital status and Mrs Bortkevičienė was known in all her spheres of activity as simply Bortkevičienė). They lived in Vilnius and joined the national movement in 1900, as well as participating in the activities and meetings of an intellectual Lithuanian club that later acquired the name of 'The Twelve Apostles.' Bortkevičienė was the first and only woman to participate in all the meetings of this club. Though her Lithuanian was weak, she participated in the national movement and organized the distribution of banned journals such as *Varpas* (Bell) and *Ūkininkas* (Farmer) in Vilnius and its district. From 1903, Bortkevičienė was actively involved in the work of *Žiburėlis* (Light), a secular association that supported gifted male and female Lithuanian students in their studies abroad.

Up until 1905, the Bortkevičienė home was a center for both Vilnius Lithuanian intellectuals and for the Lithuanian women's movement. From 1904 to 1905, Lithuanian women activists gathered secretly there to discuss public and women's issues, Bortkevičienė herself encouraging women to learn Lithuanian and join the national movement. On 22–23 September 1905, the *Lietuvos moterų susivienijimas* (Lithuanian Women's Association) was established at one such meeting of Lithuanian women and Felicija Bortkevičienė was elected to the Board of the new organization. The goals of the *Lietuvos moterų susivienijimas* were: autonomy for Lithuania within its ethnic boundaries; general, equal, secret and immediate parliamentary elections for the *Seimas* in Vilnius and equal rights for women and men. Felicija Bortkevičienė recalled the Revolution of 1905 with these words: "I participated in the revolutionary work of 1904, 1905 and 1906. Agitators needed support in obtaining literature, money, often even guns, as well as help facilitating internal communication" (Bortkevičienė "Autobiografija" 1.1). In 1902, Mrs Bortkevičienė joined the *Lietuvos demokratų partija* (Lithuanian Democrat Party) and became one of its leaders.

On 17 October 1905, the Russian Tsar Nicholas II issued a manifesto on the activities of organizations and public meetings. The manifesto expounded on the basic laws of a future constitutional government and promised to summon a *Duma* (Parliament), without which state laws would not be validated. Two days later, Lithuanian intellectuals decided to summon a Lithuanian Congress (later named the *Seimas* or Parliament) in Vilnius. Felicija was included into the organizing committee of the Congress. On 4–6 December 1905, during a meeting of the Great *Seimas* in Vilnius, the *Lietuvos valstiečių sąjunga* (Lithuanian Peasants' Union) was established with Felicija Bortkevičienė as head of the Committee of Central Affairs. On Bortkevičienė's initiative, the *Lietuvos valstiečių sąjunga* proposed that the *Seimas* include an article proclaiming the total political equality of both sexes in a *Seimas* resolution on the autonomy of Lithuania.

On 11 December 1905, the Tsar announced a law regarding State *Duma* elections, according to which women were not entitled to vote. At the end of the same month, Felicija Bortkevičienė participated in a meeting organized by the *Geležinkeliečių sąjunga* (Union of Railwaymen) as one of the Lithuanian women who had been active during the events and strikes of 1905. In a resolution passed at the meeting, women demanded equal political rights with men and a change in the social and legal status of women. After the meeting, Bortkevičienė's flat was searched by police. From 1906 to 1907, Felicija Bortkevičienė was involved in the work of the *Lietuvos moterų susivienijimas*. She helped publish the democratic newspapers *Lietuvos ūkininkas* (The Lithuanian farmer) and *Lietuvos žinios* (Lithuanian news), as well as running *Kankinių kasos* (The martyrs' support fund) from 1903 to 1914, a journal providing assistance to Lithuanian women and men in Russian prisons.

On 23–24 September 1907, Felicija Bortkevičienė participated in the First Lithuanian Women's Congress in Kaunas and, in the following year, attempted to prevent a split within the women's movement into 'Catholic' and 'liberal' wings. From 1908, her activities in the women's movement dwindled as she poured all "her happiness, soul and power" into the creation of a Lithuanian democratic press (Zenonas Toliušis, "Felicija Bortkevičienė"). Bortkevičienė was then one of the best-known editors in Lithuania. Among her many publications, of particular note is the liberal newspaper *Lietuvos ūkininkas* (Lithuanian farmer), through which Bortkevičienė sought to address the large Lithuanian population (85 percent) living in the countryside. *Žibutė* (Violet), the newspaper's supplement from 1911 to 1913, was a liberal magazine for women of both town and country.

During World War I, Felicija Bortkevičienė organized support for refugees and exiles. After her return from Russia to Vilnius in 1918, the Prime Minister of Lithuania, Mykolas Sleževičius, wanted her to head the Ministry of Food but the appointment was opposed by the presidium of the Council of Lithuania (as the Lithuanian legislative body was called from November 1918 until May 1920). In July 1919, Felicija Bortkevičienė returned to Kaunas and reactivated both *Lietuvos žinios* (Lithuanian news) and *Lietuvos ūkininkas* (The Lithuanian farmer). In 1920, together with other members of the *Lietuvos socialistų liaudininkų partija* (Lithuanian Socialist Populist Party), she established the company and printing-house *Varpas* (Bell), which she ran until 1930. In April 1920, Felicija Bortkevičienė participated in the elections of the *Steigiamasis Seimas* (Constituent Assembly) and was on the lists of the Lithuanian Peasants' Union and the Lithuanian Socialist Populist Party (both parties worked together). She also organized the publication and distribution of election material as the editor of both the *Lietuvos žinios* and the *Lietuvos ūkininkas*. Although Bortkevičienė was not elected to the *Seimas* herself, she did become a Member of Parliament in 1921, instead of ***Gabrielė Petkevičaitė*** (who stepped down for health reasons). Bortkevičienė was not part of the activities of the *Lietuvos krikščionių demokratų partija* (Lithuanian Christian Democrat Party), but helped prepare the Statute of the Lithuanian University and the Patients' Fund Law. The latter was especially important for women entering paid employment, which was happening increasingly at the time. In response to the new health risks to women, this law included maternity provisions that granted two weeks leave before, and six weeks after the birth of a child, forbade the dismissal of women from employment on the grounds of pregnancy and established hygiene standards to be maintained in women's places of work. From 1922 until 1936, Bortkevičienë was chief editor of *Lietuvos žinios* (Lithuanian news), the most popular daily in the country. Articles criticizing the policies of the right-wing conservative government and political caricatures, publicized in the daily from 1925, incurred the wrath of the authorities and Felicija Bortkevičienë was imprisoned and/or fined on several occasions.

In the summer of 1922, Felicija Bortkevičienė helped re-establish the liberal *Lietuvos moterų sąjunga* (Lithuanian Women's Union), of which she was Chairwoman until 1928 and whose main aims were to educate women and raise their social and political awareness. Her activities in the *Lietuvos valstiečių liaudininkų sąjunga* (Lithuanian Peasant Populist Union) and the newspaper *Lietuvos žinios* prevented her from devoting all her time and energy to the liberal women's movement. In 1926, she stood for election to the III *Seimas* for the Lithuanian Peasant Populist Union but was (again) not elected. After the Lithuanian Peasant Populist Union won the III *Seimas* election, Felicija Bortkevičienė ran for State President. She had been nominated by Members of Parliament but received only one vote.

In 1928, she resigned from her position as a Chairwoman of the Lithuanian Women's Union. Although staying on as a Board Member, she stated: "I give up, let the students, Mrs Baronienė [teacher and member of the *Lietuvos socialdemokratų partija*] and others do the work. ... They may be able to carry out the work we could not manage. I believe that it is necessary to teach civil duties; a woman must be acculturated [educated] but I do not know whether this should be done through women's associations or in other ways" (Manuscript Department in Lithuanian Literature and Folklore Institute, f. 30, 1143, Mrs Bortkevičienė's Letter to ***Miss G. Petkevičaitė,*** 1.12). Bortkevičienė was a committee member of the *Lietuvos moterų globos komitetas* (Lithuanian Women's Wardship Committee), Board Member of the *Lietuvos moterų, baigusių aukštąjį mokslą sąjunga* (Association of Lithuanian Women with University Education) and Chair of *Žiburėlis* (Light), reestablished in 1922. After 1930, the activities of the *Lietuvos moterų taryba* (*LMT,* Lithuanian Council of Women) were being financed by the government [formed by the conservative *Lietuvos tautininkų sąjunga* (Lithuanian Nationalist Union), the only governing party in Lithuania during the authoritarian regime of President A. Smetona], which had decided to support the liberal women's movement on the one hand, while on the other hand placing restrictions on what it could and could not do. For example, the Lithuanian Council of Women could not organize strikes protesting the dismissal of women from their jobs and it could only write petitions to the government. The government used the Lithuanian Council of Women as an organization that could raise the problems of Lithuania (such as the return of Vilnius, occupied by Polish forces from 8 November 1920, to Lithuania) in the forums of international organizations. Felicija Bortkevičienė opposed these kinds of government strategy and therefore also the activities of the Lithuanian Council of Women, which she protested in the press. Bortkevičienė, who was against the restriction of democracy, demanded parliamentary elections for the IV *Seimas* of 1936 (the III *Seimas* was dismissed in April 1927). In this period, parliamentary candidates could be selected from just one party, the *Lietuvos tautininkų sąjunga* (Lithuanian Nationalist Union).

During the Second Women's Congress from 10 to 12 December 1937, to which Felicija Bortkevičienė was invited as a guest of honor, Bortkevičienė reminded the audience of a demand made at the First Lithuanian Women's Congress of 1907, that the sale of alcohol be forbidden countrywide. Together with ***Gabrielė Petkevičaitė*** and Emilija Vileišienė [Board Member of the *Vilniaus lietuvių labdaros darugija* (Vilnius Lithuanians' Charity Association) and an active member of the *Lietuvių katalikių moterų draugija* (Lithuanian Catholic Women's Organization)], she presented a request to the Presidium of the Second Women's Congress to organize a special committee which could represent women's interests to the IV *Seimas* (1936–1940).

Gabrielė Petkevičaitė described the aims of Felicija Bortkevičienė as: the democratization of society, the formation and development of the women's movement and the creation of a free democratic press (for which she was called 'the grandmother of the press'). In Petkevičaitė's words: "I do not know any other woman able to act like Felicija Bortkevičienė, tirelessly able to strive for the achievement of one of the greatest aims of humanity: to make people conscious citizens of their motherland" (Petkevičaitė 1967). Felicija Bortkevičienė died on 21 October 1945. She was buried in the village of Troškūnai (Ukmergė district), where a monument was erected in her name. In 2004, the Lithuanian Government established a special award for socially active women: the 'Felicijos Borkevičienės Award.'

Dr. Virginija Jurėnienė
Vilnius University

SOURCES

(A) Lithuanian National Martynas Mažvydas Library, Manuscript Department, Zenonas Toliušis Fund No. 60, File Description No.15. Zigmantas Toliušis. "Felicija Bortkevičienė" (A portrait sketch of Mrs Felicija Bortkevičienė).

(A) Lithuanian National Martynas Mažvydas Library, Manuscript Department, Zenonas Toliušis Fund No. 68, File Description No. 2. Felicija Bortkevičienė. "Autobiografija."

(A) Lithuanian National Martynas Mažvydas Library, Manuscript Department, Petras Ruseckas Fund No. 25, File Description No. 530. Petras Ruseckas. "Kalinių globa ir F. Bortkevičienė" (The support of prisoners and Mrs F. Bortkevičienė).

(A) Lithuanian Science Academy, Manuscript Department, F. Bortkevičienė Fund, No. 192, File Description No. 7. "Moterys ir Lietuvos atgimimas" (Women and Lithuania's rebirth).

(A) Lithuanian Science Academy, Manuscript Department, Fund No. 192, File Description No. 25. "Advokato Zenono Toliuşio pasakyta kalba prie F. Bortkevičienės karsto" (Speech of lawyer Zenonas Toliušis delivered by Felicija Bortkevičienė's coffin).

(A) Lithuanian Science Academy, Manuscript Department, F. Bortkevičienė Fund No.192, File Description No. 31. "F. Bortkevičienės žodis visuomenei" (F. Bortkevičienė's word to society).

(A) Vilnius University Library, Manuscript Department. "F. Bortkevičienės atsiminimai" (Reminiscences of F. Bortkevičienė). *Straipsniai iš Varpo ir Ūkininko redakcijos fondo*

[Articles taken from the archival fund of the editors of newspapers *Varpas* (Bell) and *Ū kininkas* (Farmer)]. Fund No. 1-F.120, File Description No. 31.

(A) Lithuanian Literature and Folklore Institute, Manuscript Department, f. 30, 1143, Mrs Bortkevičienė's letter to Miss G. Petkevičaitė.

(B) "Felicija Bortkevičienė." *Naujasis žodis* (The new word), no. 14 (1925): 5.

(B) "Visą gyvenimą su spauda" (All life with the press). *Trimitas* (The trumpet), no. 39 (1933): 767.

(B) "Felicija Bortkevičienė." *Lietuviai* (The Lithuanians), no. 14 (1943): 4.

(B) Petkevičaitė, Gabrielė. *Raštai* (Writings). Vol. 5. Vilnius: Vaga, 1967.

(D) Butėnas, Julius. *Gyvenusi kitiems: apybraiža apie Feliciją Bortkevičienę* (She lived for others: A sketch of Mrs Felicija Bortkevičienė). Kaunas: Šviesa, 1993.

BOTEZ, Calypso (1880-?)

Leading member of several Romanian women's organizations. Dominant figure in the interwar Romanian feminist movement. Member of the National Peasant Party. One of the first women representatives on the Bucharest city council after 1929.

Born in 1880, in the Moldovan city of Bacău, Calypso Botez completed a course of study in history and philosophy at the University of Iaşi, going on to become Principal of the Lyceum for girls in Galaţi. There she married a prominent local lawyer, Corneliu Botez, an active supporter of women's rights. During World War I, Calypso Botez was President of the Red Cross in Galaţi. In 1918, she helped found the *Asociaţia pentru emanciparea civilă şi politică a femeilor române* (*AECPFR*, Association for the Civil and Political Emancipation of Romanian Women) in Iaşi, remaining a leader of this organization after the war.

After 1918, Botez became one of the leading members of several important women's organizations, among them the *Societatea Ortodoxă Naţională a Femeilor Române* (*SONFR*, National Orthodox Society of Romanian Women), the *Consiliul Naţional al Femeilor Române* (*CNFR*, National Council of Romanian Women), as well as the intellectually prominent *Institutul Social Român* (Romanian Social Institute), which led reform and policy-making during the interwar period.

As the founder of a section for women's studies ("feminine studies") within the *Institutul Social Român*, which lasted until the communist takeover, Botez helped bring visibility and intellectual viability to the debate over women's enfranchisement and women's civil equality. As part of a famous series of debates sponsored by this institute in 1921, Botez presented a sophisticated and forceful argument on behalf of women's enfranchisement in an important public lecture on women's rights and the Constitution, along the lines of the liberal philosophy of John Stuart Mill. Her arguments for the full political equality for women were based on the contention that women were already fully participating in public/national life. Although she couched her polemic in the nationalist discourse of her day, Botez was unmistakably a liberal feminist first and a nationalist second.

And yet Botez did not join the National Liberal Party, preferring to become active in, and politically committed to the National Peasant Party—a pragmatic rather than an ideological choice. Despite its name, the National Liberal Party had very little in common with liberal ideas regarding gender equality and during the debates over the Constitution, to which Botez contributed with her powerful plea for women's enfranchisement, several members of the National Liberal Party spoke out against extending full political rights to women. The only political party with a (limited) progressive agenda regarding women's rights was the National Peasant Party. After coming to power in 1929, the National Peasant Party allowed women to vote in local and municipal (but not national) elections. Botez participated as a candidate for the municipal council in Bucharest and became one of the first women to sit on that body.

In her capacity as a member of the Bucharest municipal council, Botez worked tirelessly to protect and improve employment opportunities for young women, especially on behalf of recent migrants from the villages. Like other activists, Botez was concerned about the social and personal vulnerability of these young women, who often became prey to abusive work and personal relationships. In particular, she helped found several training schools for young female workers, such as the '*Vojvode Radu*' home economics school (named after a Wallachian ruler), which helped orphans acquire skills for gainful employment.

She pursued this interest in the protection of women workers by participating in international conferences organized by the International Woman Suffrage Alliance/International Alliance of Women for Suffrage and Equal Citizenship in Rome (1923), Paris (1926), Berlin (1929) and Istanbul (1935), and traveling abroad to the League of Nations in Geneva. In addition, she regularly published articles on the protection of women at work, both in Romania and for the League of Nations, in the bulletin of the *CNFR* and in the prominent social science journal, *Arhiva pentru reforma şi ştiinţa socială* (Archive for social science and reform).

In the interwar period, Botez was a dominant figure in the Romanian feminist movement, an intellectual leader known for her astute and sophisticated analyses of women's movements abroad, and persuasive arguments vis-à-vis her Romanian audiences. Her 1920 study, *Problema feminismului. O sistematizare a elementelor ei* (The problem of feminism. A systematization of its elements), offered a thorough understanding of nineteenth-century liberal debates in Western Europe, and of the radical challenges to women's pro-suffrage activism posed by recent trends towards biologizing women's gender identities. Employing statistical data, Botez offered a strong rebuttal to those who would argue for women's inborn inferior intelligence and moral sense.

Botez was also active in mainstream politics. Her interest in politics had less to do with gaining personal power and prestige than with her belief that women could no longer depend on the kindness of male politicians to change fundamental legal and social inequalities, designed to keep women dependent on men in every walk of life. In debates over women's political engagement, whether in existing parties or new women's organizations, Botez sided with those who had joined the National Peasant Party and other established political parties. Yet she continued to work with those who advocated separate associations for women, such as ***Alexandrina Cantacuzino*** and her *Gruparea Femeilor Române* (*GFR*, Association of Romanian Women). She also maintained her position as President of the *CNFR* until 1930, when she resigned due to conflicts with Alexandrina Cantacuzino over political strategies and goals.

After 1934 however, Botez became embittered over conflicts among women activists. In what appears to have been an entirely political manouver, Botez and two other women from the Bucharest municipal council were accused of financial improprieties. The media of the ruling National Liberal Party made much of this issue and blew it out of all proportion, something that Botez and other members of the opposing National Peasant Party had in fact expected. Among the critics were also some women activists, such as Maria Castano, who placed her Liberal Party loyalties above any feminist ones and did not question the real nature of the accusations.

Although the accusations proved unsubstantiated, this scandal did not provoke women activists into defending the cause of women's enfranchisement and many chose to see it as a warning against involvement in established party politics. Botez, however, did not back off. She continued to remain active in the National Peasant Party until 1938, when, with the dissolution of regular parliamentary politics and the establishment of an authoritarian dictatorship under King Carol II, she advocated stepping back from the political arena.

Together with a number of other feminist activists, including ***Ella Negruzzi,*** Botez sought to fundamentally alter the political, economic and social status of all women in Romania. Her actions were pioneering and, although she had only limited success in the political arena, her writings and civic activities went a long way towards providing a powerful role model for other female activists, feminists in particular.

Maria Bucur
Indiana University

SOURCES

(B) Bogdan, Elena. *Feminismul* (Feminism). Timişoara: Tip. Huniadi, 1926, 78–81.

(C) Botez, Calypso. "Problema feminismului. O sistematizare a elementelor ei" (The problem of feminism. A systematization of its elements). *Arhiva pentru ştiinţa şi reforma socială* (The archive for social science and reform) 2, no. 1–3 (April–October 1920): 28–84.

(C) Botez, Calypso. "Drepturile femeii în Constituţia viitoare" (Women's rights in the future constitution). In Institutul Social Român, ed. *Constituţia din 1923 în dezbaterea contemporanilor* (The Constitution of 1923 in contemporary debates). Bucharest: Humanitas, 1990, 124–142.

(D) Bucur, Maria. "Calypso Botez: Gender Difference and the Limits of Pluralism in Interwar Romania." *Jahrbücher für Geschichte und Kultur Südosteuropas* (Yearbook for South-East European history and culture) 3 (2001): 63–78.

(E) Cosma, Ghizela. *Femeile şi politica în România. Evoluţia dreptului de vot în perioada interbelică* (Women and politics in Romania. The evolution of suffrage rights in the interwar period). Cluj: Presa Universitară Clujeană, 2002.

BUDZIŃSKA-TYLICKA, Justyna (1867–1936)

Polish physician, feminist, social and political activist; involved in the International Socialist Women's Movement, the International Woman Suffrage Alliance (IWSA) and the Women's International League for Peace and Freedom (WILPF); co-founder in 1923 of the Little Entente of Women (LEW).

Justyna Budzińska was born on 12 September 1867 in Suwałki (in numerous sources an incorrect place of birth is given: Łomża), to a family of many children. Her mother's name was Jadwiga (no other data available). Her father, Alfons, a veterinary surgeon, was deported to Siberia for his involvement in the 1863 January Uprising against Russian occupation. Justyna was sent to a girls' boarding school in Warsaw. Her family situation was complicated: her father had died and she was forced to earn her own living. Nonetheless, she managed to complete her education at the school, pass her high school final exams as an extramural student and start work as a teacher-governess at a manor in the Ukraine. By then she was eighteen, and with this first job as a teacher, also running a secret school for village children, she became involved in the kinds of social activities that would later come to characterize her life. In 1892, she found the material resources necessary to cover a period of study in Paris, where she pursued courses in medicine. During her studies she lived, as did the majority of her fellow students, in difficult financial conditions, but threw herself into social activities: helping Polish émigrés (from the Polish Kingdom) in France, participating in debates and distributing underground publications. In 1895, she briefly joined the Parisian section of the *Zagraniczny Związek Socjalistów Polskich* (Foreign Association of Polish Socialists) but soon distanced herself from the socialist movement–a distance she would maintain for almost thirty years while remaining faithful to socialist ideas throughout her life.

Around 1894, Justyna Budzińska married Stanisław Tylicki. While still a student, she gave birth to a son, Stanisław (d. 1918). In 1898, she became a doctor of medicine. Early on in her medical career, she became especially interested in the fight against pulmonary tuberculosis. As a young doctor, she set up a practice in a little town near Paris. Three years after the birth of her son, she gave birth to a daughter, Wanda (exact data unknown), whom she breastfed herself as an advocate of modern approaches to motherhood. Wanda's father was also actively involved in the care of the child.

Continuing her social activities, Justyna Budzińska-Tylicka became an Honorary Member of a local workers' society for mutual assistance. After the Russian Revolution of 1905, the Tylickis decided to return to Poland, to Cracow (under Austrian partition) since they had been denied permission to live in the Polish Kingdom because of their political activities and connections with the socialist movement. In Cracow, Budzińska-Tylicka cooperated with campaigners for women's equality such as ***Kazimiera Bujwidowa*** and Maria Turzyma-Wiśniewska. She was also active in the *Towarzystwo Szkół Ludowych* (Society of Elementary Schools) and the *Towarzystwo Opieki nad Dziećmi* (Society for Child Welfare). After two years, she and her family moved to Warsaw, where she worked as an assistant at the Hospital of the Holy Spirit from 1908 to 1916. She became involved in the temperance movement and was also active in the Society Against Tuberculosis, the Polish Society for Hygiene and the *Towarzystwo Kolonii Letnich dla Kobiet Pracujących* (Summer Camp Society for Working Women). She was one of the first female physicians to work in schools for girls and between 1910 and 1912, she worked at the girls' boarding school of Popielewska-Roszkowska in Warsaw, where she studied and promoted modern principles of hygiene and new pedagogical methods in girls' education. She wrote handbooks on female hygiene and pamphlets concerning the health and legal protection of mothers. She also had her own private practice, mainly for people suffering from lung disease. As a supporter of women's equal rights, she became an active member of the *Związek Równouprawnienia Kobiet Polskich* (Union of Equal Rights for Polish Women), led by ***Paulina Kuczalska-Reinschmit*** and legalized in 1907. From 1912, she was also active in the Society of Oarswomen, of which she became President, as well as in the *Liga Kobiet Pogotowia Wojennego* (Women's League for War Alert, whose aim was to prepare women for a possible war). During World War I, she organized first-aid training courses for women and ran a hospital for wounded soldiers. In 1918 her son, an officer with the Polish Legions, was killed. It was a devastating blow, all the more so because her marriage to Tylicki was not a happy one and her relationship with her daughter was not particularly close.

In December 1918, at the Congress of the Second International in Brussels, the *Wydzial Kobiecy PPS* (Women's Department of the Polish Socialist Party) was established as a branch of the International Socialist Women's Committee, with Justyna Budzińska-Tylicka as its Vice-President. In 1919, along with ***Teodora Męczkowska*** and ***Zofia Daszyńska-Golińska*** (among others), Budzińska-Tylicka founded the *Klub Polityczny Kobiet Postępowych* (*KPKP*, Progressive Women's Political Club), aimed at training women in Poland to exercise their voting rights (women had been granted the vote in 1918). The *KPKP* extended its activity abroad, cooperating with the International Woman Suffrage Alliance (IWSA). In 1920, the *KPKP* sent a paper *O stanie* *sprawy kobiecej w Polsce* (On the state of the woman question in Poland), to the IWSA Congress in Geneva (where it was read by M. Dolecka, according to IWSA *Congress Report*, 190–191). At the 1923 IWSA Congress in Rome, the *KPKP* (that is, its President, Justyna Budzińska-Tylicka), together with the Romanian ***Princess Alexandrina Cantacuzino,*** put forward a proposal to establish the Little Entente of Women (LEW). The congresses of this organization were held annually in a different country each year (in 1929 in Warsaw). At the Fourth LEW Congress (Prague, 1927), Budzińska-Tylicka became Chairwoman of the Little Entente and the seat of its Central Bureau was moved to Warsaw.

In 1921, also on Budzińska-Tylicka's initiative, the *Polska Liga Kobiet Pokoju i Wolności* (Polish Women's League for Peace and Freedom) was founded within the *KPKP* as a section of the Women's International League for Peace and Freedom (WILPF), established in 1919. Justyna Budzińska-Tylicka participated in many WILPF congresses: in Vienna (1921), Washington (1924), Innsbruck (1925?), Dublin (1926) and Prague (1929). The Polish branch of the WILPF also organized border Polish-German conferences about the peaceful co-existence of the German minority in Poland and the Polish minority in Germany (on 6 May 1927 at Bytom and on 8 May 1927 at Katowice), at which Budzińska-Tylicka spoke on behalf of the Polish delegates.

From 1919 until 1934, Budzińska-Tylicka was a member of Warsaw City Council: first as a representative of the *Klub Polityczny Kobiet Postępowych* (KPKP), which functioned as a political party at the local level; from 1922 as a representative of the *Polska Partia Socjalistyczna* (*PPS*, Polish Socialist Party), which Budzińska-Tylicka joined that year. From 1919 until her death, she was a member of the *Polskie Towarzystwo Medycyny Społecznej* (Polish Society for Social Medicine) and in the years 1929 and 1936, she was elected a member of its board. From 1929 to 1931, she was an officer of the *Naczelna Izba Lekarska* (Polish Medical Chamber), while working to promote the causes of maternity protection (giving a lecture on this subject at the Congress of Social Work held in Paris in 1928), birth control and the fight against alcoholism and poverty. In Warsaw, she founded the first birth control clinic in Poland, of which she also became the director. The clinic, which was opened on 25 October 1931, was visited by female physicians (from England and Sweden among other countries) wishing to acquaint themselves with the clinic's activities.

In 1926, Justyna Budzińska-Tylicka founded the *Zrzeszenie Lekarek Polskich* (Association of Polish Female Physicians); she also wrote its statute and became its Vice-President. In the same year, she entered the Central Women's Division of the Polish Socialist Party. In the 1930s, she became President of the Division. On 14 September 1930, as an opponent of the post-Piłsudkis (*Sanacja*) camp, which rose to power after the May Coup in 1926, she co-organized and participated in the demonstration of opposition parties (the so-called *Centrolew*, i.e. the Center-Left) as a protest against the imprisonment of oppositional activists (the famous 'Brest Trial') by the

Sanacja camp. In 1931, she was arrested and sentenced to one year's imprisonment but the sentence was revoked as the result of an appeal. She remained active in the Polish Socialist Party until her death, serving as a member of its Chief Council from 1931 (when the *PPS* held its 22nd Convention).

From 1930, Budzińska-Tylicka presided over an organization established in the previous year by the Polish Socialist Party: the *Robotnicze Towarzystwo Służby Społecznej* (Workers Social Service Association), in which she advocated birth control. In 1935, she was elected a member of the Chief Board of the *Polski Związek Myśli Wolnej* (Polish Union of Free Thought). In the October of that year, she signed a petition demanding amnesty for political prisoners and closure of the camp for political prisoners at Bereza Kartuska–a campaign organized by the Communist Party of Poland. On 8 April 1936, Justyna Budzińska-Tylicka died suddenly from a cerebral stroke. Her funeral became a rally of the Warsaw *PPS*.

Katarzyna Sierakowska, Ph.D.
Institute of History
Polish Academy of Science, Warsaw

SOURCES

(B) Walewska, Cecylia. *W walce o równe prawa. Nasze bojownice* (Fighting for equal rights. Our fighters). Warsaw: Kobieta Współczesna, 1930.

(B) Bełcikowski, Jan. *Warszawa kobieca* (Women's Warsaw). Warsaw: Biblioteka Nowej Cywilizacji, 1930.

(B) Szelągowska, Anna. *Międzynarodowe Organizacje Kobiece* (International women's organizations). Warsaw: Wydział Prasowy ZPOK, 1934.

(B) Bełcikowski, Jan. *Polskie kobiece stowarzyszenia i związki współpracy międzynarodowej kobiet* (Polish women's organizations and women's associations for international cooperation). Warsaw: Towarzystwo Wydawnicze "Polska Zjednoczona," 1939.

(B) IIAV, *Congress Report* of the IWSA (1920, 1923).

(C) Budzińska-Tylicka, Justyna. *Higiena kobiety i kwestie społeczne z nią związane* (Woman's hygiene and social issues relating to it). Warsaw: E.Wende, 1909.

(C) Budzińska-Tylicka, Justyna. *Świadome macierzyństwo* (Conscious motherhood). Warsaw: Towarzystwo Wydawnicze "Rój," 1935.

(C) Articles by Budzińska-Tylicka in various periodicals: *Ster* (Helm) (1907–1914); *Głos Kobiet* (Voice of women); *Robotnik* (Worker) (1929–1932); *Kurier Polski* (Polish courier) (1925).

(D) Knappe, Wilhelm. "Dr Justyna Budzińska-Tylicka w pierwszą rocznicę śmierci" (Dr. Justyna Budzińska-Tylicka on the first anniversary of her death). *Warszawskie Czasopismo Lekarskie* (Warsaw medical journal) XIV (1937): 321–323.

(D) Heydrich, Danuta. "Dr Justyna Budzińska-Tylicka w dwudziestą piątą rocznicę zgonu" (Dr. Justyna Budzińska-Tylicka on the twenty-fifth anniversary of her death). *Archiwum Historii Medycyny* (Archives of the history of medicine) XXIV (1961): 443–458.

(D) Hulewicz, Jan. *Przegląd historyczno- oświatowy* (Historical-educational review), no. 2 (1962): 306–316.

(D) Kalabiński, Stanislaw. "Justyna Budzińska-Tylicka." In Feliks Tych, ed. *Słownik biograficzny działaczy polskiego ruchu robotniczego* (Biographical dictionary of Polish workers' movement activists). Warsaw: Książka i Wiedza, 1978, 1: 343–344.

(E) Pachucka, Romana. *Pamiętniki z lat 1886–1914* (Memoirs from the years 1886–1914). Wrocław: Zakład Narodowy im. Ossolińskich, 1958.

(E) Wawrzykowska-Wierciochowa, Dionizja. *Nie po kwiatach los je prowadził* (Fate led them not along the flower path). Warsaw: Iskry, 1987.

(E) *Wielka Encyklopedia Powszechna PWN* (Great encyclopaedia of the Polish Scientific Publishers). Warsaw, 2001, 4: 565.

BUJWIDOWA, Kazimiera (1867-1932)

Polish feminist campaigner and publicist.

Kazimiera Bujwidowa (born Klimontowicz) was born on 16 October 1867 in Warsaw. She was the only child of Ludwika (*nee* Szczęśniewska) and Kazimierz Klimontowicz, the latter from a lower noble family of Lithuanian origin. Although her parents were not married, her father gave her his name and supported her financially. After the death of Kazimiera's mother, Kazimiera was placed in the custody of her aunt, Karolina Petronela Klimontowicz, who had participated in the January 1863 Uprising against Russian rule. Kazimiera Klimontowicz attended ***Justyna Budzińska***'s private boarding school for girls in Warsaw, going on to qualify as a private tutor after her graduation. Her plans to study abroad were opposed by her aunt and so, since women were not allowed to study at the Russified Warsaw University, Kazimiera Klimontowicz enrolled in a dressmaking course. In the late 1880s, she also attended classes at the secret 'Flying University'–a social initiative founded in 1885 to enable women from the Russian partition, unable to study abroad, to receive higher education. In 1886, Kazimiera Klimontowicz married the bacteriologist and social worker Odon Bujwid, with whom she formed a happy partnership. She worked in the laboratory of her husband as his assistant and laboratory technician. The Bujwid family always participated together in social and educational activities. They had six children: four daughters (Kazimiera, b.1888; Zofia, b.1890; Jadwiga, b.1892 and Helena, b.1897) and two sons (Jan, b.1889 and Stanisław, b.1895).

In 1893, the Bujwids moved to Cracow, where Odon was appointed professor at the Jagiellonian University and Bujwidowa worked as an administrator at the Institute for the Production of Sera and Vaccines, headed by her husband. In this period, Bujwidowa participated in social, educational and feminist campaigns in both Warsaw and Cracow; these aimed to reduce adult illiteracy, promote education and establish reading rooms for young people. From 1899 to 1901, Bujwidowa was a member of the Board of Directors of the *Towarzystwo Szkół Ludowych* (*TSL*, Society of Elementary Schools), in which she had been actively involved since 1893. In the Cracow Women's Circle of the *TSL*, she encountered the two feminists Maria Siedlecka and Maria Turzyma-Wiśniewska (1860–1922). Bujwidowa organized the Cracow *Czytelnia dla kobiet* (Reading Room for Women) and became its Chairwoman. She was co-organizer and Board member of the Adam Mickiewicz People's University, an educational organization that aimed to improve mass education, and published the pamphlets *Domy ludowe* (People's houses, 1903) and *Reforma wychowania i ochrona dziecka* (The reform of child rearing and child protection, 1905). Bujwidowa considered the roles of mothers and schools crucially important in the creation of a better society. Women, therefore, were to be professionally trained in pedagogy, psychology and hygiene. Bujwidowa also argued for co-education and in 1909, attended the *II Polski Kongres Pedagogiczny* (Second All-Polish Pedagogical Congress) as Vice-Chair of the Girls' Education Section.

During the 1890s, Bujwidowa officially abandoned the Roman Catholic Church and declared herself an atheist. She co-operated with the anticlerical *Komitet młodzieży krakowskiej* (Cracow Youth Committee), financing the publication of a manifesto, *Młodzież społeczeństwu* (The Young for Society). Inspired by the ideas of the Spanish freethinker Francisco Ferrear, Bujwidowa co-initiated the *Towarzystwo Etyczne* (Ethical Society). In addition to her freethinking activities, which led to certain hostilities towards her from conservative circles in Cracow, Bujwidowa led campaigns for women's higher education. As Chairwoman of the *Towarzystwo Gimnazjalnej Szkoły Żeńskiej* (Society of High Schools for Girls), she established the first High School for Girls on Polish territory where girls could take state graduation examinations.

In 1894, Bujwidowa initiated a campaign for women's university admission, coordinating the submission of women's individual and collective applications to the Galician universities in Lviv and Cracow. The campaign was not without success: in 1897, the authorities of both universities decided to open their philosophy and medicine faculties for women. In 1904, Bujwidowa signed petitions to the *Sejm Krajowy* in Lviv (Parliament of autonomous Galicia) and in 1910 to the State Council in Vienna, demanding full equality for women in university education. In the same period, Bujwidowa participated in suffrage campaigns, chairing a women's delegation to the *Sejm Krajowy* in 1896 that demanded equal voting rights for women in council elections. She also attended Polish women's congresses, where she established contacts with feminists from the Russian partition. In 1903, within the framework of the Cracow Reading Room for Women, she co-organized the *Sekcja dla Obrony Praw Kobiet* (Section for the Defence of Women's Rights), became its first Chairwoman and participated in electoral campaigns and feminist meetings. In 1908, the first general election for the Austrian Parliament (State Council in Vienna) was held for the Habsburg Monarchy as a whole, but women were excluded from voting. In protest, Bujwidowa and other suffragists pointedly nominated Maria Dulębianka as a candidate for the *Sejm Krajowy* in Lviv. In 1909, Bujwidowa joined the *Komitet Równouprawnienia Kobiet* (Committee of Equal Rights for Polish Women) in Cracow, an organization that had made contact with international suffragists at the Congress of the International

Woman Suffrage Alliance held in London in the same year. In 1910, as a representative from Galicia, Bujwidowa attended the International Congress on Women's Questions (at least this is the name given in the sources) in Paris. In 1912, she participated in the First Austrian Congress on Women's Voting Rights in Vienna, as a result of which she was chosen to join a group of delegates to the Prime Minister of Austria. The Congress also led to the establishment of the *Polska Sekcja Związku Austriackiego Praw Wyborczych Kobiet* (Polish Section of the Austrian Union for Voting Rights for Women) in Cracow.

While fighting for women's political rights, Bujwidowa also published political commentaries in the liberal *Nowa Reforma* (New reform, 1902-1907) and in the feminist *Ster* (Helm, 1907-1911). In the social and cultural review, *Krytyka* (Criticism), she had her own column entitled "Przegląd ruchu kobiecego" (Women's movement review, 1903-1904; 1907 and 1911). She edited a collection of articles by Polish feminists under the title of *Głos kobiet w kwestii kobiecej* (Women's voices on the woman question, 1903) and also wrote several short feminist pamphlets: *Prawa nauczycielek* (The rights of female teachers, 1903); *Czy kobieta powinna mieć te same prawa co mężczyzna* (On whether women should have the same rights as men, 1909); *U źródeł kwestii kobiecej* (The roots of the woman question, 1910) and *O postępowym i niepostępowym ruchu kobiecym w Galicji* (On the progressive and non-progressive women's movement in Galica, 1913). In her view, women's organizations were not progressive if they were not interested in women's political and educational emancipation. In late 1918/early 1919, Bujwidowa wrote *Deklaracja Programowa kobiet wobec nadchodzących wyborów do Sejmu Ustawodawczego* (A women's manifesto on the forthcoming parliamentary election).

During World War I, Bujwidowa and her husband organized a hospital for the wounded soldiers of the Polish Legions (Polish military formations fighting under Austro-Hungarian command until 1917). In 1918, Bujwidowa was appointed manager of the Institute for the Production of Sera and Vaccines, where she worked up until her death in 1932. After the war, Bujwidowa withdrew from social activism due to chronic illness. She died in Cracow on 8 October 1932.

Dr. Dobrochna Kałwa
Institute of History,
Jagiellonian University, Poland

SOURCES

(B) "Program I Zjazdu Kobiet Polskich w Krakowie" (Program of the First Polish Women's Convention in Cracow). *Nowe Słowo* (New word), no. 20 (1905): 409-412.

(B) "Akcja o prawa wyborcze kobiet w Galicji" (Campaign for women's voting rights in Galicia). *Ster* (Helm), nos. 7-8 (1908): 314.

(B) Kornecki, Jan. *Księga pamiątkowa II Kongresu Pedagogicznego odbytego w dniach 1 i 2 listopada 1909 roku we Lwowie* (Commemorative volume of the Second Pedagogical Congress, Lviv, 1-2 October 1909). Lviv: Komitet Wykonawczy Polskiego Kongresu Pedagogicznego, 1909.

(B) "Zjazd Austriacki Wyborczych Praw Kobiet" (Austrian Convention on Women's Voting Rights). *Ster* (Helm), no. 7 (1912): 10-12.

(B) *Pamiętnik Zjadzu Kobiet Polskich odbytego w dniach 11 i 12 maja 1913 roku* (Proceedings of the Polish Women's Convention, 11-12 May 1913). Cracow: Biuro Porady Kobiet "Gościna," 1913.

(B) Walewska, Cecylia. *W walce o równe prawa. Nasze bojownice* (Fighting for equal rights. Our fighters). Warsaw, 1930.

(B) Hulewicz, Jan. *Sprawa wyższego wykształcenia kobiet w Polsce w XIX wieku* (The question of women's higher education in Poland in the nineteenth century). Cracow: Polska Akademia Umiejętności, 1939.

(C) Bujwidowa, Kazimiera. "Cele i zadania czytelń kobiecych" (The goals and tasks of reading rooms for women). *Nowe Słowo* (New word), no. 24 (1903): 563-566.

(C) Bujwidowa, Kazimiera. "Stańmy się sobą!" (Let's become ourselves!). *Krytyka* (Critique) 2 (1907): 178-186.

(C) Bujwidowa, Kazimiera. *Czy kobieta powinna mieć te same prawa co mężczyzna?* (On whether women should have the same rights as men). Cracow: W. Kornecki i K. Wojner, 1909.

(C) Bujwidowa, Kazimiera. *U źródeł kwestii kobiecej* (The roots of the woman question). Warsaw: Redakcja "Steru," 1910.

(D) Witkowska, Helena. "Wspomnienie o śp. Kazimierze Bujwidowej" (In memory of Kazimiera Bujwidowa). *Kobieta Współczesna* (Contemporary woman), no. 40 (1932): 785-787.

(D) Hulewicz, Jan. *Kazimiera Bujwidowa*. In *Polski Słownik Biograficzny* (Polish biographical dictionary). Cracow: Polska Akademia Umiejętności, 1937, 3: 111-12.

(D) Kwiatek, Agnieszka. "*Kazimiera Bujwidowa. Poglądy i działalność społeczna*" (Kazimiera Bujwidowa. Her ideas and social activism). In Anna Żarnowska and Andrzej Szwarc, eds. *Kobieta i świat polityki. Polska na tle porównawczym w XIX i początkach XX wieku* (Women and the world of politics. Comparative studies on Poland in the nineteenth and early twentieth centuries). Warsaw: Wydawnictwo Sejmowe, 1994.

(D) Dormus, Katarzyna. *Kazimiera Bujwidowa 1867-1932. Życie i działalność społeczno-oświatowa* (Kazimiera Bujwidowa 1867-1932. Her life and social and educational activities). Cracow: Wydawnictwo i Drukarnia "Secesja," 2002.

(E) Czajecka, Bogusława. *Z domu w szeroki świat. Droga kobiet do niezależności w zaborze austriackim w latach 1890-1914* (From home to the outside world. Women's road to independence in the Austrian Partition, 1890-1914). Cracow: Towarzystwo Autorów i Wydawców Prac Naukowych Universitas, 1990.

CANTACUZINO, Princess Alexandrina (1876-1944)

One of the most important leaders of the Romanian women's movement; President of the *Societatea Ortodoxă Națională a Femeilor Române* (*SONFR*, National Orthodox Society of Romanian Women) (1918–1938); Vice-President (from 1921) of the *Consiliul Național al Femeilor Române* (*CNFR*, National Council of Romanian Women) and its only President from 1930; co-founder and first President (1923–1924) of the Little Entente of Women (LEW) (1923–1929); member of the official delegation of Romania to the League of Nations (1929–1938); Vice-President of the ICW (1925–1936) and convener of the ICW Art Committee (from 1936); President of the Romanian feminist organizations *Solidaritatea* (Solidarity) (from 1925) and of the *Gruparea Femeilor Române* (*GFR*, Association of Romanian Women) (from 1929).

Alexandrina (Didina) Cantacuzino (born Pallady) was born on 20 September 1876 in Ciocăneşti (Ilfov county, near Bucharest), a village on her family's estate. Both her parents were from old boyar families. Alexandrina's father, Theodor Pallady (1853-1916), was a career officer–a member of a Moldavian boyar family first documented in the twelfth century. In 1874, he married Alexandrina Krețulescu (1848-1881), an heiress from a well-known, wealthy Wallachian boyar family. Together they had four children but only Alexandrina survived infancy. After her mother's death, Alexandrina was adopted by an aunt and raised by the Ghica family, another famous boyar family. As a young woman, Alexandrina was sent to France to study.

In 1899 (?), Alexandrina Pallady married the conservative politician Grigore Gheorghe Cantacuzino (1872-1930), son of Gheorghe Grigore Cantacuzino ('the Nabob'), the wealthiest Romanian landowner of the time and leading figure of the Conservative Party. Her husband's family was of Greek origin and claimed to be descended from the Byzantine imperial family of Cantacuzino. For this reason, some of the Cantacuzinos used the aristocratic title of prince/ss, a title also adopted by Alexandrina after her marriage to Grigore Cantacuzino. The couple had three sons (born between 1900 and 1905) and the marriage lasted until 1930, when Grigore Cantacuzino died. Alexandrina Cantacuzino never remarried.

Cantacuzino was an ambitious and enterprising woman. Proud of her boyar origins and affiliation to a family that had once produced rulers of the Romanian provinces, she saw her purpose in life extending beyond the roles of wife and mother. Identifying with Romantic ideas on the historic mission of the Romanian upper classes in the creation and defence of the nation, Cantacuzino sought to translate them into practical endeavours that would strengthen the nation. This was an approach that resonated with the ideology of (upper-class) women's organized assistance for the socially disadvantaged as a way of serving the country and the nation. Her social activities began in 1910, when she helped establish the *Societatea Ortodoxă Națională a Femeilor Române* (*SONFR*, National Orthodox Society of Romanian Women), a Christian Orthodox women's philanthropic society. Cantacuzino also enrolled in the Red Cross and during World War I, dedicated most of her time and energy to helping the wounded, providing support to Romanian prisoners and opening canteens. In that period, she organized and led the largest hospital in Bucharest. Her determination to remain in the capital, then under German occupation, and to offer help to Romanian soldiers in spite of warnings received from the occupation regime, almost cost her her liberty.

In recognition of her war activities and enterprising character, Cantacuzino was elected President of the *SONFR* in 1918. Under her presidency, which lasted until 1938, the *SONFR* became one of the most important Romanian women's organizations with branches all over the country. It was the organization Cantacuzino seemed fondest of, and into which she invested most of her material resources and energy. The *SONFR* founded numerous educational establishments, hospitals, workers' and students' restaurants, and organized public lectures with a view to propagating a moral, patriotic and religious spirit. Cantacuzino and the *SONFR* were inspired by the wish to create an educational and cultural movement among the masses that would strengthen the nation and instill the moral and ethical values of Christian Orthodoxy into society. To achieve these goals, 'Romanian women' were called on to appropriate public space, drawing upon the symbolic and social value of their mothering roles. Cantacuzino's passionate discourse of 'women's social mission' attracted many upper- and middle-class women aspiring to an active role in public life to the ranks of the *SONFR*. Alexandrina Cantacuzino also established contacts with members of two newly formed feminist organizations: the *Liga Drepturilor și Datoriilor Femeilor* (*LDDR*, League for Women's Rights and Duties, founded in 1911) and the *Asociația pentru Emanciparea Civilă și Politică a Femeilor Române* (*AECPFR*, Association for the Civil and Political Emancipation of Romanian Women, founded in 1917). In 1919, Cantacuzino unsuccessfully tried to bring the *SONFR* into an alliance with the *LDDR* and, in the same period, became a member of the *AECPFR*. From then on, she became a dominant figure in the emerging Romanian women's movement. In 1921, she helped create the *Consiliul Național al Femeilor Române* (*CNFR*, National Council of Romanian Women), a federation of women's organizations which aimed to bring together and coordinate the work of all the Romanian women's associations in Romania, acting as the representative national body of the Romanian women's movement at home and in the International Council of Women (ICW). Cantacuzino was elected one of the Vice-Presidents of the *CNFR* and in this capacity became actively involved in lobbying for women's civil and political rights. In 1923, Cantacuzino took part in the Rome Congress of the International Woman Suffrage Alliance (IWSA, from 1926 the International Alliance of Women for Suffrage and Equal Citizenship, IAWSEC) as a representative of the *LDDR*. She took the opportunity on this occasion to create, together with other East European representatives, the Little Entente of Women (LEW), an alliance of women's organizations from Romania, Poland, Czechoslovakia, Yugoslavia and Greece, which sought to design common strategies for peace and the improvement of women's position in the region. Cantacuzino became the LEW's first President, serving a one-year term. In 1925, she was elected one of the Vice-Presidents of the ICW and became, in Romanian public opinion, the leading light of Romanian feminism. The title of ICW Vice-President further strengthened Cantacuzino's authority in the *CNFR*. She became the second President of the organization, responsible for external affairs alongside ***Calypso Botez,*** who, as President, was responsible for internal affairs.

In 1925, another Romanian feminist organization, *Solidaritatea* (Solidarity) was created, from 1926 under Cantacuzino's presidency. *Solidaritatea* soon became the third Romanian organization–after the *Liga Drepturilor şi Datoriilor Femeilor Române* in 1913 and the *Asociaţia pentru Emanciparea Civilă şi Politică a Femeilor Române* in 1924–to be affiliated to the IAWSEC. The new organization increased existing animosities towards Cantacuzino and her dominant role in the Romanian women's movement. Older feminists from the *AECPFR* and *LDDR* accused Cantacuzino of attempting to monopolize and misrepresent the Romanian women's movement at home and abroad. After 1930, when ***Calypso Botez*** resigned from her position as *CNFR* President and other important feminists withdrew from the organization, Cantacuzino remained the only President of the *CNFR*. Between 1934 and 1937, Cantacuzino's critics tried repeatedly but unsuccessfully to create a separate federation of Romanian women's organizations that could have replaced the *CNFR* as a representative body abroad and counteracted Cantacuzino's ambition to represent the Romanian women's movement. In the *SONFR* too, Cantacuzino's ambitions and preoccupation with 'internationalism' in 1935 caused significant elements within the organization to vehemently contest her leadership. Cantacuzino handled the situation resolutely, forcing protesters to withdraw from the organization.

Despite criticism at home however, Cantacuzino's 'international career' continued successfully. Her energy and rhetorical skills were appreciated in the International Council of Women and she was chosen to represent the organization on numerous occasions (in 1927 and 1933 at the League of Nations; in 1936 at the Congress of the National Council of Women of India; in 1936 as convener of the ICW Committee on Fine and Applied Arts). At the League of Nations, Cantacuzino also acted as IAWSEC rapporteur (1926, 1928 and 1938). From 1929, she was a technical councilor for the Romanian delegation on committees formed to address issues such as trafficking in women and child protection. From 1938, as an official delegate of the Romanian government, she participated in discussions on international legislation, dealing with such issues as abandoned and illegitimate children, a Children's Charter and the protection of children in wartime (together with Spanish and French delegates, Cantacuzino supported the idea of the establishment of neutral zones for the protection of children).

At the same time, Cantacuzino began supporting women's social work as a member of the financial commission of the Bucharest municipality (1927), and from 1928, as municipal councilor of Bucharest. Preoccupied with the professionalization of social work, she invested a great deal of energy into opening one of the first Romanian schools for women social workers (1929). In 1930, the school was affiliated to the *CNFR* under the name of *Şcoala de Auxiliare Sociale* (The School of Social Auxiliaries). Cantacuzino's social activity resulted in her being awarded the *Meritul Cultural* (Cultural Merit) with the rank of officer–the first Romanian woman to receive that distinction.

In 1929, certain women of 21 years or over became entitled to elect and be elected to local councils (those with primary or secondary education, vocational training, bureaucrats, members of leading cultural and charity societies, war widows and women who had received war decorations). At this time, Cantacuzino established and became President of the *Gruparea Femeilor Române* (*GFR*, Association of Romanian Women), which aimed to mobilize women in the exercise of their municipal rights, to forge solidarity among them and to support women's initiatives and interests at local council levels. Unlike the older feminist organizations, the *GFR* forbade its members to enroll in political parties because of women's lack of political rights, in particular, suffrage. The organization also strongly criticized the Romanian political party system. In the 1930s, under the auspices of the *GFR*, Cantacuzino's attitude to Romanian democracy harshened, displaying a virulent nationalism with strong xenophobic accents. In that period, Cantacuzino and the *GFR* demanded women's political rights within the framework of a corporatist reform of the parliament that would restrain the free competition between political parties. (In 1938, in accordance with the new Romanian Constitution, Romanian women were granted parliamentary voting rights and the first women MPs were elected.) There is no clear evidence of Cantacuzino's support for the extreme-right legionary movement before the establishment of the legionary regime in 1940. However in 1938, Cantacuzino was put under permanent surveillance of the police at her residence, accused of having connections to the legionary movement. Not long before her home arrest, Cantacuzino's youngest son, an important supporter of the legionaries, had been shot dead, together with the leader of the movement. This episode apparently is not related to Cantacuzino's show of support for the legionary regime in 1940. Cantacuzino died of old age in September/October 1944.

An authoritarian but extremely enterprising woman, Alexandrina Cantacuzino was probably the most important and controversial figure to dominate the Romanian women's movement. Throughout her public career, she combined nationalist beliefs with women's rights activism. As a result of her active involvement in a number of national and international activities to improve the situation of women and children, she became publicly identified with the image of the interwar Romanian women's movement.

Roxana Cheşchebec
Ph.D. Candidate,
Central European University, Budapest

SOURCES

(A) Romanian National Archives, Fond familia Cantacuzino, 1853–1965.

(A) Romanian National Archives, Fond *SONFR*, 1910–1948.

(B) *Bulletin. International Council of Women* IV–XV (September 1925–December 1936).

(B) *1e Conference de la Petite Entente des Femmes. Discours prononcés aux séances publiques de 3 et 4 Novembre 1923* (The first conference of the Little Entente of Women. Public speeches held on November 3-4 1923) Bucharest: Tipografia "Dorneanu," 1923.

(B) *La deuxième conference de la Petite Entente des Femmes à Belgrade. Discours et rapports de 1-4 novembre 1924* (The second conference of the Little Entente of Women at Belgrade. Speeches and reports presented on 1-4 November 1924). Bucharest: L'imprimerie des livres religieux, 1925.

(C) *Discours tenue par la Princesse Alexandrine Gr. Cantacuzene à la réunion publique organisée par l'Association de la "Petite Entente des Femmes" à Belgrad, november 1924* (Speech held by Princess Alexandrina Gr. Cantacuzino at the public meeting organized by the Association of the "Little Entente of Women" in Belgrade). Bucharest: Imprimerie du Ministčre des Arts et Cultes, 1924.

(C) *Conferinta tinuta de D-na Alexandrina Gr. Cantacuzino in ziua de 31 Ianuarie 1926 la Fundatia Carol I asupra lucrarilor Conferintei Micii Intelegeri Feminine de la Atena in zilele de 6-13 Decemvrie 1925 si asupra calatoriei D-sale in Egipt si Ierusalim* (Lecture held by Mrs Alexandrina Gr. Cantacuzino on 31 January 1926 at the Carol I Foundation on the work of the conference of the Little Entente of Women between 6 and 13 December 1925 and on her trip to Egypt and Jerusalem). Bucharest: Tipografia Cartilor Bisericesti, 1926.

(C) Cantacuzino, Alexandrina. *Cincisprezece ani de muncă socială şi culturală. Discursuri, conferinţe, articole, scrisori* (Fifteen years of social and cultural activity. Discourses, conference papers, articles, letters). [Bucharest]: Tipografia românească, 1928.

(C) Cantacuzino, Alexandrina. *Femeileîn faţa dreptului de vot. Programul de luptă al grupului femeilor române. Cuvîntare ţinută in ziua de 10 aprilie la Casa Femeii pentru Constituirea grupului femeilor române* (Women facing the right to vote. The action program of the Association of Romanian women. Speech held at Woman's House on 10 April for the establishment of the Association of Romanian Women). Bucharest: Tipografia Capitalei, [1929].

(E) Predescu, Lucian. *Enciclopedia României "Cugetarea". Material românesc. Oameni si înfăptuiri* (The encyclopedia of Romania "Cugetarea." Romanian material. People and facts) Bucharest: Editura Saeculum I. O., Editura Vestala, 1999 (first edition 1940).

CHEKHOVA, Mariia Aleksandrovna Argamakova (1866–1934)

Russian feminist activist. Founder (1905) of the *Soiuz Ravnopraviia Zhenshchin* (Women's Equal Rights Union) and editor (1907–1909) of the journal *Soiuz Zhenshchin* (Union of Women), the official organ of the *Soiuz Ravnopraviia Zhenshchin*. President (1909–1917) of the Moscow branch of the *Liga Ravnopraviia Zhenshchin* (League for Women's Equal Rights).

Mariia Chekhova was born Mariia Argamakova on 18 January 1866, into a gentry family in St Petersburg. Both her maternal and paternal grandfathers were teachers, as was her father, Aleksandr Pavlovich Argamakov, who taught at St Petersburg's First Military *Gimnazium* (high school). Mariia had a younger sister Sophia (married name Kemnits), born in 1869. Her mother, Ekaterina Ivanovna Mertsalova, died in 1872.

In 1877, Mariia's father remarried. Mariia had a difficult relationship with her stepmother (Serafima Alekseevna Popova) and when Aleksandr Pavlovich took a job in Irkutsk in 1880, Mariia happily moved in with her maternal grandmother, remaining there for the next ten years. She attended *gimnaziia* and later teachers' courses, graduating in 1886. She majored in mathematics, established her own school in St Petersburg (which existed from 1889 to 1916) and in 1890 married fellow educator Nikolai Chekhov.

Theirs was a companionate marriage; relations based on reciprocity and mutuality were idealized by the Russian intelligentsia of the time and the couple, heavily influenced by the ideas of Leo Tolstoi, sought to live out their ideals in the Russian countryside. From 1890 to 1904, the Chekhovs resided in several provincial towns and cities, where they established day and Sunday schools and ministered to victims of the 1891 famine. Mariia gave birth to seven children in succession: Ekaterina (b.1891), Liudmila (b.1892), Anna (b.1894), Aleksandr (1895–1916), Vladimir (1896–1900), Lev (1897–1899) and Sophia (b.1901).

Moving to Moscow in 1904, the Chekhovs became active participants in the Liberation movement and the Teachers Union. The outbreak of the 1905 Revolution made demands for political rights possible, but male liberals sought the vote solely for men and socialists only paid lip service to women's suffrage. In response, Chekhova, along with about thirty other women of the small Russian educated class, founded the *Soiuz Ravnopraviia Zhenshchin* (Women's Equal Rights Union) in Moscow in February 1905. Chekhova was the Secretary of the *Soiuz* and a member of its Central Bureau. Her husband was the only man in the *Soiuz* leadership. Chekhova's ties with the provinces aided the organization in its outreach to women outside Moscow and St Petersburg; by 1906, the *Soiuz* boasted a membership of eight to ten thousand and chapters throughout the Russian Empire.

In addition to her involvement with the *Soiuz Ravnopraviia Zhenshchin*, Chekhova taught Russian language and literature courses to workers of both sexes and helped organize the first Moscow children's club (a philanthropic and educational organization modeled on the US women's clubs). From 1906 to 1910, the Chekhov family lived in St Petersburg, where Mariia kept up her activism in the *Soiuz* and joined the *Russkoe Zhenskoe Vzaimno-Blagotvoritel'noe Obshchestvo* (Russian Women's Mutual Philanthropic Society). She also organized petition campaigns for women's suffrage to the Second *Duma* (Russian Parliament). As editor (1907–1909) of the journal *Soiuz Zhenshchin* (Union of Women), she took a socialist feminist line, arguing in the journal's third issue that the full liberation of women was possible "only when all exploitation of one person by another is ended; that is, under socialism" (Chekhova October 1907, 4). She was especially critical of the radical feminism of Mariia Pokrovskaia. Pokrovskaia, who in her journal *Zhenskii Vestnik* (Woman's herald) had emphasized the primacy of sexual oppression–especially in connection with prostitution–was accused by Chekhova of having "unfounded dreams and [using] idealistic airy sentences" (Chekhova December 1907, 18).

Representing the *Soiuz*, Chekhova served on the organizing committee for the first All-Russian Women's Congress in 1908. When the *Soiuz* disbanded and its journal ceased publication in December 1909, Chekhova found a new venue for her feminist activity as President of the Moscow branch of the *Liga Ravnopraviia Zhenshchin* (League for Women's Equal Rights). Despite having moved to Moscow, she continued to be active in St Petersburg as well. She attended congresses on prostitution and education such as the *Pervyi Vserossiiskii S'ezd po Bor'be s Torgom Zhenshchinami* (First All-Russian Congress on the Struggle against the Trade in Women; held on 21–25 April 1910) and the League-organized Women's Education Congress (held in the tsarist capital from 26 December 1912 to 4 January 1913). Focusing on 'small deeds' in a time of political reaction, she joined the lobbying of the very conservative Third and Fourth Dumas for suffrage and equal rights and rejoiced in the modest victories won for women: the granting of equal inheritance rights to daughters and sons regarding moveable and real urban property (1912) and the rights of wives to have separate passports from their husbands (1914). She also kept up her educational work, initiating a course on pre-school education at the Moscow Teachers Courses, becoming the head of the pre-school education section of the Moscow Pedagogical Circle and organizing a daycare center for children of students at the Women's Higher Courses.

After the February 1917 Revolution and the formation of the Provisional Government, the *Liga Ravnopraviia Zhenshchin* spearheaded a successful campaign for women's right to vote. Chekhova was prominent among those who lobbied the new Provisional Government and its Minister of Justice, Alexander Kerensky, for women to be included in the electorate. A large feminist-led demonstration on 19 March won a promise from Provisional Government leaders that women would be given suffrage rights and, with the passing of the July 1917 suffrage law, Russia became the first world power to extend ballot rights to women. Chekhova continued to promote feminist political involvement, prompting a split at the All-Russian Congress of Women (held in April 1917) and the creation of the *Respublikanskikh Soiuz Demokraticheskikh Zhenskikh Organizatsii* (Republican Union of Democratic Women's Organizations). Chekhova was on the *Liga Ravnopraviia Zhenshchin*'s electoral list for the Constituent Assembly, along with the *Liga*'s President ***Poliksena Shishkina-Iavein,*** historian ***E. N. Shchepkina,*** political activist ***E. Kuskova,*** historian and *zemstvo* statistician A. Efimenko and A. Kalmykova (a supporter of 'legal Marxism'). The list received 7676 votes.

Mariia Chekhova and her husband remained in Russia after the Bolshevik Revolution. Nicholai Chekhov became a prominent Soviet educator and, with feminist organizations banned, Mariia Chekhova also devoted herself to educational activity and to the writing of her memoirs (never published but presently located in the Moscow City Historical Archive). Chekhova died in Moscow on 8 April 1934, her significance as a feminist pioneer consigned by the Soviets to the dustbin of history. Besides her husband and daughters, she was survived by four grandchildren: Vladimir and Liudmila Dervis and Elena and Nataliia Stefanovich.

Rochelle Goldberg Ruthchild
The Union Institute and University
and the Davis Center for Russian and Eurasian Studies,
Harvard University

SOURCES

(A) Mariia Chekhova's personal archive is located in the *Tsentral'nyi Istoricheskii Arkhiv gorod Moskvy* (*TsIAM*), Fond 2251 (Mariia Aleksandrovna Chekhova). It contains her extensive autobiography (covering her life from birth to the 1890s) and a sixty page biographical sketch by her daughter, Ekaterina Nikolaevna Chekhova (which includes useful information about her mother's life in the late nineteenth and twentieth centuries both before and after the Bolshevik Revolution, as well as reminiscences about mother and daughter working together on the journal *Soiuz Zhenshchin*). Other materials include correspondence with Liubov Gurevich, Anna Miliukova, Anna Shabanova and Poliksena Shishkina-Iavein, as well as Chekhova's exchange with Kerensky in March 1917 on the subject of women's suffrage.

(A) Materials about Mariia Chekhova and Nikolai Chekhov's activities in the *Soiuz Ravnopraviia Zhenshchin* (Women's Equal Rights Union) can be found in the *Gosudarstvennyi Arkhiv Rossiiskoi Federatsii* (*GARF*), Fond 516 (*Soiuz Ravnopravnosti Zhenshchin*).

(B) Numerous articles and editorials in *Soiuz Zhenshchin* (Union of Women) (1907-1909).

(B) Mirovich, N. (Z. S. Ivanova). *Iz istorii zhenskago dvizheniia v Rossii* (From the history of the women's movement in Russia). Moscow: Tipografiia I. D. Sytina, 1908.

(C) Chekhova, Mariia. "Bor'ba za pravo, kak nravstvennaia obiazannost' zhenshchiny" (The struggle for rights as the moral obligation of women). *Soiuz zhenshchin* 3 (October 1907).

(C) Chekhova, Mariia. "Khronika zhenskogo voprosa v Rossii" (Chronicle of the woman question in Russia). *Soiuz zhenshchin* 5 (December 1907).

(D) Arian, Praskovia N. "M. A. Chekhova." In Praskov'ia N. Arian, ed. *Pervyi zhenskii kalendar' na 1912 god* (First Women's Calendar for 1912). St Petersburg, 1912, 8-11.

(D) Ruthchild, Rochelle Goldberg. "Chekhova, Mariia Aleksandrovna Argamakova." In Norma Corigliano Noonan and Carol Nechemias, eds. *Encyclopedia of Russian Women's Movements*. Westport, Connecticut: Greenwood Press, 2001, 13-15.

(D) Ruthchild, Rochelle Goldberg. "Writing for Their Rights. Four Feminist Journalists: Mariia Chekhova, Liubov' Gurevich, Mariia Pokrovskaia, and Ariadna Tyrkova." In Barbara T. Norton and Jehanne M. Gheith, eds. *An Improper Profession: Women, Gender, and Journalism in Late Imperial Russia*. Durham and London: Duke University Press, 2001, 167-195.

(E) Goldberg, Rochelle (Ruthchild). *The Russian Women's Movement 1859-1917*. Doctoral Dissertation. University of Rochester, 1976.

(E) Grishina, Zoia V. *Zhenskie Organizatsii v Rossii (1905 g.-fevral'/mart 1917 g* (Women's organizations in Russia, February 1905-March 1917). Doctoral Dissertation. Moscow State University, 1978.

(E) Edmondson, Linda. *Feminism in Russia*. Stanford: Stanford University Press, 1984.

(E) Stites, Richard. *The Women's Liberation Movement in Russia: Feminism, Nihilism, and Bolshevism 1860-1930*. Princeton: Princeton University Press, 1978; 1991.

ÇOBA, Shaqe (Marie) (1875-1954)

The first woman intellectual of the city of Shkodra (Shkoder in Albanian); founder (in Shkodra, 1920) of the organization *Gruaja Shqiptare* (The Albanian Woman); activist of the women's and national independence movements.

Shaqe (Marie) Çoba was born in Shkodra in 1875 to the distinguished Shiroka family, traditionally active in the social life of the city. Her father's name was Zef Shiroka. She had one brother, Loro, and one sister whose name, like that of her mother, is unknown. Shaqe Shiroka's nephews and grandchildren—namely Filip Shiroka and his son Angjelini (an architect in Beirut), as well as Ejlli, Zefi, Dr. Frederiku, Emili and Tonini Shiroka–became well known for their social activities. Shaqe Shiroka's intelligence was noted from an early age. She attended the elementary school in Shkodra, an ancient town in northern Albania, and completed middle school at an Austrian convent school in Zagreb, where she studied Italian, German and Serbo-Croat. In 1904, she went to Italy to continue her studies (in Venice). On the way, she met Ndoc Çoba (1865-8 March 1945), who was impressed by Shiroka's intelligence and later asked her family for her hand in marriage. In the Çoba family, Shaqe found a stimulating intellectual environment and a home for her national ideas. Ndoc Çoba was an affirmed Albanian nationalist and involved in a great number of cultural and political projects. The couple had one son, Karlo Çoba (November 1907-27 January 1968).

On 3 August 1920, Shaqe Çoba founded *Gruaja Shqiptare* (The Albanian Woman), for upper-class women of Shkodra interested in issues of emancipation. Shaqe Çoba led the organization and Habibe Bekteshi was Honorary Chair; Paulina Leka was secretary and Albina Ashiku, bookkeeper. *Gruaja Shqiptare* was formed principally to raise and distribute funds on behalf of the National Army during the 1920 Koplik war (against Yugoslav forces pushing for the annexation of Albanian territories). The program of *Gruaja Shqiptare* stated that "our aim has always been [...] to serve our Patria, which our ancestors have preserved from the countless invasions of enemies." Members of *Gruaja Shqiptare* collected money and other donations from families in Shkodra, which they then distributed among soldiers, volunteers and poor families (e.g. the families of those lost in the war). Those women who served *Gruaja Shqiptare* as volunteers wore a strap of white cloth on their arms with the initials "G Sh" in red letters. Rich documentation, which has been well preserved by the Çoba family, sheds light on the diverse activities of these women in this period.

In order to publicize the work of *Gruaja Shqiptare*, the organization also ran a magazine, *Gruaja Shqiptare* (The Albanian woman), from November 1920 to July 1921. The magazine informed readers about donations–including the exact sums and names of donors–and published articles on the problems of 'the Albanian housewife.' *Gruaja Shqiptare* strove to show ways in which Albanian women might function 'properly' in their society and many articles discussed women's 'rights' and 'duties.' Articles such as "Zakonet Tona" (Our customs) called for the "ladies of Shkodra" to lead their "co-citizen sisters towards development" and rid the country "of those undesirable customs which we have inherited from our ancestors, but which today we have no reason to keep in the face of the ray of civilization that has begun to flame among us" (*Gruaja Shqiptare*, no. 2). In articles such as "Detyrat e nanes" (Mother's duties), mothers were instructed how best to educate their children: parents were to emulate the moral and national ideal; to instill in their children a love of work; to send girls to school and set them a good and virtuous example. For the first time in Albanian history, women's opinions on their own rights, education and culture had acquired a public forum through the pages of *Gruaja Shqiptare*; for the first time, their thoughts on a new moral awareness and a new understanding of modern Albanian womanhood could be heard. "We should convince ourselves that woman is ... the spirit of human society and the center of the family" (*Gruaja Shqiptare*, no. 6). "'The Albanian Woman' must be strong and prosper ... not only in Shkodra but in all regions of Albania, if only to tell the civilized world [*sic*] that even 'The Albanian Woman' knows how to act, knows how to love and honor her patria" (*Gruaja Shqiptare*, no. 9). The magazine closed for financial reasons within a year.

According to her grandson Ndoc Çoba, Shaqe Çoba was equipped with an unusually strong memory, as well as an interest in the preservation of different documents, events and stories (she kept an encyclopedic diary). She was a very good economist, a skill that she demonstrated in her administration of the family estates and Ndoc, who lived with his intelligent and knowledgeable grandmother for some years, recalls how remarkable it was that Çoba's husband often accepted her opinions on political matters. Ndoc also remembers how she encouraged him to attend university which, for 'biographical reasons,' (i.e. opposition to the communist regime), would never happen.

In November 2002, on the occasion of the ninetieth anniversary of Albanian Independence, the President of the Republic of Albania, Alfred Moisiu, posthumously awarded Marie Çoba the "*Naim Frasheri*" Order (named after a great Albanian national writer), for her participation in the 1920s independence movement as a fighter "against the division of Albania and for the emancipation of the Albanian woman."

Shaqe Çoba was the first woman intellectual of Shkodra and one of the first activists of the women's and national independence movements.

Zenepe Dibra
President of the Association
"Intellectual women of Shkodra"

Translated from the Albanian by Artemisa Celanji, MA student, Department of Gender Studies, CEU, Budapest.

SOURCES

(A) *Arkivi Qendror Shteteror* (State Central Archives), Fund 847, year 1920, file 177.
(A) *Arkivi Qendror Shteteror* (State Central Archives), Fund 152, year 1920, file 184.
(B) *Gruaja Shqiptare* (The Albanian woman) (November 1920–July 1921).
(B) Shiroka, Filip. *Zani i Zemres* (Voice of the heart), 1932.
(E) Bushati, Hamdi. *Shkodra dhe motet* (Shkoder through the years). Vol. 1. Shkoder, 1998.
(E) Bushati, Hamdi. *Shkodra dhe motet* (Shkoder through the years). Vol. 2. Shkoder, 1999.
(E) Musaj, Fatmira. *Gruaja ne Shqiperi (1912-1939)* [Woman in Albania (1912-1939)]. Tirana: Academy of Science, 2002.
(E) Dibra, Zenepe. *Bijat e Rozafes' (gra te shquara te hapsires shkodrane)* [Children of Rozafa (famous women of Shkodra)]. Shkoder, 2004.
(E) Xhevat, Rrepishti. *Lufta per mbrojtjen e Shkodres ne vitet 1918-1920* (The war for the defense of Shkoder in the years 1918-1920).

DASZYŃSKA-GOLIŃSKA, Zofia (1866–1934)

Polish socialist, suffrage campaigner and social activist; economist, sociologist, professor at the *Wolna Wszechnica Polska* (Free Polish University), publicist and member of the Polish Senate (1928–1930). Pseudonyms: Jaskółka, 'Z. D.,' 'ZDG (Dr ZDG),' 'Z,' 'z,' 'PD,' 'ZP,' 'Z. G.' and 'S. P. Dański.'

Zofia Daszyńska-Golińska (*nee* Poznańska) was born in Warsaw on 6 August 1866, to an impoverished landowning family. Her parents, Damian Poznański–an agronomist and estate administrator–and Aniela born Puternicka (no further data), created an atmosphere conducive to intellectual development at home (where Zofia, her sister Wanda and brother Michał were all educated). In 1878, having graduated from a state grammar school for girls in Warsaw (finishing the last two years of secondary education in Lublin), Zofia Poznańska became a private tutor. In 1885, she took up studies in political economy and economic history at the University of Zurich, which she completed in 1891 with a doctorate in demography entitled *Zürichs Bevölkerung im XVIII Jahrhundert* (Zurich's population in the eighteenth century). The following year she moved to Vienna to continue her studies in economics and history, later–after several years in Warsaw–becoming an assistant professor at the Humboldt University in Berlin (1894–1896).

While studying abroad, Poznańska encountered socialist activists, one of whom, Feliks Daszyński (1863–1890), she married in 1888. Her husband was the brother of Ignacy Daszyński (1866–1936), an outstanding socialist figure, leader of the *Polska Partia Socjaldemokratyczna Galicji i Śląska Cieszyńskiego* (*PPS*, Polish Social Democratic Party of Galicia and Teschen Silesia) and, in the interwar period, Prime Minister (1918) and Deputy Prime Minister (1920) of the Polish Republic. In 1890, Feliks Daszyński died unexpectedly and several years later, Daszyńska married Stanisław Goliński (1868–1931), a botanist. The Golinskis did not have their own children but brought up Stanislaw's son Jan from a previous marriage (Jan would later become a doctor and independence activist).

Daszyńska-Golińska was active in many spheres of life: research, politics, social activism and publishing. Upon her return from Germany, she settled in Cracow (then in autonomous Habsburg Galicia), where she associated herself with the *PPS*. She wrote for the socialist periodicals *Naprzód* (Forward), *Prawo Ludu* (People's right), *Gazeta Robotnicza* (Workers' gazette), *Światło* (Light), the progressive democratic review *Krytyka* (Criticism), *Głos* (Voice), *Prawda* (Truth), *Przegląd Tygodniowy* (Weekly review), *Przegląd Poznański* (Poznan review), the scientific *Ateneum, Biblioteka Warszawska* (Warsaw library), *Ekonomista* (Economist) and *Czasopismo Prawne i Ekonomiczne* (Journal of law and economics)–winning appreciation as a versatile and adept social researcher.

Politically, Daszyńska-Golińska departed from orthodox Marxism, moving gradually towards a revisionism inspired by the works of Eduard Bernstein. She was interested in Hegel and Nietzsche, read the works of Karl Kautsky and Ferdinand Lassalle, admired the intellectual achievements of the Fabians and rejected the ideas of Malthus in his *Essay on the Principle of Population* (1798). Her creative thinking formed the basis of lectures she gave at various educational institutions where women made up a substantial part of the student body. (From all three Polish partitions, these were female students who had been refused admission to institutions of higher education. In 1897, the Polonized Galician Universities in Lviv and Cracow opened their faculties of philosophy and medicine to women). From 1892 to 1894, Daszyńska-Golińska worked at the Flying University–a secret academy for women founded in 1885. In 1907, the Flying University was legalized and renamed the *Towarzystwo Kursów Naukowych* (Society for Scientific Studies) and in that year Daszyńska-Golińska lectured for the new Society. Later (1910–1911), she lectured at the Adrian Braniecki Courses in Cracow, at the School of Household Economics in Lviv and at the Adam Mickiewicz People's University in Cracow (an organization aimed at raising levels of education, particularly among the poorer social strata). In 1919, she became professor of economics at the *Wolna Wszechnica Polska* (Free Polish University) in Warsaw (a private higher education institution, formed in 1919, which had evolved from the Society for Scientific Studies).

Early on in her career, Daszyńska-Golińska began to associate herself with the Polish and international women's and feminist movements. From the mid-1890s, she was affiliated with the *Koło Pracy Kobiet* (Women's Labor Society), an organization coordinating women's activities (mainly practical handicrafts) on Polish territory. In 1896, she attended the International Women's Congress in Berlin, where she met Lilly Braun and Lina Morgenstern. Later, through these contacts, she wrote for the German periodical *Die Gleichheit* (Equality). She also attended national Polish women's meetings in Zakopane (1899), Cracow (1905) and Warsaw (1907, 1917). In 1907, together with ***Paulina Kuczalska-Reinschmit***, she organized the *Związek Równouprawnienia Kobiet Polskich* (Union of Equal Rights for Polish Women).

By the early twentieth century, Daszyńska-Golińska was combining feminist activities with work on behalf of temperance and abolitionist associations such as *Trzeźwość* (Sobriety), *Eleuteria* and *Przyszłość* (Future). In journalistic commentaries published in *Prawda* and *Krytyka*, as well as *Świat Kobiety* (Woman's world), she addressed women's social and political inequality and promoted campaigns to combat social problems such as alcoholism, venereal disease and prostitution. In 1908, she joined the campaign for women's political rights in Galicia, after the first general election for the State Council in Vienna (the Austrian Parliament) violated the voting rights of women. In protest, Daszyńska-Golińska, supported by various feminist groups, nominated herself as a candidate for the *Sejm Krajowy* in Lviv (the Parliament of autonomous Galicia). Eventually, her candidature was cancelled in favor of Maria Dulębianka. Though the actions of the Polish women were primarily symbolic gestures, they generated widespread debate and were not without influence on younger generations of Polish women. Daszyńska-Golińska presented a comprehensive review of issues relating to women's citizenship in the ideological manifestos *Kobieta jako obywatelka* (Woman as a citizen, 1903), and *Prawo wyborcze kobiet* (Women's voting rights, 1918). Despite her commitment to equal citizenship for women, Daszyńska-Golińska refrained from any feminist stance advocating separation from other democratic trends and openly voiced this position in her writings.

During World War I, Daszyńska-Golińska joined the *Liga Kobiet Pogotowia Wojennego* (Women's League for War Alert, an independent women's organization dedicated to supporting the Polish military formations fighting under Austro-Hungarian command). In 1917, she was appointed editor-in-chief of the legionary periodical, *Na posterunku* (At the post). After Poland became independent in 1918, Daszyńska-Golińska became a senior official at the Ministry of Labor and Social Welfare. She supported Józef Piłsudski's May Coup in 1926 and, two years later—nominated by a women's electoral committee on behalf of the *Bezpartyjny Blok Współpracy z Rządem* (Non-Party Bloc for Cooperation with the Government, a political base of Piłsudski's regime)—she became a member of the Polish Senate (1928–1930).

During the interwar period, Daszyńska-Golińska was active in several women's organizations, including (from 1921) the *Klub Polityczny Kobiet Postępowych* (Progressive Women's Political Club) and (from 1928) the *Związek Pracy Obywatelskiej Kobiet* (Women's Association for Civil Labor). These organizations cooperated with the Little Entente of Women (LEW, an international organization of women from Czechoslovakia, Romania, Greece, Yugoslavia and Poland) and, from 1926, with the *Stowarzyszenie Kobiet z Wyższym Wykształceniem* (Association of Women with Higher Education). She also led the Polish section of the Women's International League for Peace and Freedom (WILPF). Throughout these years, she remained a productive scholar, completing around seventy published books and several hundred articles.

In recognition of her achievements, Daszyńska-Golińska was awarded the *Krzyż Oficerski Orderu Polonia Restituta* (Officers' Cross of the Order of Polonia Restituta)

(1923), the *Krzyż Niepodległości* (Independence Cross) (1933) and the *Złoty Krzyż Zasługi* (Golden Cross of Merit). She died on 11 February 1934 in Warsaw.

Grzegorz Krzywiec
Institute of History,
Polish Academy of Science

SOURCES

(B) *Ateneum* (1892-1896).
(B) *Krytyka* (Criticism) (1899-1914).
(B) *Prawda* (Truth) (1894-1899).
(B) *Światło* (Light) (1894-1896).
(B) *Na posterunku* (At the post) (1917).
(B) *Świat Kobiety* (Woman's world) (1905-1906).
(B) *Życie* (Life) (1898).
(C) Daszyńska, Z. "Współczesny ruch kobiecy wobec kwestii robotnic" (The contemporary women's movement and the question of working women). *Krytyka*, no. 3 (1897).
(C) Daszyńska, Z. "Dokąd dąży dzisiejszy ruch kobiecy?" (Where is the present-day women's movement heading?). *Krytyka* 1, no. 2 (1901): 217-224.
(C) Daszyńska, Z. "Społeczne zadania naszej kobiety" (The social tasks of our women). *Tydzień* (Week), nos. 18-20 (1904): 22.
(C) Daszyńska, Z. *Kwestia kobieca a małżeństwo* (Marriage versus the woman question). Warsaw: Wydawnictwo im. Wacława Męczkowskiego, 1925.
(C) Daszyńska, Z. "W poczuciu obywatelskiego obowiązku" (Out of a sense of civic duty). *Kobieta Współczesna* (Modern woman), no. 24 (1928): 4-5.
(C) Golińska, Z. *Dr. Zofia Golińska, pionierka wiedzy gospodarczo-społecznej w Polsce. Notatki autobiograficzne* (Dr. Zofia Golińska, pioneer of socio-economic knowledge in Poland. Autobiographical notes). Cracow: Wydawnictwo Stowarzyszenia 'Służba Obywatelska,' 1932.
(D) "Golińska 1 v. Daszyńska Zofia." In *Polski Słownik Biograficzny* (Polish biographical dictionary), vol. 8, no. 2, 1959-1960, 223-5.
(E) Stegmann, Natali. *Die Töchter der geschlagenen Helden. 'Frauenfrage,' Feminismus und Frauenbewegung in Polen (1863-1919).* (The daughters of fallen heroes. 'The woman question,' feminism and the women's movement in Poland, 1863-1919). Wiesbaden: Harrassowitz Verlag, 2000.

DEJANOVIĆ (Dejanovich), Draga (born Dimitrijević) (1840–1871)

Serbian feminist, actress, poet; prominent member of the *Ujedinjena omladina srpska* (United Serbian Youth).

Draga Dimitrijević was born on 18 August 1840 in Stara Kanjiža (Habsburg Monarchy, now in Serbia). Her parents were Živojin and Sofija Dimitrijević. As the daughter of a well-to-do lawyer, Draga received an education in her native town and, later, at the Vinčikov Institute in Timisoara (today in Romania). Due to her poor health (she had problems with her eyes), Draga's education was interrupted. Together with her family, she moved from Stara Kanjiža to Bečej, where she married the young schoolmaster Mihajlo Dejanović against her father's will. Soon afterwards, she resumed her education in Pest (Hungary), where she met a group of Serbian students (Giga Geršić, Laza Kostić and Jovan Turoma among them) and began writing poems. These were first published in the magazine *Danica*, and later collected and published as a book under the title *Spisi Drage Dejanović* (Writings of Draga Dejanović, 1869).

In the 1860s, Draga Dejanović joined the recently established Serbian National Theater in Novi Sad. It was a bold break with established rules–a move resisted by her family. One year later, Draga moved to Belgrade where she translated some plays for the National Theater. In 1864, Dejanović returned to Bečej, where she continued to live with her husband. Despite her private obligations she did not abandon public work and the task she had devoted herself to: "prosvećivanje Srpstva" (the enlightenment of Serbdom, an expression she often used in her texts). She wrote three important studies: *Nekoliko reči srpskim ženama* (A couple of words to Serbian women), *Emancipacija Srpkinja* (The emancipation of Serbian women) and *Srpskoj majci* (To the Serbian mother), in which she expressed her dissatisfaction with the inert behavior of Serbian women.

Draga Dejanović loved her family (children and husband) dearly and suffered a sense of great personal tragedy when her son died in infancy in 1867. She herself died in 1871, while giving birth to a daughter.

Some of Draga Dejanović's writings remained unpublished. The most important of these include her play "Deoba Jakšića" (The succession of Jaksić), "Svećenik u Morlaku" (The priest of Morlak) and a pedagogical study, "Mati" (Mom). Perhaps her most well-known works were her feminist writings. She saw the enlightenment of women as necessary for "the awakening of the people's self-consciousness," [Hlapec (Chlapec)-Đorđević 1935, 73] and sought to contribute to this "awakening." The roles of 'woman'–in family life and as "a teacher of children" [Hlapec (Chlapec)-Đorđević 1935, 68]–were burdened with a great responsibility since it was women who would determine whether or not the family home was "prosperous or ruined. The liberation of women should be taken as the liberation of our people from all the backward habits which still imprison them. Therefore we should not dismiss the woman question as unimportant" (Stojaković 2001, 101).

Draga Dejanović was imbued by romantic patriotism, but pointed at formidable problems facing women in society. She considered a poor education to be the greatest obstacle to a woman's emancipation. In her article "Zla sreća devojačka" (The ill fortune of a girl), she concluded that financial independence and modern education were the basis of women's independence. Dejanović was a prominent member of the *Ujedinjena omladina srpska* (United Serbian Youth) which existed from 1866 to 1872. This was a Serbian organization modelled after Mazzini's United Youth of Italy. Its purpose was to enlighten Serbian people through education and culture. The founders of the *Ujedinjena omladina srpska* were the first Serbian socialists and liberals: Svetozar Marković, Svetozar Miletić and Vladimir Jovanović. The *Ujedinjena omladina srpska* was among the first organizations to raise the question of women's emancipation and had a women's section that coordinated various related activities. The newspaper *Mlada srbadija* (Young Serbs) published articles which presented the situation of women in various European countries and the USA, and compared them with the position of women in Serbia. Dejanović called for the *Ujedinjena omladina srpska* to stand openly behind the demand for equal education for both girls and boys. Her attitude caused negative reactions from some conservative circles.

In all her texts, Draga Dejanović also expressed dissatisfaction with what she considered to be the passivity of Serbian women. She publicly criticized the majority of women for believing that the responsibility for the material support of the family should rest entirely with men. She pointed out that women had a legal right to public education and argued that there were no formal obstacles preventing women from acquiring education and enabling them to become equally trained for both intellectual and manual work. Draga Dejanović criticized women for not being organized, for being satisfied with men's alleged superiority, and for not undertaking anything to change their situation. Dejanovic's early death ended her sincere and energetic struggle for women's emancipation.

Ivana Pantelić
Belgrade Women's Studies and Gender Research Center

SOURCES

(B) *Matica* (1869–1871).

(B) *Mlada Srbadija* (Young Serbians), no. 21 (1871).

(B) Marković, Ljubica. *Počeci feminizma u Srbiji i Vojvodini* (The origins of feminism in Serbia and Vojvodina). Belgrade: Narodna misao, 1934.

(B) Hlapec (Chlapec)-Đorđević, Julka. *Studije i eseji o feminizmu* (Studies and essays on feminism). Belgrade: Život i rad, 1935.

(C) Dejanović, Draga. *Spisi Drage Dejanović* (Writings of Draga Dejanović). Novi Sad: Platonova stamparija, 1869.

(D) Petrović Radmila. "Milica Stojadinović Srpkinja i Draga Dejanović o ženama" (Milica Stojadinović Srpkinja and Draga Dejanović on women). *Glasnik istorijskog društva u Novom Sadu* (The herald of the Novi Sad historical society), knj. III, no. 1 (Novi Sad, 1930).

(E) Božinović, Neda. *Žensko pitanje u Srbiji u XIX i XX veku* (The woman question in Serbia in the nineteenth and twentieth centuries). Belgrade: Feministička '94, 1996.

(E) Vuletić, Vitomir. "Ujedinjena omladina srpska i društveni položaj žene" (The United Serbian Youth and the position of women in society). In *Srbija u modernizacijskim procesima XIX i XX veka* (Serbia in the modernization processes of the nineteenth and twentieth centuries). II. Belgrade: Institut za noviju istoriju, 1998.

(E) Stojaković, Gordana. *Znamenite žene Novog Sada* (The renowned women of Novi Sad). Novi Sad: Futura publikacije, 2001.

DERVİŞ, Suat (Saadet Baraner) (1905-1972)

Turkish novelist, journalist and translator; leftist political activist; co-founder (1970) of the *Devrimci Kadınlar Birliği* (Socialist Women's Association).

Suat Derviş was born in 1905 (1904 according to some sources), to an aristocratic family in Istanbul. Her father, gynecologist İsmail Derviş (?-1932), was a professor at the Medical Faculty of Istanbul University and the son of chemist Müşir Derviş Pasha and his second wife, Şevkidil. Suat Derviş' mother was Hesna Hanım, a daughter of Kamil Bey (1830-1876) from the entourage of Sultan Abdülaziz and a former slave girl from the Palace of the Sultan known as *Perensaz*. [NB: In the Ottoman era there were neither surnames nor official birth records. The 'paterfamilias' would occasionally record names of new-borns on the family Quoran but, since this was by no means regular and did not usually include names of females, collating accurate data on women is difficult. The tradition of marrying off former slave girls of the Palace to 'pashas' (military/civil officers), has added to the difficulty of tracing particular family genealogies.]

Suat had a sister, Hamiyet (1902?-1968), who studied music (singing) at the *Sternisches* Conservatory in Germany. Her parents' relationship was monogamous and they were committed to one another, providing Suat with a liberal and enlightened family background. She enjoyed the support of an unusually tender father and a highly respected, well-educated mother. Towards the end of her life she was to stress that having been brought up in a house where there was no gender segregation and discrimination had helped her cope with the difficulties of later years. She was privately tutored in French and German, and also in literature and music. After World War I, she spent the years 1919-1920 in Germany with her sister, where she attended the Berlin School of Music and Berlin University (Faculty of Letters). She began her literary career writing pieces about Turkey for German magazines (among them *Die Berliner Zeitung*). Her first book, *Kara Kitap* (Black book), was published in 1920 in Istanbul. Between 1920 and 1932, Derviş published over ten novels while working as a freelance journalist; in this latter capacity, she reported on the Lausanne Conference in 1922-1923, an event which would determine the future of the young Turkish Republic.

Suat Derviş's early novels reveal a deep interest in psychology, especially women's psychology. The works do not depict 'Anatolian peasants' (the fashion of the period) but marginals and representatives of the urban poor. As a novelist who spent her youth in Istanbul and in the metropols of Europe (Paris, Berlin, Lausanne), Derviş was a distinctively 'urban' writer concerned with processes of individualization—a theme which ran quite contrary to the period's dominant solidarist/corporatist ideology. Her sincere depictions of human psychology and her exceptional ability to 'look inside' herself and others appeared as a stylistic quality in her writing and added to her popularity. One critic wrote that "[Suat Derviş], who is more objective and modern than ***Halide Edib*** [the most famous woman writer of the time], is by no means less profound" (Uraz 1941, 282). Her 'profundity' owed much to her ability to combine analyses of gender and class issues, as in her novel *Emine* (1931), in which a poor woman eventually kills her rich, bullying husband.

In 1932, when her father died, Suat Derviş returned to Turkey for good and took up a place in intellectual and political circles, participating in their debates. In 1930, after having joined the oppositional *Serbest Cumhuriyet Fırkası* (Liberal Republican Party), which advocated women's suffrage, she ran in the local elections together with ***Nezihe Muhittin***, a leading political figure. Both were unsuccessful in the elections and the party itself was soon banned. During the 1930s, Suat Derviş moved closer to a Marxist position and participated in debates on the creation of a social realist literary current. The magazine *Yeni Edebiyat* (New literature) formed the ground for these debates and Suat Derviş was one of its prominent writers, together with famous male writers such as Nazım Hikmet, Sabahattin Ali and Sadri Erten. Derviş was a proponent of social realism but, as her friend and publisher ***Sabiha Zekeriya Sertel*** put it, "she combined a socialist approach with a deep sensitivity towards women's issues" (Sertel 1987, 182).

1935 saw Derviş reporting on the Congress of the International Alliance of Women for Suffrage and Equal Citizenship (IAWSEC) in Istanbul for the daily paper *Cumhuriyet* (Republic). In 1936, working as a freelance journalist, she followed events at the Montreux Conference in Switzerland, which was to decide the fate of the Turkish straits. She traveled widely in Western Europe and twice to the Soviet Union. From these visits came a book entitled *Niçin Sovyetler Birliği'nin Dostuyum?* (Why am I a friend of the Soviet Union?), which caused great controversy in Turkey. In the meantime, Suat Derviş married no less than three times. She is said to have had a short but passionate marriage to the wrestler Seyfi Cenap Berksoy (who participated in the Turkish team that represented Turkey in the 1924 Paris Olympic Games). Her other two husbands—Selami İzzet Sedes (1896–1964) and Nizamettin Nazif Tepedelenlioğlu (1901–1970)—were prominent intellectuals of the time and witnessed Suat Derviş develop intellectually from a liberal, to a more socially-oriented and socialist position. In 1941, she married a fourth time, to Reşad Fuat Baraner (1900–1968), the leader of the illegal Turkish Communist Party. From 1942 to 1944, the magazine *Yeni Edebiyat* assumed a new profile and became a journal of the Communist Party. On 10 March 1944, Suat Derviş and her husband, along with other party functionaries, were detained on the grounds of their "illegal communist activity" (Berktay 2003, 206). Derviş was sentenced to eight months imprisonment. During the investigation period of the trial Derviş, who was pregnant, lost her child. She was released on 6 November 1944 (after which she could not find a job with any newspaper because of her declared political views and had to use pseudonyms for every piece that she wrote–one of the reasons why a full bibliography of her works cannot be given). Her husband, Reşad Fuat Baraner, was kept in prison until the general amnesty of 1950 but in 1951 (having since become the General Secretary of the Communist Party), he was arrested again. Suat Derviş stayed in Turkey until the trial formally began in 1953, and then left the country due to increasing pressure and harassment from the regime (pressures which had been mounting since 1943 and which forced Derviş to use different pseudonyms in order to publish).

Between 1953 and 1963, Suat Derviş lived abroad (mostly in France) and published novels in French, which were well received. Among them were *Le prisonnier d'Ankara* (The prisoner from Ankara, 1957) and *Les Ombres du Yali* (The shadows of the Yali, 1958). In Turkey however, there was a silence over this prolific and famous writer, first and foremost because of her political views but also because of her feminism, which was not easily accepted in leftist circles either. Suat Derviş was a woman who had an independent and critical mind and was courageous enough to live on her own terms. These traits did not make her popular in communist circles and she was much criticized for leaving her husband in prison and going abroad (although her husband had supported and admired her as an intellectual). Party members were critical of her behavior, which they defined as unwomanly!

From 1963 until the death of Reşad Fuat Baraner in 1968, Derviş and her husband had a happy, albeit difficult life together. In 1970, Suat Derviş was among the founders of the *Devrimci Kadınlar Birliği* (Socialist Women's Association), which aimed to create a revolutionary women's movement and raise women's consciousness. Meanwhile, she completed her most popular novel, *Fosforlu Cevriye* (Radiant Cevriye, 1968), a wonderfully sensitive and humanist account of Istanbul life, in particular the life of a marginal woman of the streets. Although she lived to see the success of the film version of the novel, her work was for the most part dismissed, or met with silence. An independent and critical woman writer, Derviş intentionally chose to remain outside the dominant power loci–irrespective of whether they represented ruling or suppressed oppositional parties. When she was presented as "the wife of Reşat Fuat Baraner, the General Secretary of the Turkish Communist Party," at a meeting (in 1970) of the *Demokratik Devrim Derneği* (Association for a Democratic Revolution), she was quick to rise up and say "No, I am Suat Derviş, the writer!" (Berktay 2003, 205). On another occasion, she replied to sarcastic sexist remarks from rightists about her gender and profession by saying "I am not ashamed of being a woman, and I am proud of being a writer. That title is my sole wealth, my only pride and my bread" (Tahir, Derviş and Cevad 1936, 22). Suat Derviş died on 23 July 1972, having written herself into the history of feminism in Turkey. The new interest in her work by feminist researchers and the republishing of her books in the last decade stand witness to this fact.

Fatmagül Berktay
University of Istanbul

SOURCES

(B) Tahir, Kemal, Suad Derviş and Ahmed Cevad. "Namık Kemal'i Bir Tarafa Bırakalım; İktidarınız Varsa İlmi Münakaşaya Geçiniz." (Let's leave aside Namık Kemal and get into scientific debate–if you have the power!). In *1936 Modeli Gençler ve Zavallı Peyami Safa* (1936 model youngsters and poor Peyami Safa), a polemical booklet. Akış Library Publishing no. 1, 1936.
(B) Anadol, Zihni. "Suat Derviş ile Konuşmalar" (Interviews with Suat Derviş). *Gerçekler Postası* (Magazine of truths) (September 1967); republished in *Yazın* (Literature), no. 59 (March 1994): 16-18.
(B) İleri, Rasih Nuri ed. *Records of the Turkish Communist Party, 1944 Trial.* Istanbul: Tüsdav Publishing, 2003.
(C) Derviş, Suat. *Neden Sovyetler Birliği'nin Dostuyum*? (Why am I a friend of the Soviet Union?). Istanbul: Arkadaş Publishing, 1944.
(C) Derviş, Suat. *Le prisonnier d'Ankara* (The prisoner from Ankara). Paris, 1957.
(C) Derviş, Suat. *Les Ombres du Yali* (The shadows of the Yali). Paris: Les Editeurs Français Réunis, 1958.
(C) Derviş, Suat. *Fosforlu Cevriye* (Radiant Cevriye). May Yayınları, 1968.
(C) Derviş, Suat. "Hayatımı Anlatıyorum" (I'm telling my life). *Tarih ve Toplum* (History and society), no. 29 (May 1986): 18-24; no. 30 (June 1986): 51-56.
(D) Haşim, Ahmet. "Edebi Bir Seyahat" (A literary journey). *Güneş* (The sun), no. 10 (15 May 1927).
(D) Sülker, Kemal. "Çileli, Onurlu Yaşamın Temsilcilerinden Biri: Suat Derviş Baraner" (Representative of a dignified, enduring life: Suat Derviş Baraner). *Sanat Edebiyat 1981* (Art and literature) 2, no. 15 (1981): 23-27.
(D) İleri, Rasih Nuri. "Suat Derviş–Saadet Baraner." *Tarih ve Toplum* (History and society), no. 29 (May 1986): 17-18.
(D) Sertel, Sabiha. *Roman Gibi* (Like a novel). Istanbul: Belge, 1987.
(D) Paker, Saliha and Zehra Toska. "Suat Derviş'in Kimlikleri" (The different identities of Suat Derviş). *Toplumsal Tarih* (Social history), no. 39 (March 1997): 11-22.
(D) Berktay, Fatmagül. "Yıldızları Özgürce Seyretmek İsteyen Bir Yazar: Suat Derviş" (A writer who claims the right to watch the stars freely: Suat Derviş). In Fatmagül Berktay. *Tarihin Cinsiyeti* (The gender of history). Istanbul: Metis, 2003, 204-217.
(E) Uraz, Murat. *Kadın Şair ve Muharrirlerimiz* (Our women poets and writers). Istanbul, 1941, 181, 182, 231, 282, 452.

(E) Interview with Suat Derviş's closest friends Rasih Nuri İleri (a well-known leftist activist and intellectual) and his wife Bedia İleri, conducted by Fatmagül Berktay and kept in Berktay's personal archive. Istanbul, 1988.

(E) Interview with Neriman Hikmet (a close friend of Suat Derviş), conducted by Fatmagül Berktay and kept in Berktay's personal archive. Istanbul, 1988.

DESPOT, Blaženka (1930–2001)

Croatian philosopher, feminist theorist and lecturer at the University of Zagreb; the first person from Yugoslavia to write and publish books, essays and critical studies in the field of philosophical anthropology on the position of women, feminism and the New Age.

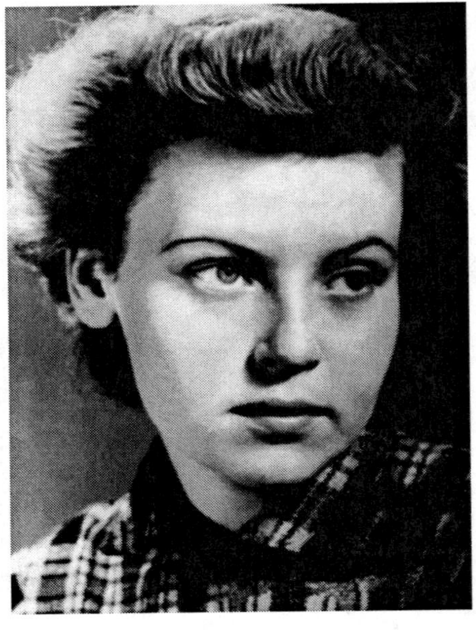

Blaženka Despot (*nee* Lovrić) was born on 9 January 1930 in Zagreb (then the Kingdom of Yugoslavia, today Croatia), to a typical middle-class Zagreb family–the eldest child of Dr Stjepan and Melanija Lovrić. Her father held a Ph.D. in law and for many years was the director of a hospital in Zagreb. Her mother was a piano teacher. Together with her younger brother Zlatko, the young Blaženka was brought up and educated in a family that had enjoyed middle-class status over several generations. Upon graduation from high school in 1948, she married a doctor, Pavle Gugić, and soon gave birth to a daughter, Iris. After five years, the marriage broke up and she went to work as an office clerk while studying 'pure' philosophy at the University of Zagreb. She graduated in 1954.

Thus the life of Blaženka Lovrić began as a single mother, accompanied by a tragedy–her daughter's lifelong illness–which she had to endure alone and for which she sacrificed a great deal. Upon her graduation from the University of Zagreb, she began teaching at Zagreb gymnasiums, which she did for almost ten years. She taught philosophy, sociology, psychology and logic, establishing a reputation for herself as one of the most highly regarded high school teachers of philosophy in Zagreb. A second marriage, to a colleague Ivo Mimica, was also short-lived.

In 1964, Blaženka Lovrić-Mimica began working as a lecturer at the University of Zagreb, where she also conducted research. She taught sociology and other mandatory social sciences. The mid-1960s was a productive period for her: she published extensively in almost all Zagreb's major social science journals, especially in *Praxis*, but belonged to no particular circle and remained an independent thinker, strongly criticizing dogmatic and patriarchal approaches to theory. It was during this period of her life that she married again–this time to a philosophy professor, Dr. Branko Despot–but the marriage ended after approximately five years. From 1968, she conducted all her work and published all her writings under the name of Despot.

In 1968, Blaženka Despot acquired a postgraduate degree in the philosophy of anthropology from the University of Ljubljana. It was here, in 1970, that she defended her doctoral thesis, entitled *Humanitet tehničkog društva* (The humanity of a technical society). She published a book with the same title in 1971, in which she used Marxian and Hegelian philosophy to explore the threat to humanity and freedom posed by technical society. The first philosopher in Yugoslavia to examine these issues with regard to women's freedom and subjectivity, Blaženka Despot radicalized basic Marxist tenets and the discipline of philosophy. In her second book, *Plädoyer za dokolicu* (A plea for leisure, 1976), Despot drew still more radical approaches from Marxist theory, positing perceptions of culture and leisure time as important historical manifestations of human existence. She addressed the negative implications of dogmatism and the political imposition of ideas in contemporary debates, journals and a variety of social and political forums.

Despot won an Alexander von Humboldt scholarship to study in Frankfurt am Main at the *Institut für Sozialforschung* (Institute for Social Research) in 1971–72. Two years later, she became an associate professor at the *Veterinarski fakultet Sveučilišta u Zagrebu* (Faculty of Veterinary Medicine, University of Zagreb), receiving tenure in 1980 and teaching sociology, political economy, introductions to Marxist philosophy and the social sciences, as well as the theory and practice of self-management. In 1977, she founded the *Zavod za društvene znanosti u veterinarstvu* (Institute of Social Sciences in Veterinary Medicine), which she headed until she left the University in 1989 to join the *Institut za društvena istraživanja Sveučilišta u Zagrebu* (Institute for Social Research, University of Zagreb). She won the Humboldt scholarship twice more, this time to study at the *Fakultät für Sozialwissenschaften* (Faculty for Social Sciences) in Konstanz, and later at the *Lehrschul für Philosophie* (School of Philosophy) in Bamberg. At the latter institution, she carried out a research project entitled *Der Begriff der Emanzipation in der neuen sozialen Bewegung und in Technologie* (The concept of emancipation in the new social movement and in technology). She regularly attended conferences and international symposiums; her most notable appearances were in Dubrovnik and Cavtat, where she spoke on "Socialism in the World," and at an international symposium in Ludwigsburg, where she presented a paper, "Die Möglichkeit der Begründung des marxistischen Feminismus" (The possibility of a foundation for Marxist feminism).

Despot's creative and theoretical engagement with the social standing of women and feminism culminated in journal articles and books published in the 1980s, reaching its ultimate expression in her *Žensko pitanje i socijalističko samoupravljanje* (The woman question and socialist self-management, 1987). In this work (for the first time in Yugoslavia), feminist questions were posed within the framework and domain of philosophy, establishing a basis for the critique of Hegel's philosophy of liberty. "Critical analysis of Hegel," wrote Despot, "ought to contribute to the raising of consciousness among women ... Acquaintance with the dialectico-speculative method of the philosophy of freedom leads to the realization that the problem of the emancipation of women is indistinguishable from the idea of freedom" (in Bosanac, ed. 2004, 137). In Despot's reformulation of Hegelian thought, "[t]he servant has a history; to be a servant is not a destiny," whereas "[w]oman does not possess this history; her sex is her destiny; she cannot liberate herself; she cannot mediate; she cannot establish herself in relation to her husband as consciousness in relation to consciousness" (in Bosanac, ed. 2004, 32). In this important work, Despot asked: "what do women call masculine thinking?" and interrogated meanings surrounding "the history and nature of woman." She also established points of departure for the exploration of the historical and social essence of patriarchy as a specific form of the 'will to power' (Despot 1987, 7–38; 89–106). Deconstructing Hegelian gender dialectics—which establish the individual as a subject but distinguish between the sexes (man is granted freedom and acknowledgement within the state, in society and at work; woman is left to "the piety of the family")—Despot exposed with irony the reduction of woman to an "ahistorical birth-giver" (in Bosanac, ed. 2004, 35).

In her book *Emancipacija i novi socijalni pokreti* (Emancipation and the new social movements, 1989), Despot delivered a radical thesis of emancipation, elaborating the relationship between Marxism and feminism and the difference between emancipation as 'the woman question' and feminist emancipation. Feminism, she argued, was a realization of freedom, criticism of the will to power and, together with the New Age movement, an expression of the movement of 'the Other' towards emancipation.

In all Despot's writings (she published six books and more than one hundred articles in all), she remained a sharp critic of official ideology, particularly of self-management (a system of full worker participation in the management of enterprise and of public affairs). Despot argued that real self-management did not exist and that the system had betrayed its principles. In *Emancipacija i novi socijalni pokreti*, she critiqued Marxism, focusing on its neglect of important aspects of 'the woman question' and patriarchal practices, which she regarded as the cultural and civilizational axes of the will to power. Her final work, *New Age i Moderna* (New age and modernity, 1995), synthesized Despot's unique conceptualization of freedom and emancipation and integrated fundamental themes of our times: the relationship between technology and humanity; critiques of ideology and self-management; women's issues; the significance of new social movements and the development and significance of new paradigms. Like her *Žensko pitanje i socijalističko samoupravljanje*, *New Age i Moderna* employed feminism as an integrative mode of historical vision and insight.

In addition to her theoretical endeavors, Despot also helped found, and was active in a new women's group, *Žena i društvo* (Woman and Society), set up in 1979 under the auspices of the *Sociološko društvo Hrvatske* (Croatian Sociological Society). Her theoretical work represented a breakthrough into a marginalized area of philosophy hitherto neglected by mainstream philosophical currents—a breakthrough founded upon a critique of the philosophy of liberty and its legacy in Marxism, and one which constituted a significant contribution to feminist theory. From 1977 until her death, Despot lived with (and in 1990 married) Dr. Zoran Žugić, professor at the Faculty of Kinesiology. In 1988, she had a severe car accident and her vocal cords were seriously damaged, forcing her to abandon teaching. She retired in 1993. Distinguished by her tactfulness and finesse in communication and by an extraordinary eloquence, Blaženka Despot was regarded highly by both her peers and her students as a teacher and thinker of strong convictions and originality. She was endowed with a brilliant intelligence and great physical beauty, as well as an unpretentious spontaneity. After a severe illness, Blaženka Despot died on 18 February 2001 in Zagreb.

Dr. Gordana Bosanac
Retired full professor of the University of Zagreb

Translated from the Croatian by Nataly Anderson.

SOURCES

(C) Despot, Blaženka. *Humanitet tehničkog društva* (The humanity of a technical society). Zagreb: Centar za društvene djelatnosti omladine RK SOH, 1971.

(C) Despot, Blaženka. *Ideologija proizvodnih snaga i proizvodna snaga ideologije* (The ideology of productive forces and the productive force of ideology). Osijek: Glas Slavonije, 1976.

(C) Despot, Blaženka. *Plädoyer za dokolicu* (A plea for leisure). Belgrade: Predsedništvo Konferencije SSOJ, 1976.

(C) Despot, Blaženka. *Žensko pitanje i socijalističko samoupravljanje* (The woman question and socialist self-management). Zagreb: Cekade, 1987.

(C) Despot, Blaženka. *Emancipacija i novi socijalni pokreti* (Emancipation and the new social movements). Osijek: Međuopćinska konferencija SKH–Centar za idejno-teorijski rad, 1989.

(C) Despot, Blaženka. *New Age i Moderna* (New age and modernity). Zagreb: Hrvatsko filozofsko društvo, 1995.

(C) Bosanac, Gordana, ed. *Izabrana djela Blaženke Despot* (The selected works of Blaženka Despot). Zagreb: Institut za društvena istraživanja–Ženska infoteka, 2004.

(D) Bartoluci, Sunčica. "Bibiliografija knjiga, članaka i ostalih priloga Blaženke Despot te radova o njoj" (A bibliography of works by and on Blaženka Despot). In Gordana Bosanac, ed. *Izabrana djela Blaženke Despot* (The selected works of Blaženka Despot). Zagreb: Institut za društvena istraživanja–Ženska infoteka, 2004, 49-63.

DJIONAT, Elena (1888-?)

Teacher, journalist and activist of the Romanian feminist movement; founder and leader of the *Organizația Femeilor Basarabene* (Organization of Bessarabian Women), renamed *Uniunea Femeilor Basarabene* (League of Bessarabian Women) in 1933.

Born in 1888 in the village of Bozieni, at that time part of the Russian Empire, Djionat pursued a career in medicine at the University of Odessa but only completed two years of study. She became a teacher and went on to become Principal at the Princess Elena Primary School in Chişhinău in 1919, after Bessarabia became part of Romania. She retained this position until 1935.

In addition to pursuing her career as an educator of young girls, Djionat also became active in the feminist movement. She had her first encounter with feminist ideas in 1907 but up until 1919, her activities were focused more on Romanian nationalist cultural endeavors than on feminist ones. After the unification with Romania, Djionat and many other Bessarabian women activists–such as the prominent Elena Alistar (1873–1955), the single female signatory of the act of unification with Romania in March 1918–had high expectations regarding women's enfranchisement and civil rights. Yet the promise to extend these rights to women, spelt out in the act of unification, failed to materialize. It was only in 1928, under the National Peasant Party government, that women in Romania finally gained limited political rights in local elections. This moment gave fresh impetus to the revitalization of the feminist movement in Bessarabia. In November 1928, Djionat called a meeting that led to the establishment of the *Organizația Femeilor Basarabene* (Organization of Bessarabian Women), headed by Djionat herself. This new initiative was designed to counter the actions of Elena Alistar, who was less involved in local Bessarabian activism. Alistar had become affiliated with organizations in Bucharest such as ***Alexandrina Cantacuzino***'s *Societatea Ortodoxă Națională a Femeilor Române* (*SONFR*, National Orthodox Society of Romanian Women) and took Cantacuzino's disapproving view of women's activism in, and membership of, traditional political parties.

By 1933, Djionat had succeeded in generating several branches of the new Organization of Bessarabian Women, now renamed the League of Bessarabian Women, and she held a major Congress. Some of the most important feminist organizations and personalities from Moldavia, Transylvania and Wallachia sent representatives and messages of solidarity, including ***Maria Baiulescu***, ***Elena Meissner*** and ***Calypso Botez***. The Congress formulated a motion to be submitted to King Carol II of Romania, requesting full political and civil equality for all citizens, regardless of sex, class, income or title, and the abolition of various restrictions on women's education. The statement also carried a strong pacifist message.

In the pursuit of her goals, Djionat joined the National Peasant Party and also published a short-lived feminist journal, *Mişcarea feministă* (The feminist movement), which she personally financed from her meager teacher's salary. As Djionat's efforts came into conflict with those of Alistar, the small Bessarabian feminist movement found itself split along lines drawn up in Bucharest, to the detriment of the local concerns of women activists. Elena Djionat's activities after 1936 remain unknown.

Maria Bucur
Indiana University

SOURCES

(B) Alistar, Elena. "Mişcarea femenistă din Basarabia. Începuturi şi realizări. Spre un viitor mai frumos" (The feminist movement in Bessarabia. Beginnings and accomplishments. Towards a more beautiful future). *Mişcarea femenistă* (The feminist movement) 1, no. 1 (1933): 2.

(B) "Congresul Ligei femeii basarabene" (The Congress of the Bessarabian Woman's League). *Mişcarea femenistă* 1, no. 2 (1933): 1.

(E) Colesnic, Iurie ed. *Femei din Moldova. Enciclopedie* (Women from Moldova. Encyclopedia). Chişinău: Museum, 2000.

(E) Cosma, Ghizela. *Femeile şi politica în România. Evoluţia dreptului de vot în perioada interbelică* (Women and politics in Romania. The evolution of suffrage rights in the interwar period). Cluj: Presa Universitară Clujeană, 2002.

EDİB ADIVAR, Halide (1884–1964)

Distinguished writer and novelist of late Ottoman and Republican Turkey; advocate of women's rights and nationalism.

Halide Edib was born in Istanbul in 1884 and brought up in an Ottoman mansion house, for the most part by her grandmother (a member of the Mevlevi sufi order). Her mother, Fatma Bedirfem Hanım, died of tuberculosis when Halide was a child. Her father, Edib Bey, a secretary of Sultan Abdülhamid II (1842–1918), greatly admired the principles of the English education system and tried to have Halide educated accordingly.

Halide attended the American College for Girls, a missionary school in Istanbul (becoming one of its first few Muslim graduates). She also received home tutorials in the Islamic sciences, as well as in the Arabic and Persian languages. After graduating in 1901, she married one of her tutors, Salih Zeki Bey (1863–1921), an eminent professor of mathematics and philosophy. The couple had two sons: Ayetullah and Zeki Hikmetullah. An intellectual woman of the Ottoman elite, Halide Edib had continuous social interaction with prominent male, and a few female reformers of the time. The nationalist clubs, or *Türk Ocakları* (Turkish Hearth), founded in 1911, functioned as cultural clubs for the Young Turks (revolutionaries who became the leading cadre within the Committee of Union and Progress, the party of the Constitutional Revolution). Halide Edib was among the few female intellectuals to participate in the activities of the Young Turks, contributing articles to the influential journals *Vakit* (Time), *Akşam* (The evening) and *Tanin*; signing her name Halide Salih.

Just after the 1908 Young Turks Revolution, which ushered in the Ottoman Empire's 'second constitutional period,' Halide Edib fled to Egypt with her sons, fearing the counter-revolutionary reprisal (the so-called '31 March uprising'). In 1909, she went to England and visited Isabel Fry (1869–1958), an education reformer from a famous Quaker family in London with whom Edib shared ideas about women's education and maintained an enduring friendship.

The intellectually, socially and politically lively public discussions that preceded the 1908 Young Turk Revolution inspired Halide Edib to write. Although she belonged to a literary canon of writers such as Ziya Gökalp, a leading proponent of Pan-Turanism (an extremist nationalist project to unite Turks living in different states), Edib critically acknowledged the failings of Pan-Turanism in her memoirs, especially after 1915.

Halide Edib's efforts to reconcile the philosophies of 'East' and 'West' can be observed with regard to the female protagonists of her novels *Seviye Talip* (1910) and *Handan* (1912). These were women admired by men for their highly educated and cultivated characters, usually contrasted with women of more conservative morals and manners. The theme of 'forbidden love' was transformed in her early novels into a renouncement of self in her later works: stories of virtuous women patriots related in *Yeni Turan* (New Turan, 1912), *Ateşten Gömlek* (Turkish ordeal, 1922) and *Vurun Kahpeye* (Strike down the whore, 1923) were mostly inspired by accounts of the War of Independence (1919-1922) against the occupation of Anatolia by the Allied Forces after World War I.

Although she was critical of certain social practices in Muslim societies such as polygamy, Halide Edib maintained that Islamic law had, on the whole, been more favorable to women than Western law codes because it accorded property and economic rights to women. At the same time, she tried to explain the social and economic rationale for Islamic practices like polygamy, arguing that they kept men away from prostitutes and mistresses and legalized the position of the second wife and her children. Halide Edib had suffered personally from the polygamous marriage of her father, experiencing a divided reality of different 'homes' during her childhood years. Edib Bey had taken a second and third wife after the death of Halide's mother and Halide Edib had four sisters: older sister Mahmure, from her mother's first marriage to Ali Şamil Pasha; Nilüfer and Nigar Hanım, from her father's second wife and stepsister Belkıs Hanım, as well as step-brother Said Bey, from her father's third wife. When Halide Edib's husband, Salih Zeki Bey–at that time director of *Galatasaray Sultani* (Galatasaray Lycee)–decided to take a second wife, the reality of polygamy in her own marriage came as a blow to Edib's integrity and sense of self. Without hesitation, Edib divorced her husband in 1910, after nine years of marriage.

After her divorce, Halide Edib dedicated her life to educational activities, teaching, organizing and directing schools. She worked in the *Darülmuallimat* (Teachers' College for Women), the *Kız İdadisi* (High School for Girls) and as an inspector for the *Evkaf Kız Okulları* (Girls' Schools under the Directorate of the Pious Foundation, to which all the mosque schools belonged). She was the founder of a women's organization, the *Teali Nisvan Cemiyeti* (Association for the Elevation of Women), which organized various courses for women and ran a small hospital, where Halide Edib and other women served as nurses during the first Balkan War (1912). She was later sent to Syria by Cemal Pasha (1916) to set up orphanages and girls' schools in the Arab regions of the Empire. Her second marriage–to Dr. Adnan Adıvar (then a professor at the Medical College and a deputy to the Ottoman Assembly)–took place in 1917.

Halide Edib became well-known as a public speaker and her speech at the Sultanahmet Meeting (6 June 1919) against the occupation of Izmir by Greece has served as a powerful icon of Turkish resistance and the fight for independence. An active member of the *Wilson Prensipleri Cemiyeti* (Society for Wilsonian Principles, founded in 1919) and an important networker between the Nationalists in Ankara and the American government, she was regarded as an advocate of the American mandate in Turkey. Along with her husband, Edib joined the National Forces led by Mustafa Kemal after the occupation of Istanbul by the Allies (1920). Adnan Adıvar served as the Vice-President of the Nationalist Parliament during the Greek–Turkish War (1919–1923) and Edib worked as a press officer and English interpreter at the parliamentary headquarters. Both were members of the inner circle of the leader, Mustafa Kemal; Edib was known as Corporal Halide, later awarded the rank of Sergeant-Major. Paradoxically, just after the war, the couple had to leave the country because of Adnan Adıvar's involvement in the establishment of an opposition party, the *Terakkiperver Cumhuriyet Fırkası* (Progressive Republican Party, 1924–1925), banned on 5 June 1925.

In 1926, Halide Edib and Adnan Adıvar left for Western Europe, where they lived in quasi/ self-imposed exile for about fourteen years (mostly in England and France, with a few months spent in Vienna and Karlsbad, where Edib received medical treatment for chronic bowel and bladder problems). The couple did not return to Turkey until after the death of Atatürk (1939). Halide Edib was invited to the United States in 1928 and 1930 as a guest lecturer to a number of universities. In lecture tours of both America and India (1935), she emphasized historical continuity between Republican and late Ottoman reforms in women's rights, presenting a new image of women in modern Turkey. As part of the enlightened Islamic perspective that she had adopted, Halide Edib reinterpreted Islamic verses and Islamic institutions (such as those of family law) to argue for a higher status for women in Islamic societies.

On her and her husband's return to Turkey, Halide Edib was appointed professor of English language and literature at Istanbul University (1940), where she worked until becoming a Member of Parliament on the list of the Democrat Party (1950–1954). Adnan Adıvar worked on the editorial board of the *Encyclopedia of Islam* and wrote his famous book, *Tarih Boyunca Din ve İlim* (Religion and science throughout history). He also became an MP for the Democrat Party (1946–1950). Halide Edib's life with Adnan Adıvar combined personal attachment, strong friendship and intellectual and political companionship, a relationship to which Halide Edib paid tribute in a book she wrote in her husband's memory following his death in 1955. She died in Istanbul on 9 January 1964.

Ayşe Durakbaşa
University of Muğla

SOURCES

(C) Edib Adıvar, Halide. *Memoirs of Halide Edib*. New York, London: The Century Co., 1926.

(C) Edib Adıvar, Halide. *The Turkish Ordeal*. Memoirs of Halide Edib. New York, London: John Murray Publications, 1928.

(C) Edib Adıvar, Halide. "Dictatorship and Reforms in Turkey." *The Yale Review* XIX (September 1929): 27-44.

(C) Edib Adıvar, Halide. *Turkey Faces West–A Turkish View of Recent Changes and Their Origin*. New Haven: Yale University Press; London: H. Milford; Oxford University Press, 1930.

(C) Edib Adıvar, Halide. *The Clown and His Daughter*. London: George Allen and Unwin Limited, 1935.

(C) Edib Adıvar, Halide. *Conflict of East and West in Turkey*. Jamia Millia Extension Lectures. Lahore: S. M. Ashraf, 1935.

(C) Edib Adıvar, Halide. *Inside India*. London: George Allen and Unwin Limited, 1937.

(C) Edib Adıvar, Halide. *Dr. Abdülhak Adnan-Adıvar*. Istanbul: Nurgök Matbaası, 1956.

(D) Sönmez, Emel. "Halide Edib Adıvar and Turkish Feminism." *Die Welt des Islams* 14, nos. 1-4 (1973): 81-115.

(D) Enginün, İnci. *Halide Edib Adıvar'ın Eserlerinde Doğu ve Batı Meselesi* (The question of East and West in Halide Edib's works). Istanbul: İstanbul Üniversitesi Edebiyat Fakültesi Yayınları, 1978.

(D) Durakbaşa, Ayşe. *Reappraisal of Halide Edib for a Critique of Turkish Modernization*. Unpublished doctorate thesis. University of Essex (Sociology), 1993.

(E) İz, Fahir, Khalide Edib'. *Encyclopedia of Islam*. Vol. IV. Leiden: E. J. Brill, 1978.

ENGELGARDT, Anna (1838–1903)

Russian writer, publicist, translator and activist in the Russian women's movement.

Anna Engelgardt (*nee* Makarova) was born on 2 June 1838 in the village of Aleksandrovka in the Kostroma province of the Russian Empire. Her father, Nikolai Makarov (1810–1890), was a member of the gentry and owned a small estate. In addition to being a famous Russian lexicographer—author of several dictionaries—he was also a writer, composer and actor. Anna's mother, Alexandra Makarova (*nee* Boltina, data unknown), died when Anna was six years old.

In 1845, wishing to give his daughter a comprehensive education, Nikolai Makarov sent Anna to the Catherine Institute in Moscow (the only Russian educational institution for girls in the 1840s). In 1853, Anna graduated from the Institute with honors and returned to her father's estate. She felt dissatisfied with the knowledge she had acquired, feeling that it was practically inapplicable. In order to expand it, she turned to the books in the family library (mainly European writers of the seventeenth and eighteenth centuries) and learned English, French and German. A student who spent his holidays in the neighboring estate acquainted Anna with the ideas of Alexander Hertsen, Nikolai Chernyshevskii, Nikolai Dobroliubov (the famous Russian publicist and literary critic) and Charles Darwin, whose works convinced her that only a thorough knowledge of contemporary ideas could give her social status equal with men. It was then that her life's credo was formed: "I only love two things: labor and knowledge" (Engelgardt 1910, 544). In 1859, she married Alexander Engelgardt (1832–1893), a young 'scientist-artilleryman,' graduate from Mikhailovskoe Artillery College, and later a doctor of chemistry. They had three children: Mikhail (b. 1861), Vera (b. 1863) and Nikolai (b. 1867), all of whom became writers.

The 1860s saw the rise of a democratic movement and the emergence of the Russian women's liberation movement. Following her life's credo, Anna Engelgardt began to participate actively in public and cultural life. In 1862, she began the practical application of her ideas on women's emancipation. In that year, Engelgardt became the first upper-class Russian woman to work 'publicly' as a shop assistant, in a recently founded bookstore in St Petersburg with strong connections to revolutionary underground circles. In Russian patriarchal society of the 1860s with its caste prejudices, Engelgardt's activities were considered scandalous by members of her own social class. In 1863, Engelgardt was one of the founders of the first Russian *Zhenskaia Izdatel'skaia Artel'* (Women's Publishing Cooperative), which aimed to give women the opportunity to earn their own income and gain financial independence. At the same time, the first of Engelgardt's translations into Russian appeared. Altogether, she translated more than seventy novels, essays and stories (including works by Zola, de Maupassant, Rousseau, Flaubert, Collins, Stevenson and Elliot). She became well known for her collection of pedagogical essays, *Ocherki Institutskoi Zhizni Bylogo Vremeni* (Essays on the institutional life of bygone times, 1870) and as the compiler of the *Polnyi Nemetsko-Russkii Slovar'* (Complete German–Russian dictionary, 1877). Other writings reveal Engelgardt's deep interest in women's history and literary work; among the manuscripts to be found in Engelgardt's archival collection is "Zhenschina v Obschestve i Sem'ie" (Woman in society and the family): a study of women's status from ancient to modern times (delivered as a lecture in St Petersburg on 27 March 1900). Engelgardt also wrote articles on the two Russian women-writers Kokhanovskaia (pen-name for Nadezhda Sokhanskaia) and Krestovskii (pen-name for Nadezhda Khvoschinskaia). Engelgardt's article on Kokhanovskaia, "Zabytaia pisatel'nitsa" (A forgotten woman writer), was published in the *Vestnik Evropy* (European herald) in 1899. Her article on Khvoschinskaia (which was unfortunately never published) dealt with issues raised in Khvoschinskaia's work, such as the sham of bourgeois marriage.

In 1870, both Anna Engelgardt and her husband were arrested for their active participation in the students' circle, a group of socialist students at the *Zemledel'cheskii Institut* (Agricultural Institute) in St Petersburg, who were opposed to the government and led by Alexander Engelgardt. Anna Engelgardt spent a month and a half in prison, her husband a year and a half. Since there was no direct evidence of Anna Engelgardt's guilt she was released, but her husband was found guilty and exiled from St Petersburg for life. Anna Engelgardt remained in St Petersburg with her children. Although she had three children to maintain almost alone, working as translator and writer, Engelgardt did not give up her public activity.

The 1880s and 1890s marked the peak of Engelgardt's involvement in the women's movement: she focused on issues of women's employment, marriage rights and (especially) education. Engelgardt was active in almost all the undertakings of Russian feminists. At the end of the 1870s, she helped found the *Vysshie Zhenskie Kursy* (Women's Higher Education Courses, the famous "Bestuzhev Courses") and in 1897, she co-founded the *Zhenskii Meditsinskii Institut* (Women's Institute of Medicine). Engelgardt also headed, and was chief librarian of the biggest women's charity organization in Russia, the *Russkoe Zhenskoe Vzaimno-Blagotvoritel'noe Obshchestvo* (Russian Women's Mutual Philanthropic Society). She wrote the editorial policy for the organization's journal *Zhenskii Trud* (Women's labor), with the aim of elucidating the development of the women's movement in Russia and abroad, as well as women's position in the labor market and issues surrounding women's education. It was assumed that Anna Engelgardt would be the editor-in-chief of this journal but she died in 1903, before the first issue appeared in print.

The life of Anna Engelgardt was devoted to showing, by her own example, that both knowledge and active participation in social work could free women from the burdens of patriarchal society; that a woman could be not only a devoted mother and wife, but also an active public and cultural figure. She deserves an honorable place in the annals, along with other Russian women who devoted their lives to the cause of women's liberation and enlightenment.

Igor' Shkol'nikov
Russian State University of Trade and Economy,
Ivanovo

SOURCES

(A) *Rossiiskii gosudarstvennyi arkhiv literatury i iskusstva* (Russian State Archive of Literature and Art), stock no. 572 (Engelgardt's archival collection).

(C) Engelgardt N. A. "Davnie epizody" (Long standing episodes). *Istoricheskii vestnik* (Historical herald), no. 2 (1910): 544.

(D) Mazovetskaya E. *Anna Engelgardt. Sankt-Peterburg vtoroi poloviny XIX veka* (Anna Engelhardt. St Petersburg in the second half of the nineteenth century). St Petersburg: Akademicheskii proekt, 2001.

(E) Pavlyuchenlo E. *Zhenschiny v russkom osvoboditel'nom dvizhenii ot Marii Volkonskoi do Very Figner* (Women in the Russian liberation movement: from Maria Volkonskaya to Vera Figner). Moscow, 1988.

EZERA, Regīna (born Šamreto) (1930–2002)

Latvian prose writer, journalist and public figure.

Regīna Šamreto was born on 20 December 1930, into a working-class family in Riga. Her father, Robert Šamreto, was a carpenter. Her mother, Lūcija Šamreto, was a housewife who had been educated at Riga Polish gymnasium and trained as a nurse after World War II. Regina's family members lived in a small flat in a working-class district of Riga. They included Regīna's grandmother, who had lost four children, and Felicija, one of her three surviving daughters. Regīna's maternal family came originally from Latgale in southeastern Latvia, a region characterized by ethnic pluralism, Catholicism (as opposed to Protestantism in other regions) and a distinctive set of cultural traditions. Regīna later recalled early memories of Belarussian folksongs and witticisms, Catholic prayers in Polish and Latin, as well as the specific Polish dialect spoken in her family. Up until the age of six, she had been practically without a mother tongue and had learned Latvian at school as a foreign language. Regīna also vividly remembered craving the countryside, in place of the shabby townscape of her childhood neighborhood. Once she had become a professional writer, she would spend the summers working at her country house *Brieži* (Deer) near Ķegums, a small town in the vicinity of Riga. In the late 1970s, she settled there permanently. Long walks in the forest, swimming and picking mushrooms were her favorite pastimes, in which she was always accompanied by her beloved Alsatian.

In 1938, Regīna Šamreto entered Riga Elementary school No. 28. During World War II, she and her family spent long periods outside Riga with distant relatives near Kaibala and Rembate, where the young Regīna took part in various forms of agricultural work and came into intimate contact with nature: a "dark-haired barefoot girl," in her own words, "who, standing beneath the huge dome of heaven, a shepherd's twig under her arm, suddenly discovered the human relation to Time and Space and sensed the transience of life, the eternity of Living–the basic themes for the would-be writer" (Tabūns 1980, 21; S. M., trans). In 1944, the family was deported by the retreating German army to a labor camp at Acken on the Elbe near Magdenburg. They returned to Latvia (which had come under Soviet rule) in 1945 and Regīna Šamreto enrolled in the N. Draudziņa Riga Secondary School No. 7. After leaving school, she studied journalism at Latvia State University (1950–1955), married twice and gave birth to three daughters: Inese (b. 1951); Ilze (b. 1955) and Aija (b. 1957). Neither of her marriages were successful and Regina Lasenberga (first marriage)/Kindzule (second marriage) assumed the responsibility for raising her daughters alone.

It was during her student period, in 1954, that she began working at the editorial office of the youth magazine *Draugs* (Friend), as well as for the children's newspaper *Pionieris* (Pioneer). In 1955, she published her first literary piece, a poetic sketch entitled "Pat īkšķis nepalīdzēja" (Even the thumb did not help) under the pen-name of Ezera (meaning lake), a name inspired by her attachment to the natural world. She also engaged extensively in literary criticism and review. In 1957, Ezera became a professional writer, making her living by writing so-called 'interior' reviews (reviews of literary works for publishing houses). Some of these reviews were later compiled and published in 1989 under the title *Virtuvē bez pavārgrāmatas* (In the kitchen without a cookery book). In 1961, Ezera published a collection of stories, *Un ceļš vēl kūp* (Dust on the road still unsettled) and the novel *Zem pavasara debesīm* (Under the spring skies), after which she joined the *Latvijas Padomju Rakstnieku Savienība* (Latvian Soviet Writers' Union), thus confirming her status as a professional writer. From 1965, she was a member of the Board of the Writer's Union and Chair of its committee for the enrolment of new members (1965–1977). She was active throughout the 1960s in the *Rīgas Deputātu padome* (Riga Council of Deputies) and a member of the Riga Communist Party Committee (1976–1978). In the late 1970s and 1980s, she represented Latvia as a member of the USSR Writers' Union.

Ezera portrayed human existence in a rich, inimitable and poetic literary style. During her most prolific period (the late 1960s and 1970s), she published a book a year; for Ezera, writing was a laborious daily task. In 1971, she received the *Ordenis Goda Zīme* (Order of the Honorary Sign); in 1972, the Latvian SSR State Prize; in 1974, the honorary title of *Latvijas PSR Nopelniem bagātā kultūras darbiniece* (Latvian SSR Cultural Official) and in 1981, the title of *Tautas Rakstniece* (National writer). When Ezera first began writing, the literary scene in Latvia had been dominated by socialist realism. Prose following realist traditions developed in Latvian literature from the late nineteenth century onwards. This changed with the advent of a new generation of young writers that included Visvaldis Lāms, Dagnija Zigmonte and Ilze Indrāne. Inspired by the new literary milieu, Ezera called for a psychological engagement in literature that might serve to counteract overbearing ideological schemes and promote diverse textual-poetic elements. No doubt Ezera was using her authority as a talented and recognized writer to emphasize such ideas, exemplified in her own work. The psychological focus of her prose is inseparable from the search for new forms of poetic expression in the modernist and post-modernist traditions. More specifically, Ezera's writing was inspired by the lives, loves and complex dilemmas of women, often central dramatic themes in Latvian literature in the second half of the twentieth century. Feminine worlds and awareness of feminine difference were issues raised by Ezera and her generation of women writers, writing from a 'closed' Soviet sociocultural space which nevertheless drew from, and reproduced, the new feminist consciousness emerging in works by non-Soviet writers such as Doris Lessing, Toni Morrison and Margaret Atwood. Ezera depicted women's lives across several generations in her second novel *Viņas bija trīs* (There were three of them, 1961). Questions of female happiness and its limitations are raised in Ezera's novel Aka (The well, 1972) and in the story "Vasara bija tikai vienu dienu," (The summer lasted but a day, 1974). In *Nakts bez mēnesnīcas* (Night without moonlight, 1971), feminine and masculine worlds meet in ironic confrontation; in *Slazds* (a collection of "Zoological short stories," 1979), Ezera explores ecological issues, relational values and global responsibility. Among her masterpieces are the novels *Zemdegas* (Underground fire, 1977), *Varmācība* (Violence, 1982), and its sequel *Nodevība* (Betrayal, 1984); the latter two works formed parts of an unfinished tetralogy *Pati ar savu vēju* (With her own wind), in which Ezera addressed women's victimization, motherhood and issues of feminine creativity.

In 1988–1989, Ezera, along with other outstanding intellectuals and creative figures, became politically active in the re-awakened national movement for Latvian independence (declared in 1990). In 1995, Ezera was awarded the *Trīszvaigžņu ordenis* (Three Star Order), the most prestigious national award of the Republic of Latvia. In the early 1990s, amid economic restructuring, sudden material changes took place in the spheres of arts and culture which, having been previously funded by the state, were now reorganized on a commercial basis. The dramatic effects of these changes was experienced mostly by an older generation, including the aging Ezera who spent her later years in difficult material circumstances, struggling with health problems and depression. Her final works–fragments of the third novel of her tetralogy *Esamība* (Being) and the miniature cycle *Odas skumjām* (Odes to sadness)–were published posthumously in 2003. Regīna Ezera died on 11 June 2002 and was buried in Tome Cemetery.

Sandra Meshkova
Daugavpils University and The University of Latvia

SOURCES

(C) Ezera, Regīna. "Par vai pret psiholoģismu?" (For or against psychology?). *Literatūra un māksla* (Literature and art) (22 April 1967): 3.

(D) Kokorevich, N., ed. *Regīna Ezera*. Riga: Cīņa, 1980 [in English].

(D) Tabūns, Broņislavs. *Regīna Ezera. Dzīves un jaunrades apskats–mozaīka* (Regina Ezera. Review–mosaic of her life and work). Riga: Liesma, 1980.

(D) Gulēns, Māra. *(Re)defining Limits: Women's Search for Identity in Regīna Ezera and Margaret Laurence's Prose.* University of Stockholm, 1990.

(D) *Regīna Ezera 60: bibliogrāfisks rādītājs* (Regina Ezera sixty: bibliographic directory). Riga: Latvijas Valsts bibliotēka, 1990.

(E) Miške Ezergailis, Inta. *Nostalgia and Beyond.* Langham, 1998.

FICKERT, Auguste (1855–1910)

School teacher and leading figure in the radical wing of the women's movement in Habsburg Austria.

Auguste Fickert (also known as Gusti) was born on 25 May 1855 in Vienna. Her mother, Louise Fickert (born Luhde, died 1907), was a housewife; her father, Wilhelm Fickert (d. 1881), was a foreman at the Court and State printers. They had two daughters (Auguste and Marianne) and two sons (Emil and Willy). Two of Auguste Fickert's siblings were later to become involved in her projects: Marianne Fickert committed herself to the *Allgemeiner Österreichischer Frauenverein* (General Austrian Women's Association) for many years and, after Auguste Fickert's death, her younger brother Emil Fickert (1870–1957, bank director) held a leading position with the periodical *Neues Frauenleben* (New woman's life), as well as with the women's cooperative housing project *Heimhof.*

Auguste Fickert attended primary school in Vienna. From 1869/70, she studied at the *Englische Fräulein* convent school in Burghausen, Bavaria and in 1872, was admitted to the *Lehrerinnen-Bildungsanstalt St. Anna* (St Anna's teacher training institute for women) in Vienna, where she graduated with honors on 9 July 1876. Much of her diary (preserved in manuscript form) dates from this period and tells in particular of girls' friendships, of an intensive crush on a (male) teacher and of the burning wish to become an actress. Auguste Fickert worked continuously as a school teacher from 1876 until her death in 1910, beginning her teaching career at a girls' school in Schulgasse (in Vienna's eighteenth district), where she also lived. Having been involved in the (politically moderate) *Verein der Lehrerinnen und Erzieherinnen* (Association of Women Teachers) since the early 1880s, Auguste Fickert faced grave confrontations with her superiors throughout the 1890s, due to her public criticism of the religious nature of school instruction. She left the Catholic Church in 1893. In 1899, she was transferred to the Grüne Thorgasse (a primary school in the ninth district). Hostilities *ad personam* from the clerical, anti-Semitic *Christlich-Soziale Partei* run all the way through her political career.

The launch of a petition by Auguste Fickert in 1889—against the disfranchisement of (taxpaying) women in Lower Austria, who had lost their communal suffrage as a consequence of municipal restructuring–is generally regarded as her first public appearance. The political basis of her work was provided by the *Allgemeiner Österreichischer Frauenverein* (General Austrian Women's Association, hereafter the *Frauenverein*). The *Frauenverein* committed itself to women's labor and employment, to education for working-class women and rights for female domestic servants; it raised the question of prostitution from an abolitionist perspective, created legal protection centers for impoverished women and rallied a large number of female civil servants, particularly post and telegraph office clerks. As the radical wing of the Austrian women's movement, the *Frauenverein* displayed closer rapport with activists of proletarian women's organizations (e.g. ***Adelheid Popp*** or ***Therese Schlesinger-Eckstein***) than with the moderate, liberal bourgeois wing (under the aegis of ***Marianne Hainisch***). From the first assemblies in 1893, including those of the board committee, Auguste Fickert was actively involved in the *Frauenverein*, becoming its Chair in 1897. In 1906, at her instigation, the *Frauenverein* left the moderate *Bund Österreichischer Frauenvereine* (Union of Austrian Women's Associations)–a member of the International Council of Women. Personalities who worked closely with Auguste Fickert include Marie Beyer-Mus(s)ill, Caroline Gronemann and Indra Weishan. For a time, she cooperated closely with Therese Schlesinger-Eckstein, Marie Lang and ***Rosa Mayreder***; later with Adele Gerber, Leopoldine Kulka and Ida Mayer, Sophie Regen, the Hug sisters Antonie and Hermine, as well as Christine Touaillon. As delegates of the *Frauenverein*, Marie Lang participated in the International Abolitionist Federation meeting in London (July 1898) and Leopoldine Kulka and Adele Gerber in the founding congress of the International Woman Suffrage Alliance in Berlin (June 1904).

The political practice of public textual production formed a crucial part of Auguste Fickert's activities. From 1893 to 1898, she edited *Das Recht der Frau* (The right of woman), an insert of the periodical *Volksstimme* (People's voice), published by the Democratic Party. In 1899, she founded–together with Marie Lang and Rosa Mayreder–the fortnightly *Dokumente der Frauen* (Documents of women), the periodical of the *Frauenverein*. From 1902, she acted as the single editor of the monthly *Neues Frauenleben* (New woman's life), at that time the organ of the *Frauenverein*. Its insert *Die Staatsbeamtin* (The woman civil servant) became a separate periodical for and by civil servants in the *Frauenverein* after 1908.

A decisive event in the history of the radical wing of Austria's women's movement, as well as in the political biography of Auguste Fickert, was the discord and final rupture with Marie Lang over the publication of *Dokumente der Frauen*. The exuberant friend and effusively enthusiastic colleague who would lovingly call Fickert "Bille," rapidly became an opponent to whom Fickert handed over the entire project (following Rosa Mayreder's advice) so as to limit further damage to the feminist cause. Subsequently, Auguste Fickert appeared to regard herself more markedly as a figure of autocratic leadership. She demanded absolute dedication from the new generation of activists she had recruited, leaving it uncertain whether such dedication was to be to her or to the cause. To admiration she reacted constantly with rejection and—eventually—with rituals of reconciliation such as joint mountain hikes. Thus, most of the younger activists related to her as a leader, both gruff and adorable.

Auguste Fickert's partner for decades was Ida Baumann (1845–1913). Baumann, also known as Baumännchen, was the daughter of a Jewish teacher who grew up in the principality of Schwarzburg-Sondershausen (present day Thüringen). She was a kindergarten teacher before moving to Vienna in 1872 to become a school teacher. She and Auguste Fickert met at the *Lehrerinnen-Bildungsanstalt* (teacher training institute) in 1881 and, after the death of Fickert's father, Baumann moved in with her. When, in 1887, Auguste Fickert got entangled in a complicated love affair with a man in Breslau, it was supposedly Ida Baumann—nicknamed "Hekuba" in Fickert's diary—who acted as her level-headed adviser. The two women jointly undertook their first steps into political territory, namely active participation in the organization of progressive women teachers, in the women's suffrage movement and in public debates on prostitution. Yet while Fickert grew into an increasingly prominent personality, Baumann remained a background figure. Regarded as a burden, suffering from her partner's coldness and impatience and with relations between Baumann and Fickert's colleagues growing tense, Ida Baumann drowned herself in the Danube near Greifenstein in Lower Austria, not quite three years after the death of Fickert.

The founding of the housing cooperative *Heimhof* was to be Auguste Fickert's last achievement. She did not live to see the residential home for professional women, the renowned *Einküchenhaus* (one kitchen house), open in 1911. After a few weeks of suffering, purportedly as a result of internal organ failure, Auguste Fickert died on 9 June 1910 in the Wällischhof sanitorium (near Maria Enzersdorf, Lower Austria), without having formally settled the succession to her position in the *Frauenverein*. The burial took place on 11 June 1910 at the Neustift am Walde cemetery. In addition to representatives of women's organizations, Julius Ofner and Engelbert Pernerstorfer—eminent progressive members of the *Reichsrat* (the Austrian monarchy's legislative body)—also attended the funeral service. A statue was erected in memory of Auguste Fickert in the *Türkenschanzpark* in Vienna in 1929.

Hanna Hacker
University of Vienna

SOURCES

(A) Wiener Stadt- und Landesbibliothek, Handschriftensammlung, Auguste Fickert: Manuscripts including her diary 1871/72–1910 (124 pp.) and c. 2000 unpublished letters.

(D) Flich, Renate. "Der Fall Auguste Fickert—eine Lehrerin macht Schlagzeilen" (The case of

Auguste Fickert–A woman teacher makes the headlines). *Wiener Geschichtsblätter* 45, no. 1 (1990): 1-24.

(D) Hacker, Hanna. "Wer gewinnt? Wer verliert? Wer tritt aus dem Schatten? Machtkämpfe und Beziehungsstrukturen nach dem Tod der 'großen Feministin' Auguste Fickert (1910)" (Who will win? Who will lose? Who steps out of the shadow? Power struggles and relations after the death of the 'great feminist' Auguste Fickert, 1910). *L'Homme-Zeitschrift für Feministische Geschichtswissenschaft* 7, no. 1 (1996): 97-106.

(E) Anderson, Harriet. *Utopian Feminism. Women's Movements in fin-de-siècle Vienna*. New Haven-London: Yale University Press, 1992.

(E) Hacker, Hanna. "Zeremonien der Verdrängung: Konfliktmuster in der bürgerlichen Frauenbewegung um 1900" (Ceremonies of suppression: conflict patterns in the bourgeois women's movement around 1900). In Lisa Fischer and Emil Brix, eds. *Die Frauen der Wiener Moderne* (The women of Viennese modernism). Vienna-Munich: Verlag für Geschichte und Politik und Oldenbourg Verlag, 1997, 101-109.

(F) ARIADNE: Projekt "Frauen in Bewegung"–Fickert, Auguste, 1855-1910. www.onb.ac.at/ariadne/vfb/bio_fickert.htm.

FILOSOFOVA, Anna Pavlovna, born Diaghileva (1837–1912)

Russian women's movement activist; philanthropist; driving force behind the establishment of the famous St Petersburg Higher Women's Courses (the *Bestuzhev* courses); Chairwoman (1861–1863; 1867–79) of the *Obshchestvo Dostavlenniia Deshevykh Kvartir i Drugikh Posobii Nuzhdaiushchimsia Zhiteliam Sankt-Peterburga* (Society for Cheap Lodging and Other Aid to the Residents of St Petersburg); Vice-President of the International Council of Women (1899–1911); Chairwoman of the First All-Russian Women's Congress (1908).

Anna Pavlovna Diaghileva was born on 5 April 1837 into a wealthy and longstanding noble family in St Petersburg. Her father, Pavel Dmitrievich Diaghilev (1808–1883), was a successful official at the Ministry of Finance who retired in 1850 and started his own distillery business at his family estate in Perm. Around 1855, he became obsessively religious and Anna's mother, his wife Anna Ivanovna (born Sul'meneva) (1818–1888), took over the family business. The eldest of nine children (she had five brothers and three sisters), Anna Diaghileva received her education at home (as was customary in Russian noble families) and received a strict upbringing from her mother. Anna herself found classes, governesses and teachers dull. In 1855, at the age of eighteen, she married Vladimir Dmitrievich Filosofov (1820–1894), then a powerful official at the Ministry of War and Defence. Like many feminists of her time, Anna Filosofova managed to combine extensive public activities with childbearing and childrearing. She had six children (three boys and three girls). Her youngest son, Dmitry (1872–1940), together with his cousin Sergey Diaghilev–the son of her younger brother Pavel (1848–1914)–established the famous magazine *Mir Iskusstva* (World of art) and the two became prominent cultural figures in early twentieth-century Russia.

Anna Filosofova spent the first years of her married life (1855–1861) leisurely, making short visits to her husband's family estate of Bogdanovskoe in Bezhanitsy (the Pskov region). Her husband was from typical country gentry that lived off serf labor; his father was a tyrannical figure, known to sexually exploit peasant women on the estate. Filosofova was struck by this lifestyle since her family had never used serf labor. She began reflecting on social problems, especially those relating to peasant life. Her first philanthropic efforts involved providing poor peasants with medicine and food. The emancipation of the serfs on 19 February 1861 was a real turning point for Anna Filosofova, as was meeting ***Mariia Trubnikova***, who gave her books to read on 'the woman question' and with whom she often discussed her reading. In 1860, Mariia Trubnikova, Anna Filosofova and ***Nadezhda Stasova***–collectively known as 'the Triumvirate'–established the *Obshchestvo Dostavlenniia Deshevykh Kvartir i Drugikh Posobii Nuzhdaiushchimsia Zhiteliam Sankt-Peterburga* (Society for Cheap Lodging and Other Aid to the Residents of St Petersburg), based on a new approach to philanthropy. Filosofova believed that instead of giving relief or cash benefits to the needy, it was necessary to create conditions that would enable the poor–through education, training and moral development–to earn their own incomes. The society rented an apartment where poor women could live at affordable rent and provided them with sewing work at workshops, also organized by the society. Under Filosofova's leadership as Chairwoman, the society acquired its own building and a large contract to make uniforms for the army (1871). The society also opened a cheap canteen and hired a doctor.

'The Triumvirate' set up many other philanthropic projects, the two most important being the *Obshchestvo Organizatsii Zhenskogo Truda* (Society for the Organization of Work for Women) and the *Zhenskaia Izdatel'skaia Artel'* (Women's Publishing Artel). By the late 1860s, these organizations had difficulties remaining operative: the *Obshchestvo Organizatsii Zhenskogo Truda* suffered from internal disagreements and the *Zhenskaia Izdatel'skaia Artel'*, from a lack of funds. The most ambitious initiative of 'the Triumvirate' was the one launched on behalf of women's education. Stasova and Filosofova zealously promoted plans to allow women to attend lectures at St Petersburg University. In 1868, they managed to collect four hundred signatures on a petition to Tsar Alexander II, asking for permission to open the first Higher Education Courses for Women at St Petersburg University. Filosofova was elected Chairwoman of the committee organizing the women's Higher Education Courses. Resistance among conservative circles was strong and the Minister of Education, Count Tolstoi, did not support the admission of women into universities. However, he did allow women to attend public lectures by university professors and this subsequently took place, often for free. In 1871, these informal courses obtained the name *Vladimirskii* (after the name of the college institution in which the courses were held). At the same time, Filosofova managed to open a small village school at the *Bogdanovskoe* estate (which she then represented and which, after the death of her husband in 1894, she would later inherit). The school exists today. The reaction of upper layers of Russian society to the Vladimirskii courses was exceedingly hostile and many articles appeared in the press on the harm done to girls through education. Many female students decided to go abroad (mostly to Zurich) in order to complete an education. In the face of this out-flow of women, the government consented to keep the courses open, but as revolutionary ideas spread among female students–some of them members of revolutionary organizations–the courses were closed down in 1875. Filosofova campaigned for their re-opening and, in 1876, managed to get official permission to open the first women's university in Russia, known as the *Bestuzhev* Courses (after the name of the nominal founder of the courses, Professor Bestuzhev-Riumin).

Filosofova was now at the height of her career, a member of many societies and committees. But her sympathy with the revolutionaries did not make her popular at the official level, especially since her husband was then a public prosecutor. Known to be kind and open, Filosofova was often approached by the families of convicted and exiled revolutionaries who appealed to her for help. When, in 1879, tsarist police discovered that she had been collecting money for certain revolutionary organizations, she was exiled abroad and only permitted to return in 1881. The assassination of Tsar Alexander II produced a wave of strong conservative reaction and Filosofova, having been exiled as an accomplice of revolutionaries, found no friends and supporters for her further undertakings. Her family situation was disturbing too; her husband was not promoted as a result of her activities and the couple, with their six children, had to move and assume a more modest way of life.

Filosofova returned to active public life in the late 1880s/early 1890s, when she began providing assistance to starving people in the Volga region (1892–93), later joining the *Sankt-Peterburgskii Komitet Gramotnosti* (St Petersburg Committee for the Promotion of Literacy) in 1892. In 1895, she became a founder member of the *Russkoe Zhenskoe Vzaimno-Blagotvoritel'noe Obshchestvo* (Russian Women's Mutual Philanthropic Society); in 1905, she actively participated in the Revolution of 1905 (joining the *Kadets* or the Constitutional Democrats) and pushed determinedly for permission to hold the First All-Russian Women's Congress, which finally took place in 1908. In those years, her dream was to create an all-Russian National Council of Women that could bring Russia officially into the International Council of Women–to which she was elected Vice-President in 1899. Support for this dream was not forthcoming, given the number of different factions within the Russian women's movement. In the aftermath of the 1908 Congress, the ultra-right Duma deputy V. M. Purishkevich dispatched letters to Filosofova, ***Anna Shabanova*** and Mariia Pokrovskaia, comparing the Congress to a gathering of whores. Filosofova created a sensation by making the letter public and successfully taking Purishkevich to court, whereby the deputy was subsequently sentenced to a month in jail.

In the later years of her life, Filosofova became interested in theosophy and joined the Russian Theosophical Society, set up (with her help) in 1908. 1911 marked the fiftieth Jubilee of Filosofova's public activities, which represented the achievements and real progress of the women's movement in Russia. More than a hundred women's organizations from all over Russia presented addresses to Filosofova, joined by several foreign women's organizations. She was also honored by Russian deputies at Mariinskij Palace, then the building of the State *Duma* (Russian Parliament) in St Petersburg. For many members of the younger generation she was a living legend: a symbol of feminism and the gains made by women campaigners of the 1860s generation. Prior to her death on 17 March 1912, at the age of 75, she had been the last living founder of the women's movement in Russia; thousands of people attended her funeral and paid tribute to her memory.

Ariadna Tyrkova called Anna Filosofova the first Russian feminist: "a woman who, deep in her heart and in her clear, enlightened mind, realized that humanity would never be free until women had full rights." [in *Vestnik Evropy* (European herald) 6 (1912): 321]. Having been likened to a Russian "Mme Roland" in the 1870s, working to open universities for women and helping women to find their way in a new hostile world of nascent capitalism, Filosofova personifies many of the achievements of Russian feminism.

Marianna Muravyeva
Herzen State Pedagogical University,
St Petersburg

SOURCES

(A) St Petersburg Central State Historical Archive, collection no. 1075, f. 1075 [Anna Pavlovna Filosofova's papers and documents of the *Russkoe Zhenskoe Vzaimno-Blagotvoritel'noe Obshchestvo* (Women's Mutual Philanthropic Society)]. Contains thousands of documents collected by Filosofova herself and later donated to the society, including her autobiography, family correspondence and official documents (relating to the work of the society).

(A) National Library of Russia, collection nos. 124, 146, 157, 297, 391, 475, 585 and 1033 (various correspondence).

(A) Russian Academy of Sciences, Institute of Russian Literature / *Pushkinsky Dom*, collection no. 102 (Diaghilev MSS). Contains the manuscripts of the Diaghilev family, information on Filosofova's early life, family genealogies (on both maternal and paternal sides) and the correspondence and recollections of family members.

(B) Benua A. *Moi Vospominaniia* (My memoirs). Moscow, 1980, I: 499–508.

(B) Schtakenschneider E. *Dnevnik i Zapiski. (1854–1886)* (Diary and memoirs). Moscow: Academia, 1934.

(B) Diaghileva E. V. *Semeinaia Zapis' o Sem'ie Diaghilevyh* (Family records of the Diaghilev family). St Petersburg, Perm: Dmitry Bulanin, 1998.

(C) Filosofova, Anna Pavlovna. *Zaiavlenie Predsedatel'nitsy Obshchestva Deshevykh Kvartir* (Statement of the Chairwoman of the Society for Cheap Lodging). St Petersburg, 1873.

(C) Filosofova, Anna Pavlovna. "Mezdunarodhyi Sovet Zenschin" (International Council of Women). *Soiuz Zenschin* (Union of Women) 2 (1907): 14–16.

(C) Filosofova, Anna Pavlovna. "O Natsional'nykh Sovetakh Zenschin" (On the National Councils of Women). *Zenskii Vestnik* (Women's herald) 11 (1908): 263–264.

(D) Pisareva, E. *Pamiaty Anny Pavlovny Filosofovoi* (In memory of Anna Pavlovna Filosofova). Moscow: Russkoe Teosofskoye Obschestvo, 1912.

(D) Tyrkova, A. "Anna Pavlovna Filosofova i Eio Vremia" (Anna Pavlovna Filosofova and her times); "Stat'i i materialy" (Articles and materials). In *Sbornyk Pamiaty A. P. Filosofovoi* (Articles in memory of A. P. Filosofova), vols. 1/2. Petrograd: Tovarischestvo R. Golike i E. A. Vil'borg, 1915.

(D) Rabkina, N. "Real'naia Istoriia I Slovestnost'. Anna Pavlovna Filosofova v Bol'shoi Literature" (Realist narrative and literature: Anna Pavlovna Filosofova in Russian literature). *Voprosy Literatury* (Literary questions) 9/10 (1991).

(E) Laskin, A. S. *Neizvestnye Diaghilevy* (Unknown Diaghilevs). St Petersburg: Novaya Literatura, Petropol', 1994.

FRUMKIN, Esther (real name Malka Lifschitz, Esfir' Frumkina in Russian, known as Esther Frumkin in English) (1880–1943)

The best known woman activist in the Russian Jewish revolutionary movement.

Esther Frumkin, 1908 (seated second from the left) with delegates to the Chernovits Conference

Throughout her notorious–often celebrated–career, Esther Frumkin led a life full of paradoxes. Criticized for opposing the study and popularization of Yiddish at a 1908 conference in Czernowitz (in Ukrainian Bukovina, then part of the Austro-Hungarian Empire), she later embraced the Bolshevik Revolution and lobbied for Yiddish as the revolutionary language of Jews. She led virulent anti-religious campaigns in the 1920s as the leader of the Communist Party's Jewish Section, only to be cast aside as party policies shifted. The granddaughter of rabbis, she passionately attacked rabbinical authority. A gifted linguist and advocate for Yiddish, she helped undermine the bases for a distinct Jewish language. An advocate for a separate Jewish working-class culture, she supported policies which accelerated assimilation. A fervent Communist, she spent the last years of her life in a Stalinist labor camp.

Born Malka Lifschitz in 1880, into a wealthy merchant's family in Minsk, she and her two sisters received both Jewish and secular educations. Malka's revolutionary inclinations were primarily responses to the widespread Jewish poverty she had witnessed in the Minsk of her youth. She taught a women's circle in Minsk before leaving, at the age of seventeen, for St Petersburg, in order to attend the Bestuzhev Higher Women's Courses, a hotbed of radical activity. Her interest in philology led her eventually to become fluent in six languages. Malka returned to Minsk in 1900 as a member of the *Bund* (the Jewish revolutionary socialist party, founded in 1897) and married a fellow Bundist, the engineer Boris Frumkin, who died soon after she gave birth to their only child, a daughter.

By the Russian Revolution of 1905 and the Duma elections of 1906, Frumkin (now using the name Esther) had become the only female member of the *Bund* in a policy-making position. A pedagogue and linguist, Frumkin advocated the establishment of Yiddish schools, modeled on the Montessori schools she had seen in her pre-war travels in Switzerland and Austria. She saw such schools as a means of teaching socialism to Jewish children, as well as preserving Jewish identity. Esther Frumkin first came to prominence in 1908 at the Yiddish Language conference in Czernowitz, during a period of political exile. She (and others) advocated keeping Yiddish as the language of the Eastern European Jewish proletariat, defeating a proposal by the renowned Yiddish writer I. L. Peretz to establish Yiddish as the national language for all Jews. The Zionists, who supported the revival of Hebrew, also vigorously opposed the Peretz proposal.

Unlike many Bundists, Esther Frumkin did not see a contradiction between raising the consciousness of Jewish workers and the observance of religious customs in the home. Initially, her vision of the ideal Jewish proletarian home resembled a traditional vision, with the mother lighting the Sabbath candles and the father blessing the wine. The difference was that this Jewish worker family would form the core of a secular Jewish society. From 1917 to 1920, Frumkin's attitude towards the Bolsheviks developed from an initial position of outright hostility into one of open support and solidarity. Following the February Revolution of 1917, which toppled the Tsar, she became a 'revolutionary defensist', supporting Russia's continued involvement in the War. She joined the *Bund* Central Committee in April and in May became the editor of the important Yiddish journal *Der Vekert* (The awakener). In 1918, Frumkin accepted the education post offered her by the Bolshevik majority of the Minsk Revolutionary Council. But at the eleventh *Bund* conference in March 1919, Esther Frumkin criticized Bolshevik terror and censorship.

The Soviet government sought to co-opt Jewish socialism. Esther Frumkin became the only woman in the eleven person strong Central Bureau of the Communist Party's *Evsektsiia* (Jewish Section), established in the fall of 1918. For nine years she led efforts to bring "the revolution to the Jewish street" (Gitelman 2001, 111). Frumkin is especially known for her ardent campaign against the religious establishment, exemplified by her pamphlet *Doloi ravvinov* (Down with the rabbis!). Although at times she admired the tenacity of her opponents, "wrapped in their prayer shawls" (Levin 1990, 72), Frumkin the commissar approved attacks on Jewish communal institutions and decried religious leaders as *lishentsy* (superfluous), depriving them of their civil and economic rights. Frumkin was part of the *Evsektsiia* effort to create a "Red Judaism" and was instrumental in having Yiddish designated a national language and establishing a system of Soviet Yiddish schools. By the end of the 1920s, in Belarus and Ukraine, half the Jewish children attended such schools. But many Jews identified Yiddish with the culture of the backward *shtetl* (Jewish village), not with a bright industrial and Soviet future. Higher education in Yiddish was not allowed; Russian was the language of the colleges and universities. In 1926, over seventy percent of all Soviet Jews gave Yiddish as their first language; by 1939, this number was down to less than forty percent.

In 1930, Stalin disbanded the *Evsektsiia*. Esther Frumkin became the head of the Jewish Department and then rector of the University of the National Minorities of the West, training foreign student cadres. The University was closed in 1936, as the purge trials began in earnest, and Frumkin moved to the Institute of Foreign Languages. In January 1938, she was arrested and imprisoned and in August 1940, sentenced to eight years forced labor in the notorious Stalinist *gulag* Karaganda, in Kazakhstan. Her daughter and son-in-law were also imprisoned. Released in 1943, following the intervention of Party comrades, she died in June of that year from the effects of her imprisonment.

Esther Frumkin's early defense of women's role in preserving cultural traditions in the home helped honor women's critical contribution to Jewish continuity and to the building of the progressive Jewish family. She articulated the basic concepts of the *Folkschule*, the secular progressive Jewish school; she argued the case for a proletarian Jewish culture; she was a skilled and dedicated teacher. As a journalist, as the only woman in a leadership position in the *Bund* and the Jewish Section, as a proponent of social change in a Jewish context, Esther Frumkin made an important contribution to the development of a secular alternative to Jewish religious culture. By centering that alternative in the family and in the school, two areas in which women were prominent, Frumkin highlighted women's role as both preservers and transformers of Jewish culture. As an activist, Frumkin provided Jewish women with a significant role model. As Naomi Shepherd observes, by emphasizing women's importance in passing down Jewish culture from generation to generation, Frumkin remained "'a true daughter of the Jewish tradition'" (quoted in Shepherd 1993, 171).

Rochelle Goldberg Ruthchild
The Union Institute and University
and the Davis Center for Russian and Eurasian Studies,
Harvard University

SOURCES

(B) Reisen, Zalmen. *Leksikon fun der yiddisher literature* (Lexicon of Yiddish literature). Vilna, 1926–1929.

(C) Frumkina, Maria Y. *Doloi ravvinov* (Down with the rabbis!). Moscow, 1923.

(D) Falkovich, E. "Ester–der lebensveg fun der groiser revolutsyonern" (Esther: the life path of the great revolutionary). *Folkstimme* (People's voice) 20, nos. 1–6 (1965).

(D) Shepherd, Naomi. *A Price Below Rubies: Jewish Women as Rebels and Radicals*. Cambridge: Harvard University Press, 1993, 137–171.

(D) Goldberg Ruthchild, Rochelle. "Esther Frumkin: Jewish Woman Radical in Early Soviet Russia." *Di froyen (The Women), Women and Yiddish: Tribute to the Past Directions for the Future*. New York: National Council of Jewish Women New York Section, 1997, 58–63.

(E) Nathans, Benjamin. *Beyond the Pale: The Jewish Encounter with Late Imperial Russia*. Berkeley: University of California Press, 2002.

(E) Gitelman, Zvi. *Jewish Nationality and Soviet Politics: The Jewish Sections of the CPSU, 1917-1930*. Princeton: Princeton University Press, 1972.

(E) Gitelman, Zvi. *A Century of Ambivalence: The Jews of Russia and the Soviet Union, 1881 to the Present*. Second extended edition. Published in association with the YIVO Institute for Jewish Research. Bloomington: Indiana University Press, 2001.

(E) Levin, Nora. *Paradox of Survival: The Jews in the Soviet Union Since 1917*. 2 vols. London: Taurus, 1988.

(E) Levin, Nora. *The Jews in the Soviet Union Since 1917*. Vol. 1. London and New York: Tauris, 1990.

GALDIKIENĖ, Magdalena (1891-1979)

Teacher and leader of the *Lietuvių katalikių moterų draugija* (Lithuanian Catholic Women's Organization); editor of *Moteris* (Woman); member of the Lithuanian Parliaments (1920–1926). Pseudonyms: 'Feminist' and 'Mokytoja M. D.' (Teacher M[agdalena] D[raugelyte]).

Magdalena Galdikienė, between 1931 and 1935

Magdalena Galdikienė (maiden name Draugelytė) was born on 26 September 1891 in the village of Bardauskai, in Vilkaviškis County. Her father, Petras Draugelis (1849-1914), was a primary school teacher who illegally distributed Lithuanian books (Lithuanian Latin script books were prohibited by the tsarist regime from 1864 to 1904). Her mother (little data available) gave birth to twelve children of which only seven reached adulthood. Magdalena was one of the younger siblings, influenced not only by her parents, but also by her older brothers and her sister, Apolonija Draugelyte-Cemarkiene.

Magdalena attended the girls' gymnasium in Marijampole. She graduated in 1910, and immediately went on to teach at the Lithuanian school in Liepaja, taking up a new post at the Obeliai Girls' Farming School a year later. In this way, she managed to earn a living independently while saving for her studies. In 1912, she enrolled at the Higher Pedagogy School in St Petersburg, graduating in 1915. In 1917, after having worked as a teacher in a number of educational establishments across Russia, she married Adomas Galdikas (1893-1969), who would become a celebrated Lithuanian painter. They formed a happy couple and had no children. By 1918, they had returned to Lithuania, to the city of Kaunas; life in the Soviet Union was becoming dangerous and both wished to contribute to social and political developments in the newly established Lithuanian State. From 1923 to 1940, Magdalena Galdikienė was head of the Gymnasium of the Holy Christ's Heart Congregation, where she also taught German.

Galdikienė was already involving herself in public activities by the early age of fourteen, when she organized discussion groups at her school on issues related to the Lithuanian culture and language. She came to see a value in special organizations for women and, after the *Lietuvių katalikių moterų draugija* (*LKMD*, Lithuanian Catholic Women's Organization) had been founded in 1908, helped her sister organize a local Marijampole *LKMD* branch the same year. Later, in St Petersburg, she led the *Ateitininkai* (People of the Future), a Catholic Lithuanian youth group whose credo was "to renew everything in Christ." In 1919, she became the elected head of the *LKMD*, which she led with only one brief interruption until the suppression of the organization in 1940. In addition to organizing women of the towns, she was especially interested in drawing lower-class Lithuanian women from the countryside into the *LKMD*, which, under her guidance, grew to 410 branches and united 42,000 members. For ten years, Galdikienė edited the first women's newspaper in Lithuania, *Moteris* (Woman), the newspaper of the *LKMD*. In 1940, the publication reached subscription rates of eighteen thousand in a population of just two to three million. Galdikienė emphasized women's important role in promoting 'Lithuanian' and 'Catholic' virtues, for which task they had to organize for empowerment through professional work, an independent income and participation in public/national life–the last was essential if women were to defend their interests as Catholic/Lithuanian mothers.

Magdalena Galdikienė's political career began in 1919, when she was elected onto the Board of the Kaunas Municipality. She was an advocate of Christian democratic values and, as a member of the Christian Democratic Party, was elected to all four democratically elected Parliaments between 1920 and 1926. She worked on parliamentary commissions on education, social security policy and public libraries. In 1922, Galdikienė was one of four female Catholic Members of Parliament to initiate changes to the old civil code. The new code, effective from 1922, eliminated most civil legal inequalities, including those in inheritance law whereby daughters inherited less than sons.

In 1925, Galdikienė was elected the Secretary of Parliament and in 1926, the second Vice-Chairperson. In her parliamentary speeches, she advocated separate education for girls and boys but insisted on equal school syllabi. Later, she suggested that women be granted eight weeks of paid maternity leave and that widows be provided with state pensions. In 1926, the government decided to issue a law allowing only one spouse to be employed in the civil service, effectively sacking all women civil servants whose husbands also worked for state institutions. Galdikienė gave a highly animated speech defending women's employment rights, arguing that a profession was a necessary precondition for women to secure adequate living standards and a future. She signed all memorandums protesting women's discrimination written by the Lithuanian Women's Council to the government.

Her organizational work was not restricted to the *LKMD*. In 1923, aware of the benefits of cross-institutional cooperation, she founded the *Katalikių organizacijų sąjunga* (Union of Catholic Women's Organizations) and in 1934, the union's section for intellectuals, *Moteru talka* (Women's Aid). She also participated in the work of another fifteen, mostly women's organizations.

During the German occupation, Magdalena Galdikiene, who was a German teacher, taught at the Kaunas Art Institute, as did her husband. As the Soviet Army approached Lithuania, she and her husband fled westwards. From Germany, the couple went to Paris and in 1952, on to the USA, where Adomas Galdikas hoped for better working conditions as an artist. Galdikiene strongly supported her husband in this period, even completing evening courses in order to be able to work in a bank and thus earn a living for both of them. Despite her endeavors, they found themselves in difficult circumstances, although this did not deter Galdikienė from participating in public activities in the Lithuanian community. She became head of the Catholic Women's Union in New York and New Jersey and a Board Member of the *Ateitininkai* Federation. After her husband's death in 1969, she arranged for his paintings to be donated to a Lithuanian gallery and contributed to a book on his work, *Adomas Galdikas: A Color Odyssey* (1973). But Galdikienė was less influential within the Lithuanian American community than she had been back home and it seems that her husband's lasting (posthumous) fame as a painter was not enough to ensure her own public standing, even though it had been she who had supported him throughout his artistic career and had created the conditions necessary for him to work. She died on 22 May 1979 in a nursing home in Putnam, Connecticut.

Throughout her life, Magdalena Galdikienė encouraged women to promote Christian ideals by participating in public life. She was as devout a believer in the equality of women and men as she was in the authority of the Catholic Church, and openly denounced the many ways in which the state discriminated against women in both public and family life, taking the pseudonym of 'Feminist.' For her, Catholic principles meant helping the needy and bringing happiness, peace and love to both home and parish through organized action. Thus it was her deep religious beliefs that motivated her to organize women. On the basis of equality-in-difference, she encouraged women to play an active role in society and the church, that their 'female qualities' might be of benefit to all.

Indrė Karčiauskaitė
Vytautas Magnus University, Kaunas

SOURCES

(C) Willard, Charlotte. *Adomas Galdikas: A Color Odyssey*. New York: October House, 1973. Contains extracts about the life of Adomas Galdikas by Magdalena Galdikienė.

(D) *Moteris* (Woman), no. 3 (1935). This issue is dedicated to the life and activities of M. Galdikienė, celebrating her fifteen years of *LKMD* leadership.

(D) Liulevičienė, Monika. "Magdalena Draugelytė-Galdikienė–visuomenininkė" (Magdalena Draugelytė-Galdikienė–public figure). *Tėvynės sargas* (Guardian of the fatherland) (1977): 58-67.

(D) Vailionytė, Danutė. "Nenuilstanti Lietuvos pilietinės visuomenės kūrėja" (Tireless creator of Lithuanian civil society). *XXI amžius* (Twenty first century), no. 31 (25 April 2001).
(D) Butkuvienė, Anelė. "Tiesos, meilės, meno vardan" (In the name of truth, love and art). *Šeimininkė* (Housewife), no. 40 (3 October 2001).
(E) *Lietuvių enciklopedija* (Lithuanian encyclopedia). Vols. 5/6. Boston: Lietuviu enciklopedijos leidykla, 1955.

GÁRDOS, Mária (Mariska Gárdos, Mrs György Pintér, likely born M. Grünfeld) (1885-1973)

Leader of the social democratic women's movement in Hungary before World War I; active in social democratic organizations as an émigré in Vienna (after 1919) and in Budapest (from 1945); member of the Communist Party; women's activist; appointed Permanent Member (1971) of the *Magyar Nők Országos Tanácsa* (Hungarian Women's National Council).

Mariska Gárdos, 1965, sitting (right) with close friend and famous Hungarian poet, Zseni Várnai (1890–1981) (left) at the Congress of the *Magyar Nők Országos Tanácsa,* where Gárdos was made a Permanent Member of the organization.

Mariska Gárdos was born on 1 May 1885 (one source claims 1 October 1884), in Nagyberény, Hungary, south of Lake Balaton. She was one of many children, yet only three of her siblings reached adulthood: her much younger sister Frida (born mid-1890s–died in a Soviet prison around 1926) and her elder sister and brother Giza and Sándor (data unknown). Her father, originally a tailor's assistant, moved to Budapest with his family in 1886, where he became a casual worker and canvas repairer in the Óbuda Dockyard Factory. Mariska's mother worked hard to maintain her large family. In the interwar period, she and her husband died relatively young, at the ages of 54 and 60 respectively. Mariska, having finished lower-level secondary school, successfully concluded a preparation course for trade employees. However, she found her (short-lived) experiences of positions available to women of her social class sexually humiliating. In 1905/1906, she moved to Kolozsvár (Cluj, today Cluj-Napoca, Romania), where, with the help of leftist intellectuals and social democratic comrades, she built up a career as a professional journalist. Back in Budapest after a few years, possibly in 1908, she also accepted a part-time position as an employee in the lawyer's office of a socialist comrade. After her emigration years (1919-1932), Gárdos lived from her activities as a party educator and journalist; in the 1930s, she also wrote novels and did translation work.

In 1909, Gárdos married the socialist journalist Ernő Bresztovszky (1882-1922). Not long after the death of their child Márta, who did not live to see her first birthday, the couple divorced. In 1913, Gárdos remarried and, years later, had a second child (Marianne, born 1922) with her second husband, György Pintér, also a socialist and white-collar worker. She lived with Pintér until his death in 1941. Gárdos, who was of Jewish origin, belonged to the Lutheran confession in the interwar period and had her daughter baptized a few days after the birth.

Mariska Gárdos's relationship to the social democratic workers' movement reached back to her childhood years, when she became acquainted with the organized workers' milieu through her father and her brother Sándor. Mariska became a member of the party as a teenager in 1900 and, soon after, we find her a founding member and public activist of the *Kereskedelmi Alkalmazottak Szakegylete* (Union of Trade Employees). In these early years, Mariska's comrade Sándor Garbai wrote to her: "As I look around ... I ask: where are the women? But I do see one woman, you, who possesses the power and the talent to awaken millions of your sex. Therefore set out for the battlefield, to the great task!" (Kende 1985, 9). These lines indicate two crucial points of departure for Mariska Gárdos's involvement in organizing women within the workers' movement: one was the masculinism of the party, the identification of the real worker with the male worker and of the interests of the working class exclusively with those of male workers; the other was the sexualized and marginalizing labor and social relations into which working women were systematically drawn. Gárdos's earliest monograph, *Az igazság az élet* (Justice is life, 1906), a letter-novel addressed to her younger sister, is a masterly elaboration of her radically critical attitude towards the latter experiences. From 1902, Gárdos worked–initially in close cooperation with representatives of the unfolding non-socialist feminist movement–for the foundation of a woman workers' association which, in 1904, was formally established as the *Magyarországi Munkásnők Országos Egyesülete* (*MME*, National Association of Woman Workers in Hungary). The *MME* very soon ceased to be related to the non-socialist women and it was in the course of these changes that Gárdos became President of the association. Although she only retained this position until 1906, the *MME* remained an important organizational basis for her activities. After a separate organization for women was founded within the Social Democratic Party in 1905, Gárdos became active at this level as well. Lively organizational and political endeavors, with a focus on trade unionism and on feminized professions without access to trade unions such as servants and washer-women, formed a crucial focus of the activities of the socialist women's movement in this period. While the Social Democratic Party of Hungary did not give Gárdos an opportunity to become formally involved in international organization before World War I, she made contacts and exchanged letters with Klara Zetkin in 1909, as the secretary of the social democratic *Országos Nőszervező Bizottság* (National Women's Organizing Committee), the follow-up organization of the women's organization within the party.

From 1912, after a period of deep crisis in social democratic women's activities, women's organizing was completely mainstreamed into, and controlled by, the highly masculinist party. The group around Mariska Gárdos, which had kept up resistance to this unprecedented form of subordination within the party, did not play an important role in the social democratic women's movement after these reforms. The 'compromises' which Gárdos had made over the years as an expression of loyalty to the party (intellectually, for example, by making sure in her writings that horrifying gendered/sexualized experiences of working-class women were blamed exclusively on 'bourgeois men'; politically, for example, by following the party line of temporarily 'setting aside' the struggle for woman suffrage, which she had done in 1905) had been largely in vain. From 1916, Gárdos withdrew from the socialist women's movement, having failed to productively connect her two basic strategies: one to ensure relative organizational autonomy for women towards and within the party; another to ensure that women's strategies and action would not endanger their (organized) status within "the big community" (Gárdos 1975, 124). The latter strategy of remaining formally within the wider workers' movement was regarded by Gárdos as the only possible basis for meaningful leftist political activism, whether on behalf of women or otherwise.

Yet Gárdos's political and professional engagement within and on behalf of the workers' movement had never been restricted to women's organizing. In 1905, she became the first editor of the newly founded journal *Nőmunkás* (Woman worker) for a few months. Later on, yet only for certain periods, she remained an important contributor to this journal and she also published in *Népszava* (People's voice) and various progressive journals. Gárdos continued to be deeply involved in party activities, often as a high-ranking public speaker. In 1912, she traveled to Paris and, during an extended tour through the USA in 1912/1913, she gave a number of public speeches on 'the situation in Hungary,' 'the workers' question,' 'organization' and the 'election'–all in Hungarian.

In the revolutionary period of late 1918, Gárdos remained a member of the Social Democratic Party. Under the short-lived Hungarian Council Republic of 1919, she was one of the editors of the communist *Vörös Újság* (Red journal), a move that symbolized the integrative appeal of the Communist Party, with which the Social Democratic

Party had been unified. In the same period, she was a member of the leading committee of the party's newly established women's organization. After the fall of the Communist regime in August 1919, Gárdos had to hide for months until she was finally able to leave the country by ship to Vienna. She spent most of the emigration period in the Austrian capital, working closely with the Austrian and emigrants' social democratic milieu and organizations, particularly those on the left wing of the social democratic workers' movement.

Gárdos returned to Budapest in October 1932. She soon became active in the social democratic women's movement and a member of the Social Democratic Party's women's organizing committee, agitating for a leftist turn in party politics and advocating active resistance to fascism. In 1936, Gárdos was sentenced to five months imprisonment for 'incitement,' which she served in 1937. In the early 1940s, she was put under police supervision, detained in 1943, but set free after two months (upon the intervention of high-ranking representatives of the Social Democratic Party). Gárdos could now no longer remain politically active in public. In 1944, she went into hiding from the Nazi-German occupying forces. Her name appeared on a list of 'Jewish authors' whose writings were banned. Her daughter (who survived the war) was arrested, kept in a number of Hungarian prisons as a member of the organized resistance, and subsequently taken to two concentration camps in Germany.

Upon the liberation of Pest, Gárdos's first step was to become a member of the Hungarian Communist Party in early 1945. She co-founded and became the second President of the *Magyar Nők Demokratikus Szövetsége* (Democratic Alliance of Hungarian Women, hereafter *MNDSz*), the new, formally independent and inter-party, leftist women's alliance. From its beginnings in the summer of 1945 to March 1948, she was also a member of the editorial board of the *MNDSz* journal *Asszonyok* (Women), which was composed of the highest ranking *MNDSz* representatives. Soon, however, Gárdos ceased to be visibly active in this capacity. As early as the summer of 1945, after having actively shaped the first activities of the *MNDSz* and feeling that the organization was up and running, Gárdos resigned from her position in the *MNDSz* and reoriented her activities towards cooperative societies with only a very partial focus on women. From the summer of 1949 onwards, she found working difficult–except for occasional public lecturing–due to serious eye problems. From 1955, after a period in which she had been politically regarded with mistrust, Gárdos became publicly esteemed, officially respected and, gradually, a 'Grand Old Dame' of the Hungarian socialist women's movement. In 1965, she became an Honorary, in 1971 a Permanent Member of the *Magyar Nők Országos Tanácsa* (Hungarian Women's National Council).

One comrade's memory of Gárdos in the 1930s reflects a crucial element of her self-presentation: "Tiny 'aunt Mariska' still stands before my eye, weighing herself down on the lecturer's desk, bending over it, her head the only visible part of her body. In these moments, she gave the public the impression of being an allegory for revolution" (cited in Kende 1985, 9). Mária Gárdos died in Budapest on 23 January

1973. The tiny little street in Óbuda in Budapest, which had for many years borne her name, was renamed after 1989.

Susan Zimmermann
Department of Gender Studies, Department of History,
Central European University, Hungary

SOURCES

(A) *Politikatörténeti Intézet Levéltára* (Archive of the Institute of Political History), 940 f., 24. ő.e. Mariska Gárdos.
(B) *Nőmunkás* (Woman worker) (1905–1938).
(B) *Népszava* (Voice of the people) (1900–1940s).
(B) *Asszonyok* (Women) (1945–1949).
(B) *Államrendészeti zsebkönyv. Kiadja a m. kir. Belügyminisztérium közbiztonsági osztálya* (Handbook of public supervision. Published by the Public Security Department of the Hungarian Royal Ministry of the Interior), *sine loco, sine anno.*
(C) Articles in *Nőmunkás* (1905–1938) and *Népszava* (1900–1940s).
(C) Gárdos, Mariska. *Az igazság az élet* (Justice is life). Kolozsvár: Ujhelyi M. és tsa Könyvsajtója, 1906.
(C) Gárdos, Mariska. *A nő a történelem sodrában* (Woman in the stream of history). Budapest, 1942.
(C, D) Gárdos, Mariska. *Százarcú élet* (One hundred faces of life). Budapest: Szépirodalmi Könyvkiadó, 1975.
(D) Pintér, Marianne. "Gárdos Mariska." In Ágnes Bakó, ed. *A szocialista forradalomért. A magyar munkásmozgalom kiemelkedő harcosai* (For the socialist revolution. Outstanding fighters of the Hungarian revolutionary workers' movement). Budapest: Kossuth Könyvkiadó, 1975.
(D) Kende, János, ed. *Gárdos Mariska*. Budapest: Kossuth Könyvkiadó, 1985 (includes documents and a biographical essay).
(D) Zimmermann, Susan. "How they became feminists: the origins of the women's movement in Central Europe at the turn of the century." *Central European University History Department Yearbook* (1997/1998). Budapest, 1999, 195–236.
(E) Trócsányi, Zoltán. "A budapesti német könyvhurcolás" (German book-hauling in Budapest). *Magyar Könyvszemle* 69 (1945): 1–21.
(E) *Munkásmozgalomtörténeti lexikon* (Dictionary of the history of the workers' movement). Budapest, 1976.
(E) Zimmermann, Susan. *Die bessere Hälfte? Frauenbewegungen und Frauenbestrebungen im Ungarn der Habsburgermonarchie 1848 bis 1918* (The better half? Women's movements and women's aspirations in Hungary in the Habsburg Monarchy, 1848 to 1918). Vienna/Budapest: Promedia Verlag–Napvilág Kiadó, 1999.
(E) *Új magyar életrajzi lexikon* (New Hungarian biographical dictionary). Vol. 2. *sine loco*, 2001.
(E) *Magyar életrajzi lexikon, 1000–1990* (Hungarian biographical dictionary). CD-Rom edition.
(E) Oral information provided by Marianne Pintér, January 2005.

GEŐCZE, Sarolta (1862–1928)

Pioneer in the fields of girls' education and Christian social work in Hungary; founder (1906) of the *Magyar Keresztény Munkásnők Országos Egyesülete* (Hungarian National Association of Christian Women Workers); director (1907–1917) of the State Institute for the Instruction of Women School Teachers, Budapest.

Sarolta Geőcze was born on 27 December 1862, in Bacska (Zemplén County, named Bačka in 1920; today in Slovakia), into a middle-class, intellectual, Catholic family. Her mother, Erzsébet Bertha (died 1869), was from the small town of Felsőőr (today Oberwart, Austria). Her father, Bertalan Geőcze (dates of birth and death unknown), was a lawyer with a practice in Zemplén County. Sarolta Geőcze had siblings including a sister, Berta (later Mrs László Krötzer). Nothing is known of the others.

Some sources state that it was 1882 when Geőcze entered the *Állami Elemi Tanítónőképző* (State Institute for the Instruction of Women Primary School Teachers) in Buda (hereafter the Buda Institute), and 1883 when she entered the *Állami Polgári Iskolai Tanítónőképzőintézet* (State Institute for the Instruction of Women Secondary School Teachers) in Pest (hereafter the Pest Institute). Geőcze did become a qualified primary and intermediate school teacher in 1883, but it is possible that several years passed between Geőcze finishing at the Buda Institute and continuing her teacher training at the Pest institute; in all probability this time was spent at home looking after siblings.

In 1886, Janka Zirzen, a pioneer in the field of women's education in Hungary, recommended Geőcze for a position at an intermediate school for girls in Brassó County (today in Romania). Geőcze became the first female director of this school in 1888 and began publishing miscellaneous articles on education in school newsletters and national journals, including *Budapesti Hírlap* (Budapest news), *Az Egészség* (Health), *Az Iskola és a Szülőház* (School and home), *Magyar Szalon* (Hungarian salon), *Pesti Napló* (Pest journal) and *Természettudományi Közlöny* (Journal of natural science).

In 1885, Geőcze helped found the *Mária Dorothea Egyesület* (*MDE*, Mária Dorothea Association), which aimed to improve women's higher education and the social status of female teachers. Around 1890, Geőcze joined the associates of *Nemzeti Nőnevelés* (National women's education), a journal edited by ***Ilona Stetina***, and in 1892 she joined the *Magyar Paedagógiai Társaság* (Hungarian Pedagogical Society). In the period 1890–1910, Geőcze wrote articles for *Nemzeti Nőnevelés* and *Magyar Paedagogia* (Hungarian pedagogy) on girls' education, pedagogical methods used in France, England and Switzerland and the need for *Hungarian* pedagogical methods able to strengthen national identity and morality.

In 1892, Geőcze joined the Board of an intermediate school for girls in Komárom County (western Hungary), later becoming director of 'the Sarolta Geőcze school,' as it became famously known. She retained this position until 1897, during which time she studied English and French and spent a year in Italy (to improve her health). In 1896 (a year after women were admitted to university courses in Hungary), she lectured on women's education and employment at the Second National University Education Congress, Budapest. In 1897/98, she traveled to France, Switzerland and England to research pedagogical methods at different religious institutions. In 1898, she was appointed by the Hungarian Culture Ministry to teach at the Pest Institute.

Throughout the 1890s, Geőcze began to lay greater emphasis on the role of women's education as a means of advancing Hungary as a Christian nation. By the turn of the century, she was seeking to protect women she thought morally and economically vulnerable–migrants, domestic servants, factory workers–through education and material assistance. In 1904, she established the *Magyar Keresztény Munkásnők Szakosztálya* (Hungarian Christian Women Workers' Section), a wing of the *Budapesti Keresztény Munkásegylet* (Budapest Christian Workers' Association). In open competition with Social Democracy, the Women's Section sought to improve material conditions for female (wage) workers but, in Geőcze's formulation, without Social Democracy's "destructive, anti-family" approach (cited in Mona 1998, 175). In 1906, Geőcze founded a separate organization, the two hundred-strong *Magyar Keresztény Munkásnők Országos Egyesülete* (Hungarian National Association of Christian Women Workers). She was now one of the key figures in the Christian Socialist women's movement. The first significant project of the new organization was the establishment of a home for women workers in Budapest (1907).

Geőcze's relationship to the women's movement was ambiguous. In an 1899 article published in *Nemzeti Nőnevelés*, "A nő a modern társadalomban" (Woman in modern society), Geőcze presented the Christian faith as both enlightening and liberating for women, enabling them to realize their potential as educated individuals without abandoning their duties as wives and mothers. (Geőcze never married nor had children.) But after the turn of the century, as Geőcze became more ensconced in Christian Socialism, she began to consciously oppose feminist demands for women's economic independence. Taking an interest in new left-liberal constellations in Hungary, Geőcze summarized these views in a long essay published as a book, *Modern feminizmus* (Modern feminism, 1907).

In 1907, Geőcze was made director of the Buda Institute (the state teacher-training institute for women primary school teachers). The decision was a controversial one: the Crown Inspector of Schools, Imre Mosdossy, expressed doubts that Geőcze was qualified to hold the position; the socialist poet Endre Ady saw the appointment of "sanctimonious Sarolta Geőcze"–"feudal Hungary's guardian angel"–as a victory for the forces of clericalism [Ady, letters to *Budapesti Napló* (Budapest journal) (26 July and 6 October 1907)]. Nevertheless, Geőcze took up the post and kept up a public profile in other spheres of activity as well. She was a member of the *Magyarországi Nőegyesületek Szövetsége* (*MNSz*, Alliance of Women's Associations in Hungary), founded in 1904 and affiliated with the International Council of Women in that year, as well as of the *Magyar Gyermektanulmányi Társaság* (Hungarian Child Study Association), founded in 1906, which encouraged her to oppose single-child families. In September 1908, Geőcze traveled to London to attend the first International Moral Education Congress (organized by Felix Adler and his Society for Ethical Culture), where she spoke on the damaging effects of pornography. By this time her perspective saw 'national decline' as directly related to a lack of Christian family values–more specifically to birth control, single-child families, divorce, inadequate facilities for working women, pornography and alcohol.

By World War I, Geőcze was embracing rightist discourses sweeping Hungary. "We must develop patriotism to the point of fanaticism," she had written in 1912 (Geőcze 1912, 232). After the war, she joined the right-wing *Magyar Asszonyok Nemzeti Szövetsége* (*MANSz*, Hungarian National Women's Union), founded in 1918. Geőcze and another *MANSz* member, Emma Ritoók, led a Foreign Affairs Committee formed by *MANSz* to communicate "the truth" of Hungary's territorial losses after World War I to Western countries and "win the understanding of women abroad" [*Magyar Asszony* (Hungarian woman) (15 July 1921): 25–26]. The war seems to have effected Geőcze deeply; colleagues like ***Ilona Stetina*** noted signs of nervous exhaustion and Geőcze was relieved of her position at the Buda Institute in 1917, later returning to the Pest Institute to teach until her retirement in 1926. Throughout the 1920s, she continued to lecture, speaking at the *MANSz* Women's Education Congress (held under the umbrella of the Women's Education Section of the Third National University Congress) in 1924. She also traveled to international congresses but the data is unfortunately vague. According to *Magyar Asszony* (Hungarian woman), the official organ of *MANSz*, she attended international women's congresses in Washington (1924) and Geneva (1926). It seems unlikely that Geőcze would have attended the left-oriented Women's International League for Peace and Freedom Congress held in Washington in 1924, given her outright equation of Bolshevism and Social Democracy with 'anti-family' values. It is recorded that prior to the 1926 Geneva congress, Geőcze attempted to gather statements of commitment to the international "fight against Bolshevism" from various Hungarian women's and social organizations, arriving in Geneva with a statement to that effect from the *MDE*'s section for women teachers (Stetina 1928, 448).

Right up until her death, Sarolta Geőcze worked to facilitate women's greater social and economic integration as workers and teachers, yet her later work was full of attacks on feminism, which she considered individualistic and (like Social Democracy) 'immoral'–views which gained dominance in the formerly diverse women's movement of interwar Hungary. She died in Budapest on 23 September 1928, after a brief illness.

Anna Loutfi
Ph.D. Candidate, Department of History,
Central European University, Budapest

SOURCES

(B) *Egyesült Erővel* (With united strength). (September / October 1909).
(B) *Magyar Asszony* (Hungarian woman) (1921-1928).
(B) *Magyar Paedagógia* (Hungarian pedagogy) (1892-1921).
(B) *Nemzeti Nőnevelés* (National women's education) (1897-1909).
(B) Thuránszky, Irén. *Magyar tanítónők. Mária Dorothea Egyesületek félszázados története, 1885-1935* (Hungarian women teachers. The fifty year history of the Mária Dorothea Association, 1885-1935). Budapest, 1935.
(C) Geőcze, Sarolta. *Külföldi nevelésügyi tapasztalatok* (Pedagogical experiences from abroad). Budapest, 1899.
(C) Geőcze, Sarolta. "A nő a modern társadalomban" (Woman in modern society), parts I and II. *Nemzeti Nőnevelés*, no. 20 (February 1899): 49-56; 104-108.
(C) Geőcze, Sarolta. *Modern Feminizmus* (Modern feminism). Budapest, 1907.
(C) Geőcze, Sarolta. *Erkölcsi nevelés a tanítóképzőben s a nemzeti élet* (Moral instruction in teacher training and national life). Budapest, 1912.
(D) Szinnyei, József. "Geőcze Sarolta." *Magyar írók* (Hungarian writers). Budapest, 1894, 3: 1135-1137.
(D) Stetina, Ilona. "Geőcze Sarolta." *Magyar Asszony* (December 1928): 444-449.
(D) "Geőcze Sarolta temetése" (Sarolta Geőcze's funeral). *Magyar Tanítóképző* (Hungarian teacher training), no. 5 (1928): 271-272.
(D) Deák, Gyula. "Geőcze Sarolta." In *Polgári iskolai író-tanárok élete és munkái* (The lives and literary production of lower-level secondary school teachers). Budapest: Az Országos Polgári Iskolai Tanáregyesület, 1942, 138-139.
(D) Gulyás, Pál. "Geőcze Sarolta." In *Magyar írók élete és munkái* (Hungarian writers and their lives and works). Budapest, 1992, 10: 676-679.
(D) Mona, Ilona. "Geőcze Sarolta, 1862-1928." In *Tanulmányok, cikkek a fővárosi gyermekvédelem köréből* (Essays on child protection in the capital city of Budapest). Budapest: Fővárosi Önkormányzat Főpolgármesteri Hivatal, 1992, 163-175.

(D) Hegedűs, Judit. "Tanítónői karriertörténetek a dualizmus korában" (Careers of women teachers in the dualist period). *Iskolakultúra* (School culture) 3 (2003): 47-49.

(E) Mona, Ilona. "A Magyar Katolikus Munkásnőmozgalom története, 1897-1952" (The history of the Hungarian Catholic women's movement, 1897-1952). In István Bárdas and Margit Beke, eds. *Nemzetközi történész konferencia előadásai, 1995 Május 24-26* (Lectures delivered at the International Historical Conference, 24-26 May 1995). Esztergom, 1998, 173-176.

(E) *Ady Endre összes művei* (The collected works of Endre Ady). CD-rom. Arcanum Adatbázis, 1999.

GJIKA, Elena (Elena Ghica, pen-name **DORA D'ISTRIA)** (1828?-1888?)

Romanian writer of Albanian descent, known in Romania as Elena Ghica and throughout Europe under her pen-name of 'Dora d'Istria.' Campaigner for national minorities in the Habsburg Empire and for the cause of women's equality.

Elena Gjika was probably born on 28 February 1828. While some of her biographers give Bucharest or Constanta (a city on the Black Sea, currently in Romania) as her birthplace, in the first volume of her book *Les femmes en Orient*, published in Zurich in 1859, Elena includes a letter to one of her friends in which she writes: "I was born on the shores of South Albania, not far from the Suli mountains, in the city of Parga, whose misfortunes, after the fall of Napoleon, concerned the whole of Europe. My dear Parga, which for centuries had not seen the half-moon [i.e. the Ottoman Empire] above her walls, Parga was surrendered to the merciless Vezir [?] of Janina, Ali Pasha, who had long been attacking this Christian city" (Vehbi Bala 1967, 18). The aristocratic Gjikas, like the Lupujt and Dukajt families, were of Albanian origin and had settled in Wallachia and Moldavia.

From 1835 until 1842, Elena's father, Mihail Gjika (1792–1850), was Minister of Interior Affairs for Wallachia in Bucharest, and during this period his brother, Aleksander Gjika, was ruler of Wallachia. Mihail was a well-known collector of antiques who left a considerable heritage to the Bucharest Museum of Antiquities. Elena's mother, Katerina, was a knowledgeable woman who passed on her outstanding literary skills to her daughter. From childhood, Elena received instruction from the Macedonian philosopher and psychologist Grigor Papadhopulli and Elena became known for her intelligence (as well as for her beauty). Around 1841, she emigrated for political reasons to Vienna, Berlin and Dresden with her father and her uncle. A little later, she translated Homer's *Illiad* from Greek into German. While abroad, she was instructed in the fine arts by Cikareli, Persiani, Ronkonin and Balfa, and took classes with Papadhopulli. Later, she studied painting with Felice Skavioni, who painted a beautiful portrait of her (as did Adolf Salmoni). According to the French *Larousse Encyclopedia,* "Princess Elena had excellent knowledge of Italian, French, English,

Romanian, Greek, Latin, Russian and Albanian" (Larousse 1870, 6: 1107). Some biographers have compared Elena Gjika with three well-known French authors: namely Madame de Staël, George Sand and the Countess Marie d'Agoult. By 1876, when the latter two passed away, Elena had reached the height of her fame. It was around this time that Prince Carl I of Romania awarded her the *Bene merenti*, an honor awarded exclusively to outstanding and learned individuals, which had never before been awarded to a woman.

At the age of twenty, Elena married the Russian Prince Alexander Masalsky (also Massalsky and Koltzoff-Massalsky, d. around 1855). In St Petersburg, where she spent some of her married years, she participated in an exhibition of Fine Arts, winning a silver prize. Around 1855, she gave birth to a son. Not long thereafter, her husband died and she left St Petersburg for Belgium. After the death of her child (date unknown), she went to Switzerland, where on 13 June 1855, she climbed the Monch/Jungfrau mountain, later recording the experience in "La Suisse Allemande et l'ascension du Monch." In 1857, she published a collection of Romanian oral literature, *La literature roumaine-chants et recits populaires* (Romanian literature, folk songs and poetry), establishing herself as one of the first researchers of Romanian folklore. She also published her travel impressions in various journals, including *L'Illustration* (Illustration) in Paris and *Le Jour* (The day) in Trieste.

An "ardent champion of the rights of nationalities" (Davenport Adams 1906, 46), Dora d'Istria defended the independence of all nations and their democratic development. She was against absolute monarchy and supported intense collaboration between nations in the cultural field. Inspired by these philosophical ideas, she wrote on the different peoples of Southeastern Europe on the basis of their oral folklore, and promoted their right to national independence and free development. On 15 March 1859, she published a study called "La nationalité roumaine d'après les chants populaires" (The Romanian nationality according to folk songs) in the well-known Paris magazine *Revue des deux Mondes*. It was the beginning of a series of seven articles written over a period of fourteen years on the different nationalities in South Eastern Europe and the songs of their respective ethno-national communities. In 1859/60, she also published her two-volume *Les femmes en Orient* (Women in the East) and (according to Davenport Adams 1906, 25) there was a *Les femmes d'Occident* (Women from the West) as well. Other works on women by Dora d'Istria include her *Des femmes, par une femme* (Women, seen by one of them, 1869), in which she expressed admiration for the audacious courage of Jeanne d'Arc, and her last work on women (as far as we know), *The Condition of Women among the Southern Slavs* (1878) (original title unknown).

From 1865, Elena Gjika/Dora d'Istria settled permanently in Italy. She followed the Albanian cause from Italy at a time when the country, under the leadership of Giuseppe Garibaldi (to whom she was close), was fighting for national unification. She acted as an intermediary between Albania and Albanian colonies in Italy (and elsewhere) and established contacts with foreign researchers of Albanian history and the Albanian national cause, thus facilitating the growing independence and Albanian cultural movements. Through the Albanian writer Jeronim De Rada (with whom she corresponded; 109 letters exchanged between them are kept in the Archives of the Albanian State), she was put in touch with personalities and artists throughout Europe and the United States. From Villa Kaprilli in Livorno, Elena Gjika/Dora d'Istria expressed her vehement national sentiments in a letter to De Rada on 14 June 1866: "A nation like ours will not be destroyed and I want to believe that we will not die before seeing our country freed from the barbarians." She also suggested that De Rada create an Albanian Academy and an Albanian Literary Association in Calabria. In 1873, she published a history of her own family, *Gli Albanesi in Rumenia: storia dei principi Ghica nei secoli XVII, XVIII e XIX* (The Albanians in Romania: a history of the Ghica Princes in the seventeenth, eighteenth and nineteenth centuries), based on unpublished documents from archives in Venice, Vienna, Paris, Berlin and Constantinople. She continued to publish on Balkan cultures in Italy and elsewhere–for example in *Le Spectateur d'Orient* (The spectator of the Orient), *L'Esperance d'Athène* (The hope of Athens) and in Germany. She was honored by many international institutions, elected a Member of Honor of "Minerva" Trieste and Vice-Director of the "Association of Greek Women for Female Education" (see Vehbi Bala 1967; more precise information is unavailable), among many other positions.

Elena Gjika/Dora d'Istria died in the Vila d'Istria, Florence, it is thought on 20 November 1888. A number of scholars, Albanians and others, her own contemporaries as well as present-day researchers, have considered her to be one of Europe's most distinguished women.

Zenepe Dibra
President of the Association "Intellectual women of Shkodra."

Translated from Albanian by Aurora Elezi, MA student, Department of Gender Studies, CEU, Budapest.

SOURCES

(A) *Arkivi Qendror Shteteror* (*AQSH*, State Central Archives) (SCA), file N. 338-536, 54/1: "Letrat e Dora d'Istrias derguar J. De Rades" (Letters of Dora d'Istria sent to J. De Rada), Archives De Rada.

(C) Istria, Dora d', comtesse. *Les femmes en Orient* (Women in the East). Zurich: Meyer & Zeller, 1859/60.

(C) Istria, Dora d', comtesse. *Des femmes, par une femme* (Women, seen by one of them). Paris: Librairie Internationale; Bruxelles: A. Lacroix [etc.], 1869. Also available on Microfilm. New Haven, Conn.: Research Publications, Inc., 1975 (History of Women: 2310).

(D) Entry about Dora d'Istria in *Larousse. Grand Dictionnaire Universel du XIX-e siècle*. Paris, 1870, 6: f.1107.

(D) Davenport Adams, W. H. "Countess Dora d'Istria." In *Celebrated Women Travellers of the Nineteenth Century*. London: Swan Sonnenschein & Co, ninth edition, January 1906, 17–47.

(D) Iorga, Nicholai. "Letres de Dora d'Istria" (The letters of Dora d'Istria). *Revue historique du Sud-Est-Europe* IX (1932): 134–209.

(D) Iorga, Nicolae. "Despre Dora d'Istria" (On Dora d'Istria). *Revista Istorică* 21 (1935): 4–6; 103–104. This refers to the work of the Venetian historian Bartolomeo Ceccheti, *Bibliografia della principessa Elena Ghika, Dora D'Istria*, published in 1868.

(D) Fishta F. "Dora d'Istria." *Shkendija* (Sparkles) 2, nos. 7/8 (1942).

(D) Kastrati J. "Letrat e Dora d'Istrias" (The letters of Dora d'Istria). *Arsimin Popullor* (Popular education), no. 3 (May–June 1963).

(D) Vehbi Bala. *Jeta e Elena Gjikes-Dora d'Istrias* (The life of Elena Gjika-Dora d'Istria). Tirana: Publishing house "Naim Frasheri," 1967.

(E) The Academy of the Albanian Popular Socialist Republic. *Fjalori Enciklopedik Shqiptar* (Albanian encyclopedic dictionary). Tirana, 1985.

(E) Elsie, Robert, ed. *Historical Dictionary of Albania*. Lanham/Maryland/Oxford: The Scarecrow Press, 2004.

(F) Letters written (in French) by Dora d'Istria can be read online at: http://www.bcu-iasi.ro/biblos/biblos9/doraistria.pdf

GLÜCKLICH, Vilma (1872-1927)

First woman in Hungary to receive a degree from the Faculty of Philosophy, Budapest State University; advocate of pedagogical reform and theoretician of pedagogy and girls' education; eminent figure of the left-liberal wing of the Hungarian women's movement and internationalist; head of the *Feministák Egyesülete* (Feminist Association) from 1904 to her death; suffrage and peace activist; holder of high-ranking positions in the Women's International League for Peace and Freedom (WILPF) in the 1920s.

Vilma Glücklich, 1912, with an issue of *A Nő és a Társadalom,* the journal of the *Feministák Egyesülete (FE)* in her hands.

Vilma Glücklich was born on 9 August 1872, in Vágujhely (Nové Mesto, today Slovakia) into a Jewish family, the youngest of four children (including a brother named Emil). Her father was a high school teacher, her mother from an educated family. Vilma grew up in Budapest. After completing lower-level secondary school, Vilma combined high school with teacher training and in this way received her final exam certificate (*maturita* or *abitur*: a necessary condition for entering formal academic education). In addition to Hungarian, Vilma Glücklich spoke German, Italian, English and French fluently.

From 1893, Glücklich worked as an upper-level secondary school teacher in Fiume (Rijeka, today Croatia). Upon the partial opening of Hungarian universities to women, she resigned from her position and enrolled in the Budapest State University in 1896, completing a course of study in physics and mathematics and becoming the first woman to graduate from the Faculty of Philosophy. From 1898, she worked continuously as a lower-level secondary school teacher of girls for a municipal school in Budapest. Soon after being promoted to teach at a *gymnázium* (high school) in 1914, she requested to be reinstalled as a lower-level secondary school teacher, convinced that the pedagogical work she could carry out for girls at this level would yield greater rewards. By 1917, she had become a headmistress. Between 1913 and 1917, she was an officer of the *Országos Polgári Iskolai Tanáregyesület* (National Association of Lower-Level Secondary School Teachers). In late 1918, the National Council (a transitional representative political body established prior to, and lasting through the first short-lived democratic regime in Hungary) appointed Glücklich as one of two female members of a Supervision Committee for the municipal administration of Budapest. When, in 1921 (under the semi-authoritarian right-wing Horthy regime), Glücklich protested the continuous involvement of girls in glove knitting for the military, she lost her post and pension entitlement as a result of disciplinary proceedings.

Glücklich became a leading figure in the women's movement after she had been elected a Board Member of the *Nőtisztviselők Országos Egyesülete* (*NOE*, National Association of Woman Employees) in May 1902. Together with *NOE* President ***Róza Schwimmer***, Glücklich soon became involved in establishing a women workers' organization. Glücklich was to be Schwimmer's closest co-worker in Hungary for over a decade, as well as a key figure in bringing Hungarian and international developments into entangled relations with one another.

Leading the Constituting General Assembly of the *Feministák Egyesülete* (*FE*, Feminist Association) in December 1904, Glücklich's speech, prior to becoming Executive President of the new organization, received wide attention in the Hungarian press. (In an anti-formalistic and anti-hierarchical move, Glücklich refused to accept the title of President, while remaining the formal head of the *FE* until her death.) In 1906, Glücklich edited *Feminista Értesítő* (Feminist bulletin), the first journal of the *FE*. Over the years, her activities and articles–published in *A Nő és a Társadalom* (Woman and society), later renamed *A Nő. Feminista Folyóirat* (Woman. A feminist journal), and educational periodicals–focused on pedagogy (school reform, coeducation and child protection). Glücklich also actively participated in suffrage work and other activities organized by the *FE*. She played a key role, for example, in the running of the "Select a Profession" counseling system for girls and their parents, established in 1905 by the *FE* in close cooperation with the reform-oriented head of the municipal education department, the later Major of Budapest, István Bárczy.

The outbreak of World War I caused irreparable damage to Glücklich's faith in the educability of humankind, changing her for life. From this period onwards, she continued to work for the women's movement and for the pacifist cause, employing "her full power, but with clipped wings," to cite one of many similar recollections by Glücklich's co-workers [Mrs Oszkár Szirmai, cited in *A Nő. Rendkivüli szám* (1927/28): 36]. In Budapest, Glücklich was involved in what became known as 'the banned 1916 Feminist Congress,' organized by the *FE* as a public demonstration against the war but finally forbidden by the authorities. Internationally, Glücklich participated in the famous International Congress of Women in The Hague in 1915. She was a member of the International Committee of the Congress and later, of the International Committee of Women for Permanent Peace established by the Congress. She was also present at the follow-up International Congress of Women in Zurich in May 1919, when the organization adopted its permanent name: the Women's International League for Peace and Freedom (WILPF). From 1922, Vilma Glücklich was Headquarters Secretary of the WILPF in Geneva. Work at the international office was beset with difficulties (not only for her) and she formally retired in May 1924, only to be elected Secretary General of the WILPF in the same month, and member of the Executive Committee of the international organization in 1926. Glücklich also cooperated, as a representative of the WILPF, with the International Institute for Intellectual Cooperation in Paris, founded in 1926 in connection with the League of Nations' *Commission de cooperation intellectuelle*; the mission of the latter was to overcome post-World War I isolation between national cultures in education and scholarship.

In addition to having a good sense of humor and sharp intellect, Glücklich was regarded as a very balanced, modest and supportive person; an ideal counterpoint to the more flamboyant and controversial ***Róza Schwimmer*** (the other prominent leader of the self-declared feminist movement in Hungary). Making efforts to "conceal her own self," [*A Nő. Rendkivüli szám* (1927/28): 37], Glücklich wholeheartedly adopted a professional, pedagogical attitude to children and co-workers alike. Upon her return to Budapest in late 1925, she became the executive editor of *A Nő* and shared the position of head of the *FE* with Mrs Oszkár Szirmai. A prolonged and serious illness followed and, in the final stages of her suffering, Glücklich moved to Vienna, managing to keep her co-workers in Budapest unaware of her condition. She died on 19 August 1927 in the Viennese Rudolfspital. At her cremation in Vienna, representatives of the Budapest and Viennese women's movements, as well as a group of Hungarian émigré women paid her their respects. Her ashes were buried in her parents' grave in Budapest on October 1927. Two days later, the *FE* held an extraordinary general meeting in memory of its long-standing President, at which Anna Kéthly (1889-1976)–an eminent social democratic Member of Parliament and women's movement representative–declared, in a remarkable tribute, that her party considered Glücklich "as one of its own deceased," (i.e. as one of their own), going on to describe her as a person with an "unshakable trust in the 'better human being.'" Róza Schwimmer wrote that "in the history of our century of slaughter, the name of Vilma Glücklich will take its place besides those whose lives give others the right to call our epoch a civilized one." Emily Greene Balch, leading personality of WILPF, stated that Vilma Glücklich "was one of those people for whom small things remained small, and for whom personal pleasure was entirely unimportant. Yet she could be merry and did not (as Anglo-Saxons are said to do) 'take her pleasures sadly'" [all three citations taken from *A Nő. Rendkivüli szám* (1927/28): 9, 13, 32].

Susan Zimmermann
Department of Gender Studies, Department of History,
Central European University, Budapest

SOURCES

(A) *Magyar Országos Levéltár* (Hungarian State Archive), P999: *Feministák Egyesülete* (Feminist Association).

(A) *Politikatörténeti Intézet Levéltára* (Archive of the Institute for Political History), IV. 940.f.24.ő.e. Obituary by Mariska Gárdos.

(B) *A Nő és a Társadalom* (Woman and society) (1907-1913).

(B) *A Nő. Feminista Folyóirat* (Woman. A feminist journal) (1914-1928, published intermittently).

(B) International Women's Committee of Permanent Peace, ed. *International Congress of Women. The Hague, 28th April-May 1st 1915*. Amsterdam: International Women's Committee of Permanent Peace, *sine anno*.

(B) *Az 1916 junius havában betiltott feminista kongresszuson el nem mondott beszédek* (Speeches undelivered at the banned 1916 feminist congress). Budapest, 1916.

(B) *Reports of the Congresses of the Women's International League for Peace and Freedom*.

(B) *Women's International League for Peace and Freedom: Newsletters from Geneva*, May and August 1925.

(B) Deák, Gyula. *Polgári iskolai író-tanárok élete és munkái* (The lives and literary production of lower-level secondary school teachers). Budapest: Az Országos Polgári Iskolai Tanáregyesület, 1942.

(C) Articles by Vilma Glücklich in *A Nő és a Társadalom* and *A Nő*; *Nemzeti Nőnevelés* (National women's education); *Népművelés* (People's education) and *Izraelita Tanügyi Értesítő* (Israelite educational bulletin).

(D) *A Nő. Rendkivüli szám Glücklich Vilma emlékének* (Woman. Special commemorative edition in remembrance of Vilma Glücklich) (1927/28).

(E) *Magyar életrajzi lexikon* (Hungarian biographical dictionary) (1000-1990). CD-Rom edition.

(E) Bussey, Gertrude and Margaret Tims. *Women's International League for Peace and Freedom 1915-1965. A Record of Fifty Years' Work*. London: Allen & Unwin, 1965.

(E) Rupp, Leila. *Worlds of Women. The Making of an International Women's Movement*. Princeton: Princeton University Press, 1997.

(E) Zimmermann, Susan. *Die bessere Hälfte? Frauenbewegungen und Frauenbestrebungen im Ungarn der Habsburgermonarchie 1848 bis 1918* (The better half? Women's movements and women's aspirations in Hungary in the Habsburg Monarchy 1848 to 1918). Vienna/Budapest: Promedia Verlag/Napvilág Kiadó, 1999.

(E) Papp, Claudia. *'Die Kraft der weiblichen Seele.' Feminismus in Ungarn 1918-1941* ('The strength of women's soul.' Feminism in Hungary 1918-1941). Münster: Lit-Verlag, 2004.

GREGOROVÁ, Hana (1885–1958)

Writer, editor and prominent literary figure in Bratislava; founder of the first literary salon in Slovakia (in her own home); first woman writer in Slovakia to show a strong interest in women's emancipation and feminism; briefly (after 1945) Chairwoman of the *Zväz slovenských žien* (Union of Slovak Women).

Hana Gregorová was born Anna Božena Lilgová on 30 January 1885, to a middle-class family in the town of Turčiansky Svätý Martin (T. Sv. Martin) in northern Slovakia, at that time a center of national culture. Her father Jan Lilge (d. 1900) was a dyer. Her mother Maria, born Jamnická (1849–1926) was a housewife. Anna Lilgová had five siblings. Her sister Ľudmila Thurzová (born Lilgová) (1881–1971) was a famous herbalist, co-author of *Malý atlas liečivých rastlín* (Small atlas of herbs, 1936). Her brother Ivan Lilge (1886–1918) was a writer, translator and publicist. Anna attended primary school in T. Sv. Martin. Later, especially in the period following her marriage (in 1907) to the outstanding critical realist writer Jozef Gregor Tajovský (1874–1940), she worked hard to provide herself with a good education. After 1907, bearing the name Hana Gregorová, she accompanied her husband to Nadlak (Romania), then to Prešov, later returning to T. Sv. Martin. In 1916, she gave birth in Budapest to an only daughter, Dagmar. Dagmar Gregorová (later Prášilová) would become a well-known actress and author, writing several books about her parents. Her descriptions of them are full of admiration, love and respect, while revealing contrasts and also some tensions between the two: he was a realist, she a romantic; he a pragmatist, she an idealist; he was an introvert, she liked to organize social events, debates on literature and art; he was more traditional in his thinking, she desired to live as an 'emancipated woman,' and to write.

From 1919 to 1920, Gregorová lived in Košice and edited the journal *Slovenský východ* (Slovak east). She lived in Bratislava from 1921 until 1940 when, upon her husband's death, she left for Prague, remaining there for the rest of her life with her daughter's family. In addition to her literary work, Gregorová was involved in several organizations and cultural institutions: prior to 1940, she organized lectures on Slovak and Czech literature and art for the *Umelecká beseda* (Society of Artists) and she was also a member of the *Spoločnosť pre kultúrne styky so Zväzom SSR* (Society for Cultural Contacts with the USSR); after 1945, she briefly became Chairwoman of the *Zväz slovenských žien* (Union of Slovak Women). In 1936, Gregorová took part in the Congress of Slovak writers held at Trenčianske Teplice, where she delivered a speech on children's literature, arguing that it needed to show social reality as it was, with its social problems, and not in an idealized form. During World War II, she mediated between Czech and Slovak anti-fascists and cooperated with Czech women and writers in the field of culture and women's issues, thus helping to strengthen the relationship between Slovak, Czech and other women writers.

Hana Gregorová published several books of fiction and many articles while working as a children's author and translator. In her first book of stories, *Ženy* (Women, 1912), as well as in *Môj svet* (My world, 1920), *Pokorní ľudia* (The humble ones, 1924), *Zo srdca* (From the heart, 1930) and *Vlny duše* (The waves of the soul, 1933), she revealed a deep empathy with women and a great interest in women's emancipation. Gregorová explored the lives of women across the spectrum of social classes and generations, protesting against gender and other social inequalities. At the same time, she attempted to describe the inner, emotional lives of her female protagonists, primarily focusing on marriage and partnerships with men and the desire of women for alternatives, for more independent means of living. Addressing the array of emotional responses felt by women about their intimate relationships and social roles—from hope and expectation to frustration and disillusionment—Gregorová's works provided sophisticated psychological analyses of love and were critical reactions to idealized representations of womanhood: i.e. female happiness acquired through marriage or motherhood (an idealism that could be found in the novels of ***Terézia Vansová*** or ***Elena Maróthy-Šoltésová***, two of the most important contemporary Slovak women writers). Gregorová also focused on women's emancipation, education and issues of equality, linking these issues to women's dissatisfaction with the roles of 'wife' and 'mother' and the constraints placed on women by gender stereotypes and the prescriptions of tradition. Many of her heroines experienced difficulties as single women. Through their stories, Gregorová strove to highlight the lack of support available to young women seeking education and independence in families and communities where such women were seen as 'unfeminine' or 'abnormal' and whose ambitions were usually characterized as an 'illness' or as going against 'women's nature.' Criticized by conservative literary critics, Gregorová nevertheless had her defenders. In a review of Gregorová's book *Ženy*, ***Elena Maróthy-Šoltésová*** defended the work as a truthful representation of women, whose unhappy marriages, suffering and frustration were products of social circumstances determined by worn gender stereotypes.

In her important work *Slovenka pri krbe a knihe* (Slovak woman by the fireplace with a book, 1929), Gregorová analyzed particular social norms governing women in Slovak society and described the lives of several women she thought to have made a contribution to the development of Slovak culture. In the context of the national movement (against forced 'magyarization' of the country), Gregorová also paid attention to the social impact of World War I and economic crisis upon the life of 'ordinary' people, particularly women. Hana Gregorová's literary contribution followed existing traditions in Slovakian women's writing (i.e. those of ***Elena Maróthy-Šoltésová***, ***Terézia Vansová***, and ***Ľudmila Podjavorinská***) but also initiated important changes regarding the representation of women's lives in prose–in this respect following a tradition closer to that of the outstanding woman writer (and critical realist) Božena Slančíková-Timrava. In her critique of gender stereotypes and support of women's emancipation, Hana Gregorová was, in many ways, more radical than her predecessors. Her books, articles and cultural activities formed part of important developments in Slovakian literature, helping generate new horizons for women and encouraging modern Slovak women in the struggle for education and the right to participate in social and public life. She died on 11 December 1958.

Etela Farkašová
Department of Philosophy and History of Philosophy,
and *Centrum rodových štúdií* (Center for Gender Studies),
Comenius University, Bratislava

SOURCES

(D) Gregorová-Prášilová, Dagmar. *Gregorovský dům* (The house of the Gregors). Prague: X-Egem, 1995.

(E) Pišút, Milan, et. al. *Dejiny slovenskej literatúry* (The history of Slovak literature). Bratislava: Osveta, 1962.

(E) Rosenbaum, Karol, ed. *Encyklopédia slovenských spisovateľov* (Encyclopedia of Slovak writers). Bratislava: Obzor, 1984.

(E) Rudinsky, Norma L. *Incipient Feminists: Women writers in the Slovak national revival.* With an appendix of Slovak women poets, 1798-1875 by Marianna Prídavková-Mináriková. Ohio: Slavica Publishers, Inc., 1991.

(E) Maťovčík, Augustín, ed. *Slovník slovenských spisovateľov 20. storočia* (Dictionary of Slovak writers of the twentieth century). Bratislava and Martin: Publishing House of the Association of Slovak Writers and the Slovak National Library, 2001.

(E) Cviková, Jana. "Po boku muža a národa" (Side by side with man and nation). *Aspekt*, no. 1 (2003-2004): 71-78.

GUREVICH, Liubov' Iakovlevna (1866-1940)

Russian literary critic, writer and feminist activist; founding member (1905) of the *Soiuz Ravnopraviia Zhenshchin* (Women's Equal Rights Union); pamphleteer and publicist on women's rights from 1905 to 1908 and in 1917.

Liubov' Gurevich was born in St Petersburg on 20 October 1866. She grew up in a progressive urban intellectual household with a mixed social background. Her mother, Liubov' Ivanovna Il'ina, was of the gentry class. The sister of the writer Ekaterina Tsekina-Zhukovskaia, she encouraged her daughter to take an interest in literature. Her father, Iakov Gurevich (1843-1906), was of Jewish parentage but had converted to Russian Orthodoxy. A lecturer in history at St Petersburg University, as well as at the Bestuzhev Higher Women's Courses, he also edited the liberal Russian pedagogical journal *Russkaia Shkola* (Russian school).

In a short autobiography written in 1911, Gurevich claimed that from an early age she was aware of the inequality of the sexes: "I cursed myself for being a woman, as a result of which I couldn't go wherever I wanted, couldn't run into the most diverse kinds of people, experience with the very essence of my being all that was most vital and important in life" (Fidler 1911, 190; R.R., trans). Gurevich began to question the existence of barriers to women's achievement, seeking recognition as an equal to men in the world of literature and culture.

After having commenced a period of study at the Bestuzhev Higher Women's Courses, she read an excerpt from the diary of Mariia Bashkirtseva, a Russian émigré artist who had died young in Paris. Gurevich described burning with passionate love for the dying Bashkirtseva, "feeling strikingly close to her in spirit" (Fidler 1911, 188; R. R. trans). Later, when Gurevich was sent abroad to receive treatment for a serious illness, she traveled to Paris (1886), met Bashkirtseva's mother, visited the late artist's studio and wrote about her experience in her first published article for a populist 'thick journal,' *Russkoe Bogatsvo* (Russian wealth). ('Thick journals' were large volumes–as the name implies–of material on contemporary literary, political and social debates, deliberately bulky so as to foil the censors.)

Upon returning from Paris, the twenty-year-old Gurevich began frequenting the salon of Alexandra Davydova, where the talk of old populists such as Nikolai Mikhailovskii felt "foreign" to her but where she made contacts with such young and upcoming writers as Dmitrii Merezhkovskii, Nikolai Minskii and Akim Volynskii. Aided by loans from family members, Gurevich purchased, and became the publisher of the journal *Severnyi Vestnik* (Northern herald) in 1891. Volynskii was the editor but Gurevich, just 25 and a recent graduate of the Bestuzhev Courses, was the driving force behind the journal. As its publisher, she managed its affairs until 1899 (when it ceased publication because of financial problems and the personal hostility of the head censor). Under Gurevich and Volynskii's stewardship, *Severnyi Vestnik* made its mark publishing modernist writers such as Merezhkovskii, Zinaida Gippius, Mirra Lokhvitskaia and Fedor Sologub, as well as famous women such as Annie Besant, Sophia Kovalevskaia, Lou Andreas-Salomé, Zinaida Vengerova and ***Ol'ga Shapir***. The journal included many articles on women's status in society and works by populist economists such as Alexandra Efimenko. It also published the work of established writers such as Chekhov and Tolstoi (the wife of Tolstoi accused the writer of having an affair with Gurevich).

When *Severnyi Vestnik* ceased publication, Gurevich was left with a mass of debts; she later described this as the "most difficult period of my life" (Fidler 1911, 194; R. R, trans). She does not mention in any of her autobiographical pieces that she gave birth at this time to a daughter (Elena Nikolaevna). Gurevich did not marry the father, probably the poet Nikolai Molostov. In choosing to be a single mother, she showed great courage in flouting prevailing social norms and living out her feminist ideals.

While Gurevich's literary achievements have been highlighted in most surveys of her life, her involvement in feminist organizations has been minimized or ignored. Yet her connection to women's organizations dates to her early membership in the *Russkoe Zhenskoe Vzaimno-Blagotvoritel'noe Obshchestvo* (Russian Women's Mutual Philanthropic Society). Founded in 1895, the society–limited under strict tsarist laws to charitable and educational pursuits–attempted to model itself on US women's clubs. Gurevich's public feminist activity blossomed with the Revolution of 1905 when, for the first time, political rights became a possibility in Russia for both men and women. A left feminist, close to her Bolshevik sister Anna, Gurevich reacted to the opposition of liberal males and the hypocrisy of socialist males regarding women's suffrage, calling for a close tie between 'the woman question' and the revolutionary movement.

Stung by the sexism of liberal and left men, Gurevich was a founding member of the *Soiuz Ravnopraviia Zhenshchin* (Women's Equal Rights Union), established in Moscow in February 1905. She attended the organization's first and subsequent delegate congresses, spoke at meetings and penned such pamphlets as *Pochemu Nuzhno Dat' Zhenshchinam Vse Prava i Svobody* (Why women ought to be given all rights and freedoms). She offered the *Soiuz* her publishing and distribution experience and volunteered to distribute feminist pamphlets in St Petersburg and to Trudovik Party

Duma (Parliament) deputies, writing to *Soiuz* founder ***Mariia Chekhova*** that she was "working all the time for the cause of women's equal rights" (*TsIAM*, f. 2251, op.1, d. 163, p. 2). Gurevich was one of four women (along with ***Ekaterina Shchepkina***, Olga Klirikova and Gromnitskaia) to work with the Committee on Equal Rights of the First Russian Duma on laying the legal groundwork for women's equality. On 7 July 1906, the women presented their completed report but the next day the Tsar dissolved the Duma. No further comprehensive review of women's equal rights was considered until after the 1917 Bolshevik Revolution.

Gurevich continued to write for women's rights, contributing several articles to *Soiuz Zhenshchin.* Discouraged by the feminists' lack of success, the force of the tsarist regime's repression and her growing debts, she dropped out of political activity in 1908, writing to ***Mariia Chekhova***: "I have spent too much of my energy all my life trying to resolve the *zhenskii vopros* (woman question) in practice, fighting my way with a child in my arms and without any help" (*TsIAM*, f. 2251, op. 1, d. 163, p. 34). She returned to her literary activities in 1908, devoting much of her time to working with Konstantin Stanislavskii; she was the first editor of his theoretical works and an enthusiastic supporter of the Moscow Art Theater.

After the February Revolution toppled the Tsar in 1917, Gurevich resumed her public advocacy for women's rights, writing enthusiastically about the large women's suffrage demonstration of 19 March 1917, which had called for Provisional Government leaders to enfranchize Russian women. Gurevich withdrew from public advocacy of feminism after the Bolshevik (October) Revolution and again began devoting her time to theater, expounding on Stanislavskii's theoretical works, as well as editing and publishing them. Although maintaining friendships with such pre-revolutionary feminist comrades as ***Mariia Chekhova*** and ***Praskov'ia Arian***, she stopped advocating women's rights in print. Liubov' Gurevich died in Moscow on 14 October 1940 after a long illness.

Rochelle Goldberg Ruthchild
The Union Institute and University
and the Davis Center for Russian and Eurasian Studies,
Harvard University

SOURCES

(A) *Institut russkoi literatury* (*IRLI*, Institute for Russian Literature) or Pushkinskii Dom, St Petersburg, Fonds 89.

(A) *Russkaia Gosudarstvennaia Biblioteka* (Russian State Library), Moscow, Fond 489, no. 3939.14, and Fond 154, no.1.26. These files contain Gurevich's autobiographies from the years 1866 to 1927.

(A) *Rossiiskii gosudarstvennyi arkhiv literatury i iskusstva* (*RGALI*, Russian State Archive of Literature and Art), Moscow, Fond 131.

(A) *Tsentral'nyi Istoricheskii Arkhiv gorod Moskvy (TsIAM)*, Fond 2251 (Mariia Aleksandrovna Chekhova).

(B) *Soiuz ravnopraviia zhenshchin: Otchety i Protokoly* (Women's Equal Rights Union: reports and proceedings). St Petersburg, 1905-1907.

(B) *Ravnopravie zhenshchin: Tretii s'ezd soiuza ravnopravnosti zhenshchin, otchety i protokoly* (Equal rights of women: third congress of the Women's Equal Rights Union: reports and proceedings). St Petersburg, 1906.

(C) Gurevich, Liubov. *Zhenskoe dvizhenie poslednikh dnei* (The women's movement in recent times). Odessa, 1905.

(C) Gurevich, Liubov. *Pochemu nuzhno dat' zhenshchinam vse prava i svobody* (Why we must give women all rights and freedoms). St Petersburg, 1906; reprinted and updated, 1917.

(C) Gurevich, Liubov. *9-e ianvaria po dannym "anketnoi kommissii"* (9 January, taken from the evidence of the formal commission). St Petersburg: izdano zhurnalom "Temy zhizni," ezhened. no. 4, vyp., 1906; reprinted, 1926.

(D) Gurevich, E. N. "L. Ia. Gurevich–Teatral'nyi kritik" (L. Ia. Gurevich–theater critic). In *Bestuzhevki v riadakh stroitelei sotsializma*. (Bestuzhev students in the ranks of the builders of socialism). Moscow: Mysl', 1969, 187-190.

(D) Rabinowitz, Stanley. "Gurevich, Liubov Iakovlevna." In Marina Ledkovsky, Charlotte Rosenthal and Mary Zirin, eds. *Dictionary of Russian Women Writers*. Westport, CT: Greenwood Press, 1994, 235-238.

(D) Ruthchild, Rochelle Goldberg. "Writing for Their Rights. Four Feminist Journalists: Mariia Chekhova, Liubov' Gurevich, Mariia Pokrovskaia, and Ariadna Tyrkova." In Barbara T. Norton and Jehanne M. Gheith, eds. *An Improper Profession: Women, Gender, and Journalism in Late Imperial Russia*. Durham and London: Duke University Press, 2001, 167-195.

(D) Kittel, Dina. "Chelovek bol'shoi i skromnoi dushi: rakursy odnoi biografii" (A short biography of a person with a great and modest soul). In *Adam i Eva: Al'manakh gendernoi istorii* (Adam and Eve. An almanac of gender history). Moscow: Rossiiskaia akademiia nauk, Institut vseobshchei istorii, 2002, 4: 63-77.

(D) Kittel, Dina. "Ljubov Jakovlevna Gurevii als Vorkämpferin des russischen Frauenwahlrechts" (Liubov' Iakovlevna Gurevich as a pioneer of the struggle for Russian women's suffrage). In Grigorii A. Tishkin, ed. *Zhenshchina v grazhdanskom obshchestve: Istoriia, filoso-fiia, sotsiologiia* (Woman in civil society: history, philosophy, sociology). St Petersburg: St Petersburg Philosophical Society and the Konrad Adenauer Fund, 2002, 131-139.

HAINISCH, Marianne (1839–1936)

Leader of the Austrian liberal women's movement. Founder (1902) and President (until 1918) of the *Bund österreichischer Frauenvereine* (*BÖFV*, Union of Austrian Women's Associations); President (from 1929 until her death) of the *Österreichische Frauenpartei* (Austrian Women's Party); honorary Vice-President for Austria–Hungary in the International Council of Women (appointed 1899), later ICW Vice-President (1909–1914).

Marianne Hainisch (*nee* Perger) was born on 25 March 1839 in Baden, a summer resort close to Vienna. Her father Josef Perger (1806–1886), a merchant, owned a metal plant and a cotton mill in Hirtenberg, Lower Austria. Marianne Hainisch's memories of her mother Maria (1820–1903), with whom she had a close relationship and who influenced her views on the significance of the mother for the family, are insightful. Education was all-important for Maria Perger, who taught her children herself (Marianne had two brothers and three sisters), in addition to employing tutors. In 1857, Marianne Perger married Michael Hainisch (1832–1889), the owner of a cotton mill in Aue bei Schottwien, Lower Austria. The couple had two children: a son Michael (1858–1940), who was to become President of Austria (1920–1928), and a daughter Maria (born 1860). In 1868, the Hainisch family moved from Lower Austria to Vienna.

Marianne Hainisch's interest in the women's movement reflected the economic crises of the 1860s and 1870s, when many cotton mills were closed down. Increasingly, men could not afford to marry and women's (cheaper) labor became a focal point of discussion. Hainisch repeatedly mentioned one personal experience that showed how inadequate women's education was for any profession or trade: A young friend whose husband had fallen ill had sought an occupation in order to be able to support her family. In spite of her language and musical skills, she had been unable to find a profession in keeping with her social status: "It became clear to me that middle-class girls needed preparation for gainful employment. I was deeply moved and became a champion of women on that day" (cited in Laessig 1949, 12–13). Marianne Hainisch joined the *Wiener Frauenerwerbsverein* (Viennese Women's Employment Association, founded in 1866), which sought to give lower middle-class women vocational training and thus save them from impoverishment. The *Wiener Frauenerwerbsverein* organized courses in sewing, stitching, tatting, hairdressing, dressmaking, cooking and homemaking. It also established a commercial school and a school for office jobs. In her book *Die Brodfrage der Frau* (Women and employment, 1875), Marianne Hainisch complained how difficult it was to find adequate jobs for skilled women. Well-paid jobs clashed with gender roles, according to which 'nature' supposedly restricted the kind of work women could perform. In her first public speech, "Zur Frage des Frauen-Unterrichtes" (On the issue of women's education), given at the third general meeting of the *Wiener Frauenerwerbsverein* in 1870, Hainisch demanded secondary schooling for girls that might enable them to pursue higher education and to enter the professions.

As a member of the *Verein für erweiterte Frauenbildung* (Association for Extended Women's Education, founded in 1888), Marianne Hainisch was able to further her goals. In 1892, the first grammar school for girls in the German-speaking region was established in Vienna. Besides higher education and the opening of universities for women, the general improvement of the school system was one of Hainisch's causes. She deplored dry, uninspiring, and gender-specific instruction for girls, favoring co-education–see for example her *Aufwand und Erfolg der Mittelschule vom Standpunkte der Mutter* (Input and results of secondary school education from the perspective of a mother, 1904). Hainisch was also active in the abolitionist movement (against state regulation of prostitution); she demanded protective laws and higher wages for working women; campaigned for the appointment of women as factory inspectors and poor relief functionaries; supported the settlement movement, which provided relief (e.g. day-care) and education for working-class mothers; demanded the abolition of the celibacy requirement for female teachers and criticized marriage and family laws, in particular the exclusion of women from guardianship of their own children, the absence of divorce laws and lack of protection for unmarried mothers. In addition to works mentioned above, Hainisch published *Ein Mutterwort über die Frauenfrage* (A mother's word on the woman question, 1892), *Seherinnen, Hexen und die Wahnvorstellungen über das Weib im 19. Jahrhundert* (Prophetesses, witches and delusions regarding women in the nineteenth century, 1896), *Frauenarbeit* (Women's labor, 1911) and *Die Mutter* (The mother, 1913). She also published articles in leading Austrian women's journals such as *Dokumente der Frauen* (Documents of women) and *Der Bund* (The union).

Women's suffrage was not among Hainisch's early goals–she did not wish women to be sucked into the 'muck' of politics–but from 1896 onwards, witnessing the difficulties experienced by the women's movement, she gradually came to see the vote as an instrument of power. During the electoral reform movement of 1905/06, Marianne Hainisch founded the *Wiener Frauenstimmrechtskomitee* (Viennese Women's Suffrage Committee). She regarded the time ripe for such a committee, in spite of the fact that the Social Democrats had deferred women's enfranchisement in favor of adult male suffrage. Due to the association law of 1867, women were not allowed to become members of political associations and therefore the committee could not become a regular suffrage organization.

Marianne Hainisch is well known for initiating the *Bund österreichischer Frauenvereine* (*BÖFV*, Union of Austrian Women's Associations) in 1902, following the International Council of Women's (ICW) move to admit new national associations. The *BÖFV* became the ICW's official representative for Austria in 1903. Both the *BÖFV* and the ICW were confronted with the problem of national strife in the Habsburg Monarchy. Czech, German, Hungarian, Polish and Slovenian women organized in separate committees and associations. Within the ICW, Hainisch–appointed honorary Vice-President for Austria-Hungary in 1899 and serving as ICW Vice-President from 1909 to 1914–was careful to observe the official Habsburg government position of an externally unified representation of the Monarchy. As President of the *BÖFV* until 1918, she made no special attempt to bridge ethnic barriers, accepting the dominantly German-speaking composition of the *BÖFV*. In addition, ideological and social barriers largely prevented liberal women joining forces with social democratic or Catholic–less so Jewish–organizations, and Hainisch found it especially difficult to collaborate with feminist groups more in line with social democratic goals for social change, such as the *Allgemeiner österreichische Frauenverein* (General Austrian Women's Association) led by ***Auguste Fickert***.

With the implementation of women's suffrage in Austria after the fall of the Habsburg Empire in 1918, Marianne Hainisch joined the *Bürgerlichdemokratische Arbeiterpartei* (Civil Democratic Labor Party) and ran (unsuccessfully) as a parliamentary candidate at the first February elections in 1919. Over the following years, she became particularly active in issues such as public welfare, temperance, popular education and the peace movement, having participated in the International Congress of Women for peace at The Hague in 1915. Often portrayed as a model wife and mother, Hainisch initiated Mother's Day in Austria in 1924. Women's parliamentary marginalization, as well as general political strife in the 1920s, led Marianne Hainisch to join a new women's initiative at the age of ninety. She became President of the *Österreichische Frauenpartei* (Austrian Women's Party, founded in 1929). Among its goals were peace and equality with an emphasis on homemaking as a viable profession that would entitle housewives to social security.

Marianne Hainisch died on 5 May 1936 at the age of 97, having led an immensely active and influential life in the Austrian women's movement. She is buried in Eichberg am Semmering. A monument in her memory was erected in Baden, the town of her birth, in 1967. Marianne Hainisch's visions for women were closely connected to the social class she had been born into. She was not a radical, she did not applaud social upheaval nor challenge power relations. Arguing her cause "in a matter-of-fact and pragmatic way," her goal was equality for women "in marriage, in civil, social and political life." To her, the women's movement was essential if women were to become aware of their collective task: to "lift all humanity to a higher moral and intellectual level and relieve its suffering" (Hainisch 1901, 22).

Birgitta Bader-Zaar
University of Vienna

SOURCES

(A) *Bund Österreichischer Frauenvereine* (Union of Austrian Women's Associations). Marianne Hainisch's papers here have not yet been catalogued.

(A) *Handschriftensammlung der Wiener Stadt- und Landesbibliothek* (Manuscript collection of the Vienna City Library). The collection consists of over 800 letters written by/addressed to Marianne Hainisch.

(C) Hainisch, Marianne. *Bericht über den International Council mit einem Rückblick auf die österreichische Frauenbewegung an der Jahrhundertwende* (Report on the International Council with a review of the Austrian women's movement at the turn of the century). Vienna, 1901.

(C) Hainisch, Marianne. "Die Geschichte der Frauenbewegung in Österreich" (The history of the women's movement in Austria). In Helene Lange and Gertrud Bäumer, eds. *Handbuch der Frauenbewegung* (Handbook of the women's movement). Berlin, 1901, 1: 167-188.

(C) Hainisch, Marianne. "Zur Geschichte der österreichischen Frauenbewegung. Aus meinen Erinnerungen" (On the history of the Austrian women's movement. Memories). In Martha Braun et al., eds. *Frauenbewegung, Frauenbildung und Frauenarbeit in Österreich* (The women's movement, women's education and women's labor in Austria). Vienna, 1930, 13-24.

(D) Laessig, Hildegard. *Marianne Hainisch und die österreichische Frauenbewegung* (Marianne Hainisch and the Austrian women's movement). PhD dissertation, University of Vienna, 1949.

(D) *Österreichisches biographisches Lexikon 1815-1950* (Austrian biographical dictionary 1815-1950). Graz/Köln, 1959, 2: 152.

(D) *Neue Deutsche Biographie* (New German biography). Berlin, 1966, 7: 525.

(E) Anderson, Harriet. *Utopian Feminism. Women's Movements in fin-de-siècle Vienna*. New Haven/London, 1992.

(E) Wallner, Viktor. *Zwischen Fächer und Bubikopf* (Between fan and Eton crop). Baden, 1993, 34-39.

(E) Czeike, Felix. *Historisches Lexikon Wien* (Historical encyclopaedia Vienna). Vienna, 1994, 3: 29.

(E) Friedrich, Margret. *"Ein Paradies ist uns verschlossen ...". Zur Geschichte der schulischen Mädchenerziehung in Österreich im "langen" 19. Jahrhundert* (A paradise is closed to us ... On the history of schooling for girls in Austria in the long nineteenth century). Vienna/Cologne/Weimar, 1999.

(E) Zimmermann, Susan. "The Challenge of Multinational Empire for the International Women's Movement: The Habsburg Monarchy and the Development of Feminist Inter/National Politics." *Journal of Women's History* 17, no. 2 (Summer 2005): 87-117.

(F) Publications by Marianne Hainisch can be viewed online at Austrian Literature Online <http://www.literature.at/webinterface/library>

(F) Iconographical representations: *Frauen in Bewegung. Diskurse und Dokumente der österreichischen historischen Frauenbewegung 1848-1918* (Women on the move. Discourses and documents of the Austrian women's movement 1848-1918) under Hainisch, Marianne <http://www.onb.ac.at/ariadne/vfb/bio_hainisch.htm>, "4. Bildernachweis."

HORÁKOVÁ, Milada (1901-1950)

Czech lawyer (JUDr.) and politician; colleague and co-worker (from 1923) of ***Františka Plamínková*** in the *Ženska národní rada* (National Council of Women); founder and head (1945–1948) of the *Rada československych žen* (Council of Czechoslovak Women).

Milada Horáková, maiden name Králová, was born in Prague on 25 December 1901, to a middle-class, patriotic Czech family. Her parents, Čeněk Král (1869-1955) and Anna Králová, maiden name Velíšková (1875-1933), had four children (Marta, Milada, Jiří and Věra). Her father was a pencil factory owner in České Budějovice; her mother took care of the children at home, as was customary in middle-class families at that time. In 1913, tragedy struck the family when Marta and Jiří died of scarlet fever. This sad event had an impact on Milada´s later life; from that moment she felt that practical assistance rather than pity was needed to alleviate suffering. The sadness in the Král family was soothed by the birth of Věra in 1915.

Through her father, a supporter of the philosopher and future Czechoslovak President Tomáš Garrigue Masaryk (1850-1937), Milada Králová became familiar with Masaryk's ideas and activities. Later on, during the course of her own study of Masaryk's work, his ideas greatly influenced her own thinking concerning the position of women in society and the family. Masaryk's democratic and humanist ideas became a key with which Králová could interpret the world, including issues of Czechoslovak statehood.

Milada Králová grew up during World War I and other important historical turning points: the collapse of the Habsburg Monarchy and the establishment of the independent Czechoslovak State (1918). After graduating from the *Gymnázium* (high school) for girls in Prague (1921), she needed to make a decision about her future career. Although she had wanted to study medicine, thinking that as a medical doctor she would be in a better position to help relieve suffering, her father dissuaded her from this course, convinced as he was that doctors had been partly responsible for the death of his two children. Instead he persuaded his daughter to study law, believing that as a lawyer she would also be able to help people. During her studies at the law faculty of Charles University in Prague, she joined the Czechoslovak Red Cross in order to participate in voluntary social work. In 1923, she met the leader of the Czechoslovak women's movement, ***Františka Plamínková***, and became involved in activities of the *Ženska národní rada* (National Council of Women). Králová (Horáková from 1927) and Plamínková remained colleagues until 1940, Horáková taking care of the legal and social agenda within the *Ženska národní rada*. At that time, the civil code was about to be changed and the *Ženska národní rada* tried to insert equality of the sexes into its paragraphs (especially those dealing with the relations between spouses and their children) on the basis of the fact that the equality of women and men in all spheres of life had already been made part of the Czechoslovak Constitution. Horáková proposed the modification of relevant family law paragraphs. She discussed her suggestions with the women's organization of each political party, with clubs that worked with mothers and children and with politicians and Ministry officials. She tried to find a compromise that deputies and senators from the conservative parties would be willing to vote for as well. Despite her efforts however, the proposals made by the *Ženska národní rada* were not accepted during the hearing of the amendment in Parliament.

Horáková strove for absolute equality between women and men. In her view, all aspects of a woman's life, her profession, public activity and motherhood, should be harmonized. She advocated that women have paid employment, not in order to maintain their families but so that they might realize their own needs. The education of women should not only prepare women for later employment, but also for motherhood. She perceived the role of mother to be irreplaceable. For this reason she promoted the idea that women who decided to devote their lives solely to the family should be eligible for both legal and social security.

In the fall of 1926, Králová finished Law School and received her doctoral degree on 22 October. She married Dr Bohuslav Horák (1899–1976) early in 1927 and it was to be a happy union. In 1933, she gave birth to their only child, a daughter named Jana (currently living in the U.S.). In March 1927, Horáková began working for the Welfare Department of Prague City Council, thus fulfilling her dream of helping people in need. At this time, social work still remained under the authority of voluntary organizations, which in the majority of cases were funded from private sources. Horáková publicly declared this situation untenable and demanded a legally anchored, well-organized and good quality public welfare system, which could then be supplemented by voluntary forms of social welfare.

In 1929, she joined the *Československé strany socialistické* (Czechoslovak Socialist Party), which connected socialist and patriotic ideas but did not become politically active (in the sense of party politics), and began focusing on her professional career and the women's movement. This changed during World War II, when she actively participated in an antifascist resistance organization called *Petiční výbor "Věrni zůstaneme"* (Petition Committee "We stay faithful"). In 1940, she and her husband were arrested by the Gestapo and transported to the transit camp in Terezín, where she met ***Františka Plamínková*** for the last time. Horáková's trial took place in October 1944 in Dresden and she received an eight-year sentence. After that, she was transported to the women's prison in Ainach near Munich, from which she was liberated by Allied forces in the spring of 1945.

After her release from prison, Horáková promptly returned to her work and public activities. This time, in contrast to the pre-war years, she considered it necessary to enter politics and participate actively in the creation of a democratic and socially just society that would guarantee truly equal rights for all citizens without exceptions based on origin or sex. The first domain in which she became publicly active was the new women's organization *Rada československych žen* (Council of Czechoslovak Women), which she founded and headed until it was abolished in 1948. Her second forum was the Parliament. She joined the Provisional National Assembly and, in the elections of 1946, was elected deputy to the Constituent National Assembly. She submitted a range of law proposals and interpellations dealing with the position of women in the family and society. She also proposed the version of the family law bill that was passed in 1949, following the Communist take-over in February 1948.

After the Communist regime came to power, Horakova resigned from her position in the National Assembly and took part in the anti-Communist movement. Although she was aware of the danger of arrest and imprisonment, she refused to leave Czechoslovakia due to concern for her elderly father. On 27 September 1949, she was arrested (her husband having managed to escape under dramatic circumstances) by the Communist secret police, and imprisoned. In the Czechoslovak version of the Stalinist show trials, she was sentenced to death and, on 27 June 1950, executed by hanging in Prague, the trials' only female victim in Czechoslovakia. Before the execution, Milada Horáková wrote eleven farewell letters to her family and closest friends, which served as her personal and political testament. Most of the letters did not reach the addressees but were later discovered in 1990 and given to the bereaved.

Horáková represents a third generation of feminists in the Czechoslovak women's movement–a generation that tried first to complete the fight for actual equality between women and men and second to harmonize women's careers with their public activities and motherhood. She saw her own professional, public and political activities as embedded in the struggle for freedom, democracy and social justice. She projected these principles into her proposal of the family law bill that became–with some later modifications–part of the Czech legal code, still operative today.

Dana Musilová
University of Hradec Králové

Translated from the Czech by Jitka Kohoutková, MA student at the Department of Gender Studies, Central European University, Budapest.

SOURCES

(A) Národní archiv Praha, fondy: Politické procesy, Komise 1955–1957, Rehabilitační komise ÚV KSČ 1968 (State Central Archive in Prague, collection: Political processes, Commission 1955–1957, Rehabilitation Commission UV KSC 1968).
(A) Archiv Ministerstva spravedlnosti ČR, fond: K. Klos (fond K) [Archive of the Ministry of Justice of CR, collection: K. Klos (Collection K)].
(B) *Československá žena* (Czechoslovak woman) (1945–1948).
(B) *Rada žen* (The Women's Council) (1945–1946).
(B) *Svobodné slovo* (Free word) (1945–1948).
(C) *Dopisy Milady Horákové* (Milada Horáková's letters). Prague: Lidové noviny, 1990.
(D) Kaplan, K. *Největší politický proces, M. Horáková a spol* (The greatest political process: Horáková and co.). Brno: Doplněk, 1995.
(D) Dvořáková, Z. and J. Doležal. *O Miladě Horákové a Milada Horáková o sobě* (On Milada Horáková and Miladá Horáková on herself). Prague: Nakladatelství Eva, 2001.

IVANOVA, Dimitrana (1881-1960)

Teacher, journalist, and editor; leader (from 1926 to 1944) and ideologist of the feminist *Bulgarski Zhenski Sujuz* (Bulgarian Women's Union); member of the Board of the International Alliance of Women for Suffrage and Equal Citizenship (1935–1940).

Dimitrana Ivanova (born Petrova) was born on 1 February 1881 into a middle-class family in the town of Rousse, a prosperous commercial and business center with a cosmopolitan outlook located on the river Danube. Her parents, the craftsman and trader Petur Drumev and Stanka pop Todorova (about whom nothing further is known), had three children. After graduating from the girls' high school in Rousse in 1896, Dimitrana studied philosophy at the University of Zurich, Switzerland (Sofia University, the only Bulgarian university at the time, did not accept women). With only the final examination to complete, she had to return to Bulgaria in 1900 due to family misfortunes. She became a teacher and taught at several institutions before managing to transfer in 1906 to her native town of Rousse (where her parents had been living alone since the deaths of her two brothers). In 1914 she married Doncho Ivanov (1877-1961), then a secretary of the Chamber for Trade and Industry, assuming his family name. She continued to teach at the girls' high school in Rousse until 1916, when her family moved to the capital Sofia.

Well educated and with a keen sensitivity to sexual inequality, having more than once encountered discrimination because of her sex, her involvement in the women's movement seems only logical. From 1908 to 1911 Dimitrana Petrova chaired the women's association *Dobrodetel* (Virtue) in Rousse. She took part in the congress of the Bulgarian Women's Union in 1911, where the constitutional provisions for women's voting rights were debated, and became a member of the special committee appointed by the congress to study the electoral rights of women from a legal perspective. In addition, she engaged in wider public and cultural activities, showing a deep involvement with the problems of teachers and women. From 1905 onwards she contributed regularly to the newspaper *Uchitelska probuda* (Teachers' awakening) and *Zhenski glas* (Women's voice), the organ of the Bulgarian Women's

Union. She also wrote for the professional journals *Uchitel* (Teacher) and *Uchilishten pregled* (School review), the official journal of the Ministry of Education.

Dimitrana Petrova worked as a nurse during the Balkan Wars of 1912–1913. Though she gave birth to her three children in Sofia during World War One (in 1916, 1917, and 1918), she nevertheless managed to participate in the activities of the women's educational society *Suznanie* (Conscience). She also briefly worked as an under-secretary in the Social Care Department of the Ministry of Internal Affairs and Public Health.

After World War One, Ivanova devoted herself entirely to social and political activism. From September 1920 until 1944 she was editor-in-chief of *Zhenski glas* and wrote articles for almost every issue. Her uncompromising character, self-sacrifice and firm espousal of the women's cause elevated her to the highest position in the so-called 'bourgeois' women's movement. From 1926, until the communist takeover in September 1944, she was chairwoman of the Bulgarian Women's Union, the largest and best-known feminist organization in the country. In the early 1920s–while being married with three young children–she decided that an education in law would enable her to do more for the women's cause. She tried to enroll at the Law Faculty of Sofia University but was rejected on the grounds that she "did not have a complete secondary education" (all high schools in Bulgaria by then had eight grades, while she had only had to complete six) (National Library "Cyril and Method," Bulgarian Historical Archive, collection No. 584, a. e. 1, l. 65). It was then, as she wrote in her autobiography, that "the persuasion became deeply seated within me that I should fight injustices against women and against formalism" (National Library "Cyril and Method," Bulgarian Historical Archive, collection no. 584, a. e. 1, l. 68). After 'completing' her eight-year high school education by taking the necessary final exams (at the same high schools where she had been teaching for sixteen years), Ivanova enrolled in the Law Faculty and graduated in 1927. She then founded (1928), and for two years edited, the journal *Zhenata* (The woman), which specialized in legal aspects of women's subordinate status.

Under Dimitrana Ivanova's leadership, the Bulgarian suffragists achieved partial success in 1937, when married, divorced and widowed women from 21 years of age were enfranchised. In the 1920s and 1930s, Ivanova demanded equality between the sexes in the sphere of education, reacting against government attempts to establish different types of school for girls and campaigning for the right of women-jurists to appear as defense lawyers in courts (commitments that were intimately connected to her personal life). The Bulgarian Women's Union, under her outstanding leadership, grew in influence among the civic organizations and helped shape social and ideological trends. In 1925, Ivanova became co-founder of the national *Druzhestvo za zashtita na detsata* (Union for the Protection of Children) and a member of its Board until 1935. In the 1930s she was involved in social-reformist legislative projects, as well as in the peace movement. She also gained recognition for her public lectures, which were subsequently published as pamphlets.

Dimitrana Ivanova maintained extensive foreign contacts and contributed to the international standing and representation of the *Bulgarski Zhenski Sujuz.* From 1929 onwards, she participated in almost all the congresses of the International Alliance of Women for Suffrage and Equal Citizenship (IAWSEC) and of the International Council of Women (ICW). She became a Board member of the IAWSEC at its Congress in Istanbul in 1935 and was re-elected at the Copenhagen Congress in 1939. Up until the outbreak of World War II, Ivanova actively participated in all IAWSEC meetings and activities and implemented its strategies, priorities and arguments in the Bulgarian context. She also worked to eliminate tensions with other Balkan women's movements.

The communist regime was a turning point in her life. Initially, she became a victim of personal revenge, like other socially prominent figures of the 'ancien regime.' She was arrested and spent four months in prison, accused of having "carried out pro-fascist and pro-nazi activities" as the leader of the *Bulgarski Zhenski Sujuz* (National Library "Cyril and Method," Bulgarian Historical Archive, collection no. 584, a. e. 1, l. 96). She narrowly escaped a death sentence–i.e. an arbitrary decision to murder her without trial–in the manner of the new regime. The last years of her life were hard. The communists banned her from the right to practice law because she was deemed 'untrustworthy.' Moreover, in 1944 she was excluded from the *Sujuza na jurnalistite* (Union of Journalists) after having been a member since 1922. In November 1959, only six months before her death on 29 May 1960, she finally received notification that her membership had been restored.

Dimitrana Ivanova's life story, like the history of the women's movement in Bulgaria, was shaped by powerful political trends–leftist, nationalist and authoritarian–as well as by particular political situations. The compulsory end of her public activities in 1944 marked the end of the autonomous women's movement in Bulgaria, her life story merging once again with the wider history of the Bulgarian women's movement.

Krassimira Daskalova
St. Kliment Ohridski University of Sofia

SOURCES

(A) National Library SS. "Cyril and Method," Bulgarian Historical Archive, collection no. 584 (f. 584, Dimitrana Ivanova). Dimitrana Ivanova's personal archival collection at the National Library in Sofia contains several thousand pages of materials which have not been fully catalogued. It includes an autobiography, official documents (both personal and relating to the Bulgarian Women's Union), newspaper cuttings and correspondence.

(B) *Zhenski glas* (Women's voice) (1899-1944).

(B) *Zhenata* (The woman) (1928-1930).

(E) Daskalova, Krassimira. "The Women's Movement in Bulgaria in a Life Story." *Women's History Review* 13, no. 1 (2004): 91-103.

JARNEVIĆ, Dragojla (1812–1875)

Croatian diarist, poet, writer and teacher; prominent figure in the 'Illyrian revival' (the nineteenth-century Croatian national movement).

Dragojla Jarnević was born on 4 January 1812, in the prosperous merchant town of Karlovac (also known in German as Karlstadt), a military center fifty km southwest of Zagreb, close to the Habsburg military border. She was baptized in the Catholic Church as Carolina and also had a nickname, Lina, but following the rise of the Illyrian movement and the vogue for 'Croatizing' personal names, she later used the Croatian version of her name, Dragojla.

Her father, Janko Jarnević (1753-1819), was a hardware tradesman from a bourgeois family—a man of strong patriotic sentiments. When he died, he left his wife and six children considerable wealth. Dragojla's mother, Ana (born Mlinac, 1784-1843), was a housewife with no experience in trade or farming; as a widow, she struggled to manage finances without much success and the family grew impoverished. Ana could not breastfeed Dragojla (unlike the rest of the children) and withdrew her love. Dragojla thus became her father's darling and his death was an immense loss for the girl. She attended the German language primary school for girls in Karlovac and by the age of twelve had completed her formal education.

Of her five siblings (two older sisters, one younger sister and two younger brothers), Dragojla Jarnević thought of herself as having received the worst health but the best intellect: "Nature wished to compensate the spirit for what it refused to the body" (in Lukšić, ed. 2000, 9). Jarnević was a charming girl with beautiful brown hair and young men loved her company, but she suffered from nocturnal enuresis (bed-wetting) up until her forties. This problem provoked much affliction in her childhood and a fear of rejection by men in adult life. It was one of the reasons, together with her sense of superiority, for her decision never to marry and her dedication to intellectual pursuits. Determined to combat her disability and at great cost to her health, she spent most of her nights reading and writing—having devoted herself to housework and professional sewing by day. At the age of 21, Jarnević fell deeply in love with printer Franz Redinger, a Moravian German from Brün. Knowing that Redinger had a fiancée back home, Jarnević stepped back from a full-blown affair, but she continued to treasure memories of Redinger throughout her life, comparing subsequent lovers to the romantic idealization of Redinger she had built for herself.

Under the influence of German romantic literature, Jarnević wrote her first poem—in German—in 1830. On New Year's Day 1833, she began keeping a diary and continued to do so for 41 years, right up until her death. The first eight years of her diary were originally written in German, the language of culture and everyday communication among the Croatian middle-class prior to the rise of the Croatian national movement (or the 'Illyrian revival') in 1830s Zagreb. Later, in 1872–73, Jarnević edited these early diary years herself, translating them into Croatian. In 1839, dissatisfied with provincial life, Jarnević went to Graz (Austria) to acquire knowledge of ladies fashion, or so she wrote in her diary (in Lukšić, ed. 2000, 114). There, she met the young Croatian poet Ivan Trnski (1819–1910), who stirred her patriotic feelings and urged her to write in Croatian. Jarnević's first Croatian poem was published that same year (1839) in the national newspaper, *Danicza horvatzka, slavonzka y dalmatinzka* (The Croatian, Slavonian and Dalmatian morning star). In spite of having received a post in Venice to work as a governess for a noble family, she returned to her 'homeland' after fifteen months abroad, ready to devote herself to the national cause.

Jarnević soon became known in Illyrian circles as the author of numerous romantic and patriotic poems (composed between 1839 and 1843). Her work seemed to respond to the nationalist call (to the 'daughters of Illyria') for women to abandon German literature and adopt a Croatian vernacular, educating their children in the national language and spirit. From her modest home in Karlovac, Jarnević kept in contact with leaders of the new national movement, as well as publishers. She publicly called for subscribers to put up the money for the publication of her stories, and was in this way able to publish her first collection, *Domorodne poviesti* (Patriotic stories, 1843). She became a prolific writer of stories (nineteen altogether, written between 1843 and 1875; the most noted of these appeared in newspapers between 1853 and 1870). Her work dealt with contemporary topics (in contrast with the historical epics of her male counterparts), combined with romantic plots. In 1864, she published a novel, *Dva pira* (Two weddings)—the second novel to enter modern Croatian literature. She was also the author of three plays that were neither published nor staged. She wrote painstakingly, especially at the beginning of her writing career, and twentieth-century critics (especially those who dismissed her literary merits and excluded her from the literary canon) have argued that she never quite mastered the Croatian language, describing her stories as sentimental and weakly characterized (Slavko Ježić, 1944; Jakša Ravlić, 1965; Slobodan Prosperov Novak, 2003). In fact, her writing was quite comparable with that of her well-known contemporaries.

Jarnević felt strongly that writing was her vocation but professional writing was not a particularly profitable career for a single woman. Most of the Jarnević family resources had been used to pay for the education of her brothers and to provide dowries for her sisters, forcing Dragojla Jarnević to earn a living as a seamstress and private teacher. Her attempt to open a school for girls in Karlovac in 1850 was unsuccessful, but she taught twelve girls privately. From 1853 to 1866, she lived in the village of Pribić, first with her sister and brother (a priest with whom she did not get along) and later with her niece. In Pribić, she taught religion, basic economics and agriculture to peasant children of both sexes—again privately. The last fourteen years of her life were spent in poverty but marked by ongoing creativity, including the production of several pedagogical essays on girls' education, a topic she became preoccupied with in the later years of her life. As a respectable public figure, Jarnević was invited to participate in the debate on the reform of education launched by a new generation of Croatian teachers in the early 1870s. She emphasized the importance of moral education for girls, a strong national identity acquired through the study of national literature and the need to prolong girls' compulsory education and improve teacher training. In 1872, Jarnević became a member of the *Hrvatski pedagoško-književni zbor* (Croatian Pedagogical-Literary Union).

Dragojla Jarnević is primarily remembered for her 1094-page *Dnevnik* (Diary). For decades treated in a sensationalist manner—as the personal record of "our greatest spinster," "material for psychologists and physiologists" and "pornography" (Lukšić, ed. 2000, 773)—professional readers and editors have tended to focus on Jarnević's intimate accounts of her personal life and struggle, in particular her frank discussions of her sexual longings and experiences. With the publication of the complete diary in the year 2000, a fuller picture of Jarnević's writing—her reflections on the writing process, its role in shaping her identity, the complexity of her approach—has started to emerge, moving away from the tendency (which Jarnević herself displayed) to encode her life as a struggle between body and mind. Jarnević's work presents a rich panorama of social, cultural and political life in nineteenth-century Croatia and a valuable insight into the challenges facing independent women of her generation: "My heart is boldly alarmed when I think that I should submit to a man ... I, who do not know what submission is! In leaving behind the restrictions imposed as duties upon every woman, I am neither a mother, nor a wife, nor a homemaker—but I can't help myself" (in Lukšić, ed. 2000, 205).

She maintained a life-long interest in politics, the national movement and female education, yet on several occasions declared herself to be against political rights for women—insisting first upon the education of women and the attainment of intellectual equality. Towards the end of her life, Jarnević became more bitter, conservative and alienated from the emancipatory movements of younger generations of women. Notwithstanding this, her singular personality and the precious legacy she left in the form of her diary make her an important figure in Croatian women's history. A text which can be read as a most poignant critique of female subordination and patriarchal attitudes, her diary has become an inspiration for Croatian feminists today, some of whom have chosen to identify with Dragojla Jarnević's striving for achievement and independence alongside her personal struggle for self-fulfilment and happiness.

Dragojla Jarnević died in Karlovac on 12 March 1875, four months after the last entry in her diary. She was buried in Dubovac cemetery on 14 March 1875, her passing marked by leading figures of the city's social, cultural and political life.

Sandra Prlenda

Ph.D. student at the University of Zagreb and at the *École pratique des hautes études*, Paris, Associate of the Center for Women's Studies in Zagreb

SOURCES

(C) Jarnević, Dragojla. "Uzgojivanje žene" (Education of woman). *Napredak* (Progress) 14, nos. 28 and 29 (1873): 433–437; 449–452.

(C) Jarnević, Dragojla. *Dnevnik* (Diary). Irena Lukšić, ed. Karlovac: Matica hrvatska Karlovac, 2000. Includes a comprehensive bibliography of works by and on Dragojla Jarnević.

(C) Jarnević, Dragojla. *Izabrana djela* (Selected works). Dunja Detoni-Dujmić, ed. Zagreb: Matica hrvatska, 2003.

(D) Tomić, Janko. *Dragojla Jarnevićeva kano hrvatska spisateljica i učiteljica, prijateljica i vatrena rodoljubka* (Dragojla Jarnević: Croatian writer and teacher, friend and fervent patriot). Karlovac, c. late nineteenth century.

(D) Milčinović, Adela. *Dragojla Jarnevićeva* (Dragojla Jarnević). Zagreb, 1907.

(D) Zečević, Divna. *Dragojla Jarnević*. Zagreb: Zavod za znanost o književnosti - Sveučilišna naklada Liber, 1985.

(E) Hays, Meghan. "Valjane majke i blage kćeri. Odgoj i izobrazba žena u nacionalnom duhu u Hrvatskoj 19. stoljeća" (Worthy mothers and treasured daughters: Educating women in the national spirit in nineteenth-century Croatia). *Otium* (Leisure) 4, nos. 1/2 (1996): 85–95.

(E) Detoni-Dujmić, Dunja. *Ljepša polovica književnosti* (The prettier half of literature). Zagreb: Matica hrvatska, 1998.

JESENSKÁ, Milena (1896–1944)

Czech journalist and translator who challenged gender stereotypes. Pseudonyms include 'A. X. Nessey,' 'Marie Kubešová,' 'M.,' 'Mi.,' 'Milena,' 'Milena J.' and 'M. J.'

Milena Jesenská was born on 10 August 1896 in Prague. Her father, Jan Jesenský, a professor of dentistry at the Faculty of Medicine of Charles University, was one of the top professionals in his field and also a prominent member of Czech society in Prague. Milena Jesenská's childhood and youth were marked both by the illness of her mother (also Milena, born Hejzlarová), who was for a long time bedridden, and by the usurpatory and unbalanced love of her father. Milena was enrolled in the "Minerva" Czech high school for girls, attended by the first generation of emancipated and educated women. After completing the final exam in 1915, she began studying medicine, but soon interrupted her studies with a short intermezzo at the conservatoire, later embarking on an extravagant life-style as one of Prague's 'gilded youth'–none of this was unusual for a young woman of her social background, but it did bring her the criticism and condemnation of Prague social elites.

Intellectual interest, inquisitiveness and resistance to her father's nationalism directed Jesenská to a circle of German-Jewish writers (including Max Brod, F. Werfer, W. Haas and Franz Kafka) that met regularly at the Arco café. There, Jesenská met her future husband, Ernst Polak, a bank plenipotentiary who, though knowledgeable about literature, was not a writer himself. Intensified conflicts with her father, along with her 'irreverent' lifestyle on the margins of the law (arrested on one occasion for picking state-owned magnolias), resulted in Jesenská's forced placement in a mental hospital in 1917. After she had legally come of age, and having obtained the agreement of her father, she married Ernst Polak and moved with him to Vienna. In the early months of post-war impoverishment, she began writing texts for Czech newspapers about life in Vienna: first for the *Tribuna* (Tribune) and later (probably with the help of her aunt, the writer Růžena Jesenská), for the important Prague daily newspaper *Národní Listy* (National paper). The intellectual environment of discussions in the cafés *Herrenhof* and *Central* became a school for this young journalist and significantly influenced her style of writing. At that time, probably at the suggestion of Ernst Polak, she also started translating. Her work on a translation of Kafka's short story "Topič" (The stoker) evolved into an intense romantic friendship with the writer, expressed in the form of "written kisses" in their mutual correspondence (1920–23). The later publication of Kafka's *Dopisy Mileně* (Letters to Milena, 1961) made the addressee of his letters world famous. However Jesenská's subsequent categorization as 'Kafka's friend Milena' has also resulted in a prevailing ignorance of her life, particularly her work as a journalist, and her death in a Nazi concentration camp.

After the break-up of her marriage with Ernst Polak, Jesenská spent a short time in Buchholz (near Dresden) with her new partner, the communist Count Xaver Schaffgotsch. There, they stayed at the home of Otta Rühle and his wife Alice Gerstl. By 1925, she was back in Prague. She was already well known as a journalist and established herself firmly within the Czech avant-garde camp organized around *Devětsil* (Butterbur), a radical group of artists. Through this circle, she met her second husband, the architect Jaromír Krejcar (whom she married in 1926). She wrote for the women's section of the *Národní Listy* (National paper) and for the *Lidové Noviny* (People's newspaper), cooperating with women such as Slávka Vondráčková on pioneering projects that advocated avant-garde ideas of emancipation in the spheres of modern housing design, lifestyle and fashion for women. Jesenská became one of the most prominent women journalists of her time, yet her sphere of influence was nevertheless limited to women's sections in journals, newspapers and feuilletons. She later published her writings in two books: *Cesta k jednoduchosti* (The way to simplicity, 1926) and *Člověk dělá šaty* (Human makes dress, 1927).

The birth of her daughter Honza in 1928, severe illness (resulting in a paralyzed right knee), together with a drug addiction, resulted in the decline of Jesenská's career in journalism and also in the break-up of her second marriage in 1933. During the early 1930s, Jesenská's life was marred by material deprivation, mediocre journalistic work and an alliance with the Communist Party (from which she radically dissociated herself in 1935, during the Moscow trials). With Czechoslovakia facing a growing threat from Nazi Germany, Jesenská finally found an opportunity to profile herself as a political journalist and reporter in the weekly paper *Přítomnost* (Presence), under the leadership of the excellent Czech journalist Ferdinand Peroutka. Her reportage and articles for *Přítomnost* in the years 1937–1938/9 may be counted among the best in modern Czech journalism for their political prescience, the strength of the messages and their empathy.

After the annexation of the Czech borderlands by Nazi Germany in the autumn of 1938, Jesenská became a link in a chain of people helping antifascists and Jews to escape abroad. When the rest of Czechoslovakia was annexed on 15 March 1939, she began working for the resistance organization *Obrana národa* (The Defense of the Nation) and published her articles in its illegal newspaper *V boj* (Let's fight). Jesenská was arrested in Prague on 11 November 1939, but could not be sentenced due to lack of evidence. She was deported to the Ravensbrück women's concentration camp (Germany) in August 1940, where she met many former friends from the artistic avant-garde circles of the 1920s, as well as the antifascist and former communist Margarete Buber-Neumann, who had already experienced the Soviet Gulag and with whom she developed an intense friendship. Buber-Neumann later became Jesenská's first biographer. In May 1944, Jesenská underwent an operation on an infected kidney in the hospital section of the camp where she had been previously working, as a result of which she died on 17 May 1944.

Alena Wagnerová

Translated from the Czech by Alice Szczepanikova, Ph.D. student at the Department of Gender Studies, Central European University, Budapest.

SOURCES

(B) Kafka, F. *Briefe an Milena* (Letters to Milena). Willy Haas, ed. New York: Schocken Books, 1952.

(C) Jesenská, Milena. *Cesta k jednoduchosti* (The way to simplicity), 1926.

(C) Jesenská, Milena. *Člověk dělá šaty* (Human makes dress), 1927.

(C) Jesenská, Milena. *Alles ist Leben (Reportagen u. Artikel aus den Jahren 1920–1939*) Edited with biographical notes by D. Rein. Frankfurt am Main, 1984.

(C) Wagnerová, Alena, ed. *Die Briefe von Milena* (The letters of Milena). Mannheim, 1995; Frankfurt, 1999.

(D) Buber-Neumann, M. *Milena, Kafkas Freundin* (Kafka's friend Milena). Munich, 1977. Also published as *Milena: the story of a remarkable friendship*. Ralph Manheim, trans. New York: Schocken Books, 1989.

(D) Černá, Jana. *Adresát Milena Jesenská* (Adressee Milena Jesenská). Prague, 1991.

(D) Vondráčková, Jaroslava. *Kolem Mileny Jesenské* (Around Milena Jesenská). Prague: Torst, 1991.

(D) Marková-Kotyková, Marta. *Mýtus Milena* (The Milena myth). Prague, 1993.

(D) Wagnerová, Alena. *Milena Jesenská: Biographie*. Mannheim: Bollmann, 1994.

(D) Abeles Iggers, Wilma. *Women of Prague. Ethnic Diversity and Social Change from the Eighteenth Century to the Present*. Providence and Oxford: Berghahn Books, 1995, chapter nine.

(D) Steenfatt, Margret. *Milena Jesenská, Biographie einer Befreiung*. Hamburg: Europäische Verlagsanstalt, 2002.

(D) Hockaday, Mary. *Kafka, love and courage: the life of Milena Jesenská*. London: A. Deutsch, 1995.

(E) Jirásková, Marie. *Zpráva o trojí volbě* (Report on a triple choice). Prague, 1996.

JOVANOVIĆ, Biljana (1953–1996)

Serbian writer, feminist and peace activist

Biljana Jovanović was born in Belgrade on 28 January 1953. Her father, Batrić Jovanović, was a politician and her mother, Olga Jovanović, a journalist. She had a brother named Pavle Jovanović and a sister named Ana Jovanović. The family lived in Belgrade, where Biljana Jovanović attended gymnasium, changing schools several times and graduating in 1972. In that year, she enrolled as a student at the Faculty of Philosophy, University of Belgrade, where she graduated from the Department of Philosophy.

Even as a student, Jovanović was already engaged in literary life. Her first book was a collection of poetry entitled *Čuvar* (Keeper, 1977) and her first book of fiction, a novel, followed almost immediately. *Pada Avala* (Avala is falling, 1978; second ed. 1981) gave Jovanović a name among the younger generation of writers and it was at this time that she decided in favor of a professional writing career. She published two more novels, *Psi i ostali* (The dogs and the others, 1980) and *Duša, jedinica moja* (My soul, my only child, 1984). In addition, she wrote extensively for the theater, including the plays "Ulrike Meinhof" (1976; staged as "Stemmheim" in Belgrade in 1982), "Leti u goru kao ptica" (Flies into the woods like a bird, staged in Belgrade in 1983), "Centralni zatvor" (The central prison, staged in Bitola in 1992) and "Soba na Bosforu" (A room in Bosphor, published in the journal *ProFemina* in 1994).

Biljana Jovanović married twice: first when she was still a student, to a philosopher from Belgrade named Dragan Lakićević; later to the Slovenian sociologist Rastko Močnik. From her second marriage in the late 1980s until her premature death in 1996, she divided her time between Belgrade and Ljubljana. Her husband Rastko Močnik was actively involved with her in many peace initiatives of the 1990s.

Biljana Jovanović was active on the public scene not only as a writer, but also as a critical intellectual. Throughout the 1980s, she took part in debates about intellectual freedom and freedom of speech. Particularly important was her involvement in the foundation and early work of the *Odbor za zaštitu umetničkih sloboda* (Committee for the Defense of Artistic Freedoms), which was established in 1982 within the framework of the *Udruženje književnika Srbije* (Association of Serbian Writers). Jovanović was one of its founders and for a period of time, its President. Towards the end of the 1980s, the *Udruženje književnika Srbije* became increasingly nationalistic and Jovanović distanced herself from its activities.

By the late 1980s and early 1990s, it was obvious that various forms of nationalism had become dominating ideologies among the peoples of Yugoslavia, threatening to tear the country violently apart. Jovanović became actively involved in the civic movement and anti-nationalist actions, initiating a number of events and public protests herself. She organized a number of public actions against the war calling for peace and tolerance and was one of the founders of the *Civilni pokret otpora* (Civil Resistance Movement, founded in Belgrade on 29 February 1992). In November 1992, she was among the founders of the *Leteća učionica radionica, LUR* (Flying classroom workshop), an alternative theoretical and artistic project connecting Yugoslav spaces in an already partly dismembered country. Despite the war, various kinds of cultural activities took place in Ljubljana, Belgrade, Priština, Skopje and Titograd (today Podgorica), in which people from all over the country participated in various languages of the former Yugoslavia: Slovenian, Serbian, Croatian and Macedonian. Biljana Jovanović was also involved in a number of antiwar actions carried out in cooperation with women's and feminist groups, in particular with *Žene u crnom* (Women in Black) and the *Ženski lobi* (Women's Lobby) from Belgrade.

Accounts of some of these activities for the period June 1991 to November 1992 are chronicled in detail in a book of letters exchanged between four women writers: Biljana Jovanović, Rada Iveković, Maruša Krese and Radmila Lazić. The book was first published in German, under the title of *Briefe von Frauen über Krieg und Nationalismus* (Women's letters on war and nationalism, 1993) and a year later in Belgrade. In the letters–written across old, newly established, national and international borders–the four women express feelings of unhappiness, disbelief and rage, as well as the need to take action against dangerous forces destroying the country and pushing people into war, hatred and death.

Biljana Jovanović was among the first women writers to introduce a new kind of self-conscious female character to South-Slavic literature. In her novels, a range of themes characteristic of Anglo-American women's writing of the 1970s and 1980s are clearly recognizable, including an interest in women's bodies and women's sexuality; relationships with men, but also with women; mother–daughter relations and women's psyche. The novels are peppered with references to everyday life under former Yugoslav 'soft communism' and in this respect, her two early novels *Pada Avala* and *Psi i ostali* are of particular importance. Both employ quasi-autobiographical narratives, bringing the main character close to the writer, but any real identification between character and author is virtually impossible. In *Pada Avala*, the narration centers upon a young woman who refuses to accommodate dominant, traditional perceptions of 'proper' womanhood and allow social expectations to mould her body and behavior.

The novel has an open, dual ending that brings the heroine to a mental institution as a schizophrenic and sends her off into utopian seclusion with an ideal lover, parodying the genre of trivial romance. The mentally unstable heroine in *Psi i ostali* cannot solve the troubled and complicated relationship she has with her mother. She is also the first openly lesbian character in modern Serbian literature.

Biljana Jovanović was diagnosed with a brain tumor in 1994. She died on 11 March 1996 in Belgrade and was buried in the central city cemetery: Novo Groblje. After her death, a yearly literary prize for women's fiction bearing her name was institutionalized by the Belgrade magazine *ProFemina* in 1996. In 2005, a street in Belgrade was also named after her. Not an organized feminist, but close to feminist circles in Belgrade, Zagreb and Ljubljana from the early 1970s, when feminists started to be active on the public scene, Biljana Jovanović's civic resistance to the nationalism and wars of the late 1980s and 1990s was also strongly permeated with feminist ideas and often realized in close cooperation with organized feminists. Her literature too, is strongly rooted in an overtly feminist world-view.

Jasmina Lukić
Department of Gender Studies,
Central European University, Budapest

SOURCES

(C) Jovanović, Biljana. *Čuvar* (Keeper). Belgrade: KOS, 1977.

(C) Jovanović, Biljana. *Pada Avala* (Avala is falling). Belgrade: Prosveta, 1978.

(C) Jovanović, Biljana. *Psi i ostali* (The dogs and the others). Belgrade: Prosveta, 1980.

(C) Jovanović, Biljana. *Duša, jedinica moja* (My soul, my only child). Belgrade: BIGZ, 1984.

(C) Jovanović, Biljana, Rada Iveković, Maruša Krese and Radmila Lazić. *Briefe von Frauen über Krieg und Nationalismus* (Women's letters on war and nationalism). Frankfurt a/M.-Berlin: Edition Suhrkamp, 1993.

(C) Jovanović, Biljana, Rada Iveković, Maruša Krese and Radmila Lazić. *Vjetar ide na jug i obrće se na sjever* (The wind goes to the south and turns to the north). Belgrade: Radio B92, 1994.

(C) Jovanović, Biljana. "Soba na Bosforu" (A room in Bosphor). *ProFemina*, no. 1 (1994/95): 193–219.

(D) Slapšak, Svetlana. "Biljana Jovanović (28. 1. 1953–11. 3. 1996.)." *ProFemina*, nos. 5/6 (1996): 285.

(D) Lukić, Jasmina. "Svemu nasuprot" (Against all restrictions). *ProFemina*, no. 7 (1996): 126–134.

(D) Šop, Ljiljana. "Dok je neznanog junaka, Avala ne sme pasti" (While the unknown warrior is there, Avala cannot fall). *ProFemina*, no. 7 (1996): 135–138.

(D) Jevremović, Zorica. "Ram za sliku Ulrike Majnhof" (Frame for a picture of Ulrike Meinhof). *ProFemina*, no. 7 (1996): 139–143.

(D) Stojanović-Pantović, Bojana. "Beskrajna: zapisi o pesmama Biljane Jovanović" (Herself, endless: a note on the poems of Biljana Jovanović). *ProFemina* 9/10 (1997): 244–247.

JURIĆ, Marija (1873-1957)

Croatian novelist and feminist; one of the first woman political journalists in Southeast Europe (1896–1910); editor of *Ženski list* (Woman's magazine) (1925–1938) and *Hrvatica* (Croatian woman) (1938–1940); founder of the *Kolo radnih žena* (Working Women's Circle, 1897) and leader of the first women's demonstrations in Zagreb (1903). Pseudonym: Zagorka.

Marija Jurić, known by her pseudonym 'Zagorka,' was born on 2 March 1873 on the Negovac estate near the city of Križevci. She was given the name Marianna and baptized in a Roman Catholic Church on 3 March 1873. Her mother, Josipa Domin, and father, Ivan Jurić (data unknown), were wealthy and had three children besides Marija: two sons (names and data unknown) and a daughter, Dragica (1879-1896), who died of tuberculosis.

Marija Jurić spent her childhood in the Zagorje region of Croatia, where her father owned the Golubovec estate (near the city of Varaždin) and managed Šanjugovo, the estate of Baron Geza Rauch. Marija attended three different elementary schools: one at Rauch's manor house, another in the city of Varaždin and the third at the Sisters of Charity Convent in Zagreb. Marija was both a precocious child and an excellent student, and her father planned to send her to university in Switzerland (with Rauch's financial support). Her mother emphatically opposed this proposal, protesting that she would "never allow [Marija] to drag herself around some institution of higher education where she would be exposed to men" and withdrew Marija from school in her final year (Lasić 1986, 34). The Jurić household was a turbulent one and Marija's childhood often violent; during the constant arguments and physical fights between her parents she would often run away from home, seeking consolation and protection from the local people of the village.

Marija Jurić exhibited literary talent, a deep sense of social justice and a 'revolutionary nature' at an early age. At twelve, she was reprimanded for her first literary endeavor: *Samostanske novine* (Convent newspaper), in which she set down folk stories and legends. At the age of eighteen, she established an amateur theater company with her cousin and, in 1891, a school newspaper: *Zagorsko proljeće* (Zagorje spring). Her first (and male) pseudonym as editor was 'M. Jurica Zagorski.'

Prevented from continuing her education, Marija Jurić expressed ambitions to become an actress. To 'discipline' their unruly daughter, Marija's parents married her off for a large dowry to one Lajos Nagy (it is not known whether that was his real name), a bachelor eighteen years her senior. The marriage took place towards the end of 1891, most probably in Varaždin. In early 1892, the newly-weds left Croatia and went to live in Szombathely, a provincial Hungarian town. Once married, Jurić described feeling as though she was being "subjected to a moral inquisition" (Prohaska 1921, 267). She regarded the national chauvinism of her Hungarian husband negatively, but nonetheless learned the language of 'her colonizer' and even completed a course in telegraphy. Throughout her marriage, she continued to write secretly in the small room of her attic.

Later, in her memoirs, Jurić described in detail the following period of her life: from escaping her husband in 1895 to becoming a contributor to the newspaper *Obzor* (Horizon) in the October of 1896. In her autobiographical *Kamen na cesti* (A stone on the road, 1937–1939), the fictional heroine commits suicide in circumstances strikingly similar to those of Jurić during this episode of her life. Bishop Josip Juraj Strossmayer, an owner of the newspaper *Obzor*, supported Jurić's move into journalism but *Obzor*'s editor-in-chief, Šime Mazzura, declared that a "woman in the editorial offices" was a "cultural and moral scandal," complaining that "not even in London, where suffragettes drag officers through the streets, do women edit political news" (Lasić 1986, 68). Mazzura did not hide his misogyny and antifeminist sentiments and, in the years to come, attached labels to Jurić that would follow her to her grave: "a crone with no name or reputation, a cowgirl from Zagorje and, what's more, infected with a socialist mentality and feminist notions" (Lasić 1986, 69). It was obvious that Jurić was being, as she put it later, "treated everywhere with distrust and disdain because a woman in politics in the nineteenth century was seen in the same way as a woman in a public house. And I stood in the front lines, spreading feminism and awakening in women the desire to take part in public life" (Đorđević 1979, 161). In the course of her ten-year career (1895–1905) covering the work of the Hungarian-Croatian Parliament in Budapest, Jurić nevertheless managed successfully to establish herself as one of the first woman political journalists in Southeast Europe. She was publicly supported by Tomáš Masaryk and the Croatian politician Frano Supilo, who reportedly told her that she was, in his view, "a decent man [*sic*]" (Zagorka 1953, 40).

In 1903, Jurić became the sole editor of *Obzor* for five full months. She also participated in the work of the *Glavni narodni odbor* (Central National Committee), which in 1903 organized socialist demonstrations against Khuen's right-wing government. When members of the *Kolo radnih žena* (Working Women's Circle)—an association of female typographers founded by Jurić in 1897—were arrested, Jurić led the first demonstrations of women in Zagreb (approximately 1800 women took part), for which she was imprisoned. From prison, she wrote the play "Evica Gupčeva" (1903), in which she 'reinterpreted' national history from a feminist standpoint, suggesting that the leader of the Peasants' Revolt of 1573 had in fact been a woman. The work, also a commentary on the history of Jurić's own writing process and anticipating the future direction of her work, was censured and remained unpublished. Nevertheless, it was successfully performed (from the manuscript) in Dubrovnik (1903–1904) and Split (under Austrian rule), as well as in Zagreb after the fall of the Khuen regime (1906).

Jurić was a prolific writer who wrote with ease, yet to this day not one complete bibliography of her work exists. In 1910, encouraged by Bishop Josip Juraj Strossmayer, she began writing feuilleton novels, which dramatically helped raise *Obzor*'s circulation. She was also the editor of the informative column "From a woman's world," which appeared in the magazine *Domaće ognjište* (Domestic fireplace) and for which she wrote texts with feminist and polemic overtones under the pseudonym 'Iglica' (Little needle). In 1909, Jurić, together with Mira Kočonda and ***Zofka Kveder***, publicly debated issues of sexual equality with the influential writer Antun Gustav Matoš, attacking his presumption of fixed 'roles' for women—embodied by the trope of *Kinder, Küche, Kirche* (children, kitchen, church)—upon which prevailing arguments for women's inferiority rested. Jurić promoted women's equality in education, employment and suffrage rights in over 200 public panels and journalists' meetings, and as a participant in the Woman's Slavic Congress in Prague (1917).

In 1910, Jurić married Slavko Amadej Vodvařka, a popular writer of humorous sketches and comedies, and began using (from 1911) two surnames: Jurić Vodvařka. That same year, her book *Kneginja iz Petrinjske ulice* (Princess from Petrinjska street) was published, the first in a series of some forty historical novels that brought her popularity and a large readership. Later, she published a collection of works between 1912 and 1918 under the title of *Grička vještica* (A witch from Grič), namely: *Tajna Krvavog mosta* (Secret of the bloody bridge); *Kontesa Nera* (Countess Nera); *Malleus Maleficarum, Suparnica Marije Terezije* (Maria Theresa's rival); *Dvorska kamarila* (The court camarilla) and *Buntovnik na prijestolju* (A rebel on the throne). After completing *Grička vještica*, Jurić Vodvarka (or 'Zagorka') wrote *Crveni ocean* (Red ocean, 1918), a social-utopian novel inspired by the events of the Russian October Revolution, and *Tozuki* (1918), as well as the historical novels *Kći Lotrščaka* (Daughter of Lotrščak, 1922), *Kameni križari* (Stone crusaders, 1928–1929) and the twelve volume *Gordana* (1934–1935). *Kraljica Hrvata* (Queen of the Croats, 1937, which became one of her nicknames) and the autobiographical novel *Kamen na cesti* (A stone on the road, 1937–1939) followed soon after.

Jurić Vodvařka adapted a number of her novels for the stage and by 1940, fourteen of her adaptations had been shown at the Croatian National Theater. She continued her feminist journalism, setting up *Ženski list* (Women's magazine) in 1925, for which she wrote until 1938, and founding the journal *Hrvatica* (Croat woman, 1938), which was dissolved in 1941 by the *Ustasha* under the Independent State of Croatia (the newly formed fascist puppet-state). Jurić Vodvařka's belongings were confiscated because she refused to collaborate with the new regime and she was barred from public life—a situation that led to her attempted suicide in 1941. Thus silenced, she remained in Zagreb until 1945, after which she resumed her public activities in newly formed socialist Yugoslavia, mainly participating in panels on behalf of the *Antifašistički front žena* (Antifascist Women's Front).

Jurić Vodvaŕka ('Zagorka') died in Zagreb on 29 November 1957 and was buried in Mirogoj cemetery on 4 December 1957, in the crypts of the most eminent members of the Croatian political and cultural elite. Today, though recognized for her literary achievements and journalism (a prestigious award for Croatian journalists carries the name of "Marija Jurić Zagorka"), her pioneering "Amazonian feminism" (Sklevicky 1996, 245) still awaits the same recognition.

Slavica Jakobović Fribec
Cultural and Information Center, Zagreb

Translated from the Croatian by Jelena Primorac.

SOURCES

(A) The State Archive in Zagreb, Republic of Croatia. Rakovac Parish: register of births and baptisms (1858–1878), year 1873, p. 224.

(A) *Arhiv Instituta za književnost i teatrologiju* (*HAZU*, Literary and Theatrical Institute Archives), Croatian Academy of Arts and Sciences, no. 1416. Jurić Zagorka, Marija. "Evica Gupčeva." Written in 1903, unpublished.

(A) National and University Library in Zagreb, no. R 7601, Jurić Zagorka, Marija. *Što je moja krivnja* (The fact of my faults). Manuscript, 1947.

(B) *Domaće ognjište* (Domestic fireside) [Zagreb: Hrvatski pedagoško-književni zbor—Klub učiteljica (Croatian Pedagogical Association and Croatian Women Teachers' Club), 1900–1914].

(B) Prohaska, Dragutin. *Pregled savremene hrvatsko-srpske književnosti* (An overview of contemporary Croato-Serb literature). Zagreb: Matica hrvatska (special edition), 1921.

(C) Jurić Zagorka, Marija. *Kneginja iz Petrinjske ulice* (Princess from Petrinjska Street). Published in 147 installments in *Hrvatske novosti* (Croatian news) (1910); Zagreb: Prva hrvatska radnička tiskara, 1910.

(C) Jurić Zagorka, Marija. *Kamen na cesti* (A stone on the road. A woman writer's novel). *Ženski list* (Women's magazine) (1932, 1933, 1934); Zagreb: Tiskara Merkantil, Jutriša i Sedmak, 1938.

(C) Jurić Zagorka, Marija. "Tko ste vi?" (Who are you? Autobiographical notes). *Hrvatica* (Croat woman). (Zagreb, 1939–1940).

(C) Jurić Zagorka, Marija. "Mala revolucionarka" (Little revolutionary girl). *Hrvatica* (Croat woman) (1939–1940).

(C) Jurić Zagorka, Marija. *Iz Zagorkinih memoara* (From Zagorka's memoirs). *Ilustrirani vjesnik* (Illustrated news). Zagreb, 1952. For 'technical reasons,' publication of the memoirs ceased suddenly on 5 April 1954, which are thus incomplete.

(C) Jurić Zagorka, Marija. *Kako je bilo* (How it was). Belgrade: Redakcija Zabavnog romana, 1953.

(C) Jurić Zagorka, Marija. *Sabrana djela* (Collected works). Vols. 1-7. Zagreb: Stvarnost, 1963.

(D) Hergešić, Ivo. "Marija Jurić Zagorka." Preface to *Grička Vještica* (A witch from Grič). In *Sabrana djela* (Collected works). Vol. 1. Zagreb: Stvarnost, 1963.

(D) Đorđević, Bora. *Zagorka–kroničar starog Zagreba* (Zagorka–chronicler of the old Zagreb). Sisak: Grafička radna organizacija Joža Rožanković, 1979.

(D) Lasić, Stanko. *Književni počeci Marije Jurić Zagorke (1873-1910), Uvod u monografiju* (The literary beginnings of Marija Jurić Zagorka, 1873-1910, an introduction to the monograph). Zagreb: Znanje, 1986.

(E) Horvat, Josip. *Povijest novinstva Hrvatske od 1771. do 1939* (History of journalism in Croatia from 1771 to 1939). Zagreb: Stvarnost, 1962.

(E) Sklevicky, Lydia. *Konji, žene, ratovi* (Horses, women, wars). Zagreb: Ženska infoteka, 1996.

KÄER-KINGISEPP, Elise (1901-1989)

Founder (1926) of the *Eesti Akadeemiliste Naiste Ühing* (*EANÜ,* Estonian Association of University Women); pharmacologist and physiologist; university lecturer; science historian.

Elise Käer was born on 3 October 1901 in the vicinity of Tartu (in Metsaküla, Estonia) the first of the two daughters of farmers Gustav Käer (1861-1932) and Liisa (born Rosin) Käer (1878-1977). [Elise's sister Helene Käer (born 1906), married name Helene Sultson, is a musician living in Montreal, Canada.] The family moved to Tartu and Elise studied at the Second elementary school there and later, at the elite Girls' Gymnasium (high school), named after A. S. Pushkin and established in 1899. In 1918, after German military forces had occupied Tartu, the Pushkin Gymnasium was evacuated to Russia. Most Russified students and professors of the Pushkin Gymnasium left Tartu and Elise continued her education at the Russian gymnasium of the Tartu Schoolmasters' Society, finishing her studies in the spring of 1919. In the autumn of that year, she applied to the medical faculty of Tartu University. Since her diploma–issued by the Russian gymnasium–was not sufficient for enrollment at the university, Elise Käer was initially admitted as an auditor student, later passing additional exams in mathematics, physics and Latin. In May 1920, she enrolled as a fully qualified student in medicine at the University of Tartu. Inclined towards research, her work on the curative properties of Estonian mud attracted the attention of medical scientists and was published in the journal *Eesti Arst* (Estonian doctor), which had thus far only published studies by male doctors. Elise Käer graduated from Tartu University as a physician in 1924. At the end of this year, inspired by her interest in theoretical medicine, she decided to continue her studies at the university's Department of Chemistry of the Faculty of Mathematics and Natural Sciences while teaching at the Girls' Gymnasium and the Ninth elementary school in Tartu. During the summer months, she applied her theoretical knowledge practically, as a doctor on duty at the mud bath and mud cure center in the town of Haapsalu.

In 1923, she joined the *Eesti Naisüliõpilaste Selts* (Society of Estonian Women Students, founded in 1911) and in September 1924, was elected to its Board as Chair of the committee for foreign relations. Elise Käer mastered German, Russian, English and French; these skills not only gave her an advantage when communicating with students' organizations from various European universities, but resulted in Käer becoming a representative of Tartu University to a number of international students' forums in Riga, Kaunas (Kovno), Helsinki and Warsaw. She was a member of the Central Bureau of the *Eesti, Läti, Leedu ja Soome Üliõpilasliit, Keskbüroo* (*SELL*, Association of Estonian, Latvian, Lithuanian and Finnish Students), an organization of students from the Baltic countries that existed from 1923 to 1939, and (after 1926) joined the Board of the *Confédération Internationale des Étudiants* (*CIE*, International Students Confederation).

Elise Käer was on the Editorial Board of the Tartu students' *Üliõpilasleht* (Student newspaper) and, thanks to her, articles addressing issues relevant to female students were also published. It was Käer who, during a 1925 meeting of the *Eesti Naisüliõpilaste Selts*, proposed setting up an association of university women. The founding meeting of the *Eesti Akadeemiliste Naiste Ühing* (*EANÜ*, Estonian Association of University Women) took place in Tartu on 1–2 May 1926. Elise Käer read out the statutes of *EANÜ* and raised the possibility of *EANÜ* joining the International Federation of University Women (established in 1919). Käer was among the seven members elected to the *EANÜ* Board and became the first *EANÜ* Vice-Chairwoman (1925–1936), Chairwoman of its medical committee (1936–1940) and the organization's main coordinator. In 1927, the *Üliõpilasleht* initiated a discussion about the university education of women. Käer's popularity as a student leader led to the appearance of a number of friendly cartoons and other doggerel in the *Üliõpilasleht*.

In 1931, Elise Käer married Georg Kingisepp (1898–1974) who, after having graduated from Heidelberg University, had been working in Germany for a couple of years before coming to work as an assistant at the Institute of Pharmacology at Tartu University. In 1927, Georg Kingisepp obtained his M.D. degree and in 1938, was nominated for a professorship. Elise Käer-Kingisepp, who defended her M.D. degree in 1934, was the second Estonian female scientist to qualify from Tartu University. [The first woman was the Baltic German Renata Beckmann (born 1901; *dr med*, 1929); the first Estonian woman was Liidia Poska-Teiss (1888–1956)]. Elise and Georg Kingisepp had a daughter, Aime-Reet Kingisepp (b. 1931, Tartu), and a son, Peet-Henn Kingisepp (b. 1936, Tartu). Aime-Reet Kingisepp graduated from the medical faculty of Tartu University in 1956 and worked as a lecturer at various vocational medical educational establishments, as well as at Tartu University. She is a member of the *EANÜ* (reestablished in 1991), is currently a researcher of the history of academic women and since 1991, has been the Chairwoman of the *EANÜ Ajaloo Toimkond* (the section of the historians within the Estonian Association of University Women). Peet-Henn Kingisepp is a physiologist and science historian based at the Institute of Physiology, University of Tartu.

In 1936, Elise Käer-Kingisepp was involved in the work of the medical committee attached to the *EANÜ*, focusing on the development of the professional and research work of female doctors. The committee was central to the drafting of a new law on childcare and drafted its own bill on medical doctors, including doctors specializing in women's diseases.

Throughout the 1930s, Estonia was subjected to ongoing discussion about the so-called 'overproduction of intellectuals.' As a recognized scientist and lecturer at the university, Elise Käer-Kingisepp mobilized academic women in protest against cuts in the number of students (especially women students of pharmaceutics and philology). Elise Käer-Kingisepp herself tenaciously pursued an academic path, and was held in high esteem by her colleagues. In January 1939, she successfully applied for an assistant professor position in pharmacology, which she received on 20 March 1939, after having delivered her *venia legendi* lecture. Two years later, in 1941, she was given a senior post within the Chair of Pharmacology. During the war years, she worked in the laboratory of a medicine-producing joint-stock company and, in the autumn of 1944, became professor and head of the Chair of Physiology and Biological Chemistry. From 1948 to 1975, she was professor and head of the Chair of Physiology of Tartu University and from 1953 to 1980, Chairperson of the Estonian Society of Physiology. Elise Käer-Kingisepp investigated sportsmen's cardiac and circulatory functions as well as respiratory functions and it was on her initiative that, after World War II, Tartu University became one of the few educational establishments for sport-medics in the so-called 'Eastern bloc.'

After withdrawing from active teaching, Elise Käer-Kingisepp devoted herself to the history of medicine (particularly of physiology). Her heroes were the medical scholars from the golden era of Imperial Tartu University (1802–1889) who had promoted various research schools. She enjoyed observing the natural world and had a keen interest in classical music, along with an extensive record collection at home. Her love for her native town is reflected in the abundant collection of photographs and postcards of old Tartu that she kept.

Professor Elise Käer-Kingisepp, Estonian female intellectual and leader of the university women's movement in Estonia, died on 10 February 1989 in Tartu.

Sirje Tamul
Tartu University

Translated from the Estonian by Leili Kostabi, Tartu University.

SOURCES

(A) *Eesti Ajalooarhiiv* (Estonian History Archives, hereafter EHA), Stock 2100, Series 1, Collection 6668 (Elise Käer).

(A) EHA, Stock 2100, Series 19, Collection 376, 409 (Student societies in the 1920s at Tartu University).

(A) EHA, Stock 3713, Series 1, Collection 1-105, *Eesti Akadeemiliste Naiste Ühendus, 1926-1940* (Estonian Association of University Women, 1926-1940).

(A) EHA, Stock 1781, Series 1, Collection 157, *Eesti Naisüliõpilaste Selts 1911-1940* (Society of Estonian Women Students, 1911-1940).

(B) *Üliõpilasleht* (Student newspaper) (Tartu, 1925-1927).

(C) Käer-Kingisepp, Elise. "Theatrum anatomicum Universitatis Tartuensis. Lehekülgi Tartu ülikooli arstiteaduskonna õppetööst XIX sajandi algusaastail" (Theatrum anatomicum Universitatis Tartuensis. Tuition at the Medical Faculty of Tartu University at the beginning of the nineteenth century). *Nõukogude Eesti Tervishoid.* [(Soviet Estonian) Journal of Health] 2 (1985): 118-122.

(D) Kingisepp, Peet-Henn. "Elise Käer-Kingisepp Tartu ülikooli füsioloogiaprofessorina" (Elise Käer-Kingisepp—Head of the Chair of Physiology). In *Elise Käer-Kingisepp 100.* Tartu, 2001, 9-33.

(E) Siilivask, Karl, ed. *History of Tartu University 1632-1982.* Tallinn: Perioodika, 1985, 177-180.

(E) Käbin, Ilo. *Medizinische Forschung und Lehre an der Universität Dorpat/Tartu 1802-1940* (Medical science research and tuition at Tartu University, 1802-1940). Stockholm, 1986, 438.

(E) Tamul, Sirje. "Üliõpilaskonna organiseerumisest 1920. Aastatel" (The formation of student societies and corporations in the 1920s). In *Tartu Ülikooli ajaloo küsimusi XXII (I)* (Issues relating to the history of Tartu University). Tartu: Tartu Ülikooli Kirjastus (Tartu University Press), 1989, 68-89.

(E) Lindström, Lauri and Toomas Hiio. "Statistilisi andmeid kommentaaridega Tartu ülikooli 1918-1944 immatrikuleeritud üliõpilaste kohta Album Academicum Universitatis Tartuensis 1918-1944 andmestiku põhjal" (Some statistical data with notes on students admitted to Tartu University between 1918 and 1994). In *Tartu Ülikooli ajaloo küsimusi XXIX.* (Issues related to the history of Tartu University). Tartu: Tartu Ülikooli Kirjastus, 1997, 28-38.

(E) Barkala, Ester, ed. *Eesti Akadeemiliste Naiste Ühing, 1926-1940* (Estonian Association of University Women, 1926-1940). With archival research by Reet-Aime Kingisepp. Tartu: Tartu Ülikooli Kirjastus, 2001, 26-28.

KAIJA, Ivande (born Antonija Millere-Meldere, married name Antonija Lūkina) (1876–1941)

Latvian prose writer, journalist, public and political figure; co-founder (1918) of the *Latvijas Sieviešu Asociācija* (Latvian Women's Association).

Ivande Kaija (Antonija Millere-Meldere) was born on 12 October 1876 in Jumpravmuiža, to middle-class parents. Her father, Miķelis Millers-Melders, was originally a tradesman. He made a fortune and became a proprietor and landlord in Riga, where, in 1879, the family settled in the pleasant suburban district of Torņakalns. Her mother, Matilde Millere-Meldere (born Flintman), was a housewife. The family lost three children but three daughters survived. In 1881, Antonija entered Torņakalns Elementary school; later, she studied at the Riga Lomonosov Women's Gymnasium. In 1895, she travelled to the Caucasus before spending a couple of years in Switzerland and Germany, where she studied philosophy and art history at the universities of Bern and Leipzig. This was a period of rapid intellectual development for Antonija Millere-Meldere; she frequented libraries, museums and art galleries and learned German, Russian, Latin, French, English and Italian. After her marriage in 1901 to Felikss Lūkins, a successful oculist, she gave up her studies and settled down with her husband in Riga. They had three children: a daughter Silvia (b. 1903) and sons Haralds (b. 1905) and Ivars (b. 1907).

In 1910, with her husband remaining in Latvia with the children, Antonija Lūkina went to France to study journalism at the Sorbonne. She wrote editorials for the *Collège de France* (what this entailed is not clear) and traveled the country, also making trips to Italy and Switzerland. When in Switzerland, Antonija Lūkina visited the Latvian émigrés ***Aspazija*** and Rainis (Jānis Pliekšāns), outstanding Latvian poets and playwrights who were active supporters of the social democratic movement and who had fled from the violent aftermath of the Revolution of 1905, settling down at Castagnola near Lake Lugano. Lūkina had wanted to meet the poet Aspazija, whom she greatly admired. The two women developed a deep friendship, sustained by intimate correspondence throughout their years away from Latvia (1910–1920), and lent each other mutual support. Lūkina began a donation-collection scheme to support

Aspazija and Rainis financially and the sum raised was presented to them in the form of a national award upon their return to Latvia in 1920. In the 1920s, Lūkina used her relations with leading politicians and the President, Kārlis Ulmanis, to reconcile Rainis with liberal political circles, mitigate the effects of hostilities caused by his social democratic interests and promote him in public life. Rainis and Aspazija became her literary foster-parents to whom she showed her draft manuscripts. During their first meeting in 1910, Rainis suggested she turn from drama to prose, advice that may well have contributed to the development of an unorthodox woman and a unique, early twentieth-century writer.

After her return to Riga in 1913, Lūkina published her first novel, *Iedzimtais grēks* (The innate sin), under a pen-name, 'Kaija,' inspired by the image of a seagull with broken wings on a gravestone she had seen in Castagnola cemetery (*Kaija* means seagull in Latvian). The book was controversial; it touched upon issues such as free love and openly dealt with a woman's disillusionment in marriage and her right to personal happiness through sexual liberation. Kaija was instantly acknowledged as an emancipated woman writer, a view sustained by her articles on women's and other social and political issues in the newspaper *Dzimtenes Vēstnesis* (Homeland gazette) and *Latviešu izglītības biedrības gadagrāmata* (The almanac of the Latvian Educational Association). During World War I, Kaija left Latvia with her children and followed her husband, who had been called up to serve as a surgeon in the Russian army. They lived in Moscow, St Petersburg and the Crimea.

In 1918, Kaija actively supported the idea of an independent Latvian Republic; she was a deputy candidate on the government list to the first *Saeima* (Latvian Parliament) and helped assemble the ministerial cabinet. In 1918, she was also one of the founders of the *Latvijas Sieviešu Asociācija* (Latvian Women's Association), a political party for the promotion of women's rights (especially suffrage). It was she who wrote up its statement of purpose and agenda. In 1919-1920, Kaija (among others) set up the Gold Foundation to assist Latvian independence, to which women donated their family treasures and jewellery. Kaija participated in the organization of the *Kultūras fonds* (Culture Foundation), as well as international events such as the Entente Cordiale Conference of the Baltic States.

During these years of active political and public life, Kaija had to support her family due to her husband's illness and difficult material conditions in the post-war period. She worked in the Foreign Office of the Republic of Latvia as a commentator on the French press, became head of the department of art and literature for the periodical *Latvijas Sargs* (Latvian guard) and continued to publish extensively. This period of her life (1918-1921) is reflected in her published autobiography which, given Kaija's involvement in public life, constitutes a significant historical text. In 1917, Kaija completed her second novel, *Jūgā* (In bondage, 1919), a critical examination of the institution of marriage. This was followed by the novel *Sfinksa* (Sphinx, 1920), which dealt with femininity, the psyche of the modern woman and the search for perfect love. In

1920, Kaija wrote a historical novel about the ancient Baltic people *Dzintarzeme* (Amber land), which was published the following year. She actively participated in public life–namely in the development of the new Latvian state and raising national awareness–and gave public presentations and lectures on diverse topics in different parts of Latvia. On 17 April 1921, on a lecture trip to Valmiera (northeast Latvia), Kaija had a stroke which left her partially disabled with grave hearing problems. Of the life that was to follow the stroke, Kaija wrote in 1936: "Fate has put an end to my writing and public career. (...) For fifteen years I have merely been observing all that is going on, without participating. Do you know what it means to keep silent for so many years? No words can describe all that I have suffered. First it was terrible despair, but then time cured me and I gradually reconciled myself to the inevitable" (cited in Ķelpe 1936, 53–54; S. M., trans). In 1927, Kaija was awarded Latvia's most prestigious national award, the *Trīszvaigžņu ordenis* (Three Star Order) for her participation in founding the independent Latvian state. She died in a car accident. The official date of her death is 2 January 1942, although in her published diaries Astrīda Muchka, a family friend, states that the fatal incident happened on 24 December (Christmas Eve) 1941. Kaija was buried in Meža kapi Cemetery in Riga. Nowadays she is mostly remembered in Latvia as a feminist writer and appreciated for the contemporary relevance of her writing, yet little attention has been paid to her public and particularly her political activities.

Sandra Meshkova
Daugavpils University and the University of Latvia

SOURCES

(C) Kaija, Ivande. "Autobiogrāfijas vietā" (Instead of autobiography). *Atziņas: latvju rakstnieku autobiogrāfijas* (The autobiographies of Latvian writers). Rīga: sast. K. Egle, Cēsis, 1923.

(D) Tālmane, E. "Ivande Kaija: biogrāfisks apcerējums" (Ivande Kaija: a biographical sketch). In Ivande Kaija. *Kopoti raksti* (Complete works). 9 vols. Rīga, 1928.

(D) Ķelpe, Jānis. "Ivande Kaija par sevi" (Ivande Kaija on herself). Jānis Ķelpe, ed. *Sieviete latvju rakstniecībā* (Woman in Latvian writing). Jelgava, 1936.

(D) Muchka, Astrīda. "Par Ivandes Kaijas pēdējām dienām un bērēm" (The last days and funeral of Ivande Kaija). In *Literārā gadagrāmata Zari* (Literary almanac Branches). Stockholm: The Baltic Scientific Institute in Scandinavia, 1986.

(E) Jēger-Freimane, Paula. *Atziņu ceļi: teātris, literatūra, dzīve* (The routes of ideas: theater, literature, life). Rīga, 1936.

KAL'MANOVICH, Anna Andreevna (dates of birth and death unknown)

Russian feminist activist from Saratov; one of the first to speak out publicly for women's equal political rights in the period leading up to the 1905 Revolution and one of the few Jewish women active in the movement. Steered an independent course between women's rights advocates aligned with liberal or socialist parties; supporter of suffragism; attended the congress of the International Council of Women (ICW) in Berlin (1904), as well as congresses of the International Woman Suffrage Alliance (IWSA).

Anna Andreevna Kal'manovich (personal and family data unknown) had a public career which by the 1905 Russian Revolution had moved from philanthropy in the 1890s to radical feminism. In 1893, she founded the *Saratovskoe Evreiskoe Popechitel'stvo o Bol'nykh* (Saratov Hebrew Society for the Care of the Sick), remaining its President until 1904. She also founded a children's committee and served as liaison to the local society for poor relief before becoming immersed in feminist activities. She gave her first public speech–a report on the 1904 Berlin Congress of the International Council of Women, originally written for Mariia Pokrovskaia's *Zhenskii Vestnik* (Women's herald)–in December 1904, in which she elaborated upon key elements of her feminist politics: her interest in, and ties to the international feminist movement; her advocacy of an independent feminist position distinct from those defined by 'male politics,' and her proud description of herself as a feminist.

Kal'manovich's husband was Samuil Eremeevich Kal'manovich, a prominent defense lawyer involved in many of the major political trials leading up to, and during the 1905 Revolution. They had children but names, birthdates and numbers are unknown. Barely escaping the wrecking of their apartment in 1905, as the extreme nationalist and anti-Semitic *Chernosotentsy* (Black Hundreds) was scapegoating Jews for the failures of the tsarist regime at home and abroad, the Kal'manoviches fled Saratov and soon after left Russia. Two years in exile gave Anna Kal'manovich the opportunity to strengthen her contacts with foreign feminists and develop her talents as a public speaker. She attended International Woman Suffrage Alliance (IWSA) congresses in Copenhagen (1906) and Amsterdam (1908). She lectured on the women's movement to Russian groups in Geneva, Lausanne and Zurich, and took part in a debate on women's rights organized by professors at the University of Geneva. Kal'manovich observed that women encounter hostility only when they seek democratic rights for themselves: they were not, she argued, "fighting against men, but against ignorance, selfishness and prejudice" (Kal'manovich 1908, 35, 37; R. R. trans). It was around this period that two of Kal'manovich's daughters emigrated–at least temporarily–to Argentina.

Returning to Russia, Kal'manovich participated in meetings of the *Soiuz Ravnopraviia Zhenshchin* (Women's Equal Rights Union) and wrote for the leading feminist periodicals *Soiuz Zhenshchin* (Union of women) and *Zhenskii Vestnik* (Woman's herald). She also gave lectures, of which her most notable and controversial was delivered to the 1908 All-Russian Women's Congress. Entitled *Zhenskoe Dvizhenie i Otnosheniia Partii k Nemu* (The women's movement and how the parties relate to it), the lecture marked one of the clearest arguments by a Russian feminist for the primacy of women's oppression. For Kal'manovich women, like the proletariat, were oppressed as a class and as such, they had to fight for their own liberation. Facing vocal opposition from socialists and liberals, Kal'manovich, citing her husband and sons, decried those who called her a man-hater and declared herself a "patriot for women" (lecture reprinted in Aivazdova, ed. 1998, 205–219).

After the 1908 Congress, Kal'manovich and many other *Soiuz* activists (such as ***Mariia Chekhova***, ***Zinaida Mirovich***, Liudmila Ruttsen and ***Ariadna Tyrkova***) joined the *Liga ravnopraviia zhenshchin* (League for Women's Equal Rights), continuing their feminist agitation as the democratic hopes kindled by the 1905 Revolution faded further from view. Kal'manovich spoke at the *Pervyi Vserossiiskii S'ezd po Bor'be s Torgom Zhenshchinami* (First All-Russian Congress on the Struggle against the Trade in Women), held on 21–25 April 1910. She contested the claims of both government representatives, who defended state regulation of prostitution, and Marxists, who argued that prostitution was an outgrowth of capitalism–demanding that attention be paid to gender discrimination in prostitution and calling for the abolition of state-regulated prostitution.

During this time, Kal'manovich's interest in the suffrage movement intensified, particularly in the militant struggle of English suffragettes such as the Pankhursts. Her pamphlet *Suffrazhistki i Suffrazhetki* (Suffragists and suffragettes) was published in 1911 and her translation of Christabel Pankhurst's condemnation of male immorality, *The Great Scourge and How to End It*, appeared in 1914 in Russian (under the title *Strashnyi bich i sredstvo ego unichtozhii*).

Kal'manovich's fate after the 1917 Bolshevik Revolution is unknown.

Rochelle Goldberg Ruthchild
The Union Institute and University and the Davis Center for Russian and Eurasian Studies, Harvard University

SOURCES

(A) A short autobiographical sketch written by Kalmanovich in 1913 can be found in the *Rossiiskii gosudarstvennyi arkhiv literatury i iskusstva* (*RGALI*, Russian State Archive of Literature and Art), Moscow, Fond 1018, "Praskov'ia Ariian," opis 1, delo 116. Kalmanovich says nothing about her family but the autobiography is written on stationery from her husband's law practice.

(C) Kal'manovich, Anna Andreevna. *Otchet o zhenskom mezhdunarodnom kongresse 1904g* (Report on the 1904 International Congress). Saratov: G. K. Shel'gorn, 1905.

(C) Kal'manovich, Anna Andreevna. *Zhenskoe dvizhenie i ego zadachi* (The woman's movement and its aims). St Petersburg: Rabotnik, 1908. Excerpts from pages 1-4, translated by Karen L. Myers, can be found in Robin Bisha, Jehanne M. Gheith, Christine Holden, and William G. Wagner, eds. *Russian Women, 1698-1917: Experience and Expression. An Anthology of Sources*. Bloomington: Indiana University Press, 2002, 321-324.

(C) Kal'manovich, Anna Andreevna. *Pretenzii k zhenskomu dvizheniiu voobshche i k I-mu Vserossiiskomu zhenskomu s'ezdu v chastnosti* (Demands of the women's movement in general and of the First All-Russian Women's Congress in particular). St Petersburg: Tip. TS. Kraiz, 1910.

(C) Kal'manovich, Anna Andreevna. *Suffrazhistki i suffrazhetki* (Suffragists and suffragettes). St Petersburg: Tip. B. M. Vol'f, 1911.

(C) Kal'manovich, Anna Andreevna. *Zhenskoe dvizhenie i otnoshenie partii k nemu* (The woman's movement and the attitude of the parties to it). St Petersburg: B. M. Vol'f, 1911. Reprinted in Svetlana Aivazova, ed. (with introductory essay) *Russkie zhenshchiny v labirinte ravnoproviia. Ocherki politicheskoi teorii i istorii. Dokumental'nye materialy* (Russian women in the labyrinth of equal rights. Essays on political theory and history. Documentary materials). Moscow: RIK Rusanova, 1998, 205-219.

(E) Goldberg, Rochelle (Ruthchild). *The Russian Women's Movement, 1859-1917*. Doctoral Dissertation. University of Rochester, 1976.

(E) Grishina, Zoia V. *Zhenskie organizatsii v Rossii (1905g.-fevral'/mart 1917 g)* (Women's organizations in Russia, February 1905-March 1917). Doctoral Dissertation. Moscow State University, 1978.

(E) Stites, Richard. *The Women's Liberation Movement in Russia: Feminism, Nihilism, and Bolshevism, 1860-1930*. Princeton: Princeton University Press, 1978; 1991.

(E) Edmondson, Linda Harriet. *Feminism in Russia 1900-1917*. Stanford: Stanford University Press, 1983.

(E) Aivazova, Svetlana, ed. *Russkie zhenshchiny v labirinte ravnoproviia. Ocherki politicheskoi teorii i istorii. Dokumental'nye materialy* (Russian women in the labyrinth of equal rights. Essays on political theory and history. Documentary materials). Moscow: RIK Rusanova, 1998.

KALNIŅA, Klāra (born Veilande) (1874–1964)

Activist in the *Latvijas Sociāldemokrātiskā strādnieku partija* (Latvian Social Democratic Labor Party) and member of its Central Committee; spokeswoman for women's rights and member of the Latvian Constitutional Assembly; member of the Women's Committee of the Socialist International (1923).

Klāra Kalniņa in emigration in Stockholm

Anna-Luize Klāra Veilande was born in Vanci on 24 February 1874, into a family of farmers. She became interested in women's emancipation and rights early on while a student at the Doroteja (four-grade) school for girls in Jelgava, which she attended from 1887 to 1890. The language of instruction at the school was German; the teachers of the Baltic German elite did not support the education of Latvians but sought to cultivate "Germanness," as Klāra Veilande put it, writing of herself that "I, on the other hand, was intent on emphasizing that I was Latvian." Regarding the instruction of women however, it was not only German teachers who "opposed women's education and participation in public life ... the Latvian intelligentsia also considered women's aspirations for higher education and equal rights with men as damaging to family values" (Kalniņa 1964, 20).

The idea that women could struggle for equal rights with men and develop higher aspirations was becoming popular among students, yet many "were unable to specify these goals" (Kalniņa 1964, 25). A priority for many was the struggle for the highest possible welfare of humanity as a whole, which included full rights for women (following the ideas of revolutionary thinkers such as Klara Zetkin). Together with other Latvian students–e.g. Anastasia Cikste and Late Veibele–Klāra Veilande organized a literary group named *Austra* (Aurora), whose aim was to struggle against mainstream views regarding women and against the German bourgeois '4K' model (*Kinder, Kuche, Kirche, Kleider*). The group's journal *Vārpas* (Wheat ears, 1889–1890) circulated among students; later, its editorial team included Olga Liberte, Milda Liberte, Olga Bērtule and Lūcija (among others). In 1894, Klāra Veilande was admitted to the sixth grade of the newly opened Jelgava women's gymnasium, graduating in 1897 after having successfully completed the seventh grade. At the same time, she became actively involved in *Jaunā Strāva* (The Young Latvians' Movement 'The New Current'), as well as in workers' educational group meetings. As she wrote later in her memoirs, the organizers of such groups found it difficult to attract women because of the 'double burden' women were expected to carry: i.e. duties both at work and at home. In 1895, Veilande met Pauls Kalniņš (1872–1945), a student of medicine at Tartu University, who in time would become the great love of her life and her husband (1898).

The end of the 1890s was a time of new ideological currents influencing youth movements and the intelligentsia across the Russian Empire. In Latvia, new ideas were sifted through illegal socialist literature from Germany, as well as legal German and Russian periodicals. Together with her husband Pauls Kalniņš, Klāra Veilande–now Kalniņa–participated in the meetings of the first social democratic groups. Later, like many young women from Latvia, Kalniņa went to St Petersburg to continue her education, although, as she wrote in her memoirs, "[t]raining in dentistry was not compatible with my interest in philosophy and the social sciences" (Kalniņa 1964, 39). She actively participated in the activities of the Social Democrats in St Petersburg but in 1896, financial difficulties forced her to abandon her studies in St Petersburg and she returned home to continue her studies there.

From 1901 to 1903, Kalniņa was active in the organization of the social democratic group in Kurzeme (one of the four regions of Latvia). In 1903, she emigrated from Russia to live in Germany and Switzerland. Kalniņa and her husband were still in emigration during the Russian Revolution of 1905, when strikes and mutinies by both the rural and urban proletariat broke out in the Baltic littoral. The couple immediately returned to Latvia, where they witnessed revolution, repression and counter-revolution. They emigrated again in 1906, but were later invited back to Latvia by the *Latvijas Sociāldemokrātiskā strādnieku partija* (*LSDSP*, Latvian Social Democratic Labor Party) to carry out illegal revolutionary activities. Klāra Kalniņa joined the editorial group of the social democratic newspaper *Cīņa* (Struggle, 1907–1910) and from 1911 to 1914, worked in a legal capacity for other social democratic newspapers. In 1917, Kalniņa represented the *LSDSP* as a member of Riga City Council. In the period 1918–1922, she was a member of the Central Committee of the *LSDSP*, participating in the meeting held on 18 November 1918 at the National Theater of Riga, at which Latvian independence was proclaimed. In 1922, Kalniņa became an elected member of the Latvian Constitutional Assembly.

When the Constitution of The Republic of Latvia was adopted in 1922, the Constitutional Assembly was dissolved. In her memoirs, Kalniņa wrote: "my political work in the upper ranks of the Parliament and party was over. The party leadership acknowledged that in terms of tactics, it would be wrong to promote three members of the Kalniņa family (Paul, [my son] Brūno and myself) as candidates to the elections of the First Parliament. My candidacy was thus withdrawn and I was not elected to the Central Committee of the party. As we had party lists for the elections, women-candidates were crossed off by the voters. This happened to ***Aspazija*** as well" (Kalniņa 1964, 135).

In the 1920s, Klāra Kalniņa was relegated to the political margins as a woman and later, as a leftist. But she remained a long-term member of the Riga Committee of the *LSDSP*, as well as establishing and leading the women's section of the party and working for the health committee of Riga City Council. For many years, she was a member of the *Kopēja arodbiedrības valde* (United Trade Union Board), and she frequently represented the *LSDSP* at the congresses of the Socialist International (Hamburg, 1923; Marseilles, 1925; Brussels, 1928). In 1923, she became an elected member of the Women's Committee of the Socialist International and from 1930, a member of its Presidium.

From 1923 to 1930, Klāra Kalniņa worked as editor-in-chief of the Latvian journal *Darba Sieviete* (The working woman) and translated several key socialist texts into Latvian: K. Kautsky's *Sozialismus und Kolonialpolitik* (Socialism and colonial policy); K. Marx's *Bürgerkrieg in Frankreich* (The civil war in France) and A. Bebel's *Die Frau und der Sozialismus* (Woman and socialism). She also published widely on gender politics and other political and social issues in the journal *Jaunais Laiks* (New times). After the proclamation of Kārlis Ulmanis's authoritarian regime in 1934, Kalniņa's husband and son were imprisoned (as were many other Social Democrats), her husband later emigrating to Austria and her son Bruno, to Finland. Klāra Kalniņa participated in the activities of the illegal National Council of Latvia under the Nazi regime in Latvia. After the death of her husband in 1945, she herself emigrated to Sweden, where she continued her political activities as a Social Democrat and a political figure in the Latvian community-in-exile until her own death in 1964.

Irina Novikova
University of Latvia

SOURCES

(B) Brant, Līlīja. *Latviešu sieviete* (The Latvian woman). Riga: A/S Valters un Rapa Ģenerālkommisijā, 1931.

(C) Kalniņa, Klāra. *Liesmainie Gadi* (Flaming years). Stockholm: LSDSP Ārzemju Komitejas izdevums, 1964.

KÁNYA (Kanya), Emilia; Mrs Mór Szegfi (1830-1905)

Hungarian writer, publicist and translator; first female editor in the Austro-Hungarian Empire; advocate of the women's cause. Pen-name: 'Emilia.'

Emilia Kánya, 1847. Photograph of a painting attributed to Miklós Barabás (1810–1898).

Emilia Kánya was born on 10 November 1830 into a highly educated middle-class family in Pest-Ofen, Hungary. Little is known about her family background and early years. Her mother was Zsuzsanna Buro (no data); her father, Pál Kánya (1794-1876), was a teacher, later the director of a local Protestant secondary school and parish notary. Emilia received the same education as her father's students and was taught French, English, music and drawing.

In 1847, after an unhappy experience in love at the age of seventeen, she married Gottfried Feldinger, the son of a rich businessman. The couple moved to Temesvár (today Timisoara, Romania). From 1851, they published a journal in German entitled *Euphrosine*. Mrs Feldinger had an active role in editing the journal, partially due to her husband's blindness, and in this way entered contemporary circles of men of letters, making connections which would prove invaluable to her editorial activity later on. The marriage ended in divorce in 1857 and she moved to Pest to her father's residence.

In 1857, to support herself and her children, Emilia Kánya (no longer using her former husband's name) began publishing short stories, translations and biographies. She soon became an acknowledged writer and published in journals such as *Napkelet* (Sunrise), *Hölgyfutár* (Women's courier), *Szépirodalmi Közlöny* (Literary gazette) and *Divatcsarnok* (Hall of fashion) under her pen-name 'Emilia.' Her short stories were later collected in edited volumes and she also wrote etiquette books for girls. In 1860, she married Mór Szegfi (1825-1896), a well-educated Jewish literary man and journalist without means. From her two marriages she had eight children, almost all of whom went on to receive higher education.

Although not the first woman in pre-1867 Hungary who intended to establish a journal, 'Emilia' was the first to succeed in doing so. Reportedly, this was a suggestion made by the male editor of a popular weekly and she took up the idea. In October 1860, after a long and arduous struggle with the authorities, she finally received permission to launch *Családi Kör* (Family circle), a weekly journal that ran until 1880.

The journal *Családi Kör* published many articles by 'Emilia' herself, as well as the writings of young literary talents and amateurs; it included biographies with wood-engraved portraits, journalistic pieces, short stories, events listings, entertainment, poems, news, needlework and dressmaking patterns, housekeeping and cooking. 'Emilia' often performed services for rural subscribers such as shopping (for example once, at the request of a regular woman reader, she bought and shipped three dresses with the same pattern for a special occasion).

In addition to editing the journal (with the help of her husband as co-editor), Mrs Mór Szegfi born Kánya also compiled volumes of her short stories, published novels and created a series entitled *Magyar Hölgyek Könyvtára* (Library of Hungarian Ladies), consisting of more than one hundred volumes. The series started from 1867 with a novel of her own entitled *Búvirágok* (Flowers of sadness, 1867). In the years 1861, 1862, 1863 and 1864, she edited the *Magyar Nők Évkönyve* (Hungarian Women Yearbook), which contained biographies of famous Hungarian women from the past and was designed to contribute to the patriotic education of Hungarian women. She also translated books for girls.

The activities of this female writer and editor in the 1860s stirred sometimes hostile debates between her and famous literary male figures over the role of women in society and in literary life. As the editor of *Családi Kör*, 'Emilia' believed women could perform an important role in society, animating the public sphere and especially the field of literature, which she regarded as a main vehicle for conveying patriotic ideas. Her approach should be understood in the political context of the pre-1867 neo-absolutist era, when the extended family circle served as an autonomous public sphere for the preservation of Hungarian national values. In this milieu, she advocated the rights of women to education and to an independent living from their intellectual work, as well as the general advancement of women in Hungarian society. She was involved in founding and raising funds for various organizations and associations: the *Magyar Gazdaasszonyok Egyesülete* (Association of Hungarian Farmer Women); the *Országos Nőképző Egyesület* (*ONKE*, National Association for Women's Education) and the *Országos Nőipar Egyesület* (*ONE*, National Women's Trade Association) with its *Nőipariskola* (Women's Trade School). She is considered to be the founder of the *Magyar Írók Segélyegylete* (Hungarian Writers' Aid Association) and of the *Petőfi Társaság* (Petőfi Society), though she was not a member of these organizations. From 1864 onwards, her weekly *Családi Kör* became the official journal of the *Pesti Jótékony Nőegyesület* (Charity Association of Women in Pest).

As the political climate in Hungary liberalized, following Austro-Hungarian reconciliation in 1867, Mrs Mór Szegfi born Kánya benefited from the changes. She translated texts from the international women's movement (e.g. by Fanny Lewald), participated as a representative of Hungarian women, along with ***Hermin Beniczky*** (Mrs Pál Veres), in an International Women's Congress in Vienna in 1873 (exact details unknown) and lectured in German and Hungarian, advocating 'proper' family life alongside a woman's right to education and wage-earning intellectual activities.

After 1867, Mór Szegfi, who had hitherto assisted his wife with editing work, took up a post with the Ministry of Trade. In 1876, he lost his job and became a teacher in a secondary school in Lőcse (Levoča, today Slovakia). 'Emilia' remained with her children in Budapest and continued to edit the journal alone, remaining loyal to her previous ideas about women's patriotic role in society. The agenda of her journal became gradually outdated due to increasing competition between women's journals and their editors and *Családi Kör* began to lose subscribers, entering deep financial crisis. In 1880, 'Emilia' was forced to sell the journal and became the secretary of the *ONE* (National Women's Trade Association). While continuing to translate articles for a smaller journal, she had to move in with one of her married daughters, later moving again (in 1881) to the provinces, where cultural constraints and financial difficulties led to her separation from her husband. In September that year, she moved with her younger unmarried daughter–then working as a teacher–to a province in northern Hungary. In December 1884, they left the poor and culturally unstimulating environment of the small town for Fiume (Rijeka, today Croatia), where her daughter was offered another teaching position and where her son was living with his family. Emilia Kánya lived in Fiume until the end of her life, relying on the material support of her youngest daughter to supplement her insufficient pension from the *Magyar Írók Segélyegylete*. There, she published a work (in German) on the death of Crown Prince Rudolf, who had previously asked her to serve as a private tutor for the royal family. This piece was later also published in Hungarian to collect money for a monument to the Prince. When her oldest daughter Irén died in 1892, Kánya fell into deep depression and from 1899, her health began to deteriorate. From 1904, she worked on her memoirs and diaries. On 10 November 1905, she died (in Fiume) and was buried in the Campo Santo Cemetery. Although her life and achievements were gradually forgotten in the periods of her life she spent away from the capital, Emilia Kánya was acknowledged at the time of her death as the first Hungarian feminist. A monument was erected upon her grave in June 1907 by the Hungarian sculptor Béla Gerenday.

Éva Bicskei
Ph.D. Candidate in History,
Central European University, Budapest

SOURCES

(A) *Evangelikus Országos Levéltár* (Hungarian National Evangelical Archive). *Kánya Emilia emlékiratai* (The memoirs of Emilia Kánya). Vols. 1-3.

(A) *Országos Magyar Széchenyi Könyvtár Kézirattára* (Manuscript Collection of the Hungarian National Széchenyi Library): XX sz. Fol. Hung. 3314. Kánya Emilia, "'Szanaszét' Napló" ('Far and wide.' Diary); *Levelestár* (Collection of letters), Szegfi Mórné, Kánya Emilia, Emilia; Fol. Hung. 2157. 11. Fasc. 18/1-9. Rozsnyai Kálmán. "Emilia."

(B) Hentaller, Mariska Faylné. *A magyar irónőkről* (On Hungarian women writers). Budapest, 1889.

(B) Harmath, Lujza. *Magyar írónők albuma* (Album of Hungarian women writers). Budapest, 1890.

(C) Emilia. *Sziv és élet* (Heart and life). Pest: Emich, 1859. Vols. 1-2.

(C) Emilia. *Beszélyek* (Short stories). Pest: Khór, 1860. Vols. 1-2.

(C) Emilia. *Válságos napok* (Days of crisis). Pest: self-published, 1860. Vols. 1-2.

(C) Emilia. *Beszélyek az ifjúság számára. Vachot Sándornéval* (Short stories for young people. With Mrs Sándor Vachot). Pest: Engel, 1861.

(C) Emilia. *Szeretet könyve* (Book of love). Pest: Emich, 1863-1864. Vols. 1-2.

(C) Emilia. *Authentische Enthüllungen über den Tod des Kronprinzen Rudolph von Österreich* (Authentic revelations of the death of Crown Prince Rudolph of Austria). Leipzig, 1889; second (Hungarian) edition. *Rudolf trónörökös emléke* (In memory of Crown Prince Rudolf). Budapest, 1905.

(D) Szaffner, Emília. "Az első magyar szerkesztőnő és lapja, a Családi Kör" (The first Hungarian female editor and her weekly, the Family Circle). *Magyar Könyvszemle* 114, no. 4 (1998): 353-371.

(E) Orosz, Lajos. *A magyar nőnevelés úttörői* (The pioneers of the education of women in Hungary). Budapest: Tankönyvkiadó, 1962.

(E) Fábri, Anna. *A nő és hivatása. Szemelvények a magyarországi nőkérdés történetéből 1777-1865* (Woman and her vocation. Selections from the history of the woman question in Hungary, 1777-1865). Budapest: Kortárs, 1995.

(E) Fábri, Anna. '*A szép tiltott táj felé.' A magyar írőnők története két századforduló között (1795-1905)*" ['Toward a nice, forbidden land.' The history of Hungarian women writers between two turns of century (1795-1905)]. Budapest: Kortárs Kiadó, 1996.

KARACS, Teréz (1808-1892)

Hungarian writer, pedagogue, teacher and memorialist; advocate of female emancipation through education.

Teréz Karacs was born on 18 April 1808 in Pest-Ofen, Hungary. Her family was highly educated and Protestant, of modest means. Her father, Ferenc Karacs (1770-1838), was an engineer and qualified engraver of maps and illustrations. Her mother, Éva Takács (1779-1845), was a publicist and active participant in debates over the role of women in society in the 1820s.

From 1814 to 1819, Teréz attended the Protestant elementary school for boys and girls in Pest, missing one year due to illness. As the second of six children (three died in early childhood, two elder and one younger), she had to nurse her younger brothers and sisters and assist her mother in the household. Since her parents could not afford to pay for private lessons, she taught herself Hungarian and German literature, and history.

Growing up under the influence of a 'Protestant work ethic' and enlightened ideas regarding the role of women in society, the Karacs daughters received practical training in skills that would secure their material independence, such as needlework or coloring their father's engravings (typical female wage-earning activities in the eighteenth and nineteenth centuries). Apart from these activities, Teréz also participated in heated discussions and other educational events at her home, a meeting place for intellectuals and artists. In October 1824, she was invited by a family friend to spend ten months in Vienna, an experience that enhanced her education.

Teréz Karacs's memoirs allude to love affairs, but it seems none led to marriage. From 1822, she published riddles in entertaining and literary journals such as *Kedveskedő* (Endearing) and *Hasznos Mulatságok* (Useful entertainments). She translated poems from German and wrote her own (love) poems, published in journals such as *Hébé* (Hebe, 1824); *Urania* (Urania, 1829); and *Regélő* (Storyteller, 1833; 1836). In the 1830s, she published a series of short stories with moral lessons, sympathetically dealing with transgressions of love beyond class and ethnic barriers. These were published in the journals *Koszorú* (Wreath, 1833) and *Rajzolatok* (Sketches, 1835; 1838). Throughout her publishing career, Karacs always stressed her intellectual freedom, rejecting stylistic or thematic changes by male editors and asking for financial reward for her intellectual work, which was uncommon at the time. She was a regular contributor to several literary journals at a time when the female writer was still regarded as an exceptional phenomenon. In 1838, she published the humorous *Játékszini terv* (Plan for a playwright); in the preface to this work, she presented writing as a test or riddle, asking her readers which tool they thought provided a woman with a more successful living: "the needle or the pen?"

In 1838, her father and brothers died. These misfortunes were coupled with financial losses caused by the 1840 flood and Karacs moved to Máramarossziget (Sighetu Marmației, today Romania). There, she worked as a housekeeper on an aristocratic estate but did not stop publishing in literary journals. Her works appeared in *Regélő* (1842), *Pesti Divatlap* (Pest fashion magazine, 1844), *Honderű* (Brightness of the homeland, 1843–1846) and *Életképek* (Subject pictures, 1844–1846). Her writings focused on women's education, a topic of patriotic debate in the period, and she pleaded for equal curricula for girls and boys, emphasizing the patriotic and practical education of middle-class girls in institutions run by local communities. She also advocated the right of unmarried women to become self-reliant by entering trade or gaining positions of office.

In 1844, Karacs was invited by the local Protestant community to run a school for girls in Miskolc (northern Hungary). Yet prior to taking up the position with the Miskolc school (August 1846) and after the death of her mother (1845), Karacs was invited by Countess Blanka Teleki–who wished to open a patriotic and enlightened school for girls of the aristocracy–to come to Pest as her guest. Karacs opposed Teleki's ideas about private schools and education for upper-class girls; her goal was the patriotic and practical education of young middle-class girls in institutions supported by local communities. Therefore when Teleki offered her a position at her school, Karacs refused, proposing Klára Leövey instead. Nevertheless, she called for public support for Teleki's institution and spent half a year with Teleki visiting educational institutions, attending conferences and preparing to teach in Miskolc.

Countess Blanka Teleki was born on 5 July 1806 in Hosszúfalva (Săcele, today Romania). A talented woman, she prepared herself for a professional artistic career, which was unusual for the times. She pursued her studies in painting in Munich and Paris (at the Cogniet studio) and learned sculpture from the Hungarian István Ferenczy in Buda (Ofen). In addition, she became a renowned female pedagogue, dedicating her life to and advocating the higher education of young girls, influenced heavily by her aunt, Teréz Brunswick (Brunszvik, 1775–1861), the founder of the first kindergarten in Hungary in 1828. After publishing her views on the education of women, Teleki opened her institute for young girls in 1846. In 1848, Teleki's pupils signed the first petition on the equality of men and women in Hungary, demanding the rights of women to attend university and to vote. For her patriotic public and revolutionary activities, Teleki was sentenced to prison after the fall of the revolution, where she created several small sculptures, including self-portraits (it is believed that one of them was sent to Michelet in France). After her release in 1857, Teleki left Hungary. She died in Paris on 23 October 1862.

Klára Leövey (Löwey, Lövei, Lővei, born Máramarossziget, 25 March 1821–died Budapest, 8 April 1897), pedagogue, writer and teacher of girls, was employed at Karacs's suggestion as governess at Blanka Teleki's institute from its inception. After the school closed in 1848, Leövey left for Debrecen (eastern Hungary), the new center of the revolution, where she worked as a nurse with other renowned Hungarian women. After the fall of the revolution, Leövey taught at schools for girls in Transylvania while participating in the patriotic resistance, as a result of which she was imprisoned in Kufstein (Austria) with Blanka Teleki (1851). Leövey was released in 1856 and returned to Máramarossziget, where she ran her own educational establishment for young girls. In 1862, she left for Paris with Blanka Teleki and, upon her return, taught the children of the Teleki family in Máramarossziget, contributing regularly to a local journal called *Máramaros* (Maramureş).

Teréz Karacs ran her school for girls in Miskolc until June 1859. It was financed by the local Protestant community and parent contributions, but did not automatically exclude students who could not pay. Karacs taught all subjects with the exception of German, needlework, singing and drawing. From the 1850s onwards, French, dance and music were added to the curriculum and taught by specialists. School exams were held on American Independence Day, symbolically linking the freedom of the nation to the liberation of women. In the thirteen years between 1846 and 1859, Karacs educated around 860 to 885 pupils, many of whom would subsequently become teachers.

Karacs attended the important 1848 Teachers Congress in Pest, although she did not deliver a speech. Her school functioned during the 1848 revolution too, when her students prepared clothing for the army. In 1853, her short stories were edited in two volumes.

After 1859, Karacs left for Kolozsvár (Cluj, today Romania) to lead the Protestant community school for girls there. When Protestant leaders refused to accommodate pupils comfortably (in terms of space), Karacs left Kolozsvár in December 1863, having taught an estimated 430 to 460 girls. For about two years, she was tutor to the daughters of Count Miksa Teleki (the younger brother of Blanka Teleki) in Doboka (Dăbâca, today Romania) and Kendi Lóna (Luna de Jos, today Romania) while Klára Leövey was in Paris. In 1865, Karacs left for Pest, where she gave private lessons in grammar, female etiquette, history and geography to between 96 and 140 girls of aristocratic and upper middle-class backgrounds.

In 1877, due to her age and low income, Karacs retired to the provincial town of Kiskunhalas to stay with the daughters of her eldest sister (who had at one time been her pupils in Miskolc, later becoming teachers themselves). In the summer of 1885, Karacs suffered a stroke that left her paralyzed down her left side and she moved to Békés to stay with her nephew. In 1886, she received an invitation from the *Mária*

Dorothea Egyesület (*MDE*, Mária Dorothea Association, an organization assisting women teachers) to live in *MDE* lodgings. Karacs declined, preferring to remain with her family. She supported herself with a pension from Count Miksa Teleki and a meager sum from the *Magyar Írók Segélyegylete* (Hungarian Writers' Aid Association). In the 1880s, her memoirs–in which she presented her childhood, her parents, her activities in the field of women's education, life in old Pest, her lifelong interest in the Hungarian theater and famous literary men–were acclaimed by literary personalities. They were published in *Fővárosi Lapok* (News from the capital city) in 1880, 1881, 1885 and 1888; and in *Nemzeti Nőnevelés* (National women's education) in 1885. These publications provided Karacs with some additional income.

In 1888, on her 80th birthday, Teréz Karacs was celebrated for her contribution to female education in different journals and a modest local celebration was held in Békés. Her literary merits have not, however, been fully recognized to this day. Karacs died on 2 October 1892 in Békés.

Éva Bicskei
Ph.D. Candidate in History,
Central European University, Budapest

SOURCES

(A) *Tiszántúli Református Egyházkerületi és Kollégiumi Nagykönyvtár. Kézirattár* (Library of the Tiszántúl Reform Church and Collegium. Manuscript collection). *Karacs Teréz életéből jegyzetek* (Notes from the life of Teréz Karacs). Kézirat, 1885. R759/3.

(A) *Országos Magyar Széchenyi Könyvtár Kézirattára* (Manuscript Collection of the Hungarian National Széchenyi Library). *Levelestár* (Collection of letters): Karacs Teréz.

(B) Naményi, Lajos, ed. *A régi magyar szinészetről* (On old Hungarian theater). Arad: Széchenyi Irodalmi Intézet, 1888.

(B) Hentaller, Mariska Faylné. *A magyar irónőkről* (On Hungarian women writers). Budapest, 1889.

(B) Harmath, Lujza. *Magyar írónők albuma* (Album of Hungarian women writers). Budapest, 1890, 184.

(C) Karacs, Teréz. *Játékszini terv* (Plan for a playwright) (1834). Esztergom, 1838.

(C) Karacs, Teréz. "Néhány szó a nőnevelésről" (Some words on the education of women). *Életképek* (Life subjects) II (1845): 549–555; 581–586; 613–618; 645–648.

(C) Karacs, Teréz. "Viszhang a magyar főrendű nők neveltetése ügyében emelt 'Szózatra'" (Echo of the 'Manifesto' calling for the education of Hungarian aristocratic women). *Honderű* (Brightness of the homeland) I (1846): 21–24.

(C) Karacs, Teréz. "Még egy hang a társadalmi összeforrásról" (One more word on social unity). *Életképek* I (1846): 349–356.

(C) Karacs, Teréz. "Nyilt levél a magyar nőkhöz" (Open letter to Hungarian women). *Életképek* II (1846): 11–13.

(C) Karacs, Teréz. "Erdélyi Róza jegyzeteinek átnézése" (Review of the notes of Róza Erdélyi). *Honderű* I (1846): 189-191; 209-212.

(C) Karacs, Teréz. "Egy veterán irónő emlékezései" (Memories of an old woman writer). *Magyarország és a Nagyvilág* (Hungary and the world) (1881): 710.

(C) Karacs, Teréz. "Egy igaz magyar nevelőnő életéből" (From the life of a true Hungarian governess). *Nemzeti Nőnevelés* (National women's education) (1882).

(C) Karacs, Teréz. *Karacs Teréz összes munkái* (The collected works of Teréz Karacs). Ádám Takács, ed. Vols. 1-2. Miskolc, 1853.

(C) Karacs, Teréz. *Karacs Teréz művei* (The works of Teréz Karacs). Gyula, 1889.

(D) Evva, Gabriella. *A magyar nőnevelés két úttörője. Karacs Ferencné és Karacs Terézia nőnevelési nézetei* (Two pioneers of the education of women in Hungary. Mrs Ferenc Karacs and Terézia Karacs on the education of women). Szeged: Ferenc József Tudományegyetem Pedagógiai Intézete, 1933.

(D) Evva, Gabriella. *Karacs Teréz centennáriumi emlékfüzet* (Centennial commemorative booklet for Teréz Karacs). Miskolc: Tóth Pál Ref. Tanitóképző Intézet Karacs Teréz Önképzőköre, 1948.

(D) Sáfrán, Györgyi. *Teleki Blanka és köre. Karacs Teréz, Teleki Blanka, Lővei Klára* (Blanka Teleki and her circle. Teréz Karacs, Blanka Teleki, Klára Lővei). Budapest: Szépirodalmi Könyvkiadó, 1963.

(E) Orosz, Lajos. *A magyar nőnevelés úttörői* (The pioneers of the education of women in Hungary). Budapest: Tankönyvkiadó, 1962.

(E) Fábri, Anna. *A nő és hivatása. Szemelvények a magyarországi nőkérdés történetéből 1777-1865* (Woman and her vocation. Selections from the history of the women's question in Hungary 1777-1865). Budapest: Kortárs, 1995.

(E) Fábri, Anna. *'A szép tiltott táj felé.' A magyar írónők története két századforduló között (1795-1905)* ['Toward a nice, forbidden land.' A history of Hungarian women writers between two turns of the century (1795-1905)]. Budapest: Kortárs, 1996.

(E) Kereszty, Orsolya. "Az 1848-as forradalom sajtója a nőkérdésről" (The press and the woman question during the 1848 revolution). *Magyar Könyvszemle* (Hungarian book review) 115, no. 1 (1999): 106-113.

KARAMICHAILOVA, Elissaveta Ivanova (Kara-Michailova, Elizabeth) (1897-1968)

Nuclear physicist; first woman Associate Professor at Sofia University; member of the *Druzhestvo na Bulgarkite s Visshe Obrazovanie* (DBVO, Association of Bulgarian Women with Higher Education).

Elissaveta Karamichailova was born on 22 August 1897 in Vienna, one of the three children of the Bulgarian surgeon Ivan Karamichailov (1866-1961) and Mary Slade, an English pianist born in Oxfordshire. The cultural atmosphere in the family was augmented by the presence of Ivan's sister, Elena Karamichailova, the first Bulgarian post-impressionist painter (who studied in Germany). Elissaveta Karamichailova was also greatly influenced by her father, who was descended from an old merchant family from Shoumen and believed in national and Enlightenment ideals. He financed the education of his two sisters and three children and, instead of making a career in Austria, returned to Bulgaria to establish a private clinic, as well as founding and running a Red Cross hospital on a voluntary basis.

Elissaveta thus spent her childhood in Vienna, receiving her education at home from her mother and mastering English and German. In 1917, after the family had returned to Bulgaria in 1907, she completed her six years of study at the most elite girls' secondary school in the country (in Sofia), where–her teachers being feminist activists–she became acquainted with the Bulgarian feminist movement.

Elissaveta Karamichailova subsequently enrolled at the University of her native Vienna, where she studied physics and mathematics (1917-1920). She managed to alternate between compulsory lectures and classes in philosophy, history of art and astronomy. She was good company and her broad general knowledge strongly impressed her colleagues.

In 1922, Karamichailova defended a doctoral thesis in nuclear physics and began working for the *Institut für Radiumforschung* (Vienna Radium Institute), a significant moment in her professional and personal development. Over the following thirteen years, Karamichailova hoped that Vienna would become the leading center for nuclear research, ahead of Paris or Cambridge. With determination and dedication, she began expanding her scientific field of expertise, specializing in electrical and radio engineering (at the Vienna *Polytechnic*), the only fields that were accessible to women. The research she carried out and published in association with her colleagues–on radioluminescence, gamma radiation and the radiation of polonium–is relevant to this day and at the time represented a giant step forward in physics. According to specialists Georgi Nadjakov and Hristo Hristov, Karamichailova and her co-author Marietta Blau were only a step away from the discovery of neutrons, but since they did not publish their results immediately, preferring to check them once more, the fame went to someone else. Karamichailova's work at the *Institut für Radiumforschung* brought her into a close circle of friends, including Elizabeth Róna, Marietta Blau and Berta Karlik. These were internationally renowned researchers who socialized together, supported one another professionally and were strongly attached to each other. This atmosphere of mutual support encouraged the women physicists to seek support from international organizations in the form of scholarships, thereby enabling them to enter scientific units known to be conservative with regard to applications from women. Karamichailova (probably as a member of the Austrian branch of the IFUW) became a member of the International Federation of University Women (then under the leadership of the physician Professor Ellen Gleditsch) and applied for a scholarship. In 1935, the IFUW, together with the Yarrow and Rockefeller Foundations, granted Karamichailova a three-year scholarship to Girton women's college in Cambridge (from which women could not graduate until 1947), where she worked in the Cavendish Laboratory run by Lord Rutherford. Karamichailova published important research on the energy of gamma rays emitted by actinium and on the ionization of gasses under pressure; she also discovered the division of nuclei under the impact of slow neutrons (1938). In 1939, towards the end of her stay in Britain, she taught at Girton College and visited colleagues in Norway, Sweden, Denmark, the Netherlands, Belgium and France, meeting Elizabeth Róna (among others). She rejected an invitation to work at the University of Halle in Germany.

Elissaveta Karamichailova stated in her autobiography (published in Lazarova in 1995) that her main reason for coming back to Sofia was to obtain an associate professorship at Sofia University (to which position she was elected on 12 December 1939), after having sought a permanent position there for eleven years. She required security in order to finance her research, but her return to Bulgaria was also in part due to her explicit (patriotic) wish to work in Bulgaria. After having been appointed an associate professor in experimental nuclear physics (1939), Karamichailova suppressed disappointment at not being able to continue her research work due to both lack of materials and lack of support. A deeply dedicated professional, she turned her own room at the university into a laboratory, letting the students use her own equipment for practicum, preparing appliances with materials at hand and teaching them modern scientific methods.

In reaction to the sexism of male colleagues, who refused to admit women into the seminars at the Faculty, she attempted to create a new collective culture by holding weekly tea gatherings at her own place with her students and doctoral candidates, modeled on the tea parties held at the Vienna Radium Institute. The rejection on the part of the male scientific community also led her immediately to the *Druzhestvo na Bulgarkite s Visshe Obrazovanie* (*DBVO*, Association of Bulgarian Women with Higher Education, the Bulgarian branch of the IFUW). Karamichailova had been a member of the IFUW in Austria since 1922. Her aunt, Elena Karamichailova, had been a member of the Women Artists' Section of the *DBVO* for a long time and her old classmates from the Sofia secondary school managed the organization. The *DBVO*–from 1937 headed by Tiha Bozhilova-Genova, a teacher and the wife of a Bulgarian politician–had as its goal the abolition of discriminatory rules and practices at Sofia University. It had close connections to the IFUW-Head Office and to its Chairwoman, professor Gleditsch. In the 1940s, the *DBVO* organized a series of popular lectures at which Elissaveta Karamichailova discussed contemporary scientific achievements in her field. The lectures were an occasion for the feminist press–*Zhenski glas* (Women's voice), *Zhenata* (The woman), *Vestnik na zhenata* (Woman's newspaper), among others–to praise these events, the first of their kind in Bulgarian cultural history.

The academic career and personal life of Elissaveta Karamichailova took a different turn after the Communist *coup d'état* on 9 September 1944. Along with many other prominent scientists, she was dismissed from the Faculty of Physics; her brother was forced to leave the capital and she herself was put on a list of 'unreliable scientists,' consisting of German graduates, anti-communists and non-party persons. She was accused of being under the influence of fascist ideology, of praising Germany, of valuing 'reactionary' over 'progressive' scientists and of insulting Soviet science and calling Russians "Barbarians" (Scientific Archive, Bulgarian Academy of Sciences, f.1, op. 11, a.e. 20, l.25, 36–37). While, according to her friends, Elissaveta was indeed an anti-communist, she was not opposed to Soviet science but to Soviet Party control of scientific research. At a time when her friend Róna had become a celebrity in the United States, Karamichailova–behind 'the Iron Curtain'–was prohibited from publishing, corresponding and traveling for scientific reasons. In the course of time, she was deprived of the Nuclear Physics Department she had headed (as the only nuclear specialist) and her communications with students were discontinued. Due to the protection of Georgi Nadjakov, a communist and world-famous physicist, she was given an appointment at the new Institute of Physics of the Bulgarian Academy of Science. Although she was not physically destroyed, even becoming a professor in 1962, she tended to be assigned minor practical projects researching the radioactivity of mineral spas, rocks, curative mud and soils–part of efforts to keep her away from the authorities, the university, young people and the scientific press. Censorship was lifted slightly in the 1960s, when she was able to publish some of her reports (but only as part of collective projects).

With dignity and stoicism, Karamichailova overcame her utter marginalization and tried instead to concentrate on caring for her family. Just before she died of cancer on 22 May 1968, she bequeathed all her property to the Bulgarian Academy of Science, demonstrating 'in deed' her sophisticated and generous approach to learning. This gesture did not stop the institution from continuing its prohibition of her legacy, even into the 1980s. Only two articles from the 1990s mention her, but they merely describe her activity as a physicist, not as a feminist and university professor.

Georgeta Nazarska
Higher School of Library Studies and
Information Technologies, Sofia

SOURCES

(A) Scientific Archive–Bulgarian Academy of Sciences, f. 1 (Bulgarian Academy of Sciences).
(A) Sofia State Archive, f. 994k (Sofia University).
(D) Hristov, H. "El. I. Karamichailova 1897-1968." In *Belezhiti balgarski fizici* (Eminent Bulgarian physicists). Sofia 1981, 103-112.
(D) Lazarova, P. "*Parvata: prof. d-r Elisaveta Karamichailova*" (The first one: prof. dr. Elissaveta Karamichailova). *Nauka* (Science) 2 (1995): 10-12.
(D) Tsoneva-Mathewson, Sn., M. F. Rayner-Canham and G. W. Rayner-Canham. "Elizaveta Karamihailova: Bulgarian Pioneer of Radioactivity." In M. F. Rayner-Canham and G. W. Rayner-Canham, eds. *A Devotion to their Science. Pioneer Women of Radioactivity*. Montreal-London-Buffalo: McGill University Press, 1997, 205-208.
(E) Bachmeier, P. "Die Bedeutung Wiens für die bulgarische studierende Jugend 1878-1918." In *Wegenetz europäischen Geistes*. Munich, 1987, 2: 344-361.
(E) Sretenova, N. *Universitetat I fizicite. Nachalo* (The university and the physicists. A beginning). Sofia, 2000.

KARAVELOV, Lyuben Stoychev (1834–1879)

Celebrated Bulgarian writer, poet and publicist; liberal and national revolutionary; advocate of women's equality, especially with regards to education.

Lyuben Karavelov was born in 1834 in the mountainous village of Koprivshtitsa, to Stoycho Karavelov, a well off trader, and Nedelya Doganova, a woman from a rich and educated family. Slightly literate, the parents educated the four boys of their seven children. Lyuben, the first-born, studied at the local monastery school and at the primary and middle schools of Koprivshtitsa and Plovdiv.

After the Crimean War, Russia continued its offensive with regard to 'the Eastern Question' by peaceful means. Lyuben Karavelov made use of scholarships established by the Russian Slavophils (right-wing Russian political groups supporting expansion of the Great Russian Empire into the territories of all the European Slavonic nations and Russian domination in the Straits). With a scholarship from the Slavonic Committee, he enrolled as an auditing student at the Faculty of History and Philology of Moscow University in 1859, but did not pass any examinations. He went on to educate himself further, establishing contacts with public figures (Slavophiles such as M. P. Pogodin, I. S. Aksakov, A. V. Rachinskii, V. I. Lamanskii and V. A. Kokarev; and Revolutionary Democrats such as I. G. Prizhov, I. A. Hudiakov, and A. A. Kotliarevskii), as well as working as a publicist. Karavelov felt close to the ideas expressed in newspapers such as *Kolokol* (Bell), published by Alexander Hertsen and the Revolutionary Democrat N. P. Ogaryov (1813–1877), and in the magazine *Sovremennik* (Contemporary), published by N. G. Chernishevskii, N. A. Dobroliubov and D. I. Pisarev, ideologists of the *Narodnitsi* movement. Through these publications, he became acquainted with the ideas of the Western Enlightenment, liberalism and positivism. Informed by the works of K. Foht, L. Buchner, Charles Darwin, John Draper and H. Bocl, Karavelov saw knowledge as a road to individual and collective prosperity and liberation from political and religious oppression. He admired the natural sciences, was sharply critical of the priesthood and superstition, and supported the fight to keep scientific thought independent of political and church power. The populist slogan of 'going amongst the people,' interpreted by Karavelov as an interest in traditional culture, inspired him to compose the collection *Pamjatniki narodnogo bita bolgar* (Records of Bulgarian popular customs, 1861). Later, he would fill his short novels with scenes from Bulgarian rural life, as in his *Balgari ot staro vreme* (Bulgarians of past times, 1867).

The Revolutionary Democrats' conception of national education, which opposed different levels of education on the basis of class, wealth, age or sex, also appealed to Karavelov. His sensitivity to gender developed with his reading on 'the woman question,' which was widely discussed in Russia in the 1850s and 1860s. While the Russian intelligentsia was acquainted with the works of John Stuart Mill, George Sand and the sociologist Bocl, Russian populist ideas had even greater currency—ideas which opposed low levels of girls' education and the placement of women under male guardianship. Chernishevskii wrote about women's equality and freedom in his famous *Chto delat?* (What is to be done, 1863) and Dobroliubov depicted a strong woman who opposed the conservatism of the patriarchal family and followed the impulses of her emotions.

In 1868, a year after he moved from Russia to Serbia, Karavelov explored similar ideas. He published the short novel *Kriva li e sadbata?* (Is fate wrong? 1868–1869), with the intention of presenting a new type of philosophical polemic. Through the novel's central characters, Kalmich and Tsaya, Karavelov presented woman not as a thing and a slave, but as a rational and independent person of value to society, not merely there to satisfy the caprices of men. Tsaya is a 'real Serbian woman' with common sense and an aptitude for intellectual achievement. Kalmich criticizes the notion of difference between the minds of women and men, remarking that divergences in their education caused the sexes to think differently, and that enlightened women would request equal treatment and freedom. This short novel received a great deal of attention, not only because Karavelov had taken Chernishevskii's novel *Chto delat?* as his example, but also because he was close to the leaders of the patriotic cultural organization *Omladina* (Society of Young People), which was then gathering liberal members of the intelligentsia. Thus it was a Bulgarian man who placed 'the woman question' at the center of public discussion in Serbia. The year before he published his novel, Karavelov married Nataliya Petrovich. She was the widowed sister of a friend of his from the village of Maktse (in the region of Pozharovets), a hardworking and intelligent woman without formal education. She gave him invaluable support in the difficult years to come, which would see his imprisonment in Budapest (1868–1869; Karavelov was accused of plotting and taking part in the murder of Prince Mikhail Obrenovich in 1868) and emigration to Romania (1869–1878).

This drastic turn in Karavelov's life was generated by his political activity in Serbia. In 1867, having assimilated populist revolutionary ideas based on the granting of power to the people and the creation of a Balkan-Danubian Federation, he founded a committee in Belgrade and recruited a detachment for action in the Bulgarian lands. Thereafter, he was compelled to move to Bucharest where, together with other emigrants, he founded the *Bulgarski revolyutsionen tsentralen komitet* (Bulgarian Revolutionary Central Committee) in 1869. As its ideologist and the author of its manifestos, *Program* and *Bulgarski glas* (Bulgarian voice, 1870), Karavelov still preserved the convictions he had formed in Russia. It is therefore not surprising to find references to 'the woman question' in the very first issue of *Svoboda* (Freedom), the organ of the *Bulgarski revolyutsionen tsentralen komitet*. As the newspaper's editor-in-chief, Karavelov insisted that above all, women "needed education like men: human, positive; a real education not a fashionable one," and that "everything depend[ed] on woman" [*Svoboda* 1, no 1, (7 November 1869)].

Over the next few years, Karavelov devoted himself to predominantly political activities related to the *Bulgarski revolyutsionen tsentralen komitet*, until the disintegration of the organization in 1875. In the same year, he began editing the magazine *Znanie* (Knowledge), in which he popularized contemporary scientific discoveries, printed folklore and works of art and returned to the topic of feminism. In a series of articles entitled "Za zhenskoto vospitanie" (On women's education, 1876), he expounded on progressive arguments in contemporary debates over Bulgarian women's education. Like their counterparts in other European countries (e.g. Rousseau in France), Bulgarian writers who supported the idea of women's education (K. Fotinov, P. Beron, P. R. Slaveikov) insisted for the most part on the traditionalist arguments that women be educated in order to become better mothers and housewives, pleasant companions for their husbands and useful to the nation. Only a few Bulgarian male intellectuals perceived the education of women as a natural right pertaining to women as individual human beings, Lyuben Karavelov among them. Insisting that both women and men needed to undergo complete physical, moral and intellectual cultivation, he contested notions that women should be housewives and mothers; that they only be educated to perform manual labor and housekeeping, and that education should reflect fundamental differences between the sexes. According to Karavelov, "the education that is provided for men should also be provided for women" (cited in Daskalova ed. 1998, 60); he saw the educational deprivation of women not as an advantage for the male sex, but as a form of moral impoverishment for the entire nation. He also opposed the double standards of men who approved of prostitution for their own pleasure but stigmatized women who practiced it as a means of subsistence–just as he opposed men who spoke of women's education but sought uneducated wives who conformed to more traditional 'feminine' stereotypes. Karavelov concluded that only the American coeducational model would lead to "the two sexes developing physically, morally and mentally" [*Znanie* (Knowledge) 2, no. 2 (29 February 1876); no. 3 (15 March 1876)]. After the establishment of the Bulgarian National State in 1878, Karavelov returned to Bulgaria, became involved in social activities and continued publishing *Znanie*. He later planned to found a new magazine called *Nachalo* (Beginning), but this was never realized due to his death on 21 January 1879.

Karavelov left a huge literary heritage and introduced new genres to Bulgarian literature: travel notes, memoirs, literary criticism and the short novel. The author of poems which were turned into songs ["Hubava si moja, goro" (You are so beautiful, my forest)], he was also the author of over thirty short stories and a symbol of the revolutionary movement. After his death, his wife edited his complete works in eight volumes. His life has been researched by philologists, literary scholars, journalists, historians and philosophers, yet his feminist ideas have been only sporadically mentioned and usually dismissed as odd divergences from more traditional opinions.

Georgeta Nazarska
Higher School of Library Studies and
Information Technologies, Sofia

SOURCES

(B) *Svoboda* (Freedom) (1869).
(B) *Znanie* (Knowledge) (1876).
(C) Lyuben Karavelov, "Za zhenskoto vazpitanie" (On women's education). In Krassimira Daskalova, ed. *Ot siankata na istoriata. Zhenite v balgarskoto obstestvo i kultura* (From the shadow of history: women in Bulgarian society and culture 1840s–1940s). Sofia: LIK, 1998, 53–64.
(C) Karavelov, L. *Izbrani sachinenia* (Selected works), vol. 2. Sofia, 1955.
(D) Lekov, D. "Lyuben Karavelov I zapadnoevropejskoto prosvetitelstvo" (Lyuben Karavelov and the West European enlightenment). *Izvestia na instituta Botev-Levski* (Yearbooks of the Botev-Levski Institute), no 3 (1959): 61–89.
(D) *Izsledvania I statii za Lyuben Karavelov* (Studies and essays on Lyuben Karavelov). Sofia, 1963.
(D) Arnaudov, M. *Lyuben Karavelov*. Sofia, 1964.
(D) Konev, I. *Beletristat Lyuben Karavelov* (The novelist Lyuben Karavelov). Sofia, 1970.
(D) *Lyuben Karavelov. Sbornik po sluchai 150 godini ot rozhdenieto mu* (Lyuben Karavelov. Collection in honour of 150 years of his birth). Sofia, 1990.
(D) Lekov, D. *Lyuben Karavelov. Tvorecat, grazhdaninat, savremennikat* (The creator, the citizen, the contemporary). Plovdiv, 1998.
(E) Daskalova, Krassimira. "Women, Nationalism and Nation-State in Bulgaria (1800–1940s)." In Miroslav Jovanovič and Slobodan Naumovič, eds. *Gender Relations in South Eastern Europe: Historical Perspectives on Womanhood and Manhood in 19th and 20th Century*. Belgrade–Graz: Zur Kunde Südosteuropas, vol. II / 33, 2002, 15–37.

KARAVELOVA, Ekaterina (1860-1947)

Bulgarian teacher, translator, publicist and public figure; Vice-Chairwoman of the *Bulgarski Zhenski Sujuz* (*BZhS*, Bulgarian Women's Union) (1915–1925); Chairwoman (from 1925) of the Bulgarian branch of the Women's International League for Peace and Freedom (WILPF).

Ekaterina Karavelova (*nee* Peneva) was born on 21 October 1860 into a lower middle-class family in Rouschuk (now Rousse), then one of the biggest towns in the European part of the Ottoman Empire and the center of *Tuna vilaet*, an administrative unit. She was the youngest of the four children of Stoyanka and Veliko Penev, who had three girls (Anastasiya, Mariola and Ekaterina) and one boy (Athanas). Her father died very young. In June 1870, Ekaterina left for Russia with her aunt, Kiryaki Nikolaki Minkova (her father's sister and mother of Todor Minkov, founder of a Southern Slav boarding house attached to the High School in Nikolaev). In January 1871, Todor Minkov took Ekaterina to Moscow to the family of the retired General Vsevolod Nikolaevitch Lermontov, his wife Elisaveta Andreevna and their daughters Sofia and Julia (the first woman chemist in Russia). There she met the famous mathematician Sophia Kovalevskaja. Ekaterina lived with Lermontov's family for several years during the course of her education in Moscow. In August 1878, after graduating (with a gold medal) from the Fourth Girls' High School in Moscow, Ekaterina Peneva returned to the newly established Bulgarian State and by autumn had begun teaching in Rousse (1878-1880).

In 1880, instead of following plans to study medicine and join the "learned women" of St Petersburg (Bowden 2004, 10), Ekaterina Peneva married Petko Stoichev Karavelov (1843-1903), a Bulgarian politician, lawyer by training, leader of the Liberal Democratic Party, President of the First Bulgarian National Assembly, several times Prime Minister of Bulgaria and brother of ***Lyuben Karavelov***. After the marriage, she followed her husband to Sofia. They had three daughters: Rada (1880-1883), Viola (1884-1934) and Lora (1886-1913).

Thanks to the good education and upbringing she had received from the aristocratic Russian Lermontov family and her husband's position, Ekaterina Karavelova soon became part of the political elite of the young Bulgarian State. The first part of her life was closely related to her husband's political activity, through which she came to support the democratic struggles of her husband's Liberal Party (against the Bulgarian Conservatives). After the Bulgarian Prince Alexander von Battenberg had suspended the Constitution in 1881, the Karavelov family had to leave Bulgaria and went to Plovdiv, the capital of the semi-autonomous province Eastern Rumelia, then still part of the Ottoman Empire. Both Ekaterina and Petko Karavelov worked as teachers in Plovdiv (1881–1882). In 1884, they managed to return to Sofia, where she continued to teach at the Girls' High School. As wife of the Prime Minister however, she did not receive a salary. She traveled around the country with her husband, kept his correspondence and supported his decisions in critical moments during the days of the Unification of the Kingdom of Bulgaria with Eastern Rumelia in September 1885 and during the subsequent Serbian–Bulgarian war. She coordinated medical aid in Sofia during the war and, while some of the Bulgarian statesmen lost their nerve under the Serbian threat, Karavelova managed to preserve a sense of security, impressing many people with her efficient approach to the crisis. Her life continued to be related to political events in Bulgaria: the abdication of Alexander von Battenberg; the nomination of Petko Karavelov as one of the three regents; Petko Karavelov's resignation and the subsequent dictatorship (1887–1895) of Stefan Stambolov (1854–1895). During Stam-bolov's rule, Karavelova's family suffered persecution: her husband was arrested (1887, 1892), put to jail and tortured, while she was tried for publishing political pamphlets against the regime. She was accused of telling lies about the Government to foreign diplomats (though found innocent) and when she tried to find a job as a teacher, people were afraid to hire her—with the exception of the Catholic School in Rousse, where she worked from 1892 to 1894 and which paid her a very low salary. After the change of the government, Karavelova managed to obtain a reasonably paid teaching position at the Girls' High School in Rousse (1894–1896). Upon the release of Petko Karavelov, she returned to Sofia and taught at the Girls' High School there until the death of her husband (1896–1903).

In 1899, Ekaterina Karavelova established the women's cultural organization *Maika* (Mother) in Sofia, serving as its Chairwoman for thirty years. Believing that women's independence and equality required giving them opportunities to earn a living, she strongly supported women's professional and vocational education and led *Maika* campaigns to open the vocational girls' school, "Maria Louisa." She also was among the founders (in 1901) of the *Bulgarski Zhenski Sujuz* (*BZhS*, Bulgarian Women's Union), together with ***Anna Karima***, ***Julia Malinova***, ***Vela Blagoeva*** and ***Kina Konova***. Her own professional success led Ekaterina Karavelova to think that every person could succeed if in possession of the necessary qualities. She even thought that it was too early to think of gender equality in Bulgaria, where most women were not yet 'ready.' She felt that if women were made equal before being adequately prepared, the results might not be desirable. Nonetheless, she supported the educational and emancipation activities of the *BZhS*. Because of her knowledge of foreign languages and her connections with people in other countries, she maintained the foreign correspondence of the *BZhS*. In 1915, she became Vice-Chairwoman of the *BZhS* and remained so until 1925. In 1926, she was made an honorary member of the *BZhS* (together with ***Julia Malinova***, ***Kina Konova*** and Rada Staliiska) in recognition of her outstanding work.

A new period in her life began after the death of her husband in 1903. She withdrew from participation in the Democratic Party but continued, as the entries in her diary show, to take a great interest in politics (though not as a member of a political party). She dedicated her time to public charity work, national endeavors and the causes of education and peace. After the defeat of the *Ilinden* uprising in 1903 (of Bulgarians from Macedonia and Thracia, then still under the Sultan), Ekaterina Karavelova worked in charge of a Ladies' Committee in Sofia for the release of Macedonian women from prison. At international forums she protested against the indifference of the Great Powers to Bulgarian national interests and to the fate of the tens of thousands of refugees who could not easily be absorbed by small and underdeveloped Bulgaria. In 1904, she traveled to London as a delegate to the Macedonian Conference summoned by the "Balkan Committee," under the chairmanship of James Bryce (later Lord Bryce) and Noel Buxton (1869-1948): both members of the Labor Party and supporters of the Bulgarian national cause. Invited to attend by the organizers of the conference, Ekaterina Karavelova was also asked by the Macedonians to go as their delegate. On her return journey she stayed in Paris and informed the French public of the dreadful living conditions of Macedonian and Thracian refugees. In the same year, as Secretary-Treasurer of the Ladies' Committee, she organized and dispatched a Bulgarian Sanitary Commission to Russia during the Russian-Japanese War and during the Balkan Wars (1912-1913), organized a hospital at the Military Academy. Between November 1913 and April 1914, while in Russia, she received the news of her daughter Lora's tragic death (it was never clarified whether she killed herself or was killed).

Ekaterina Karavelova became one of the symbols of the Bulgarian movement for peace and freedom. Both the Bulgarian association *Traen mir* (Durable peace)–of which she was Chair–and the *Makedonski Zhenski Sujuz* (Macedonian Women's Union) in Bulgaria became members of the Women's International League for Peace and Freedom (WILPF) upon its foundation in 1919. After the communist September uprising in 1923, Karavelova headed a committee set up to provide relief to victims, even though she did not sympathize with the communists. She also contributed to *Vik na svobodni hora* (Cry of free people), the magazine of her liberal son-in-law, the journalist Josif Herbst. Following the communist bombing of the church "Sveta Nedelia" in Sofia in 1925 and government reprisals, Josif Herbst 'disappeared' like many other progressive Bulgarian intellectuals. In 1925, Karavelova helped the French author Henri Barbusse, who had arrived in Bulgaria, to gather information about the political terror of the regime for his book *Les Boureaux* (The hangmen).

In 1924, Karavelova traveled to Washington as a Bulgarian delegate to the Fourth Congress of the WILPF, participating in the WILPF Summer School in Chicago. Upon her return to Bulgaria, she wrote articles on women's attitudes to war and peace. She claimed that women and men were different: women had "an entirely different area of activity in life from men" and "no woman wants war" (Bowden 2004, 96). She argued that in the new epoch after World War I, men were having to respect "new ways of action through peace and friendship, towards an understanding between the peoples" (Bowden 2004, 97). In 1925, Karavelova became President of the Bulgarian section of the WILPF and participated in a committee to the League of Nations; in 1926, she attended a WILPF congress in Dublin and she was Vice-Chair of the Bulgarian branch of the Union *Panevropa* (Pan-Europe). During the interwar period, Karavelova led the activities of the Bulgarian section of the WILPF: she attended congresses and summer schools, met political prisoners, gave talks and contributed to newspapers and magazines. In 1926, her close friend Camille Drouet (of the French Section of the WILPF and Secretary of the Central Office) visited Bulgaria. The fiftieth anniversary of Karavelova's public activities was commemorated in November 1928 and a jubilee publication appeared. From 25 August to 10 September 1930, Karavelova hosted a WILPF Summer School in Bulgaria. The second congress of the Bulgarian Section of WILPF took place in 1931. Ekaterina Karavelova was one of the co-founders of the Bulgarian–Romanian Association in Bucharest (1932), which was part of contemporary attempts to bring about unity in the Balkans. In May 1933, during the third general meeting of the Bulgarian Section of WILPF (again with the participation of Camille Drouet), a committee for the defence of Jews in Germany was set up. (Various newspapers published articles against the Committee and wrote that it was not Bulgarian business to interfere in the affairs of "Great Germany.")

In 1934, Karavelova's daughter Viola Karavelova-Herbst died (she had been suffering from depression since the disappearance of her husband in 1925). But in spite of family misfortunes and her advanced age, Karavelova continued to be involved in public activities. In 1935, she headed a delegation to the Prime Minister asking for the abolishment of death sentences of political prisoners. She was elected President of the *Bulgarski Pisatelski Sujuz* (Bulgarian Writer's Association, created on her initiative) and in 1938 was put in charge of a committee opposing the closure of Bulgarian schools in Romania. In addition to her public activities, she continued with her literary work and by the end of her life had authored over fifty (mainly but not only political) pamphlets and articles, translated works (from Russian and French into Bulgarian) by L. N. Tolstoi, F. M. Dostoevskii, V. Hugo, Guy de Maupassant, G. Flaubert and Charles Dickens, as well as having edited Bulgarian editions of world classics. She also wrote on women's issues in *Zhenski glas* (Women's voice), the newspaper of the *BZhS*.

Ekaterina Karavelova died in Sofia on 1 April 1947. On the personal orders of Georgi Dimitrov (1882–1949)—activist of the international communist movement prior to WWII; later a Bulgarian politician but then Prime Minister of Bulgaria–she was buried next to her husband, Petko Karavelov, in the graveyard of The Holy Seven Church, previously the Black Mosque (and at one time the main prison in Sofia). There is no cemetery near this church, only the two graves of Ekaterina and Petko Karavelovi. For her extraordinary contribution to Bulgarian public life, Ekaterina Karavelova was awarded many distinctions, including the medal *Za chovekoljubie* (For love of humanity), the highest medal for civic virtue. She also received a silver medal for culture and art, the cross for independence and a decoration from the Red Cross.

In old age, Ekaterina Karavelova often said that the struggle of the Bulgarians against foreign domination had strengthened national cohesion, safeguarded families and given women an equal standing in society. These were ideals which sustained her avid interest in life and the world until the end of her days.

Reneta Roshkeva
Rousse Historical Museum

SOURCES

(A) *Durzhaven Istoricheski Archiv* (State Historical Archive), f. 834 (Ekaterina Karavelova).

(B) *Zhenski glas* (Women's voice) (1899–1944).

(B) *Yubileen sbornik Ekaterina Karavelova. 1878–1928* (Jubilee volume on Ekaterina Karavelova). Sofia: Durjavna pechatnitza, 1929.

(B) *Bulgarski jenski sujuz (po sluchaj 30-godishninata mu). 1901–1931* (On the occasion of the thirtieth anniversary of the Bulgarian Women's Union. 1901–1931). Sofia: Pechatnitza "Pravo," 1931.

(C) *Spomeni na Ekaterina Karavelova* (The memoirs of Ekaterina Karavelova). Sofia: Izdatelstvo na Otecheestvenia front, 1984.

(D) Drenkova, Fani, ed. *Kato antichna tragedia. Sudbata na Ekaterina Karavelova i neinito semeistvo v pisma, dnevnitzi,fotografii* (An ancient tragedy. The life of Ekaterina Karavelova and her family in letters, diaries, pictures). Sofia: Nauka i izkustvo, 1984.

(D) Bowden, Regine. *Ahead of her time*. Rousee: Primax Ltd, 2004.

KARIMA, Anna (born Anna Todorova Velkova) (1871-1949)

Teacher, writer, translator, journalist and editor. Co-founder of the *Bulgarski Zhenski Sujuz* (Bulgarian Women's Union) (1901–1944) and its first head (1901–1906). Founder of the union *Ravnopravie* (Equal Rights) (1908–1921).

Anna Karima (seated, in black, on the left) among participants at the founding congress of the *Bulgarski Zhenski Sujuz* in Sofia, 10–14 July 1901.

'Anna Karima' was the pseudonym of Anna Todorova Velkova (whose married name, from 1888 to 1903, was Janko Sakuzova). Other pseudonyms were 'Vega,' 'Mamin,' and 'Samurov.' She was born in 1871 in Berdjansk (Russia), the daughter of Stepanida Mouzhichenko, a Ukrainian woman whose sensitivity to patriarchy and gender power relations Karima adopted, and Todor Velkov, a Bulgarian emigrant who settled in Izmail (Russia) to trade in wheat, after having participated as a volunteer in the Crimean War (1853-1856). Mouzichenko and Velkov had six children: three girls and three boys.

After the establishment of the autonomous Bulgarian state in 1878, the family moved to Todor Velkov's native town of Shumen, where he was appointed district prefect. Anna finished middle school and was sent to the girls' high school in Sofia. Owing to the good school library there and the influence of some of her teachers (especially ***Ekaterina Karavelova***, who later became one of the activists of the Bulgarian women's movement), Karima developed certain intellectual tastes, particularly for Russian literature. After completing her secondary education, she returned to Shumen to begin her professional life as a teacher. In 1888, she married Janko Sakuzov (1860-1941), a journalist and editor of socialist periodicals, a founder of the socialist movement in Bulgaria, one of the first socialist MPs in the country and an influential socialist politician. They had two daughters, Nadezhda and Evelyna, and a son, Ivan. Anna Karima highly valued her husband's opinion and intellectual judgement but it seems that his praise was not forthcoming and that he paid little attention to her literary works, which came to be highly regarded by some of the most eminent Bulgarian men of letters. His political activities took him away from Shumen and Anna Karima remained at home with her mother-in-law, who, according to Karima's memoirs, was one cause of her unhappy family life. Karima's first short story, "Obiknovena istoria" (A common story), was published in 1891. From 1891 to 1892, Karima taught in

Pleven, where she established a society for women's education called *Razvitie* (Development).

In 1894, the family moved to Sofia. Negative experiences of married life, as well as sensitivity to gender hierarchies within Bulgarian society more generally, spurred Anna Karima on to become one of the most active participants in the capital's women's movement. In 1897, she established a society for women's education called *Suznanie* (Conscience), which added the acquisition of civil and political rights for women to the charitable and educational goals of women's organizations of the time. She also led campaigns for the admission of women to Sofia University and began preparations for a national women's organization. It was at this time that Karima's literary career took off in earnest and she published several well-received short stories dealing with gender relations and other social questions. In 1898, due to family problems, Anna Karima left Sofia with her two small children and became a teacher in Edirne (today in Turkey). She returned to Sofia the following year and, together with ***Julia Malinova,*** edited the newspaper *Zhenski glas* (Women's voice), which became the organ of the *Bulgarski Zhenski Sujuz* (Bulgarian Women's Union) in 1901. In 1900, Karima went to Paris, where, with the support of Princess Vichnevskaja (the granddaughter of Victor Hugo), she held a meeting in support of 'the Macedonian cause.'

Anna Karima was among the founders of the *Bulgarski Zhenski Sujuz* (Bulgarian Women's Union) in 1901, the first national women's organization in Bulgaria. In that same year, Karima became the *Bulgarski Zhenski Sujuz*'s first elected head. Over the course of time, two oppositional positions developed within the *Bulgarski Zhenski Sujuz*: that of the more traditional 'bourgeois' feminists (in this case the 'broad' socialists or Social Democrats) and that of the orthodox ('narrow') socialists. Anna Karima belonged to the 'broad' socialists, insisting that the *Bulgarski Zhenski Sujuz* transcend class and party, and she opposed attempts by 'narrow' socialists to change the organization's broad, feminist orientation towards women of all classes (the orthodox socialist women split from the *Bulgarski Zhenski Sujuz* on this account in 1903). A large part of Karima's journalistic writings from this time deal with the problems of the Bulgarian women's movement. Between 1903 and 1906, tensions again developed within the *Bulgarski Zhenski Sujuz*–a result of both ideological differences and personal struggles for leadership. In 1906, Karima and some of her supporters left the *Bulgarski Zhenski Sujuz*–the second big split–on the grounds that the organization did not pay enough attention to the issue of equal rights. In 1907, Karima became editor of the journal *Nova struia* (New current) and in 1908, her group of 'progressive' women formed a separate organization called *Ravnopravie* (Equal Rights, also known as the Union of Progressive Women), devoted specifically to the pursuit of civil and political rights for women. Anna Karima argued in the periodical of *Ravnopravie* (also called *Ravnopravie*, 1908–1921), that her new group did not intend to divide, but to strengthen the Bulgarian women's movement. She directly addressed members of the *Bulgarski Zhenski Sujuz*, insisting that "ours is not hostile action but represents a movement along a different road toward a common goal" [*Ravnopravie* 1, no. 3 (1908): 2]. From 1908 onwards, Karima undertook regular tours of the country, giving talks on 'the woman question' and formulating the goals and priorities of the Bulgarian women's movement as she then saw them.

From 1912 to 1918, Anna Karima dedicated herself to patriotic and charitable activities. She worked as a nurse in the Balkan Wars (1912–1913), helping the wounded and fulfilling different missions. In 1913, at a big meeting of Bulgarian women in Sofia, Karima was elected as a 'deputy' and sent to France, where she organized a rally in support of the Bulgarian national cause. In the same year, back in Sofia, she was among the founders of the *Sujuz na bulgarskite pisateli* (Union of Bulgarian Writers). In 1917, she began publishing a newspaper, *Bulgarka* (Bulgarian woman), and established a charitable organization with the same name. In 1916, she established the first private commercial school for girls (later to become a gymnasium) and, upon the death of her daughter Nadezhda in 1918, she opened the first Bulgarian day-care home for the children of working mothers. After World War I, Karima was among the founders of a society, *Invalid* (Disabled), and of an orphanage.

Her fiftieth birthday, also the thirtieth year of her public and literary activities, was celebrated at the Bulgarian National Theater in 1921. Anna Karima left for Paris when reprisals against left-wing opponents were carried out under the right-wing regime of Alexander Tsankov (established in 1923), coming to a head after 1925, when the St. Nedelia church was blown up by a communist group and many liberal Bulgarian intellectuals were subsequently tortured and killed. In Paris, Karima participated in rallies organized by the famous leftist 'League for the Rights of Man and Citizen' and an international group of intellectuals called the Balkan Committee. She worked in close cooperation with Henri Barbusse, providing him with materials for his book *Les Boureaux* (The hangmen, 1926), which she later translated into Bulgarian. In August 1926, she wrote and published "An Appeal for Peace in Bulgaria," sending it to members of the League of Nations in Geneva and to many French intellectuals and political activists. For her political activity in Paris against the rule of Alexander Tsankov, Karima was considered a traitor and tried under the *Zakon za Zashtita na Durzhavata* (Law for Defence of the State), leaving her unable to return to Bulgaria. Towards the end of 1926, she traveled to Soviet Russia with the help of the communist functionary Krustiu Rakovski. After a short stay in Moscow she had to leave due to disagreements with the Bulgarian political émigrés and influential communist functionaries, Georgi Dimitrov and Vassil Kolarov. She spent the next couple of months in Harkov, Ukraine, where she made a living translating books from Russian into Bulgarian. She was only able to return home in 1928, when her sentence was repealed. Although not a communist herself, Karima published a book, *V dneshna Rusiya* (In contemporary Russia), in which she spoke highly of women's emancipation in Soviet Russia. She also published a brochure, *V Parizh* (In Paris), describing her patriotic activities. Back in Bulgaria however, the government seized every opportunity to limit Karima's public activities so that she could only work as a writer and translator. Personal tragedy compounded Karima's problems when her son, the promising young scholar Ivan J. Sakuzov, died in 1935. Between 1928 and 1939, Karima translated several Russian, French and German novels into Bulgarian for publication. She published short stories in the journals *Ikonomia I domakinstvo* (Economy and household), *Domakinia I maika* (Housewife and mother) and the newspaper *Vesnik za zhenata* (For women), as well as editing the journal *Put* (Road).

Anna Karima was the author of some fifty books and brochures that included literary criticism, political journalism, books and plays for children, novels, plays and short stories in which she portrayed women's lives of her time. Her works dealt with moral, psychological and social questions, focusing on the subjective experiences of women. She often gave her protagonists complex, delicate and sensitive dispositions, making some resort to suicide. Suffering was treated as a constitutive element of women's social experience and Anna Karima related this suffering to the limited professional opportunities that existed for women and the harnessing of women to traditional roles and identities. Her works include: *Pod natiska na zhivota* (Under the pressure of life, 1901); *Probuzhdane. Piessa iz suvremenniya zhivot* (Waking up. A play about contemporary life, 1906); *Edna velika ideia* (A great idea, 1907); *Otritnata. Zhertva na golemia grad* (The rejected woman. A victim of the big city, 1930); *Ubiitsa* (A woman murderer, 1933); *Murtvo surtze* (Dead heart, 1940) and *Panagiurskata deva* (The virgin from Panagiurishte). Several of her plays were staged at the National Theater in Sofia. Prior to 1917, one of her plays, *V Balkana* (On the mountain), was written in Russian and staged in St Petersburg.

The persona of Anna Karima provided the playwright St. L. Kostov with a 'real' basis for the main character in his 1914 comedy, *Androfoba* (Man hater). Kostov, a conservative critic of women's emancipation, presented his 'feminist' as a divorced female teacher whose unfulfilled search for marital happiness results in her taking refuge in political activities. Contributing to the polemics that followed performances of *Androfoba* (National Theater, Sofia, 1914), the well-known Bulgarian scholar, professor Asen Zlatarov, offered a Freudian interpretation of women's activism as the sublimation of unsatisfied sexual energies.

Anna Karima died in Sofia on 7 March 1949, alone and forgotten in a room at the *Slavianska besseda* hotel. She left a great legacy as a writer, publicist, feminist and social activist. As a feminist leader (of the *Bulgarski Zhenski Sujuz* and *Ravnopravie*), she dedicated her life to building a strong and powerful women's movement in Bulgaria, fighting determinedly for equal rights and the full emancipation of women. In her restless search for individual and social justice, Anna Karima remains an emblematic figure of Bulgarian feminism.

Krassimira Daskalova
St. Kliment Ohridski, University of Sofia

SOURCES

(A) Durzhaven Istoricheski Archive (State Historical Archive–Sofia), f. 22 (Anna Karima).
(A) NBKM-BIA (National Library "Cyril and Method"–Bulgarian Historical Archive), f. 807 (Janko Sakuzov).
(B) *Zhenski glas* (Women's voice) (1899-1944).
(B) *Ravnopravie* (Equal rights) (1908-1921).
(C) Karima, Anna. *Zhenskoto dvizhenie v Bulgaria* (The women's movement in Bulgaria). Sofia, 1910.
(C) Karima, Anna. *Kurvaviat rezhim na Al. Tsankov I deinostta mi v Parizh (po povod moia protses)* [The Bloody Rule of Al. Tsankov and My Activity in Paris (On my Trial)]. Sofia, 1934.
(C) Karima, Anna. *Kum prosveta i kultura. Spomeni* (Towards education and culture. Memoirs). Sofia, 1943.
(D) *Iubileen sbornik "Anna Karima"* (Jubilee Volume "Anna Karima") (1891-1921). Sofia, 1924.
(D) Ovcharova, Maria. "Maika na tova, koeto shte doide..." ("A mother of something that will come ..."). *Septemvri*, no. 8 (1973): 23-30.

The comic poem below, dedicated to Anna Karima, was read out to her at a writers' dinner on 17 December 1932, when she was given a paper medal in the shape of a hedgehog.

To Anna Karima

And finally, in her honor,
We pronounce from today,
In perpetuity, for ever,
The only cavalier - a woman;
An oratress, playwright, a woman poet,
And still so young - thirty years old.
Pilgrim in Paris, Moscow,
And everywhere, with lifted head,
Roaming today along the "Road"
Between village and city.
And on the way, she discards her mask
Of a would-be man hater.

That's why, oh convivial assembly -
Your attention please -
In this lightning excitement
We give happily
Our last hedgehog

To the hottest woman
In this frosty Winter,
To the rejuvenated Karima.
(What a rhyme!)

Sofia Writers' dinner 17 December 1932

Committee "Hedgehog" Dim. Panteleev Svet. (Minkov)

Translated by Krassimira Daskalova.

KAŠIKOVIĆ, Stoja (c.1865-?)

Bosnian Serb editor, teacher, writer and women's cultural activist.

Very little is known of Stoja Kašiković's early childhood. She was born Stoja Zdjelarević in 1865 in Bosanski Novi, Bosnia, though the precise day and month of her birth are unknown. It is likely that she was orphaned at an early age because she did not know either of her birth parents' names, only that she had been born to Bosnian Serbs and that her father had been a merchant. She had one brother named Simo, who eventually moved to Kovač in Slavonia to work as a blacksmith.

Stoja Zdjelarević began her education in 1879, one year after Bosnia-Herzegovina became an occupied territory of the Austro-Hungarian Empire (ending five centuries of Ottoman rule). She enrolled in the country's only school for girls, established in Sarajevo in 1869 by the English Protestant humanitarian Miss Adeline Paulina Irby (1833-1911). (This school was not, however, the first of its kind; the first girls' school was established by ***Staka Skenderova*** in Sarajevo in 1858, but closed due to financial difficulties in 1875.) Stoja Zdjelarević was thus one of very few Bosnian women to learn to read and write at a time when just three percent of the population was literate. By 1886, she had finished four years of elementary education and received her teacher training at Miss Irby's school. She went on to work as a tutor for a time and taught at Miss Irby's school for the last few years of Irby's life.

In 1886, the same year that she graduated from Miss Irby's school, Stoja Zdjelarević married a Bosnian Serb teacher named Nikola T. Kašiković (1861-1927). Nikola Kašiković taught at Miss Irby's for two years, and it is very likely that the two met one another there. Among Zdjelarević's attractions were her brown eyes and hair and her cheerful countenance [*Srpkinja* (The Serbian woman) (1913): 38]. Together, the couple had three sons (Predrag, Relje and Sreten) and a daughter (Tankosava). All four children went on to become well educated. The two eldest, Predrag and Relje, became physicians. Sreten graduated from an Orthodox seminary in Belgrade, received teacher training and later became an officer in the Austro-Hungarian Army. Like her mother, Tankosava graduated from Miss Irby's school and went on to further her education in Montenegro.

Stoja Kašiković's husband became one of Bosnia-Herzegovina's most important cultural figures. In 1885, he and three other teachers–Božidar Nikašinović (b. 1863), Nikola Šumonja (1865-1927) and Stevo Kaluđerčić (1864-1948)–founded the first Bosnian Serb literary-cultural journal, *Bosanska vila* (The Bosnian nymph) (1885-1914). It rapidly became the most popular journal in the country, as well as a leading cultural journal among South Slavs outside the country. *Bosanska vila* published folklore, poetry, short stories, translations and reported on (mainly Serb) cultural events from across the Balkans. In 1887, Nikola Kašiković became the journal's editor-in-chief and retained this position until the outbreak of World War I, when the journal ceased publication. (In 1996, the journal was revived in a new series of the same name in Sarajevo.)

Like many other married Bosnian women, Stoja Kašiković's main priority was to support her husband's work. In 1891, when Nikola became ill and bed-ridden, she became *Bosanska vila*'s acting editor-in-chief, moving the journal's administrative headquarters from the Serb elementary schoolhouse to the Kašiković family home. She also received assistance from a more experienced administrator, Stevo Kaluđerčić. But like other women of her time, her work went mainly unrecognized and it was Kaluđerčić's name that appeared on the 1891 issues as the journal's editor-in-chief. After her husband's recovery the following year, Stoja Kašiković continued to act as his trusted co-editor and collaborator, occasionally contributing to the journal. Over the years, her work for *Bosanska vila* brought her into contact with leading Serb intellectuals in Bosnia-Herzegovina (such as Dimitrije Mitrinović (1887–1953) and ***Jelica Belović-Bernadzikowska***). Because a large number of *Bosanska vila*'s subscribers lived in Belgrade, she was also well known among the thriving literary-cultural circles of that city. Among her contacts were Belgrade intellectuals Dr. Milorad Pavlović (b. 1865) and ***Isidora Sekulić***.

Stoja Kašiković eventually did receive public recognition for her cultural work among the Serbs. At the 25th anniversary celebration of *Bosanska vila* in 1910, Stoja and Nikola Kašiković received decorations from the governments of Serbia and Montenegro. Two years later, in 1912, the Belgrade-based humanitarian aid association *Kolo srpskih sestara* (Circle of Serbian sisters, founded in 1903) wrote about Stoja Kašiković's cultural activities in the *Narodnih novina* (National newspaper). Although known mainly for its charitable work, the *Kolo srpskih sestara* also supported the liberation of Serbs under foreign domination in the Balkans and its popular almanac *Vardar*, named after the main river in Macedonia, did not conceal the political ideals of the organization.

During World War I, a substantial number of Serb intellectuals and politicians from Bosnia-Herzegovina were tried for various acts of treason. Among them were Nikola, Stoja and Predrag Kašiković, all of whom were tried and convicted in 1917–1918. They were found guilty of having provided information about Austro-Hungarian military maneuvers to Serbia's spies, with whom they were thought to have conspired to unite the Serbs in a 'Greater Serb' state. Members of the Kašiković family were absolved of their crimes in 1918, when the Austro-Hungarian Empire ceased to exist and Bosnia-Herzegovina joined the Kingdom of Serbs, Croats and Slovenes.

Almost nothing is known of Stoja Kašiković's life following World War I. In 1927, her husband died and she began receiving a widow's pension. She was just 62 years old. A trailblazer among her contemporaries, Stoja Kašiković was one of the first women editors of a major literary-cultural journal. She supported women's social and cultural activism through her work as a teacher and was a member of the *Kolo srpskih sestara*. With these activities, she contributed to the growth of women's cultural activism both in Bosnia and Serbia. Like so many of her Serbian contemporaries, she remains an important yet almost forgotten figure.

Jelica Zdero
Ph.D. Candidate, The University of Western Ontario, Canada

SOURCES

(A) Historical Archives of Bosnia-Herzegovina, Provincial Government of Sarajevo, Treason Trial of Nikola T. Kašiković. (These numerous official documents related to Nikola's conviction and trial contain a lengthy interrogation that reveals a number of details regarding his and his wife's cultural activities.)

(A) Historical Archives of Bosnia-Herzegovina, Provincial Government of Sarajevo, Treason Trial of Stoja and Predrag Kašiković. (This file contains numerous official documents related to Stoja and Predrag's conviction and trial, including letters and lengthy interrogations that provide biographical details of Stoja's personal and professional life.)

(A) Historical Archives of Bosnia-Herzegovina, Government of the Kingdom of Serbs, Croats and Slovenes, Collection of Personnel Files, Kašiković, Nikola T. (This brief, three-page file contains official approval for Nikola's pension in 1926, followed by the official approval for his wife's widow's pension in 1927.)

(A) Historical Archives of Sarajevo, Family and Individual Archival Collection, ***Belović-Bernadzikowska, Jelica*** (1875–1909), Box 1. (Jelica Belović-Bernadzikowska was a contemporary and friend of Stoja Kašiković. This personal archival collection contains a memoir revealing details of cultural life in Sarajevo prior to World War I, as well as references to women's literary-cultural circles and Stoja's work on *Bosanska vila* [The Bosnian nymph] (1885–1914).

(B) *Srpkinja* (The Serbian woman) (1913).

(B) Đuričković, Dejan. *Bosanska vila: 1885–1914* (The Bosnian nymph: 1885–1914), 3 vols. Sarajevo: Svjetlost, 1975.

KOBRYNSKA, Natalia (born Ozarkevych) (1851-1920)

Ukrainian feminist writer, publicist and social/political activist, founder in 1884 of the *Tovarystvo Rus'kykh Zhinok* (Association of Ukrainian women).

Natalia Ozarkevych was born on 8 June 1851 in Beleluia, in the Halychyna Province of the Habsburg Monarchy (Galicia), to the Reverend Ivan Ozarkevych (1826-1903) and Teofilia Okunevska. She was the eldest of five children. At her death, the territory of her birth was being contested among Poles, Ukrainians and Russians. Kobrynska identified with Ukrainians, who sometimes still used the older name Rusyn or (in the Latinized version) Ruthenians. Galician Ukrainians recognized a kinship with Ukrainians then living in the Russian Empire but denied being Russian and bitterly resisted Polonization. Ukrainian democratic forces in Halychyna were trying to wrest political power from the Polish nobility, which controlled local government there.

Natalia Ozarkevych was educated at home, benefiting from close interaction with her four university-educated brothers. (Although they too were active in Ukrainian community life, none of her four brothers was as prominent as Kobrynska.) Her father, a social and political activist who lobbied the Austrian Parliament in Vienna for higher education for women, encouraged the participation of his daughter in public life. He, like his forebears, was a priest of the Greek Ukrainian Catholic Church (which had special relations with the Papal See) and could marry. Many of these priests actively promoted educational and social progress as leaders of a western Ukrainian upper-middle class that possessed intellectual aspirations and a social conscience. In 1871, Natalia married Teofil Kobrynsky (1852-1882), who also became a priest. Kobrynsky was very supportive of his wife's views on women's liberation, to which cause the couple dedicated themselves: they decided not to have children and worked jointly on a Ukrainian translation of J. S. Mill's *On the Subjection of Women* (never published). After Kobrynsky's death, Natalia did not remarry. Both her family and married life were marked by close and happy relationships. The family home served as a center for social life, in particular as a meeting place for democratic- and socialist-minded youth. With the exception of a short period in Lviv, travels in Western Europe and a trip to the Ukrainian lands in the Russian Empire, Kobrynska spent her life in the picturesque low Carpathian towns of Beleluia, Bolekhiv and Sniatyn. She lived modestly, and what little she had she channeled into publishing on women's issues.

Physically, Kobrynska was attractive: relatively tall, with dark abundant hair and a stately bearing. She was eloquent and seemed aloof. Her rejections of marriage proposals from her socialist colleagues were considered a sign of her class superiority. Although she paid *de riguer* intellectual respect to contemporaries such as writer Ivan Franko (1856–1916), like many women of her generation who were largely self-taught and who grew up surrounded by strong women, Kobrynska insisted that she had arrived at her own ideas by her own efforts, through her own life and experiences "without the help of men" (Kobrynska 1980, 402).

While her social and political views were formed under the direct impact of socialism, both directly through the works of Marx, Engels and Lassalle and through their Ukrainian interpreters, Kobrynska was a practitioner of democratic liberalism. She remained firmly committed to persuasion and gradualism as guarantors of genuine systemic change. Kobrynska felt that social and civic consciousness would be best promoted through literature, and for that reason she channeled her energy into journals that addressed a primarily middle-class female readership, in contrast to the socialists who agitated for direct action in the villages. Kobrynska thought of middle-class women as transmission belts of new ideas and as the most effective agents of change in the villages. Her refusal to see the family as purely an object of oppression and her arguments against 'free love,' seeing in the practice merely new ways of exploiting women, made her relations with socialists difficult. Moreover, she maintained that women should articulate their own philosophical space, since all existing philosophical theories had hitherto overlooked women. "It is a pity that the age-old slavery of women is etched like a scar in the way men think. Since that is the case, women must struggle not only against the social order, which keeps them in slavery, but against concepts articulated by men" (Kobrynska 1895, 10). Yet her belief in the power of 'human will' remained undaunted: "Weakness and despair are the worst enemies of humanity, be they called pessimism or religion or resignation" (Kobrynska 1893, 69).

Kobrynska saw that economic necessity had already pushed women into the labor market, yet for her the roots of women's inequality lay not in the economic, but in the social sphere. Among Ukrainian women, she introduced the notion of the 'double burden,' refusing to assume that paternalism would automatically vanish in a socialist society. "It would be more realistic for women workers, while admitting that the victory of the workers will also be their victory, to ensure their own rights and not become dependent upon the grace of men" (Kobrynska 1895, 16–17). Steady pressure mounted by women on public life was, for Kobrynska, essential for the progress of society as a whole. She championed the cause of women within the socialist community, promoted higher education and self-help societies, as well as attentively studying American and British women's social work and working tirelessly for the establishment of day-care centers and educational outreach at home. The older clergy supported her day-care plans, while the younger sons of clerical families opposed them as frivolous.

Kobrynska began her intellectual journey in the classic fashion of male members of the Eastern European intelligentsia. Under the direct influence of the works of Henry T. Buckle, Ludwig Buchner, Charles Darwin, and Herbert Spencer, as well as of Russian radicals Nikolai Dobroliubov (1836–1861) and Nikolai Chernyshevskii (1828–1889), she went through a reorientation of values and for a time denied the existence of a spiritual realm. Like the men of her milieu who had undergone similar crises, Kobrynska—after further study of the works of Nikolai Gogol (1809–1852), Ivan Turgenev (1818–1883), Ernst Renan and eventually Karl Marx and Ferdinand Lassalle—reconciled philosophical modernism and social radicalism with a very liberally interpreted Catholicism. The Ukrainian Greek Catholic (Uniate) Church was largely self-administrated and all the works Kobrynska read, she either owned or had borrowed from other clerical families who paid no attention to the recently proclaimed Vatican *Index of Forbidden Books.*

Kobrynska came to feminism through socialist theory and positivist philosophy. She presented her views through two forums: fiction and articles. Her short stories poignantly described the difficult life of middle-class women in Halychyna. Her writing impressed the leaders of the Ukrainian democratic movement and Kobrynska became something of a celebrity, participating in the first Ukrainian openly political rally for free elections and universal suffrage held in August 1884. Having witnessed the impact of the rally, she decided to organize a women's society that could also become a major political force. She pioneered the first secular women's organization in western Ukraine and forged closer relations between Ukrainian and other women (though unable to reach a consensus with the Poles). Since she wrote in Ukrainian however, she did not reach too broad an audience and, because she was critical of the tactics of the socialists, she received bad local press and did not gain the support of young people.

On 8 December 1884—several months after the rally—Kobrynska assembled 96 women from across the territory of Halychyna to create the *Tovarystvo Rus'kykh Zhinok* (Association of Ukrainian women). The founding meeting was held in Stanislaviv (currently Ivano-Frankivsk) and the goal of the society was to encourage women to pursue public interests unrelated to church activities (thus breaking with the conventions of earlier Ukrainian women's organizations). She met with opposition from the left for not being radical enough, and from the right for not cooperating with the Church. Nor could she obtain the support of like-minded Polish women, who would not admit to the separate existence of Ukrainians. There were other difficulties too. The initial funds collected for the proposed women's journal were used for a church donation and the flare-up of terrorist activity in the Russian Empire made Ukrainian women wary of open politics as a possible incentive to violence. The original idea of a journal was replaced by a women's Almanac, the *Pershyi Vinok* (First wreath, 1887), edited by Kobrynska and ***Olena Pchilka***. It was both the first almanac in Ukrainian that represented Ukrainian authors from both the Russian and Austrian Empire, and the first Ukrainian women's almanac. Ivan Franko, a leading Ukrainian socialist, supported this endeavor. Nevertheless, as the political situation among Ukrainians grew increasingly complex, Kobrynska was unable to pursue journalistic activities. She did however, edit three volumes of women's writing without any organized support: *Nasha Dolia* (Our fate) appeared in 1893, 1895 and 1896. In its pages, Kobrynska elaborated on social and feminist theory, promoted cooperation with Jewish women in Halychyna, published original short stories and the poetry of women writers (as well as translations), and shared with readers her special interest in the practical achievements of women in the United States and Great Britain.

At the turn of the century, Kobrynska tried to draw young women in Lviv to feminism but the new generation rejected her political moderation in favor of their own radical organizations. World War I, fought literally in her 'back yard,' and the subsequent Ukrainian and Polish wars made her last years difficult. She died alone on 22 January 1920 and was buried in Bolekhiv. Immediately upon her death, she became an icon for newly organized Ukrainian women, though her ideas (with the exception of those promoting general equality for women) were neither studied nor implemented.

Martha Bohachevsky-Chomiak
Director, Fulbright Office in Ukraine

SOURCES

(B) Almanac *Pershy Vinok* (First wreath), facsimile edition. New York: The Ukrainian National Women's League of America, 1988.

(C) Kobrynska, Natalia. Articles published in *Nasha Dolia* (Our fate) (1893, 1895, 1896).

(C) Kobrynska, Natalia. *Vybrani tvory* (Selected works). O. Moroz, ed. Kiev: Dnipro Publishing, 1958.

(C) Kobrynska, Natalia. *Vybrani tvory* (Selected works). I. O. Denysiuk and K. A. Kril, eds. Kiev: Dnipro Publishing, 1980.

(D) Bohachevsky-Chomiak, Martha. "Natalia Kobrynska: A Formulator of Feminism." In Andrei S. Markovits & Frank E. Sysyn, eds. *Nation Building and the Politics of Nationalism: Essays on Austrian Galicia*. Cambridge, MA: Harvard Ukrainian Research Institute, 1982, 196–219.

(E) Bohachevsky-Chomiak, Martha. *Feminists Despite Themselves: Women in Ukrainian Community Life, 1884–1939*. Edmonton: Canadian Institute of Ukrainian Studies, 1988, 71–102.

(E) Sonia Morris, ed. *Women's Voices in Ukrainian Literature*. Vol. I. Saskatchewan: Language Lanterns Publications, Inc., 1998.

KOBYLIANSKA, Olha (Kobylians'ka, Ol'ha) (1863–1942)

Activist in the Ukrainian women's movement in Bukovyna (present day southwest Ukraine); writer; leader of the fin-de-siècle Ukrainian modernist movement.

Olha Kobylianska was born on 25 November 1863 in the town of Gura-Gumora in southern Bukovyna, a beautiful, mountainous and ethnically diverse region, then part of the Austro-Hungarian (Habsburg) Empire. Today, Bukovyna is located in Ukraine proper: it shares international borders with Romania and Moldova to the south and east, is bounded regionally to the west and north by Carpathian Ukraine and Galicia (western Ukraine) and by central Ukraine in the east–all lands formerly under Russian, Polish, or Austrian rule. Her mother, Maria Kobylianska (1837–1906), and her father, Iulian Kobyliansky (1827–1912), had seven children: Maksymilian (1858–1922), Iulian (1859–1922), Evhenia (1861–1917), Olha, Stepan (1866–1940), Oleksandr (1875–1933) and Volodymyr (1877–1909). Olha spent her childhood and youth in Gura-Gumora, but when her father, a minor Austrian civil servant, became a pensioner, the family moved to the village of Dymka in northern Bukovyna. In 1891, she moved to the city of Chernivtsi in the heart of Bukovyna, where she lived until her death.

Although Olha Kobylianska now holds a prominent place in the Ukrainian literary canon as the leader of a new modernist school at the turn of the century, her path to writing was fraught with difficulties. She received a limited formal education and the four years of primary schooling that she did receive were exclusively in the German language. It is known that her family spoke German among themselves–Kobylianska's mother was of German-Polish background–but little is known about the extent to which Ukrainian was used at home. After her schooling had ended, she continued to read hungrily and through the influence of German positivist classics, became concerned with the causes of the day, especially the peasantry. Not surprisingly, Kobylianska's first works were written in German; she submitted these to German-language newspapers and journals in Berlin and Vienna.

In 1894, Kobylianska's first work in Ukrainian, a story "Liudyna" (A person), appeared in the magazine *Zoria* (Dawn) and in 1896 a novel, *Tsarivna* (The princess), appeared in *Narod* (The people), the leading Ukrainian journal of the day. The first drafts of both of these works had been written in German in 1886 and 1888–1893 respectively and the Ukrainian versions reflect the influence of German Romanticism, particularly the ideas of Friedrich Nietzsche. Kobylianska was also inspired by George Sand. While many critics disparaged her use of German technique, the writer and feminist ***Lesia Ukrainka*** praised its influence on Kobylianska's writing: "It led you to recognize *world* literature, it transported you out into the broader world of ideas and art–this simply leaps out at one, when one compares your writing with that of the majority of Galicians" (Pavlychko 1996, 88). Kobylianska's temperament was indeed modernist, inclined towards the burgeoning neo-romantic and symbolist currents of the day rather than the realist and populist.

Kobylianska's decision to write in Ukrainian was greatly influenced by her acquaintance with three feminist writers: Sofiia Okunevska, ***Natalia Kobrynska*** and Ukrainka. In general, her contemporaries among the Ukrainian literati–important writers, poets, critics and editors like Ivan Franko, Osyp Makovey and Ukrainka–gave impetus to Kobylianska's development and helped popularize her work. Most likely Kobylianska's conscious embrace of feminism was linked to Kobrynska's request, in 1890, that she collect signatures in Chernivtsi for a petition in favor of women's higher education and make contact with various Romanian and German women's organizations. In 1894, having met up with other Ukrainian women keen to form a secular women's organization, Kobylianska helped found the *Obshchestvo ruskykh zhenshchyn* (Society of Ruthenian women), hoping that it would draw in Ukrainians from Bukovyna. For several years, she worked to expand the role of the society in the community and to attract younger women to its membership, but these attempts were largely unsuccessful; young and politically-aware women were drawn to the progressive left-wing socialist intelligentsia, which rejected feminist issues in favor of radical, anti-church and revolutionary concerns, and united girls in a *Hromada* (Women's Community) in support of these agendas.

In 1897, Kobylianska's story "Valse melancolique" was published in Ukrainian (the French title is its original one). "Valse" provoked debates over whether the intelligentsia was an appropriate subject for Ukrainian literature and, more importantly, whether the three heroines were Ukrainian at all, being "creations of purely European culture" (Pavlychko 1996, 88). Whatever view Kobylianska's contemporaries took of her "Valse," it was at least apparent that her heroines transcended traditional boundaries, especially in their romantic relationships: one character recalls her relationship with a man with hatred; another sees only humiliation for women in their relationships with men; all benefit from the empathy born of genuine emotional understanding among women.

In 1899, Kobylianska first met, and subsequently became close friends with ***Lesia Ukrainka,*** through whom she came to know more about the Ukrainian people. They shared much in common: both had a love of knowledge and were very well-read. Further more, both felt a painful lack of formal education; both were harsh critics of their own works; both regretted that Ukrainian literary criticism was in its infancy, which they saw as the reason for their both being misunderstood (their literary acclaim based on lesser works); both suffered from ill health and unhappy personal lives and both challenged social norms in life and in literature (after a prolonged love affair with Osyp Makovey–who felt threatened by Kobylianska's talent and ideas and finally married a more 'traditional' woman–Kobylianska never married). Artistically the temperaments of Kobylianska and Ukrainka were modernist and complemented one another: both valued technique and aestheticism, cosmopolitanism and intellectualism, artistry above the dominant populist credo of realism, the depiction and glorification of folk life, cultural isolationism and patriotism. Their correspondence, begun in 1899, reveals all these aspects of their spiritual closeness and mutual sympathy and, as their professional and personal friendship grew, a loving tone clearly enters their letters: for example, the repeated avowals that "someone loves someone" (Pavlychko 1996, 98). While such declarations were a common feature of the European avant-guard movement, they were highly atypical in the very traditional and conservative climate of late nineteenth-century Ukrainian cultural life.

In the late 1890s, about a decade after the appearance of the first female literary almanac, *Pershyi vinok* (First wreath), both Kobylianska and Ukrainka voiced a concern that such endeavors supported an artificial artistic separation of feminism and poetry. This was not a denial of feminism, rather recognition that literature was broader than any given ideology, and in spite of Kobylianska's reservations about serving 'two masters,' her portrayal of profound gender conflicts in Ukrainian society throughout the half-century of her creative work was unflinching. In fact, her *Tsarivna* has been called "the first and most consistently feminist novel in Ukraine literature" (Bohachevsky-Chomiak 1988, 105).

Kobylianska's feminism was founded on the sanctity of individual autonomy. The middle-class heroines of *Tsarivna* and "Liudyna," stifled by their milieu, proclaim feminist ideas and fight for their rights; the heroine in "Liudyna" is unsuccessful but in *Tsarivna*, the heroine marries for love and becomes a writer. Although *Tsarivna* is about a woman's search for autonomy and was, at least initially, viewed as being about female liberation, it has subsequently been critically read as "a model for the attainment of personal autonomy" (Bohachevsky-Chomiak 1988, 109). Kobylianska abandoned exclusively feminist themes after *Tsarivna*, turning to explore the human condition in more general terms, but the attainment of individual autonomy by her heroines remained paramount even as she continued to search for new forms of expression.

Because of her interest in the lives of the Ukrainian peasantry, she was in tune with the connection between people, nature and the land. Two of Kobylianska's important novels *Zemlia* (The land, 1902) and *V nediliu rano zillia kopala* (She gathered herbs on Sunday morn, 1909) treat the forces of nature sympathetically. Predestination, magic and the irrational are central to both novels. Moreover, nature and music are both symbols of the erotic. Kobylianska was the first Ukrainian writer to deal with sexuality "as an experience and as a problem" (Pavlychko 1996, 95); her heroines are aware of their bodies, their sensuality and their physical needs, which sometimes conflict with their spiritual or intellectual needs. In *V nedilie rano zillia kopala*, Tetiana poisons her lover who has left her for another, and the reader is shown that nature does not always ennoble or promote individual autonomy. Despite its rural setting and peasant protagonists, *Zemlia* was an unveiled attack on a number of myths about the peasantry that underlay the prevalent populist view of country life as a harmonious, organic and patriarchal existence. Just as Kobylianska demythologized the Ukrainian village as an ideal social system, she showed that the idealized Ukrainian peasant woman, unchecked by education or culture, revealed little of the purity of the populist view; in Kobylianska's work, village life was crude, cruel and controlled by raw human instincts.

A solemn, austere woman with serious dark eyes, hair pulled back in a bun, and always dressed in black, Kobylianska introduced strong, self-sufficient female protagonists into a Ukrainian literature that lacked any corresponding male counterparts. She became one of the most popular writers of her time, mentored several important young modernists and incurred the wrath of literary critics who considered her elitist, inaccessible and feminist (Ukrainian cultural populists thought modernism elitist and inaccessible, thus it was but a small step to dismiss 'non-Ukrainian' feminism with the same refrain). Yet Kobylianska rarely engaged in argument; she almost always let her works speak for themselves, and by the turn of the century was at her creative zenith, becoming an icon of her time in spite of her solitary nature. She was a unifying figure for *Moloda muza* (Young Muse), an umbrella group of new Ukrainian poets and by 1910, had become a figurehead for the next generation of Ukrainian modernists. She continued to publish and these later works were by no means her most insignificant: the short stories *Iuda* (Judas, 1915), *Nazustrich doli* (Meeting one's fate, 1915) and *Ziishov z rozumu* (He went mad, 1923) reflect her horror at the violence of World War I. She was quite sympathetic to the 1917 Bolshevik revolution, particularly since the dissolution of the Habsburg monarchy in 1918 had placed Bukovyna under Romanian rule, worsening the cultural, political and economic hardships of the Ukrainians in that region. Under these circumstances, her moral indignation continued to grow and she felt that Soviet rule in eastern Ukraine was a positive force for Ukrainians there. When western Ukraine was annexed by the Soviet Union in September 1939, Kobylianska wrote an article entitled "Tsvit kul'tury rozvyvaiet'sia" (The fruit of culture is developing), which welcomed the event; in the summer of 1940, Bukovyna was also annexed. From the late 1920s, her writing–mainly of a publicist nature–was increasingly celebrated for its social criticism and she became a member of the Writers Union of the USSR. In June 1941, when German Nazi and Romanian fascist troops entered Bukovyna (now part of the Soviet Union), Kobylianska's reputation caused her to be singled out; the occupiers viewed her as a dangerous communist writer and she was scheduled to be tried by court martial. Her death on 21 March 1942 intervened.

In 1944, a literary and memorial museum dedicated to Kobylianska was opened in Chernivtsi in the building in which she lived from 1938 to 1942. Another museum to her legacy is to be found in the village of Dymka, where she spent a number of years during her youth.

Teresa Polowy
Department of Russian and Slavic Studies,
University of Arizona

SOURCES

(C) Kobylianska, Olha. *Tvory* (Works). Five vols. Kiev: Derzhavne vydavnytstvo khudozhnoi literatury, 1962–1963.

(C) Kobylianska, Olha. *Slova zvorushenoho serdtsia* (Words of a passionate soul: diaries, autobiographies, letters, reminiscences). F. Pohrebennyk, ed. Kiev: Vydavnytstvo khudozhnoi literatury "Dnipro," 1982.

(D) *Olha Kobylianska v krytytsi ta spohadakh* (Olha Kobylianska: criticism and reminiscences). Kiev: Derzhavne vydavnytstvo khudozhnoi literatury, 1963.

(D) Haag, John. "Kobylianska, Olha." In Anne Commire, ed. *Women in World History: A Biographical Encyclopedia*. 17 vols. Waterford, CT: Yorkin Publications, 2001, 8: 742–743.

(E) Shabliovsky, Yevhen. *Ukrainian Literature through the Ages*. Abraham Mistetsky, et. al., trans. Anatole Bilenko, ed. Kiev: Mistetsvo Publishers, 1970.

(E) Bohachevsky-Chomiak, Marta. *Feminists Despite Themselves: Women in Ukrainian Community Life, 1884–1939*. Edmonton: Canadian Institute of Ukrainian Studies, 1988, 103–110.

(E) Luckyj, George S. N. *Ukrainian Literature in the Twentieth Century: A Reader's Guide*. Toronto: Shevchenko Scientific Society, University of Toronto Press, 1992.

(E) Pavlychko, Solomea. "Modernism vs. Populism in Fin de Siecle Ukrainian Literature." In Pamela Chester and Sibelan Forrester, eds. *Engendering Slavic Literatures*. Bloomington: Indiana University Press, 1996, 83–103.

KOLLONTAI, Alexandra (1872–1952)

Publicist, writer, first woman-diplomat; leader and ideologist of the socialist women's movement in Russia (1907–1922); *Narodnyi Kommissar Obshchestvennogo Prizreniia* (People's Commissar / Minister of Social Welfare) in the first Soviet Government; leader of the *Zhenotdel* (Women's Bureau), attached to the Central Committee of the Bolshevik Party (1920–1922).

Alexandra Kollontai (nee Domontovich) was born on 1 April 1872 in St Petersburg, to a wealthy family, though her father and mother came from different social classes. Her father, Mikhail Domontovich (1830–1902), was a nobleman and officer whose family lineage went back to the thirteenth century. Her mother, Alexandra Domontovich (born Masalina; first married name Mravinskaya), was the daughter of a tradesman from Finland. Later, she became involved in founding the first girls' high school in Sofia. In order to marry Mikhail Domontovich, Alexandra's mother had to apply for a divorce, having had three children from her previous marriage. At the time, this was an unusual thing for a woman to do. Alexandra had two sisters and a brother from her mother's first marriage: Adel (data unknown); Euginia (1864–1914), who became a leading opera singer, and Alexander (data unknown), who became a lawyer. Alexandra was the only child from her mother's second marriage. By her own account, she inherited a keen and active nature from her parents. All the children lived together with their mother and her second husband and, after she left home, Alexandra would stay in contact with all of them, especially with Euginia.

After the armistice in San-Stephano had been signed between Russia and Turkey (19 February 1878), Alexandra's father was appointed governor of Turnovo, one of the oldest towns in Bulgaria. Later that year, he became business-manager to the Russian deputy in Bulgaria (1878–1879) and joined the political circle of Dragan Tsankov and Petko Karavelov (the husband of ***Ekaterina Karavelova***), who were preparing the constitution of the newly-established Bulgarian State. In May 1879, he was urgently recalled to St Petersburg when his liberal views were seen to conflict with those of the Russian government.

Alexandra Domontovich was educated at home. In the fall of 1888, she sat exams at the boys' high school in St Petersburg and obtained a school-leaving certificate. She later continued her education by means of private courses. Since childhood, she had always displayed a great interest in foreign languages and it was her knowledge of many European languages that shaped her career as a public figure and diplomat.

In 1893, Alexandra Domontovich became Alexandra Kollontai when she married her second cousin–Vladimir Kollontai (1867-1917), an engineer–in St Petersburg. Though she loved him and the couple had a son (Mikhail, born 1894), she saw her marriage as a prison, an obstacle to the leading of a socially useful life. In 1898, under the pretext of further pursuing her education, Alexandra Kollontai left her husband and child permanently and went abroad. She never lost touch with her son however, and they maintained close relations throughout her life.

Abroad, Kollontai began to read Marxist theory. She attended the lectures of famous academics: Professor Gerkner at Zurich University (1898) and Beatrice and Sydney Webb in England (1899); independently, she studied the life of workers in Finland and wrote "Zemel'nyi vopros v Finliandii" (The agrarian question in Finland, 1902) and "Sotsializm i Finliandiia" (Socialism and Finland, 1907). Acquaintance with the likes of Klara Zetkin, Rosa Luxemburg and Paul and Laura Lafarge (whom she met in Stuttgart, Zurich and Paris between 1901-1907) drew her deeper into socialist 'party work.' At this time, 'the woman question' was becoming increasingly central to her interests.

During the first Russian Revolution (1905-1907), Kollontai distributed propaganda among Russian women workers and tried to convince leaders of the Social Democratic Party of the need to involve women in the socialist movement. At the same time, she actively collaborated with activists of the Western socialist women's movement: Klara Zetkin, Lilly Braun, ***Adelheid Popp*** and Angelika Balabanoff. She worked in the International Women's Socialist Secretariat (IWSS), established during the international conference in Stuttgart (1907), and in 1910, became a member of the IWSS's governing body.

In Russia, Kollontai focused primarily on trying to dissuade women workers from joining liberal / feminist women's organizations, which had become very influential during the revolutionary years. Her Marxist views held that it was impossible to obtain full gender equality through reform. Only the destruction of capitalism–the basis of patriarchy–could lead to real equality; for women workers to be drawn into liberal women's organizations was, according to Kollontai, harmful to their interests. The fight against patriarchy had to be waged not by women, but by women as workers. At the first All-Russian Women's Congress (December 1908), Kollontai discussed the role of class in the Russian women's movement, wishing to prevent an alliance developing between women workers and liberal feminists. Tensions were indeed exacerbated and the women workers' delegation left the congress.

From the end of 1908 to March 1917, Alexandra Kollontai lived as an émigré, working as a fulltime agitator for the German Social Democratic Party and traveling to England, Denmark, Sweden, Belgium, Switzerland and the USA in the period before World War I. In early 1911, she taught at a socialist school in Italy organized by

Maxim Gorky (1868–1936), while maintaining her contacts in Russia. Her first significant work, *Sotsial'nye Osnovy Zhenskogo Voprosa* (The social bases of the woman question), was published in St Petersburg in 1909. In 1913, Kollontai cooperated with the Fourth State Duma as an expert on 'the woman question,' from which came the work *Obshchestvo i Materinstvo* (Society and maternity, 1916). In this study, Kollontai elaborated upon state-levels forms of support for children and mothers, discussing aspects of insurance, paid antenatal and post-natal maternity leave and the workings of a state-implemented system of childcare institutions (day nurseries and kindergartens etc.). For Kollontai, only the recognition of maternity as a socially significant function could free women from the 'double burden' of being both mothers and workers.

After the 1917 February Revolution, when the Temporary Government had declared a total political amnesty, Kollontai returned to Russia and with great enthusiasm took up Bolshevik Party work among women. After the October Revolution, Alexandra Kollontai entered the first Soviet Government as *Narodnyi Kommissar Obshchestvennogo Prizreniia* (People's Commissar / Minister of Social Welfare), a post she held from 8 November 1917 until 19 March 1918. She took part in the preparation of several laws: divorce laws, civil marriage laws, equalization of illegitimate children's rights and several provisions on the protection of maternity and childhood. In 1919, she helped set up the *Zhenskii Otdel or Zhenotdel* (Women's Bureau), attached to the Central Committee of the Bolshevik Party and introduced at every level of the party hierarchy. The aim of the Bureau was to organize cultural and educational work among women. Kollontai was the head of the Bureau from 1920 to 1922.

Having returned to Russia, Kollontai's personal life underwent certain changes. In 1917, she met Pavel Dybenko (1889–1938), a seaman of peasant origin who, in 1917, became Chairman of the Central Committee of the Baltic Fleet. Dybenko became Kollontai's second (civil) husband but their life together was fraught with difficulties: frequent partings, Civil War, age differences. Kollontai decided to part with Dybenko when she found out he was having an affair with a young woman. Their break up coincided with other changes in Kollontai's career.

From 1921 to 1922, Kollontai participated in the so-called workers' opposition: a group of Bolsheviks who believed that industrial administration should be in the hands of the trade unions, not the Party. Because of this involvement, Kollontai was discharged from the Party administration at the tenth congress of the Russian Communist Party in 1922. The same year, she was transferred to diplomatic service in Norway (1923–1925; 1927–1930) and became the first woman ambassador in the world. While there, she established trade, economic and cultural contacts between Norway and Soviet Russia and secured the diplomatic recognition (*de jure*) of Soviet Russia (16 February 1924). In 1926–1927, Kollontai became a trade delegate to Mexico. She was a member of the Soviet delegation to the League of Nations (August 1935–autumn 1936) and, during World War II, carried out peace negotiations with

Finland. From 1942, Kollontai was the head of diplomatic corps in Sweden. During her diplomatic service, her views on the status of women were marginalized and trivialized in the USSR. She returned to the Soviet Union in March 1945. From 1946 until her death in 1952, she was an advisor to the Soviet Ministry of Foreign Affairs.

Throughout her life Alexandra Kollontai wrote fiction. She published several stories and short novels on the theme of women's emancipation which caused, and still cause burning debates: *Liubov' i Novaia Moral'* (Love and the new morality, 1918); *Dorogu krylatomu Erosu* (Give way to winged Eros, 1923); *Zhenschina na Perelome* (Woman at the crossroads, 1923); *Liubov' Pchel Trydovykh* (The love of working-bees, 1923) and *Bol'shaia Liubov'* (The great love, 1927). Her prose–in many respects autobiographical–aimed to expose "bourgeois hypocrisy in moral values" (Kollontai 1927, 1) and explored the psychological problems that a woman faced in trying to build a harmonious union with a man (a union ideally to be based on the principles of equality and freedom).

Kollontai's works of the 1920s anticipate contemporary discussions on morality, sexuality and the family as instruments of patriarchal subjection. Kollontai did not see economic conditions under communism as leading automatically to harmonious relations between the sexes. For this latter progression, it was necessary to transform the three key spheres of morality, sexuality and the family. The 'new morality,' in contrast with 'bourgeois morality' had to be based on comradeship between men and women as individuals. Sex, for Kollontai, was not something shameful or, as in 'bourgeois mentality,' heartless, but in need of liberation. Communist society would recognize a variety of conjugal and extra-marital sexual unions, family life would be transformed and the state would free woman from housework (through the creation of day nurseries, kindergartens and canteens), providing the necessary assistance to mothers bringing up their children as future members of a communist society.

Alexandra Kollontai died in Moscow on 9 March 1952, leaving a huge epistolary heritage, including scientific works, belle-lettres and correspondence–much of which has been published. Her name has since become legendary, though her activities in the field of women's emancipation have been largely silenced, in favor of a focus on her diplomatic work. Contemporary research is now reopening debates on Kollontai's feminism.

Natalia Gafizova
Ivanovo State University

SOURCES

(A) *Rossiskii Tsentr Izucheniia I Khraneniia Dokumentov Noveishei Istorii* (Russian center for the study and maintenance of documents on modern history). Moscow, collection no. 134 (Alexandra Kollontai).

(C) Kollontai, Alexandra M. *Red Love*. New York: Seven Arts Publishing Co., 1927.

(C) Kollontai, Alexandra M. *Iz moei zhizni i raboty. Vospominaniia i dnevniki* (From my life and work. Memoirs and diaries). Moscow, 1974.

(C) Kollontai, Alexandra M. *"Revoliutsiia–velikaia miatezhnitsa." Izbrannye pis'ma 1901-1952* (Revolution and turmoil. Selected letters 1901-1952). Moscow, 1989.

(D) Itkina A. M. *Revoliutsioner, tribun, diplomat* (Revolutionary, tribune, diplomat). Moscow, 1970.

(D) Porter, Cathy. *Alexandra Kollontai: A Biography*. London: Virago, 1980.

(D) Olesin, M. *Pervaia v mire. Biographicheskii ocherk ob A. M. Kollontai* (The first in the world. A biographical essay about A. M. Kollontai). Moscow, 1990.

KONOVA, Kina (1872–1952)

Bulgarian teacher, translator, journalist and public figure; co-founder (1889) and subsequently leader of the *Prijatelska druzhinka. Zhenski klon* (Society of Friends. Women's branch) in Sevlievo, the first local women's socialist organization and founder (1897) of the local women's society *Nadejda* (Hope); co-founder (1901) of the *Bulgarski Zhenski Sujuz* (*BZhS,* Bulgarian Women's Union); member of the *Zhenski Sotsial-demokraticheski Sujuz* (Women's Social Democratic Union, established in 1921); honorary member of the *BZhS* (from 1926).

Kina Konova (left, first row) and Julia Malinova (second from left, first row) after Konova was made Honorary Member and Malinova Honorary President of the *Bulgarski Zhenski Sujuz* in 1926.

Kina Konova was born as Kina Moutafova in September 1872 in the small town of Sevlievo. She had two brothers: Sava (1864–1943) and Hristo (1872–1942) (one of them a teacher, the other a well-known bookseller and printer in Sevlievo, both socialists).

Kina Moutafova finished middle school in her native town and in 1889, graduated from the girls' high school in Gabrovo, where she led the female high school-students' organization. From 1889 to 1890, she worked as a teacher and became one of the founders (1889) of the socialist organization, *Prijatelska druzhinka. Zhenski klon* (Society of Friends. Women's branch) in Sevlievo, the first local women's socialist organization in Bulgaria. This society organized the translation of books into Bulgarian (mostly from Russian), some dealing with 'the woman question.' Moutafova's translations of *Zagubata ot neznanieto* (Loss of ignorance) by I. Shelgunov, *Za os-*

vobozhdenieto na zhenata (On the emancipation of woman) by I. T. Tarassov, as well as two chapters of S. S. Shashkov's *Istoricheskata sudba na zhenata* (The historical fate of woman) made a great impact on the Bulgarian reading public at the time. In 1890, she became leader of the *Prijatelska druzhinka. Zhenski klon*. That same year, she left for Geneva to study (1890–1891), since the Bulgarian national university did not yet admit women. In July 1891, she returned to Sevlievo to arrange a period of further study in Switzerland, but had to stay longer in Bulgaria than she had intended. She began teaching in her native town and, in 1892, married Andrei Konov (1865–1933), a teacher, socialist, lawyer and MP from Sevlievo. Soon after, they both left for Switzerland, where she continued her studies (in the social sciences according to her memoirs; in midwifery–in Lausanne–according to other sources). Upon the couple's return home, Kina Konova resumed teaching in Sevlievo and, in 1897, established a women's organization there called *Nadejda* (Hope). As its Chairwoman, she organized Sunday schooling for illiterate people, a reading room for women and public lectures on various (mostly educational) topics.

Access to education constituted one of the earliest women's demands worldwide. The new male Bulgarian political elite after 1878 (like their counterparts elsewhere), acted in tune with a powerful "two-sex model" and developed opinions of men as "properly political and women as naturally domestic" (Landes 1996, 4), supporting different policies for the separate education of girls and boys. Once introduced, differences in high-school curricula served as a convenient pretext to prevent girls from attending university. Consequently, the unification of the curricula for girls and boys at secondary schools became an important demand of the new women's societies established in the 1890s. Women's efforts in this regard provoked heated debate on women's education. Konova was among those who fought for the equalization (in years and programs) of women's and men's high schools, for the admission of women to Sofia University and for equal salaries for female and male teachers. She submitted petitions to the National Assembly, the government and the academic council of Sofia University. Finally, in 1897, a law equalized high school education for girls and boys (fixing it at seven grades above the primary four-year level). Thus the formal preconditions were created for women's admission to university, which happened in 1901.

Kina Konova was among the initiators and founders of the *Bulgarski Zhenski Sujuz* (*BZhS*, Bulgarian Women's Union) in 1901, together with ***Vela Blagoeva***, ***Anna Karima***, ***Julia Malinova*** and ***Ekaterina Karavelova***. At the founding congress of the *BZhS*, she delivered a paper entitled "Woman's position in society, woman's work and exploitation" (Bradinska 1969, 69–70), in which she posed the question of the social composition of the *BZhS* and insisted on its proletarization: i.e. that the *BZhS* should be composed primarily of working class women. This was to become a bone of contention within the *BZhS* in the years to come and, in 1903, led to the first major split of the organization. The socialist women (with Vela Blagoeva and Kina Konova in charge) left the *BZhS*, dissatisfied with its 'above-class' and 'above-party' stance.

Gradually, Konova became more moderate in her views on the women's movement and joined the 'reformist' *Zhenski Sotsialdemokraticheski Sujuz* (Women's Social Democratic Union) in 1921. The main goal of this organization was to work toward the civic and political education of working women and to prepare them for the realization of socialist ideas. In her talks and political pamphlets, Konova defended the idea of women's economic independence and insisted on the necessity of professional and vocational women's education as a way of building women's independence. The *Zhenski Sotsialdemokraticheski Sujuz* wanted the "conscious part of society" to transform social reality and share its benefits with all the people, unlike the Communist women's union which, according to social democratic women, wanted "to destroy present life and build a new life on its ruins" (*Sotsialdemocraticheskiat zhenski suiuz*, 4). At the same time, social democratic women tried hard to dissociate themselves from the 'separatist feminists,' i.e. the 'bourgeois' *Bulgarski Zhenski Sujuz*, even though, in retrospect, it seems that the goals of the socialist and feminist women were quite similar.

This context helps to explain Kina Konova's peculiar position within the Bulgarian women's movement. Belonging to the socialist founders of the feminist *BZhS*, she soon openly articulated her disagreement with its 'above-class' and 'above-party' stance. But her revolt against the character of *BZhS* notwithstanding, she maintained permanent contacts and participated in most of the important events and actions undertaken by the Bulgarian feminists. In spite of her affiliation (after 1921) to the *Zhenski Sotsialdemokraticheski Sujuz*, she remained a passionate and faithful follower of the activities of the *BZhS* as well. Judging from her texts, it seems that she was equally attracted to both feminist and socialist emancipation ideologies. It was not by chance, therefore, that in 1926 (together with ***Julia Malinova***, ***Ekaterina Karavelova*** and Rada Staliiska), Kina Konova was pronounced an 'honorary member' of the feminist *Bulgarski Zhenski Sujuz*.

Kina Konova wrote extensively on various aspects of women's emancipation in Bulgaria. Her sober analyses of (educational and professional) injustices against women appeared in *Zhenski glas* (Women's voice), the organ of the *BZhS*, and in the publications of the *Zhenski Sotsialdemokraticheski Sujuz*: the newspapers *Blagodenstvie* (Prosperity) and *Nedovolnata* (Unsatisfied).

Little is known about the last two decades of Konova's life. She worked as a teacher in her native town, took part in public activities as a member of the school board and continued to publish on the position of women in Bulgarian society. She died on 2 May 1952 in Sofia.

Reneta Roshkeva
Rousse Historical Museum

Krassimira Daskalova
St. Kliment Ohridski, University of Sofia

SOURCES

(A) *Tsentralen Partien Archiv* (Central Party Archive), f. 15 (Kina Konova).
(B) *Zhenski glas* (Women's voice) (1899-1944).
(B) *Zhenski glas* 1, no. 3 (1 December 1899): 7-8; no. 11 (1 April 1900): 4-6; nos. 23-24 (15 September 1900).
(B) *Blagodenstvie* (Prosperity) (1921-1924).
(B) "Sotsialdemocraticheskiat zhenski suiuz I negovite zadachi. Rezume ot referata na drugarkata J. Sultanova" (The Women's Social Democratic Union and its goals. A summary of the paper by comrade J. Sultanova). *Blagodenstvie* 1, no. 7 (12 September 1921): 4.
(B) *Nedovolnata* (Unsatisfied) (1931).
(B) *Bulgarski Zhenski Sujuz (Po sluchai 30-godishninata mu). 1901-1931* (On the thirtieth anniversary of the Bulgarian Women's Union. 1901-1931). Sofia: Pecahtnitsa "Pravo," 1931.
(D) Bojadjieva-Fol, Vera. "Po putia na edin zhivot" (Along the way of one life). *Vestnik na zhenata* (Woman's newspaper), no. 603 (9 March 1935): 2.
(E) Vulchanov, Haralampi. *Sevlievo, 1842-1942. Chast 2* (Sevlievo, 1842-1942. Part 2). Sofia: 1942, 240, 307, 336.
(E) Bradinska, Radka. *Zarazhdane I oformiavane na zhenskoto sotsialistichesko dvizhenie v Bulgaria* (The beginning and development of the women's socialist movement in Bulgaria). Sofia, 1969.
(E) Landes, Joan. *Women and the Public Sphere in the Age of the French Revolution*, Ithaca/London: Cornell University Press, 1996.

KRÁSNOHORSKÁ, Eliška (born Alžběta Pechová) (1847-1926)

Feminist, poetess, librettist, critic, translator and founder of the first girls' high school in the Austro-Hungarian Empire; President of the *Ženský výrobní spolek český* (Women's Czech Production Society). Pseudonyms: 'Bětka Rozmarná' (Jolly Betty), 'Soliman Řetkvička' (Soliman the Radish), 'Reader of the Journals,' 'A. Temná' (A. Dark).

Krásnohorská was born Alžběta Pechová in Prague on 18 November 1847, to craftsman Ondřej Pech (1802-1849?), who died when she was two years old, and Dora Vodvářková, who supported the talents of her five children, particularly their musical interests. Alžběta was the fourth child. Since her older brothers took care of her education and taught her at home, she acquired a somewhat broader education than was usual for a woman at that time. Nevertheless, in her memoirs *Co přinesla léta* (What the years brought to me, 1928), Krásnohorská expressed regret over not having had a solid, formal education.

Her family home hosted many members of Prague bourgeois circles, including the composer Karel Bendl. Pechová wrote one of her first librettos (1868) for Bendl's opera, *Lejla*. She was soon introduced to important Prague intellectuals such as the Kantian aesthetician Josef Durdík (1837-1902), who drew her attention to the ideas of the philosopher Johan Friedrich Herbart (1781-1841), and to the prominent writers ***Karolína Světlá*** and Vítězslav Hálek (1835-1874). At the age of sixteen it became clear that, since she suffered from serious and painful joint illness, Pechová was not going to be able to devote herself to her beloved music. Partly under the influence of Karolína Světlá and partly as a way of resisting her incurable illness, the young, pretty and petite Pechová chose to live a life of self-imposed celibacy, dedicating her energy to the Czech cultural and national revival then sweeping the literary scene. It was at this time that she took the slightly ironic pseudonym of 'Eliška Krásnohorská,' inspired by her imaginary father, the knight of *Krásná Hora* (meaning 'beautiful mountain').

In 1863, she began publishing her early poems in the most important literary magazine of her time *Lumír*, edited by the respected poet Vítězslav Hálek. In 1871, she published a collection of poems called *Z máje žití* (From the spring of living) which, along with other collections of poems such as *K slovanskému jihu* (Towards the Slavonic south, 1880) and *Ze Šumavy* (From the Šumava mountains, 1873), formed her best poetic works. These intellectual poems exceeded the traditional expectations of nineteenth-century Czech readers and critics and Krasnohorská was criticized for her eroticism, which was deemed unsuitable for women. She put her sense of irony to good use in the epigrams, fables and satirical sketches she wrote for the satirical journal *Paleček*, as well as in her witty books for young girls.

In the 1860s, Krásnohorská witnessed the foundation and was involved in the activities of the *Americký klub dam* (American Ladies' Club), an elite philanthropic-educational organization that emerged around Vojtěch Náprstek (1826–1894), an admirer of modernization, American democracy and the women's movement. The *Americký klub dam* brought together prominent Prague women to organize educational and philanthropic programs with the support of Czech male liberals. Countess Jenny Taxis, ***Karolína Světlá*** and her sister Sofie Podlipská were among the founding members. The activities of the *Americký klub dam* continued until the Communist takeover in 1948.

Krásnohorská's feminist activities included leadership of the *Ženský výrobní spolek český* (Women's Czech Production Society), established in 1871. This organization aimed to alleviate poverty among the female population through educational programs (in response to conditions created by the Prussian–Austrian war of 1866). Krásnohorská led the *Ženský výrobní spolek český* from 1891, after the death of the long-standing director Emilie Bártová, who had taken over the organization after Karolína Světlá's resignation in 1880. Krásnohorská's active involvement in the *Ženský výrobní spolek český* dates from 1873, when the organization took over *Ženské listy* (Women's letters), a supplement for the magazine *Květy* (Flowers). Světlá made Krásnohorská editor-in-chief of *Ženské listy* in 1875 and from then on, Krásnohorská's status as a professional writer and editor and her financial independence from her family helped assuage any social stigma she might have suffered as an ill and unmarried woman.

Under Krásnohorská's editorial leadership, *Ženské listy* was transformed from an illustrated and entertaining 'light read' for women into a monthly periodical influenced by liberal philosophy; thus she managed to create a forum that not only monitored women's movements in Bohemia, Austria, Europe and the USA, but also tried to cultivate the spiritual horizon of Czech women by means other than the *belles lettres* found in the majority of 'women's magazines.' Throughout the 1870s, *Ženské listy* became a comprehensive source of literary and feminist analysis, alongside reviews of domestic and worldly affairs and often combined with pieces of a nationalist and romantic hue. Krásnohorská gradually surrounded herself with a wide circle of contributors, often 'recruited' from the ranks of the new female-teacher intelligentsia and including personalities such as Vilma Sokolová-Seidlová, Anna and Eliška Řeháková and Pavla Maternová. Through *Ženské listy*, Krásnohorská continued to develop her ideas on feminism and literature. She considered her writing to be a tool for achieving the intellectual, legal and civic freedom of women. The concept of 'woman' that she promoted all her life emphasized women's responsibilities towards their nation and the importance of women's equal education with men, of their sharing civic duties. She summarized her feminist ideas, clearly inspired by John Stuart Mill (1806-1873), in a booklet *Ženská otázka česká* (The Czech woman question, 1881).

Krásnohorská soon attracted the ambivalent attention of Prague intellectual circles, whose members often criticized her for having crossed the border 'out' of what they called the 'female zone.' At the same time, her ideas caught the attention of Josef Emler, editor of the prestigious academic periodical *Časopis muzea království českého* (The journal of the Czech Royal Museum). Although he was accused of having lent a scientific magazine to "Misses and Ladies" (Krásnohorská 1928, 2:81), Emler invited her to become the sole female contributor to the journal. Despite her active involvement with *Ženské listy* and other periodicals such as *Hudební listy* (Music letters), it was only after the publications of her first pieces in the *Časopis Muzea království českého* that her work generated considerable response and Krasnohorská was offered to contribute to the prestigious magazine *Osvěta* (Public education). (By this point she had already published a study on the Czech women's movement–inspired by ***Světlá***–in *Osvěta* in 1874.)

The culmination of Krásnohorská's feminist efforts was the foundation (1890) of the *Minerva* Society in Prague, which helped establish (also in 1890) the first girls' gymnasium (high school) in the Austro-Hungarian Empire. This school provided women with a final exam certificate (maturita or *abitur*), a necessary condition for entering formal academic education. The first institution of its kind, with a curricula taught in the Czech language, the school raised a new generation of Czech female intellectuals (such as ***Jesenská***) in the twentieth century.

Two spheres of activity particularly close to Krásnohorská's heart were translation and music. Her first large, ambitious translation project was of Adam Mickiewicz's *Pan Tadeáš* (Master Thaddeus), begun as a young woman and continued over a period of almost ten years (1872-1882). Through this work, along with other translations of several world-famous romantic poets of the 1880s, she tested the expressive capacities and linguistic idiosyncrasies of the Czech language. She also translated Pushkin's *Boris Godunov* and Byron's *Child Harold*. By 1863, Krásnohorská's brother Jindřich had introduced her to the most prominent nineteenth-century Czech musician, Bedřich Smetana (1824-1884). Her first review of Czech music, based on her study of the Wagnerian aesthetician Otakar Hostinský (published in 1871), had included critical remarks about Smetana–a national icon at the time. Although offended by these remarks, Smetana, familiar with her libretto for Karel Bendl, invited her to work on his operas *Hubička* (The kiss, 1876), *Tajemství* (A secret, 1879) and *Čertova stěna* (The devil's wall, 1883). In *Hubička*–based on a story by ***Světlá***–Smetana and Krásnohorská created a new type of Czech national comical *Singspiel*, transforming folk culture into a unique artistic form. Not even her working relation with Smetana was free of public controversy however, and she was accused of damaging national heritage when, after his death and upon his instructions, she burned his letters (see Očadlík 1940).

Many of the attacks Krásnohorská was subjected to throughout her life clearly contained gendered subtexts, even when they were not directly targeting her feminist activities. She faced scepticism concerning her critical judgment, which was considered unusual and unnecessary for a woman, and was exposed to social disapproval based on her status as an unmarried woman. Krásnohorská was also implicated in many local cultural and literary controversies from the 1870s. In her first pieces for the *Časopis Muzea království českého*, she accused the poetic generation grouped around the literary periodical *Lumír* of eclecticism and dependence on 'foreign' literary forms. They fought back by references to her 'unfeminine' nature and intellect. In the late 1880s, Krásnohorská participated in polemics over the modernist character of Czech culture, thereby contributing to an emerging modernism and modernist aesthetic, based on decadence, symbolism and naturalism, which came to challenge nineteenth-century Czech national myths and educational ideals (especially in the 1894 debates over the poetry of Vitězslav Hálek–see Lexikon České literatury 1993).

Despite all the controversies, Krásnohorská remained a respected and generally acknowledged critic, translator and feminist, whose contributions to Czech culture were formally recognized when she received an Honorary Doctorate from Charles University in 1922. She was a woman of multiple talents who occupies a special place in Czech cultural and intellectual history. She recorded her long and fruitful life in memoirs and reflective writings (*Co přinesla léta*) that have served as reference materials for the study of nineteenth-century Czech society, including the Czech women's movement. Krásnohorská's life and works represented a feminism encapsulated by the fight for women's intellectual equality, including demands for women's secondary and university education. She died in Prague on 26 November 1926.

Libuše Heczková
Charles University of Prague

SOURCES

(B) *Ženské listy* (Women's letters) (1872–1926).
(B) *Časopis muzea království českého* (The journal of the Czech Royal Museum) (1871–1890).
(B) *Osvěta* (Public education) (1871–1921).
(B) *Lumír* (1865–66; 1873–1940).
(B) Očadlík, Mirko. *Vzájemná korespondence, E. Krásnohorská a B. Smetana* (Correspondence between E. Krásnohorská and B. Smetana). Prague: Topičova edice, 1940.

(C) Krásnohorská, Eliška. "Z mého mládí" (From my young days). In *Co přinesla léta* (What the years have brought me). Prague: Vaněk a Votava, 1928.

(D) Strejček, Ferdinand. *Eliška Krásnohorská*. Prague: Melantrich, 1922.

(D) Antošová, Pavla, ed. *Eliška Krásnohorská*. Brno: Knihtiskárna a nakladatelství Pokorný, 1947.

(E) David, Katherine. "Czech Feminists and Nationalism in the Late Habsburg Monarchy: "First in Austria." *Journal of Women's History*, 3, No. 2 (Fall 1991): 26–45.

(E) *Lexikon české literatury, K–L. Osobnosti, dila, instituce* (Lexicon of Czech literature, K–L). Prague: Academia, 1993.

(E) Pynsent, Robert. *Questions of Identity: Czech and Slovak Ideas of Nationality and Personality*. Budapest/London: CEU Press, 1994.

(E) Neudorflová, Marie L. *České ženy v 19. století* (Czech women in the nineteenth century). Prague: Janua, 1999.

(E) Hawkesworth, Celia, ed. *A History of Central European Women's Writing*. Basingstoke: Palgrave, in association with School of Slavonic and East European Studies, University College, London, 2001.

KRONVALDE (born Roloff), Karolīne Liznete (1836–1913)

Teacher; early spokeswoman for women's rights in Latvia.

Very little is known of Karolīne Kronvalde's life and work, apart from the fact that she was the wife of Atis Kronvalds (1837–1875), a prominent leader of the Latvian nationalist movement in the 1870s. Much has been published on his life and work, yet very little has been published on his wife, Karolîne Kronvalde, one of the first spokeswomen for women's rights in Latvia.

Karolīne Kronvalde was born Karolīne Roloff on 2 April 1836, in Legramzda, Kurzeme. Her father was a doctor and her mother was an educated Polish woman. Karolīne was largely responsible for her own education; as an external student, she obtained a teaching qualification from the Jelgava gymnasium in the spring of 1855. In 1860, she took up work as a private teacher in the small town of Durbe. There, she met her future husband, Atis Kronvalds (1837–1875), who at that time was also working as a private teacher in Durbe.

Together with her future husband, Karolīne Roloff moved to Tērbata. Later, in 1867, the couple moved for a second time to Vecpiebalga, where Atis Kronvalds again took up work as a private teacher. In 1868, after waiting eight years for her fiancé to finish his studies, Roloff finally married Kronvalds. After his death in 1875, Karolīne Kronvalde worked in Riga as a language teacher and managed the boarding school of the Riga Latvians' Association. From 1889 until her death, she lived in Vecpiebalga with her daughter Milda Sliede, where she was an active participant in the social and cultural life of the town. Some sources say that Karolīne Kronvalde had a daughter and a son, others maintain that she brought up four children.

Serious debate on the subject of women's rights began to enter Latvian public discourse in the 1870s. Earlier (from the late 1860s onwards), such issues were for the most part playfully dismissed in the press; stories of North American women studying medicine and law or elsewhere working in offices and shops were treated as humorous anecdotes. In the Latvian press, the first debate on 'the woman question' appeared somewhat incidentally in the *Baltijas Vēstnesis* (Baltic herald) in 1870. It was triggered by an article entitled "Piektdienas vakarā" (On Friday evening), whose author, someone named Garrs, had mocked (particularly rural) women: "a man is and always will be smarter than a woman, and the thicker his beard, the stronger his mind" (Garrs, 1870). By way of reply, Kronvalde published a letter in the same periodical, signed *Kar. K.*, in which she called for women's equal rights in the spheres of education, an end to restrictions on women's personal freedom and for a general intellectual awakening among women and the nation as a whole. Since in Kronvalde's view it was a national responsibility to have women properly educated, the current situation, in which schools and (text)books were designed with men and not women in mind, had to change. With regards to the superior wisdom of men, Kronvalde added: "You say 'that is what we men believe in, and will continue to believe'—so be it, we shall not forbid it. And you, being superior in mind, let us hold to our beliefs" (Kronvalde, 1870).

Karolīne Kronvalde's reply "To the Honorable Garrs" has since been regarded as the spark igniting women's activism and movements in Latvia thereafter. Her ideas, unique for the time, were not enthusiastically accepted by national leaders but nevertheless managed to generate a number of essays in support of the stand she had taken: see the argument by 'Anonymous' in *Baltijas Vēstnesis* (24 December 1870) and K. M.'s "Vēl kāds vārds par un priekš tautietēm" (One more word for and about women) in *Balss* (Voice) (16, 20, 23 June 1879), as well as the various related commentaries published at the time in the popular newspaper *Rīgas Lapa* (Riga news).

Karolīne Kronvalde died on 23 October 1913 and was buried in Vidus cemetery alongside her husband.

Irina Novikova
University of Latvia

SOURCES

(B) Garrs. "Piektdienas vakarā" (On Friday evening). *Baltijas Vēstnesis* (Baltic herald) (29 October 1870).

(B) Brant, Līlija. *Latviešu sieviete* (Latvian woman). Riga: A/S Valters un Rapa Ěenerālkommisijā, 1931.

(B) Kronvalds, A. *Kopoti raksti* (Collected works). A. Goba, ed. Riga: Valters un Rapa, 1936/37.

(C) Kronvalde, Karolīne. "Zeenigam Garram" (To the Honorable Garrs). *Baltijas Vēstnesis* (Baltic herald), nos. 46-47 (1870).

(E) Zelče, Vita. *Nezināmā. Latvijas sievietes 19. gadsimta otrajā pusē* (The unknown. Latvian women in the second half of the nineteenth century). Riga, 2002.

KRUPSKAIA, Nadezhda Konstantinovna (1869–1939)

Russian revolutionary; teacher; Soviet bureaucrat in the field of education; wife of V. I. Lenin (Ul'ianov)

Nadezhda Krupskaia (Krupskaya) was born in Petersburg on 14 (26) February 1869. Her father was descended from the Polish nobility. Her grandfather fought with the Russian army in the War of 1812 and then settled in the *Gubernia* (province) of Kazan. Her father was well-educated and for a time served as a regional bureaucrat in a Polish province, but lost his position when Nadezhda was a child. Although her father was later cleared of the charges against him, Nadezhda never forgot the injustice. Her mother, Elizaveta Tistrova, was poor but descended from nobility. Educated in St Petersburg at the Pavlovsky Institute as a governess, Elizaveta Tistrova also wrote children's poetry. Nadezhda Krupskaia's early life was uneventful until the loss of her father's position. She was a rather lonely child who read a great deal; later, she attended the Obolensky *Gymnazium* (high school) in St Petersburg, where she was an outstanding student. Her father died in 1883 after a lingering illness. The 1880s were also a time when she grew acquainted with the ideas of Tolstoi and became a Tolstoian; in those years she read a number of radical works. She attended the *Bestuzhev* Higher Women's Courses in St Petersburg but did not complete them, becoming active in the *kruzhki* (circles) and reading widely throughout the summer of 1890, including Marxist works. In 1891, she began teaching at the "Evening Sunday School" in St Petersburg, established by factory owners to provide workers with elementary education. She taught there three nights a week and her work was respected. Over time, the school came under Marxist influence and Krupskaia again became active in Marxist circles, through which (in February 1894) she met a young Marxist from the Volga: Vladimir Il'ich Ul'ianov (1870–1924), who used the pseudonym V. I. Lenin, among other names. Over the following year, Lenin and Krupskaia gradually became friends. Lenin taught briefly at the Sunday elementary school in 1894.

In 1895, Krupskaia began working as a copyist for the railroad administration, while continuing to teach at the evening school. Krupskaia and Lenin saw each other frequently for about two months in 1895, when the Group of Social Democrats was formed. Lenin was one of the leaders of the Group arrested in December 1895. He was briefly released from jail in 1897, before being sent into Siberian exile. Krupskaia was arrested in August 1896 as a member of the *Soiuz Bor'by za Osvobozhdenie Rabochego Klassa* (Union of Struggle for the Liberation of the Working Class). She was released in 1897 but sentenced to a term in Siberia. Some sort of agreement between Lenin and Krupskaia occured (via correspondence) regarding their 'engagement.'

Nadezhda Krupskaia, 1922, with Vladimir Il'ich Lenin, nephew Viktor Ul'janov and Vera (daughter of a worker) in Gorki.

In January 1898, Lenin asked the authorities to permit his fiancée (Krupskaia) to join him in Shushenskoe, Siberia. She was given permission on condition the couple marry and so they did–shortly after her arrival. In Siberia, Krupskaia became Lenin's secretary and assistant, roles she would assume for the entire duration of their marriage. During this period Krupskaia, encouraged by Lenin, wrote on 'the woman question.' In her brochure addressed to women workers entitled *Zhenshchina-Rabotnitsa* (The woman worker), composed during Siberian exile, Krupskaia argued that only a proletarian regime could liberate women. By becoming workers, women could free themselves from the drudgery of the home. Her views later became the centerpiece of the Soviet position on women. Some scholars believe that Lenin contributed significantly to Krupskaia's writings on women since some phrases appear to be his. Krupskaia's theoretical approach did not depart from a two-dimensional perspective:

woman-as-mother and woman-as-worker. The emphasis on woman-as-mother is embedded deeply in Russian history; the emphasis on woman-as-worker is a reflection of Krupskaia's commitment to Marxism and the working class. There is little feminism in her conception of women's roles, if compared with the writings of ***Alexandra Kollontai*** or Klara Zetkin.

Lenin was released from exile in 1900 and given permission to go abroad but he remained in Russia for a while because Krupskaia had fallen ill. In April 1901, she joined Lenin in Munich. Over the next few years, the couple lived in Munich, London and Geneva. Krupskaia worked for *Iskra*, the publication of the Russian Social Democrats. In 1903, after the Bolshevik–Menshevik split within the editorial board of *Iskra*, Lenin, and later Krupskaia withdrew from the board. They returned to Russia in 1905 and resided in St Petersburg and in nearby Finland until 1907. Early in 1908, they went to Geneva; later to Paris, remaining there until 1912, when they left for Poland. In either 1909 or 1910, Lenin met ***Inessa Armand*** but their friendship did not blossom until the winter of 1910–1911. There was a great contrast between Armand and Krupskaia. Armand was beautiful, glamorous and feminine. Krupskaia was a plain woman who cared little about beauty or glamour but devoted herself entirely to the cause. Armand, although not openly feminist like Alexandra Kollontai, had stronger feminist leanings than Krupskaia, who appears to have overlooked any marital problems and was a loyal wife to Lenin, as well as his principal aide. Armand and Lenin remained friends and correspondents and there has been considerable scrutiny of the surviving parts of their correspondence. In 1919, Armand was put in charge of the new *Zhenskii Otdel* (Women's Department) of the *Rossiiskaia Kommunisticheskaia Partiia/Bolshevikov* (Russian Communist Party/Bolsheviks), successor to the Russian Social Democratic Labor Party. It was a difficult assignment and often frustrating. In 1920, ***Armand*** traveled to the south to recover from an exhausting period of work; conditions were poor and after coming into contact with cholera victims, she contracted the fatal disease. Lenin was devastated. After Armand's death, Krupskaia and Lenin assumed some responsibility for her younger children.

Krupskaia was first and foremost an educator, who believed that the key to developing a socialist society was the education and upbringing of children. She was especially devoted to libraries and encouraged reading at all levels of society. Since reading was already popular in Russia among the well-educated, Krupskaia saw her mission as one of spreading the message among the masses. She strongly believed in the power of socialization through education and reading and is credited with being a major force behind the establishment of the Soviet library system.

Krupskaia's life with Lenin after the Bolshevik Revolution was relatively brief. Lenin was seriously wounded in an assassination attempt in 1918 and perhaps never fully recovered. During his years in power (1917–1922), the couple lived in a modest apartment within the Moscow Kremlin. After Lenin suffered a major stroke in 1922, Krupskaia devoted herself to his care. She was also the intermediary between him, the government and the Communist Party. Ioseph Stalin, General Secretary of the Party, was delegated to stay in touch with Lenin, who lived in Gorky during his illness. Stalin's behavior toward Krupskaia was dismissive and rude and Lenin wrote a letter to Stalin in which he admonished him. Lenin also wrote to the Party his famous *Pis'mo k S'ezdu* (known in English as his Last Testament), composed in 1923, in which he proposed Stalin be dismissed as General Secretary. After Lenin's death (1924), Krupskaia insisted that the *Pis'mo k S'ezdu* be published but Stalin was able to prevent publication because of his support within the Central Committee. He warned Krupskaia he could produce another woman who would claim to be Lenin's wife.

During her years as a widow, Krupskaia lived in a Kremlin apartment and worked in the *Kommissariat Obrazovaniia* (Ministry of Education), serving as Deputy Commissar (Minister) from 1929 until her death on 27 February 1939, the morning after her seventieth birthday. During the last ten years of her life, she became an important symbol of continuity with Lenin and was thus asked to speak on public holidays such as International Women's Day (8 March). Since she and Stalin shared certain views on the importance of education and the goal of socialization, she was allowed to continue her work.

Krupskaia's life as Lenin's widow was not easy. There was rivalry with Lenin's sisters as to who should maintain his papers and his legacy and Stalin played on the rivalry among the women. Krupskaia resisted an official biography of Lenin on the grounds that Marxism eschewed the glorification of the individual, but finally acquiesced to producing *Vospominaniia o Lenine* (Reminiscences of Lenin) as a children's book.

The Soviet library system and also the educational system owed much to her diligence. Her early theories on women became official policy as Soviet women were pushed into the workplace and yet continued to function as homemakers and mothers, despite the promise to free them from domestic slavery. A strong, yet dogmatic woman, Krupskaia's life was dedicated entirely to the Marxist movement, Lenin and the Soviet system. Since the fall of the USSR, there has been some new research on Krupskaia which has tended to focus on the Lenin–Armand–Krupskaia triangle, rather than on the work of Krupskaia herself.

Norma C. Noonan
Augsburg College, Minneapolis, Minnesota, USA

SOURCES

(B) Lenin, V. I. *Sobranie Sochinenii* (Collected works). Moscow: Izdatel'stvo politicheskoi literatury (Politizdat). 1964, 45: 345.

(C) Krupskaia, Nadezhda K. *Vospominaniia o Lenine* (Reminiscences of Lenin). Moscow: Politizdat, 1957.

(D) McNeal, Robert H. *Bride of the Revolution*. Ann Arbor: University of Michigan Press, 1972.

(D) Raymond, Boris. *Krupskaia and Soviet Russian Librarianship, 1917-1939.* Metuchen, N.J.: Scarecrow Press, 1979.

(D) Noonan, Norma C. "Two Solutions to the *Zhenskii vopros* in Russia and the USSR– Kollantai and Krupskaia: A Comparison." *Women and Politics* 11, no. 3 (1991): 77-99.

(D) Sokolov, Boris. *Armand i Krupskaia: Zhenshchiny vozhdia* (Armand and Krupskaia: the leader's wives). Smolensk: Rusich Press, 1999.

(D) Noonan, Norma C. "Nadezhda Konstantinovna Krupskaia." In *Encyclopedia of the Russian Women's Movement*. Westport, CT: Praeger, 2001.

(E) Vasil'ieva, Larissa. *Kremlin Wives*. New York: Arcade Press, 1992.

(E) Elwood, R. C. *Inessa Armand: Revolutionary and Feminist.* New York: Cambridge University Press, 1992.

(F) Brooke, Caroline. "What Shall We Tell the Children?" http://www.voiceoftheturtle.org/show_printer.php?aid=18

(F) Gould, Bob. "Lenin, Krupskaia, and Inessa Armand." Ozleft. September 2003 http://members.optushome.com.au/spainter/Armand.html

KUCZALSKA-REINSCHMIT (Reinschmidt), Paulina Jadwiga (1859-1921)

Polish feminist, publicist and editor; founder (1907) and activist of the *Związek Równouprawnienia Kobiet Polskich* (Union of Equal Rights for Polish Women); co-founder (1899) of the *Unia* (Union), the Polish section of the *Alliance universelle des femmes*. Literary pseudonyms: 'PK,' 'PKR,' 'PRT,' 'PR.' and 'R.'

Paulina Kuczalska-Reinschmit was born on 15 January 1859 in Warsaw, into a noble family. She grew up in the country, on estates in the Ukraine (Kośkowice in Volhynia and Bereźniaki). After the death of her father (date unknown), she moved to Warsaw with her mother and sister Helena (1854-1927, a pioneer of women's physical education). Here, the family settled and the girls received secondary education at a private girls' boarding school. From an early age, Paulina was raised in a patriotic spirit under the strong influence of her mother, Ewelina Porczyńska born Jastrzębiec (data unknown), who belonged to ***Narcyza Żmichowska***'s emancipation circle: 'The Enthusiasts.'

Initially, there were little signs that Kuczalska–who was short in stature, physically weak and suffered from chronic asthma and a heart condition–would become a leading personality of the early twentieth-century Polish women's movement. Set to become a wealthy noblewoman on the Polish eastern frontier, her unhappy marriage in 1879 to a private clerk, Stanisław Reinschmit (Reinschmidt), was to change her life. Reinschmit squandered what was left of Kuczalska's family wealth and–as a result of his dissipated lifestyle–infected his wife with venereal disease, leading to complications (loss of an eye) from which Kuczalska suffered greatly. The only child from the marriage, a son Leon (later a publicist), was brought up by Stanisław Kuczalski.

With the help of her family, Kuczalska went to Geneva to study the natural sciences (1885-1887), which she continued to study in Brussels (1887-1889). While studying abroad, she first joined the life of the Polish émigré community, later establishing contacts with the women's emancipation movement developing in Western Europe. Together with ***Maria Szeliga-Loevy***, Kuczalska attended the Second International Women's Congress in Paris (1889).

During these early activist years, Kuczalska-Reinschmit divided her time between political journalism and organizational work for the women's movement in the Polish territories. In 1881, she made her writing debut in the Warsaw periodical *Echo* (Response), later (1884–1887) writing for the progressive women's magazine *Świt* (Dawn). By the end of the 1880s, she had established a collaborative partnership with the biggest Polish daily, the *Kurier Warszawski* (Warsaw courier), in which she continued to publish until the end of her life. By the 1890s, she was publishing in the progressive periodicals *Prawda* (Truth), *Głos* (Voice) and *Przegląd Tygodniowy* (Weekly review); later in *Ogniwo* (Link), *Nowa Gazeta* (New gazette) and *Kurier Codzienny* (Daily courier).

The future direction of Kuczalska-Reinschmit's work was influenced strongly by the Women's Congress held in Paris, 25–30 June 1889, which she attended as Vice-President of the section on "Women's work and organizations" and where she delivered a talk on the social and political situation of women in the Polish territories. In Paris she became acquainted with numerous activists of the European women's movement and later maintained correspondence with such illustrious personalities as Marie Deraismes, Lina Morgenstern and Anita Augsburg. Upon her return to Poland, Kuczalska-Rein-schmit and another Paris Congress participant, Aleksandra Korycińska, established the *Unia* (Union) in Warsaw: the Polish section of the *Alliance universelle des femmes* (founded by ***Maria Szeliga-Loevy*** in 1889). The *Unia* was the first Polish organization to be affiliated with the *Alliance* and although it only existed until 1892, it provided the women's movement in the Polish territories with a strong impetus resulting, among other things, in the establishment of the first Polish feminist journal, *Ster* (Helm).

Up until the mid-1890s, Paulina Kuczalska-Reinschmit was ideologically influenced by Warsaw Positivism, a peculiar variety of Central European liberalism which espoused, among other things, women's civil rights, the development of women's activities in a wide range of professional fields and modern education for girls. The most far-reaching principle of this group of publicists was that university education be made available to women. Kuczalska-Reinschmit was closer to the more radical faction of the Warsaw Positivists, especially in matters relating to women, as shown by her column on women's issues entitled *E pur si muove* (Yet things are in motion), published in the leading Warsaw periodical of the progressive intelligentsia, the *Przegląd Tygodniowy* (Weekly review). She also inspired many initiatives to increase women's participation in social and professional life. In Warsaw, she ran a school of handicrafts for women and in 1894 founded the *Delegacja Pracy Kobiet* (Women's Labor Delegation), an organization established to coordinate the economic and professional activities of women in the Russian partition. From 1895 to 1897, she published the Polish territories' first feminist periodical, *Ster* (Helm) in Lviv (then under Austrian partition).

By the end of the 1890s, part of the Polish women's movement underwent radicalization due to, among other things, the progressive movement's incomprehension and devaluation of the importance of 'the woman question'. Younger women activists, usually those with a Western European education and experience of social movements and activism headed the new radical circles, at the heart of which was a Warsaw salon led by Kuczalska-Reinschmit: the so-called *Koło Emancypantek* (Circle of Emancipationists). Through this circle, Kuczalska-Reinschmit met co-worker Józefa Bojanows-ka, from whom she would become inseparable and who would take care of her in the later years of her life. The new emancipation movement demanded access for women to university education and voting rights for women. The appearance of women in public life was considered a sign of general social progress as well as being necessary for Polish cultural enrichment and national revival, and the radicalization of the movement resulted in new kinds of publication for women such as the feminist periodical, *Nowe Słowo* (New word), issued in Cracow (under Austrian partition) in 1902–1907 and edited by Maria Turzyma. In Russian Poland, feminism, like many other social movements, emerged in the context of the Revolution of 1905; the First Congress of Polish Women held in Warsaw on 20–23 October 1905 was organized by Paulina Kuczalska-Reinschmit, who also opened the Congress and delivered a talk on marriage reform.

In 1907, on Kuczalska-Reinschmit's co-initiative and under her leadership, the *Związek Równouprawnienia Kobiet Polskich* (Union of Equal Rights for Polish Women) was established with the revived *Ster* (Helm) as its journal (1907–1914). In that first year (1907), a group of activists (among them ***Teodora Męczkowska*** and Cecylia Walewska) broke away from the *Związek Równouprawnienia Kobiet Polskich* and formed a separate organization: the *Polskie Stowarzyszenie Równouprawnienia Kobiet* (Polish Women's Rights Association). What caused the split is not entirely clear; an accusation frequently made against Kuczalska-Reinschmit was that her feminism was too extreme, even eccentric in view of her 'radical' demands for women's suffrage before independence for the country as a whole had been attained.

In spite of this split, Kuczalska-Reinschmit continued to be unquestioningly regarded as an authority in feminist circles. A Jubilee Celebration was held in her honor in 1911 on the occasion of her thirty years work for the women's movement, attended by a large group of women's activists. Although ill in the last years of her life, Kuczalska-Reinschmit remained deeply involved in publicist activity (primarily writing for *Ster*) and organizational activity (working for the Union of Equal Rights for Polish Women). Kuczalska-Reinschmit always defended the integrity and autonomy of women's interests, gaining the nickname of 'Hetwoman' (Commander in Chief). She died on 13 September 1921.

Grzegorz Krzywiec
Institute of History, Polish Academy of Science

SOURCES

(B) Walewska, Cecylia. *W walce o równe prawa. Nasze bojownice* (Fighting for equal rights. Our fighters). Warsaw: Kobieta Współczesna, 1930.

(C) Kuczalska-Reinschmitt, Paulina. "Nasze cele i drogi. Szkic do programu działalności kobiecej" (Our targets and strategies. A draft program for women's activism). *Ster* (Helm) (Lviv, 1897).

(C) Kuczalska-Reinschmitt, Paulina. "Z historii ruchu kobiecego" (From the history of the women's movement). In Maria Turzyma, ed., with an introduction by Kazimiera Bujdwidowa. *Głos kobiet w kwestii kobiecej* (The voices of Polish women on the woman question). Cracow: Stowarzyszenie Pomocy Naukowej dla Polek J.I. Kraszewskiego, 1903, 232–272; 273–338.

(C) Kuczalska-Reinschmitt, Paulina. *Młodzież żeńska a sprawa kobieca* (The female youth and the woman question). Warsaw: Koło Pracy Kobiet, 1906.

(C) Kuczalska-Reinschmitt, Paulina. "Wyborcze prawa kobiet" (Voting rights for women). *Ster* (Warsaw, 1908).

(C) Kuczalska-Reinschmitt, Paulina. "Siostry. Sztuka psychologiczna" (Sisters. A psychological play). *Ster* (Warsaw, 1908).

(D) Hulewicz, Jan. "Kuczalska-Reinschmit Paulina." In *Polski Słownik Biograficzny* (Polish biographical dictionary). Cracow: Zakład Narodowy im. Ossolińskich & Instytut Historii PAN, 1969, 16: 69–70.

(E) Pachucka, Romana. *Pamiętniki z lat 1886–1914* (Memoirs from the years 1886–1914). Wrocław: Zakład Narodowy im. Ossolińskich, 1958.

(E) Stegmann, Natali. *Die Töchter der geschlagenen Helden. 'Frauenfrage,' Feminismus und Frauenbewegung in Polen 1863–1919* (The daughters of fallen heroes. The woman question, feminism and the women's movement in Poland, 1863–1919). Wiesbaden: Harrassowitz Verlag, 2000.

(E) Górnicka-Boratyńska, Aneta. *Stańmy się sobą. Cztery projekty emancypacji (1863–1939)* (Let us become ourselves. Four projects of emancipation, 1863–1939). Warsaw: "Świat Literacki" Publishing House, 2002.

KUSKOVA, Ekaterina Dmitrievna (born Esipova) (1869–1958)

Russian journalist, editor and publisher; independent Marxist and feminist political activist.

Ekaterina Dmitrievna Esipova was born on 8 December 1869 in the provincial Southern Ural capital of Ufa, the first of two children in her family. Her father, Dmitrii Petrovich Esipov (probably a member of Russia's untitled nobility; date of birth unknown), taught language and literature in the local secondary school and was subsequently an excise tax collector until his suicide in the mid-1880s. Her mother, Liudmila Mikhailovna Esipova (date of birth unknown), a Tatar whom Ekaterina resembled physically, died of tuberculosis in 1884. In 1885, Ekaterina graduated with highest distinction from the Mariinskii secondary school for girls in Saratov, a provincial capital on the lower Volga. Either that year or the next, she married her former physics teacher, Ivan Petrovich Iuvenaliev (1853?–1889), the son of a civil servant and member of the Saratov lesser nobility. She had two sons, Nikolai Ivanovich (1887–?) and Aleksandr Ivanovich Iuvenaniev (1888?–1890). After her husband's premature death from tuberculosis in 1889, and with few career options open to a single mother, Ekaterina resumed her education in the early 1890s, studying midwifery at Moscow's *Vospitatel'nyi Dom* (Foundling Hospital). (In Russia women could only obtain paramedical training, since they were barred entry to university medical courses.) It is not known whether Ekaterina ever completed her program.

In Moscow, Ekaterina was drawn to the fight against tsarist oppression and in 1893 married fellow radical Petr Ivanovich Kuskov (1868–?), a law student of peasant origin. Although this was a so-called fictitious marriage (arranged for political reasons—not uncommon among Russian radicals seeking to mislead the police), she would retain Kuskov's name after separating from him a year or so later. Kuskova was soon attracted to Marxism and, from 1895 to early 1896, lived abroad among Russian social democratic émigré communities in Switzerland (Geneva and Baugy sur Clarens). In mid-1896, she moved to Brussels, where she remained until late 1897; towards the end of 1897, she moved to Berlin, where she remained until late 1898 or early 1899. Like many radicals from Russia, where political parties were illegal, Kuskova found a safe haven in these European refuges. In these years, Kuskova entered into what would be a life-long political and journalistic collaboration with fellow Marxist and common law husband, Sergei Nikolaevich Prokopovich (1871–1955), a nobleman of modest income who worked as a statistician and economist (he would later become a well known economist both in Russia and in emigration after 1921).

Kuskova embarked on a career in journalism in the late 1880s or early 1890s, publishing her first articles in the liberal newspaper *Saratovskii Dnevnik* (Saratov journal) (the precise dates are not known). She then worked with the Russian social democratic émigré press in Berlin during 1897–98 (all opposition press was illegal in Russia before 1905). Upon returning to Russia at the end of the century (in late 1898 or early 1899) and settling in St Petersburg, Kuskova played a central role in the Liberation Movement, a coalition of radicals and liberals dedicated to winning civil liberties and constitutional government. After Tsar Nicholas II granted Russia a constitution in October 1905, making political parties legal for the first time, Kuskova joined the *Kadet* (Constitutional Democratic) Party for a brief period, serving on its Central Committee. However it was journalism rather than party politics that was her weapon of choice in the struggle for democracy and equality. From 1903 to 1907, she operated her own publishing house, producing monographs on critical economic and social issues of the day. She also worked as editor, publisher and/or contributor to a variety of short-lived liberal and radical periodicals in these years.

Kuskova joined the ranks of Russia's burgeoning women's movement in 1906, signing an appeal for women's rights published that year in the newspaper *Nasha Zhizn'* (Our life), of which she was a founder and editor. In 1908 (either shortly before or soon after moving to Moscow), she attended the *Pervyi Vserossiiskii Zhenskii S'ezd* (First All-Russian Congress of Women) as a delegate. Kuskova's feminism, born of numerous encounters with discrimination in both her personal and political life, found frequent expression in her journalism. She championed the demand for women's equality in the liberal Moscow newspaper *Russkie Vedomosti* (Russian news, 1908–1918), as well as in journals such as *Soiuz Zhenshchin* (Union of women, 1909) and *Obrazovanie* (Education, 1909). On the eve of World War I, she penned the entry on "The Woman Question" for the seventh edition of the prestigious *Entsiklopedicheskii Slovar'* (Granat encyclopedia, vol. 20). Her articles focused on women's educational needs and emphasized the importance of women's political participation as a means of redressing their economic subordination.

In the years leading up to 1917, Kuskova was a central figure in the Russian cooperative movement, viewing consumer cooperatives as a way to broaden the economic opportunities of working women. Her articles demanding equality and democracy for both women and men appeared in the cooperative press, in such publications as *Kooperativnaia Zhizn'* (Cooperative life) and *Vestnik Kooperatsii* (Cooperative herald), as well as in radical journals, including the prominent *Sovremmenik* (The contemporary, 1912–1915). With the outbreak of World War I, Kuskova participated in the voluntary organizations formed to aid in the wartime distribution of resources. She also took a leading role in the oppositional activities as a member of Russia's political Masonic organization *Velikii Vostok Narodov Rossii* (Grand Orient of Russia) (a highly secret organization dedicated to establishing democracy) that eventually precipitated the downfall of the Romanov dynasty in 1917.

Immediately following the February Revolution, Kuskova worked to strengthen the new Provisional Government's commitment to women's suffrage prior to elections for the Constituent Assembly, which was to determine Russia's future government (the Assembly was dissolved prematurely by the Bolsheviks in early 1918). She spoke with passion in defense of women's enfranchisement at the 1917 *Vserossiiskii Zhenskii S'ezd* (All-Russian Congress of Women); and afterwards she collaborated with the *Liga Ravnopraviia Zhenshchin* (League for Women's Equal Rights) to promote civic education among women in order to enable them to become informed and responsible voters. During this revolutionary year, Kuskova also served on the Council of the Republic (a temporary legislature that functioned until the Constituent Assembly convened), headed the Moscow *Kommissariat po Obespecheniiu Svobody Pechati* (Commissariat for the Protection of the Freedom of the Press) and continued her political journalism. As a contributor to, as well as editor of, several new and established periodicals, she frequently articulated her views on women's suffrage and civic responsibility stressing, in particular, women's duty to safeguard the freedoms of the February Revolution. She also very briefly joined the Menshevik Party.

Kuskova's outspoken journalistic opposition to the Bolsheviks, both before and after their seizure of power in October 1917, led eventually to her arrest in connection with relief efforts during the 1921 famine (she had been arrested by the tsarist police in the mid-1890s and again in 1905). She was sentenced to death in 1922, along with a number of other prominent intellectuals (including Prokopovich), but the national and international outcry forced the Soviet government to commute her sentence and expel her from Russia. Together with Prokopovich, she went first to Berlin and then in 1924 to Prague, where she was active in the émigré *Respublikansko-Demokraticheskoe Ob'edineniie* (Republican-Democratic Association), an organization of like-minded intellectuals interested in seeing democracy restored in Russia. In 1938, as the Germans moved into Czechoslovakia, Kuskova made another move to Geneva. In emigration, she continued to work as a journalist. Her articles urging cooperation among liberal and socialist opponents of the Soviet regime appeared in a variety of émigré newspapers and journals, including the Berlin/Paris-based *Dni* (Days, 1923–1928), the Paris-based *Poslednie Novosti* (Latest news, 1924–1940), the New York-based *Novyi Zhurnal* (New journal, 1942–1958) and *Novoe Russkoe Slovo* (New Russian word, 1945–1958). Kuskova remained a passionate supporter of equality and democracy for Russia until her death in Geneva on 22 December 1958.

The consolidation of Bolshevik power in the early 1920s marked the end of Kuskova's involvement in the Russian women's movement. Yet her ideas and efforts, like those of all early Russian feminists, laid the foundations for the resumption of an independent women's movement after the collapse of Soviet communism at the end of the twentieth century.

Barbara T. Norton
Widener University

SOURCES

(A) A considerable number of Kuskova's letters, written to friends and acquaintances during her emigration and bearing on her biography both before and after her expulsion from Russia, are to be found among the papers of other leading émigrés. See, for example, the Lidiia O. Dan Archive, XII–XVIII in the International Institute for Social History (Amsterdam); the S. P. Mel'gunov Collection, Groups 15–45 in the British Library of Political and Economic Sciences Archives (London); the B. I. Nikolaevskii Collection, Nos. 93, 109, and 209; the N. V. Volskii Collection in the Hoover Institution on War, Revolution and Peace (Stanford, CA), boxes 5 and 8; and the B. A. Bakhmetev Archive, Boxes 4 and 5 at Columbia University (New York). Kuskova's own papers have long been inaccessible. Those from the years up to 1938 are in the former Communist Party archives (now *Rossiiskii Tsentr Khraneniia i Izucheniia Dokumentov Noveishaia Istoriia* and *Gosudarstvennyi arkhiv Rossiiskoi Federatsii* in Moscow) and apparently not yet indexed; her papers from the period after 1938 are in the *Bibliothéque Nationale* (Paris), until very recently under embargo.

(B) *Nasha zhizn'* (Our life) (1904–06).

(B) *Russkie vedomosti* (Russian news) (1908–1918).

(B) *Vlast' naroda* (Power of the people) (1917).

(B) *Novoe russkoe slovo* (New Russian word) (1945–1958).

(B) *Bez zaglaviia* (Untitled) (1906).

(B) *Soiuz zhenshchin* (Union of women) (1909).

(B) *Obrazovanie* (Education) (1909).

(C) Kuskova, E. D. "Davno minuvshee" (From the Past) *Novyi zhurnal* (New journal) 43 (1955): 96–119; 44 (1956): 121–142; 45 (1956): 149–180; 47 (1956): 154–176; 48 (1957): 139–162; 49 (1957): 145–170; 50 (1957): 173–197; 51 (1957): 137–172; 54 (1958): 117–147.

(D) Norton, Barbara T. "The Making of a Female Marxist: E. D. Kuskova's Conversion to Russian Social Democracy." *International Review of Social History* 34 (1989): part 2, 227–247.

(D) Norton, Barbara T. "Laying the Foundations of Democracy in Russia: E. D. Kuskova's Contributions, February-October, 1917." In Linda Edmondson, ed. *Women and Society in Russia and the Soviet Union*. Cambridge: Cambridge University Press, 1992, 101–123.

(D) Norton, Barbara T. "Journalism as a Means of Empowerment: The Early Career of E. D. Kuskova." In Barbara T. Norton and Jehanne M. Gheith, eds. *An Improper Profession: Women, Gender and Journalism in Late Imperial Russia*. Durham, NC: Duke University Press, 2001, 222–248.

KVEDER, Zofka (first married name, Kveder-Jelovšek; second married name, Kveder-Demetrović) (1878–1926)

Slovene writer, journalist, editor and feminist.

Zofka Kveder was born on 22 April 1878 in Ljubljana (Slovenia), the first child of assistant railway conductor Janez Kveder (1846–1908) and Neža Kveder, born Legat (1851–1915). She spent her childhood in the country after her father—restless by nature and prone to changing jobs—decided to leave Ljubljana. Two sons were later born to the Kveders: Alojzij (1882–1932) and Viktor (1884–1939). After Zofka had finished her four-year village elementary schooling (in 1888), her father sent her to Ljubljana to a convent school. She stayed there until she was fifteen, when she returned to her parents in the small village of Retje in southern Slovenia. By that time, her father had taken to drinking and Zofka could not bear to be at home. Barely sixteen, she fled to Kočevje, the nearest large town, where she worked as a secretary in a landsurveyor's office. After several months she returned home, but the family did not welcome her. Her father's alcoholism had driven her mother to religious fanaticism and Zofka, who resented any form of religiosity after having been schooled by nuns, drifted apart from her. Both her parents often abused her physically and she decided to break away from home for good.

In August 1897, Zofka Kveder went to Ljubljana and found a job in a law practice copying out files. In the late 1890s, she began to write and in the beginning of 1898, sent some of her texts to five newspapers and magazines. The magazine *Slovenka* (Slovene woman, 1897–1902) was the first Slovene magazine for women and the first to publish Kveder's short stories. In the years to come, Kveder also published many articles in which she touched upon numerous issues affecting women, including the situation of women wage earners and women's university education. In January 1899, she moved to Trieste, where she worked in the *Slovenka* editorial office. Late nineteenth-century Trieste was a vibrant port but Kveder felt she could not settle there and longed to study. She decided to go to Switzerland, since she had not yet graduated from secondary school. After a successful interview with the rector, she was able to enrol at Bern University in October 1899. Up until then she had been earning her own living but she soon realized that in Switzerland it was impossible to survive (let alone study) on what money she made writing literary works, articles and feuilletons (many of the latter she wrote in German). After a while, she dropped out of university.

During Kveder's stay in Switzerland, she wrote an interesting short story, "Študentke" (Women students, 1899), in which she vividly depicted the lives of Russian and Bulgarian students whose company she had enjoyed. In January 1900, she left Switzerland and headed for Munich. Newspapers and magazines paid even less for her articles there than in Switzerland and so, after a month, she went to Prague (Bohemia), where she met her future fiancé Vladimir Jelovšek (1879–1931), a Croatian student of medicine and regarded by some to be a rather decadent poet. In the spring of 1900, she published her literary debut, a book of stories called *Misterij žene* (The mystery of woman). This work irritated Slovene literary critics because of its preoccupation with specifically female experiences of exploitation, violence and pain. In 1901, three short stories from the collection were published by the Viennese magazine *Dokumente der Frauen* (Documents of women).

As a result of *Misterij žene* and other articles published in Slovene magazines and newspapers, Zofka Kveder became a central figure in the emerging Slovene women's movement. She differed from other Slovene feminists of the time because of her network of contacts with women from various countries of Central and Southeastern Europe, including the Austrian feminists Martha Tausk and Marie Lang and the Czech politician, editor and feminist Karla Máchová. It is therefore unsurprising that the board of the *Splošno slovensko žensko društvo* (General Slovene Women's Association) asked her to deliver a lecture in Ljubljana (on 29 September 1901) to mark the founding of the organization. The lecture, entitled "Ženska v družini in družbi" (Woman in the family and society), addressed the need for women's education and made arguments in favor of women's equal pay with men for equal work, as well as calling for women to organize themselves and define common goals. Kveder qualified these demands with assurances that women also needed to promote 'family life,' that girls needed to be properly prepared for marriage and motherhood and that feminists were not 'man-haters.'

In 1901, Kveder gave birth in Prague to a daughter, Vladoša, but her civil marriage to Jelovšek only took place in 1903. In 1906, when Jelovšek had completed his studies, the family moved to Zagreb (Croatia), where Kveder became the editor of a supplement to the *Agramer Tagblatt* (Zagreb daily newspaper) named *Frauenzeitung* (Women's newspaper). Her daughters Marija and Mira were born in 1906 and 1911, but at this time her marriage to Jelovšek—who was having extramarital affairs—fell apart irreparably. In 1913, soon after Kveder's attempted suicide and the divorce (1912), she remarried. Her second husband, with whom she had a church wedding, was the Croatian journalist Juraj Demetrović (1885–1946). In 1914, she wrote her first novel *Njeno življenje* (Her life), which departed from unifying definitions of womanhood, exploring instead the complex and multi-faceted layers of 'femininity.'

In 1915, during World War I, Croatian women chose Kveder as their delegate to the International Women's Congress at The Hague. Although she could not attend this important event because she was pregnant, she continued to write in this period and produced her best-known novel, *Hanka*. In 1917, she began publishing the magazine *Ženski svijet* (Women's world), in which she published articles on women's movements in Slovenia, Croatia and other Slavonic countries. She was grief-stricken when her eldest daughter Vladoša (a student in Prague) died in 1919. The absence of her husband, who became an important politician in the postwar Yugoslav government, and the death of her daughter took a heavy toll on her health and she spent the following years in various spas. In 1926, when her health had somewhat improved, her husband informed her that he wanted a divorce because another woman was expecting his baby. Friends, both male and female, supported her but Kveder no longer saw any meaning in life and on 21 November 1926, she committed suicide. Two days later, she was buried in Mirogoj Cemetery, Zagreb. At the funeral, representatives of Slovene, Croatian and Serbian women's organizations paid their respects.

Contemporaries and friends of Zofka Kveder (among them Martha Tausk, who made a career in Austrian politics after World War I) admired her determination, courage and lively interest in the problems of women of different ages and social backgrounds. To Kveder, the modern emancipatory goals of women were not mere phrases on paper; she consistently strove to realize those goals in her own lifetime, including, among other things, financial independence, which she retained from the age of sixteen until the day she died. In her literary works, Kveder gave her readers multi-layered and varied presentations of motherhood, as well as captivating explorations of female identity and sexual desire. Her writing reflected wider trends shaping the work of German authors such as Hedwig Dohm, Franziska zu Reventlow and Gabriele Reuter, as well as that of Swedish feminist Ellen Key.

Today, interest in the life and work of Zofka Kveder is growing. Already well established as part of the national literary canon, several international scholars are currently conducting research on Kveder's work and a first edition of her collected works is forthcoming.

Katja Mihurko Poniž
Freelance researcher, Ljubljana

SOURCES

(A) *Zapuščina Zofke Kveder in zapuščina Erne Muser. Rokopisni oddelek. Narodna in univezitetna knjižnica Ljubljana* (The legacies of Zofka Kveder and Erna Muser. Manuscripts Department of the National and University Library in Ljubljana). Kveder (Ms 1113) and

Muser (Ms 1432). These collections contain personal documents, letters, manuscripts, photographs and newspaper cuttings.

(D) Boršnik, Marja. "Zofka Kveder." In *Študije in fragmenti* (Studies and Fragments). Maribor: Obzorja, 1962, 319–334.

(D) Mihurko Poniž, Katja. *Drzno drugačna. Zofka Kveder in podobe ženskosti* (Daringly different. Zofka Kveder and images of femininity). Ljubljana: Delta, 2003.

(E) Borovnik, Silvija. *Pišejo ženske drugače?* (Do women write differently?). Ljubljana: Mihelač, 1995, 47–59.

LEICHTER, Käthe (1895–1942)

First social scientist to specialize in women's and gender studies in Austria. Journalist, editor and leftwing ideologist of the *Sozialdemokratische Arbeiterpartei* (*SDAP*, Social Democratic Workers' Party of Austria).

Käthe Leichter was born Marianne Katharina Pick on 20 August 1895 in Vienna, into a bourgeois-liberal, intellectual and assimilated Jewish family familiar with enlightenment ideals of liberty, equality and social justice. Her parents were the attorney Dr. Josef Pick (1849–1926), who came from a northern Bohemian textile factory family, and Charlotte Rubinstein (1872–1939), the multilingual daughter of a Bucharest banking family. They were married in 1893 and had two daughters. Käthe was the second girl and not the longed for son, as she says in her autobiographical scripts. She attended the Viennese *Beamtentöchter-Lyceum* from 1906 until 1912 and after receiving her diploma, enrolled in *Staatswissenschaften* (a combination of political science, law, economy and sociology) at the University of Vienna, aiming to be one of the first female graduates in that field. In 1917, she relocated to the University of Heidelberg (since women in the Habsburg Monarchy could not yet graduate in law). The following year, she graduated *magna cum laude* under the direction of Max Weber.

Prior to the outbreak of World War I in Vienna, Käthe Pick had been involved in the radical anti-authoritarian and left-wing *Wiener Jugendbewegung* (Viennese Youth Movement). This movement was influenced by socialist ideals and psychoanalysis—corresponding in its ideals and structure with the later left-wing student movements of 1968. Käthe Pick was competitive, self-confident and led by a strong aptitude for work. Nevertheless, she suffered from personal problems with her looks (which did not meet conventional feminine ideals), as well as from her subordinated position as a woman in political, social and sexual life. A socialist, she later became a member of the *Parteischüler-Bildungsverein 'Karl Marx'* ('Karl Marx' Society for Party Scholars and Education), a forum for war opponents within the *SDAP* (Social Democratic Workers' Party). In Heidelberg, she joined the student-driven Social Revolutionary movement. After the foundation of the Republic of Austria in 1918, she became a member of the *SDAP*'s *Neuen Linken* (New Left) as a representative of the *Rätemodell* (System of Workers' Councils). As a fresh university graduate and one of the first female political scientists to have specialized in economics, she became a member of the *Reichswirtschaftskommission der Arbeiterräte* (State Economic Committee of the Workers' Councils) and the *Sozialisierungskommission* (State Committee on the Socialization of Industry), as well as working as a consultant for the Federal Ministry of Finance and the *Zentralverband für Gemeinwirtschaft* (the umbrella organization for Public Goods and Corporations). On 10 December 1921, she married the socialist and journalist Otto Leichter (Vienna 1897–New York 1973). They had two sons, Heinz (b. 1924) and Franz (b. 1930).

From 1925, Käthe Leichter worked in the *Frauenreferat der Wiener Arbeiterkammer* (Women's Department of the Viennese Institutionalized Workers' Chamber), which she led until February 1934 (when the *SDAP* was banned). Up to then, she had been better known as an economist rather than someone interested in women's rights. Käthe Leichter belonged to a generation of women who were already enjoying the successes of the older women's movement—access for women to higher education, voting rights etc—and who distanced themselves from the so-called 'bourgeois women's movement.' Leichter considered herself a Marxist and, with respect to the *Frauenfrage* ('the woman question'), took the theoretical Marxist position that the oppression of women, along with all 'super-structure' phenomena, was derived from the primacy of the economy. The 'female worker,' not 'woman,' was the focus of both her political career and her major scientific research projects, of which there were four: *Frauenarbeit und Arbeiterrinnenschutz in Österreich* (The work of women and the protection of female workers in Austria, 1927); *Wie leben die Wiener Heimarbeiter? Eine Erhebung über die Arbeits–und Lebensbedingungen von 1000 Wiener Heimarbeitern* (How do Viennese homeworkers live? An investigation into the working and living conditions of 1000 Viennese homeworkers, 1928); *Handbuch für Frauenarbeit in Österreich* (Handbook for female workers in Austria, 1930) and *So leben wir. 1320 Industriearbeiterinnen berichten über ihr Leben* (This is how we live. 1320 female industrial workers talk about their lives, 1933). To this day, her studies are used in social science courses on living and working conditions in 1920s Austria, as well as providing useful source material regarding typical hopes and fears of the period, including the attractions of National Socialism for the 'ordinary' woman. Leichter's scholarship was aimed at abolishing the dual system of wage labor and housekeeping under capitalism. Choosing to combine an academic with a 'non-academic' commitment to those whose working and living conditions she wrote about, Leichter tried to bridge scientific research and political principles—an institutionally and discursively innovative approach.

While working on, and with, female workers, Leichter's political activism with regard to women's issues took place within the social democratic *Freien Gewerkschaften* (Free Unions). Leichter held that 'equal pay for equal work' should not be rejected as a 'bourgeois feminist' demand but accepted as a solution for all organized workers. That Leichter distanced herself from 'separate women's interests,' which were seen to neglect the proletarian position, was compatible with her thinking as a leftist within the social democratic movement, resisting any rapprochement by 'bourgeois' groups in the context of increasing authoritarian-conservative trends in the country (from the end of the 1920s onwards). In 1932, the social democratic women's organization debated which social class of women should be brought into the *SDAP*, and how. Leichter criticized the delivery of non-political propaganda to women, such as at meetings on cookery and other domestic activities. That women were not afraid of political radicalism had been demonstrated by the dramatic growth of women's votes for the National Socialist Party at the 1932 Local Council elections, even in 'Red Vienna.'

In this period, Käthe Leichter found herself becoming increasingly sensitive to women's issues extending beyond class, a development informing her stance in debates over the orientation of social democratic women's politics. She was outraged by the use of discriminatory language against women and by practices within the party that relegated women to secondary positions; thus, she came to reassess her earlier view of 'the woman question' as a 'superstructure phenomenon' derived from the economic base. At the same time, she personally experienced what it meant to be discriminated against on the basis of her sex and "race." Typists in the *Arbeiterkammer* (Institutionalized Workers' Chamber) for example, were advised not to work for the "Frau Doktor" (meaning Leichter). It was only in 1932, following a 'Palace Revolution' of lower female employees, that Leichter was nominated (and elected) to the *Betriebsrat* (Workers' Committee) in the Viennese *Arbeiterkammer*, the first woman to hold such a position. In 1933, Leichter's 'elders,' the female politicians ***Therese Schlesinger*** and ***Adelheid Popp***, retired from the leadership of the *SDAP*. Prominent *SDAP* leaders wishing to form coalitions with conservative parties prevented the radical (and Jewish) female academic Leichter from being nominated for one of the free positions on the board. Yet Leichter consistently denied the role that anti-Semitic sentiments might have played against her.

With the ban on the *SDAP* as of 12 February 1934 (the Parliament having been dissolved in 1933) and the development of the authoritarian *Christlicher Ständestaat* (Christian corporatist state), the political persecution of Käthe and Otto Leichter began. Returning to Austria after a stay in Switzerland, they both joined the clandestine socialist organization (formed to replace the banned *SDAP*), the *Revolutionäre Sozialisten* (Revolutionary Socialists) and wrote leaflets and coordinated relief actions for others suffering persecution. Carrying out scientific work as émigrés for the Frankfurt Institute for Social Research and the International Labor Organization (the umbrella organization for unions) in Geneva, the couple tried to secure a basic existence. After the Nazi take-over in 1938, Käthe Leichter's two sons and husband managed to leave Austria but Käthe Leichter was betrayed by a Gestapo infiltrator of the *Revolu-*

tionäre Sozialisten shortly before she was due to depart, and issued with threats that her mother would be murdered if she did not give herself up.

On 30 May 1938, Käthe Leichter was arrested by the Gestapo in Vienna. While in solitary confinement she wrote her memoirs (edited by Herbert Steiner in 1973). In 1940, she was deported to the Ravensbrück concentration camp. In February 1942, she was murdered in a 'trial gassing' along with 1500 other Jewish prisoners in an unknown place.

Gabriella Hauch
Johannes Kepler University, Linz, Austria

Translated by Melanie Morgan.

SOURCES

(C) Leichter, Käthe, ed. *Handbuch der Frauenarbeit in Österreich* (Manual of women's work in Austria). Vienna: Verlag Carl Ueberreuter, 1930.

(C) Leichter, Käthe. "Lebenserinnerungen" (Memoirs). In Herbert Steiner, ed. *Käthe Leichter. Leben und Werk* (Käthe Leichter. Her life and work). Vienna: Europa Verlag, 1973, 233-385.

(D) Steiner, Herbert, ed. *Käthe Leichter. Leben und Werk* (Käthe Leichter. Her life and work). Vienna: Europa Verlag, 1973.

(D) Hauch, Gabriella. "Käthe Leichter, geb. Pick. Spuren eines Frauenlebens." (Käthe Leichter, born Pick. Traces of a woman's life). *Archiv. Jahrbuch des Vereins für Geschichte der Arbeiterbewegung* (1992): 97-122.

(D) Hauch, Gabriella. *Man ist ja schon zufrieden, wenn man arbeiten kann. Käthe Leichter und ihre politische Aktualität* (One is satisfied when one can work. Käthe Leichter and her present-day political meaning). Institut für Gewerkschafts- und AK-Geschichte. Vienna: Mandelbaum Verlag, 2003.

LJOČIĆ (Ljotchich)-Milošević, Draga (1855–1926)

First female medical doctor in Serbia and women's rights activist; founder of many medical organizations, including the *Materinsko udruženje* (Maternity Society) and the *Prva ženska bolnica u Beogradu Dr. Elise Inglis* (Dr. Elise Inglis First Women's Hospital in Belgrade); one of the founder members of the *Srpskog lekarskog društva* (Serbian Medical Society).

Draga Ljočić was born in Šabac (Serbia) on 25 February 1855. She graduated from the Lyceum of Belgrade and was the first Serbian woman to be admitted (in 1872) to the Zurich Medical School. At that time her brother Đjura Ljočić, a prominent socialist and editor of the journal *Radenik* (The worker, 1871–1872), had already graduated (1870) in technical engineering from the same university. While in Zurich, Draga Ljočić became influenced by Russian women nihilists (e.g. Sophia Bardina, Sophia Perovskaya and the Subbotina sisters), who shaped her feminism. Her education was interrupted by the Serbian–Turkish Wars of 1876–1878 and she joined the Serbian army as a medical assistant, taking part in the battle of Šumatovac (after which she was promoted to the rank of second lieutenant). Marija Fjodorovna Siebold (originally from Riga), a like-minded socialist colleague of Ljočić's from Zurich University, joined her friend in Serbia during the Serbian–Turkish War, after which Ljočić returned to Zurich. She graduated there in 1879, becoming the first female medical doctor in Serbia and one of the first female medical doctors in Europe at the time.

After her return to Serbia, Draga Ljočić tried unsuccessfully to find employment. In a letter addressed to officials at the Ministry of Interior, she requested a licence based on recognition of her diploma from Zurich. After a detailed review of the case by a committee of prominent Serbian male doctors, it was decided that Ljočić's diploma entitled her to work as a medical assistant in Serbia (she was only permitted to practise privately as a doctor from 1881). During the Serbian–Bulgarian War (1885), the Balkan Wars (1912–1913) and World War I (1914–1918), Ljočić worked alongside her fellow male medical practitioners as a doctor of equal status in the war hospitals. In the Serbian–Bulgarian War, Ljočić remained the only General Practitioner in the State General Hospital while others were stationed out on the battlefield. As her full rights as a practising doctor were gradually recognized, her career took off and, together with Laza Lazarević, a prominent Serbian medical doctor (and poet), Ljočić treated students of the *Ženska radenička škola* (Female Workers School, founded in November 1879). She herself founded (1904) the *Materinsko udruženje* (Maternity Society), joined (1872) the *Srpsko lekarsko društvo* (Serbian Medical Society) and co-founded the *Prva ženska bolnica Dr. Elise Inglis* (Dr Elise Inglis First Women's Hospital) in Belgrade.

Draga Ljočić would play an important role in the history of feminism in Serbia after her return from Zurich. She joined several of the private circles around Lujza and Gavra Vitaković, where issues of feminism and socialism were discussed, and ardently promoted gender equality in the professions. In 1903, in defense of a proposed bill to the National Assembly, she wrote that professional competence and moral virtues should be the sole preconditions for employment. The bill, signed by women doctors and teachers in girls' high schools, was rejected by the National Assembly but nevertheless generated a considerable stir among Serbian women.

Draga Ljočić also supported universal suffrage for men and women. In March 1911, at one of the regular meetings of the *Srpski narodni ženski savez* (Serbian National Women Alliance, founded on 18 October 1906), Ljočić and fellow feminist Jelena Spasić informed delegates that they were preparing a petition demanding equal voting rights for women and men (never submitted). Although the demands were rejected by delegates of the *Srpski narodni ženski savez*, Ljočić's petition drew attention to several important issues related to women's rights and equal citizenship.

In 1883, Draga Ljočić married Raša Milosević, one of the founders of the *Narodna radikalna stranka* (People's Radical Party) and organizer of the "Timočka buna" (Timok Peasant Mutiny). Milosević was subsequently arrested, an event he describes in his memoirs–also entitled *Timočka buna* (Timok Peasant Mutiny, 1883). The couple had a daughter, Radmila Milosević, who also graduated from the Zurich Medical School. Draga Ljočić died in 1926. Today she is only remembered within a small academic circle.

Ivana Pantelić
Belgrade Women's Studies and Gender Research Center

SOURCES

(B) *The International Woman Suffrage Alliance. Report of Sixth Congress.* Stockholm, Sweden. June 1911. London: Women's Printing Society, Ltd., 1911, 4, 125.

(E) Gavrilović, Vera. *Žene lekari u ratovima 1876-1945 na tlu Jugoslavije* (Women medical doctors during the Yugoslav wars, 1876-1945). Belgrade: Naučno društvo za istoriju zdravstvene kulture Jugoslavije, 1976.

(E) Milutinović, Kosta. "Prve srpske socijalistkinje i ruske nihilistkinje u Cirihu» (Early Serb female socialists and Russian female nihilists in Zurich). *In Zbornik istorijskog muzeja*

Srbije (Essays of the Serbian Historical Museum). Vols. 15/16. Belgrade: Istorijski muzej, 1979.

(E) Božinović, Neda. *Žensko pitanje u Srbiji u XIX i XX veku* (The woman question in Serbia in the nineteenth and twentieth centuries). Belgrade: Feministička 94, 1996.

(E) Pelcer, Olga. "Obrazovanje i/ili brak: prilog istraživanju o obrazovanim ženama u Srbiji" (Education and/or marriage: a contribution to the biographies of educated Serbian women). *Rani radovi polaznika Alternativne akademske obrazovne mreže 1998-2001* (Book of essays of the Alternative Academic Educational Network). Belgrade: Alternativna akademska obrazovna mreža, 2002.

(E) Trgovčević, Ljubinka. *Planirana elita* (The Elite Planned). Belgrade: Istorijski insitut, 2003.

MALINOVA, Julia (also Julie Malinoff) (1869-1953)

Co-founder (1901) and head (1908–1910; 1912–1926) of the *Bulgarski Zhenski Sujuz* (Bulgarian Women's Union), and Honorary President from 1926; editor of *Zhenski glas* (Women's voice), the official newspaper of the *Bulgarski Zhenski Sujuz*.

Julia Malinova was born Jakovlevna Scheider, of Russian Jewish parents. She received her university education in France and Switzerland, where she became attracted to contemporary liberal ideas. No data exists regarding her parents or the life she led before moving to Bulgaria. She came to Sofia at the invitation of the family of professor Mykhailo Drahomanov (1841-1895), a Ukrainian historian who taught at Sofia University from 1889 until his death (See also ***Olena Pchilka*** and ***Lesia Ukrainka***)). She converted to Orthodoxy (***Anna Karima*** was her godmother) before marrying Alexander Malinov (1867-1938). Malinov was a lawyer, leader of the Democratic Party, Prime-Minister of Bulgaria (1908-1911, 1918, 1931) and Vice-President of the Bulgarian Parliament (1931-1934). The couple had five children: three daughters and two sons.

Julia Malinova was a founder of the *Bulgarski Zhenski Sujuz* (*BZhS*, Bulgarian Women's Union) and a member of its first board, positions befitting a woman imbibed with the spirit of the revolutionary Russian intelligentsia and who had received her education in the liberal milieu of the French and Swiss Universities. From 1899, together with Anna Karima (the first head of the *BZhS*), Malinova co-edited *Zhenski glas* until 1901, when it became the mouthpiece of the *BZhS*. Malinova was then appointed editor-in-chief. She was twice elected President of the *BZhS* (1908-1910 and 1912-1926) and in 1908, under her leadership, the *BZhS* became a member of the International Council of Women (ICW) and the International Woman Suffrage Alliance (IWSA later IAWSEC/IAW), with Malinova attending the Stockholm Congress of the IAW in 1911. After some initial years of instability, as well as ideological and personal tensions and rivalries, the *BZhS* gradually took shape under Malinova's leadership as an organization "transcending class and party" to become "truly feminist" (as the congress literature put it). Clarifying its goals and strategies, the *BZhS* incorporated the agenda of the international women's movement, including issues such as political and civil rights for women, equal education for women and men, access of women to all professions and posts in the civil service, equal pay for equal work, equal moral standards, campaigns against the traffic in women and state regulation of prostitution, married women's nationality, peace and disarmament. Like many other women activists during the Balkan Wars and World War I, Julia Malinova led the wives of soldiers in a wide range of charitable initiatives. In 1925, she was a delegate to the Washington Congress of the ICW. In 1926, the *BZhS* (which at that time consisted of around 7,000 women, including housewives, teachers and state employees) celebrated its 25th anniversary and the 25th year of Julia Malinova's public activity. Soon after, Malinova was targeted as a foreigner by the *Bulgarski Zhenski Sujuz 'Lujbov kum Rodinata'* (Bulgarian Women's Union 'for the Love of the Motherland'), a small nationalistic and right-wing organization affiliated to the male army officers' union, 'National Defence.' The Women's Union 'for the Love of the Motherland' employed the same, extreme nationalist and xenophobic rhetoric of its male parent organization. In order to preserve the unity of the *BZhS* (the oldest Bulgarian feminist organization), Julia Malinova resigned in July 1926 at the *BZhS*'s twentieth Congress. The Congress pronounced her Honorary President of the *BZhS* and established a fund in her name: *Julia Malinova - podslon za zheni* (the Julia Malinova Women's Shelter). In her capacity as Honorary President, Malinova continued to follow and participate in the activities of the *BZhS* throughout the late 1920s and 1930s. She managed an orphanage run by the society *Milosurdie* (Charity) and founded *Suiuz na siratsite* (an Orphanage Union), as well as a summer recreation house for orphans in the town of Berkovitsa. She set up a service, *Zhenski trud* (Women's Labor), granting opportunities to women seeking employment and financial independence, and also worked for *Suiuz za obshtestvena podkrepa* (the Social Support Union), providing assistance to orphans and the elderly. Julia Malinova's house was always open to women in need, a hallmark of her generosity and great humanity. She died in 1953.

Krassimira Daskalova
St. Kliment Ohrodski, University of Sofia

SOURCES

(A) *Narodna Biblioteka Kiril I Metodii, Bulgarski Istoricheski Archiv, NBKM-BIA* (National Library "Cyril and Method", Bulgarian Historical Archive), f. 807 (Janko Sakuzov), a. e. 1, l. 85.

(A) *Narodna Biblioteka Kiril I Metodii - Bulgarski Istoricheski Archiv, NBKM-BIA*, f. 584 (Dimitrana Ivanova), a. e. 562, l. 410–413.

(A) *Narodna Biblioteka Kiril I Metodii - Bulgarski Istoricheski Archiv, NBKM-BIA*, f. 703 (Alexander Malinov), a. e. 6, 7, 8.

(B) *Zhenski glas* (Women's voice) (1899–1944).

(B) *Jubileina broshura "Bulgarski zhenski Suiuz" (Po sluchai 30-godishninata mu).* (Jubilee brochure of the Bulgarian Women's Union. On the occasion of its thirtieth anniversary) 1901–1931. Sofia, 1931, 28–33.

(B) "Bulgaria. Woman's Rights Alliance. Mrs. I. Malinoff, President." In *The International Woman Suffrage Alliance. Report of Sixth Congress.* Stockholm, Sweden, London: Women's Printing Society, Ltd., 1911, 84–85.

MALINSKA-ḰOSTAROVA GEORGI, Veselinka (1917–1988)

Socialist active on behalf of women's rights and partisan; co-founder and Secretary of the Central Committee of the *Antifasisticki front na ženite na Makedonija* (Antifascist Front of the Women of Macedonia); first editor-in-chief of the journal *Makedonka* (Macedonian woman), issued by the *Antifasisticki front na ženite na Makedonija.*

Veselinka Malinska's father, Georgi Kole Malinski (1878–1951), was born in Kumanovo and also lived in Tetovo (Macedonia), Vienna and Paris (in the latter two cities between 1913 and 1918). A merchant, photographer and social activist, he was an innovative, broad-minded and free-spirited man, the first Esperantist in the Balkans (1897), as well as the founder (1898) and President of the first merchant society in the Macedonian part of the Ottoman Empire. In 1900, he opened the first bookstore in Kumanovo, later opening a photography shop (1922). He participated in the *Ilinden* uprising against Ottoman rule (1901–1903) and remained politically active into the 1930s and 1940s.

Veselinka's mother, Persida Malinska (born Apostolova) (1885–1935), was a teacher at the Central School in Kumanovo. After marrying Georgi Malinski, she gave up teaching to work alongside her husband. She was the first woman Esperantist in Macedonia and fought for the improvement of girls' education and the greater economic and political independence of women. Persida and Georgi Malinski had seven children, of which three died very young. Veselinka, born on 15 January 1917, was their fifth child.

After completing primary education in Kumanovo, Veselinka was to start work in her father's photography workshop like her older siblings but refused, wishing to continue her education at the *Trgovachka skola* (a high school) in Skopje. Although her father strongly opposed this idea and even forbade further discussion of the topic, her mother used her own dowry money to take Veselinka to Skopje and enrol her in the school. It is unknown how Veselinka's father reacted upon her mother's return to Kumanovo, but it seems he assented to Veselinka's higher education without further objection. It is also likely (according to Veselinka Malinska's daughter, Lina Ḱostarova-Unkovska) that the rebellion of Veselinka's mother triggered Veselinka's later involvement in the women's movement.

As a student at Skopje high school, Veselinka Malinska joined the communist youth movement and was soon expelled from school. She continued her education in Niš (Serbia) and became a member of the Communist Party of Yugoslavia (*KPJ*) in 1936. During her two years of study at the Zagreb Faculty of Economy, she became acquainted with members of the *Makedonski nacionalen pokret* (*MANAPO*, Macedonian National Movement).

In 1938/39, Malinska worked in Belgrade as a bank clerk and became active in the bank workers' union, as well as in the youth section of the *Ženski pokret* (Women's Movement), a feminist and non-party organization established in April 1919 in Belgrade as the *Društvo za prosvećivanje žene i zaštitu njenih prava* (Society for Women's Enlightenment and Protection of their Rights). The organization was established in all the Yugoslav countries and attracted outstanding feminists such as Mileva Milojević, Milena Atanacković, Zorka Kasnar-Karadžić, ***Isidora Sekulić***, Paulina Lebl-Albala, Katarina Bogdanović, Delfa Ivanić, Mileva Petrović, Ruža Vinterštajn-Jovanović, ***Ksenija Atanasijević***, Ružica Stojanović and others.

Malinska also became Secretary of the local committee of National Aid, better known as Red Aid, established by the *Narodni front* (People's Front) to assist antifascist, communist and leftist individuals. The signing of the Triple Pact by the Yugoslav government (25 March 1941) and Yugoslavia's joining the Axis Powers provoked large antifascist demonstrations in Belgrade on 27 March 1941, at which Malinska spoke passionately against war and fascism. Germany's attack on Yugoslavia on 6 April 1941 led to the capitulation of the Kingdom of Yugoslavia. At the beginning of the German occupation of Belgrade (May/June 1941), Malinska and Slobodanka Đjorđjević bought a dairy plant (on 5 Francuska St., Belgrade), which became a meeting place for the Yugoslav resistance movement.

In this period, Malinska acted as a messenger and point of connection between the Central Committee (CK) of the Communist Party of Yugoslavia and its Regional Committee for Serbia from Belgrade. She transferred fighters to the partisan squads and sent messages into the Serbian mountains. In September 1941, together with Davorjanka Paunćovic-Zdenka (1921–1946) and Jašha Rajter, she illegally transferred the General Secretary of the *CK* of the *KPJ* and the Commander of the Headquarters of the National Liberation War, Josip Broz-Tito, from Belgrade to the town of Užice in western Serbia (territory liberated by the partisans). The Gestapo discovered her activities and she went undercover in Čačak (Serbia), later returning to Belgrade under an assumed German identity.

In May 1942, Malinska returned to Skopje, where she became Secretary of the Local Committee of the *KPJ*, as well as founder and editor of *Vesnik* (News), the organ of the clandestine partisan organization from Skopje. In October 1942, she joined the Skopje partisan squad, taking her typewriter with her. She held numerous meetings with the women from the Skopska Crna Gora and Shara mountain villages, with whom she discussed women's rights and equality in a future (liberated) Macedonia.

Her remarkable propaganda activism on 20 June 1943 earned her the position of Secretary of the Department for Campaigning and Propaganda, *Agitprop*, at the central Headquarters of the National Liberation War. She held the same function as a member of the Central Committee of the Communist Party of Macedonia (*KPM*).

Veselinka Malinska as a member of the Yugoslav Press delegation visiting the Trade Union Congress in London, March 1952. Malinska is trying the new model of a tractor produced in the famous Ferguson factory

On 6–8 December 1942, the Yugoslav *Antifasisticki front na ženite* (*AFŽ*, Antifascist Women's Front) was founded and in September 1943, Malinska was appointed member of the Initiative Board of the *Antifasisticki front na ženite na Makedonija* (Antifascist Front of the Women of Macedonia), of which she subsequently became Secretary. The Macedonian *AFŽ* was the first women's organization founded by women in Macedonia; previous organizations, such as the *Ženski Pokret*, had been Yugoslav organizations. Mara Naceva, a member of the Central Committee of the *KPM*, was President of the Board; other Board members were Nada Achkova, Nada Bogdanova, Stojka Dogandjiska, Lenche Jovanova-Zhunich, Maria Korobar, Olga Petrusheva and Vaska Ciriviri. Malinska formulated the goals of the Macedonian *AFŽ* in an article entitled "8 mart i uchastieto na zenata vo Narodnoosloboditelnata borba"

(8 March and women's participation in the National Liberation War), published in the People's Front magazine *Ilindenski pat.* Malinska celebrated 8 March (International Women's Day) as a day of struggle against fascism by "women all over the world." Describing fascism as "the greatest foe of all peaceful people and women's fiercest enemy," she noted the participation of women "alongside their male comrades [in a struggle that was] not only for equality, but predominantly against fascist imperialism" (Malinska 1944, 18–22).

Early in November 1944, the Initiative Board of the Macedonian *AFŽ* launched its monthly magazine *Makedonka* (Macedonian woman), the first women's magazine to be published in Macedonia in the Macedonian language. Malinska was editor-in-chief of *Makedonka* and Nada Achkova, Nada Bogdanova and Lenche Jovanova-Zhunich were all contributors and members of the editorial staff. As the Secretary of the Central Committee of the *AFŽ* in Macedonia, which existed from December 1944 until 1953, Malinska remained active in the women's movement, combining the struggle for emancipation–women's struggle for national liberty, an independent state and full human rights–with antifascist resistance. *AFŽ* documents indicate that, though the Communist Party of Yugoslavia monitored the organization, it nevertheless played an important role in women's struggle for political rights, providing the representational quota of women in social and political forums. The *Deklaracija za osnovnite prava na graganinot na Demokratska Makedonija* (Declaration of the Basic Rights of the Citizen of Democratic Macedonia), enacted by the first Macedonian Parliament on 2 August 1944 (when the Macedonian State was established), approved the *AFŽ* and supported its goals. The first article of the Declaration read: "Every citizen of the Macedonian Federal State is equal before the law, regardless of nationality, sex, race and religious beliefs." Although women and men had become legally equal, only six of the 122 MPs first elected to the Macedonian Parliament were women. Malinska was one of them.

Malinska's first husband was Dobrivoje Radosavljević-Orce (1915–1984), a high-ranking *KPJ* official who came to Skopje in August 1942, where they married in November 1944. They divorced immediately after the end of the war. Malinska's second husband was Dimitar Ḱostarov (1912–1997), a Bulgarian actor and director who, together with a group of Bulgarian actors and the director of the National Theater in Sofia, came to Macedonia during the occupation in 1942. In 1944, Ḱostarov joined the Macedonian partisans on condition that he would not have to bear arms. At that time, he met Malinska who, as the head of *Agitprop*, asked him to prepare a play for the villagers in honor of *ASNOM* (the Antifascist Assembly of the National Liberation of Macedonia). Ḱostarov was wounded in the so-called 'May offensive' of 1944. He met Malinska again after the war and they married in 1948, although the *KPM* made recommendations against it. Malinska and Ḱostarov's marriage lasted for 39 years, until the death of Malinska from heart failure in Skopje on 11 December 1988. They had a daughter Lina (1949) and two sons Stefan (1952) and Ivan (1955).

Veselinka Malinska was decorated with the *Partizanska spomenica 1941* (Partisan

Medal 1941) for her work during the National Liberation War, as well as other medals and certificates of achievement for her efforts on behalf of women's emancipation. After the liberation, she became an important political and public figure. She was director of Radio Skopje for twelve years, Vice-President of the Executive Board of the Socialist Republic of Macedonia, MP in the Federal National Assembly (two terms), President of the University Council of the Cyril and Method University in Skopje, member of the Presidency of the Central Committee of the Macedonian Communists' Union and a member of the Federal Council of the Socialist Federal Republic of Yugoslavia. Throughout this later period of her life, her interest in women's issues remained important to her.

The historical importance of Veselinka Malinska is beyond any doubt and not only as the co-founder of the Macedonian *AFŽ*; she may also be credited with (indirectly) inspiring contemporary women's NGOs in Macedonia. The *AFŽ*'s tradition may be discerned in the character of the *Organizacija na Organizaciite na ženite na Makedonija* (Organization of Women's Organizations in Macedonia, 1990) and that of the *Sojuz na ženskite organizacii vo Makedonija* (*SOZM*, Union of Women's Organizations in Macedonia). Founded in 1995, the *SOZM* explicitly describes its work as continuing that of the *AFŽ*.

Vera Vesković-Vangeli
Professor, Senior Scientific Researcher,
Institute of National History, Skopje

Translated from the Macedonian by Nevenka Grceva, MA student at the Department of Gender Studies, Central European University, Budapest.

SOURCES

(A) State Archives of the Republic of Macedonia. Collection: Central Board of the *AFŽ*.

(B) Vesković-Vangeli, Vera and Marija Jovanović, eds. *Zbornik na dokumenti za ucestvoto na zenite od Makedonija vo Narodnoosloboditelnata vojna i revolucijata 1941–1945* (Collection of documents on women's participation in the People's Liberation War 1941–1945). Skopje: Institut za nacionalna istorija & Konferencija za opstestvena aktivnost na ženite na Makedonija, 1976.

(C) Malinska, Veselinka. "8 mart i uchastieto na zenata vo Narodnoosloboditelnata borba" (8 March and women's participation in the National Liberation War). *Ilindenski pat* (The path of Ilinden) 4, no. 1 (April 1944).

(E) Vesković-Vangeli, Vera. *Ženata vo vitelot na antagonizmot na tradicijata* (Woman in the whirl of antagonistic tradition). Veles: Drustvo za nauka i umetnost, 1999.

MARÓTHY-ŠOLTÉSOVÁ, Elena (1855-1939)

First Slovak woman writer to be accepted into the national literary canon; literary critic, essayist and national activist; from 1894 President, Vice-President and Honorary President of the Slovak women's association *Živena*; promoter of women's education.

Elena Maróthy was born on 6 January 1855 in Krupina (upper Hungary, Austria-Hungary; today Slovakia), to Protestant pastor and poet Daniel Maróthy (1825-1878) and Karolína Maróthy, born Hudecová (1834-1857). Shortly after the family moved to Ľuboreč (in the district of Novohrad), Elena's mother died. An unusually strong relationship developed between Elena and her father, who in 1858 married Lujza Bauerová (1839-1879). The initially warm relationship between stepmother and daughter changed after the births of Elena's stepbrother and stepsister. As an adult, Maróthy-Šoltésová bitterly recollected how her stepmother had forced her to do so much housework that she had had no time for school work. After completing the first years of her education at a Slovak elementary school, the young Elena Maróthyová began learning Hungarian in Lučenec; later German in Lučenec and in the district of Spiš. She completed her school education in June 1867, then just twelve years old.

Her own experiences made her realize the importance of education for girls. In 1869, at the age of fourteen, she visited the constituent assembly of the women's association *Živena* (named after an old Slavic goddess of life), which would play a major role in the Slovak national revival movement. After she became a member of the *Živena* committee in 1880, Maróthyová, together with ***Terézia Vansová***, made plans to improve the education of Slovak girls through the founding of a Slovak language school for girls. The project not only met with resistance from the 'magyarizing' authorities (Slovakia was then part of 'magyar' Hungary, whose authorities suppressed the growth of Slovak nationalism), but also from parents who considered a 'proper' girls' education to be one based on conversation classes in Hungarian and German. The *Živena* school, the first Slovak higher vocational school for women, was finally established in 1919 in Martin, after the formation of the Czechoslovak Republic in 1918. Thanks to the tireless efforts of Maróthy-Šoltésová, the Milan Rastislav Štefánik

Institute was founded in 1926, also in Martin. This institute aimed to provide education in social care and teacher training for girls' schools.

While the first arguments for women's education in Slovakia were often made by men [e.g. journalist Ambro Pietor (1843–1906)], Maróthy-Šoltésová's 1898 essay "Potreba vzdelanosti pre ženu, zvlášť zo stanoviska mravnosti" (The moral need for women's education) was highly significant: "the major essay on women, and certainly the best by a woman," according to American Slovakist, Norma Rudinsky (Rudinsky 1991, 128).

In 1875, Elena Maróthyová married a merchant, Ľudovít Michal Šoltés (1837–1915). The couple lived in Turčiansky Svätý Martin, where Maróthy-Šoltésová raised her two children and which was the center of the Slovak national revival movement. The deaths of her daughter Elenka, when she was just eight years old, and her son Ivan, when he was 33, deeply affected Maróthy-Šoltésová and her writing. The diary-novel *Moje deti* (My children), first published in 1885, became a major work of Slovak literature. In 1885, Maróthy-Šoltésová also published extracts from the novel dealing with her daughter Elenka's death under the title, *Umierajúce dieťa* (The dying child). Although the piece was criticized by writer and editor Svetozár Hurban Vajanský for being excessively emotional, it was this work which took her closer to the realism she had been striving for. *Moje deti* gained wide international recognition and was published as a book in 1923 and 1924, forming part of her *Zobrané spisy* (Collected works). Although the novel focused mainly on her children and Maróthy-Šoltésová's relation to them, the writer reflects on her lack of space and time in the contradictory roles of 'writer' and 'mother.' ***Terézia Vansová*** was Maróthy-Šoltésová's contemporary and closest collaborator. In a letter to Vansová from 1 January 1885, Maróthy-Šoltésová described what it meant to her to have Vansová's supportive friendship after the death of Elenka: "You are crying with me because of my sorrow, so you are close to me. To give oneself to sorrow is the most unpleasant thing and you do so because of me ..." (cited in Handzová 1989, 79). Maróthy-Šoltésová's carer, who looked after her prior to her death, recalled that the writer's last words had been meant for her friend Vansová. The mutual support of the two women lent great impetus to both the Slovak women's movement and Slovak women's writing. As editors, literary critics and as friends, they also provided support for other women such as the Slovak prose writer Božena Slančíková-Timrava (1867–1951). That Maróthy-Šoltésová recognized the innovative qualities of Timrava's fiction suggests that she was a perceptive and able literary critic. In 1896, she began cooperating with the Czech magazine *Ženský svět* (Women's world). Contacts with Czech women were key to the support network and morale of the growing Slovak women's movement. Maróthy-Šoltésová also worked closely with *Živena* in the USA–founded in 1891 by Slovak-Americans–whose goals and activities were similar to those of *Živena* in Slovakia.

Maróthy-Šoltésová's most concise account of the emancipation of women appeared in the above-mentioned 1898 essay on women's education "Potreba vzdelanosti." In this work, the emancipation of women and the emancipation of the nation are intertwined. Written as Slovak nationalism was gaining strength in the Austrian-Hungarian Empire, Maróthy-Šoltésová saw the education of women as a significant part of the national struggle for emancipation; as part of the struggle for the national (Slovak) language. The role of women in the family (more often than not as mothers) also acquired its legitimacy through its usefulness to the national struggle. Women's education was important because of their primary roles within the family as educators and carers.

Maróthy-Šoltésová only partially addressed gender power asymmetry, though she criticized differences in the schooling of women and men. She dismissed emancipation that threatened the 'natural' division of labor between men and women in the public and private spheres as "nonsensical caprice" (Maróthy-Šoltésová 1934, 108). Women, she argued, were to invest their efforts and talents in the service of their nation (and their men) as 'helpers,' not as independent individuals. In this respect, Maróthy-Šoltésová's views, shaped by a Lutheran background, did not differ significantly from those of her male contemporaries who called for the (instrumental) emancipation of women in the interest of national revival.

Maróthy-Šoltésová made her literary debut with the short story "Na dedine" (In the village, 1881) and subsequently went on to make a significant contribution to Slovak literature as a writer, literary critic and as editor of the *Almanach Živeny* (1885), the *Letopis Živeny* (*Živena* Yearbook/Almanac, 1896, 1898, 1902, 1906) and the magazine *Živena* (1910–1922). She belonged to a generation that considered literature to be visible evidence of the nation's existence. At the end of the nineteenth century, attempts to follow the realist path sometimes turned to sentimentality, as with the idealized heroine of Maróthy-Šoltésová's novel *Proti prúdu* (Against the current, 1894), who persuades a count who has become Hungarian to 'convert' back to his 'original' Slovak national identity. Despite the critical reception of the novel, Slovak novelist Martin Kukučín recognized the author's engagement with women's issues: "The writer steps forward as an ardent advocate of her sex" (cited in Handzová 1989, 157). At the same time, although the fiction of Šoltésová was undoubtedly constrained by the idealism and sentimentality of the national revival movement, her activities in literary criticism were more progressive and played a key role in the development of modern Slovak literature.

As part of celebrations marking Šoltésová's seventieth birthday, the writer was encouraged to write an autobiography, later published under the title of "Sedemdesiat rokov života" (Seventy years of life), in a 1925 issue of the magazine *Slovenské pohľady* (Slovak views). Her writing, social work and public education activities received public recognition and several awards. Alice Masaryková, the daughter of ***Charlotta Garrigue Masaryková*** and Tomáš Garrigue Masaryk (the first Czechoslovak President), asked her to become a member of the honorary committee of the Red Cross (1933). In 1930, Elga Kern, a German author, included her in a book on "25 leading women in Europe" (*Führende Frauen Europas*).

In her declining years, Elena Maróthy-Šoltésová struggled with blindness. She died in Martin (Czechoslovakia, now Slovakia) on 11 February 1939 at the age of 84, and was laid to rest at the National Cemetery in Martin.

Jana Cviková
ASPEKT, feminist publication and educational project
www.aspekt.sk

SOURCES

(B) Gregorová, Hana. *Slovenka pri krbe a knihe* (Slovak woman by the fireplace with a book). Prague: Mazáčova slovenská knižnica, 1929.

(B) Kern, Elga. *Führende Frauen Europas* (Leading women in Europe). Munich: Verlag Ernst Reinhardt, 1930.

(C) Maróthy-Šoltésová, Elena. *Sedemdesiat rokov života. Autobiografická rozprava* (Seventy long years of life. Autobiographical discourse). Martin: Matica slovenská, 1925.

(C) Maróthy-Šoltésová, Elena. *Začatá cesta. Výbor z článkov E. Šoltésovej* (A journey begun. Selected articles by E. Šoltésová). Lea Mrázová, ed. Martin: Vydavateľstvo Živeny, Turč. Sv., 1934.

(C) Maróthy-Šoltésová, Elena. *Proti prúdu* (Against the current). In *Výber* (Selected works), vol. II. Bratislava: Tatran, 1978.

(C) Maróthy-Šoltésová, Elena. *Moje deti* (My children). Bratislava: Tatran, 1983.

(D) Kaššayová, Terézia, ed. *Elena Maróthy-Šoltésová. Zborník z vedeckej konferencie 14.-15. mája 1985 vo Zvolene* (Elena Maróthy-Šoltésová. Papers from the scientific conference of 14-15 May 1985, in Zvolen). Martin: Matica slovenská, 1987.

(D) Handzová, Želmíra. *Elena Maróthy-Šoltésová. Život a dielo v dokumentoch* (Elena Maróthy-Šoltésová. Her life and work in documents). Bratislava: Osveta, 1989.

(E) Pišút, Milan a. i. *Dejiny slovenskej literatúry* (The history of Slovak literature). Bratislava: Obzor, 1984.

(E) Šmatlák, Stanislav. *Dejiny slovenskej literatúry. Od stredoveku po súčasnosť* (The history of Slovak literature from the middle ages until the present). Bratislava: Tatran, 1988.

(E) Rudinsky, Norma. *Incipient Feminists: Women Writers in the Slovak National Revival.* (With an appendix of Slovak women poets, 1798-1875, by Marianna Prídavková-Mináriková). Columbus/Ohio: Slavica Publishers, Inc., 1991.

(E) Mikulová, Marcela. *Ženy a národ na prelome 19. a 20. storočia* (Women and the nation at the turn of the nineteenth and twentieth centuries). *Aspekt*, no. 1 (1994): 72-74.

(E) Mikulová, Marcela. "Vlastne je to všetko problém písania" (In fact all that is an issue of writing). *Aspekt*, no. 1 (1995): 30-33.

(E) *Lexikón slovenských žien* (Lexicon of Slovak women). Martin: Slovenská národná knižnica, Národný biografický ústav, 2003.

(E) Tokárová, Anna. *Vzdelanie žien na Slovensku. Spoločenské bariéry a stimuly v historickom priereze* (The education of women in Slovakia. Social barriers and impulses in historical perspective). Prešov: Project VEGA no. 1/0457/03. Akcent print, 2003.

(E) Cviková, Jana. "Po boku muža a národa" (Side by side with man and nation). *Aspekt*, no.1 (2003–2004): 71–78.

(E) Cviková, Jana. "Sinnlose" und "sinnvolle" Emanzipation. Über die Entstehung des feministischen Bewusstseins in der Slowakei ("Senseless" and "meaningful" emancipation. On the rise of feminist consciousness in Slovakia). Thesis. Vienna: Rosa Mayreder College, May 2004.

MASARYKOVÁ GARRIGUE, Charlotta (1850–1923)

Activist for women's equality, Social Democrat and wife of the first President of the Czechoslovak Republic, Tomáš Garrigue Masaryk (1850–1937).

Charlotta Garrigue was born in Brooklyn, New York on 20 November 1850. Her father, Rudolf Garrigue (1822-1891), was of Huguenot descent, born in Kodan (Denmark). While working for the publisher Brockhouse in Leipzig as a young man, he had been sent to the United States to carry out market research there and had remained in New York, becoming a bookseller and later on, a chief executive in an insurance company (Germania). Charlotta's mother, Charlotte Lydia Garrigue (1825-1891), born Whiting, was from a family that had come to America from England in the seventeenth century. The family was very religious and Charlotta, the third of eleven children, was a member of the Unitarian Church (which proclaimed individual freedom of belief). She was eleven when the Civil War began, an experience that affected her deeply and contributed to her aversion to discrimination of all kinds, including discrimination against women. Her father's mother Cecilie, a modern and emancipated woman who invited African Americans to her house to read them the latest news from the battlefields and discuss the politics of Abraham Lincoln and the future of Southern slavery, was also a great influence on the young Charlotta.

On account of Charlotta's musical talent, her father sent her to Leipzig in 1874 to stay with his friends Mr and Ms Göring and study piano at the Leipzig Conservatory. However, her musical career was disrupted as a result of the partial paralysis of one of her hands. In 1877, during her second visit to Leipzig, she met Tomáš Masaryk (1850-1937), then working on his habilitation in philosophy. Masaryk later said of Charlotta Garrigue: "She had a magnificent intellect, better than mine ... she loved mathematics. All through her life she desired exact knowledge, but did not lack feeling on that account. She was deeply religious" (Čapek 1936, 73). The two became close while reading English classics together such as John Stuart Mill's *The Subjection of Women* (1869). Masaryk asked her to marry him and the wedding took place on 15 March 1878 in Brooklyn Town Hall. Unusually, Tomáš Masaryk attached Garrigue's name to his own and thereafter signed his name Tomáš Garrigue Masaryk.

The newly-weds returned to Europe and settled in Vienna. Masaryk became an unsalaried tutor at Vienna University, earning his money giving private lessons and teaching at a secondary school. In 1879 a daughter, Alice, was born, followed a year later by a son, Herbert. The family income in Vienna was insufficient and Masaryk gladly accepted a professorship at the Czech University in Prague, where the family lived from 1882. Two more children were born in Prague: a son, Jan (1886) and a daughter, Olga (1891). They were happier in Prague than in Vienna and their standard of living also improved. Charlotta Garrigue Masaryková soon learned Czech and within a short time had adjusted to her new surroundings. She began writing articles on Czech culture for American and European newspapers, including texts on the composer Bedřich Smetana, whom she greatly admired. She also wrote an erudite essay on Smetana's work for the Czech magazine *Naše doba* (Our era).

It became habitual in the Masaryk family home to organize evening discussion sessions attended by Tomáš's university colleagues, writers, artists, scientists and students. Garrigue Masaryková was the hostess and the heart and soul of these gatherings, avidly entering into discussions with the guests. The topics of morality, love, marriage and the family were discussed openly without constraint. Garrigue Masaryková felt especially close to students and young people in general; she enjoyed giving them advice and even financial assistance. Her activities were not restricted to the 'private' sphere however and, like her husband, she became an active participant in public life.

Tomáš Garrigue Masaryk served in the Austrian Parliament (1891–1893; 1907–1914), first representing the *Mladočeská strana* (Young Czech Party), later the more moderate *Česká strana pokroková* (Czech Progressive Party). Both parties fought for an independent Czech state. On several occasions, Masaryk took a stand against the dissemination of racist and nationalistic mythologies. He defended Leopold Hilsner, a Jewish man who had been falsely accused of ritual murder (1899). During the case, Masaryk and his family were much criticized and slandered: Prague residents harassed Garrigue Masaryková and their children were insulted on the street. Garrigue Masaryková was a pillar of support to her husband, who felt harassed by the claims of his opponents, and she even managed to dissuade the disgusted Masaryk from going abroad.

With the help of her husband, Garrigue Masaryková translated Mill's *The Subjection of Women* into Czech and had it published (1890). Mill's trenchant arguments in favor of women's emancipation significantly influenced local intellectual women, such as members of the *Ženský klub český* (Czech Women's Club), which Garrigue Masaryková joined upon its establishment in 1903, participating in many of its programs. While she got along well with most of the members, some Czech feminists found it difficult to deal with her forthright and critical manner. In 1905, the writer ***Božena Viková-Kunětická*** published a piece in the *Narodní listy* (National newspaper), in which she wrote that Garrigue Masaryková's directness and impatience made her seem insensitive; that Garrigue Masaryková had been responsible for a heart attack suffered by one member of the association and that, as a foreigner, Garrigue Masaryková was unable to understand the problems of Czech women. Both Tomáš Garrigue Masaryk and the poet Svatopluk Machar came to Garrigue Masaryková's defence, as did other notable Czech intellectuals. Nevertheless, the incident led to a rupture between the *Ženský klub český* and Garrigue Masaryková and her supporters.

For Charlotta Garrigue Masaryková, 'the woman question' was part of 'the social question.' In 1905, she became a member of the *Československá sociálně-demokratická strana* (Czech-Slavic Social Democratic Party). The goals of the party were the elimination of poverty and illiteracy and the achievement of equality for women. However, she strongly disagreed with the party's Marxist perspective on the labor question. In 1906, together with Karla Máchová–a teacher and editor of a magazine for working women called *Ženský list* (Women's paper)–Garrigue Masaryková organized a lecture series for women on socialism. Garrigue Masaryková also supported women's and girls' associations in Moravia. She was an activist member of *Domovina* (Homeland), an association for the salvation of 'fallen girls' in Žižkov and a member of *Sokol* (Falcon), the Czech national civic organization for physical education, as well as of the *Ústřední spolek českých žen* (Central Association of Czech Women). Just before World War I, she helped found the *Spolek žen a dívek zaměstnaných při domácké výrobě a práci* (Association of Women and Girls Employed alongside their Domestic Production and Work) and co-edited (with Karla Machova) the journal *Ženský list*. An idealist who tried to live in accordance with her faith, she supported poor families even when it meant giving away the property of her own family.

Garrigue Masaryková considered the enfranchisement of women a priority and worked to this end with the *Výbor pro volební právo žen* (Committee for Women's Suffrage) run by ***Františka Plamínková***. Enfranchisement, the right to have a say in public affairs, was for Garrigue Masaryková the basic precondition for equality between men and women. Her views strongly influenced her husband and Tomáš Masaryk openly declared himself a distributor of his wife's ideas. It was most certainly to her credit that Masaryk, as soon as he became President, fought for the inclusion of section 106 of the Czechoslovak Constitution, which introduced universal suffrage and outlawed discrimination on the basis of sex, birth and occupation.

In 1914, after the outbreak of World War I, Tomáš Garrigue Masaryk went abroad with their daughter Olga to work on the establishment of an independent state for Czechs and Slovaks. For Garrigue Masaryková, this was the most difficult time of her life. Her husband's activities against the Habsburg Monarchy left her under constant police surveillance and she was obliged to ask for permission every time she wanted to leave Prague. The police often searched her apartment and her mail was censored. Her daughter Alice was imprisoned for nine months in Vienna and her son Jan was forced into military service and detached to Halic, a region bordering Poland, the Ukraine and Slovakia. Her son Herbert, a painter, caught typhus and died on 15 February 1915. Alone, Garrigue Masaryková came to rely upon the help of friends. Her health deteriorated and she began to suffer from depression; later, she was sent to a sanatorium in Veleslavin. She wrote frequently to her daughter Alice, then in prison, of which correspondence around two hundred letters remain. Some of these were later published under the title *Listy do vězení* (Letters to prison, 1947 and 1948) and *Milá mama/Dear Alice* (Dear mama/dear Alice, 2001). They reveal a deep moral strength, as well as the mutual love between Garrigue Masaryková and her daughter.

On 28 October 1918, the independent Czechoslovak Republic was declared and Tomáš Garrigue Masaryk was elected its first President. Garrigue Masaryková had significantly contributed to her husband's achievements–among other things by willingly devoting their personal life to politics–but now did not have the energy to enjoy this celebrity as First Lady and as a key public figure. She lived in seclusion, residing either at Hradčany Palace (Prague) or at the smaller presidential palace in Lány. When her condition worsened, she returned to the Veleslavin sanatorium. Masaryk visited her there frequently and arranged a study for himself next to her room where he often worked. The duties of First Lady were undertaken by the couple's daughter Alice. Charlotta Garrigue Masaryková died on 13 May 1923 and was buried in Lány Cemetery.

Anna Nedvědová
Gender Studies Prague, o.p.s., Library

Translated from the Czech by Jitka Kohoutkova, MA student at the Department of Gender Studies, Central European University, Budapest.

SOURCES

(B) *Masaryk a ženy, sborník k 80. narozeninám prvního presidenta republiky* (Masaryk and women, symposium published on the eightieth birthday of the President of the Republic). Vol. I., third edition. Prague: Ženská národní rada, 1930.

(B) Čapek, Karel. *Hovory s T. G. Masarykem* (Conversations with T. G. Masaryk). Prague: Fr. Borový a Čin, 1936.

(C) Masaryková, Charlotta G. *Listy do vězení* (Letters to prison). Prague: Vladimir Žikeš, 1948.

(C) Garrigue Masaryková, Charlotta. *Milá mama–Dear Alice: korespondence Alice a Charlotty Masarykových 1915-1916* (Dear mama–dear Alice: correspondence between Alice and Charlotta Masaryková 1915-1916). Dagmara Hájková and Jaroslav Soukup, eds. Prague: Masarykův ústav Akademie věd ČR, 2001.

(D) Bělohlávek, B. *Charlotte G. Masaryk and the Czechoslovak Nation*. London: The Czechoslovak Red Cross, 1941.

(D) Skilling, H. Gordon. *Matka a dcera–Charlotta a Alice Masarykovy* (Mother and daughter–Charlotta and Alice Masaryk). Prague: Gender Studies, o.p.s., 2001.

(D) Neudorflová, Marie, ed. *Charlotta G. Masaryková–Sborník příspěvků z konference k 150. výročí jejího narození, konané 10. listopadu 2000* (Charlotta G. Masaryková–Commemorative volume from the conference held on the 150th anniversary of her birthday, 10 November 2000). Prague: Masarykův ústav Akademie věd ČR, 2001.
(E) Soubigou, A. *Tomáš Garrigue Masaryk*. Prague: Paseka, 2004.
(E) Kosatík, P. *Devět žen z hradu* (Nine women from the Castle). Prague: Maldá Fronta, 1999.

MAŠIOTIENĖ, Ona (1883-1949)

Lithuanian feminist, social worker and teacher; founder and leader (1929–1934) of the *Lietuvos moterų taryba* (Lithuanian Council of Women); participant in the meeting of the Executive Committee of the International Council of Women (London, 1929).

Ona Mašiotienė born Ona Brazauskaitė (or Brzezowska; Brazauskaitė is the Lithuanian version of the latter and this is how she always referred to herself) was born on 29 January 1883, into a noble family from Šlavėnai (in the parish of Anykščiai, today northern Lithuania), one of eight children. Her father, Gustaw Brzezowski (1841-1906), was involved in the 1863 Uprising against Russian rule, wounded and later imprisoned. In prison, he met Jadwiga Michailowska (1845-1915), the daughter of one of his inmates, Enrik Michailowski, who had been sentenced to death. The young woman was to become his wife and the mother of Ona.

At the couple's home an atmosphere of Lithuanian patriotism prevailed, despite their speaking Polish. The father distributed Lithuanian books (an activity banned by the Russian occupiers) and later became an outspoken advocate of Lithuanian-Polish equality and unity in one state. While Ona's brothers retained a Polish identity, some of her sisters turned towards a Lithuanian cultural identity. Ona found this national division within her family painful. She graduated with distinction from the Kaunas Girls' High School in 1900 (?) but considered this education insufficient, since she had hoped to become a qualified schoolteacher. Moving to Moscow, she enrolled in higher education courses in the natural sciences. Though her parents were well off, it was Olga's aunt who financially supported her studies–her parents adopting a fairly typical (negative) attitude towards girls' higher education.

During her studies, Ona Brazauskait˙e became interested in social work and helped establish the Lithuanian Student Society in Moscow, an organization of male and female members. She also became interested in Western European women's movements, particularly those based in England, and began advocating equal rights for women. On 22 and 23 September 1905, she became a founder member of the *Lietuvos moteru˛ susivienijimas* (Lithuanian Women's Association), the first women's organization in Lithuania. She was elected as a delegate to what must have been the second Congress of the *Soiuz ravnopraviia zhenshchin* (Women's Equal Rights Union; also known as the All-Russian Union for Women's Equality). On 4 and 5 December 1905, Ona Brazauskait˙e participated in the Lithuanian Great *Seimas* in Vilnius: the first Lithuanian National Congress. The participation of women in the congress demonstrated women's interest and active involvement in national affairs.

While studying in Moscow, Ona Brazauskaitė met her future husband, Jonas Mašiotas, a fellow Lithuanian. They married in 1906 (?) and in 1909, she gave birth to their only child, Ona (Anulė). Ona Mašiotienė's (apparently happy) marriage did not stop her from participating in public events such as the first Lithuanian Women's Congress (23-24 September 1907). After completing her studies, she moved to Vilnius–the center of Lithuanian as well as of Polish cultural life–where she took up teaching at Vilnius High School (1911-1914). During World War I, the family fled to Moscow, where Ona Mašiotienė established the *Lietuvos moterų laisvės sąjunga* (Lithuanian Women's Freedom Union) and became its Chairwoman. In 1917, she represented the Lithuanian Women's Freedom Union at the *Lietuvių seimas Peterburge* (the Lithuanian Parliament in St Petersburg), where she delivered a speech on women's rights.

Lithuania gained its independence in 1918. Returning with her family to Vilnius in 1918, Ona Mašiotienė set up and led the first Lithuanian language high school for girls in Vilnius, as well as a high school, arranged as evening courses, in the Russian language (the aim of the latter school was to give young Lithuanians, returning home from Russia after the war, the opportunity to complete their education in the language in which they had started it: i.e. Russian). In 1919, the Polish army marched into Vilnius, at that time an important center of Polish, Jewish and Lithuanian culture. Vilnius/Wilno became an 'apple of discord' between Lithuania and Poland, which only established diplomatic relations in 1938. Despite Mašiotienė's efforts to find able teachers for her schools, Polish officials closed them after just a year and a half of existence. In 1919, Mašiotienė was elected to the Board of the *Lietuvių mokytojų sąjunga* (Lithuanian Teachers' Union) and to the *Laikinų lietuvių tarybą Vilniuje* (Temporary Committee of Lithuanians in Vilnius), which promoted Lithuanian culture under Polish rule. During the Lithuanian Independence Wars (1918-1920), Mašiotienė rallied popular support for the causes of national independence and women's involvement in national defense, founding and leading the *Moterų karo komitetas* (Women's War Committee).

After the Lithuanian State's Land Reform of 1922 (implemented by the then ruling Christian Democrats and aimed at stripping noble families–often of Polish cultural identity–of their land-base), Mašiotienė's family lost half its lands. Mašiotienė herself was left eighty ha of land in Šlavėnai, where she spent most of her summers. During the rest of the year, she lived in Kaunas where, besides teaching the natural sciences in various Kaunas secondary schools, she participated in cultural and public life and created a reputation for herself as one of the capital's most educated and intelligent women. In the municipal elections of 1921 and 1924, Mašiotienė was elected to the Utenos regional council (her estate was in Šlavėnai, in the region of Utenos). In this capacity, she worked for the Education Committee (until ca. 1928).

At the end of 1928, Mašiotienė established the *Lietuvos moterų taryba* (*LMT*, Lithuanian Council of Women). It is certain that the visit of International Council of Women (ICW) Board Member Louise C. A. van Eeghen in September 1928 had something to do with this development, but it is not known who invited Van Eeghen to Lithuania. Thanks to Mašiotienė's efforts, the *LMT* joined the ICW immediately (i.e. in 1929; although ICW sources record the date as being 1930. See *Women in a Changing World* 1966, 284). Mašiotienė designed the *LMT* program as well as delivering lectures and speeches on behalf of the organization to various women's congresses. As a result of her efforts, the *LMT* managed to unify a host of Lithuanian women's organizations in support of women's rights. As Chairwoman of the *LMT*, Mašiotienė participated in the Executive Meeting of the ICW in London (1929) and in 1933 founded a special club for women, the *Moterų seklyčia* (Women's Salon), which was closely linked to the *LMT*. The club premises provided women with cultural entertainment and a meeting place and were free for the use of all organizations belonging to the *LMT*; profits from the club (which was partly subsidized by Mašiotienė herself) went to the *LMT*. During this period, Mašiotienė was one of the most dedicated members of both the *LMT* and the *Moterų seklyčia*, seeing the organizations as crucial to the success of ongoing women's rights campaigns in Lithuania–in particular campaigns for women's employment rights.

In 1930, Mašiotienė began hosting a radio show, "Onos ir Marijonos pasikalbejimai" (The conversations of Ann and Marian), which mainly discussed household and health issues. From 1933, she also edited the radio newspaper *Namai ir Moteris* (Home and woman), which gained popularity among radio listeners. She was involved in a children's health organization called *Pieno lašas* (The milk drop) and, in 1930, her public work was acknowledged by the state (she received the Third Order of Gediminas, awarded for sincere and dedicated work in the service of the Lithuanian nation). At the second Lithuanian Women's Congress in 1937, organized as a commemoration of the first women's congress of 1907, Mašiotienė presented a paper (later published as a book) entitled *Moterų politinis ir valstybiniai tautiškas darbas 1907-1937* (The political and national work of women from 1907 to 1937). The congress discussed changes that had taken place in women's situation in Lithuania in the previous thirty years, emphasizing women's achievements while taking note of their persisting economic disadvantages.

World War II transformed Mašiotienė's life completely. In 1944, her only daughter fled Lithuania, leaving Mašiotienė and her husband without information as to her whereabouts for a long and worrying period. Under communist rule (from July 1944),

Mašiotienė was no longer permitted to teach, since she was seen as ideologically 'unreliable.' She lived with her husband at their farm in Šlavėnai, and 'voluntarily' joined a Soviet agricultural collective. After her husband's death in 1948, she felt lonely and isolated. Materially, as well as emotionally, she faced many difficulties: she lacked food and even firewood. These severe living conditions contributed to the deterioration of her health and she died, aged 66, on 29 December 1949, in a hospital in Kaunas. She was buried in the Petrašiūnai cemetery in Kaunas.

Ona Mašiotienė's activities supported both national and feminist causes. It seems that she perceived a certain kind of reciprocity in the relationship between national and women's freedom: the nation required the increased participation of women while women desired greater participation in national life as citizens. Throughout her life, Mašiotienė held to these overarching ideals. In her work as a teacher, as well as in her other public activities, she consistently emphasized the equality of both sexes. She also campaigned for women's organization and cooperation at both the national and international levels.

Indrė Karčiauskaitė
Vytautas Magnus University, Kaunas

SOURCES

(A) Lithuanian Academy of Sciences Library (*LMAB*), Fund 181. Archive O. Mašiotienė.

(A) Lithuanian National Library (*LNB*), Fund 64, file 146. O. Mašiotienė's letters to M. Čilvinaitė.

(A) *LNB*, Fund 14-583. O. Mašiotienė's letters to Marija Urbsienė Mašiotienė.

(A) *Lietuvos Valstybes Istorijos Archyvas* (*LVIA*, Lithuanian State Historical Archive), Fund 669, ap.19, b.64, l.250. Anykščiai Parish book.

(A) *LNB*, Fund 66. Typescript written between 1945 and 1956: Zigmas Toliušis. *Atsiminimai ir apybraižos* (Memoirs and essays), 182-186.

(C) Mašiotienė, O. "L. M. T. pirm. O. Mašiotienės pranesimas" (Report of O. Mašiotienė, head of the Lithuanian Women's Council). In *Lietuvos Moteru Taryba Neperiodinis Biuletenis No 1* (Lithuanian Women's Council, supplementary bulletin no. 1). Kaunas, 1930.

(C) Mašiotienė, O. "Lietuvos Moterų Taryba–jos reikšmė ir uždaviniai" (The Lithuanian Council of Women–its significance and its tasks). *Moteris ir Pasaulis* (Woman and the world), no. 1 (1937): 4-5.

(C) Mašiotienė, O. *Moterų politinis ir valstybiniai tautiškas darbas* (The political and national work of women from 1907 to 1937). Kaunas: 'Vilnius' publishers, 1938.

(D) Novickienė, Birutė. "Ona Mašiotienė (Brazauskaitė)." *Lietuvių enciklopedija XVII* (Lithuanian encyclopedia, vol. XVII). Boston: Lietuvių enciklopedijos leidykla, 1959.

(D) Butkuvienė, Anelė. "Feministė" (Feminist). *Šeimininkė* (Housewife), no. 14 (March 2001): 10.

(E) *Women in a Changing World. The Dynamic Story of the International Council of Women since 1888.* London: Routledge and Kegan Paul, 1966.

(E) Karosaitė-Gimbutienė, Elena. "Atostogos Šlavėnuose" (Holidays in Šlavėnai). *Anykščiai*, no. 9 (1995): 47–53; no. 10 (1996): 36–39.

(E) Račkaitis, Vygantas. "Gustaw Brzozowski." *Kultūros paminklų enciklopedija, Rytų Lietuva* (Encyclopedia of cultural monuments in eastern Lithuania), part I. Vilnius: Mokslo ir enciklopediju leidybos institutes, 1996, 36.

(E) Jureniene, Virginija. "Lietuvių Moterų Judejimas XIX a pabaigoje–XX a pirmoje puseje" (The Lithuanian women's movement at the end of the nineteenth century and in the first half of the twentieth century). Dissertation manuscript. Vilnius, 2004.

MATEJCZUK, Vera (first married name, Maslouskaya; second married name, Karczeuskaya) (1896–1981)

Activist of the Belarussian national movement; considered to be one of the founders of the Belarussian women's movement. Pen-name: 'Murashka.'

Vera Matejczuk was born on 24 March 1896 in Suprasl (now in Poland, then a Northwestern Province of the Russian Empire), into a poor peasant family–one of twelve children. She spent her childhood in the village of Aharodniczki, near Suprasl, where she attended an elementary school but could not continue her education for economic reasons. Later she wrote: "I read any book I could get my hands on, but I was most fascinated by the lives and struggles of outstanding individuals who had fought for the rights of the poor and the victimized. And while reading these books I would plunge into thought and remain like that until roused by someone–usually my father–who would say that I'd never be able to make a living from those books ... Oh, how my soul would ache at such times ..." (Kekeleva 1997).

Vera Matejczuk began working at a textile factory in Byalystok, but was fired for initiating a strike and was only able to find work as a maid. At the same time, she studied at the teacher-training seminary in Swislacz, from which she received her diploma in 1914. Before she could begin teaching however, World War I broke out. In 1917, she completed short-term courses at the Swislacz Belarussian teaching seminary that had been opened during the German occupation as part of German attempts to invoke and support anti-Russian (i.e. national) sentiments among the peoples living on the fringes of the Russian Empire. She went to the village of Hrabavets (currently in Poland), where she founded one of the first elementary schools to employ Belarussian as the language of instruction.

In 1919, Matejczuk lived in Wilno (now Vilnius), then occupied by the Polish army. There, she took part in the first Belarussian teacher-training courses and it was then that she became involved in politics and joined the *Belaruskaya partyja satsyjalistau-*

revalyutsianerau (Belarussian Party of Socialist Revolutionaries), which opposed the Polish government. After completing the teacher-training courses, she worked as a teacher and a school instructor (a 'teacher of teachers'), and married a Polish officer named Maslouski, who was killed at the front after several months. In the spring of 1920 in Minsk, Vera Maslouskaya set up the *Tsentral'ny sayuz Belarusak* (Central Union of Belarussian Women), operational until the Red Army (the Bolsheviks) arrived in Minsk in the summer of 1920. No exact information about the activities of this organization exist, but it is likely that they focused on women's education as part of the national 'awakening' of women as Belarussians (since many women considered themselves Polish, Lithuanian or Russian).

For a time, Vera Maslouskaya worked as an inspector at the Komissariat (Ministry) of Education of the Belarussian Socialist Republic in Minsk, but in 1920, she returned to Aharodniczki. The government of the Belarussian People's Republic (both anti-Soviet and anti-Polish and promoting the idea of an independent Belarussian state) was at that time working in Kaunas (Lithuania) and the *Belaruskaya partyja satsyjalistau-revalyutsianerau* entrusted Maslouskaya with setting up an underground organization to fight for Belarussian independence, alongside other partisan and underground groups in Belarus (divided between Poles and Soviets). The organization soon had a developed structure and incorporated a powerful partisan detachment.

In September 1921, Vera Maslouskaya went to the Belarussian national and political convention in Prague as a delegate from the Byalystok area. She explained her participation in the following way: "I could not look without indignation at the injustice and humiliation inflicted upon the Belarussian people. And I believed that it was not through evolution, but revolution that we should fight for our rights!" (Kekeleva 1997). The resolutions of the conference cautioned the Belarussian people against bloodshed, but called for them to unite until it was time for revolution–i.e. the fight for independence. The conference denounced The Treaty of Riga of 1921, which had divided Belarus between Poland and Soviet Russia.

The resolutions of the Prague conference frightened the Polish government and in 1922, Vera Maslouskaya and a number of underground activists were arrested. At the so-called "Process of the 45," Maslouskaya was tried as one of the organizers of partisan activities, accused of organizing and participating in the underground resistance, as well as of taking part in the Prague conference. In court, she declared that she had been "the one and only organizer of the movement ... Our work is pure, inspired by the [national] idea, and we are not guilty of spying on behalf of Lithuania, nor did we have any ammunition depot ... In the future, the possibility of armed struggle might emerge, but we believed that Poland would understand us, that it would not destroy our nationality and that we would not have to revert to arms" (Kekeleva 1997). Vera Maslouskaya was sentenced to six years imprisonment and spent the term in Byalystok and Warsaw. While in prison, she began contributing verses to the Belarussian newspapers *Vol'ny styah* (The free banner), published in Vilnius, and *Rassvet* (The dawn), published in the USA. In 1927, she married Uladzimir Karczeuski, whom she had met in prison.

As former political prisoners, the Karczeuskis were not allowed to teach; they would return to teaching only in 1939 (after western Belarus had been incorporated into the Belarussian Soviet Socialist Republic). In this year, they organized a Belarussian intermediate school in Aharodniczki. In December 1941, the German occupiers of Belarus closed the school, but the couple continued to teach children underground. This work continued after the war, but Vera Karczeuskaya had to leave the Byalystok area for Silesia in 1946, because the Polish patriotic underground had begun persecuting former Belarussian activists. She returned in 1951 and worked as a librarian. She participated in the activities of the so-called Women's League (probably Communist, but the exact name and other data are not available), worked for local government and in the Belarussian Cultural Association (in Poland), as well as writing verse published in Belarussian newspapers in Poland. She died on 23 January 1981 in Suprasl near Byalystok.

Aleh Hardzienka
Editor of the weekly *Nasha niva* (Our soil)

Translated from the Belarussian by Elena Gapova.

SOURCES

(D) "Maslouskaya Vera." In *Entsyklapedya historyi* (Encyclopedia of Belarussian history). Minsk: BSE, 1999, 5: 90.

(E) Turonak J. "Nepakornaya vera" (Untamed faith). In *Belaruski kalyandar* (Belarussian calendar). Bielystok (Poland), 1990.

(E) Kekeleva, T. "O, jak mne balela dusha" (Oh, how my soul suffered). *Belarus*, no. 7 (1997).

MAYREDER, Rosa (1858–1938)

Theorist and activist of the Austrian women's movement; co-founder and later Vice-President of the *Allgemeiner Österreichischer Frauenverein* (General Austrian Women's Association) (1893–1903), leader of the *Österreichische Frauenliga für Frieden und Freiheit* (Austrian Women's League for Peace and Freedom); writer of novels, short stories, sonnets, essays and sociological and political studies.

Rosa Mayreder, 1928, on her seventieth birthday

Rosa Mayreder (nee Obermayer) was born in Vienna on 30 November 1858, and grew up in a family of thirteen children. Her father, Franz Obermayer (1811–1893), was the owner of the famous *Winterbierhaus* in Vienna. He embodied contemporary values, a mixture of patriarchal authority and liberal middle-class views. Magdalena Bösch, Obermayer's first wife, died after giving birth to her eighth child. His second wife, Maria Engel (1840–1929), the mother of Rosa, bore Obermayer five more children. Since Obermayer was a Protestant and both wives Catholics, the boys were raised in the religion of their father, the girls in that of their mother. Rosa's favorite brothers were Adolf (1853–1940), an architect, and Friedrich (1861–1924), a physician in Vienna. Though not studious types, the Obermayer boys were allowed to pursue higher education–a privilege refused to the girls. At a time when women had little opportunity to participate in public life, Rosa Obermayer tried to break out of the constraints imposed on her sex by acquiring knowledge and education. She saw herself as an exception, while believing that her behaviour would become the norm for women at some time in the future. Apart from studying subjects deemed suitable for middle-class women and girls, she also took private painting lessons and persuaded her parents to allow her to study Greek and Latin alongside her brothers.

Rosa Obermayer married the architect Karl Mayreder (1856–1935) in 1881. They had known one another for ten years and had been engaged for four. Her husband worked in the studio of Heinrich Freiherr von Ferstel, professor and rector of architecture at the *Technische Hochschule*. Karl Mayreder retired from the studio in 1924, after suffering from mental illness. Inheriting substantially from her father's estate, Rosa

Mayreder was always financially independent. With her husband, she tried to sustain a marriage based on non-hierarchical ideals. Following a miscarriage in 1883, the couple remained childless.

Rosa Mayreder was an enthusiastic painter and the first woman to be admitted to the Aquarellist Club. In 1891, one of her watercolors was exhibited for the first time at the annual exhibition of the Viennese *Künstlerhaus* (House of Artists). She complained about the amateurish state of art education for women and–together with Olga Prager and Karl Federn–founded the *Kunstschule für Frauen und Mädchen* (Art School for Women and Girls). She also composed the libretto for Hugo Wolf's opera, *Der Corregidor* (The corregidor). Under the pseudonym Franz Arnold, Mayreder wrote art reviews for the Viennese daily, the *Neue Freie Presse* (New free press). In her naturalist novels and novella, Mayreder draped her theoretical ideas in literary forms. She placed her ideal figures in realistic settings and did not succumb to sentimental realism. Her greatest literary contribution however, was her collection of critical cultural and philosophical essays, devoted to contemporary themes such as the constrictions placed upon girls by their education, nineteenth-century ideas of femininity, the tyranny of convention and the double standards of bourgeois marriage. She also wrote critically on the representation of masculinity and paternal rights and was an advocate of international peace.

Rosa Mayreder held her first public lecture in 1894–criticizing discrimination against prostitutes. She co-founded and was later Vice-President of the *Allgemeiner Österreichischer Frauenverein* (General Austrian Women's Association) (1893–1903), Chairperson of the *Österreichische Frauenliga für Frieden und Freiheit* (Austrian Women's League for Peace and Freedom) (from 1919) and a member of the *Österreichische Friedensgesellschaft* (Austrian Society for Peace)–activities demonstrating Rosa Mayreder's commitment to radical change in the status of women and international peace. From 1899–1900, Mayreder co-edited the journal, *Dokumente der Frauen* (Documents of women), issued from 1899 to 1902.

Rosa Mayreder was deeply engaged in the main intellectual debates of her time. Her favourite prose form, the essay, was subjective, but she used it to criticize the scientific community and reveal the contradictions in various schools of thought claiming to be 'objective.' She focused her critique on traditional ideals of femininity and contemporary scientific and public discourses on 'woman's nature.' Her two volumes, *Zur Kritik der Weiblichkeit* (A critique of femininity, 1905) and *Geschlecht und Kultur* (Sex and culture, 1923) presented a radical approach to the concepts of femininity and masculinity, exploring their cultural history and the constructions in which they were embedded. Mayreder eschewed essentializing narratives, taking historical processes as well as cultural norms into account and exploring the approaches of individual men and women to their own, and the opposite, sex. For Mayreder, 'male' did not represent a standard against which 'female' was to be measured and evaluated; on the contrary, the two constructs had no place in Mayreder's vision of a different, progressive humanity: an androgynous utopia based on love as the expression of a relationship between two independent individuals. Femininity–neither an extension of masculinity, nor the performance of household duties–was only knowable through the emancipation of both sexes, in a society where women participated in public life. The women's movement was therefore, in Mayreder's eyes, a political and social necessity; she saw demands for gender equality in the workplace, as well as in society as a whole, as a pressing historical commitment and a prerequisite for human emancipation–not an end in itself, nor a call for women to conform.

Like many of her generation engaged with 'the woman question,' Rosa Mayreder interpreted the end of the Austro-Hungarian Empire in 1918 as the failure of male domination, as a crisis in patriarchal values. She criticized traditional family structures, demanding the transformation of the authoritarian role of the father, in particular regarding children. She thus attacked the power structures inherent in the bourgeois family. In Mayreder's view this implied neither the abolition of the family nor a negation of motherhood and fatherhood, but rather the advocation of measures to alleviate the alienation experienced in even the most intimate of human relationships. From this it followed that women might begin to demand a different kind of sexuality. Rosa Mayreder was a strong opponent of prostitution, but she saw little difference between the objectification of sex and eroticism in conventional marital arrangements–with women functioning as child-bearing machines–and the treatment of the (prostituted) female body as a commodified sex object. Thus, she vehemently opposed any moral condemnation of prostitutes. In countering the view that women were property, Rosa Mayreder held that the best strategy was to remove the taboo placed on sexuality in the education of boys and girls and to promote a non-dualistic culture of eroticism in relations between the sexes.

Rosa Mayreder's commitment to human emancipation was also evident in her struggle for peace between the nations, her avowal of internationalism and her condemnation of racial discrimination. During her long life, Rosa Mayreder became a well-known and respected public figure: she was made a honorary citizen of Vienna on the occasion of her 70th birthday in 1928, and received a book published in her honour: *Aufstieg der Frau* (Rise of woman). Rosa Mayreder died on 19 January 1938 from a cerebral stroke. Her name gradually fell into obscurity until a revival of her life and work was made possible by the 'second wave' feminist movement of the 1970s. In 2002, prior to the introduction of the Euro in Austria, Rosa Mayreder's portrait graced the 500 Schilling banknote.

Edith Leisch-Prost
Historian, Vienna

SOURCES

(C) Mayreder, Rosa. *Idola. Geschichte einer Liebe* (Idola. Story of a love). Berlin, 1899.

(C) Mayreder, Rosa. *Zur Kritik der Weiblichkeit* (Criticism of femininity). Jena/Leipzig, 1905.

(C) Mayreder, Rosa. *Pippin, ein Sommererlebnis* (Pippin, a summer experience). Leipzig/Vienna, 1908.

(C) Mayreder, Rosa. *Zwischen Himmel und Erde, Sonette* (Beween heaven and earth, Sonnets). Jena, 1908.

(C) Mayreder, Rosa. *Der typische Verlauf sozialer Bewegungen* (The typical progress of social movements). Vienna, 1917.

(C) Mayreder, Rosa. *Fabeleien über göttliche und menschliche Dinge* (Fables about divine and human things). Leipzig/Vienna, 1921.

(C) Mayreder, Rosa. *Die Frau und der Internationalismus* (Woman and internationalism). Vienna, 1921.

(C) Mayreder, Rosa. *Geschlecht und Kultur* (Sex and culture). Jena, 1923.

(C) Mayreder, Rosa. *Mensch und Menschlichkeit* (Man and humanity). Jena, 1928.

(C) Mayreder, Rosa. *Die Krise der Ehe* (The crisis of marriage). Jena, 1929.

(C) Mayreder, Rosa. *Der letzte Gott* (The last God). Stuttgart, 1933.

(C) Mayreder, Rosa. *Aschmedai's Sonette an den Menschen* (Aschmedai's sonnets to mankind). Vienna, 1937.

(C) Mayreder, Rosa. *Das Haus in der Landskrongasse* (The house in the Landskronlane). Käthe Braun-Prager, ed. Vienna, 1948.

(C) Mayreder, Rosa. *Krise der Väterlichkeit* (Crisis of fatherhood). Käthe Braun-Prager, ed. Vienna, 1963.

(C) Mayreder, Rosa. *Tagebücher 1873-1937* (Diaries 1873-1937). Harriet Anderson, ed. Frankfurt/M: Insel Verlag, 1988.

(D) Braun-Prager, Käthe, ed. *Der Aufstieg der Frau. Festgabe zu Rosa Mayreders 70. Geburtstag* (The rise of woman. Commemorative volume for Rosa Mayreder's 70th birthday). Jena, 1928.

(D) Schnedl-Bubenicek, Hanna. "Grenzgängerin der Moderne" (Crossover artist? A transgressor of modernity): Rosa Mayreder." Autorinnengruppe Uni Wien, ed. *Das ewige Klischee* (The eternal stereotype). Vienna/Köln/Graz, 1981.

(D) Schnedl-Bubenicek, Hanna. "Rosa Mayreder—Eine Sympathisantin des Lebendigen" (Rosa Mayreder—A sympathizer of vitality). Hanna Schnedl, ed. *Zur Kritik der Weiblichkeit* (Criticism of femininity). Munich: Frauenoffensive, 1981.

(D) Prost, Edith. *Weiblichkeit und bürgerliche Kultur, am Beispiel: Rosa Mayreder-Obermayer* (Femininity and bourgeois culture, the case of Rosa Mayreder-Obermayer). Dissertation. Vienna, 1983.

(D) Prost, Edith, ed. *Rosa Mayreder 1858-1938. Texte zum Symposion* (Texts from the symposium). IWK-Mitteilungen 1, 1989.

(D) Bubenicek, Hanna. *Rosa Mayreder oder Wider die Tyrannei der Norm* (Rosa Mayreder or against the tyranny of norms). Vienna/Köln/Graz: Böhlau, 1986.

(D) *Aufbruch in das Jahrhundert der Frau? Rosa Mayreder und der Feminismus in Wien um 1900* (An Awakening in the Century of Woman? Rosa Mayreder and feminism in Vienna 1900). *Katalog zur 125. Sonderausstellung des Historischen Museums der Stadt Wien 1989/1990*

(Catalogue of the 125th special exhibition in the Historical Museum of Vienna). Vienna, 1989.

(D) Sokolosky, Jane. "Promitive or differentiated? Constructions of femininity in Rosa Mayreder's theoretical and fictional texts." *Modern Austrian Literature: Journal of the International Arthur Schnitzler Research Association* 30, no. 2 (1997): 65–83.

(D) Schmölzer, Hilde. *Rosa Mayreder: ein Leben zwischen Utopie und Wirklichkeit* (A life between utopia and reality). Vienna: Promedia, 2002.

(E) Anderson, Harriet. *Utopian Feminism. Women's Movements in fin-de-siècle Vienna*. New Haven and London: Yale University Press, 1992. (German edition: *Vision und Leidenschaft. Die Frauenbewegung im Fin-de-siècle Wiens*. Vienna: Deuticke, 1994.)

MĘCZKOWSKA, Teodora (1870–1954)

Polish social activist, feminist, teacher; co-founder of numerous social, professional and women's cultural and educational organizations.

Teodora Maria Męczkowska (*nee* Oppman) was born on 5 September 1870 in Łowicz, a small town in the Polish Kingdom (under Russian partition). Her father, Jan Adolf Oppman, was the pastor of an Evangelical church; her mother, Teodora born Berlińska, was a teacher. In 1888, Teodora graduated from high school in Warsaw. Two years later, she left for Switzerland. From 1892 to 1896, she studied at the Faculty of Natural and Physical Sciences at the University of Geneva, gaining a *Bachelier des Sciences Physique et Naturelles* (B.A. in the natural sciences).

In 1895, Teodora married Wacław Męczkowski (1863–1922), a physician and national independence activist (whom she probably met in Geneva). The couple settled in Warsaw. Theirs was a modern marriage, bound by deep emotional attachment, friendship, common interests and ideals. Both participated fully in social and public life. By choice they had no children.

Męczkowska's interests and activities were connected mainly with women's emancipation, equality and questions of education. She was a member or co-founder of almost all the women's organizations established in the Russian partition from the 1890s onwards, including the most radical feminist organization of the period, the *Związek Równouprawnienia Kobiet Polskich* (Union of Equal Rights for Polish Women), founded in 1907 and led by ***Paulina Kuczalska-Reinschmit***. In 1907, Męczkowska left the *Związek Równouprawnienia Kobiet Polskich* and formed the more moderate *Polskie Stowarzyszenie Równouprawnienia Kobiet* (Polish Women's Rights Association), which combined the goals of women's equality with other social and political goals. Męczkowska participated in all the Polish women's congresses (held in 1905, 1907, 1917 and 1938) and, as the President of the *Centralny Komitet Równouprawnienia Kobiet Polskich* (Central Committee of Polish Women's Rights, founded in 1917), worked on legislation to improve women's political and civil rights in the independent Polish State.

In 1919, Męczkowska co-founded, along with (among others) ***Justyna Budzińska-Tylicka*** and ***Zofia Daszyńska-Golińska***, the *Klub Polityczny Kobiet Postępowych* (*KPKP*, Progressive Women's Political Club). The organization aimed primarily to increase women's participation in political life, to campaign against women's discrimination in the workplace–i.e. for the equal pay of women and men for equal work and for women's promotion to higher positions–and for greater legal protection of mothers and children. In 1927, Męczkowska became Vice-President of the *Demokratyczny Komitet Wyborczy Kobiet Polskich* (Democratic Electoral Committee of Polish Women, founded in 1927). This organization cooperated with the *Bezpartyjny Blok Współpracy z Rządem* (Non-Party Bloc for Cooperation with the [right-wing] Government): a political party comprised of the followers of Prime Minister Józef Piłsudski, the leading figure in Polish political life after 1926. In 1928, in spite of its efforts, the *Demokratyczny Komitet Wyborczy Kobiet Polskich* only managed to have three of its candidates elected to the Polish Parliament: Zofia Daszyńska-Golińska to the Senate and Maria Jaworska and Ewa Waśniewska to the *Sejm* (Lower Chamber).

In 1926, Męczkowska co-founded the *Polskie Stowarzyszenie Kobiet z Wyższym Wykształceniem* (Polish Association of Women with Higher Education), the Polish section of the International Federation of University Women. She was its President between 1927 and 1948. In a manifesto published in 1926, *Do czego dążymy?* (What are our aims?), she laid out the mission of the Association: to defend university women's professional interests and to campaign for women's equality with men in high-ranking positions. Męczkowska saw universal social benefits in including women in all aspects of social life and regarded women's entry into the professions as a way for them to satisfy material needs and achieve self-realization. Awareness of women's rights was thus linked by Męczkowska to women's inner development and liberation from the prescribed roles of 'wife' and 'mother.'

Męczkowska devoted many of her publications and speeches to ethical issues: she criticized prostitution, double moral standards and inadequate sex education. She initiated a campaign against state-regulated prostitution and, in 1900, founded the secret *Towarzystwo Abolicjonistyczne* (Abolitionist Society). After the Russian Parliament had begun work to ensure that domestic laws met international obligations (accepted by Russia) to curb the traffic in women for prostitution, Męczkowska participated in a campaign organized by the *Związek Równouprawnienia Kobiet Polskich* (1909, 1913), delivering lectures on both prostitution and trafficking in women. Years later in her memoirs, she described the change in public opinion regarding these issues as her success. She summarized her views on the ethical issues involved and programs of moral reform in her pamphlet *Ideały etyczno-społeczne ruchu kobiecego* (The ethical and social ideals of the women's movement, 1907).

Teodora Męczkowska's main focus, from 1900 until her death in 1954, was education. Prior to the outbreak of World War I, she taught in a girls' school in Warsaw and from 1903, was an active member of the *Towarzystwo Pedagogiczne w Warszawie* (Warsaw Pedagogical Society). During the Russian Revolution of 1905 to 1907, she participated in a school strike for the restoration of Polish schools in the Polish Kingdom. As one of the first teachers of the natural sciences, she introduced aspects of human reproduction into biology lessons at the girls' school run by Jadwiga Sikorska. Like many feminists and social activists of the so-called progressive intelligentsia, she was an advocate of sex education for both children and young people. She also promoted co-educational schools, as in her pamphlet *Szkoły mieszane (czyli koedukacyjne)* (Mixed or co-educational schools, 1905). In later years, she also introduced and popularized modern methods for teaching the natural sciences in specialist books and periodicals.

In independent Poland, Męczkowska was the first woman to be employed by the then Ministry of Education as a school inspector. She occupied this position from 1918 until 1934, contributing, among other things, to the unification of school syllabi and standards of teaching in boys' and girls' schools, as well as to the modernization of the Polish education system. Męczkowska was also a trade union activist, devoted to the question of the professional status of teachers, particularly women teachers. She was a member of various teachers' labor organizations, including the (still operative) *Związek Nauczycielstwa Polskiego* (Polish Teachers' Union).

During the Nazi occupation, Męczkowska participated in clandestine education. After the defeat of the Warsaw Uprising, she moved to Zakopane (1944–1945), where she wrote her memoirs. Immediately after the end of the war she returned to Warsaw, where she taught biology at a high school until the end of her life. She died at the age of 84 on 11 December 1954, and was buried in a Roman Catholic cemetery at Powązki in Warsaw.

The life of Teodora Męczkowska coincided with great social and political changes in Poland and Europe. She began her work and activities in partitioned Poland and later participated in the development of educational systems in independent Poland. She witnessed two world wars, the German occupation of the Polish territories and the first ten years of Communist Poland. Throughout these changes she carried out social work, fulfilling her individual need and capacity for activism. She left numerous books, pamphlets and articles on social issues such as feminism and pedagogy (in particular the teaching of the natural sciences) and published in many forums, ranging from specialist periodicals such as *Przegląd Pedagogiczny* (Pedagogical review) to feminist ones such as *Ster* (Helm). She also contributed to social review journals such as *Głos* (Voice) and *Ogniwo* (Link). For a long time she was remembered solely for her activities in the field of education. Thanks to the institutionalization of women's studies in Poland, her feminist involvement has also come to light.

Jolanta Sikorska-Kulesza
University of Warsaw

SOURCES

(A) National Library (Warsaw), Manuscript Department, T. Męczkowska. "Pamiętnik pisany w r. 1944/45 na wygnaniu" (Memoirs written in exile in Zakopane, 1944/45), no. II 10303.

(A) National Library (Warsaw), Manuscript Department, T. Męczkowska. "50 lat pracy w organizacjach kobiecych (1890–1950)" (Fifty years of working for women's organizations, 1890–1950), no. II 10302.

(B) *Głos* (Voice) (1900–1914).

(B) *Ogniwo* (Link) (1903–1905).

(B) *Ster* (Helm) (1905–1914).

(C) Męczkowska, T. *Szkoły mieszane (czyli koedukacyjne)* (Mixed or co-educational schools). Warsaw: M. Arct, 1905.

(C) Męczkowska, T. *Ideały etyczno-społeczne ruchu kobiecego* (The ethical and social ideals of the women's movement). Warsaw: Wyd. Jubileuszowe im. Orzeszkowej, 1907.

(C) Męczkowska, T. *Do czego dążymy? Ideologia Stowarzyszenia Kobiet Polskich z Wyższym Wykształceniem* (What are our aims? The mission of the Polish Association of Women with Higher Education). Warsaw: Druk "Kobiety Współczesnej," 1926.

(C) Męczkowska, T. *Wychowanie seksualne dzieci i młodzieży* (Sex education of children and the young). Warsaw: Nasza Księgarnia, 1934.

(C) Męczkowska, T. *Służące a prostytucja* (Domestic servants and prostitution). Warsaw: publisher unknown, 1935.

(D) Więckowska, Helena. "Teodora Męczkowska." In *Polski Słownik Biograficzny* (Polish biographical dictionary). Warsaw-Wrocław-Cracow: Zakład Narodowy im. Ossolińskich, 1975, vol. XX/3, no. 86, 503–504.

MEISSNER, Elena (1867?–1940?)

Co-founder (1918) and leader of the *Asociația pentru emanciparea civilă și politică a femeilor române* (*AECPFR*, Association for the Civil and Political Emancipation of Romanian Women); active in the international women's movement in the interwar period.

Born Elena Buznea in the Moldavian city of Huşi in 1867(?), Meissner was one of the first female students to attend the University of Iaşi in the mid-1880s, where she graduated in literature. In 1905, she married Constantin Meissner (1854–1942), a prominent political personality and General Secretary to the Ministry of Arts and Public Education prior to World War I. After the war, Constantin Meissner became a member of several short-lived political parties, including the center-right People's Party led by the World War I hero, Marshal Alexandru Averescu.

Elena Meissner first worked as a teacher in Iaşi, later becoming Principal of the Institute for Young Ladies for ten years. During her very active political life, she remained dedicated to this vocation and to younger generations of women, continuing her teaching into later life. In 1929, she retired from her teaching post at the Lady Oltea Lyceum in Iaşi, where she had taught history, philosophy and pedagogy whilst continuing to participate in, and encourage the creation of new educational opportunities for women. In 1932, at an important feminist Congress organized by the *Uniunea Femeilor Române* (Union of Romanian Women) in Iaşi, she made a special plea to all participants to focus more actively on educating peasant women as to their rights and responsibilities in their communities, especially given that the 1932 Civil Code had extended full civil rights to all women. These educational activities were to encourage a sense of responsibility towards the family, promote a strong work ethic and discourage rural-to-urban migration of women under the age of twenty.

In addition to her activities as a teacher and leader in the movement for women's education, Meissner was also a prominent civic leader and an ardent feminist. She helped found several organizations for the protection of poor and young women and participated actively in many prominent organizations such as the Red Cross, the School Cafeteria, the *Reuniunea Femeilor Române* (Reunion of Romanian Women) and the *Societatea Ortodoxă Națională a Femeilor Române* (*SONFR*, National Orthodox Society of Romanian Women).

Meissner is best known for her pioneering and tireless campaigns for women's political and civil rights. In 1917, she was among the handful of women who signed a petition asking for the extension of political and civil rights to all ethnically Romanian women. In 1918, together with ***Maria Baiulescu***, ***Ella Negruzzi*** and ***Calypso Botez***, Meissner co-founded the *Asociația pentru emanciparea civilă și politică a femeilor române* (*AECPFR*, Association for the Civil and Political Emancipation of Romanian Women). Together with Ella Negruzzi, she remained the leader of this organization throughout the interwar period and saw it through some tough battles, both with the patriarchal establishment and with other feminist organizations (which parted ways with the *AECPFR* in the 1930s).

In the early 1920s, Meissner worked with ***Alexandrina Cantacuzino***, a prominent women's leader in Wallachia and President of the *SONFR*, and Maria Baiulescu, an important leader of the women's movement in Transylvania. Through the *Consiliul Național al Femeilor Române* (*CNFR*, National Council of Romanian Women), Meissner worked to strengthen exchange between women of all regions and political outlooks. The *CNFR* was to be an umbrella organization that would welcome every kind of women's organization, feminist or otherwise. The aim was to facilitate conversation, debate and cooperation between women in the hope of increasing women's public visibility and creating a platform for women to voice their concerns. In 1923, Meissner and other women leaders organized a series of important protests through the *CNFR* to draw attention to the fact that women would not be enfranchised in the new Constitution. Meissner spoke eloquently of the lack of consideration given Romanian women, in comparison with "the 138 million women [in other countries, Eds.] who participate in the public administration of their countries with very satisfactory results" (Mihăilescu 2002, 41). Yet the protests were to no avail.

Following this blow to the feminist movement, a split into two camps occured. One believed, like Alexandrina Cantancuzino, that all women needed to join forces as a single political affiliation. The other believed that working with existing political parties was the best strategy for gaining the vote. Meissner considered that women needed to become members and active participants in existing party political life in order to gain prominence and to win actual political and civil rights. She did not join a party herself, since she was married to a politician whose party did not support women's rights and she did not believe in spouses supporting different political parties. Furthermore, as the leader of the *AECPFR*, which embraced feminists from across the political spectrum, Meissner did not feel entitled to become actively involved in the politics of any one particular party without compromising the organization's principle of political tolerance. Meissner saw this feminist association as a place where women could gain a political and civil education, where they might comfortably discuss different political ideologies and build bridges across ideological differences.

Nevertheless Meissner, in all her public speeches and writings, continued to advocate women's participation in existing political parties.

Meissner and ***Alexandrina Cantacuzino*** conflicted on this issue, the latter advocating the organization of a separate women's political club so as not to marginalize women within the larger framework of an established party. In 1929, when women gained the vote in local elections, this conflict intensified and politically informed women were forced to choose between the two camps. Cantacuzino and her group separated from both the *CNFR* and the *AECPFR*, forming a new organization, the *Gruparea Femeilor Române* (*GFR*, Association of Romanian Women). Meissner, together with ***Maria Baiulescu***, ***Calypso Botez*** and ***Ella Negruzzi***, remained dedicated to working within the existing political parties. Most of the women in this second camp joined the National Peasant Party but Meissner remained politically unaffiliated.

In addition to being the heart and soul of *AECPFR*, Meissner also represented this organization abroad at numerous Congresses organized by the International Woman Suffrage Alliance/International Alliance of Women for Suffrage and Equal Citizenship in Rome (1923), Paris (1926), Berlin (1929) and Istanbul (1935). In Romania she delivered speeches, wrote passionate articles, participated in protests and held steadfast to the goal of gender equality throughout her life. She died in 1940 (?) in Iaşi.

Maria Bucur
Indiana University

SOURCES

(A) *Arhivele Naţionale Istorice Centrale Bucureşti* (The National Central Historical Archives, Bucharest). Fond Elena Meissner, dos. X/15.

(B) Bogdan, Elena. *Feminismul* (Feminism) Timişoara: Tip. Huniadi, 1926, 78-81.

(C) Meissner, Elena. *Dreptatea causei feministe* (The justice of the feminist cause). Iaşi, 1923.

(C) Meissner, Elena. *Extensiunea activităţii femeii în afară de casă* (The expansion of women's activities outside the home). No publisher, 1924.

(C) Meissner, Elena. "Lupta contra imoralităţii" (The struggle against immorality). *Buletin Eugenic şi Biopolitic* (Eugenic and biopolitical bulletin) 2, nos. 11-12 (November-December 1928): 349-353.

(E) Cosma, Ghizela. *Femeile şi politica în România. Evoluţia dreptului de vot în perioada interbelică* (Women and politics in Romania. The evolution of suffrage rights in the interwar period). Cluj: Presa Universitară Clujeană, 2002.

(E) Mihăilescu, Ştefania. *Din istoria feminismului românesc. Antologie de texte (1838-1929)* [From the history of Romanian feminism. Anthology of texts (1838-1929)]. Iaşi: Polirom, 2002.

MELLER, Mrs Artur, Eugénia Miskolczy (1872–1944)

Leading representative of the Hungarian *Feministák Egyesülete* (*FE*, Feminist Association) in the interwar period; key figure in building and maintaining relations with the international women's movement.

Mrs Artur Meller was born Eugénia Miskolczy on 14 January 1872, into a Jewish family in Budapest, the capital (then undergoing unification) of Hungary. Her parents, who had married in 1870, were Adolf Miskolczy (Miskolci), a manufacturer (born 1839), and Laura Weisz (1849–1883), who died when her daughter Eugénia was just eleven years old. Eugénia had an older brother and a younger sister, both of whom died in early childhood, as well as another sister, born in 1879. In the early 1890s, Eugénia Miskolczy married Artur Meller (born 1859), an inspector for the Hungarian National Bank. They had four children: Vilmos (b. 1896); Laura (b. 1898); Erzsébet (b. 1899) and Rózsa (b. 1901). Information on Eugenia's schooling is unavailable. In the interwar period she worked as a trained language teacher and held an academic position at the *Társadalmi Múzeum* (Museum of Society), a state institution in Budapest.

Mrs Artur Meller (as she became upon marriage; in Hungarian Meller Arturné) grew active in the women's movement in the early twentieth century. She was a founding and active member of the *Feministák Egyesülete* (*FE*, Feminist Association) from its inception in 1904 until its dissolution (it was probably banned) in the early 1940s. The liberal-progressive *FE* struggled for women's rights (including suffrage) and gender equality in all spheres of life. In the early years of the association, Meller worked for women's suffrage but she also gave regular lectures at so-called Parent Conferences (on sex-education for children, children's health and material values in education). These conferences were organized by the *FE* within the framework of its "Select a Profession" counseling system for girls and their parents. Meller also published on topics such as child protection in the *FE* journals: *A Nő és a Társadalom* (Woman and society); later *A Nő. Feminista Folyóirat* (Woman. A feminist journal). It was Meller who, on behalf of the *FE*, prepared a radical critique of the marriage regulations stipulated in the 1913 draft of the Hungarian Civil Code. She called for a balance to be drawn between the pursuit of gender equality and the conscious consideration of the existing inequalities and needs of women, as well as for greater choice (e.g. over family names) for both women and men.

By 1906, Meller had become one of the 24 (later more) members of the *FE* Board. She would be re-elected several times. In 1912/1913, she was a member of the independent committee responsible for preparing the seventh international congress of the International Woman Suffrage Alliance (IWSA) that took place in Budapest in 1913. Some time earlier, she had replaced ***Róza Schwimmer*** for longer periods as head of the Political Committee of the *FE* (focusing on suffrage); in 1912, she filled the newly created function of Head Secretary of the Political Committee.

When Schwimmer left for London in 1914, finally emigrating in 1920, Meller took over (in practice) the leadership of the Political Committee. During World War I, she was very active in pacifist work and helped organize, along with other members of the *FE*, what became 'the banned 1916 Feminist Congress': a planned public demonstration against the war that was finally forbidden by the authorities. As the national-conservative and semi-authoritarian Horthy regime of the interwar period began placing gradual limitations on suffrage, including women's suffrage as introduced in 1919 (i.e. with some complex restrictions), Meller continued to focus on suffrage issues. Prior to the parliamentary elections in March 1920, Meller, together with Executive President of the *FE* ***Vilma Glücklich***, signed and sent a letter to all members of the association in Budapest, urging them to vote and to campaign for the only female candidate, ***Margit Slachta***. Slachta, who was standing for the *Keresztény Nemzeti Egyesülés Pártja* (National Christian Union Party) was promoted by the *FE* on the grounds that "no matter how anti-feminist in her self-representation, ... natural development [would] lead [Slachta's] deeds in the national assembly in a feminist direction" (*MOL* P999/file on the 1920 elections, f. 4). Meller was also involved in *FE* activities related to education. In 1923, for instance, the *FE* sent a memorandum to the government, signed by Mrs Meller among others, urging action against the decision of the Budapest Medical University in December 1919 not to admit female students. Meller also wrote a number of articles about equal opportunities for girls and boys in different kinds of schools for the *FE* journal *A Nő* (Woman).

In the early 1920s, Meller was an active member of the Commission for Party Cooperation in the *FE*, which existed at least until 1922. She tried, with some success, to bring about a united front of activists from different political backgrounds in favor of maintaining the existing (and relatively inclusive) voting laws. In spite of these efforts, suffrage restrictions were introduced. Meller continued to propagate women's rights until the early 1940s as one of the three main leaders of the *FE*. The second most prominent *FE* leader was Mrs Oszkár Szirmai (born Irma Reinitz,

1868–1958), whose activities covered the broad fields of social education, social work and child protection. For a short period prior to the death of ***Vilma Glücklich*** in 1927, Szirmai had formally taken over the co-leadership of the *FE*, withdrawing from the organization in 1927 due to a family tragedy. After this development, Eugénia Meller became the most important representative of the *FE*.

The third most prominent *FE* leader–besides Meller and Szirmai–was Melanie Vámbéry (Vámbéri; born ?–reportedly died 1944), who had belonged to the inner circle of the *FE* from the prewar period and functioned as *FE* Secretary throughout the interwar period. From 1930, this was Vámbéry's sole position; by 1938, the first of the three 'Jewish laws' in Hungary, seeking to curtail the economic and intellectual activities of the Jewish population, "removed from her mouth" this "last bit of bread" (Zsuzsa Osváth at the re-constituting general assembly meeting of the *FE* in 1946. *MOL* P999/minutes of the *FE* meetings). Vámbéry subsequently moved to the countryside to live with her daughter, from where she was deported under the Nazi regime.

Meller's relatives as well as co-workers described her as intelligent, educated and a tireless campaigner for women's rights. Accompanying her mother to a workers' tenement in the outskirts of Budapest to distribute suffrage propaganda, Mrs Meller's daughter Erzsébet remembered that there was "just one person who did not notice" how she was ridiculed by the audience, and this was "consciously, I'm sure, my mother. On the way home she stayed serious and silent for a while ... before talking to me cheerfully about my school" [*MOL* P999/legacy of Noémi Kobor, Erzsébet (daughter of Mrs Meller) to Noémi Kobor 04.12.1958, f. 69].

Restricted by the political constellation and developments in interwar Hungary, the *FE* remained strongly involved in the international women's movement. As an *FE* representative Meller, whose English and French were flawless, participated in many congresses of the International Woman Suffrage Alliance/International Alliance of Women for Suffrage and Equal Citizenship (IWSA/IAWSEC) between 1920 and 1935, as well as in some Women's International League for Peace and Freedom (WILPF) congresses between 1924 and 1937. Reportedly (but unresearched to date), Meller was closely involved with the disarmament work of the WILPF in the mid-1920s. Early in the 1930s, she took an active role in international activities, lobbying for women's interests as the League of Nations began preparing international codification of citizenship law. In 1930, Meller was one of two members of the WILPF Committee on Statelessness to present women's demands (regarding statelessness and the codification of international law) to the League. From 1931 to 1933, she was one of two representatives of the WILPF on the Women's Consultative Committee on Nationality, formed at the invitation of the League of Nations (though not officially related to the League) by eight inter/transnational women's organizations.

Further research is required if a precise account of Mrs Meller's involvement in women's activities on the international level is to be established. However, letters from the *FE* archive demonstrate clearly that Meller's personal connections to leading figures of the IWSA/IAWSEC and the WILPF helped keep the *FE* financially afloat. In the interwar period, the association received financial support of three hundred US dollars annually from the American Leslie Woman Suffrage Commission (established with the help of a large donation to the IWSA President, Carrie Chapman Catt, in support of women's suffrage), as well as occasional help from the WILPF. The visits of well-known international women's leaders to Budapest–including IAWSEC President Margery Corbett Ashby in 1927 and 1929: a visit widely covered in the Hungarian press–strengthened the reputation of the *FE* in Hungary. In the 1930s too, the activities of the *FE* reflected Meller's international connections: in 1935 and 1936 for example, Meller organized (as part of the "People's Mandate" WILPF initiative) a collection of signatures petitioning the national government of Hungary to halt armament production and build international mechanisms for the peaceful settlement of conflicts instead. 12,800 signatures were collected and presented to the Hungarian Foreign Ministry by a Committee of Honor, comprised of high-ranking representatives of major religious denominations, Members of Parliament and public figures–a politically remarkable result in nationalist and revisionist Hungary.

There is no reliable information on Mrs Meller's activities for the period following the dissolution / political repression of the *FE* in the early 1940s. Conditions in Hungary were becoming more and more dangerous. After the Nazis had annexed Austria in 1938, Meller's co-worker from the early years, ***Róza Schwimmer*** (then living in the United States), tried to persuade former IWSA President, Carrie Chapman Catt, to sign an affidavit for Meller (and also one for feminist activist Sarolta Steinberger [1875–1966], the first female physician to graduate from a Hungarian university in 1900). The affidavit would have been one precondition enabling Meller and Steinberger to emigrate to the United States, but Catt refused one on the grounds that she had already taken too much responsibility for friends, relatives and suffragists; that she was old; and that the affidavit would "still hold against (the) estate" of the person who had signed it, even after that person had passed away (IIAV/Copy of Carrie Chapman Catt Papers, General Correspondence, Catt to Schwimmer 30.06.1938). Some years later, Meller successfully sought help for some of her relatives to emigrate, but not for herself. After the German occupation of Hungary in March 1944, Meller was arrested. "Her notes on lectures by [the Social Democrat] Anna Kéthly were found with her. ... Since July 1944, when she was taken to [the detention camp of] Kistarcsa, we have received no news of her. Where did she die? We don't know. ... She did not live passively through her martyrdom, but ... proclaimed her convictions in a way few members of this nation have matched" (Lilla Wagner at the re-constituting general assembly meeting of the *FE* in 1946. MOL P999/Minutes of the *FE*). In November 1946, a (silver) Hungarian Order of Freedom was posthumously awarded Eugénia Miskolczy Meller by the government, for her "outstanding merits in fostering the democratic spirit" [*Magyar Közlöny* (Hungarian gazette), 18 December 1946].

Claudia Papp, Ph.D.
Municipal Museum and Archive of Sachsenheim/
Baden-Württemberg, Germany

Susan Zimmermann
Department of Gender Studies, Department of History,
Central European University, Budapest

SOURCES

(A) International Information Center and Archives for the Women's Movement, Amsterdam, Copy of Carrie Chapmann Catt Papers (Washington D.C., Library of Congress). General Correspondence.
(A) *Magyar Országos Levéltár* (*MOL*, Hungarian State Archive), P999: *Feministák Egyesülete* (Feminist Association).
(B) *Feminista Értesítő* (Feminist bulletin) (1906).
(B) *A Nő és a Társadalom* (Woman and society) (1907-1913).
(B) *A Nő. Feminista Folyóirat* (Woman. A feminist journal) (1914-1928).
(B) *Magyar Közlöny* (Hungarian gazette), no. 289 (18 December 1946).
(C) Articles by Mrs Artur Meller in *A Nő és a Társadalom, A Nő* and *Jus Suffragii* (the official organ of the IWSA/IAWSEC).
(C) Miskolczy Meller, Eugenie. "Das Frauenwahlrecht in Ungarn" (Women's suffrage in Hungary). *Zeitschrift für Frauenstimmrecht* (Women's suffrage journal) 8, no. 7 (1918): 8.
(C) Miskolczy Meller, Eugenie. "Frauen von gestern–Frauen von heute in Ungarn" (Women of yesterday–women of today in Hungary). *Wort der Frau* (Woman's word) 23 (1931).
(D) Strasser, László. *Minibiography of Mrs Meller*. MS Manuscript.
(E) Bussey, Gertrude and Margaret Tims. *The Women's International League for Peace and Freedom 1915-1965. A Record of Fifty Years' Work*. London: Allen & Unwin, 1965.
(E) Szegvári, Katalin. *Út a nők egyenjogúságához* (Towards women's equal rights). Budapest, 1981.
(E) Miller, Carol. "Geneva–the key to equality: inter-war feminists and the League of Nations" *Women's History Review* 3, no. 2 (1994): 219-245.
(E) Papp, Claudia. *'Die Kraft der weiblichen Seele.' Feminismus in Ungarn, 1918-1941* ('The strength of woman's soul.' Feminism in Hungary, 1918-1941). Münster: Lit-Verlag, 2004.

MEVLAN CİVELEK, Ulviye (1893–1964)

Turkish journalist and activist; founder (1913) of the *Müdafaa-i Hukuk-i Nisvan Cemiyeti* (Association for the Defence of Women's Rights) and publisher of the journal *Kadınlar Dünyası* (Women's world, 1913–1921).

Ulviye Mevlan was a pioneering feminist in Ottoman society of the early 1900s, a time when social and political structures were undergoing important changes. Born in 1893, in Göreme, she was brought to the *harem* of the Ottoman Palace at the age of six where, like all the new incoming girls, she received her first education. Her family was Circassian, exiled from Caucasia by the Russians. Her father, Mahmut Yediç, was a farmer; her mother's name was Safiye Hanım. At the age of thirteen Ulviye, in compliance with the rules of the Palace, was given in marriage to an elderly man, Hulisi Bey, but was widowed soon after. (Hulisi Bey was a foster brother of the Sultan; his mother was the wet-nurse of the Sultan Abdülhamid II.) She married again, this time to Rıfat Mevlan (1869–1930), a well-known journalist.

Her own career as a journalist began prior to her second marriage. By the age of twenty, she was running a women's magazine, *Kadınlar Dünyası* (Women's world); in 1913, she founded an association, the *Müdafaa-i Hukuk-i Nisvan Cemiyeti* (Association for the Defence of Women's Rights). In the first few issues of *Kadınlar Dünyası*, her name–Nuriye Ulviye–appeared as the owner of the magazine; later, she took the name Mevlan, her husband's surname. After her husband was exiled for his opposition to Atatürk (the founder of the Turkish Republic), she divorced him (in 1923). In 1931, she married Ali Civelek (1904–1985), who had come to Istanbul from Antakya (a city in southern Turkey) to study medicine. He was a boarder in her house and ten years her junior. Although his family did not approve of this marriage, it was a happy one. Ulviye Mevlan Civelek did not have a child of her own but adopted a poor orphan named Lütfiye.

From 4 April 1913 to 1921, with some interruptions, Ulviye Mevlan published *Kadınlar Dünyası*. The first hundred issues came out daily, afterwards weekly. Up against enormous difficulties and at great personal cost, Mevlan worked to mobilize women and improve their position in society. She demanded rights for women in the family, in social life and at work, and considered political rights a necessary complement to these social rights. Although the editorial column of the magazine was anonymously signed "Kadınlar Dünyası," her singular style of writing is recognizable. Later, she signed the column with her own name, under the heading "Düşünüyorum" (I am thinking).

Of the approximately forty women's magazines that emerged around the end of the nineteenth century, accompanying a proliferation of women's associations, *Kadınlar Dünyası* was the only women's magazine to introduce an explicitly feminist agenda and rhetoric to the Ottoman press. Various magazines and associations–philanthropic, cultural, national, feminist (in the case of *Kadınlar Dünyası*), political (e.g. women's branches of political parties) and educational (offering opportunities for employment)–sought to enlighten and mobilize Ottoman women in a number of ways. *Kadınlar Dünyası*, which declared itself feminist and dedicated to helping women acquire the self-confidence to articulate their demands, attracted women from different sectors of Ottoman society. It was the first magazine to publish a photograph of a Muslim woman and the first owned by a woman, and whose writers, press workers and readers were all women. The journal advocated a principle of 'women writers only,' which it justified in the following way: "Until our legal equality is acknowledged in general law, until women and men are deemed equal in every respect, *Kadınlar Dünyası* will not open its pages to men. Moreover, it would be more beneficial for men who believe in the exaltation of womanhood to publish their articles in those magazines and newspapers which are not interested in women's issues" [*Kadınlar Dünyası*, no. 9 (12 April 1913): 3].

Kadınlar Dünyası was an important feminist forum in which established sex and gender norms could be questioned. It also raised issues on the agenda of the *Müdafaa-i Hukuk-i Nisvan* (Association for the Defence of Women's Rights); the journal announced the program of the association and became instrumental in the communication of the association's activities. Women from ethnic minority communities were members of the *Müdafaa-i Hukuk-i Nisvan* (though the association primarily targeted Muslim women) and European journalists such as Grace Ellison from *The Times* in London and German reporter Odett Feldmann joined the *Müdafaa-i Hukuk-i Nisvan Cemiyeti,* publishing articles in *Kadınlar Dünyası*. Between 7 December 1913 and 7 February 1914, *Kadınlar Dünyası* also published a French supplement that aimed at facilitating communication between Ottoman woman and their 'European sisters.'

Mevlan was conscious that women's emancipation could only be accomplished through the efforts of women themselves. She relied on her personal experiences as a woman and on women's sisterhood and solidarity, distinguishing her from other publicly active women of her time. She courageously defied traditional gender roles and identities imposed on women and tried to create a new 'world for women.' Not supported by wealthy and prestigious friends, due to her own modest social background and her distance from dominant political circles, she was relegated to the shadows for a long time.

Ulviye Mevlan died at the age of 71 in Istanbul in 1964. Her husband, as a mark of respect to her struggle for women's emancipation, organized a ceremony of remembrance five years after her death and erected a commemorative plaque in her honor, on which was inscribed: "Ulviye Nuriye Civelek–a leading figure of the Ottoman women's struggle for emancipation." A similar inscription was also carved on her tombstone. It is of interest that these inscriptions bear her marital name (Ulviye Nuriye Civelek) and not the name by which she was widely known (Ulviye Mevlan). Her influential husband also had a street named after his beloved wife (located in Antakya, Kırıkhan); he bought up the buildings there and turned them into *hayrats* (fountains and boarding houses for free public use), as well as having a local church restored and converted into a library, which he donated to the municipality in her memory. In the 1990s, research instigated by feminists in Turkey established Ulviye Mevlan's name as a pioneering feminist in the history of the Ottoman, and Republican women's movement.

Much of the above information on Ulviye Mevlan Civelek was collected through oral history research, conducted while carrying out a study of the Ottoman women's movement. Although her writings in *Kadınlar Dünyası* constitute primary material, they do not reveal much about her private life. The author has been able to gather data on the basis of interviews conducted with Mevlan's niece and adopted daughter, having been fortunate enough to meet both of these individuals by chance! Difficulties in tracing her life story are further compounded by the fact that her surname changed three times with consecutive marriages, and that well-known women of her time, like ***Nezihe Muhittin***, neglected to mention her in their writings because she did not belong to their social and economic milieu and held to a radical non-conformism. Ulviye Mevlan's endeavors, through *Kadınlar Dünyası*, to create a new 'world for women' without the participation of men; the constant pressure on her to moderate her feminism; the fact that her husband was an opponent of the republican regime, was a Kurdish nationalist and was sent into exile are all factors that may well have contributed to her negative reputation regarding her involvement with 'the woman question.'

Serpil Çakır
University of Istanbul

SOURCES

(B) *Kadınlar Dünyası* (Women's world) (1913-1921).
(C) Mevlan, Ulviye. "Düşünüyorum" (I am thinking). *Kadınlar Dünyası*, no. 163 (2 March 1918).
(D) Interview with her niece, Nezihe Civelek (10 March 1990).
(D) Çakır, Serpil. "Kadın Tarihinden İki İsim: Ulviye Mevlan ve Nezihe Muhittin" (Ulviye

Mevlan and Nezihe Muhittin: two women from Turkish women's history). *Toplumsal Tarih* (Social history), no. 46 (1997): 6-14.

(E) Çakır, Serpil and Zehra Toska, et al. *Eski Harfli Türkçe Kadın Dergileri Bibliyografyası* (Bibliography of women's periodicals written in Ottoman script). Istanbul: Metis Publishing, 1993.

(E) Çakır, Serpil. *Osmanlı Kadın Hareketi* (The Ottoman women's movement). Istanbul: Metis Publishing, 1994.

(E) Çakır, Serpil. "Political-Social Movements: Revolutionary Turkey." *Encylopedia of Women and Islamic Cultures*. Leiden: Brill, 2004, 2: 415-416.

MILČINOVIĆ, Adela (1878–1968)

Croatian feminist activist, novelist, critic and journalist.

Adela Milčinović (born Kamenić) was born on 14 January 1878 in the city of Sisak, the largest of the Croatian river ports, located along the rivers Sava and Kupa. Adela was the illegitimate daughter of Ludmila Kamenić (data unknown). After graduating from the girls' high school in Sisak (ca. 1892), she qualified as a teacher in Zagreb at the Sisters of Charity Convent in 1896 (this being the only way for a woman to receive teacher training until the passing of a new education law in 1888. In 1899, she married Andrija Milčinović (born 1877), a teacher and philosophy student at the University of Zagreb whom she had known since her high school days. She assumed his family name and the young couple moved to Slavonia, to the village of Zdenci near Slavonski Brod, where Andrija Milčinović accepted a teaching post.

In 1900, Adela Milčinović published a letter in *Domaće ognjište* (Domestic fireside), a magazine which had just been launched by the *Klub hrvatskih učiteljica* (Croatian Women Teachers' Club) under the umbrella of the *Hrvatsko pedagoško društvo* (Croatian Pedagogical Association). In the letter, Milčinović presented a well-formulated feminist critique, denouncing the absence of women from public life and outlining her vision of a new aesthetics. In the years 1902 to 1904, she and her husband moved to Hamburg and then to Munich. In this period they published a collection of stories together, *Pod branom* (Under the barrage, 1903) while Andrija Milčinović kept up his studies as a theater scholar and Adela attended courses in art history, also writing for the Zagreb newspaper *Narodne novine* (The nation).

Upon returning to Zagreb (where the couple settled from 1904 to 1915), Andrija Milčinović completed his studies and began working for the *Muzej za umjetnost i obrt* (Museum of Arts and Crafts). Adela Milčinović, still writing for *Narodne novine*, published a pedagogical study, *Naše ženske škole i kako nam koriste* (Our girls' schools and how they benefit us, 1904), in which she criticized clericalism and demanded the secularization and modernization of girls' education. In *Ivka*, a collection of short stories and Milčinović's literary debut (1905), she depicted a new generation of emancipated women determined to transcend the perimeters of domesticity, organized around the coordinates of 'church,' 'children' and 'kitchen.' In doing so, she attempted to regenerate women's literary expression in the early twentieth century. In *Naše hrvatske spisateljice* (Our Croatian female writers, 1905), she evaluated the work of her contemporaries, later turning to that of literary predecessors such as ***Dragojla Jarnević***: see, for example, her *Dragojla Jarnevićeva, živopisna studija* (Dragojla Jarnević, a biographical study, 1907). Milčinović's short stories explored femininity, the 'female professions,' socially prescribed gender roles, the 'female soul,' the relationship to one's own (gendered) body and the ambivalence of eroticism and motherhood. In the play *Bez sreće* (Without luck, 1912), two female protagonists become tragic rivals in a love triangle. This 'naturalistic drama' about life in Slavonia was well received, though critics emphasized its tragic elements from the perspective of the male protagonist. They applauded its treatment of the social problem of landlessness without noting the gender issues it raised. *Bez sreće* won awards in 1912 and was performed in Varaždin, Belgrade, Skopje, Prague and Chicago (in a run that lasted until the 1930s).

Adela and Andrija Milčinović often traveled around the Balkans and occasionally made trips to Vienna and Paris. They had two daughters, Vera and Deša (data unknown) and eventually divorced around 1915 (precise date unknown). It was around this time that Adela Milčinović started to become politically active. In February 1915, as part of initiatives to unite the southern Slavs, Milčinović held secret meetings in Rome with Ivan Meštrović and Ante Trumbić, émigré politicians at the head of the *Hrvatski odbor* (Croatian Committee; later the Yugoslav Committee). She spent the war years (1915–1918) in Belgrade, working in the editorial offices of the *Beogradske novine* (Belgrade news). Upon returning to Zagreb in 1918, she began working as a secretarial assistant in the financial department of the *Narodno vijeće Države Slovenaca, Hrvata i Srba* (National Council of the State of Slovenes, Croats and Serbs), where she remained until 1920. In 1919, she published the short stories *Sjena* (Shadow), *Gospođa doktorica* (Mrs Doctor) and *Sestra Marija-Liza* (Sister Marija-Liza) in the literary magazine *Savremenik* (Contemporary). In *Sjena*, she addressed the slippage between language and speech and examined the role of each in the socialization of the sexes. In a later three-volume collection of selected short stories, *Novele* (Short stories, 1921), the psychological structure of communication between the sexes surfaces again as an important focus of Milčinović's work. Contemporary critical reviews of her work focused on Milčinović's 'metaphysics of the sexes' without remarking upon the strident anti-militarism of her writing. In more recent times, her artistic language has been affirmed, here by ***Blaženka Despot***, as a "new paradigm of freedom and its values: peace, inter-culture, nature and life" (Despot 2004, 39).

On 29 September 1918 (following the collapse of the Austro-Hungarian monarchy), the State of Slovenes, Croats and Serbs was proclaimed; on 1 December 1918, the state was reunified with the Kingdom of Serbia and Montenegro—to become the new

Kingdom of Serbs, Croats and Slovenes. A month later, on 3 January 1919, the *Narodni ženski savez Srpkinja, Hrvatica i Slovenkinja* (National Women's Alliance of Serbs, Croats and Slovenes) was established in Zagreb by different women's associations and societies. The Alliance sought to represent women's political interests at the federal level, such as the right to vote and the right to participate in public decision-making. In September 1919, representatives of women's societies and associations from across the country held their first conference in Belgrade, where another organization–the *Narodni ženski savez* (National Women's Alliance)–was also established (changing its name in 1929 to *Jugoslovenski ženski savez*, the Yugoslav Women's Alliance). Under the patronage of this latter organization, Milčinović worked tirelessly for the causes of women's suffrage and child protection in her capacity as a Croatian delegate. She also took part in a number of international conferences: the Ninth Congress of the International Woman Suffrage Alliance (IWSA) in Rome (1923); the International Congress for the Struggle against White Slavery in Graz (1924) and the Eighth Congress of the International Council of Women (ICW) in Washington D.C. (1925).

In 1923, Milčinović converted from Roman Catholicism to Serb Orthodoxy (whether for private or political reasons is unknown). In the 1930s, she moved permanently to New York (the USA) with her daughters, dedicating herself, as she put it, to their artistic careers (Vera's as a dancer and Deša's as a painter). She worked with emigrants at the Serbian consulate until 1937, when she joined the American Ministry of Foreign Affairs to work in the Office of War Information. When this Office became the *Voice of America* radio station in 1943, she continued her work there as a journalist and announcer, as well as working for the Columbia Broadcasting System (C.B.S.). She retired in 1953. In 1964, she wrote a short autobiography for a Zagreb edition of her selected works. She died in New York in 1968, aged ninety. The work of Adela Milčinović is not widely recognized in modern day Croatia but in 2003, a women's group from her birthplace, Sisak, named themselves *Adela* in a tribute to the memory of this important feminist activist and thinker.

Slavica Jakobović Fribec
Culture and Informative Center, Zagreb

Translated from the Croatian by Jelena Primorac

SOURCES

(A) The State Archive in Sisak, Republic of Croatia. Holy Cross Parish, Sisak: register of births and baptisms (1868-1878), year 1878, (p.) 400, reg. no. 2176-82-04-2.
(A) The State Archive in Sisak, Republic of Croatia. Holy Cross Parish, Sisak: marriage register (1879-1900), year 1899, (p.) 366. reg. no. 2176-82-04-2.

(B) *Domaće ognjište* (Domestic fireside). (Zagreb: Hrvatski pedagoško-književni zbor—Klub učiteljica, 1900–1914).

(B) Kveder-Demetrović, Zofka, ed. *Ženski svijet. Mjesečnik za kulturne, socijalne i političke interese žena* (Woman's world. Monthly cultural, social and political magazine for women) (Zagreb, 1915–1917). Later renamed *Jugoslavenska žena* (Yugoslav women) (1918–1920).

(C) Milčinović, Adela & Andrija Milčinović. *Pod branom* (Under the barrage). Zagreb: Tisak Mile Maravića, 1903.

(C) Milčinović, Adela. *Naše ženske škole i kako nam koriste* (Our girls' schools and how they benefit us). Zagreb: self-published, 1904.

(C) Milčinović, Adela. *Ivka*. Zagreb: Tisak Milivoja Majcena, 1905.

(C) Milčinović, Adela. *Dragojla Jarnevićeva, živopisna studija* (Dragojla Jarnević, a biographical study). Zagreb: Hrvatska knjižara i industrija papira, 1906.

(C) Milčinović, Adela. *Bez sreće* (Without luck). Zagreb: Matica hrvatska, 1912.

(C) Milčinović, Adela . *Sjena* (Shadow). Zagreb: self-published, 1919.

(C) Milčinović, Adela. *Gospođa doktorica* (Mrs doctor). Zagreb, 1919.

(C) Milčinović, Adela. "Sestra Marija-Liza" (Sestra Marija-Liza). *Savremenik*, no. 3 (1919).

(C) Milčinović, Adela. *Novele* (Short stories). Book I: *Nedina ljubav* (The love of Neda), *Tajna* (Secret) and *Mati* (Mother); Book II: *Roman gospojice Maje* (A novel by Miss Maja) and *Noći* (Nights); Book III: *Listići iz dnevnika* (Papers from a diary) and *On i "on"* (He and "he"); Book IV: *S prozora* (From the window), *Naši razgovori* (Our conversations), *Pjesma Solweige* (Solweige's song) and *Sinovljeva baština* (A son's heritage). Zagreb: Naklada Stjepan Kugli, 1921.

(C) Brlić-Mažuranić, Ivana, Adela Milčinović and Zdenka Marković. *Izabrana djela Ivane Brlić-Mažuranić, Adele Milčinović i Zdenke Marković* (Selected works by Ivana Brlić-Mažuranić, Adela Milčinović and Zdenka Marković). Zagreb: Zora-Matica hrvatska, 1968.

(E) Prohaska, Dragutin. *Pregled savremene hrvatsko-srpske književnosti* (An overview of contemporary Croato-Serb literature). Zagreb: Matica hrvatska (special edition), 1921.

(E) Kecman, Jovanka. *Žene Jugoslavije u radničkom pokretu i ženskim organizacijama 1918-1941* (Women of Yugoslavia in the workers' movement and in women's organizations, 1918–1941). Belgrade: Narodna knjiga-Institut za savremenu istoriju, 1978.

(E) Sklevicky, Lydia. *Konji, žene, ratovi* (Horses, women, wars). Zagreb: Ženska infoteka, 1996.

(E) Detoni-Dujmić, Dunja. *Ljepša polovica književnosti* (The prettier half of literature). Zagreb: Matica hrvatska, 1998.

(E) Bosanac, Gordana, ed. *Izabrana djela Blaženke Despot* (Selected works by Blaženka Despot). Zagreb: Institut za društvena istraživanja-Ženska infoteka, 2004.

MIROVICH, pseudonym for Zinaida Sergeevna Ivanova (1865–1913)

Russian feminist activist, historian, critic, writer and translator; one of the founders (February 1905) of the *Soiuz Ravnopraviia Zhenshchin* (Women's Equal Rights Union). Participated in International Council of Women (ICW) and International Woman Suffrage Alliance (IWSA) Congresses. Used the pseudonyms 'N. Mirovich' and 'Zinaida Mirovich.'

Zinaida Ivanova, who was born in 1865, grew up in Moscow, the daughter of a Moscow Superintendent of Schools. Further information about her parents is not available. Like many other feminist activists, she was part of the newly emerging but small female intelligentsia. She took advantage of newly available higher education opportunities for women, graduating from Moscow's Guerrier Higher Courses for Women (which provided women with a liberal education) in 1897. Soon after graduation, she married and began to participate in the activities of the *Moskovskaia Kommissiia po Organizatsii Domashnego Chteniia* (Moscow Commission on the Organization of Home Reading), also working as a freelance writer and translator (which were among the few career opportunities for educated women in this period).

Sometimes using the male pseudonym 'N. Mirovich,' or at times 'Zinaida Mirovich,' she wrote on topics related to the *zhenskii vopros* or 'the woman question,' especially with reference to the French Revolution. She wrote about Madame Roland and St. Just. Her interest in the Norwegian playwright Henrik Ibsen led her to translate his best known plays. At the end of the nineteenth century, when she was unable to publish articles about the French Revolution, she turned to publicist writing and lecturing, speaking for example in Moscow and in several provincial towns on British feminism. Fluent in six languages (English, French, German, Norwegian, Finnish and Russian) and a seasoned world traveler, she attended several international women's gatherings, including the 1899 Congress of the International Council of Women (ICW) in London. She also reported on the Russian women's movement to the congresses of the more militant International Woman Suffrage Alliance (IWSA) (Berlin, 1904; Copenhagen, 1906). An Anglophile, she spent a great deal of time in England, spoke on several occasions at suffrage rallies in Hyde Park and translated John Stuart Mill's *On the Subjection of Women* into Russian.

When the granting of women's political rights became a possibility during the 1905 Revolution, Mirovich was among the founders (in February 1905) of the *Soiuz Ravnopraviia Zhenshchin* (Women's Equal Rights Union) in Moscow. She spoke at the *Soiuz*'s First Organizational Congress in Moscow (May 1905), attended subsequent *Soiuz* congresses, lectured, wrote in favor of equal rights and suffrage and continued to publish–translating a message from newly enfranchised white Australian women into Russian at the IWSA Congress in Copenhagen (1906). In 1908, she compiled an invaluable overview of historical sources for the Russian feminist movement, *Iz Istorii Zhenskogo Dvizheniia v Rossii* (From the history of the women's movement in Russia).

At the 1908 Women's Congress in St Petersburg, the largest such gathering in pre-revolutionary Russia, Mirovich was among the more militant feminists, advocating tactics similar to those of English suffragists (like her close friends the Pankhursts) and arguing for women's unity across party lines.

Mirovich continued her feminist activity in the years of repression after the 1905 Revolution and, after the *Soiuz* dissolved in 1908, joined other activists such as ***Mariia Chekhova*** and Olga Bervi-Kaidanova in the *Liga Ravnopraviia Zhenshchin* (League for Women's Equal Rights). She spoke at the *Liga*'s 1912 Congress on Women's Education and continued to attend international feminist congresses, such as the IWSA Congress in Stockholm in 1911. She also continued her translation work and, in 1912, published the memoirs of Countess Shauzel-Guff'e, which described the court of Tsar Alexander I. Her last years were marred by a dispute with Mariia Raikh who was, along with Mirovich, a delegate to the 1911 Stockholm Congress. Raikh charged Mirovich with anti-Semitism, an accusation backed by the Board of the Moscow *Liga*. Mirovich hotly disputed Raikh's charge and resigned from the *Liga*, causing a split which seriously weakened the organization. Mirovich never regained her standing among Russian feminists in Russia, although she continued to maintain close contacts with British feminists until her death on 24 August 1913. She died in Vladykino, near Moscow. In his tribute to her, A. A. Kizevetter praised Mirovich for her integrity, her courage in expressing her beliefs, her idealism, her commitment to democratizing education and for strengthening the connections between the Russian women's movement and its counterparts abroad.

Rochelle Goldberg Ruthchild
The Union Institute and University
and the Davis Center for Russian and Eurasian Studies,
Harvard University

SOURCES

(C) *Gospozha Rolan': istoriko-literaturnyi etiud N. Mirovicha* (Madame Roland: An historical-literary study by N. Mirovich). St Petersburg: *Panteon literatury* (Pantheon of literature), 1890.

(C) Mirovich, Zinaida. *Stranitsa iz istorii Velikoi Frantsuzskoi revoliutsii* (A page from the history of the great French Revolution). Moscow, 1905.
(C) Mirovich, Zinaida. "Otkrytoe pis'mo k chlenam 'Soiuza 17-go Oktiabriia'" (An open letter to the members of the 'Union of 17 October'). *Russkaia mysl'* (Russian thought) 3 (March 1906): 100–104.
(C) Mirovich, Zinaida. "Zhenskii vopros v soiuze 17 Oktiabriia" (The woman question in the 'Union of the 17 October'). *Russkaia mysl'* 4 (April 1906): 206–210.
(C) Mirovich, Zinaida. "Tretii congress 'Mezhdunarodnago soiuza izbiratel'nykh prav zhenshchin, v Kopengagen'e, 7–12 avgusta 1906g" (The Third Congress of the International Woman Suffrage Alliance in Copenhagen). *Russkaia mysl'* 11 (November 1906): 125–149.
(C) Mirovich, Zinaida. *Iz istorii zhenskago dvizheniia v Rossii* (From the history of the women's movement in Russia). Moscow: I. D. Sytina, 1908.
(C) Mirovich, Zinaida. "Iz istorii zhenskogo obrazovaniia v Rossii" (From the history of women's education in Russia). *Russkaia mysl'* 9 (1909).
(C) Mirovich, Zinaida. "Pervyi vserossiiskii zhenskii s'ezd" (The First All-Russian Women's Congress). *Vestnik Evropy* (European herald) 1 (January 1909): 411–415.
(C) Mirovich, Zinaida. *Vserossiiskii zhenskii s'ezd v Peterburgie:10–16 dekabriia 1908 goda* (The All-Russian Women's Congress in St Petersburg: 10–16 December 1908). Moscow: Tip. I. N. Kushnerova, 1909.
(C) Mirovich, Zinaida. "Zhenskii parlament v Londone, 26 apreliia–1 maia 1909 g" (The Women's Parliament in London, 26 April–1 May 1909). *Russkaia mysl'* 7 (1909).
(D) *Sbornik na pomoshch' uchashchimsia zhenshchinam* (Anthology for aid to women students). Moscow, 1901, 242.
(D) Kizevetter, A. A. "Pamiati Zinaidy Sergeevny Mirovich" (Remembering Zinaida Sergeevna Mirovich). *Russkaia mysl'* 9 (1913): 140–141.
(D) Pokrovskaia, Mariia. "Z. S. Mirovich." *Zhenskii vestnik* (Women's herald) (October 1913): 215–216.
(D) Ariian, Praskov'ia N. "Z. S. Mirovich." In Praskov'ia N. Arian, ed. *Pervyi zhenskii kalendar' na 1914 god* (First women's calendar for 1914). St Petersburg, 1914, opposite 306i.
(D) Ruthchild, Rochelle. "'Mirovich, N.'" In Marina Ledkovsky, Charlotte Rosenthal and Mary Zirin, eds. *Dictionary of Russian Women Writers*. Westport, Connecticut: Greenwood Press, 1994, 431–432.
(D) Ruthchild, Rochelle Goldberg. "Mirovich, Zinaida Sergeevna Ivanova." In Norma Corigliano Noonan and Carol Nechemias, eds. *Encyclopedia of Russian Women's Movements*. Westport, Connecticut: Greenwood Press, 2001, 42–44.
(E) Goldberg, Rochelle (Goldberg). *The Russian Women's Movement 1859-1917*. Doctoral Dissertation: University of Rochester, 1976.
(E) Edmondson, Linda. "Russian Feminists and the First All-Russian Congress of Women." *Russian History* 3, no. 2 (1976): 123–149.
(E) Stites, Richard. *The Women's Liberation Movement in Russia: Feminism, Nihilism, and Bolshevism, 1860–1930*. Princeton: Princeton University Press, 1978; 1991.
(E) Grishina, Zoia V. *Zhenskie organizatsii v Rossii, 1905 g.-fevral'/mart 1917 g* (Women's organizations in Russia). Doctoral Dissertation. Moscow State University, 1978.
(E) Grishina, Zoia V. "Dvizhenie za politicheskoe ravnopravie zhenshchin v gody pervoi

Rossiiskoi revoliutsii" (The movement for women's political equal rights in the years of the first Russian revolution). *Vestnik Moskovskogo universiteta* (Moscow university bulletin): *Ser. 8 Istoriia* (History), no. 2 (1982): 33–42.

(E) Edmondson, Linda. *Feminism in Russia*. Stanford: Stanford University Press, 1984.

MORACZEWSKA, Zofia (1873-1958)

Social and political activist, publicist and deputy to the Polish Parliament (1919–1922 and 1930–1935); leader and ideologist of the *Liga Kobiet Polskich* (Polish Women's League) (1916–1918), the *Związek Pracy Obywatelskiej Kobiet* (Women's Association for Civil Labor) (1928–1933) and the *Samopomoc Społeczna Kobiet* (Women's Mutual Aid Society) (1935–1939).

Zofia Moraczewska (*nee* Gostkowska) was born on 4 July 1873 in Czerniowce, Bukovina (then in the Austro-Hungarian Empire), into an intellectual family. Her father, Roman Gostkowski (1837-1912), was a professor at the Technical University of Lviv; her mother, Wanda born Dylewska (?-1912), was a housewife. They had four children, two of which (both boys) died in their early youth.

Zofia spent her first years at home in Lviv. At the age of twelve, she entered Wiktoria Niedziałkowska's school for girls. The educational atmosphere there had a considerable impact on Zofia's views, arousing her patriotic feelings, a passion for social work and an interest in the ideas of Darwin, Spencer, Buckle and Kropotkin, as well as in the work of positivists such as ***Eliza Orzeszkowa*** and Maria Konopnicka.

In 1893, Zofia Gostkowska graduated from the Teachers Seminary in Lviv (today in Ukraine) and took up a teaching post. In 1896, she married Jędrzej Moraczewski (1870-1944), assuming his name. In the same year, she joined the Polish Social Democratic Party in Galicia, to which her husband also belonged. Over the following years they moved house repeatedly, on account of Jędrzej's job as a supervisor of railway construction works. They were both politically active among workers. When in 1907, Jędrzej Moraczewski became a member of the Austrian Parliament, the couple moved to Stryj, the district from which Jędrzej Moraczewski had been elected (now located in Ukraine; in Poland before World War II; previously part of the Austrian empire). Once settled, Zofia Moraczewski set up educational activities for working-class women, organizing lectures on Polish history, geography, Polish language and the basics of bookkeeping. She established the *Związek Kobiet* (Women's Association), through which she founded a school for working women, and *Praca* (Labor); both organizations spread ideas about socialism and Polish independence. She also founded a cooperative bakery and sewing plant in Stryj. The bakery aimed to lower town prices; the sewing plant supplied goods for hospitals. The Moraczewskis had four children (b. 1901, 1903, 1905 and 1907); the youngest son, Stanislaw, died in infancy of scarlet fever.

After the outbreak of World War I, Moraczewska joined the *Liga Kobiet Galicji i Śląska* (Women's League of Silezia and Galicia), formed in 1915. The *Liga Kobiet Galicji i Śląska* aimed to involve women in the national independence movement, raise funds for the national struggle, promote national ideas and lend material support to the Polish military formations founded on Austrian territory by Józef Piłsudski. Zofia Moraczewska–straightforward, bold, adamant and decisive, a good speaker and outstanding thinker, as well as a recognized socialist activist whose husband belonged to Piłsudski's closed circle–was elected Chair of the *Liga Kobiet Galicji i Śląska* in 1916, after which she moved to Cracow. In 1918, the *Liga Kobiet Galicji i Śląska* and the *Liga Kobiet Pogotowia Wojennego* (Women's League for War Alert, operative in the Kingdom of Poland), joined forces to form the *Liga Kobiet Polskich* (Polish Women's League), the first mass organization in Poland, numbering as many as 16,000 members. Although the *Liga Kobiet Polskich* focused mainly on the issue of national independence, it also fought for women's rights and played an important role in the women's emancipation process. It saw women's public activities–whether related to the exercise of their civil rights or not–as necessary to securing women's rights in the emerging independent Polish State for which the *Liga Kobiet Polskich* now struggled.

Moraczewska openly articulated the independent goals of the *Liga Kobiet Polskich*. A statement she made on women's equal rights as a political aim of the organization, delivered during the Extraordinary Congress of the Women's League of Silezia and Galicia (held on 1 and 2 February 1917 in Cracow), triggered an adverse reaction from the Roman Catholic Church. An Episcopal letter from May 1917 reproached the *Liga Kobiet Polskich*'s leaders for interfering in politics and criticized them for advocating women's independence and 'radicalism,' even going so far as to call on Catholic members to leave the organization. The result was an internal crisis from which the *Liga Kobiet Polskich* never recovered.

When in November 1918 Poland regained its independence and the new state granted women political rights, Moraczewska moved to Warsaw, where her husband was appointed Prime Minister (November 1918–January 1919). Moraczewska became a deputy to the Polish Parliament as a representative of the *Polska Partia Socjalistyczna* (*PPS*, Polish Socialist Party). From 1919–1927, she was a member of the editorial staff of the *Głos Kobiet* (Voice of women), the official newspaper of the *PPS*'s Women's Department. In 1920, she lost another child when her sixteen-year-old son Kazimierz was killed on the Bolshevik front.

In December 1927, after Józef Piłsudski's May Coup of 1926 and the subsequent rise of the left to power, Moraczewska became Chair of the *Demokratyczny Komitet Wyborczy Kobiet Polskich* (Democratic Electoral Committee of Polish Women). After the elections in March 1928, the Committee was reorganized (on Moraczewska's initiative) into the *Związek Pracy Obywatelskiej Kobiet* (Women's Association for Civil Labor). It soon became the largest women's organization in Poland, boasting 30,000 members in 1930. Moraczewska envisioned the *Związek Pracy Obywatelskiej Kobiet* as a "school of democracy," preparing women for self-reliant political and social activities and helping them to overcome their inhibitions regarding public work (Moraczewska 1928, 1–2). Moraczewska, whose priorities were the protection of women's interests and the real achievement of equal rights for women in Poland, stressed that women needed their own political representation. Thanks to her efforts, representatives of the *Związek Pracy Obywatelskiej Kobiet* joined the official Polish delegations to the sessions of the International Labor Bureau at the League of Nations in Geneva (1931) and to the Disarmament Conference in Geneva (1932). The *Związek Pracy Obywatelskiej Kobiet* cooperated with the International Alliance of Women for Suffrage and Equal Citizenship (IAWSEC), the International Council of Women (ICW) and the Disarmament Committee of the women's international organizations. In 1930, Moraczewska participated in the Slavonic Convention in Prague, organized by the Slavonic Women's Union (founded in Czechoslovakia in 1929). In 1933, due to growing disagreement within the *Związek Pracy Obywatelskiej Kobiet*, Moraczewska resigned from her post and left the organization with a group of fellow activists. The issue in question was how the association should have reacted to the anti-democratic practices of Polish governments since 1926, practices which Moraczewska increasingly and openly criticized. In her opinion, a women's organization that was supposed to edify its members in a civil spirit could not be an instrument of government policy. "I shall always stand up for freedom of conscience and personal beliefs, as these are the most precious treasures of a free citizen in reborn Poland," she declared in one of her last statements as Chairperson of the association (National Library, *ZPOK* Collection, cat. no. 48, 26). In 1935, remaining steadfastly loyal to her ideas, she founded the *Samopomoc Społeczna Kobiet* (Women's Mutual Aid Society) for working-class women.

World War II took the rest of her family. Both her children, Wanda and Adam, died in the Auschwitz concentration camp. In 1944, when Soviet troops were taking up positions near Warsaw, her husband was killed in a bombing raid. Earlier, in April 1942, Moraczewska had written in her diary: "I want to note in these few words that all my dreams have come true and our long shared life has passed like a dream ... Today, as the sad reality–the war–has ended our work, possibly for ever, I return to our past, happy that we have spent our life as we have lived it" (National Library, *ZPOK* Collection, cat. no. 30, 39).

After the war, Moraczewska stayed out of public life, although she kept in touch with her old comrades from the *Liga Kobiet Polskich* and the *Związek Pracy Obywatelskiej Kobiet*. She received the new Communist regime with concern, while at the same time hoping for the realization of a truly working-class system. The new authorities respected her as the widow of a former socialist Prime Minister, helping to organize her husband's funeral and letting her keep the family home at Sulejówek, where they had lived since 1920. She kept herself busy with the family archives and the files from her own public activities. She died on 16 November 1958 at Sulejówek. Zofia Moraczewska was undoubtedly a charismatic leader and an intellectually influential personality in democratic women circles, yet her name and legacy remain widely unknown to this day.

Joanna Dufrat, Ph.D.
University of Wrocław, Institute of History

SOURCES

(A) Central Archives of Modern Records, Warsaw: collection of Jędrzeja i Zofii Moraczewskich. Cat. nos. 71/I-30, 71/I-89, 71/I-91, 71/I-130, 71/II-227, 71/III-6.

(A) National Library, Warsaw: archival collection of the *Związek Pracy Obywatelskiej Kobiet* and Moraczewska's personal papers (currently being catalogued so reference numbers are subject to change).

(B) *Na Posterunku* (At the post) (1916, 1917-1919).

(B) *Głos Kobiet* (Voice of women) (1919-1927).

(B) *Praca Obywatelska* (Civil work) (1928-1933).

(C) Moraczewska, Zofia. "Nasz program." *Praca Obywatelska*, no. 1 (1928): 1-2.

(C) Moraczewska, Zofia. *Do członkiń Związku Pracy Obywatelskiej Kobiet... Wyjaśnienie z jakich powodów został zwołany do Warszawy Nadzwyczajny Zjazd Delegatek Związku dnia 30 września 1934* (To the members of the Association for Civil Labor ... An explanation of the reasons for the Extraordinary Convention of the Association's Delegates called to Warsaw on 30 September 1934). Warsaw, 1934.

(C) Moraczewska, Zofia. *Mój testament pisany do ogółu kobiet polskich w roku 1945* (My testament to all Polish women in 1945). Wrocław, 1946.

(C) Moraczewska, Zofia. *Przemówienie Zofii Moraczewskiej wygłoszone na zebraniu kobiet w Warszawie dnia 13 stycznia 1928* (Speech of Zofia Moraczewska to the women's meeting in Warsaw, 13 January 1928). Warsaw, 1928.

(E) Dufrat, Joanna. *Kobiety w kręgu lewicy niepodległościowej. Od Ligi Kobiet Pogotowia Wojennego do Ochotniczej Legii Kobiet (1908-1918/1919)* (Women in the circle of the pro-independence left-wing. From the Women's League for War Alert to the Women's Voluntary Legion). Toruń, 2001.

MOSZCZEŃSKA, Iza (Izabela Moszczeńska-Rzepecka) (1864–1941)

Polish publicist, suffragist, educator and social/political activist involved in the international women's movement. Pseudonyms: M. Bell, Izydor Brzłkowski, Dora, I. M., M.

Iza Moszczeńska was born on 28 October 1864, into a noble family from Great Poland (the historical name for the Polish territories then incorporated into the Prussian State under the so-called Prussian partition). She was born on the family estate of Rzeczyca, the daughter of Alfons Moszczeński (1816–1890) and his second wife Eufemia, born Krukowiecka (b. ca. 1838). Iza Moszczeńska had three sisters and one brother: Zofia (b. ca. 1860), Anna (ca. 1865–ca. 1878), Cesia (b. 1866) and Jan (b. 1870).

Like many female members of the Polish intelligentsia unable to afford an expensive education abroad, Moszczeńska studied at home. (Women in the Prussian and the Russian parts of Poland could not enter higher education institutions. In the 1890s, universities in Lviv and Cracow, in the autonomous province of Galicia, admitted women to their faculties of medicine and philosophy). In 1878, Moszczeńska moved to Warsaw to attend Jadwiga Sikorska's boarding school for girls, well known for its innovative approach to girls' education. However in 1880, family financial troubles forred her to end her education before graduating, and she continued her studies alone at home. In this period, she read John Stuart Mill, Herbert Spencer and Henry T. Buckle, as well as learning Polish, English, German and French fluently.

Before 1890, Iza Moszczeńska lived on the family estate at Rzeczyca, where she taught the children of the village and wrote her first articles for the *Tygodnik Poznański* (Poznan weekly), the *Wielkopolanin* (Pole from Great Poland) and *Kurier Codzienny* (Daily courier). In the years 1884 to 1889, she kept a personal diary in which she recorded her views on women's emancipation and democracy. From 1880 to 1890, she traveled to Warsaw several times to attend lectures at 'the Flying University,' a secret academy established by Jadwiga Szczawińska-Dawidowa for young women unable to afford a university education outside Poland. In 1890, after her father's death and the forced sale of their family estate, Moszczeńska moved to Warsaw (at that time under Russian rule), where she and her mother established an illegal secondary boarding school for girls. (After the January Uprising of 1863 against Russia, the tsarist authorities prevented Poles from setting up private schools and associations.)

In 1894, Moszczeńska married Kazimierz Rzepecki, editor of the newspaper *Goniec Wielkopolski* (Great Poland courier), and they moved to Poznan where she worked as co-editor of the *Goniec Wielkopolski* and participated in the social activities of women's organizations in Great Poland, including the Warta Educational Association (named after the Warthe river) and the *Czytelnia dla kobiet* (Reading Room for Women), established in the 1880s. Moszczeńska's activism, modernism and anticlericalism provoked criticism from her husband's family, leading her to break off contact with them. From then on, Moszczeńska used her maiden name for public activities. In 1896, she attended the International Women's Congress in Berlin, where she delivered a talk on Polish women's activities under Russian partition. In 1897, the Rzepeckis moved to Lviv (in Galicia in the Habsburg Monarchy). Moszczeńska wrote for the Lviv newspapers *Kurier Lwowski* (Lviv courier) and *Słowo Polskie* (Polish word). She cooperated with Galician activists from the women's movement, whose campaign for women's voting rights she strongly supported.

In 1898, Moszczeńska and her husband took up residence in Warsaw, where they cooperated closely with members of the Polish Socialist Party (Moszczeńska under the pseudonym of 'Dora'). After the sudden death of her husband in 1902, she was forced to earn a living for herself and her two children: daughter Hanna (b. 1895) and son Jan (b. 1899). Despite financial difficulties and lack of support from her husband's family, she entered a period of prolific writing and other public activities after 1902, publishing translations of W. James' *Pogadanki psychologiczne* (Talks on psychology) in 1902 and Ellen Key's *Stulecie dziecka* (The century of the child) in 1904. She published in the progressive socio-political newspapers *Głos* (Voice), *Kuźnica* (Forge) and *Krytyka* (Criticism), as well as in *Przegląd Pedagogiczny* (Pedagogical review). Her articles also appeared in the feminist *Nowe Słowo* (New word), a periodical published in Cracow from 1902 to 1907, and in *Ster* (Helm), published in Warsaw between 1907 and 1914; the organ of the *Związek Równouprawnienia Kobiet Polskich* (Union of Equal Rights for Polish Women). In her writings, Moszczeńska encouraged women to organize in associations, further their education and exploit their creative potential. She proposed reform of civil laws, especially those that discriminated against married women, and introduced social issues to Polish political journalism that had previously been taboo: sexual abuse of domestic servants and double sexual moral standards and their consequences, namely venereal disease and prostitution. Rejecting biological and religious prejudices, she popularized modern educational methods. The first Polish publicist to advocate sex education for both girls and boys, she published short texts on this subject under the pseudonym M. Bell: *Co każda matka swojej dorastającej córce powiedzieć powinna* (What every mother should tell her growing daughter, 1904); *Jak rozmawiać z dziećmi o kwestiach drażliwych. Wskazówki dla matek* (How to talk to children about sensitive matters. Instruction for mothers, 1904) and *Czego nie wiemy o naszych synach. Fakta i cyfry dla wszystkich rodziców* (What we do not know about our sons. Facts and figures for all parents, 1904).

From 1904, Moszczeńska's stance became more openly political. During the Revolution of 1905 in the so-called Congress Kingdom (Polish territory under Russian partition), she joined strikes by members of the intelligentsia and workers demanding the democratization of political life, the abolition of censorship, freedom of association and the Polonization of schools (which were forbidden at that time from teaching Polish subjects). She grew ideologically close to the *Zjednoczenie Postępowo-Demokratyczne* (Progressive-Democratic Union), a liberal political party. She was imprisoned several times by the tsarist authorities for her democratic and patriotic views (in 1905, 1908 and 1912). In 1913, she co-founded and chaired the *Liga Kobiet Pogotowia Wojennego* (Women's League for War Alert), a political organization of women supporting Polish independence and full equal rights for women.

Polish women were awarded full political rights in 1918, as a result of their work for the independence movement. The first parliamentary election was held in 1919. Before the election, Moszczeńska submitted a so-called 'women's list' of social and political activists as candidates for MPs. Unexpectedly, the initiative failed completely; nobody from the list was elected. In the interwar period, Moszczeńska's politics shifted noticeably to the right. As a representative of the *Narodowa Organizacja Kobiet* (National Women's Organization)–associated with the nationalist National Democracy Party–she was a member of Warsaw City Council from 1927 to 1934. From 1926 to 1939, she worked for the *Kurier Warszawski* (Warsaw courier), also publishing articles in *Wiarus* (Veteran campaigner), *Bellona*, *Polonia*, *Placówka* (Outpost), *Szaniec* (Rampart), *Odnowa* (Revival) and *Zwrot* (Turnabout). She did not approve of Józef Piłsudski's coup in May 1926, and in the 1930s began sympathizing with the political opposition, which consisted of centrist parties concentrated around the so-called 'Front Morges.'

During the 1920s, the religious life of Moszczeńska underwent a complete transformation as she became an increasingly ardent Roman Catholic. She died on 20 March 1941 in Warsaw, after two strokes in 1934 and 1937. An outstanding political commentator who fought passionately for women's political rights and made an invaluable intellectual contribution to the project of Polish women's emancipation, her numerous activities, often independently organized, are impossible to categorize in accordance with one, overarching ideology.

Magdalena Gawin, Ph.D.
Institute of History of the Polish Academy of Science

SOURCES

(A) Warsaw University Library, Special Collections Division, MS. nr. akc. 406-a/1-8. Manuscript: Iza Moszczeńska-Rzepecka. "Wspomnienia i listy 1864-1914-1941" (Memoirs and letters 1864-1914-1941). Compiled by Hanna Pohoska. These materials also include Moszczeńska's correspondence with family and friends, fragments of her personal diaries from 1884-1889 and 1894-1897, as well as chronicles of her activities between 1914 and 1941.

(B) *Głos* (Voice) (1900-1904).

(B) *Kuźnica* (Forge) (1904-1905).
(B) *Nowe Słowo* (New word) (1902-1907).
(B) *Ster* (Helm) (1912).
(B) *Krytyka* (Criticism) (1904-1908).
(B) *Kurier Warszawski* (Warsaw courier) (1926-1939).
(D) Rzepecki, Jan. "Moszczeńska Iza." In *Polski Słownik Biograficzny* (Polish biographical dictionary). Wrocław-Warsaw: Polish Academy of Sciences, 1977, vol. XXII, no. 1, 80-85.

MUHİTTİN, Nezihe (1889–1958)

Turkish writer and activist in the early Republican period; founder (1923) of *Kadınlar Halk Fırkası* (Women's People's Party); publisher of the journals *Kadın Yolu* (Women's way) (1925) and *Türk Kadın Yolu* (Turkish women's way) (1925–1927).

Nezihe Muhittin was born in 1889 in Istanbul. Her mother was Zehra Hanım (the daughter of Ali Şevket Pasha; the name of Zehra Hanım's mother is unknown). Nezihe's father, Muhittin Bey, was a state prosecutor. Nezihe Muhittin attended the French Missionary School and her early ambition was to become a teacher. Even though she was not a graduate of the *Öğretmen Okulu* (Teacher Training College), she appealed to the Ministry of Education, succeeded in passing the entrance exam and began teaching the natural sciences at a secondary school for girls in Istanbul. In 1909, she wrote her first novel, *Şebab-i Tebah* (Lost youth), under the name Nezihe Muhlis (Muhlis being her first husband's name). She was appointed to the Teacher Training College as a teacher at the age of twenty. She wrote proposals for the reform of primary and secondary schools and sent them to the Ministry of Education. She also worked as a nurse in the First Aid Hospital of the governing *İttihat Terakki Partisi* (Union and Progress Party) in Istanbul. Nezihe Muhittin married twice. Her first marriage with Muhlis Ethem (about which no specific data exists) was short-lived. Later, she married an official of the Istanbul Municipality, Memduh Tepedelengil. The couple had a son named Malik. She never used her husband's surname, preferring to use that of her father's.

In 1913, Nezihe Muhittin founded the *Osmanlı-Türk Hanımları Esirgeme Derneği* (Association for the Protection of Ottoman-Turkish Women), which cared for orphans and women without means of material support. She was also active in the *Donanma Cemiyeti* (Association of Support to the Navy) and in the *Müdafaa-i Milliye Hanımlar Heyeti* (Women's Committee for the Defence of the Nation). These were basically nationalist and patriotic associations for the defence of the country at war. Their rhetoric stressed the need to rise against foreign invasion and to defend independence.

Muhittin's main contribution as a women's activist was her founding of a political party to fight for the (political) rights of women, which she did immediately after the

Greek-Turkish War (1919-1923). The *Kadınlar Halk Fırkası* (Women's People's Party), of which Muhittin was elected President, was founded on 16 June 1923–prior to the foundation of the *Cumhuriyet Halk Fırkası* (Republican People's Party) that was to govern the country for the entire single-party era (1930-1945). The *Kadınlar Halk Fırkası* was dedicated to the promotion of women in social, economic and political life, and to obtaining equal rights for women (including women's right to serve in the military). Yet it also emphasized the importance of women's traditional duties in the family as mothers. Official authorization of the *Kadınlar Halk Fırkası* was refused on the grounds that women did not yet have political rights and members were advised to set up a women's association, suggesting the extent to which the perimeters for the granting of social and political rights for women were largely set by men as founders of Republican Turkey. The *Kadınlar Halk Fırkası* became an association: the *Türk Kadınlar Birliği* (Turkish Women's Association), but its founding principles were in fact similar to the proposed program of the political party. In the journals that she founded–namely *Kadın Yolu* (Women's way, 1925) and *Türk Kadın Yolu* (Turkish women's way, 1925-1927)–Nezihe Muhittin worked to promote women's social status and the right to vote.

Nezihe Muhittin's position accorded with contemporary 'Western' trends in equal rights feminism in that it demanded full citizenship for women. The demand for political rights was raised again in the general meeting of the *Türk Kadınlar Birliği* convened in February 1927 in Istanbul, and a consensus was reached on the immediate need to wage a struggle for women's enfranchisement in the coming municipal elections. Although the *Türk Kadınlar Birliği*'s demand for women's voting rights was not acknowledged by the Turkish Parliament, Muhittin continued to promote suffrage as a key demand of the *Türk Kadınlar Birliği*: "We have not given up our primary goal of winning suffrage. Had we done so, our association would have no reason to exist. We will struggle for victory to the death. If our lives do not suffice, we will have at least cleared the way for future generations" (Caporal 1982, 693).

Following the above meeting, members of the *Türk Kadınlar Birliği*'s executive commitee dismissed Nezihe Muhittin from her presidential post. The official pretext used for this dismissal was a police raid on the central office of the *Türk Kadınlar Birliği* and the subsequent accusation that the women's association was engaged in illegal activity. In fact, the dismissal reflected tensions and disagreements within the *Türk Kadınlar Birliği*, the negative attitude of the press and, above all, the Republican regime's policy of banning independent civil organizations. The new executive committee was more moderate and stressed cultural, economic and philanthropic activities rather than those of a political nature. In 1930, for the first time, women gained the right to participate in (local) elections, paving the way for the later achievement of the right to vote in national elections. Most of the women elected to Parliament in the 1935 elections were members of the *Türk Kadınlar Birliği*.

In 1930, Nezihe Muhittin joined the opposition party, the *Serbest Cumhuriyet*

Fırkası (Liberal Republican Party), which included voting rights for women in its program. Together with the writer ***Suat Derviş***, Muhittin set up a women's branch of the Liberal Republican Party, which later became an association named *Kadın Varlığı* (Women's Being). Both Muhittin and Derviş were listed by the *Serbest Cumhuriyet Fırkası* for the municipal elections of 1930, but neither succeeded and the party itself was soon outlawed by Parliament. Meanwhile, Nezihe Muhittin kept writing and published a book in 1931 entitled *Türk Kadını* (Turkish woman). Although the book was not badly received, Muhittin had chosen to place herself at center stage in an attempt to guarantee herself a prominent place in the history of women in Turkey, ignoring other key women activists such as ***Ulviye Mevlan***.

When political rights were granted to women (5 December 1934), Muhittin applied to become an independent candidate in the elections. Under the single-party regime, even independent candidates required the support of the Central Commitee of the ruling *Cumhuriyet Halk Fırkası* (Republican People's Party). In spite of her long-standing dedication to the struggle for women's political rights, Nezihe Muhittin was not granted this support. She did not give in and continued to fight for her cause, but never achieved her dream of becoming a parliamentary deputy. Latife Bekir, her rival and successor as President of the *Türk Kadınlar Birliği*, did manage to enter Parliament as a deputy and it was Bekir who chaired the opening session of the Congress of the International Alliance of Women for Suffrage and Equal Citizenship (IAWSEC, later the IAW) held in Istanbul on 18–24 April 1935, in which five hundred women from thirty countries participated. Bekir's success was largely due to her close alliance with the regime; through her, the Turkish government was able to exploit the IAWSEC Congress for its own purposes, boasting improvements in women's political participation and emphasizing the number of Turkish women MPs–which then amounted to more than in some of the Western countries.

In later years, Nezihe Muhittin earned a living–with difficulty–writing novels. Her mental health deteriorated and she died in a mental hospital (La Paix, Istanbul) on 10 February 1958. As a woman who faced persistent difficulties and disappointments but nevertheless remained politically active throughout her life, Nezihe Muhittin rightfully occupies a place as a pioneer in the history of the struggle for women's suffrage in Turkey.

Serpil Çakır
University of Istanbul

SOURCES

(C) Muhittin, Nezihe. *Türk Kadını* (Turkish woman). Istanbul: Numune Matbaası, 1931.

(D) Çakır, Serpil. "Kadın Tarihinden İki İsim: Ulviye Mevlan and Nezihe Muhittin" (Two women from Turkish women's history: Ulviye Mevlan and Nezihe Muhittin). *Toplumsal Tarih* (Social history), no. 46 (1997): 6–14.

(E) Caporal, Bernard. *Kemalizmde ve Kemalizm Sonrasında Türk Kadını*, (Turkish woman in and after Kemalizm). Ankara: İş Bankası Yayınları, 1982.

(E) Çakır, Serpil. *Osmanlı Kadın Hareketi* (The Ottoman women's movement). Istanbul: Metis, 1994.

(E) Çakır, Serpil. "Political-Social Movements: Revolutionary Turkey." *Encylopedia of Women and Islamic Cultures*. Leiden: Brill, 2004, 2: 415–416.

(E) Berktay, Fatmagül. "Political Regimes: Turkey." *Encylopedia of Women and Islamic Cultures*. Leiden: Brill, 2004, 2: 370–371.

NĂDEJDE, Sofia (1856–1946)

Romanian writer, publicist, editor of militant journals, translator and model woman-citizen who fought for women's rights for almost five decades.

Sofia Băncilă was born in 1856 in the city of Botoşani (northern Moldavia), at that time a Russian protectorate still formally under Ottoman suzerainty. Her family were *răzeşi* (free peasants); her parents were Vasile Băncilă Gheorghiu and Puheria-Profira Neculce (data unknown). In 1874, at the age of just eighteen, Sofia married Ion (Ioan) Nădejde (1854–1928), a well-known socialist, lawyer, writer and, between 1893 and 1899, one of the leaders of the *Partidul Socialist Democrat al Muncitorilor din România* (Socialist Democratic Party of Workers in Romania). The couple moved to Iaşi, the largest city in northern Moldavia, where they lived for twenty years before moving to Bucharest in 1894. Sofia Nădejde joined her husband's activities in the socialist movement, first in Iaşi and then in Bucharest. During their stay in Iaşi, their six children (two boys and four girls) were born.

Sofia Nădejde had attended both primary and secondary schools in her hometown of Botoşani and began publishing at the age of 23. In her countless articles, she demonstrated a remarkable political, scientific and literary erudition, which she had largely acquired through self-study. Her socialist and feminist ideas undoubtedly took shape during her first years in Iaşi, where she and her husband transformed their home into a meeting place for young intellectuals–men and women who wished to debate the possibility of change in their country. In 1879, she published a tough polemic in the journal *Femeia română* (The Romanian woman), edited by Maria Flechtenmacher. The article, entitled "Chestiunea femeilor" (The woman question), criticized the argument that women "are incapable of any development ... that, no matter how much they try to develop their intellect, they will not succeed but rather, as civilization progresses ... tend towards idiocy" (Nădejde 1879).

After her marriage, Sofia Nădejde became involved in the socialist movement and participated in the development of the movement's first political agendas, which included equal civil and political rights for women and men, equal pay for equal work and equal access of women and men to all professions. The latter program was adopted at the Second Congress of the Socialist Party in 1894. Nădejde published many articles in socialist journals such as *Basarabia* (Basarabia), *Munca* (Work), *Drepturile omului* (Human rights), and *Lumea nouă literară și științifică* (The new literary and scientific world). Her writings covered the evolution of the family, women's role in the socialist movement, current prejudices regarding women's education, social movements and women's work in the countryside and in factories. They displayed a profound knowledge of the Western European scientific and philosophical discourses of her period, from John Stuart Mill, Herbert Spencer and Charles Darwin to Karl Marx and August Bebel.

Sofia Nădejde was part of a group of socialist intellectuals in Iaşi who, between 1881 and 1891, published the newspaper *Contemporanul* (The contemporary), with a run of 4,500 copies (an unusually high number for any paper in Romania at that time, particularly for a left-wing publication). This paper became the arena in which Nădejde launched a veritable feminist campaign against the then widespread argument of women's alleged 'smaller brains' (used to 'prove' that women were unable to attain high spiritual planes and that they should not participate in politics). Nădejde had a particularly heated debate with the prominent intellectual Titu Maiorescu. On the basis of a sophisticated reading of the latest scientific discoveries in biology, anatomy and anthropology, Nădejde demonstrated that proportionally, women's brains were actually larger than men's. Her analysis turned from biology to the socially and politically pertinent factors that helped explain women's state of inferiority: the social environment, prejudice, discriminatory laws and lack of an education commensurate with the needs of modern life. Nădejde presented the work of John Stuart Mill to the readers of *Contemporanul* (in particular his *On the Subjection of Women*, 1869), and used his arguments to advocate political and civil rights for women in Romania.

During the early years of writing for *Contemporanul*, Nădejde also rallied women of diverse social backgrounds and from various associations, groups and clubs, to raise funds for women's education and employment. After 1886, under the influence of Marxism, her articles moved towards a broader view of social inequality and its elimination, portraying women's oppression as a byproduct of capitalism and private property. In the second half of the 1890s, her Marxist radicalism modulated into democratic liberalism under the influence of the *poporaniști* (populists) and their leader, Constantin Stere. In the late 1890s, Nădejde edited and published articles in *Evenimentul literar* (The literary event), a journal affiliated with this group.

In 1899, Nădejde left the socialist movement, together with her husband and a large faction of other socialist leaders who were convinced that socialism had no social base in predominantly agrarian Romania. The group abandoned revolutionary goals, left the Socialist Party, joined the National Liberal Party and embraced a more reformist perspective. Sofia Nădejde, who did not become a member of the Liberal Party, lost her enthusiasm for political engagement in the midst of these changes and began to focus on writing fiction. Her first novel, *Patimi* (Passions, 1903), was awarded first prize (1903) in a literary competition organized by the widely circulated newspaper *Universul* (Universe). Two more novels followed: *Robia banului* (The servitude of money, 1906) and *Părinți și copii* (Parents and children, 1907); neither one was as successful as the first. The central theme of her writings was still the oppression of women and her novels were suffused with a feminist spirit. Other writings from this period, which she published in various magazines and yearbooks, focused on education, hygiene, science, gastronomy and agriculture. A concern with women's ability to function in modern society and economic life figured prominently in the kinds of general and specific advice Nădejde offered in these articles.

Her feminist activities continued through her work with the feminist publication *Revista noastră* (Our magazine), as well as through her leading role in the *Asociația pentru Emanciparea Civilă și Politică a Femeilor Române* (*AECPFR*, Association for the Civil and Political Emancipation of Romanian Women), which she helped found in 1918. She continued her work on behalf of civil and political rights and democracy in the 1930s, speaking out against the rise of fascism in Europe and trying to prevent its ascent in Romania. In this period, she was elected Honorific President of the *Frontul Feminin* (Feminine Front), an umbrella group founded by prominent Romanian women writers and artists (including Lucia Sturdza Bulandra and Izabela Sadoveanu), in order to assist the efforts of affiliated women's organizations to save civil rights and freedoms threatened by the rise of the right in Romania and across Europe. During the war years, Sofia Nădejde continued to live with one of her daughters, Amelia Nădejde Gesticone (she had moved in with Amelia upon the death of her husband in 1928), supporting herself with a modest pension from the Society of Romanian Writers. She died in her daughter's home on 11 June 1946.

Ștefania Mihăilescu
Lecturer in Women's History,
National School for Political Studies and Public Administration, Bucharest

Translated from Romanian by Maria Bucur.

SOURCES

(B) *Femeia română* (The Romanian woman) (1879).
(B) *Contemporanul* (The contemporary) (1881-1891).
(C) Nădejde, S. "Chestiunea femeilor" (The woman question). *Femeia română* 1, no. 11 (25 March 1879).
(C) Nădejde, S. *Scrieri* (Selected works). Iași: Editura Junimea, 1978.
(D) Vișinescu, V. *Sofia Nădejde*. Bucharest: Editura Politică, 1972.
(E) Mihăilescu, Șt. *Emanciparea femeii române. Antologie de texte, 1815-1918*. (The emancipation of Romanian women. An anthology of texts, 1815-1918). Bucharest: Editura Ecumenica, 2001.
(E) Mihăilescu, Șt. *Din istoria feminismului românesc. Antologie de texte (1838-1929)* [A history of Romanian feminism. An anthology of texts (1838-1929)]. Iași: Polirom, 2002.

NEGRUZZI, Ella (1876–1948)

Romanian liberal feminist and political activist in the National Peasant Party; first woman lawyer in Romania (1920); one of the first women representatives in the Bucharest city council after 1929.

Born in Hermeziu, a village in the province of Moldavia (in the young Romanian Kingdom), Ella Negruzzi was the daughter of the writer Leon Negruzzi. Details of her mother are unknown. Intellectually prominent members of her family include her uncle, Iacob Negruzzi, a professor at the University of Iaşi and twice President of the Romanian Academy (1910–13 and 1923–26). After her father passed away prematurely, Iacob Negruzzi took charge of both Ella's education and that of her brother, Mihai (who later became an army general). Ella Negruzzi was briefly married to, and later divorced Nicolae Beldiman.

Given this illustrious intellectual background, it is unsurprising that Negruzzi was both academically gifted and professionally ambitious. She graduated from the University of Iaşi in philosophy, history and law. In 1913, Negruzzi became the first woman to attempt to register for the bar exam in Iaşi. When her request was rejected, she moved to Galaţi and attempted to take the bar there, with the support of a prominent local lawyer, Corneliu Botez (see also ***Calypso Botez***). On her third attempt, in 1919, she was finally allowed to take the exam in Bucharest (Ilfov County). In 1920, Ella Negruzzi became the first woman to practice law in the capital.

During World War I, Negruzzi participated directly in the war effort in Iaşi and across Moldova, working as a volunteer nurse at a hospital in the front lines. After 1918, she continued to support women's education (especially in the countryside) and to work on behalf of women's employment rights. She became particularly vocal from the mid-1930s when, in a desperate wave of measures to address the unemployment crisis, the liberal government launched a virulent campaign against employment rights for women, such as the right to paid work and to pension benefits. In a speech given at the 1934 Congress of the *Asociaţia pentru emanciparea civilă şi politică a femeilor române* (*AECPFR*, Association for the Civil and Political

Emancipation of Romanian Women), Negruzzi emphasized the double marginalization of women in the workforce: their limited possibilities for professional advancement and their relegation to first-in-the-firing-line positions in a given moment of crisis. By way of solutions to these problems, Negruzzi focused on private and rural sectors, suggesting the development of a network of rural vocational schools attached to cooperative enterprises.

Negruzzi's concern for women's social welfare also led to a critique of prostitution. She pointed out the existence of a sexual double standard that helped perpetuate prostitution and argued that an environment of sexual permissiveness towards men increased the vulnerability of women, suggesting that prostitutes be helped, through education and rehabilitation, to enter other forms of employment.

Negruzzi was as indefatigable a feminist in the political sphere as she was in her pursuit of law and in her endeavors to provide social assistance for women. In 1917, together with a number of other prominent feminists (such as ***Elena C. Meissner***), she signed a petition demanding that the Senate grant women full civil and political rights. Though the response was resoundingly negative, Negruzzi never abandoned her resolutely suffragist position. In 1918, she helped found the *AECPFR* in Iaşi, which she led, together with Elena Meissner, throughout the interwar period. This suffragist group sought to counter prevailing prejudices against women's emancipation and fought for the right of women to participate in any and all areas of public life, including politics, the professions and education. Within a year, *AECPFR* had branches in Bucharest, Cernăuţi, Brasov and Sibiu, among other places. Negruzzi remained active in the Bucharest branch after 1918.

In the early 1920s, Negruzzi published prolifically and worked energetically to secure political rights for women in the new Constitution (passed in 1923). In the feminist debates over strategies for political empowerment (see also Elena Meissner and ***Alexandrina Cantacuzino***), Negruzzi embraced the position taken by the *AECPFR* and insisted on women's participation in existing political parties, rather than in a separate political bloc for women as Alexandrina Cantacuzino had suggested. Negruzzi became a member of the National Peasant Party and in 1929 participated in the first elections to allow women as candidates for local elections. She became one of the first group of women city councilors, together with ***Calypso Botez***, Alexandrina Cantacuzino and three others. Over the next few years, these women leaders attempted to increase women's participation in the political life of the capital, hoping that in doing so they might provide a powerful example to the rest of the country. They also addressed a wide variety of 'women's issues,' including education, employment for young migrants to the city and refuges for elderly women and war widows.

By the late 1930s, as King Carol II moved from usurping the democratic political process behind the scenes to openly declaring an authoritarian dictatorship, participation in political life became an act of simple acquiescence. Negruzzi was among those feminists who did not choose to cooperate with the new regime, retreating into opposition. Among other activities in this period, Negruzzi became a member of the *Gruparea Avocaților Democrați* (Group of Democratic Lawyers) in 1935. Little is known of her life after the outbreak of World War II. She died in 1948 in Bucharest.

Maria Bucur
Indiana University

SOURCES

(C) Negruzzi, Ella. "Educația casnică a femeii de țară" (Home education for the peasant woman). In Ministerul Instrucției, Cultelor și Artelor. Direcția educației poporului (Ministry of Instruction, Religion, and Arts. Department of Popular Education), ed. *Program de lucru pentru acțiunea culturală* (Working program for cultural activities). Bucharest, 1933, 38–39.

(E) Câncea, Paraschiva. *Mișcarea pentru emanciparea femeii în România 1848–1948* (The movement for women's emancipation in Romania. 1848–1948). Bucharest: Politică, 1976.

(E) Predescu, Lucian. *Enciclopedia României. Cugetarea* (Encyclopedia of Romania. The thought). Bucharest: Saeculum I. O., 1999.

(E) Cosma, Ghizela. *Femeile și politica în România. Evoluția dreptului de vot în perioada interbelică* (Women and politics in Romania. The evolution of suffrage rights in the interwar period). Cluj: Presa Universitară Clujeană, 2002.

NĚMCOVÁ, Božena (born Barbora Panklová) (1820?-1862)

Czech fiction writer, poet, journalist, collector and editor of folk narratives; key figure of the Czech National Revival and representative of the national literary canon; one of the first Czech women to publicly address the question of women's identity and their position in society.

Although there have been some attempts to prove her noble origins, most sources agree that Barbora Panklová was born out of wedlock in Vienna on 5 February 1820 (?), to Marie Magdalena Terezie Novotná (1797-1863), a fifteen-year-old Czech servant, and Johann Baptist Pankel (1794-1850), an Austrian coachman. She was the first of their twelve children. The Pankl family soon moved to Ratibořice, an estate in north-east Bohemia belonging to Countess Zaháňská, for whom both Barbora's parents worked. Barbora was raised in a humble rural environment. Her grandmother Magdaléna Novotná, who inspired her literary masterpiece *Babička* (The grandmother, 1855), significantly influenced her during her childhood (1825-1830). She received a basic elementary education at a local Czech Catholic school (from 1826) and spent three years (1830-1833) with a German-speaking family who worked at Chvalkovice castle. Having access to the library there, she became a passionate reader of German Romantic literature.

In 1837, at the age of seventeen, Barbora Panklová was forced into a loveless marriage with an excise officer, Josef Němec (1805-1879). Although a committed patriot, who was also persecuted for his patriotic activities, he was anything but a Romantic and over ten years her senior. Due to the nature of his job, the couple had to move frequently in the first years of their marriage, during which time Němcová also bore four of their children (Hynek, b. 1838; Karel, b. 1839; Theodora, b. 1841 and Jaroslav, b. 1842). Between 1842 and 1845, the family lived in Prague, where Němcová became familiar with the patriotic salons and growing circles of the young, pro-Czech literati. This period represented a turning point in her intellectual development. Němcová published her first lyrical poems in local journals–the first one entitled "Ženám českým" (To Czech women, 1843)–combining naive patriotism with an explicit call for women's participation in the nationalist struggle. In

1845, in keeping with her patriotic convictions, she accepted a more Czech-sounding literary name, Božena.

It was not only her unusual talent, but also the long-lasting desire of the patriotic community for an emancipated creative heroine that turned this exceptionally beautiful and charismatic woman into an idol. Němcová's (mostly male) peers soon celebrated her as the first Czech poetess. This first 'Prague period' was marked by deep friendships with leading women of Prague patriotic families, such as Bohuslava Rajská and her sisters. She began collecting and adapting folk tales for publication, resulting in her *Národní báchorky a pověsti* (Czech and Slovak folk tales, 1845–1847). Her folkloric interests developed even further after 1845, when she and her family had to move once again, this time to the west Bohemian region of Chodsko; later to south Bohemia. She also collected folkloric material during travels to Slovakia. Despite the popularity of her stories among generations of Czech and Slovak children (continuing to this day), her fellow revivalists often criticized her particular poetic renditions of the stories for distorting their 'authentic' form.

The revolutionary year of 1848 dashed the liberal and patriotic expectations of many Czechs. Němec faced further political persecutions and both he and his wife were put under secret police surveillance. They kept moving, mostly to Germanized towns in north Bohemia (Nymburk, Liberec), where Němcová suffered from intellectual and social isolation. She was becoming trapped between her literary and spiritual ambitions and pressure from close patriotic friends, who accused her of wasting her talent on folkloric material. These creative dilemmas, along with the increasing poverty of her family and the poor health of both her and her children, exacerbated growing conflicts between her and her husband, resulting occasionally in outbursts of domestic violence. These were controversies which were to shape much of her life and to which she responded in part by writing a great number of personal letters to her family members, lovers, friends and numerous key personalities of the local cultural and social scene. These texts not only form a valuable part of Czech epistolary literary culture, but also represent a unique testimony to the struggles and unresolveable conflicts experienced by a creative and independent-minded woman.

In 1850, Němcová's husband accepted a position in a removed region of Slovakia (then part of Hungary), a move which *de facto* meant the couple's first step towards separation. Despite economic misery and all the apparent social consequences, Němcová returned alone with her children to Prague. She visited her husband in Slovakia several times (1850–1855), using these journeys to collect folklore, study rural life and promote Czech–Slovak relations via her contacts with leading Slovak intellectuals. Her free lifestyle and independent nature generated a growing barrier between Němcová and the middle-class patriots of her generation, many of whom criticized her for her relaxed attitude to money, which some saw as a major reason for her poverty. She grew closer to the circles of younger patriots surrounding Josef Václav Frič (such as her last intimate friend Hanuš Jurenka) and Johanna and Sofie Rotts (otherwise known as ***Karolína Světlá*** and Sofie Podlipská), as well as Vítězslav Hálek and Jan Neruda.

The painful 1850s represented the most fruitful period in Němcová's creative writing career. She supported her family by writing journalistic pieces and fiction, as well as translating Slovenian, Serbian and Bulgarian works into Czech, but she often had to beg friends for help. Her fiction combined authentic records of country life–usually through strong female characters of lower-class origins–with her unique literary imagination. Shortly after the death of her beloved oldest son Hynek in 1853, she began work on her most celebrated piece *Babička* (1855), a key text of the Czech national revivalist literary canon which has since been published over three hundred times in Czech and translated into twenty languages. Although several shorter stories followed, none of them have been thought to compare with *Babička*, a poetic reminiscence of her childhood in an ideally happy rural setting. Its elaborate structure is built around the cycle of the seasons, accompanied by lively depictions of traditions. customs and the daily life routines of the villagers. The rich patchwork of stories and events, narrated in exceptionally cultivated Czech, are synthesized through the character of the grandmother. Her simple wisdom represents human harmony, sympathy, order and light, in contrast with the dark femininity of Viktorka who brings in motives of tragic love, protest, seduction, unwanted pregnancy, murder and madness; a figure who embodies exclusion, solitude and the unspeakable.

The year 1857 was marked by Němcová's first creative writing crisis and increasing financial desperation. These pressures forced her to produce more translation work and folkloric essays. She also published a collection of Slovak tales, escaping into letter writing for creative release. In 1861, seriously ill and weak, Božena Němcová left Prague to edit her collected works for her publisher. Shortly afterwards her husband brought her back to Prague, where she died of cancer in poverty and solitude on 21 January 1862. It was one of the bitter paradoxes of her life that what followed was a grandiose funeral decorated with national symbols, crowded with people and attended by the leading personalities of patriotic circles, aristocrats and city representatives.

Božena Němcová was certainly one of the first women in modern Czech history to explicitly articulate deep-rooted philosophical dilemmas and conflicts over definitions of femininity. Yet for almost 150 years, critics and historians have been struggling to find ways to interpret her life and work: she has been labeled a national hero; a victim of petty Czech patriotism; a tragic figure unhappily married to an insensitive man; an unstable, promiscuous woman; a congenial narrator and a slightly sentimental late-Romantic writer. Communist criticism emphasized her affiliation with early socialism and the 'fighting spirit' of her patriotic attitudes. She herself regarded her writing as a service to her nation; later however, her writing increasingly became a way of life, a means of living and a source of independence–the only possible material and spiritual survival available to a creative woman. In 1857, she wrote in a letter to her husband: "You [in plural] had my body, my actions, my honesty, but my desires went further–I myself did not understand where ... I was longing, I wanted to fill the empty space in my soul with something, but I had no idea what it could be. First I thought it could be love for a man ... now I know that this was not true. I embraced the national idea with all my heart, but even that did not bring fulfillment ...This desire has settled in my soul—a little drop which can never dry out ..." (Němcová 1960, 14: 82).

Statements like these point to the need to re-read Božena Němcová's work. We need to examine the capacity of her writings to reveal the limits of naming women's desire and experience within the dominant symbolic and social order. Such a reading would also bring to light her ability to anticipate themes elaborated in feminist theory decades later.

Jiřina Šmejkalová
University of Lincoln, UK

SOURCES

(B) *Spisy Boženy Němcové Sv.14* (The complete works of Božena Němcová, vol. 14). Prague: Knihovna klasiků, 1960.

(C) Němcová, Božena. *Národní báchorky a pověsti* (National stories and tales). Prague: Jaroslav Pospíšil, 1845-47.

(C) Němcová, Božena. *Babička* (The grandmother). Prague: Jaroslav Pospíšil, 1855.

(C) Němcová, Božena. *Pohorská vesnice* (A highland village). Prague: Jeřábková, 1856.

(C) Němcová, Božena. *Slovenské pohádky a pověsti* (Slovak stories and tales). Prague: Josef Šálek, 1857-58.

(C) Adam, Robert, ed. *Božena Němcová–Korespondence* (Božena Němcová–correspondence). Prague: Nakladatelství Lidové Noviny, 2003.

(D) Tille, Václav. *Božena Němcová*. Prague: Mánes, 1911.

(D) Novotný, Miloslav. *Život Boženy Němcové, Dopisy a dokumenty* (The life of Božena Němcová, letters and documents). I-VI. Prague: Československý spisovatel, 1951-1959.

(D) Guski, Andreas. *Zur Poetik und Rezeption von Božena Němcovás Babička* (On the poetics and reception of Božena Němcova's "Grandmother"). Wiesbaden: Harrassowitz, 1991.

(D) Morava, Georg J. *Sehnsucht in meiner Seele: Božena Němcová, Dichterin: ein Frauenschicksal in Alt-Österreich* (The desire in my soul: Božena Němcova, poetess: women's destiny in the old Austria). Innsbruck: Haymon, 1995.

(E) Iggers, Wilma A, ed. *Women of Prague*. Providence, Oxford: Berghahn Books, 1995.

(E) Wagnerová, Alena, ed. *Prager Frauen. Neuen Lebensbilder*. Prague & Furth im Walde: Vitalis, 2000.

NINKOVIĆ (Ninkovich), Milica (Todorović, Todorovich) (1854–1881)

Prominent journalist and translator; one of the first Serbian feminists; founder (1880) of the first feminist organization of local Serbs in Novi Sad.

Milica Ninković (right) with her sister Anka

Milica Ninković was born on 30 January 1854 in Novi Sad (then southern Hungary, now in Serbia), where her father Petar Ninković was a headmaster and teacher at the Serb High School. Since the University of Zurich was the first European university to admit female students, many well-to-do girls from southern Hungary entered its faculties. Together with her sister Anka (1855–1923), Milica studied at the School of Pedagogy from September 1872 to 1874.

During her Zurich years, Milica Ninković was influenced by socialism and feminism. Switzerland was then a center for the European socialist network and the leading place of exile for Russian populists, socialists and anarchists. Ninković, imbued with the ideas of Russian socialism, was especially close to several Russian female revolutionaries devoted to feminist ideas. Many of her future attitudes were also formed through her friendship with the founder of Serbian socialism, Svetozar Marković (1846–1875).

In 1874, the Ninković sisters returned from Switzerland to Serbia and decided to settle in Kragujevac. The former capital of Serbia was then a center of national education: the first Serbian lyceum and high school had been established there and it was there that the Ninković sisters planned to open a private high school for women based on modern pedagogical methods. Advertisements for the school were published in local newspapers, but since the Ninković sisters were devoted feminists and influenced by socialism as well, their efforts were soon banned and the sisters themselves threatened with expulsion from the country by the authorities. The two sisters avoided this by marrying two Serbian citizens.

Together with her husband Pera Todorović, a famous Serbian journalist and future founder of the *Narodna radikalna stranka* (People's Radical Party) who had also studied in Switzerland, Milica Ninković set up the newspaper *Staro Oslobođenje* (Old liberation) and edited its supplement.

During the Serbian-Turkish Wars (1876-1878), Milica Ninković served as a nurse. After the war, she worked for the British legation in Belgrade but the authorities pressurized the British Consul General to have her discharged. Milica Ninković left the country, traveling to St Petersburg, Zurich and Paris, where she studied medicine. Upon her return from the study abroad, Milica Ninković founded (1880) one of the first feminist organizations of local Serbs in Novi Sad. During her second study period abroad, she caught tuberculosis. She died in Kragujevac on 18 November 1881. Her sister Anka Ninković lived in Belgrade, where she worked as nursery-governess. She retreated from public life after the death of her daughter.

Milica Ninković's main interests were the history of feminism, the French Revolution and literature. She knew German, French and Russian and translated several works from Russian and French, among them: *Jedna junakinja iz Francuske revolucije* (A heroine of the French revolution) by H. Tausinski; *Istorija jednog zločina* (A history of one crime) by V. Hugo and a Russian translation of S. Marković's *Srbija na istoku* (Serbia of the East).

Ivana Pantelić

Belgrade Women's Studies and Gender Research Center

SOURCES

(B) Marković, Ljubica. *Počeci feminizma u Srbiji i Vojvodini* (The origins of feminism in Serbia and Vojvodina). Belgrade: Narodna misao, 1934.

(E) Kecman, Jovanka. *Žene Jugoslavije u radničkom pokretu i ženskim organizacijama, 1914-1941* (Yugoslav women in the labor movement and women's organizations, 1914-1941). Belgrade: Institut za savremenu istoriju, 1978.

(E) Perović, Latinka. *Srpski socijalisti XIX Veka* (Serbian socialists of the nineteenth century). Belgrade: Službeni list, 1995.

(E) Božinović, Neda. *Žensko pitanje u Srbiji u XIX i XX veku* (The woman question in Serbia in the nineteenth and twentieth centuries). Belgrade: Feministička '94, 1996.

(E) Stojaković, Gordana. *Znamenite žene Novog Sada* (The renowned women of Novi Sad). Novi Sad: Futura publikacije, 2001.

NOVÁKOVÁ (born Lanhausová), Teréza (1853-1912)

Czech feminist, writer, ethnographer and editor of *Ženský svět* (Women's world); co-founder of the *Ženský klub český* (Czech Women's Club). Pseudonyms: 'Lona,' 'Thea' and 'N. T. Fedorovič.'

Teréza Lanhausová was born on 31 December 1853, into a wealthy middle-class Czech-German family from Prague (her mother, Ernestina, was German). Along with her sister Marie, she attended the famous private Amerling school for girls, where she acquired the basic knowledge of foreign languages that she would later develop through additional private education. In 1876, she married Josef Novák (1847-1907), a liberal secondary school teacher. Five of her six children died young; only her son Arne reached adulthood to become a significant historian of Czech literature (whose work was also translated into English).

In 1876, her husband received a teaching post in the eastern Bohemian town of Litomyšl. Though it was a provincial cultural center at that time, Teréza Nováková missed the literary and intellectual environment of Prague. After several years of living in Litomyšl, during which she gave birth to five of her six children (the sixth born later in Prague), Nováková became interested in folk culture and also began organizing local middle-class women in the *Spolek paní a dívek* (Association of Ladies and Girls).

The importance of Litomyšl to Nováková is reflected in her ethnographic studies, which she later incorporated into her novels. She was inspired by the work of ***Karolína Světlá***, whom she came to think of as a literary and intellectual mother figure after meehing her in the days before Nováková's marriage, when the two women had worked together in Prague for the *Americký klub dam* (American Ladies' Club), founded in 1865 by Vojtěch Náprstek (1826-1894). Nováková dedicated one of her first articles to Světlá and wrote her literary biography in 1890. While in Litomyšl, she produced numerous short stories and novels depicting conventional middle-class life, published in the collection *Z naší národní společnosti* (From our national society, 1887). In her *Maloměstský román* (A small-town novel, 1890), she turned to realism in an attempt to condemn what she thought of as the insular national idealization of

Czech society. She eventually became so fond of Litomyšl, surrounded by the foothills of the Orlické Mountains, that she bought a cottage there, in the village of Proseč. But the years to follow would see the sad loss of her husband and no less than five of her children: her first child Marie died in 1895; her beloved son Theodor drowned in 1901, František Vladimír committed suicide and her daughter Lily died in 1905, she lost her husband Josef in 1907 and Jaroslav, her youngest son, fell in 1915 during World War I. Nováková would later call her home "the gloomiest cottage in the world" (see Svadbová 1988).

Her ethnographic studies, the results of trips to the eastern Bohemian countryside, were published in the periodical *Domací hospodyně* (Housewife). Inspired by peasant and folk culture while addressing a modern, middle-class female readership, the journal contained articles on a broad range of topics from ethnography to education. Novakova published educational articles for *Domací hospodyně* in a column headed "Hovory po práci" (Talks after work). She collected folk costumes and embroidery and also contributed to *Český lid* (The Czech people), a journal established by the founder of Czech modern positivist ethnography, Čeněk Zíbrt. Nováková was particularly interested in the Evangelical-Catholic border region that lay between Bohemia and Moravia. In her longest and in terms of composition, most complex novel, *Děti čistého živého* (Children of pure subsistence, 1909), she explored the harsh treatment meted out in this region to religious heretics of the reformist sectarian church: "the children of the spirit of pure subsistence."

Her articles for *Domací hospodyně*, particularly the regular column "Hovory po práci," did not contain radical ideas on women and their position in the family–at least not initially. Yet by the early 1890s, Teréza Nováková had published two important studies of women's social status. In the first, "J. S. Millovo Poddanství žen" (On J. S. Mill's *The Subjection of Women*), Nováková expounded on Mill's concepts of freedom and responsibility with regard to women. In the second, "L. N. Tolstojova Kreutzrova sonata ze stanoviska ženského" (L. N. Tolstoi's Kreutzer Sonata from a feminine perspective), she reviewed the debates over double moral standards for men and women that had been generated by Tolstoi's controversial work.

In 1894, Nováková published *Slavín žen českých* (A monument to Czech women's glory), a book on outstanding female figures in Czech literature and history. She returned to Prague in 1895, after the death of her eldest daughter. In 1896, the publisher Jan Otto offered her the post of editor-in-chief for a new women's magazine called *Ženský svět* (Women's world) and asked her to edit a reinstated publication called *Ženská bibliotéka* (Women's library). First edited by Sofie Podlipská (the sister of ***Karolína Světlá***) from 1872 to 1878, Nováková ran the new *Ženská bibliotéka* from 1898 to 1899. As editor-in-chief of *Ženský svět*, she transformed the magazine into a feminist monthly that reported on political and social issues and published pieces on women's literature, art and education. In 1896, together with several female teachers and activists from Prague, Novaková organized the *První sjezd žen československých*

(First 'Czechoslav' Women's Congress–the name of which stressed the *Slavic* origin of Czech women). The Congress laid the foundations for the creation of an organization which could represent the interests of Czech women, the *Ústřední spolek českých žen* (Central Association of Czech Women). A second 'Czechoslav' Women's Congress was held in 1908. When Jan Otto realized that *Ženský svět* looked unlikely to become a 'regular' women's magazine, he handed ownership of the magazine over full to the *Ústřední spolek českých žen*.

In addition to editing, Teréza Nováková was involved in other feminist activities. In 1903, along with teacher and activist ***Františka Plamínková***, she established the liberal, politically more radical *Ženský klub český* (Czech Women's Club), which campaigned for women's suffrage rights. Nováková was not particularly close to T. G. Masaryk, whose views and opinions strongly influenced the group of radical progressive feminists around Plamínková and so it was not only fatigue and poor health that led Nováková to resign from her editorial position with *Ženský svět* in 1907, but a shift in her feminism towards the stronger radicalism represented by the Czech 'suffra-gettes.' The journal *Ženský svět* was taken over by the more conservative *Ústřední spolek českých žen* and Nováková came to distance herself from it politically.

The importance of feminist ideas for Teréza Nováková was the role they might play in strengthening national identity (through the education of women) and in the development of a specifically 'feminine' rationality and aesthetics. In her writing, she was strongly influenced by the Norwegian realist Henrik Ibsen (even adopting the name of Lona Hessel, the playwright's heroine from the play *Pillars of Society,* as the pseudonym with which she signed her feminist articles). Nováková emphasized fundamental gender differences, drawing upon her own experiences of motherhood, while at the same time reclaiming for women supposedly 'male' qualities such as rationality and intellect. She was also strongly influenced by the South African feminist writer Olive Schreiner (1855–1920), some of whose works she translated, and the Swedish philosopher, reformer and pedagogue Ellen Key (1849–1926), whose concept of an emotionally-grounded 'female genius' became popular in Bohemia at the fin de siècle. Nováková expressed admiration for Key's work in her article, "Genialita citu" (The genius of feeling), published in the journal *Přehled* (Overview) in 1912. Nováková's most significant feminist works were published under the title *Ze ženského hnutí* (On the women's movement) in the same year.

Powerful personalities and a tragic sense of individuality lay at the core of the realist novels Nováková was to write between 1898 and 1910. In *Jan Jíle*k (1898), *Jiří Šmatlán* (1900), *Na Librově gruntě* (On Libra's farm, 1901) and *Drašar* (1910), Nováková created almost Wagnerian protagonists struggling to maintain their integrity and freedom. Eastern Bohemia provided Nováková with the source material from which she drew a host of archetypal characters and provincial settings for both her novels and her stories, the latter published in the collections *Úlomky žuly* (Fragments of granite, 1902) and *Z kamenité stezky* (From the stony path, 1908). In her stories, unlike her novels, the main characters were women. Her admiration for Wagner (which brought her to Bayreuth at the end of her life) generated a number of symbolist texts such as *Výkřiky a vzdechy* (Screams and groans, 1911), a particularly strong example of what Nováková herself would have regarded as 'female modernism' in which pessimism is overcome through the grandeur of woman's tragedy, her symbiosis with nature and through her ability to sacrifice for love.

One of the most influential Czech women writers, Teréza Nováková was a feminist who began by accepting women's traditional roles, later challenging them and finally, by the end of her life, embracing a utopian mystique of womanhood. She died in Prague on 13 November 1912.

Libuše Heczková
Charles University of Prague

SOURCES

(A) *Literární archiv Památníku národního písemnictví. Literání pozůstalost Terézy Novákové a Arne Nováka* (National Literary Archive, legacy of T. Nováková and Arne Novák), *uspoř* (inventory) by Karol Bilek. Prague, PNP 2000.
(B) *Domácí hospodyně* (Housewife) (Olomouc, 1883-1893).
(B) *Žensky svět* (Women's world) (Prague, 1896-1930).
(B) *Přehled* (Overview) (Prague, 1902-1914).
(C) Svadbová, Blanka, ed. *Z lidské sonáty. Teréza Nováková: Korespondence* (On the human sonata. Teréza Nováková: correspondence). Prague: Odeon, 1988.
(C) Nováková, Teréza. *Ze ženského hnutí* (On the women's movement). Prague: Přehled, 1912.
(E) Novák, Arne. *Czech Literature*. Michigan: Ann Arbor, 1976 (1986).
(E) Opelík, J., ed. *Lexikon české literatury. Osobnosti, díla, instituce, díl III.* (Lexicon of Czech literature. Personalities, works, institutions, t. III). Prague: Academia, 2000.
(E) Hayes, Kathleen. "Introduction: Concepts of Woman and the 'Woman Question' at the Fin de Siècle." In Katleen Hayes, ed. *A World Apart and Other Stories–Czech Women Writers at the Fin de Siècle*. Prague: Karolinum, 2001.
(F) http://www.hn.psu.edu/faculty/jmanis/h-ibsen/pillars-society.pdf

ORZESZKOWA, Eliza (1841–1910)

Polish fiction writer, novelist and publicist; literary pseudonyms: 'E. O.,' 'Bąk (z Wa-Lit-No),' 'Li...ka' (i.e. *Litwinka,* meaning Lithuanian woman) and 'Gabriela Litwinka.'

Eliza (real name Elżbieta) Orzeszkowa, *nee* Pawłowska (second married name Nahorska) was born on 6 June 1841 into a well-off noble family on the family estate of Milkowszczyzna (approx. forty km from Grodno; located in territory annexed to the Russian empire, but not part of the Polish Kingdom established in 1815). She was the youngest daughter of Benedykt Pawłowski (1788–1843) and his second wife, Franciszka born Kamieńska (ca. 1814–1878). Eliza's father, a lawyer by profession and Chairman of the district court of Grodno, was a man of high intellectual culture, a freethinker and a Freemason. Eliza and her older sister Klementyna (1838–1851) were brought up by their maternal grandmother, Elżbieta Kamieńska born Kaszuba. Eliza kept in contact with her mother, who in 1849 remarried (to Konstanty Widacki) and did not devote much time to her daughters. Initially, Eliza was educated at home by a governess. Then from 1852 to 1857, she attended the Catholic convent girls' school of the *Sakramentki; Benedyktynki od Nieustającej Adoracji Najświętszego Sakramentu* (Benedictins of Perpetual Adoration of the Holy Sacrament) in Warsaw, where she received an education typical for girls of her class. Shortly after her return home, she consented to a marriage arranged by her mother to Piotr Orzeszko (ca. 1825–1874), a landowner several years her senior. Following the marriage in Grodno, on 21 January 1858, Orzeszkowa moved to her husband's residence in Ludwinowo (in the Kobryn district). The marriage turned out to be a failure, and Orzeszkowa tried to leave her husband, later returning to him at her mother's request. She was in Ludwinowo when the 1863 January Insurrection against the Russian occupation broke out, which she immediately joined. Together with other women involved in the Insurrection, she delivered insurgent mail and distributed food. At her husband's residence in Ludwinowo, she sheltered the wounded and harbored Romuald Traugutt, later to become a leader of the Insurrection. In the autumn of 1863, Orzeszkowa's husband, indicted by the Russian authorities for helping the Insurgents, was arrested and exiled to Ossa (Russia, the province of Perm) in 1865. Early in 1864,

Orzeszkowa returned to her family home (Milkowszczyzna). In 1867, she requested consistorial abrogation of her marriage, which she received in 1869. The direct motivation for this request was her affection for Zygmunt Święcicki (1836–1910), a doctor whom she had met at Ludwinowo.

During her stay at Milkowszczyzna, Orzeszkowa immersed herself in modern literature on the natural and social sciences, philosophy and history (among other subjects). She subscribed to Polish and foreign papers and took an interest in new literary trends. In 1866, she made her literary debut with a novella, *Obrazek z lat głodowych* (A picture of the hungry years). In this period, she also composed several short stories and ten novels, six of which were published; the most significant of these were *Pan Graba* (Mr Graba, 1869–1870) and *Ostatnia miłość* (The last love, 1867), which raised the then daring topic of unsuccessful marriage and women's right to divorce. Around 1869, a new love entered her life in the form of a private solicitor, Stanisław Nahorski (1826–1896). Their relationship was legalized only in 1894, shortly after the death of Nahorski's first wife. In 1869, Orzeszkowa moved to Grodno, where she lived in a rented flat. In 1870, due to family debts, she sold the Milkowszczyzna estate.

Orzeszkowa's thought was greatly influenced by the Warsaw Positivists (a group of Polish publicists and writers fascinated by the ideas of Western liberalism). Since writing was becoming an additional source of income for her, she was able to develop her own ideas as a professional writer. She was interested in Jewish issues, to which she devoted her novels *Eli Makower* (1874) and *Meir Ezofowicz* (1878), as well as the short stories "Daj kwiatek" (Give a flower, 1877) and "Silny Samson" (Strong Samson, 1877). The Jewish theme, together with the idea of the assimilation of Polish Jews, would surface frequently in her writings over the following decades.

One of Orzeszkowa's major treatises in this period—*Kilka słów o kobietach* (A few words about women, 1870)—analyzes modern methods used in girls' education, with particular reference to the works of Herbert Spencer and with the deliberate omission of religion, which was then a core element of the educational system. She emphasized the necessity of overcoming restrictions on women imposed by cultural norms; what she saw as the physical and psychological weaknesses of women were, in her view, a consequence of defective upbringing rather than inherent in nature. Orzeszkowa thus considered a comprehensive education to be essential for women's development, enabling them to take up professional work and obtain financial self-sufficiency. Only then, she argued, would marriage no longer be regarded the sole means of material support for women. That women had the right to education, professional work and independence was, for Orzeszkowa, an integral element of 'the new human being,' conceived as a broad social project. She did not distance herself from men, nor decry patriarchal culture. The emancipation project presented in *Kilka słów o kobietach* did not envisage a revolution of manners, but consisted in a rejection of passive femininity. This study, along with her novel *Martha* (1873), which depicted the lack of woman's independence as a thorny social issue, won her a reputation as an advocate of women's emancipation in Poland.

In the 1880s, Orzeszkowa wrote a number of prose works in which she created many interesting portraits of women: *Niziny* (The underdogs, 1884); *Dziurdziowie* (The Dziurdzia family, 1885); *Nad Niemnem* (On the banks of the Niemen, 1887); *Cham* (The boor, 1888) and *Bene nati* (published a few years later, in 1891). From 1880, she worked on an ambitiously conceived but never completed historical study of the social standing of women across diverse cultures. In 1881, she wrote an essay "O kobiecie polskiej" (On Polish woman), of which an abridged form entitled "Poland" and signed "Elise Oresko" was included in *The Woman Question in Europe*, compiled by Theodore Stanton (1884). In this essay, Orzeszkowa related the contemporary emancipatory aspirations of Polish women to their high social standing in pre-partitioned Poland. She returned to the role of the woman-citizen in the history of Poland in her essay "O Polce Francuzom" (To Frenchmen on Polish woman), which the editor of the French periodical *Revue des Revues* commissioned from her in 1897. In 1884, she began writing a column for the Warsaw women's weekly *Świt* (Dawn) called "Listy o sprawach kobiet" (Letters regarding women's concerns), in which she demanded, among other things, access to higher education for women and public patronage for poor women studying abroad. In the 1890s, she wrote on 'the woman question' in the feminist periodical *Ster* (Helm), published in Lviv by ***Paulina Kuczalska-Reinschmit***.

In 1891, on the occasion of the 25th anniversary of Orzeszkowa's writing career, feminists in Warsaw organized an illegal convention of representatives from every group of Polish women from every Polish province, across diverse social communities. Congratulatory letters were sent to Grodno from feminist organizations from various countries and particular interest in Orzeszkowa's writings was shown by German women. In 1892, in response to this interest, she submitted an open letter, "W kwestii równouprawnienia kobiet wobec nauki, pracy i dostojności ludzkiej" (On the question of women's equality in education, work and human dignity) to Lina Morgernstern in Berlin and to Marie Stritt, President of the *Neue Frauen Reform* in Dresden. In this open letter, Orzeszkowa presented her current views on the emancipation movement, arguing that educated and conscious women were to morally improve society as a whole and to strengthen its proper ethical and civic attitudes.

A sign of her increasing literary prestige was her nomination for the Nobel Prize for Literature in 1904. Between 1904 and 1908, various celebrations were held in Orzeszkowa's honor, the most important of these undoubtedly being the Polish Women's Congress in Warsaw (9–11 June 1907), which she was unable to attend due to illness. Again, many congratulatory letters were received from abroad (including letters from the Russian Women's Equal Rights Union, the Central Association of Czech Women, the Association of French Women and the Swedish Women's Union). However since Orzeszkowa's emancipation program advocated a particular civic stance based on the philosophical categories of 'rights' and 'duties,' without demanding deeper reforms of manners, it was criticized at the 1907 Congress by younger Polish feminists, who thought her approach outdated.

In 1905, in the wake of revolutionary movements among the intelligentsia and working-class men and women, Orzeszkowa used her writing to wage a battle for the political rights of women. She demanded, among other things, that women in Lithuania be allowed to work in local self-governments–see her "O sprawiedliwość" (For justice, 1905) and "List do Wujaszka" (Letter to uncle, 1905)–and vote in the Russian *Duma*. Prior to the election of the First State *Duma*, a proclamation issued in the Vilnius press, "Do wyborców i wybrańców naszych Ziem i Miast" (To the electors and privileged of our lands and towns, 1906), appeared alongside Orzeszkowa's open letter and her article "Frazes" (The platitude, 1906). She was also involved in a campaign to introduce the Polish language in schools and offices–see her "List otwarty do społeczeństwa rosyjskiego" (Open letter to the Russian people, 1905). In 1907, she became the literary supervisor of the Vilnius daily *Kurier Litewski* (Lithuanian courier), retaining this position until the end of her life. In addition to her literary and publicist work, she also participated in philanthropic and social enterprises: she delivered a series of secret lectures to young women on the literature and history of Poland; she took young women between the ages of sixteen and nineteen into her home and organized education programs for them; she supported child welfare initiatives, especially on behalf of the Jewish poor, and she applied to influential financiers for scholarships for talented Polish youth. Her home at Grodno, open to all visitors, was a center of Polish culture which radiated across the town and its vicinity. Orzeszkowa was one of the best, most prolific Polish epistolographers of the nineteenth century and left over ten volumes of letters (the majority of which has been published). She spent the last months of her life chair- and bedridden. She died on 18 May 1910 at her home in Grodno. She had no children. All her life she was an ardent advocate of the social and political emancipation of women.

Iwona Wiśniewska
Institute of Literary
Research of the Polish Academy of Sciences, Warsaw

SOURCES

(A) *Instytut Badań Literackich Polskiej Akademii Nauk w Warszawie* (Institute of Literary Research of the Polish Academy of Sciences, Warsaw), Eliza Orzeszkowa Archives.

(C) Oresko, Elise (Eliza Orzeszkowa). "Poland." In Theodore Stanton, ed. *The Woman Question in Europe. A Series of Original Essays*. New York / London / Paris, 1884, 424–445.

(C) Orzeszkowa, Eliza. *Listy zebrane* (Collected letters). E. Jankowski, ed. Vols. 1-9. Wrocław: Zakład Narodowy im. Ossolińskich, 1954–1981.

(C) Orzeszkowa, Eliza. *O sobie...* (About myself...). Warsaw: Czytelnik, 1974.

(D) Jankowski, E. *Eliza Orzeszkowa*. Warsaw: Państwowy Instytut Wydawniczy, 1964.

(D) Żmigrodzka, M. *Orzeszkowa. Młodość pozytywizmu* (Orzeszkowa. The early years of positivism). Warsaw: Instytut Badań Literackich PAN, 1965.

(D) Żmigrodzka, M. "Eliza Orzeszkowa 1841-1910." In *Obraz literatury polskiej w XIX i XX wieku* (A review of Polish literature in the nineteenth and twentieth centuries). Series 4, vol. 2. Warsaw: Państwowe Wydawnictwo Naukowe, 1966.

(D) Jankowski, E. "Eliza Orzeszkowa." In *Polski Słownik Biograficzny* (Polish biographical dictionary), vol. 24. Warsaw: Zakład Narodowy im. Ossolińskich, 1979.

(D) Gacowa, H. "Eliza Orzeszkowa, Bibliografia Literatury Polskiej" (Eliza Orzeszkowa, bibliography of Polish literature). *Nowy Korbut* (New Korbut) 17, no. 2. Wrocław: Zakład Narodowy im. Ossolińskich, 1999.

(D) Borkowska, G. Introduction to *E. Orzeszkowa, Publicystyka społeczna* (E. Orzeszkowa, social journalism), 2005 (forthcoming).

(E) Borkowska, G. *Cudzoziemki. Studia o polskiej prozie kobiecej* (Alien women. Studies in Polish women's prose). Warsaw: Instytut Badań Literackich PAN, 1996.

(E) Górnicka-Boratyńska, A. *Stańmy się sobą. Cztery projekty emancypacji (1863-1939)* (Let us become ourselves. Four projects of emancipation, 1863-1939). Izabelin: "Świat Literacki," 2001.

OVADYA, Haim Estreya (1922-1944)

Macedonian woman of Jewish origin who worked for the emancipation of Jewish women and lost her life as a partisan fighter of the Macedonian Army during the antifascist war against the Bulgarian Army.

Haim Estreya Ovadya, August 1944 (shortly before her death on August 26) as a political commissar of a battalion on Mount Kajmakchalan

Born in Bitola on 25 December 1922, into a very poor family (no data regarding her parents exists), Estreya Ovadya was a member of the Bitola *Ženska Internacionalna Cionisticka Organizacija* (*ZICO*, Women's International Zionist Organization/WIZO) which, in accordance with Jewish traditions, provided impoverished girls with dowries and/or opportunities for education, thereby enabling them to support themselves.

In 1934, an antifascist and women's rights activist, Julia Batino (born in Bitola 1914-died in Jasenovac concentration camp, Croatia 1942) was made President of the Bitola *ZICO*. The organization became actively involved in the progressive women's movement in Yugoslavia and Batino herself directed her energies towards the emancipation of Jewish women, with a special emphasis on young women. Her connections to the Jewish community in Belgrade enabled her to send a certain number of girls to work or receive an education in Belgrade each year. This was how Estreya Ovadya, along with a group of young women from Bitola, arrived in Belgrade in 1938.

Ovadya soon adjusted to life in the Yugoslav capital. She joined the progressive Workers' Movement–a faction of the Communist Party of Yugoslavia that participated in the *URS-Ujedinjeni radnički sindikati Jugoslavije* (United Workers' Syndicates of Yugoslavia)–and became involved in the movement's women's sections, which organized lectures on syndical and women's economic and political rights.

Returning to her native town of Bitola after a German bombing raid on Belgrade (6 April 1941), Ovadya was forced to live in a ghetto under anti-Semitic legislation implemented in Macedonia immediately after the Bulgarian Occupation of 18 April 1941. Her antifascist beliefs led her, in May 1941, to become involved in preparations for what became known as the Antifascist and People's Liberation War of the Macedonians (1941–1945), fought together with the Allies (the USA, USSR and Great Britain) and the Resistance Movement in Europe. At the same time, Estreya Ovadya devotedly worked on the liberation of young Jewish women from restrictions imposed by family codes. She formed small groups of (mostly young) women–workers, high-school students and housewives–with whom she wished to share the knowledge and experience she had gained while in Belgrade. They debated and discussed women's rights to education, to free choice of employment and to the free choice of a husband or partner. Estreya Ovadya became a member of the Communist Party of Yugoslavia in 1942.

The humiliations suffered in the ghetto seem to have inspired Ovadya to organize Jewish youth resistance and encourage their participation in the antifascist and liberation war–a highly perilous activity. On 11 March 1943, the Jews of Skopje, Bitola and Stip were deported and 7,240 of them were taken to the Treblinka II death camp in Poland. On 10 March 1943, prior to the deportation of 3,276 Jews from Bitola, the Central Committee of the Communist Party of Macedonia gave the Jewish community advance warning of the deportation. Shelters were organized, as well as connections to the partisan units, but only a few Jews made use of these opportunities, unable to believe that a program for their destruction was really underway and preferring to stay together as a group. Estreya Ovadya, Adela Feradji, Zhamila Kolonomos, Stela Levi and Rosa Kamhi (among others) went into hiding and the group was accommodated in the clandestine shelter of the resistance movement and the Communist Party of Yugoslavia/Communist Party of Macedonia's Local Committee in Bitola, located in a small room belonging to the shop of Bogoja Siljanovski, a member of the antifascist resistance. While the Bitola deportation was in process, the Damjan Gruev partisan unit from Bitola offered Jews in hiding the opportunity to join the partisan unit as fighters. As a result of the poor living conditions, Ovadya had fallen sick but she nevertheless insisted on joining the partisan struggle. In April 1943 she, together with three of the four Jewish girls who had been hiding in the village of Kanino (in the region of Bitola), were taken by a partisan courier to join the Damjan Gruev unit and collect their uniforms and partisan names: 'Estreya Ovadya-Mara;' 'Zhamila Kolonomos-Cveta;' 'Adela Feradji-Kata' and 'Estreya Levi-Lena.' On 23 May 1943, Estreya Ovadya-Mara was out on the battlefield with a newly founded partisan unit, Goce Delcev. She participated in combat, showing exceptional courage. One co-fighter later remembered her as his wonderful friend "courageous nurse Mara" (Dimovski-Colev 1993).

Ovadya applied her experiences on the battlefield to her work as a member of the Stiv Naumov Battalion right from its inception on 11 November 1943. She was delegated by the Battalion to address young people (especially women) in the liberated territories, and audiences received speeches by the popular "partisan Mara" with great interest (Vesković-Vangeli and Jovanović eds. 1976, 351, 448). Soon after, the Battalion became part of the Third Macedonian Brigade and Ovadya was appointed political commissar of her squad. Her unit helped organize the *Antifašističko sobranie na narodnoto osloboduvanje na Makedonija* (*ASNOM*, the Antifascist Assembly of the People's Liberation of Macedonia) held at the St. Prohor Pcinski monastery on *Ilinden* (Orthodox Christian holiday) on 2 August 1944, when the contemporary Republic of Macedonia was founded.

On 21 August 1944, the Headquarters of the People's Liberation Army and the partisan units in Macedonia established the 7th Macedonian Brigade, also known as the Bitola Brigade (because the majority of the fighters were either from Bitola or the surrounding region). Ovadya received a high position in the partisan hierarchy and was appointed commissar of a battalion. Four days later, on 26 August 1944, she died in a bitter clash with the Bulgarian army in Kajmakchalan.

Estreya Ovadya was declared a National Hero of Yugoslavia for the courage she displayed in the Macedonian Antifascist and Liberation War. Her name has been commemorated in a folk song–"...Pomnete ja braka/i Estreya Mara/Estreya Mara/za narod zagina/za Makedonija..." (Remember brothers/Estreya Mara/Estreya Mara died for the people/for Macedonia...). The city of Bitola erected a monument in her honor and named a kindergarten and a street after her (other streets throughout Macedonia also bear her name). Ovadya, who came from a strictly patriarchal family, combined her work for the liberation of Macedonia from fascist occupation during World War II with a commitment to women's emancipation. Today, she is remembered for her dedication to both causes.

Prof. Dr. Vera Vesković-Vangeli
Senior Scientific Researcher,
Institute of National History, Skopje

Translated from the Macedonian by Nevenka Grceva, MA student, Department of Gender Studies, Central European University, Budapest.

SOURCES

(A) Macedonian State Archives, Jewish Community Collection.

(B) Vesković-Vangeli, Vera and Marija Jovanović, eds. *Zbornik na dokumenti za učestvoto na ženite od Makedonija vo Narodnoosloboditelnata vojna i revolucijata 1941-1945* (A collection of documents on women's participation in the People's Liberation War 1941-1945). Skopje: Institut za nacionalna istorija & Konferencija za opstestvena aktivnost na zenite na Makedonija (Institute of National History, Conference on the Social Activities of the Women in Macedonia), 1976.

(B) Kolomonos, Zhamila and Vera Vesković-Vangeli. *Evreite vo Makedonija vo Vtorata Svetska vojna (1941-1945)* (Macedonian Jews in World War II, 1941-1945). Documents Digest. Vols. I/II. Skopje: Makedonska akademija na naukite i umetnostite (Macedonian Academy of Sciences and Arts), 1986.

(E) Matkovski, Aleksandar. *Istorija na Evreite vo Makedonija* (A history of the Macedonian Jews). Skopje: Makedonska revija (Macedonian review), 1983.
(E) Dimovski-Colev, Gorgi. *Bitolskite Evrei–Lus Gidjos di Monastir* (The Jews from Bitola). Bitola: Drustvo za nauka i umetnosti (Society of Science and Arts), 1993.
(E) Tomovski, Mirce and Eftim Kletnikov. *Iskusenijata na Davidovata zvezda* (The temptations of the Star of David). Skopje: Menora, 2002.

ÖZTUNALI, Nurser (1947–1999)

Turkish architect, city planner, publisher; leading activist of the 'second wave' feminist movement in Turkey; founder (1984) of the *Kadın Çevresi Yayınları* (Women's Circle Publications); founder (1990) of the *Mor Çatı Kadın Sığınağı Vakfı* (Purple Roof Women's Shelter Foundation); founder (1995) and member of the *Mimarlık Vakfı* (Architecture Foundation).

Nurser Öztunalı was born on 4 February 1947 in Mersin, the eldest daughter of a middle-class family from Istanbul. Her father, Hilmi Öztunalı (1924–1990), was a customs officer; her mother, Semiha (b. 1927; maiden name Balcı), a housewife. Nurser Öztunalı had two sisters: Gülser (1952), a feminist academic and Eser (1956), an export manager. Gülser is currently a professor in the Department of Public Administration at Akdeniz University and an activist in the Turkish feminist movement (a volunteer with the Purple Roof Foundation). Öztunalı lived in Istanbul from the age of three and graduated from the *Fatih Kız Lisesi* (Fatih Girls' High School) with honours in 1968. She majored in architecture (1972) at the Fine Arts State Academy. In 1969, while still a university student, she married a doctor, Ali Şevket Bürkev (b. 1945). The couple had two daughters: Amila (1974–1996) and Beyza (b. 1970).

In the authoritarian and depoliticizing aftermath of the 1980 Military Coup–when political and social opposition had been subdued and every movement for freedom had been driven underground–Nurser joined other leftist women in publicly defining themselves as feminists and carrying out feminist political activity. After divorcing her husband (1981) on the grounds that "she had experienced systematic physical violence in her marriage" (Öztunalı, personal archival collection, doc. no. 10/2), Öztunalı's small office became a center for the new feminist movement in Turkey: a forum for heated ideological and political debates; a meeting place for consciousness-raising groups; a publishing house for feminist publications and pamphlets and a headquarters for activists planning protest activities.

Öztunalı was among the 35 women in Istanbul to set up the *Kadın Çevresi Yayınları* (Women's Circle Publications) in 1984. The Women's Circle translated and published feminist books and articles with the aim of raising women's awareness of women's issues and sexism in Turkish society. This explicitly feminist and independent publishing project responded to an increasing demand for theoretical and political knowledge about feminism. The 'feminist enlightenment' that Öztunalı herself experienced in the 1980s as an architect changed her perspective on her profession and she began contributing to the development of a new sensibility regarding women's needs in the fields of architecture and city planning. Arguing for, and applying 'woman-friendly' approaches, Öztunalı initiated and contributed to the realization of a number of architectural projects as the founder (in 1995) of the *Mimarlık Vakfı* (Architecture Foundation). Throughout the 1980s and early 1990s, feminists began addressing women's subordination–particularly in the private sphere–and politicizing problems relating to women's identities 'as women.' Öztunalı was among the first to talk publicly (and therefore courageously) about violence against women, especially domestic violence. She openly declared that, despite being an educated and professional woman of relatively high social status, she had been systematically beaten by her husband throughout her married life and she urged women to unite and say 'No!' to all forms of violence.

By 1987, the information and experience accumulated in the early 1980s–a "period of ideological preparation" (Tekeli 1989, 36)–had become a full-blown political movement in the form of campaigns and mass demonstrations. It was Öztunalı who gave the name "The Campaign against Wife Beating" to the impressive campaign against violence waged in Istanbul that year. Large numbers of women from a number of cities participated. For her part, Öztunalı argued tirelessly for a united stand among women against wife-beating, sexual harassment and sex discrimination. The campaign against violence against women was a real turning point in the development of the women's movement: it helped render 'taboo' subjects visible; it disseminated critical discussion beyond the big cities and redefined domestic violence, rape, incest and sexual harassment in the workplace as salient problems in Turkish society, thus contributing to a further politicization of the private sphere. For Öztunalı, the campaign was an important part of the broader struggle to educate women to resist violence, question their personal situations, talk frankly about the violence they may have been subjected to, demand their rights and be empowered to start new lives on their own terms.

One outcome of "The Campaign against Wife Beating" was a shelter for battered women. The *Mor Çatı Kadın Sığınağı Vakfı* (Purple Roof Women's Shelter Foundation) was set up in 1990 as an independent civil society institution that aimed to introduce the notion of women's shelters to Turkey. Öztunalı was one of its founders and also worked as a volunteer under 'the Purple Roof.' One of the most committed feminist activists in terms of organizing street demonstrations and other protests, she also reviewed the theoretical implications of her work, aiming to develop feminist theories that could complement feminist practice. Her manuscripts, kept in the archives of the *Kadın Kütüphanesi ve Bilgi Merkezi Özel Arşiv Bölümü* (Women's Library and Information Center) in Istanbul, constitute an important source of information on feminist debates of the time and shed light on the difficulties faced by activists seeking to raise feminist awareness and organize feminist campaigns.

Öztunalı, who had worked tirelessly as an activist from 1981 to 1996, retreated from the public domain following the death of her youngest daughter, Almila Bürkev (who fell off a balcony at her home in 1996). Nurser Öztunalı died of a heart attack at her home in Istanbul on 28 February 1999. Right up until her death, she had continued to serve as a volunteer with the Purple Roof Collective. Her life and struggle stand witness to, and reflect the history of 'second wave' feminism (or 'new' feminism) in Turkey. Öztunalı, along with other leading feminist women, contributed to the establishment of feminism as a political and indigeneous phenomenon in Turkey in the period spanning 1981 to 1996. She regarded feminist theory and practice as tools to be made available to women from all walks of life (i.e. beyond relatively small numbers of activists) and, by drawing attention to the problems of domestic violence and sexual harassment, helped transform women's private experiences into burning public issues. Her work paved the way for the establishment of a strong social pressure group for women's rights able to address deeper, more pervasive issues than those of 'equal rights,' and facilitate the eventual institutionalization of the feminist movement.

Sevgi Uçan Çubukçu
University of Istanbul

SOURCES

(A) *Kadın Kütüphanesi ve Bilgi Merkezi Özel Arşiv Bölümü* (Women's Library and Information Center in Istanbul, Department of Personal Archives). Nurser Öztunalı's manuscripts, doc. no. 3/2.

(A) *Mor Çatı Kadın Sığınağı Vakfı Arşivi* (Archive of the Purple Roof Foundation). Nurser Öztunalı's personal archival collection, doc. no. 10/2.

(A) *Mor Çatı Kadın Sığınağı Vakfı Arşivi* (Archive of the Purple Roof Foundation). Nurser Öztunalı's manuscripts, doc. no. 10/3, Notes on "Nurser Öztunalı's Contributions to the Women's Movement" by her sister, feminist activist and academician Gülser Kayır (15 October 2004).

(A) *Mimarlık Vakfı Arşivi* (Archive of the Architecture Foundation). Nurser Öztunalı's personal manuscripts, doc. no. 17.

(C) Öztunalı, Nurser. "Gönüllünün Not Defteri" (Notebook of a volunteer). In *Evdeki Terör, Kadına Yönelik Şiddet* (Terror at home, violence against women). Istanbul: Mor Çatı Yayınları (Purple Roof Publications), November 1996.

(D) Interview with Nurser Öztunalı's daughter, Beyza Bürkev (Istanbul, 16 October 2004). Unpublished.

(E) Tekeli, Şirin. "80'lerde Türkiye'de Kadının Kurtuluşu Hareketi'nin Gelişmesi" (The development of the women's liberation movement in Turkey in the '80s). *Birikim Dergisi* (Birikim journal), no. 3 (July 1989): 34–41.

(E) Uçan, Sevgi (Yöney). The Turkish feminist movement in the '80s. A study of two feminist journals: *Kaktüs* and *Feminist*. Master Thesis. Istanbul: Boğaziçi University, 1995.

(E) Uçan Çubukçu, Sevgi. "Contribution to Substantial Democracy: Non-Governmental Women's Organisations in Turkey." In Fatmagül Berktay, ed. *The Position of Women in Turkey and in the European Union: Achievements, Problems, Prospects*. Istanbul: Kader Press, 2004.

PAJK, Pavlina (born Doljak) (1854-1901)

Slovenian poet, author and pioneer of Slovenian 'literary feminism.'

Pavlina Doljak was born on 9 April 1854 in Pavia (Italy), where her father Josip Doljak (from Grgar near Gorizia) was a judge and (after 1848) a member of the Viennese Parliament. Her mother, Pavlina Milharčič, was the daughter of a school inspector and teacher from Gorizia who prior to her marriage had been a lady-in-waiting. She died in 1857 in Milano, following the birth of her fourth child, a daughter called Teodolina. Two years later, Josip Doljak, his son Teodor and three daughters Pavlina, Henrieta, and Teodolina (1857-?), moved to Trieste, where Josip died in 1861.

After the death of Josip Doljak, his brother Matija Doljak assumed responsibility for the children and their education. He was a landowner, a member of the provincial assembly and the Mayor of Solkan (near Gorizia). He was also the founder of the Slovene reading society in Gorizia and one of the initiators of the Slovene national movement in the Gorizia region. At the age of eleven, after finishing the Ursuline boarding school in Gorizia, Pavlina took over the housework in her uncle's house, where she met prominent Slovene politicians and writers who aroused her interest in art and culture. Her education and artistic endeavors were further influenced by her friendship with Karel Lavrič, an attorney-at-law. A widely read person and nationalist, Lavrič became her mentor, encouraging her to read Slovene poetry and prose. Pavlina also widened her horizons by reading German and Italian classics. In 1873, her brother Teodor finished his law studies and received employment at the Gorizia court of justice. Pavlina and her sisters moved in with him and she took care of the housework. Teodor Doljak saw his sister's cultural activities as dangerous since, from the 1870s onwards, rivalry between the Italian and Slovene national camps in Gorizia was increasing in severity. Pavlina Doljak had to publish her first writings anonymously. On 19 June 1872, she published her first short novel *Prva ljubezen* (First love) in the Slovene gazette *Soča* (Isonzo–the name of a river). Three months later, she published the article "Ženska v družini" (Woman in the family). In these early works she emphasized female sensitivity and criticized the restrictions on women's freedom in patriarchal society.

In writing for the literary gazette *Zora* (Dawn), edited in Maribor by Janko Pajk, Pavlina Doljak's literary creativity was released, turning towards romantic idealism. In *Zora* she published her first poems (1874) and the autobiographical prose "Odlomki iz ženskega dnevnika" (Excerpts from a woman's diary, 1876), as well as biographical notes on the contemporary French writer George Sand. In 1877, *Zora* published her "Ženska pisma prijatelju" (A woman's letters to a friend) as a feuilleton. In addition to her literary working relationship with Janko Pajk, the two developed a private friendship as well. They were married on 26 February 1876, one year after the death of Janko Pajk's first wife, Marija Wellner. In December 1876, their first son Milan was born. Janko's daughter from his first marriage was also part of the family. After their marriage, the couple lived in Maribor, where Janko had a good reputation as a successful editor and publisher and Pavlina was known as a promising artist, coeditor of *Zora* and a supporter of women's emancipation. But in the politically conservative and narrow-minded bourgeois atmosphere of Maribor, their public activities soon became the object of public disapproval. When *Zora* published "Razgovori" (Conversations) with Pavlina, the reproach became worse. The relatives of Janko's first wife withdrew most of the financial support that his deceased wife had left him, thereby forcing him to give up editing the gazette.

The end of her husband's editing and publishing career changed Pavlina's life as well. When, in 1877, her husband had to accept state employment and move to Reid, a period of isolation and increased amount of housework began for Pavlina, continuing even after she followed her husband to a new placement in Grätz, later to Brno. In Grätz, she gave birth to a daughter (1878) who died soon afterwards. In Brno their second son, Božidar, was born. Even during these hard times, Pavlina did not give up writing and kept publishing in Slovene literary gazettes, mostly prose. In 1878, she published a book of poems, *Pesmi* (Poems).

When her husband was transferred to Vienna, a somewhat quieter and more productive period began for Pavlina. In Viennese circles she could meet important Slovene writers and intellectuals and take part in cultural and social events in the Viennese Slovenski klub (Slovene Club). On 13 January 1894, she held a lecture entitled "Aforizmi o ženstvu" (Aphorisms on womanhood), published in the gazette *Dom in svet* (Home and world) later that year. During her 'Viennese period,' she wrote several novels, including *Roman starega samca* (The old bachelor's novel, 1895), *Dušne borbe* (Soul battles, 1896), *Judita* (Judith, 1896) and *Slučaji usode* (Twists of fate, 1897). She also wrote numerous stories and short novels that were published in the most prominent Slovene literary gazettes of the time, including *Ljubljanski zvon* (The Ljubljana bell). In 1893, *Dom in svet* published the first volume of her *Zbrani spisi* (Collected writings).

Despite numerous publications in notable Slovene literary gazettes and her friendship with influent editors, such as Franc Levec and Fran Lampe, Pavlina Pajk did not win the approval of Slovene literary circles. In 1885, Slovenska matica (the central

Slovene publishing house) turned down her novel *Arabela* (Arabella) and refused to publish her later works. When naturalism became the predominant literary tendency in Slovene writing, critics started to reproach Pavlina for her sentiment and idealism. Nevertheless, Pavlina Pajk remained an adherent of romanticism even after holding public debates with Slovene naturalist writers such as Fran Govekar.

As a woman poet and author, Pavlina Pajk was among the first to bring women's issues into the Slovene public sphere. In 1884, she published "Nekoliko besedic o ženskem vprašanju najprej" (First a few words on the woman question) in the gazette *Kres*, published in Gorizia as a monograph later that year. In this treatise she called for better education for women, including married women. She was in favor of elementary education for rural women, as well as access to higher education and employment opportunities in the educational, administrative and medical professions for unmarried women. She argued for sexual equality, referring to the values of liberty, progress and social welfare. Her public discussions supported women's involvement in Slovenian cultural and political life and helped pave the way for organized women's activity. Pavlina Pajk died of pneumonia on 1 June 1901 at the age of 47. That same year, a group of women founded the *Splošno žensko društvo* (General Women's Association) in Ljubljana.

Marta Verginella
Departmant of History,
University of Ljubljana (Slovenia)

Translation from the Slovenian: Jaka Andrej Vojevec.

SOURCES

(C) Pajk, Pavlina. *Iz spisov Pavline Pajkove* (From the work of Pavlina Pajk). Gorica: Goriška tiskarna, 1894.

(D) "Pajkova, Pavlina." In *Slovenski biografski leksikon* (Slovenian biographical dictionary). Ljubljana, 1933–1952, 2: 257–259.

(D) Pešak Mikec, Barbara. "Pavlina Pajk. Zagovornica ženske emancipacije" (Pavlina Pajk: supporter of women's emancipation). In Nataša Budna Kodrič and Aleksandra Serše, eds. *Splošno žensko društvo: 1901–1945* (The General Women's Society). Ljubljana: Arhiv Republike Slovenije, 2003, 63–72.

PANTELEEVA, Serafima (1846–1918)

Russian feminist, physiologist and popular science writer.

Serafima Latkina was born in 1846 in St Petersburg and brought up in a relatively well-to-do Russian Orthodox family. Her father, Vasilii Latkin (1812–1867), grew up in Ust'-Sysol'sk, a small town located in a remote northern province of European Russia and made his fortune as a result of a successful expedition to gold fields in Siberia. Serafima fondly remembered her father in her memoirs. Nothing is known about her mother. The lives of her siblings were also closely connected to the Siberian gold industry: her brother Nikolai Latkin (1832–1904) pursued the same line of business as his father and her sister married a prosperous gold field owner, Mikhail Sidorov. Serafima spent her childhood in a progressive, urban, intellectual household. In the early 1860s, her uncle, Petr Latkin, hosted gatherings of democratically minded young people at his home, as many progressives then did. It was at one such gathering that Serafima Latkina met her future husband, Longin Panteleev (1840–1919), a former law student at St Petersburg University and a frequent visitor to her uncle's home. They married when Serafima was just eighteen and remained in the capital, where Panteleev prepared himself for his final examinations and also ran a printing press owned by a popular local publisher, Nikolai Tiblen. Born into the impoverished noble family of an army officer and brought up in Vologda, Panteleev belonged to the growing body of poor students flooding into universities liberalized in the aftermath of the Crimean War (1853–1856). He had been active in the radical underground for some years and would later become a prominent progressive publicist and publisher. Serafima Latkina's relationship with Longin Panteleev was a supportive one, their marriage lasting for the duration of their lives.

Following a reversal of liberal university policies and a wave of reactionary measures, Longin Panteleev's participation in the student disturbances in the fall of 1861 brought him under the suspicion of the tsarist authorities, as did his involvement in the clandestine circle *Zemlia i Volia* (Land and Freedom)–inspired by the ideas of Alexander Hertsen (1812–1870), Nikolai Ogarev (1813–1877) and Nikolai Chernyshevskii (1828–1889). In December 1864, when Serafima Panteleeva was expecting their first child, her husband was arrested for revolutionary activity in connection with the Polish uprising, brutally crushed by the summer of 1864. Thus began the most difficult period of Panteleeva's life, vividly described in a short autobiographical essay entitled "Iz perezhitogo v shestidesiatykh godakh" (Life experiences of the 1860s, published 1905).

After staying in 1865 in Vilna (Lithuania), where Longin was awaiting trial in a prison for political convicts, Serafima followed him into Siberian exile in May 1866. Following the Decembrist rebellion of 1825, many wives of political prisoners followed their husbands to Siberia and it was an act of immense self-sacrifice to give up their privileges to live in rough conditions and freezing desolation. The Panteleevs first settled in a small gold prospecting village in the province of Eniseisk (eastern Siberia), where Panteleeva's family connections allowed her husband to secure employment as a gold-washing works supervisor. Separated from her family, friends and her little daughter Olga (b. 1864)–left in the care of her grand-parents–Panteleeva had to share all the ordeals, hardships, hazards and insecurities that came with Siberian exile. In 1867, the painful experience of their second child's birth and death, as well as the news of the sudden death of her beloved father, left Panteleeva depressed and physically weakened. On medical advice, she returned to St Petersburg.

Uncertainty regarding her husband's future and financial difficulties brought by her father's death forced Panteleeva to consider possible ways of earning a living and acquiring a profession in order to support herself and her little daughter. Her education however, typical of that of an upper-class woman, was of little help in finding a job. "The ability to chatter easily in three foreign languages, some basic information taken from bad textbooks, music, art–such was the typical baggage that young girls, including myself, received by the time we had come of age in the early 1860s," she wrote in her memoirs (Panteleev 1958, 683). But by the end of that decade, expanding educational opportunities were providing women like Panteleeva with the chance to pursue scientific study, which many young people of her generation considered a tool for achieving truth, progress, social justice and change.

In 1870, Panteleeva enrolled at the newly opened co-educational Vladimir lecture courses, where she studied chemistry, physics and botany with leading Russian scientists supportive of women's education such as the chemist Aleksandr Butlerov (1828-1886) and the botanist Andrei Beketov (1825-1902). Having reached the highest level of education available to Russian women of her time, Panteleeva resolved to go abroad in order to acquire formal medical qualifications. She made her way to Zurich where, in 1867, her compatriot Nadezhda Suslova (1843-1918) became the first woman in Europe to obtain a doctorate in medicine, inspiring dozens of young Russian women to follow her example. When Panteleeva enrolled at the medical faculty in the spring semester of 1872, 63 women–54 of them from the Russian Empire–were studying at Zurich University.

Panteleeva's memoirs provide a remarkably frank account not only of her own personal experience, but also of Zurich, its Russian émigré colony and the attitude of Swiss professors and male fellow students towards aspiring female physicians or scientists. "How shocked Swiss burghers were at the sight of young Russian women without chaperones or guardians," recalled Panteleeva. "Only a few students, and senior students at that, had learned to respect our work and tasks" (Panteleev 1958, 686).

Despite the high degree of political activism characterizing the Russian student colony, Panteleeva, unwilling to catch the eye of the authorities and thereby draw negative attention to her exiled husband, stayed away from politics during her Zurich days. After the hardships she had endured over the previous years, she found scientific research deeply satisfying, both emotionally and intellectually. Her interest in the frontiers of scientific and medical research brought her to the study of the vasomotor system and its regulation, which she carried out in the physiology department under the guidance of Professor Ludimar Hermann (1838–1915). Part of this original research was later published in the *Zentralblatt für Medizinische Wissenschaften* (Journal of medical science).

However, Panteleeva was not to defend her doctoral dissertation in Zurich. On his release from Siberian exile her husband, still banned from residence in St Petersburg, spent some time in Yalta (Crimea), where Panteleeva joined him in the summer of 1875. In November that year, all restrictions on Longin Panteleev's residence were lifted and the couple returned to St Petersburg. There, Panteleeva worked in the physiological laboratory of the Medical-Surgical Academy, later transfering to the physiological laboratory of the Russian Academy of Sciences. The latter institution had the necessary equipment for Panteleeva's experiments on blood pressure and there, in the summer of 1876, she was able to add the final touches to her doctoral dissertation.

Like many other Russian women who had benefited from foreign higher education, Panteleeva did not continue her scientific work. (Major obstacles still prevented women from becoming university lecturers, laboratory researchers or doctors in Russia.) Instead, she devoted her time to the publishing house her husband had founded on his return to St Petersburg. Putting to use her academic background and fluent knowledge of several major European languages, Panteleeva translated scientific works and wrote essays on popular science in the spirit of the progressive social activism of the 1860s (marked by a powerful faith in the natural sciences and the power of education).

By 1900, as Panteleeva became more involved in educational issues, this work had come to absorb most of her energy and interest. The area of feminist activity related to education and professional training was highly successful in Russia. Of all the issues that had absorbed the energies of the women's movement from the 1860s onwards, it was this one which proved to be the most enduring and which yielded the greatest rewards. In December 1908, Panteleeva was amongst the delegates of the *Pervyi Vserossiiskii Zhenskii S'ezd* (First All-Russian Congress of Women) held in St Petersburg by the *Russkoe Zhenskoe Vzaimno-Blagotvoritel'noe Obshchestvo* (Russian Women's Mutual Philanthropic Society). Although she did not present a paper herself, Panteleeva participated actively in the debates, as the proceedings of this Congress show. In December 1913, she attended the *Pervyi Vserossiiskii S'ezd po Obrazovaniiu Zhenshchin* (First All-Russian Congress on Women's Education), organized in St Petersburg by the *Rossiiskaia Liga Ravnopraviia Zhenshchin* (League for Women's Equal Rights), one of the largest and best-known feminist organizations in the country. Panteleeva's paper on her Zurich experiences was the only one dealing with the studies abroad of thousands of Russian women to be presented to the Section on Higher Education.

Panteleeva's absence from feminist leadership may be taken as a sign of her relative insignificance in the history of the women's movement. However, her biography offers an insight into the different paths taken by educated women in turn of the century Russia, while her earlier years allow us to examine ways in which political and social developments in Russia of the 1860s and 1870s fashioned women's lives and personalities. First as a deportee's wife and then as a student, Serafima Panteleeva exhibited extraordinary determination, energy and independence in challenging the social and political norms of her day. In the last decades of the nineteenth century and into the twentieth, this member of the intelligentsia, popular science writer, scientific translator, memoirist and feminist, worked to shape opinions, tastes and scientific priorities influencing the culture and society of her time.

Throughout their lives, Serafima and Longin Panteleev continued to show an interest in radical politics and would sometimes express their opinions publicly. In March 1901, Longin, along with 150 writers, lawyers and professionals, signed two collective petitions condemning the brutal treatment of peacefully demonstrating students by the tsarist police and demanding punishment of those responsible. This action resulted in the couple's being banished from St Petersburg for three years, which they spent in Western Europe (mostly in Italy), only returning home in 1904. They remained in Russia after the 1917 October Revolution. Panteleeva died in Petrograd (as St Petersburg was temporarily called after the outbreak of World War I) in 1918, at the age of seventy. Her husband outlived her by one year.

Natalia Tikhonov
Geneva University, Switzerland

SOURCES

(A) *Institut russkoi literatury (Pushkinskii Dom)* (Institute of Russian Literature, Pushkinskii Dom), St Petersburg, Longin Panteleev's personal archival collection.

(C) Panteleeva, Serafima. "Iz perezhitogo v shestidesiatykh godakh" (Life experiences of the 1860s). *Mir bozhij* (God's world) 12 (1905). Reprinted in Longin Panteleev. *Vospominaniia* (Memoirs). Moscow: Izdatel'stvo Khudozhestvennoi literatury, 1958, 659–681.

(C) Panteleeva, Serafima. "Iz Peterburga v Ziurikh" (From St Petersburg to Zurich). In Arian Praskov'ia, ed. *Pervyi zhenskii kalendar'* (First women's calendar) (1912). Reprinted in Longin Panteleev. *Vospominaniia*, 683–694.

(C) Panteleeva, Serafima. "Na putiah k vysshemu obrazovaniiu. V Ziurikh s 1864 po 1875 gg" (On the way to higher education. To Zurich, 1864 to 1875). In *Trudy pervogo vserossiiskogo s'ezda po obrazovaniiu zhenshchin organizovannogo Rossiiskoi Ligoi Ravnopraviia Zhenshchin v S.-Peterburge* (Proceedings of the First Congress on Women's Education organized in St Petersburg by the Russian League of Equal Rights for Women). St Petersburg: Rossiiskaia Liga Ravnopraviia Zhenshchin, 1914, 1: 63–66.

(E) Brügger, Liliane. "Russische Studentinnen in Zurich" (Russian women students in Zurich). In Peter Brang, Carsten Goehrke, Robin Kembal and Heinrich Riggenbach, eds. *Bild und Begegnung. Kulturelle Wechselseitigkeit zwischen der Schweiz und Osteuropa im Wandel der Zeit* (Pictures and meetings. Cultural exchanges between Switzerland and Eastern Europe through the ages). Basel: Helbing & Lichtenhahn, 1996, 504.

(E) Koblitz, Ann Hibner. *Science, Women and Revolution in Russia*. Amsterdam: Harwood Academic Publishers, 2000, 174.

(F) http://www.rektorat.unizh.ch/matrikel/manual/hintro.html

PAPIĆ, Žarana (1949–2002)

Sociologist-anthropologist, academic, one of the founders of the feminist movement in Yugoslavia and co-founder (1992) of the Belgrade Women's Studies Center.

Žarana Papić, 1996, at home at her computer

Žarana Papić (called Žarka by her family) was born on 4 July 1949 in Sarajevo, Federal People's Republic of Yugoslavia. She was brought up in a family that actively resisted fascism and nationalism and fought for freedom and social justice. Her parents were Milena, born Šotrić (1921–2002) and Radovan Papić (1910–1983). Her father was a high ranking Communist Party official and his position secured the family a higher standard of living and privileged social status. In 1955, her family moved from Sarajevo to Belgrade, where she graduated (in 1968) from the Fifth Belgrade gymnasium as the best student of her generation. Although her family belonged to the privileged social group, both Žarana and her older brother Žarko Papić (economist, minister and diplomat) strove to prove themselves in their chosen fields of work.

Žarana Papić belonged to the first generation of Yugoslav feminist theorists in the post-World War II socialist system, and she had a tremendous influence on the development of younger feminists. Throughout her life her appearance, like her personality, revealed strength and fragility, courage and integrity. A woman of unique style and refinement, a cosmopolitan fluent in English and French, she traveled and communicated widely with numerous colleagues from abroad and throughout Yugoslavia, including Sanja Iveković (feminist artist, Women's Studies Center, Zagreb, Croatia), Chislaine Glasson Deschaumes (coordinator of *Transeuropéene, Réseau pour la culture en Europe* [Network for European culture] Paris, France), Corrine Kumar (feminist activist from India and coordinator of El Taller International, Tunisia), Rosi Braidotti (feminist professor of philosophy, Utrecht University, the Netherlands), Vjollca Krasniqi (Women's Kosovo Network, Priština, Kosovo) and Rada Iveković (feminist professor of philosophy, Paris, France). Žarana Papić lived in a flat next to that of her parents in 16 Baba Višnjina Street, a quiet part of Belgrade. A private yet warm woman, many of her numerous friends remember the hospitality of her large room, dominated by her library.

From 1968 to 1974, Papić studied for, and obtained a B. A. degree in sociology at the Faculty of Philosophy, University of Belgrade. These years coincided with vibrant left-wing student activity in Yugoslavia, culminating in the student protests of 1968 and opening the doors to modes of intellectual thought that offered alternatives to the rigid ruling socialist ideology. Žarana Papić belonged to a circle of well-educated young people who actively participated in many of the events organized by the most significant institution of alternative thought and culture of that time, the Students' Cultural Center. On the one hand, the state took care to suppress and limit political uprising among students, but on the other hand, opportunities to act in the sphere of 'culture' through youth media were present, hence the Center, which was financed with state money, could afford a very alternative kind of cultural politics (organizing exhibitions, lectures, events, theater and so on). As a young sociologist-anthropologist, Papić was introduced to contemporary feminist theory at the Croatian Sociological Association Conference in Portorož, Slovenia, in 1976. The same year, she attended the first Women's Studies course at the Inter-University Centre in Dubrovnik, Croatia. She was inspired by feminist theory, especially by the work of feminist anthropologists, by Simone de Beauvoir's *Le Deuxième Sexe* (which she must have read in French or English since it was not available in Serbian at that time) and later, by the work of Rosi Braidotti. With Dunja Blažević (the director of the Students' Cultural Center) and other colleagues, Žarana Papić organized the first international feminist conference in Eastern Europe under the title of "Drug/ca žensko pitanje, novi pristup?–Comrade/ess" (Comrade/ess–the woman question, a new approach?). The conference, which took place in October 1978 in the Students' Cultural Center in Belgrade, was a key moment in Yugoslav feminism. Its aim was to present the new feminist movement and feminist theory to interested men and women from Yugoslavia, and to this end it invited prominent feminists from all over Europe. Among the participants were Helen Cixous, Haty Garcia and Nil Yalter from France; Jill Lewis, Helen Roberts and Parveen Adams from the UK; Dacia Maraini, Carla Ravaioli and Chiara Saraceno from Italy; Ewa Morawska from Poland; Judit Kele from Hungary; Alice Schwarzer from Germany; Nadežda Čačinović-Puhovski, Slavenka Drakulić-Ilić, Đurđa Milanović and Vesna Pušić from Zagreb; Nada Ler-Sofronić from Sarajevo; Silva Mežnarić from Ljubljana; and Rada Iveković, Dunja Blažević, Anđelka Milić, Jasmina Tešanović and Sonja Drljević from Belgrade. A courageous and challenging event, the conference was also a breakthrough since it critically examined the system, the regime and the current government (Iveković 2002, 49) and facilitated the formation of a core group of feminist theorists and activists in Yugoslavia. Members of the group believed that feminism was not to be dismissed as a 'foreign import,' but was something that their country needed. From then on, they embarked on a continuous feminist critique of patriarchy within socialism.

Žarana Papić's feminist world view was also reflected in her own academic work. From 1977, she began publishing papers dealing with women's issues, leading eventually to the publication of a book, coedited with ***Lydia Sklevicky*** from Zagreb, entitled *Antropologija žene* (Towards an anthropology of woman, 1983). It was the first book of feminist anthropology in Yugoslavia and inspired many women to take up the subject. In 1986, Žarana Papić obtained her M.A. degree with the thesis "A Feminist Critique of Sociology," submitted to the interdisciplinary Department of Anthropology at the Faculty of Philosophy, University of Belgrade. The thesis was published in 1989 as *Sociologija i feminizam* (Sociology and feminism).

In 1989, Žarana Papić was appointed to the Faculty of Philosophy at the Department of Sociology in Belgrade as an assistant in social anthropology. She obtained her Ph.D. degree in social anthropology in 1995 with the thesis *Dijalektika pola i roda–priroda i kultura u savremenoj socijalnoj antropologiji* (The dialectics of sex and gender–nature and culture in contemporary social anthropology) and was promoted to the position of assistant professor. A greatly loved teacher, Žarana Papić taught social and cultural anthropology at the Departments of Sociology and Archaeology and was one of the three women (together with her professor and mentor Anđelka Milić and the sociologist Marina Blagojević) to teach Gender Studies as an optional course for the students of the Faculty of Philosophy. Her Ph.D. thesis was published in 1997 under the title *Polnost i kultura: telo i znanje u savremenoj antropologiji* (Gender and culture: body and knowledge in contemporary anthropology).

The break-up of socialist Yugoslavia in the early 1990s brought new challenges to the integrity of intellectuals and Žarana Papić belonged to those who rejected nationalism and multi-ethnic conflict. Considering herself 'nationless,' she directed all her academic and activist energy into exposing and underlining the constructed nature of war, strongly believing that women could contribute to strengthening the cooperation between the warring nations. She published analytical papers and lectured on the contemporary situation from a feminist perspective, linking nationalism, patriarchy and war.

Having been involved in some form of feminist work since 1977, as well as having been among the first academics to write about women's studies and to reflect on the meaning of the term 'gender,' Žarana Papić was one of the eight women founders of the Belgrade Women's Study Center in 1992. She was also a member of the first Board of the Center and one of its first lecturers. The Center was conceived as an alternative forum for intellectual and anti-war women's activities. Papić taught the anthropology of gender and her lectures reflected the high standard of her teaching and inspired many students to continue working in the field.

Žarana Papić believed that women needed to take a more active role in politics and she strongly supported the founding (in 2000) of the women's group for the promotion of women's political rights, the *Glas razlike* (Voice of difference). Through her activism, Žarana Papić contributed to the visibility of a new intellectual feminist force: she appeared in 'Women in Black' anti-war vigils and in public discussions in the media; she supported the Autonomous Women's Center Against Sexual Violence and the gay and lesbian movement and its initiatives in Serbia (lecturing in Belgrade in 2001 on issues relevant to Queer studies), as well as supporting movements against discrimination of all kinds.

By combining academic work with activism, Žarana Papić was exceptionally hard working, sometimes stretching her physical and psychological resources to the limits of endurance. As a member of the Advisory Board of the Women's Study Center, she was part of the organizing committee of the First Eastern European Feminist Conference: "Šta možemo da učinimo za sebe?" (What can we do for ourselves?), held in Belgrade in June 1994. Papić was also the Country Contact for Serbia for the European Forum of Left Feminists. From 1982 to 1986, she was a Regional Representative at the Editorial Board of *Women's Studies International Forum*. She was also a member of the Editorial Board (1995–2002) of the Belgrade Women's Study Journal *Ženske studije* (Women's studies) and editor-in-chief (1995–1997) of the journal *Sociologija* (Sociology) in Belgrade. In the mid-1990s, she became an HESP Fellow affiliated to the Program on Gender and Culture at the Central European University in Budapest, and she spent the winter of 1996 at the *Laboratorie d'anthropologie sociale* (Laboratory for Social Anthropology) at the *Collège de France* in Paris. From 1998, Papić coordinated a project of cooperation between women's studies in the countries of former Yugoslavia and France entitled: "Le corps civil et politique–la nation mâle–quelle Europe pour le femmes: transition, post-socialisme, post-guerre: integrations trans-européennes" (Civil and political bodies–the bad nation–what kind of Europe for women: transition, post-socialism, post-war: trans-European integrations). She lectured at the Department of Social Sciences and Humanities of the *Alternativna Akademska Obrazovna Mreža* (Alternative Academic Educational Network), a separate NGO institution of higher education established in September 1998 in Belgrade, which opposed the University of Belgrade under President Milošević's rule.

In the spring of 2002, Papić's mother died after a long illness. In that year, Žarana Papić went on her last trip (between 25 May–9 June) as part of the *Transeuropéennes* project "Balkan Women for Peace: Women Activists Cross Borders," of which project's Advisory Board Papić was a member. During this trip she saw her beloved Mostar once again. Soon after that, on 10 September 2002, she died unexpectedly in her flat.

Honoring her long-standing association with French academic institutions, she was posthumously awarded the *Palmes Académiques* (Academic honors) and named *Chevalier dans l'Ordre des Palmes Académiques* (Bearer of the order of academic honors) by the French government on 31 October 2002. Žarana Papić will be remembered in the history of Yugoslav feminism not only as one of its pioneers, but as someone who combined theory and activism.

Vanda Perović
Belgrade Women's Studies Center

SOURCES

(A) Belgrade Women's Studies Center, Collection Žarana Papić.

(C) Žarana Papić and Lydia Sklevicky, eds. *Antropologija Žene* (Towards an anthropology of woman). Belgrade: Prosveta, 1983. Reprint 2003 (Biblioteka XX vek i Centar za ženske studije).

(C) Papić, Žarana. *Socijologija i feminizam: savremeni ženski pokret, misao o oslobođenju žena, i njegov uticaj na socijologiju* (Sociology and feminism: the contemporary women's movement, thoughts on women's liberation and its influence on sociology). Belgrade: Istraživačko-izdavački centar, 1989.

(C) Papić, Žarana. "Women as Ex-Citizens in Ex-Yugoslavia." In M. Pellikaan-Engel, ed. *Against Patriarchal Thinking–A Future without Discrimination*? Amsterdam: Vrije Universiteit Press, 1992, 326-331.

(C) Papić, Žarana. "Patrijarhat" (Patriarchy). In *Enciklopedija političke kulture* (Encyclopedia of political culture). Belgrade: Savremena administracija, 1993.

(C) Papić, Žarana. *Polnost i kultura: telo i znanje u savremenoj antropologiji* (Gender and culture: body and knowledge in contemporary anthropology). Belgrade: Edicija XX vek i Institut za sociološka istraživanja Filozofskog Fakulteta, 1997.

(C) Papić, Žarana. "From State Socialism To State Nationalism: The Case of Serbia in Gender Perspective." In Rada Iveković and Neda Pagon, eds. *Otherhood And Nation*. Ljubljana: Institutum Studiorum Humanitatis & Paris: Editions de la Maison des Sciences de L'Homme, 1998.

(C) Papić, Žarana. "Women in Serbia: Post-Communism, War and Nationalist Mutations." In Sabrina Petra Ramet, ed. *Gender Politics in the Western Balkans: Women, Society and Politics in Yugoslavia and the Yugoslav Successor States*. University Park, Pa.: Penn State University Press, 1998.

(D) *Žarana Papić. In Memoriam (1949-2002)*. Belgrade: Ženske studije i komunikacija-Centar za ženske studije, 2002.

(D) Iveković, Rada. "Žarana Papić (1949-2002)." In *Žarana Papić In Memoriam (1949-2002)*. Belgrade: Ženske studije i komunikacija-Centar za ženske studije, 2002.

(E) Popov, N. *Kontrafatum*. Mladost, Belgrade, 1989.

(E) *Ovo je studentski kulturni centar. Prvih 25 godina 1971-1996* (This is the students' cultural center. The first 25 years 1971-1996). Belgrade: SKC, 1996.

(E) Denegri, J. *Studentski kulturni centar kao umetnička scena*. Belgrade: SKC, 2003.

(E) Personal communication by the author with Žarana Papić's family members and friends.

(F) www.awin.org.yu/srp/arhiva/izarhive/ Hronologija feministički orijentisanih programa realizovanih u Studentskom kulturnom centru u Beogradu od 1975 do 1992. godine koja obuhvata podatke o radu Feminističke istraživačke grupe 'Žena i društvo' (1979-1992) [A chronology of feminist-orientated programs in the Students' Cultural Center in Belgrade from 1975-1992. Contains information on the activity of the feminist group. "Žena i drustvo" (Women and society) from 1979 to 1992].

PARREN, Callirhoe (born Siganou) (1859–1940)

Greek journalist and literary figure; editor of the *Efimeris ton Kyrion* (Ladies' journal, 1887–1917); leader of collective action campaigns to improve the situation of Greek women. The first in Greece to elaborate 'the woman question' in terms of 'emancipation;' founder (1896) of the *Enosis ton Ellinidon* (Union of Greek Women) and (1911) of the *Lykeion ton Ellinidon* (Lyceum of Greek Women); actively involved in the work of the International Council of Women; President of the Greek section of the Women's International League for Peace and Freedom (affiliated to the WILPF in 1921).

Callirhoe Parren was undoubtedly the first to introduce feminism to Greece, or rather a 'moderate' feminism (according to the poet Kostis Palamas); one which could adapt to the existing structures of Greek society at the end of the nineteenth and beginning of the twentieth centuries. Her rich, varied and untiring work in journalism and writing, as well as in the fields of education, philanthropy and social reform, her acquaintance with the intellectual 'elite' of the Greek capital, and the (often passionate) persistence with which she fought for her ideas established her as a leading public figure of her time and a privileged target of misogynist criticism and satire. Despite her public presence, mainstream historiography has systematically ignored Parren's public action; on the other hand, little is known about her parents, siblings or other aspects of her private life (no personal archives have been found) and a reliable biography of Parren is still lacking. This entry is primarily concerned with features of her public life, increasingly a subject of interest in the historiography emerging from studies of women, feminism and gender in Greece.

Callirhoe Siganou was born in 1859 in the Cretan village of Platania, not far from the city of Rethymno. The family was living in Rethymno when the outbreak of the Cretan revolution against Ottoman rule (1866–1869) radically altered the lives of its members. According to biographical information authored by Callirhoe herself, the revolution (in which her father, Stylianos Siganos, had participated) forced the family to abandon the island and begin a new life in Athens under significant financial strain. Parren recalled with gratitude how her father put the remaining financial resources of the family towards the education of his children. She wrote that her father's example taught her "to face life, not as a field of joy and pleasure, but as an arena of work and duty" (Parren 1909, 745–746). Callirhoe attended secondary-school level private classes and received a teaching qualification from Arsakeion, a private institution which trained female teachers through a system of scholarships supported by the government and the local authorities. In 1879, upon receiving her teaching certificate, Callirhoe Siganou worked for a short time as headmistress of the *Kentrikon Parthenagogeion* (Central Girls' School) of the Greek diaspora in Adrianople and in Odessa at the *Rodokanakeion* Girls' School, a salaried position funded by the Athenian *Syllogos pros diadosin ton Ellinikon Grammaton* (Association for the Diffusion of Greek Education). Following her marriage to Ioannis (Jean) Parren, a journalist of Anglo-French descent from Constantinople (Istanbul)–later to become founder of the Athens News Agency–she moved to Athens. There, inspired by the journalistic milieu, Callirhoe Parren channeled what she called her "mania for writing" (Parren 1915, 2732–2734) into the cause of women's emancipation through education and paid work.

In 1887, Parren began publishing the *Efimeris ton Kyrion* (Ladies' journal), which would soon function as an intellectual forum for scholarly women determined to occupy themselves systematically with 'the cause.' During its long life (it came out weekly from 1887 to 1907 and fortnightly from 1907 to 1917) and through a large network of subscribers and correspondents that extended beyond Greece to the Hellenic diaspora, the *Efimeris ton Kyrion* became the most successful journalistic venture of the time, held by women and devoted to the women's cause. In her frequent articles in the *Efimeris ton Kyrion*, as well as in the periodical *Estia* (Hearth) and the newspaper *To Asty* (The city), Callirhoe Parren put forward the first coherent proposals for women's emancipation in Greece. Giving priority to the civil and social rights of women, legitimized as specific duties towards the nation and civil society, Parren elaborated a feminine version of citizenship which redefined traditional gender roles within the framework of nationalist ideology. Parren's proposal for women's emancipation provoked an outcry at the end of the nineteenth century, despite the moderate terms in which it was formulated. The 1896 dispute between the writer Emmanuel Roïdis and several Greek women writers, in which Parren defended the right of her fellow women to write freely, is most telling on this matter. Having secured the support of the scholars who frequented her literary salon, the editor of the *Efimeris ton Kyrion* did not hesitate to denounce the diffuse misogyny of her time, and to involve herself in disputes, sometimes violent, with authors and politicians who appeared to oppose her vision of women's emancipation.

Although journalism undoubtedly constituted the main part of her writing activity, Callirhoe Parren also engaged in other genres: translations, interviews, epistolary journalism, diaries, travel journals, women's biographies and historical narratives. By the turn of the century, Parren was using the novel to popularize Greek emancipation–a theme which she had already begun formulating in earlier writings. She wrote a trilogy entitled *Ta vivlia tis Avgis* (The books of dawn)–consisting of *I Cheirafetimeni*

(The emancipated woman), *I Magissa* (The witch) and *To Neon Symvolaion* (The new contract) and originally published in a serialized form in the *Efimeris ton Kyrion* between 1899 and 1903 (a French translation of *I Cheirafetimeni* was published in *Le Journal des Débats,* 1907). In *Ta vivlia tis Avgis,* women's emancipation was put forward as a painful road of self-discovery, capable of releasing women from archaic social conventions and leading them to new, equal relations with the other sex. Three other novels followed, also published in the *Efimeris ton Kyrion: Choris onoma* (Nameless, 1905–1906), *To marameno krino* (The wilted lily, 1907–1910) and *To aspro triantafyllo* (The white rose, 1915–1917). The first two novels of the *Ta vivlia tis Avgis* were the basis for Parren's play *I Nea Gynaika* (The new woman), which was successfully produced for the stage in 1907 and published in 1908.

Parren's activities in the women's movement were as multifaceted as her writing and entirely complementary to it. They included, amongst others, the foundation of charities (Sunday schools, a Home for the Incurably Sick and St. Catherine's Asylum), the organization of women's craft exhibitions and the submission of petitions for the improvement of women's education. More specifically, Parren fought for equal opportunities at all levels of secondary education (offered by the state exclusively to men), for women's right of access to universities (it was only in the 1890s that certain faculties–philology, medicine and mathematics–accepted the first female students), as well as to the various professions from which women had been barred for social reasons and because civil law forbade a married woman to enter paid employment without her husband's permission. Parren also campaigned for legislation to protect women in paid employment, a drafting process that in Greece would actually begin in 1912 under the Venizelos' government and which was further developed in 1920. Interestingly, and in tune with the dominant political ideas of the Greek society of the time, Parren did not initially envisage the franchise for Greek women. Later (between 1910–1920), she began to gradually accept demands for female suffrage; finally, in the 1920s, she came to adopt a clear pro-suffrage position.

Parren participated in European and North American women's conferences: the *Congres des oeuvres et institutions feministes* (International Congress on Women's Charities and Institutions) and the French and International Congress on Women's Rights held in Paris (1889); the Congress of the International Council of Women (ICW) in Chicago (1893); three women's movement conferences held in Paris (1900) and the International Congress of Lyceum Clubs in Paris (1914). These activities were in keeping with her general plan to coordinate the Greek national women's movement with the first enduring international feminist network, the ICW. Thanks to her activities the *Ethniko Symvoulio ton Ellinidon* (National Council of Greek Women) was founded in 1908 and became affiliated to the ICW in the same year. Of special importance in this regard was Parren's foundation, in 1896, of the *Enosis ton Ellinidon* (Union of Greek Women) and later, in 1911, of the *Lykeion ton Ellinidon* (Lyceum of Greek Women). These two organizations contributed to the identification of feminism in Greece with 'nation enhancing' women's activism.

This most productive period of Parren's activity was interrupted by the suspension of the *Efimeris ton Kyrion* at the end of 1917 and Parren's exile to Hydra (a small island not far from Athens in the Argolikos Bay), imposed by the Venizelos administration (ostensibly as a result of her opposition to the participation of Greece on the side of the Entente during World War I). Upon her return from exile, Parren decided to organize the Women's Conference of the *Lykeion ton Ellinidon*, which took place in 1921. The conference was attacked for being too conservative by most of the new feminist organizations which had been formed in the interim, and which would shape Greek feminism in the interwar years. The 1921 conference signaled the end of the Greek women's movement as represented by the founder of the *Efimeris ton Kyrion* and from then onwards, Callirhoe Parren would embody the most conservative elements within the interwar women's movement. The *Lykeion ton Ellinidon*, over which she presided until her death, increasingly poured its energies into activities of a 'national' and philanthropic nature. In 1936, on the occasion of the fiftieth anniversary of her public activity, Parren was decorated with the Silver Medal of the Athens Academy, the Red Cross Silver Medal and the Medal of the Municipality of Athens and her activities were deemed "beneficial to the nation." Such activities did not, however, prevent Parren from cooperating frequently with other women's organizations of the time such as the *Syndesmos gia ta Dikaiomata tis Gynaikas* (League for Woman's Rights) and the *Ethniko Symvoulio ton Ellinidon* (National Council of Greek Women); nor from participating in attempts to reach a trans-Balkan women's accord, and in the creation of the *Mikri Entent Gynaikon* (Little Entente of Women, LEW) during the Congress of the International Woman Suffrage Alliance (IWSA) in Rome, in 1923; nor from forming contacts with the energetic Women's International League for Peace and Freedom (WILPF), which she represented in Greece. (She was the President of the Greek section during the interwar period.)

Callirhoe Parren had no children and lived with Ioannis Parren until her death in Athens on 16 January 1940. She was buried at public expense in the First Cemetery of Athens.

Angelika Psarra
Historian and journalist, Athens

Eleni Fournaraki
Historian, Department of Sociology,
University of Crete

Translated from the Greek by Martha Michailidou.

SOURCES

(A) Athens, Historical Archives of the *Lykeion ton Ellinidon* (Lyceum of Greek women).

(B) Parren, Callirhoe, ed. *Efimeris ton Kyrion* (Ladies' journal) (1887-1917).

(C) Parren, Callirhoe. *Istoria tis Gynaikos apo ktiseos kosmou mechri simeron* (The history of woman from the creation of the world until today). Athens: Anastasios Trimis' printing press, 1889.

(C) Parren, Callirhoe. *Zoi enos etous. Epistolai Athinaias pros Parisinin, 1896-1897* (A year's life. Letters of an Athenian lady to a Parisian lady, 1896-1897). Athens: Paraskevas Leonis' printing press, undated.

(C) Parren, Callirhoe. *I Cheirafetimeni* (The emancipated woman). Printed by Paraskevas Leonis, Athens, 1900. Originally published in the *Efimeris ton Kyrion*, nos. 559-618 (17 January 1899-30 April 1900).

(C) Parren, Callirhoe. *I Magissa* (The witch). Printed by Paraskevas Leonis, Athens, 1901. Originally published in the *Efimeris ton Kyrion*, nos. 630-688 (10 September 1900-16 December 1901).

(C) Parren, Callirhoe. *To Neon Symvolaion* (The new contract). *Efimeris ton Kyrion*, nos. 689-761 (23 December 1901-28 September 1903).

(C) Parren, Callirhoe. *Istoria tis Gynaikos. Synchroni Ellinides 1503-1896* (The history of woman. Contemporary Greek women 1503-1896). Athens: Paraskevas Leonis' printing press, 1903.

(C) Parren, Callirhoe. "Choris onoma" (Nameless). *Efimeris ton Kyrion*, nos. 819-906 (16 January 1905-4 June 1906).

(C) Parren, Callirhoe. *I Nea Gynaika. Drama is praxeis tessaras* (The new woman. A four-act play). Athens: Paraskevas Leonis' printing press, 1908.

(C) Parren, Callirhoe. "Empros is ton nekron patera mou" (Before my dead father). *Efimeris ton Kyrion* 23, no. 970 (15-30 June 1909): 745-746.

(C) Parren, Callirhoe. "To marameno krino" (The wilted lily). *Efimeris ton Kyrion*, nos. 906-987 (4 March 1907-15 May 1910).

(C) Parren, Callirhoe. "To aspro triantafyllo" (The white rose). *Efimeris ton Kyrion*, nos. 1057-1105 (15-31 January 1915-November 1917).

(C) Parren, Callirhoe. "Pos egina dimosiografos. Apo tin omilian tis k. Parren eis to Lykeion ton Ellinidon" (How I became a journalist. From the speech of Mrs C. Parren to the Lyceum of Greek Women). *Efimeris ton Kyrion* 29, no. 1062 (1-15 April 1915): 2732-2734.

(D) *Eikosipentaetiris tou Lykeiou ton Ellinidon (1911-1936)–Pentikontaetiris tis draseos tis idrytrias kai Proedrou aftou Callirhoes Parren (1886-1936)* [The 25th anniversary of the Lyceum of Greek Women (1911-1936)–the fiftieth anniversary of the action of its founder and President Callirhoe Parren (1886-1936)]. Athens, 1937.

(D) Tarsouli, Athina. "Callirhoe Parren." *Nea Estia* (New hearth) XXVII, no. 315 (1940): 173-176.

(D) Anastasopoulou, Maria. "Feminist Awareness and Greek Women Writers at the Turn of the Century: The Case of Kallirhoe Parren and Alexandra Papadopoulou." In Philip Carabott, ed. *Greek Society in the Making, 1863-1913. Realities, Symbols and Visions*. Hampshire: Variorum Ashgate Publishing Ltd., 1997, 161-175.

(D) Polykandrioti, Rania. "Callirhoe Parren." In *I palaioteri pezografia mas. Apo tis arches tis os ton proto pagkosmio polemo* (Our earlier prose works. From their beginnings to World War I). Athens: Ekdoseis Sokoli, 1997, 7: 338–363.

(D) Psarra, Angelika. "To mythistorima tis cheirafetisis i 'syneti' outopia tis Callirhoes Parren" (The novel of emancipation or the 'moderate' utopia of Callirhoe Parren). In Callirhoe Parren. *I Cheirafetimeni* (The emancipated woman). Second edition. Athens: Ekdoseis Ekati, 1999, 407–486.

(D) Anastasopoulou, Maria. *I syneti apostolos tis gynaikeias cheirafesias. Callirhoe Parren. I zoi kai to ergo* (The moderate apostle of women's emancipation. Callirhoe Parren. Life and work). Athens: Ekdoseis Iliodromion (undated).

(D) Psarra, Angelika. "'Few women have a history:' Callirhoe Parren and the beginnings of women's history in Greece" (forthcoming).

(E) Bompou-Protopappa, Eleni. *To Lykeio ton Ellinidon 1911–1991* (The Lyceum of Greek Women 1911–1991). Athens, 1993.

(E) Varikas, Eleni. *I exegersi ton kyrion. I genesi mias feministikis syneidisis stin Ellada (1833–1907)* [The Ladies' Revolt. Creation of a feminist consciousness in Greece (1833–1907]. In *Idrima Erevnas kai Paidias Emporikis Trapezas tis Ellados* (The Foundation for Research and Culture of the Commercial Bank of Greece). Athens, 1987; second edition Katarti, Athens, 1996.

(E) Psarra, Angelika. "Mitera i politis? Ellinikes ekdoches tis gynaikeias cheirafetisis (1870–1920)" (Mother or citizen? Greek versions of women's emancipation, 1870– 1920). In *To fylo ton dikaiomaton. Exousia, gynaikes kai idiotita tou politi, Evropaďko Synedrio, Athina 9–10 Fevrouariou 1996, Praktika* (The gender of rights. Power, women and citizenship. European Conference Proceedings, Athens 9–10 February 1996). Kentro Gynaikeion Erevnon kai Meleton Diotima (Centre of Women's Studies and Research 'Diotima'). Athens: Ekdoseis Nefeli, 1999, 90–107.

(E) Avdela, Efi and Angelika Psarra. "Engendering 'Greekness:' Women's Emancipation and Irredentist Politics in Nineteenth-Century Greece." *Historia. Journal of the Historical Society of Israel* 5 (2000): 109–121 (in Hebrew).

(E) Fournaraki, Eleni. "The Olympism of the Ladies. The International Olympic events in Greece (1896, 1906) and the *Ladies' Journal*." In Christina Koulouri, ed. *Athens, Olympic City, 1896–1906*. Athens: International Olympic Academy, 2004, 333–376.

(E) Psarra, Angelika. "A Gift from the New World: Greek feminists between East and West (1880–1930)" (forthcoming).

PASHKEVICH, Alaiza; pen-name **'TSIOTKA'** ('Auntie' in Belarussian) (1876–1916)

The most famous Belarussian revolutionary woman poet; advocated ideas of women's independence.

Alaiza Pashkevich was born on 3 July 1876 into a wealthy peasant (Catholic) family on the Peszczyn estate in western Belarus (the Belarussian-Lithuanian ethnic and linguistic territories), in the Northwestern Province of the Russian Empire. She was one of the six children of Styapan/Stephan and Hanna Pashkevich. For one year, Alaiza was taught at home by a female pedagogy student, who served as a vivid example of the new educational and professional opportunities that were becoming available to women. In 1894, at the age of eighteen, Alaiza Pashkevich entered the fourth grade of the seventh-grade private school for girls run by Vera Prozorova in Wilno (currently Vilnius, the capital of Lithuania; the town is considered to be the birthplace of the modern Belarussian intellectual tradition). She completed the school in 1901 and went to work as a teacher in the countryside.

In 1902, Alaiza Pashkevich published her first poems, full of sympathy for the life and suffering of impoverished peasants. In that year–her education still insufficient to enter university and with most university courses, with very few exceptions, closed to women–Pashkevich left for St Petersburg, the Russian imperial capital, to begin her studies at the Lesgaft Women's Courses for Governesses and Women Physical Education Teachers. After the anti-Russian Uprising of 1863, all universities in the Northwestern Province were closed and Belarussian (mostly male) youth were forced to seek their education elsewhere. At the turn of the century, St Petersburg had a small Belarussian intellectual circle and Alaiza Pashkevich was drawn into the literati. In 1903, together with the brothers Ivan and Anton Lutskevich, Ales' Burbis and several others, she became one of the organizers of the Belarussian Socialist Union *Hramada* (Unity), established by Belarussian intellectuals receiving their higher education in St Petersburg and involved in the literary life of the city. She returned to Wilno in 1904 with an awakened class, national and women's consciousness and from that moment on, 'the woman question' was an important part of her ideas on social justice. She worked as a nurse in a mental hospital, spoke at workers' meetings, organized solidarity groups of workers and wrote revolutionary poems. In 1905, after the first Russian Revolution had been set in motion, the Tsar was obliged to consent to the establishment of a 'Parliament:' the Russian Duma. In May that year Alaiza Pashkevich attended a Women's Congress in Moscow as a delegate for the women workers of Wilno.

Early in 1906, Alaiza Pashkevich had to emigrate because of her revolutionary activities. Her apartment became a club and meeting place for Belarussian intellectuals (at a time when the Belarussian language had been forbidden by the tsarist administration). Her poem "Chrest na svabodu" (The cross for freedom) was seen as a revolutionary manifesto and the basement of the mental hospital where she worked was used to print revolutionary pamphlets. In emigration, Alaiza Pashkevich published two books of poetry: *Chrest na svabodu* (The cross for freedom) and *Dudka belaruskaya* (The Belarussian horn), both in 1906. She also published the first children's books in Belarussian. Six years of emigration became a time of intense literary work and study, first at the Philosophy Department of Lwow University (Galicia, in the Habsburg Empire; currently Lviv in Ukraine); later, after she had developed tuberculosis and left for southern Poland, at the Department of History and Philology in Cracow, where she joined a revolutionary students' organization. Alaiza Pashkevich also studied acting and exchanged regularly with Belarussian intellectuals in various parts of the empire. She traveled to Italy (1908) and Scandinavia (1914) and wrote poems and prose. One of her poems was specifically addressed to women ("To peasant women") and was inspired by Belarussian folklore.

In 1911, Alaiza Pashkevich married the engineer Steponas Kairys (1879–1964), an ethnic Lithuanian, and was able to return to her homeland under her new name. She threw herself into Belarussian cultural and intellectual life, acting in and traveling with the first Belarussian theater group—established by the actor, cultural activist and founder of the First Belarussian Society of Drama and Comedy (1917) Ihnat Buynitski. She contributed to the first Belarussian newspaper *Nasha Niva* (Our field) and participated in an underground elementary school for peasant children with Belarussian as the language of instruction, legalized in 1915. As the national cultural idea grew in strength as a means of political empowerment, teaching children in the native language came to be considered an important part of the work for the national future, as well as being work to which women in particular were suited. In 1914, Alaiza Pashkevich initiated the first Belarussian magazine for children and youth called *Luchynka* (The splinter).

Soon after the outbreak of World War I, the Belarussian ethnic territories became a battlefield at the rear of the front lines. Alaiza Pashkevich became a nurse in a soldiers' typhoid ward; she organized shelters for refugees, soup kitchens for the hungry, asylums for children and sewing shops where refugee women could earn a little money. In 1915, she also participated in setting up Belarussian elementary schools and courses for training Belarussian teachers in Wilno.

In January 1916, Alaiza Pashkevich received news that her father was sick. She rushed home but arrived too late to see him alive. She stayed in her village to help her compatriots during the epidemic of typhoid fever but became infected herself and died on 5 February 1916. She remains the most famous and brilliant woman of the Belarussian national revival: a key figure of both women's activism and Belarussian literature. In 1918, a children's asylum organized in Minsk by Paluta Badunova was named "Tsiotka." In 1931, ***Nadzeja Sznarkiewicz*** established the first Belarussian women's organization in Wilno (then in Poland) and named it after Tsiotka.

Elena Gapova
EHU-International (European Humanities University)

SOURCES

(D) "Paskevich, Alaiza (Tsiotka)." *Entsyklapedya litaratury I mastatstva Belarusi* (Encyclopedia of Belarussian literature and art). Minsk: BSE, 1984, 5: 472.

(E) Koutun, Valyantsina. *Kryzh milasernasci* (The cross of mercy). Minsk: "Mastatskaya litaratura," 1988.

PAVLYCHKO (PAVL'YCHKO), Solom'iya (Solom'ea, Solom'iia) Dm'ytrivna (1958–1999)

Ukrainian scholar and central figure in the late twentieth-century Ukrainian feminist movement; Senior Research Associate at the Institute of Literature, Ukrainian Academy of Sciences; Doctor of Philology/ professor at the National University ('Kyiv-Mohyla Academy'), Kiev.

Solom'iya Pavlychko was born in Lviv (Ukraine). Her parents were Dmytro Pavlychko (b. 1929), Ukrainian poet and influential figure in the Ukrainian movement for independence, and Bohdana Pavlychko, a doctor. Pavlychko spent most of her adult life in Kiev, where she studied English and French at the Taras Shevchenko Kiev State University from 1975 to 1985. After the completion of her doctoral studies, she began her professional career as a literary translator at the Institute of Literature, Ukrainian Academy of Sciences, Kiev. The range of Pavlychko's activities and initiatives make her a significant public figure in Ukraine: the translator of English and American writers (such as M. Twain, E. Hemingway, D. H. Lawrence and W. Golding); author of the important monograph, *Dyskurs modernizmu v ukražns'kii literaturi* (Modernist discourse in Ukrainian literature, 1997); key figure in Ukrainian literary circles of the late 1980s and 1990s and provocative feminist critic of long-established dogmas in Ukrainian society, culture and academic scholarship.

After 1986, the personal and the political became intrinsically connected in the lives of many Ukrainians, who were surviving deep trauma under the shadow of Chernobyl. In 1989, Pavlychko supported the *Narodnyi Rukh Ukraïny* (People's Movement of Ukraine), a new political party founded by members of the Writers' Union of Ukraine. As a political opposition movement, the *Rukh* united many groups: those who demanded the restoration of the Ukrainian language and political independence for Ukraine; those campaigning for the democratic freedoms of former political prisoners; religious and ethnic minorities (such as Ukrainian Catholics and Crimean Tatars), as well as anti-militarist and ecological activists (e.g. the Association of Mothers of Soldiers in Ukraine). *Rukh* was successful in the election campaign of 1990 and eventually formed a political fraction–the *Narodna Rada* (People's Council)–within the *Verkhovna Rada Ukraïny* (Supreme Council of Ukraine), emerging as a reformist opposition movement by early 1990. As a founding member of the *Zhinocha Hromada* (Women's Community), Pavlychko was instrumental in giving a voice to the women's wing of *Rukh*, establishing *Zhinocha Hromada* as an independent national organization in 1991. In her first book in English, *Letters from Kiev* (subsequently published in Ukrainian), Pavlychko captured the spirit of that turbulent time: the collapse of Soviet power accompanied by political and economic upheaval. Written to her Canadian friend Dr Bohdan Krawchenko, *Letters from Kiev* covers the period from 12 May 1990 to 25 March 1991.

Increasing discrimination against women at work and shifting women's status in Ukrainian society marked the 1990s. After a Soviet period in which feminism was thought of as 'bourgeois' ideology, Pavlychko revitalized the concept of feminism in Ukraine, organizing the first feminist seminar in Ukraine at the archconservative Institute of Literature (Kiev) in 1990. Together with Oksana Zabuzhko and Vira Aheyeva, Pavlychko laid the foundations for a revitalized Ukrainian feminist critique, embedded in two trends in contemporary Ukrainian society: the revival of nationalism in the 1990s (rooted in Ukrainian romantic nationalism of the early nineteenth century) and the rediscovery of 1960s and 1970s feminist literary criticism. In her article "Between Feminism and Nationalism: New Women's Groups in the Ukraine" (1992), Pavlychko criticized an illusory vision of womanhood imposed by those unwilling to accept new roles for women in post-Soviet Ukraine. In "Feminism in Post-Communist Ukrainian Society" (1996), she examined the backlash against women's emancipation in Ukraine during the early 1990s, concluding on a pessimistic note that revival of a Ukrainian matriarchal cultural myth: *Berehinya* (hearth mother) favored the relegation of women to the domestic sphere. Through her interviews and appearances in the media, Pavlychko helped bring feminism and modernism to the fore of public discussion. In her essay "Modernism vs. Populism" (1996), Pavlychko broke new ground, interrogating gender and feminist issues in Ukrainian literary texts and revealing deep connections between literary production and identity construction in contemporary Ukraine. Presenting an anthology *From Three Worlds: New Ukrainian Writing*, a collection of writing from sixteen young Ukrainian writers translated into English, Pavlychko concluded that it was the inner freedom felt by national writers and the intelligentsia that had led to Ukrainian independence; that the sign of that freedom was the rediscovery of the mother tongue. Pavlychko's introduction to this volume is emblematic of her efforts to support young writers (such as V. Dibrova, Yev. Pashkovsky and O. Zabuzhko) who transcended historical limitations and explored their cultural roots. The national priorities of the Ukrainian women's movement of the 'first wave' (1989 to the mid-1990s), when feminism was perceived as the only ideological alternative to communism, were inseparably tied to the process of collective identity formation in contemporary Ukraine.

In her most noted monograph, *Dyskurs modernizmu v ukražns'kii literaturi*

(Modernist discourse in Ukrainian literature), Pavlychko called for a rethinking of twentieth-century Ukrainian literary history. Paradigms in Ukrainian modernism (from 1898–1970) were indicative, in Pavlychko's view, of a conflict between modernism and folklorism. Applying contemporary theoretical standards to a discussion of literary works by ***Lesia Ukrainka***, ***Olha Kobylianska***, Hnat Khotkevych, Mykhailo Iatskov and *Moloda Muza* (Young Muse, a New York-based creative group), Pavlychko demonstrated that a 'Ukrainian feminist consciousness' had developed during the extremely complex twentieth century, under the powerful influence of women writers whose passion for beauty over social problematics, suppressed by the mainstream national critics, had been interpreted as a dangerous and pathological phenomenon in Ukrainian literature. Pavlychko's work was critical in bringing national cultural discourse into contact with broader debates on issues of sexuality and gender in literature and art. In 1998, Pavlychko co-edited an anthology of short fiction by contemporary Ukrainian and Canadian Ukrainian writers, *Two Lands, New Visions: Stories from Canada and Ukraine*, in collaboration with Canadian writer Janice Kulyk Keefer. Pavlychko's "Women's Discordant Voices in the Context of the 1998 Parliamentary Elections in Ukraine" (published in an edited volume of essays entitled *Feminisms and Women's Movements in Contemporary Europe*, 2000) explored changes in the political participation of Ukrainian feminists, who had made repeated efforts to organize themselves into a united electoral bloc, hoping to acquire greater power at the institutional level and to combat the deep cultural conservatism of Ukrainian women (especially in rural regions). Pavlychko suggested a possible convergence of identities between democratic political groups and women's organizations, capable of overcoming the archaic discourses reproduced by national male demagogues. Since Pavlychko rejected the idea of a single 'women's identity,' she also rejected the idea of a single political choice for Ukrainian women; nevertheless, she believed that a quick transition to democracy was central to the future of the Ukrainian feminist movement. An internationally recognized literary scholar, she taught courses in Ukrainian and American literature and literary theory at the Taras Shevchenko Kiev State University and the National University ('Kyiv-Mohyla Academy') in Kiev. She was also invited (as a Visiting Professor) to teach at Harvard University and the University of Alberta. For young Ukrainian writers and artists she was a unique role model, exerting a tremendous influence on their creative activities. As founder and editor-in-chief of *Osnovy* (Foundations), a publishing house in Kiev established in 1992, Pavlychko provided Ukrainian readers with translations of significant contributions to Western culture and thought, including popular feminist texts such as *The Second Sex* by Simone de Beauvoir and *Sexual Politics* by Kate Millet. Pavlychko's untimely death in Kiev on 31 December 1999, a result of an accident in her home, plunged the country into deep sorrow. She was survived by her parents, her daughter Bohdana (b. 1986), her younger sister Roxolana and her life partner Dr Bohdan Krawchenko (b. 1946, currently Vice-Rector of the Ukrainian Academy of Public Administration in Kiev). Pavlychko was buried in Baikove cemetery in Kiev on 4 January 2000.

Pavlychko generated new discussions on modernism and feminism, opening up the field of late nineteenth and twentieth-century Ukrainian literature for future research in these areas. The Solomea Pavlychko Stipend (established by George Luckyj, Slavic Department, University of Toronto) is now an award available to Ukrainian literary scholars or creative writers. The annual Solomea Pavlychko Prize in Literary Criticism, awarded by AGNI Magazine, honors a critic whose work has enlarged America's literary horizons. The Solomea Pavlychko Publishing House (*Osnovy*) has born her name since the year 2000. In her last book, *Natsionalizm, seksual'nist', orientalizm: skladnyi svit Ahatanhela Kryms'kogo* (Nationalism, sexuality, orientalism: the complicated world of Ahatanhel of the Crimea), she explores the tragic life of Ukrainian poet, scholar, translator and literary historian Agatangel Kryms'ky (1871–1942). In *Feminizm* (Feminism), a collection of her works, interviews and talks published after her death, the focus is shifted from politics to the wider objective of creating a national women's movement and developing women's individual identities in Ukrainian society. Pavlychko predicted that the future of an independent women's movement lay with non-governmental groups–later a distinctive characteristic of Ukrainian feminist movements of the 'second wave' (i.e. from the mid-1990s onwards). Her last two books have significantly contributed to the establishment of Pavlychko as an outstanding literary and feminist critic and progressive voice of Ukrainian women.

Viktoriya M. Topalova
Ph.D. Candidate, The University of British Columbia

SOURCES

(C) Pavl'ychko, Solom'iya. *Letters from Kiev*. Myrna Kostash, trans. Edmonton: Canadian Institute of Ukrainian Studies, 1992.

(C) Pavl'ychko, Solom'iya. "Between Feminism and Nationalism: New Women's Groups in the Ukraine." In Mary Buckley, ed. *Perestroika and Soviet Women*. Cambridge: Cambridge University Press, 1992, 82–96.

(C) Pavl'ychko, Solom'iya."Facing Freedom: The New Ukrainian Literature." Introduction to Ed Hogan, Michael Naidan, Oksana Zabuzhko, Mykola Riabchuk and Askold Melnyczuk, eds. *From Three Worlds: New Ukrainian Writing*. GLAS Series. Boston, MA: Zephyr Press, 1996.

(C) Pavl'ychko, Solom'iya. "Modernism vs. Populism in Fin de Siècle Ukrainian Literature: A Case of Gender Conflict." In Pamela Chester and Sibelan Forrester, eds. *Engendering Slavic Literatures*. Bloomington, Indiana: Indiana University Press, 1996, 83–103.

(C) Pavl'ychko, Solom'iya. "Feminism in Post-Communist Ukrainian Society." In Rosalind J. Marsh, ed. *Women in Russia and Ukraine*. Cambridge: Cambridge University Press, 1996, 305–314.

(C) Keefer, Janice Kulyk and Solomea Pavlychko, eds. *Two Lands, New Visions: Stories from Canada and Ukraine*. Reissue edition. Coteau Books, 1998.

(C) Pavl'ychko, Solom'iya. *Dyskurs modernizmu v ukrażns'kii literaturi* (Modernist discourse in Ukrainian literature). Kiev: Lybid', 1997; Revised second edition. Kiev: Lybid', 1999.

(C) Pavl'ychko, Solom'iya. "Women's Discordant Voices in the Context of the 1998 Parliamentary Elections in Ukraine." In Anna Bull, Hanna Diamond and Rosalind Marsh, eds. *Feminisms and Women's Movements in Contemporary Europe*. London: Macmillan, 2000.

(C) Pavl'ychko, Solom'iya. *Natsionalizm, seksual'nist', orientalizm: skladnyi svit Ahatanhela Kryms'kogo* (Nationalism, sexuality, orientalism: the complicated world of Ahatanhel of the Crimea). Kiev: Vydavnytstvo "Osnovy," 2000.

(C) Pavl'ychko, Solom'iya. *Feminizm* (Feminism). Kiev: Vydavnytstvo "Osnovy," 2002.

(D) Aheyeva, Vira P. *Intelektual'na biohrafiya Solomiż Pavlychko* (Solomiya Pavlychko: an intellectual portrait). Kiev: Dukh i litera, 2001.

PCHILKA, Olena (real name Olha Petrivna Kosach, born Drahomanova) (1849–1930)

Ukrainian writer, editor, translator, ethnographer and women's activist; corresponding member (from 1925) of the Academy of Sciences of the Ukrainian Soviet Socialist Republic.

Olena Pchilka (pseudonym of Olha Petrivna Kosach, born Drahomanova) was born in Hadiach (in the region of Poltava) on 29 July 1849, to a landed noble family steeped in liberal and intellectual traditions. Her father, Petro Yakymovych Drahomanov (1802–1866), was a graduate of the St Petersburg Law Academy who also wrote, published and translated short stories and poetry. Her mother, Yelizaveta Ivanivna Drahomanova (born Tsiatska, 1821–1895), was semi-literate (she could read but could only sign her name), yet it was she who introduced Ukrainian folklore to the Drahomanov family and instilled a love for its richness in her children. The Drahomanovs had five children altogether, among them Mykhailo Drahomanov (1841–1895), a historian, publicist, folklorist, literary critic and public activist who emigrated in 1876 and taught at Sofia University (Bulgaria) from 1889 until his death. He would play an important role in the lives of Olena Pchilka and her daughter, ***Lesia Ukrainka*** (see also ***Julia Malinova***).

Olena Pchilka received her primary education from her father and in 1861, Mykhailo Drahomanov placed her in the Kiev Institute for Girls of the Nobility, from which she graduated in 1866. In 1868, she married Petro Antonovych Kosach (1842–1909). Kosach, who was also from a noble family, received his primary education at the Chernihiv Gymnasium and entered St Petersburg University, from which he was expelled for his part in the student movement. He nevertheless succeeded in entering Kiev St. Volodymyr University, where he graduated in legal science. After they married, the couple moved to Zviagel (now Novohrad-Volynsky in the region of Zhytomyr), where Kosach held a legal position. In 1879, the family moved to Lutsk, later purchasing a land share in Kolodiazhne (in Kovel, in the region of Volyn) and building the house where they would live until the death of Petro Kosach.

In 1876, Pchilka published her first work *Ukrainskiy narodnyi ornament* (Ukrainian folk design), edited by Mykhailo Drahomanov and Volodymyr Antonovych. It was written in Russian in accordance with the so-called Emsk Decree (1876), which explicitly prohibited any kind of publishing activity in the Ukrainian language on the territory of the Russian Empire. In 1879, after the family had moved to Lutsk, Pchilka set up a publishing house: the *NHV* (Small Volyn Group). In 1880, the *NHV* published *Spivomovky* by Stepan Rudansky ("spivomovky," a word invented by Rudansky, is roughly translatable as "singing words"), thereby rescuing the forgotten poet from obscurity. A year later, Pchilka published her translations of works by Mykola Hohol and her own play, *Suzhena–Ne Ohuzhena* (She who is promised but not disgraced). In her foreword to the Hohol translations, Olena Pchilka stated explicitly that her primary goal was to develop the Ukrainian language and bring it out of the home into the public sphere. By the early 1890s, Olena Pchilka was publishing quite regularly, for example in the Lviv magazine *Zoria* (Star). She soon became an acknowledged writer and a key figure of Ukrainian literary and thus cultural life.

In her much-criticized writings, Olena Pchilka strove to transcend limitations posed by Ukrainian nationalist-populist discourses. She sought new topics that were not related to village life (conceptualized at that time as the sole basis for the Ukrainian national idea). In her own words: "...I set out in a new field–though I remain, so to speak, on the fresh ground of the very same Ukrainian field, Ukrainian literature, Ukrainian life... [My heroines] are all taken from the lives of the people; though they are not the heroines of Vovchok, Kulish, or even Shevchenko (those delicate lovers, sisters, women), they are still the figures of patriot women" (Bohachevsky-Chomiak 1999, 42). Her heroines, like herself, shaped by her ideas on the position of women and the importance of women's role in the development of the nation, went very much against the grain of the society she lived in and did not receive popular acclaim.

An energetic woman with a keen sensitivity to women's inequality in Ukrainian society (split at that time between the Russian and Austro-Hungarian Empires and regarded as two independent entities by the Ukrainians themselves), Olena Pchilka was actively involved in many spheres of Ukrainian cultural and political life. Together with ***Natalia Kobrynska,*** Pchilka edited and published an anthology, *Pershy Vinok* (First wreath, 1887). Among the works selected for *Pershy Vinok* were Pchilka's novel *Tovaryshky* (Girlfriends) and poems by ***Lesia Ukrainka,*** which had been smuggled into Halychyna. The anthology played a key role in the development of a women's literature in Ukraine, opening up a female space in literature and social life that had remained hitherto unexplored. Subsequently, both editors hoped to publish another anthology *Druhy Vinok* (Second wreath) but this plan was never realized. In the 1890s, Pchilka received with enthusiasm a proposal by M. Pavlyk, editor-in-chief of *Narod*

(Nation; the official organ of the Radical Party) to establish and publish a special newspaper for Ukrainian peasant women.

One of the few public activists to regard women's public activity to be an inseparable part of, if not a driving force behind the Ukrainian national movement, Olena Pchilka invested a great deal of energy in affairs seemingly irrelevant to 'women's causes.' She was one of five delegates to submit, in 1904, a petition to the Ministry of Internal Affairs, requesting permission to publish books in Ukrainian. In 1905, when the Revolution resulted in the liberalization of education, in particular of higher education, Pchilka urged the Ukrainian intelligentsia to raise funds for a Ukrainian people's university. Later, having moved to Poltava to edit and publish a magazine *Ridny Kray* (Homeland) and an appendix, *Moloda Ukrayina* (Young Ukraine, 1906–1914), Pchilka agreed to head the Poltava regional branch of the *Vserosiyska spilka rivnoupravlinnia zhinok* (All-Russian Union for Women's Equality), which had branches in nine cities of the Right-bank Ukraine and which worked for women's equality and the defence of national interests. Although she was not very popular in the Right-bank Ukraine due to what many perceived as her 'radical' politics, Pchilka nevertheless urged Ukrainian women to establish women's organizations as part of a broader national endeavor. Together with Maria Yanovska, she represented the *Kyivska Zhinocha Hromada* (Kiev Women's Community), a Ukrainian branch of the *Vserosiyska spilka rivnoupravlinnia zhinok*, at the All-Russian Congress of Women (organized by the *Vserosiyska spilka rivnoupravlinnia zhinok*) in St Petersburg (1908). At this event, Pchilka presented a report entitled "The Tasks of Ukrainian Women." The text itself has not been preserved but, judging from other sources, it seems likely that Pchilka discussed the role of the national women's movement for the future of Ukraine and the ways such a movement could serve the country as a whole. In other words, Pchilka's emphasis is likely to have subordinated the specific needs of women to those of 'the nation' and the national cause.

After the death of her daughter (***Lesia Ukrainka***) on 8 August 1913, Olena Pchilka moved to Hadiach and there (from 1917 to 1919) began editing the *Hazeta Zemstva Hadiatskoho* (Hadiach zemstvo newspaper). From 1921, Pchilka resided permanently in Kiev, where she worked for various (e.g. ethnographic and literary) commissions of the Ukrainian Academy of Sciences. In April 1925, she was elected a corresponding member of the Academy of Sciences of the Ukrainian Soviet Socialist Republic, in spite of the fact that she was not entirely supportive of communist rule and, after the 1917 Revolution, had avoided political life. The early 1920s–the 'korenizatsia' years during which state policy sought to establish national languages as the state languages of the corresponding republics (including Ukraine)–was a period of 'national revival' in Ukraine: a brief period in the history of the Right-bank Ukraine when Ukrainian language, culture and science were promoted by the administration. Later, in 1927, purges directed against national activists swept away many members of the cultural elite, including the families of Olga and Izydora Kosach.

After Olena Pchilka's death (from pneumonia) on 4 October 1930, she was buried in Kiev Baikhove cemetery, alongside her husband, only son Mykhailo and daughter Lesia Ukrainka. In 1944, her daughters Olga Petrivna Kosach-Kryvyniuk (1877–1945) and Izydora Petrivna Kosach-Borysova (1888–1980) left the USSR to avoid persecution. Her other daughter, Oksana Petrivna Kosach-Shymanovska (1882–1975), moved to Czechoslovakia shortly after her marriage in 1908 and remained there for the rest of her life, never to return to Ukraine.

Natalia V. Monakhova
Ph.D. Candidate (Comparative Literature),
National University "Kyiv-Mohyla Academy"

SOURCES

(C) Pchilka, Olena. *Opovidannia, z avtobiografiyeyu* (Short stories and autobiography). Rukh, 1930.

(D) Chernyshov, Andry. "Olena Pchilka." *Nevmyrushchi* (Immortal) (Kharkiv: Prapor, 1970): 137–173.

(E) Bohachevsky-Chomiak, Martha. *Bilym po bilomu: Zhinky v hromadskomy zhytti Ukrayny* (White on white: women in Ukrainian public life). Kiev: Lybid, 1999.

(E) Smoliar. L. O., ed. *Zhinochi studii v Ukraini: Zhinka v istorii i siohodni* (Women's studies in Ukraine: woman in history and today). Odessa: AstroPrint, 1999.

(E) Karmazina, Maria. *Lesia Ukrainka*. Kiev: Alternatyvy, 2003.

PEJNOVIĆ, Kata (1899–1966)

Serbian leader of the *Antifašistički front žena* (*AFŽ*, Antifascist Women's Front), Yugoslavia; co-founder (1942) of the first women's newspaper on liberated Croatian territory, *Žena u borbi* (Woman in struggle); elected to the Central Committee of the Communist Party of Croatia (1948).

Kata Pejnović (*nee* Bogić) was born on 21 March 1899, to a peasant family in the village of Smiljan in Lika, a poor rural region of Croatia with an ethnically mixed population consisting of Serbs and Croats. Her father, Dmitar Bogić, worked for the Austro-Hungarian police, retiring early to continue farming. Her mother, Jelena Bogić, was a self-taught dressmaker, whose small earnings, assisted by Dmitar's retirement income, supported a large family: Kata, her three brothers and two sisters. (Archival data suggests that Jelena may have had nine children instead of six, but this cannot be confirmed with any certainty.) Since their parents could not afford to send them to school, none of the children in the family received any substantial education. Thus, after graduating from the local elementary school in 1911, in spite of her excellent record and her lively interest in study, Kata was not given the opportunity to attend the gymnasium because she had to help feed her family, working in the houses of wealthier peasants in return for food.

Kata Bogić married early and assumed the name of her husband, of whom little is known. (In her public appearances and interviews, she took care to avoid speaking of her private affairs, preferring to concentrate upon her services to public life.) Pejnović gave birth to five children: three sons and two daughters. In 1936, Pejnović, a peasant mother and wife who supported her family by selling milk and dairy products from her house in the nearby town of Gospić, came into contact with people who had links to the Communist Party. So began a politically active life and a new intellectual environment that enabled Pejnović to explore literature for the first time. By Pejnović's own account, the first 'sophisticated' book she read was *Mother* by Maxim Gorky. She became active in the regional communist cell in Smiljan, soliciting financial and other types of logistical support for local fighters participating in the Spanish civil war. Her fierce commitment resulted in her being admitted to the *Komunistička partija Jugoslavije* (Yugoslav Communist Party) on 10 April 1938, an unusually quick ascent into the ranks of the party (others had to pass through what was called 'the period of candidacy,' during which their suitability was tested). This development further motivated her to spread the political line of the Communist Party. According to available testimonies, Pejnović was particularly successful in establishing contacts with women and enlisting their support for her political agenda. Her special fields of interest and work were twofold. She worked on attempts to alleviate increasing ethnic tensions between Serbs and Croats in the Lika region (just three years prior to World War II and the ethnic carnage that would be committed on Yugoslavian territory) and she endeavored to 'raise consciousness' among the female population concerning women's social inequality. In accordance with prevailing communist ideology, Pejnović believed that the emergence of private property had caused women to lose their freedom and equality with men. Within the framework of the Marxist-Leninist theory of revolution, discrimination against women and women's specific social interests could not be justified as issues in their own right; instead, they were regarded as inequalities that would disappear with the obliteration of private property, achieved through communist revolution. Feminism was a bourgeois relic and ideologically dangerous. These were the ideas that shaped Pejnović's political agenda.

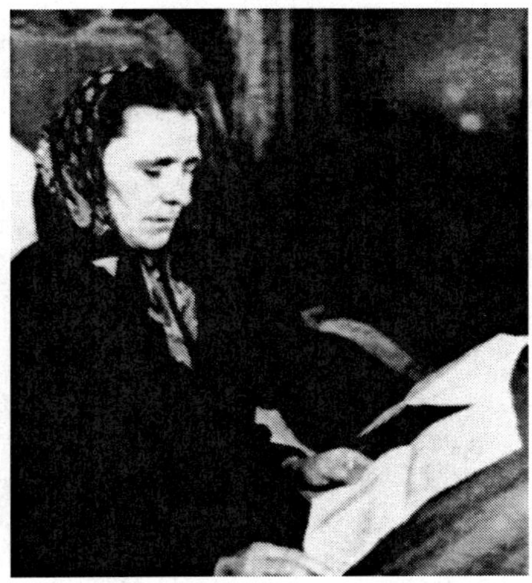

Kata Pejnović in the Croatian National Theater in Zagreb, giving a speech on the occasion of Women's Day, March 8, year unknown

Kata Pejnović's work soon aroused the suspicions of the Yugoslav police, which treated communist activity as anti-state action. Her house was searched by the police several times but real personal disaster struck during World War II. Following the proclamation of the Independent State of Croatia in April 1941—a fascist puppet-state—Pejnović became a target of police repression not only as a communist, but also as a Serb. In July of that year, during one of the bloody rampages conducted by Croatian fascist forces in the Lika region, her husband and three sons were arrested. Her husband was tortured (presumably to reveal her secret hiding place) and finally killed, together with her three sons, aged nineteen, thirteen and three. It is likely that from this time onwards, Kata Pejnović took to wearing a black scarf or kerchief, for which she later became known as 'the woman with the black scarf.'

With the Yugoslav Communist Party leading armed resistance against the fascists, it was only logical that Pejnović became a prominent name in the antifascist struggle. Her main tasks were logistics (collecting food and clothing for partisans) and helping to instigate popular uprisings against the fascists. In particular, she addressed illiterate peasant women, whom she strove to inspire and give self-esteem. In March 1942, she helped found the first women's newspaper on liberated Croatian territory, with the aim of spreading antifascist propaganda. The newspaper was called *Žena u borbi* (Woman in struggle) and Pejnović wrote for this and other women's newspapers, also gaining a reputation as a public speaker. In order to attract more women into the partisan ranks, the Communist Party decided to found an organization that could articulate women's needs: the *Antifašistički front žena* (*AFŽ*, Antifascist Women's Front), which held its first conference in Bosanski Petrovac on 6–8 December 1942, and of which organization Kata Pejnović was elected President. Earlier that year, she had been the only woman delegate to the Yugoslav war parliament's *Antifašističko vijeće narodnog oslobođenja Jugoslavije* (*AVNOJ*, Antifascist Council of the People's Liberation of Yugoslavia). Pejnović particularly advocated expanding the political, economic and social rights of women. She considered the full political freedom of women and their active political participation to be the foundation of their social equality. She was a delegate to the historic second session of *AVNOJ* in Jajce on 29 November 1943, when the second Yugoslav State was founded. She was also a delegate to the *Zemaljsko antifašističko vijeće narodnog oslobođenja Hrvatske* (*ZAVNOH*, State Antifascist Council of the People's Liberation of Croatia). In December 1944, she was heavily wounded, presumably as a result of air bombing, but recovered after two difficult surgical operations.

In the post-war years, Kata Pejnović remained politically very active. In 1948, she was elected to the Central Committee of the Communist Party of Croatia. From then until 1963, when illness left her bedridden, she was repeatedly elected to the Parliament of the People's Republic of Croatia and twice to the Federal Parliament. She served a number of public and political organizations, including the *Crveni križ* (Red Cross), of which she was President for a year. In recognition of her work, Kata Pejnović received many awards: the *Partizanska spomenica* (for partisanship); the *Orden bratstva i jedinstva prvog reda* (for brotherhood and unity of the first order); the *Orden hrabrosti* (for courage); the *Orden rada prvog reda* (for work of the first order) and the *Orden republike prvog reda* (for services of the first order to the Republic). Posthumously, she was accorded the *Orden narodnog heroja* (People's Hero Award). She died from an illness in 1966. Although Pejnović's contributions were recognized during her lifetime, her story–like those of all activists and leaders of the Antifascist Women's Front in Yugoslavia–beyond short references in collective volumes on the Yugoslav partisan fighters, was not documented during the communist years, nor after the collapse of communism.

Maja Brkljačić
Ph.D. Candidate, Central European University, Budapest

SOURCES

(A) Archival collection *AFŽ* (Antifascist Women's Front), Croatian State Archive. (Official documents and proclamations released by the *AFŽ*, as well as press coverage printed with *AFŽ* funding).

(B) Šoljan, Marija, ed. *Žene Hrvatske u Narodnooslobodilačkoj borbi* (Women of Croatia in the people's liberation struggle), vols. 1/2. Zagreb: Glavni odbor Saveza ženskih društava Hrvatske, 1955.

(E) Pulić, Nikola, ed. *Revolucija i revolucionari* (Revolution and revolutionaries). Zagreb: Naprijed, 1970.

(E) Sklevicky, Lydia. *Konji, žene, ratovi* (Horses, women, wars). Zagreb: Ženska infoteka, 1996.

PERIN-GRADENSTEIN, Karoline Freifrau von (1806–1888)

President of the first *Wiener demokratische Frauenverein* (Viennese Democratic Women's Association) (1848).

Karoline Freifrau von Perin-Gradenstein (*nee* von Pasqualati) was born on 12 February 1806 in Vienna, into an intellectual and artistic family. Her father, Joseph Andreas Freiher von Pasqualati (1784–1864), was a pomologist and wholesale trader in fruit and vegetables, whose family originally came from Trieste; her mother was Eleonore Fritsch (d. 1811). Karoline received an education typical for a girl of her social class. In 1830, she married Christian Freiherr von Perin-Gradenstein, a court secretary from a family of artistic patrons. The couple loved music and kept a salon. They had four children, one of which died in infancy. After her husband's death in 1841, Karoline von Perin lived with her children in Penzing, then a suburb of Vienna. In the mid-1840s, the musician and democrat Joseph Frischhof (1849–1857) suggested that the composer and journalist Alfred Julius Becher (1803–1848) become a piano teacher for Karoline von Perin's daughter, Marie. Von Perin and Becher became a couple and formed part of the clandestine opposition to the Metternich regime.

In the censorship-free, revolutionary months of 1848, von Perin financed Becher's newspaper, *Der Radikale* (The radical), and campaigned publicly for women's rights. In contrast to the men's discussion groups in cafes and pubs, which were held during the *Vormaerz* (Pre-March, the period between 1815 and March 1848), women–including von Perin–held political meetings in inns and pubs later, during the revolutionary 'free' months of 1848. Von Perin's political involvement and lifestyle (i.e. her relationship with Becher, to whom she was not married) gave rise to defamatory remarks regarding von Perin's character and reputation.

Among the numerous associations established at this time was the *Wiener demokratische Frauenverein* (Viennese Democratic Women's Association), which first assembled on 28 August 1848, in the *Volksgarten* (Public Gardens), Vienna. The meeting was stormed by men, antagonistic to the cause of women's rights, who destroyed furniture and threatened the participants with violence. After a number of meetings–in which internal differences were said to have emerged over positions towards the Emperor–Karoline von Perin was elected President of the organization, which passed a statute declaring its dedication to democratic principles. With the exception of similar associations in France, the statutes of this *Frauenverein* were unique, emphasizing the importance of a "political, social and human" education for girls and the political education of women, as well as arguing for children to be brought up in accordance with democratic principles such as equal rights for women. The *Frauenverein* also organized nursing for the wounded during the 1848 Revolution. The rules of the *Frauenverein*–regarding the right to introduce a motion, the right to speak and the right to nominate, elect and vote out board members–indicate a democratic structure to the organization, but men were only allowed to participate in meetings "exceptionally, as honorary members" (§. 8. *Statuten des Wiener demokratischen Frauenvereins*, 235-239). The *Frauenverein*'s statement of purpose reveals plans to expand the organization country-wide.

In the two months of its existence (until 31 October 1848), the members of the *Frauenverein* tried to establish an agreement between the different revolutionary parties and gathered signatures for a petition calling for *Landsturm* (a mobilization of the peasants), presented to the *Reichsrat* (Imperial Council) by a Women's Delegation under the leadership of von Perin on 17 October 1848. The members of the *Frauenverein* also participated in the funerals of those who had fallen victim to the militant 'August riots,' when working men and women, as well as students, fought the bourgeois *Nationalgarde* (National guard), marking the end of the united revolutionary movement of 1848 in Vienna. The fact that the *Frauenverein* co-founded the *Zentralausschluss der demokratischen Vereine* (Central Committee of the Democratic Associations)–established on 10 September 1848 in the Odeon Theater, Vienna–demonstrates the presence of a 'sisterhood' within the democratic movement of 1848 Vienna: a women's association whose members were included as partners in a bourgeois public sphere created by, and for, men. Although male supporters were, in the main, friends and relatives, this kind of unity was a European novelty, the result of the ambivalence between traditional and modern structures and mentalities that characterized the unique political culture of the Habsburg Monarchy and of its capital city in the mid-nineteenth century.

When the attack by counter-revolutionary troups against the revolutionary 'Island' of Vienna began on 22 October 1848, members of the *Frauenverein* were among the defenders. We will never know whether Karoline von Perin really did hold a black, red and gold flag (the German colors representing democracy in 1848) and fired pistols into the air at the barricades to urge the continuation of the fight, or whether these are merely the fantasies of von Perin's contemporaries. That von Perin was the only woman to be handed over to the victors, together with thirteen other revolutionaries under the capitulation terms of Prince Windischgrätz, suggests that the counter-revolutionaries considered the President of the Democratic Women's Association dangerous to the state. On 31 October 1848, revolutionary Vienna was surrounded and Becher and von Perin's plan to escape to Hungary failed. On 4 November 1848, von Perin's place of hiding was uncovered and she was arrested. On 13 November, Becher was also found and he was shot under martial law on 23 November. Pleas to let the two see each other one last time were rejected.

A few days later, after 23 days of mistreatment in prison, von Perin was released. On 17 April 1849, she received a passport and emigrated to Munich. Having transgressed the limits of both class and gender during the 1848 revolution, she had lost everything: her loved one and most of her friends were dead, or had also emigrated; her fortune had been confiscated; she had been rejected by her family and she had lost her right to custody of her eight-year-old son. After the release of her *Ungedruckte Aufzeichnungen* (Unpublished memoirs), in which she distanced herself from her 1848 engagement in the Viennese Revolution, she received permission to return to Vienna. Upon her return, she opened an employment agency so that she could live independently of her family. She did not take part in further political actions for the remainder of her life. She died on 10 December 1888.

Gabriella Hauch
Institute for Women's and Gender Studies
and Institute for Modern and Contemporary History,
Johannes Kepler University, Linz, Austria

Translated by Melanie Morgan.

SOURCES

(B) "Statuten des Wiener demokratischen Frauenvereins." In Gabriella Hauch. *Frau Biedermeier auf den Barrikaden. Frauenleben in der Wiener Revolution 1848* (Biedermeier woman at the barricades. Women's lives in the Viennese Revolution of 1848). Vienna: Verlag für Gesellschaftskritik, 1990, 235–239.

(B) Frankl-Hochwart, Bruno von. "Aus Bechers letzten Tagen. Ungedruckte Aufzeichnungen seiner Braut (Becher's last days. The unpublished memories of his bride)." *Die Zeit*, no. 201 (1898): 89.

(D) Hauch, Gabriella. *Frau Biedermeier auf den Barrikaden. Frauenleben in der Wiener Revolution 1848* (Biedermeier woman at the barricades. Women's lives in the Viennese Revolution of 1848). Vienna: Verlag für Gesellschaftskritik, 1990.

(D) Hauch, Gabriella. "Wir hätten ja gern die ganze Welt beglückt. Politik und Geschlecht im demokratischen Milieu 1948/49" (We would have made the whole world happy. Politics and gender in the democratic milieu 1848/49). *Österreichische Zeitschrift für Geschichtswissenschaften*, no. 4 (1998): 471–495.

(D) Hauch, Gabriella. "Women's Spaces in the Men's Revolution of 1848." In Dieter Dowe et. al., eds. *Europe in 1848. Revolution and Reform*. Oxford and New York: Berghahn Books, 2001, 639–682.

PETKEVIČAITĖ, Gabrielė (1861–1943)

Teacher, writer, journalist and editor; leader and ideologist of the Lithuanian women's movement before World War I; founder of the *Lietuvos moterų susivienijimas* (Lithuanian Women's Association, 1905) and the *Lietuvos aboliucionistų draugija* (Lithuanian Abolitionist Society, 1920); involved in the IWSA. Pseudonyms: 'Bitė' (Bee) and 'Vilkienė.'

Gabrielė Petkevičaitė was born on 18 March 1861, into a Catholic gentry family on the Puziniškės family estate in the Panevežys district in northern Lithuania. The family estate of Puziniškės was a local cultural center that attracted many activists of the Lithuanian national movement. During the 1863–1864 uprising against Russian domination, Petkevičaitė's parents sheltered rebels. Her father, Jonas Petkevičius (1828–?), was a doctor in the provincial Joniškis hospital and her mother, Malvina Chodakauskaitė-Petkevičienė (data unknown), organized social work and helped nurse poor patients and arrange support for their families. Gabrielė apparently inherited her parents' sense of altruism and social justice.

Gabrielė Petkevičaitė received her primary education at home from a private teacher, Laurynas Ivinskis, the author and editor of the first calendar in the Lithuanian language (from 1864 to 1904, printing in the Lithuanian language was banned). In 1873, she enrolled in a private girls' school (the *Töchterschule* 'Dorothea,' owned by Cicilija von der Osten Zalien), from which she graduated in 1876 with an elementary school teacher's license. While studying languages, history and mathematics, Petkevičaitė, who had been raised in a Catholic family, experienced a crisis of religiosity and eventually became indifferent to religious beliefs. From 1876 to 1878, Petkevičaitė continued her education at the Mintau girls' high school of St. Trinitis and received a diploma to teach domestic science. After graduating, she expressed a desire to go on and study mathematics at university, but her father objected to her leaving Lithuania because he wanted her to manage the family estate. At that time, inspired by the works of ***Eliza Orzeszkowa*** and *Swit* (Sunrise), a magazine edited by the Polish essayist Maria Konopnicka, she became excited by ideas of women's emancipation, especially the necessity of girls' education.

Using the pseudonyms 'Bitė' (Bee) and 'Vilkienė,' Petkevičaitė actively contributed to the illegal Lithuanian press. She also helped organize and distribute Lithuanian books smuggled from Prussia. In 1890, she established a secret secular school on her estate where most of the students were girls and where she taught in Lithuanian. Petkevičaitė contributed the income of Puziniškės, the estate she had inherited from her father, to the school so it could remain tuition-free and open to Lithuanian girls from the lower classes. By the end of the nineteenth century, Puziniškės had become a center of Lithuanian cultural and political life. Both her father and herself welcomed students, writers and artists.

The five women Members of Parliament in 1920
Middle: Gabrielė Petkevičaiė, sitting right ***Magdalena Galdikienė***

Petkevičaitė felt that members of the male intelligentsia of her generation were hostile towards women, considered women unreliable and refused to invite them to meetings where important decisions were made. For this reason, she decided to work independently and in 1894, together with Jadvyga Juškytė, she established the first illegal charitable women's organization *Žiburėlis* (Light), which financially and materially supported poor male and female students. She admired the British suffragettes' struggle for the vote and was influenced by the French feminist Olympe de Gouges (1748–1793), whom she read and referred to in her own writing. Petkevičaitė started discussions of women's rights in the illegal Lithuanian press, encouraging and organizing women's initiatives in Lithuania. Her article "The women's movement and its obligations," published in 1905, became a manifesto for future generations of women in Lithuania. She encouraged women to follow the women of Finland (who received the vote in 1905) by organizing a general women's strike until the right to vote was won. Her writings also prompted Lithuanian women's activism in the field of education. According to Petkevičaitė, Lithuanian women were the last in Europe to have become aware of their lack of rights, and had no time to lose in fighting for them.

In 1905, Petkevičaitė organized a women's meeting in Šiauliai, attended by some fifty women. The outcome of the meeting was the establishment of the *Lietuvos moterų susivienijimas* (Lithuanian Women's Association), a secular, left-wing organization whose main goal was the achievement of equal political rights for women. *Lietuvos moterų susivienijimas*, chaired by Petkevičaitė, began organizing women in Lithuanian provincial towns and villages and also established connections with women's organizations in Russia, such as the *Soiuz ravnopraviia zhenshchin* (Women's Equal Rights Union).

Petkevičaitė was very active during the first Lithuanian Women's Congress held in Vilnius in September 1907. She was elected Honorable Chair of the *Lietuvos moterų sąjunga* (Lithuanian Women's Union), founded in 1908. The Union's goal was to unite Catholic and secular women in the fight for equal economic, legal and political rights. Petkevičaitė was in charge of organizing the structure and practical work of the *Lietuvos moterų sąjunga*, writing and publishing its statute and program. However, the tsarist regime did not register and thus legalize the organization, and this uncertain legal status limited many Union activities. In December 1908, Petkevičaitė attended the First All-Russian Women's Congress in St Petersburg, where she gave a talk on "Lithuanian woman in the family and society." In 1909, she moved from the estate in Puziniškės to Vilnius, the then Lithuanian political and cultural center.

Her participation in the Russian Women's Congress inspired her political activities and in 1910, Petkevičaitė published a book, *Apie moterų klausimą* (The woman question). In 1912, with the help of ***Felicija Bortkevičienė,*** she established and edited the secular women's monthly *Žibutė* (Violet), but only a few issues of *Žibutė* came out due to financial difficulties.

During World War I, Petkevičaitė again lived on the Puzinišės family estate. She decided to remain there and help people instead of choosing a safer life in exile, as many had chosen to do. Petkevičaitė believed that an intellectual's duty was to be close to ordinary people and help them, a wish to serve others that she realized in practical ways, such as by passing the exams necessary to gain a paramedic's license (in 1917). On Puziniškės, Gabrielė also organized weekend classes for adults. She contributed all of her modest wealth and time to this project, but the classes had to be closed after eleven months due to financial problems. During the war, Petkevičaitė wrote her (later published) *Karo meto dienoraštis* (A wartime diary), in which she expressed pacifist views.

Lithuania established its independence in 1918 and women achieved the right to vote. Due to health problems however, Petkevičaitė was not actively involved. In 1919, she became a teacher at Panevėžys state gymnasium and shared part of her salary with poor students, returning in 1920 to the center of political events. She was elected from the *Lietuvos socialistų liaudininkų partija* (Lithuanian Socialist Populist Party) to the Constitutive *Seimas* (Parliament) of the newly independent Lithuanian State. More importantly, it was Petkevičaitė (sometimes calling herself Petkevičaitė-Bitė after 1918) who opened the first *Seimas* session, expressing her happiness–as an old protagonist of her nation and as a woman who had achieved equal rights–at being able to do so. Health problems stopped her from being an active politician but, despite her absences from the *Seimas*, Petkevičaitė remained very popular in Lithuania and was re-elected as a member of Parliament in the 1922 and 1925 elections. In 1925, she was one of the candidates for the presidential office, but received just one vote. Who proposed Petkevičaitė for the Lithuanian Presidency is not known; it might have been the Socialist Populist Party or even Petkevičaitė herself, most likely the latter, or Bortkevičienė. This move in the male-dominated Lithuanian Parliament was unusual and provoking, especially since women in Lithuania in the interwar period did not hold high positions within governmental structures.

As much as her health allowed her, Petkevičaitė was active in the women's movement. In 1920, she represented Lithuania at the Congress of the International Woman Suffrage Alliance (IWSA) in Geneva, where she became interested in abolitionist ideas. Lithuanian abolitionists used rhetoric referring to 'white slavery:' i.e. the buying and selling of women in red light districts and across national borders. She established the Lithuanian Abolitionist Society in 1920 and was a devoted organizer of awareness campaigns against prostitution in general and red light districts in particular, both of which the Society strove to abolish. During its first year, the Society organized 26 abolitionists groups in all the regions of Lithuania and attracted over a thousand members. In 1922, Petkevičaitė set up and edited four issues of the newspaper *Lietuvos aboliucionistas* (The Lithuanian abolitionist).

In 1922, Petkevičaitė also helped restore the *Lietuvos moterų sąjunga* (Lithuanian Women's Union) in opposition to right-wing Catholic women's organizations. The *Lietuvos moterų sąjunga* fought against restrictions in the job market for married women. This, however, was to be Petkevičaitė's last active year. She returned to her estate in Puziniškės where, although seriously ill, she continued to write and to encourage women's activism. In 1933, she helped establish an Orthopedic Help Society and wrote her last novel, *Ad Astra* (Latin for "To the stars"). The main theme of the novel, based on her personal biography, was the dilemma of an educated woman in Lithuanian society, forced to choose between her personal desires and the requirements of society. In 1937, almost blind, she gave her last public speech at the second Lithuanian Women's Congress. Petkevičaitė died on 14 June 1943, after having suffered from severe dementia in the last five years of her life.

Gabrielė Petkevičaitė never married and gave her life to public service. She remains *the* symbol of the Lithuanian women's movement.

Rima Praspaliauskienė
Beatrice M. Bain Research Group on Genders,
University of California, Berkeley

SOURCES

A) *Lietuvių literatūros ir tautosakos institutas* (Institute of Lithuanian Literature and Folklore), Collection No. 30 (F.30–Gabrielė Petkevičaitė-Bitė). Contains Gabrielė Petkevičaitė's letters, manuscripts and publications. A large part of this material is also published in Petkevičaitė's *Raštai* (Collected works).

A) *Vilniaus universiteto bibliotekos rankraščių skyrius* (VUB RS) (Manuscript Department at the Library of Vilnius University), Collection F.1-f.780. Contains Gabrielė Petkevičaitė's letters to ***F. Bortkevičienė.***

(B) Newspaper *Žibutė* (1912).

(B) Newspaper *Moteris ir pasaulis* (1938-1940).

(B) Newspaper *Moteris*, no. 1 (1921).

(C) Petkevičaitė-Bitė, Gabrielė. *Raštai* (Collected works). Six volumes. Vilnius, 1967-1972. Includes all Petkevičaitė's published works, letters and interviews.

(D) Jasaitis, J. *Gabrielė Petkevičaitė-Bitė*. Vilnius, 1972.

PĪPIŅA, Berta (1883-1942)

Latvian writer, editor, journalist; co-founder (1930) of the *Latvijas Sieviešu organizāciju padome* (Council of Latvian Women's Organization); first woman to be elected to the Latvian Parliament (1931).

Berta Pīpiņa (born Ziemele) was born on 28 September 1883, in the parish of Code (Latvia). Her father, Jekabs Ziemelis, was an innkeeper and also a farmer, as was her mother Liza (born Kula). Berta Ziemele attended the state school in the parish of Misa and later, the Bekeris girls' 'preliminary gymnasium' in the town of Bauska, which offered the first four grades of gymnasium proper. In 1901, she became a teacher and taught in Charkov (Ukraine). From 1904 to 1908, she studied speech therapy for disabled children at the clinic of Dr. Liebman in Berlin (Germany), later traveling to Switzerland and Russia to familiarize herself with educational issues in these countries. She returned to Latvia in 1910 to marry Ermanis Pipiņš (d. 1927), a teacher, editor, writer and critic. They had two daughters, Biruta and Nora, and a son, Jānis.

Berta Pīpiņa followed political and social developments during the formation of the independent Republic of Latvia and from 1918, when Latvia became an independent state, she began actively participating in political and social activities. Explaining in an interview what had encouraged her to become a politician, she confided that it was the smile she saw on her husband's face whenever she raised up her hand to tell him what she thought or what concerned her. "I swore that I would one day speak so well that no one would ever laugh at me" (Silvija 1933, 3). She helped found the *Demokrātiskā Centra Partija* (Democratic Center Party), became a member of the Party Council and was the first of the Party women to be elected to its Central Committee. In 1919, she was elected to Riga City Council and worked on different Council committees until 1934. From 1925 to 1928, she headed the Council Department for the Destitute and, from 1928 to 1931, was a member of the Riga Audit Commission, whose task it was to monitor the work of the Riga municipality offices (and those subordinate to them). While working for the Riga City Council, she also advocated and helped introduce legal restrictions on public (drinking) houses. One of Pīpiņa's central concerns and a focus of her work was the situation of women and the family in

Latvia. She held lectures on these issues and wrote articles for newspapers and magazines, in addition to giving public lectures on national advancement and national culture in Riga and other Latvian towns.

From 1922, Pīpiņa began participating in the activities of the *Latvju sieviešu nacionālā līga* (Latvian Women's National League/National Council of Women), formed in St Petersburg in 1917. In 1925, she became its President. The *Latvju sieviešu nacionālā līga* organized charity work, a kindergarten, Sunday school for children and library and evening courses for women. Women used the premises of the *Līga* as a place where they could perform handicraft work and, in summer, attend needlework courses. In 1928, Pīpiņa described the *Līga* as bringing Latvian women together in the national spirit: it aimed to "support the tired and desperate spirit of refugees. The national word possesses magical power ... scattered Latvians must be united by the women of this nation through national ideals in different forms" (Rubina 1992, 169). In 1922, the *Līga* became affiliated with the International Council of Women (ICW). Pīpiņa became Vice-President of the ICW in 1936, but was apparently not re-elected in 1938. She took part in ICW congresses in Vienna (1930), Stockholm (1933), Paris (1934) and Dubrovnik (1936), and visited women's groups in Russia, Hungary and Austria, among other countries.

In 1930, Pīpiņa was among the founders of the *Latvijas Sieviešu organizāciju padome* (Council of Latvian Women's Organizations). An energetic, intelligent and ambitious woman, Pīpiņa was elected onto the Board and appointed leader of the new organization, a position she retained until 1935. While the 1917 *Līga* had focused on uniting and educating women in what it perceived to be 'the national spirit,' the 1930 *Latvijas Sieviešu organizāciju padome* was an umbrella organization: it united several organizations with the aim of fostering gender equality and increasing women's political and social influence.

In 1931, Pīpiņa became the first female member of the Latvian Parliament (*Saeima*), the fourth Parliament in the Republic of Latvia. In the *Saeima*, Pīpiņa assisted the Chairman of the Commission on Self Government and was Secretary of the Petitions Commission. As the only woman in the 100-member strong *Saeima*, she worked on various law projects and frequently drew the attention of other Members of Parliament to the potential influence of legislation on women and families. She argued that married women should be able to enter paid employment, emphasized the importance of state support for families and mothers and stressed the destructive effects of poverty on the family, views often contested by male MPs. Early on in the first session of the fourth *Saeima*, Pīpiņa protested a law that would require married women to give up paid employment. In the ruckus that followed, calls for order were made and MPs were asked to give Pīpiņa attention, to which the future (authoritarian) President of Latvia, Kārlis Ulmanis, replied scornfully: "Attention to what? Have you heard what she is saying?" [*Latvijas Republikas* (1931): 126].

In 1934, Pīpiņa became one of the founders of the monthly periodical *Latviete*

(Latvian woman), to which she contributed regularly. In the first issue, she wrote that the purpose of *Latviete* was to unite women, combat patriarchal stereotypes and promote women's equality and national consciousness as women and as Latvians. She set out the three tasks of the 'woman-educator and mother.' First came self-education: women were not to follow men's example, e.g. regarding alcohol consumption; second came the education of young people, whom women were to raise in a patriotic spirit that allowed them at the same time to explore human, spiritual and aesthetic feelings; third came the moral improvement of national society, which could be achieved through greater participation of women in social life. In 1928, Pīpiņa produced a brochure for mothers entitled *Kā es runāju ar saviem bērniem par dzimumdzīvi* (How to talk to my children about sexuality). In 1935, she published a novel, *Lejaskrodznieces meitas* (The daughters of the Lejaskrogs publican).

Under the authoritarian regime of 1936 to 1940, Pīpiņa withdrew from political work but remained active in public life (mainly journalism) until 1940. In 1941, she was deported by Soviet officials to Siberia, where she died in a labor camp near the Ob river in 1942. Although Pīpiņa and her husband appear as important public figures in encyclopedias published at the time of the first independent Republic, the *Latvijas Padomju Enciklopēdija* (Latvian Soviet Encyclopedia, 1981–1987), while noting Pīpiņa's husband, did not include Pīpiņa herself, most probably because she was by then regarded as an enemy of the state, having been a member of the Latvian Parliament. Berta Pīpiņa, the first female member of the Latvian Parliament and a key figure in the women's movement, strove to bring gender equality and women's rights to the political agenda in Latvia, and to unite women around those issues.

Elizabete Picukane
Center for Gender Studies, University of Latvia

SOURCES

(A) Latvia State Historical Archive, F. 2412, 2. apr., 7.1, *Latvijas Sieviešu Organizāciju Padomes valdes protokoli* (Protocols of the Board of the Council of Latvian Women's Organizations).

(A) *Archiefcentrum voor Vrouwengeschiedenis* (Archival Center for Women's History), Brussels, Fond 3, Archive ICW, no. 24: *Verslagboek* (Report book), file 214: President's memorandum regarding the council meeting of the International Council of Women held in Dubrovnik (Yugoslavia), 28 September–9 October 1936, 22; also files 215, 216 and 1504.

(B) Kroders, P., ed. *Latvijas darbinieku galerija* (Gallery of Latvia's leading officials). Riga: "Grāmatu draugs," 1929.

(B) *Latvijas Republikas IV Saeimas stenogrammas: I un ārkārtējā sesijas, 1931. Gads* (Minutes of the IV Parliament of the Republic of Latvia: first and extraordinary meeting for the year 1931). Riga: Saeima, 1931.

(B) Šmits, P., ed. *Latvijas vadošie darbinieki* (Leading persons of Latvia). Riga: Latvju kultūrvēsturiskā apgade, 1935.

(C) Pīpiņa, B. "Ko redzējām Stokholmā" (What we saw in Stockholm). *Jaunākās Ziņas* (Latest news), no. 143 (1933).

(C) Pīpiņa, B. "Starptautiskās sieviešu konferences ziņojumi un lēmumi" (The reports and resolutions of the international women's conference). *Jaunākās Ziņas* (Latest news), no. 151 (1933).

(C) Pīpiņa, B. "Vecas un jaunas sejas starptautiskajā sievie-u kongresā Parīzē" (Old and new faces at the international women's congress in Paris). *Jaunākās Ziņas* (Latest news), no. 152 (1934).

(C) Pīpiņa, B. "Latviete: mēnešraksts sievietes dzīvei" (Latvian woman: a monthly women's periodical for life). *Latviete* (Latvian woman), no. 1 (1934).

(C) Pīpiņa, B. "Sieviete jaunajā Latvijā" (Woman in new Latvia). *Latviete* (Latvian woman), nos. 7-8 (1934).

(C) Pīpiņa, B. "Apvienošanās ideja dzīvē" (The idea of unity in life). *Latviete* (Latvian woman), no. 3 (1935).

(D) Silvija, A. "Aicinājums latvju sievietei (saruna ar Saeimas deputāti Bertu Pīpiņu)" [An appeal to a Latvian woman (a conversation with the Saeima Deputy Berta Pīpiņa)]. *Vidzemes Vēstnesis* (Vidzeme herald), no. 269 (17 August 1933).

(D) Švābe A., A. Būmanis and A. Dišlērs. "Pīpiņš: 1. Berta." In *Latviešu konversācijas vārdnīca* (Latvian encyclopaedia). Riga: A. Gulbis Publishers, 1938, XVI: 32426.

(D) Ābelnieks, R. "Codiete Berta Pīpiņa–pazīstama politīe" (Codean Berta Pīpiņa–a known politician). *Bauskas Dzīve* (Bauska life) 2 (October 1998).

(E) *Women in a Changing World. The Dynamic Story of the International Council of Women since 1888*. London: Routledge and Kegan Paul, 1966.

(E) *These Names Accuse: Nominal List of Latvians Deported to Soviet Russia in 1940/41*. Second edition with supplementary list. Stockholm: The Latvian National Foundation, 1982.

(E) *Latvijas Padomju Enciklopēdija* (Latvian Soviet encyclopaedia). Vol. 7. Riga: Galvenā Enciklopēdiju Redakcija, 1986.

(E) Rubina, V. "An Insight into Women's Movement of Latvia [sic]." In I. Trapenciere and S. Kalniņa, eds. *Fragments of Reality: Insights on Women in a Changing Society*. Riga: Vaga Publishers, 1992.

(E) Cielēns, F. *Laikmetu maiņā: atmiņas un atziņas, 4. grāmata* (In the change of epochs: memories and conclusions, part four). Stockholm: Apgāds Memento, 1999.

PLAMÍNKOVÁ, Františka F. (1875-1942)

Czech teacher and leading feminist; founder (1923) and Chairwoman of the Czechoslovak National Council of Women; member of the Senate of the Czechoslovak National Assembly; longtime Vice-President of the International Alliance of Women for Suffrage and Equal Citizenship (IAWSEC) and the International Council of Women (ICW) in the interwar years.

Františka Plamínková was born on 5 February 1875 in Prague, a descendant of farmers and weavers in Podkrkonoší, a district in the north of Bohemia. Her mother was Marie Plamínková, born Gruberová; her father, František Plamínek, had attended a craft school in Prague and started his own shoemaking business when very young. Františka had two older sisters: Růžena and Marie. As a girl, Františka enjoyed school and spending time in her father's workshop, where people discussed politics, narrated stories and read aloud (reading aloud, fiction as well as non-fiction, was a relatively common pursuit among middle-class families). After qualifying in 1894 from the teacher-training college in Prague, then one of the very few higher educational establishments for women with intellectual ambitions, she taught at elementary schools outside Prague (1894-1899) and at secondary schools in Prague (1899-1925). Extremely able, Plamínková also learned French and German, painting (at night school), played the piano, sang with a Prague choir of female teachers, as well as attending lectures at Prague University.

As Plamínková's education progressed, a sense of justice pushed her to address women's inequality, which seemed immutable in the face of thousand-year-old prejudices and traditions. In 1903, Františka Plamínková co-founded the *Ženský klub český* (Czech Women's Club), which sought to promote the cultural and political life of women through lectures. Applying her talent for organizing and for identifying urgent political issues, she designed a lecture series on the legal position of women, as well as on health and other social issues. Eminent university professors such as Tomáš Garrigue Masaryk participated in the program as lecturers.

Plamínková herself, in a lecture called "Moderní žena" (Modern woman)–held at the headquarters of the *Ženský klub český* in 1907–set forth strategies for the Czech women's movement: not to fight at any cost, but to continue to carry out good works as women, alongside men. Czech feminism, as envisioned by Plamínková and her colleagues, was to help men understand that better educated and more self-confident women also made better partners and professional colleagues.

The lectures in the *Ženský klub český* were very successful and greatly influenced public opinion, as did the other, mostly educational activities of the Association. Nevertheless, it was deemed necessary to establish a more politically oriented organization if a better position for women in society and employment were to be won. To this end, Plamínková and others, including the politician Fráňa Zemínová, founded the Czech-Bohemian *Výbor pro volební právo žen* (Committee for Women's Suffrage) in 1905. Plamínková became a leading figure in this organization and, upon discovering that electoral regulations did not explicitly exclude this option, began a campaign to get a female representative elected to the National Assembly. She herself refused to be nominated because she wanted to devote herself entirely to the campaign. In the end, the writer ***Božena Viková-Kunětická*** was nominated and in 1912, became the first woman to be elected to the *Zemský sněm Království českého* (Assembly of the Czech Kingdom). Although she never took office, the event was celebrated across Europe as well as at the Seventh Congress of the International Woman Suffrage Alliance (with which the *Výbor pro volební právo žen* had been affiliated since 1909) in Budapest in 1913.

One of the pillars of the Czech women's movement was Tomáš Garrigue Masaryk (1850–1937), political leader, philosopher, chief founder and first President of the Republic of Czechoslovakia—well known for his articles and lectures at the University and at the *Americký klub dam* (American Ladies' Club) in Prague, as well as for his support of women's admission to universities while working as a deputy in Vienna. Influenced by Masaryk's observation that there was no woman's or man's question, only a social question (Masaryk, 62), a new generation was beginning to reevaluate attitudes towards women. The Washington Declaration of 18 October 1918 that promulgated the main democratic principles of the future Czechoslovak State, and which had been drafted by T. G. Masaryk, included the principle that women would hold a political, social and cultural position equal to men. Masaryk considered the incorporation of this principle into the later Constitution of the Czechoslovak State to be the outcome of the work and prewar activities of Plamínková and her colleagues, as he stated on numerous occasions.

Meanwhile, the battle for real equality between men and women continued. One of the first tasks on the agenda was the abolition of the celibacy clause—the prohibition of paid work for married women in the civil service. Plamínková had been campaigning against the celibacy clause since the beginning of the twentieth century, but only in 1919, in the new Czechoslovak State, did she succeed in having the celibacy requirement for female teachers abolished (in 1923 she successfully intervened when this recent achievement was threatened). Her next goal was the abolition of the celibacy requirement in all civil service occupations.

In 1918, Plamínková joined the democratic *Československá strana národně socialistická* (Czechoslovak National Socialist Party). She contributed to the party program, became a member of its leadership and was elected to represent it to Prague City Council. She strove to improve housing conditions and took a particular interest in social welfare issues, especially regarding women and children. She organized an advisory center for women, job placements for disabled women or women with lower working abilities and was involved in the humanitarian institution, *České srdce* (The Czech Heart). For Plamínková, social work also included paying attention to moral health. She became head of the Czechoslovak branch of the International Bureau for the Suppression of the Traffic in Women, was active in the movement against prostitution and the temperance movement and was also an inspector of the Prague women's prison. As a member of the governmental School Committee, she aimed to implement reforms of the school system and contributed to the establishment of the first pilot reform school in Prague.

In 1923, Františka Plamínková founded the *Ženská národní rada* (Czech National Council of Women, NCW). This organization, with Plamínková as its Chairwoman, coordinated the activities of various women's organizations in Bohemia, Moravia and Slovakia and represented over sixty women's associations with more than three hundred thousand members. The Czechoslovak NCW had working groups that dealt with every kind of social issue and set up projects dedicated to the improvement of women's position in the cultural, legal, social and economic spheres.

Under Plamínková's inspiring leadership, the Czechoslovak women's movement became further integrated into the international women's movement. Plamínková first participated in a Congress of the International Woman Suffrage Alliance in Amsterdam in 1908. She was Vice-President of this organization (then called the International Alliance of Women for Suffrage and Equal Citizenship, IAWSEC) from 1926 until World War II. The Czechoslovak National Council of Women became a member of the International Council of Women in 1924. Plamínková was Vice-President of the ICW from 1925 until World War II. She was also actively involved in the International Federation of Business and Professional Women, the Open Door International (an organization aimed at "the economic emancipation of the woman worker") and (as representative of the *Výbor pro volební právo žen*) in the Little Entente of Women (LEW), an alliance of women's organizations from Romania, Poland, Czechoslovakia, Yugoslavia and Greece. Plamínková participated in and held speeches at LEW meetings in Bucharest (1923), Belgrade (1924) and Prague (1927); it is unclear whether she attended the Warsaw meeting (1929). The proceedings from the 1927 Prague meeting lists Plamínková as the main organizer and an important figure in the Czech women's movement. Peace was high on the agenda of the international feminist movement between the two world wars and Plamínková was also involved in the Czechoslovak branch of the Women's International League for Peace and Freedom (WILPF).

In 1925, Plamínková became a Senator in the Czechoslovak National Assembly. She was repeatedly re-elected. She foresaw the danger of Hitler's regime in neighboring Germany and tried, via lectures, open letters and other public presentations, to convey the threat of German Nazism–not only to Czechoslovakia, but to the whole world. In September 1938, she wrote an open letter to Hitler in her capacity as Senator to protest against his attacks on Czechoslovakia.

In the summer of 1939, that is after Nazi-Germany had invaded and occupied Bohemia and Moravia, Plamínková participated in the Thirteenth Congress of the IAWSEC in Copenhagen, Denmark. Her friends abroad pleaded with her not to return home but she refused; she was against emigration at that particular time, convinced that nothing could be done abroad and that it was necessary for people to work from home. Immediately after the outbreak of World War II on 1 September 1939, Plamínková was arrested by the Nazis for the first time, but released after a couple of weeks. She continued to work for the Czechoslovak NCW and organized literary seminars on nineteenth-century Czech female writers, with titles such as "Spisovatelky o sobě" (Female writers on themselves) and "Krásy českého jazyka" (The beauty of the Czech language). The goal of the seminars was to strengthen national consciousness. The last seminar she prepared (on religion) never took place. On 11 June 1942, as part of a wave of reprisals after the assassination of Reich Protector Reinhard Heydrich, the Nazis arrested Plamínková for the second time, imprisoned her in the *Kleine Festung* (Small Fort) in Terezín, and on 30 June 1942, executed her in Prague.

At the first postwar Congress of the International Alliance of Women in 1946, the IAW President remembered Plamínková personally as "Františka Plamínková, our Plam, ... as big in mind and soul as she was big and lovely in body. How splendidly she combined the virtues of the 'old' and the 'new' woman. ..." (IAW 1946 *Congress Report*, 8). According to the International Council of Women, "Senator Plamínková" left "to the women of her country and of the world a precious legacy of 'courage, fortitude and faith'" (*Women in a Changing World*, 78, citing from *ICW Records* 1947, 67). It should be noted that during the Communist era, silence surrounded her life and achievements, mainly because of her close relation with Masaryk. Today, in the twenty-first century, we still do not even have a comprehensive biography of Františka Plamínková.

Soňa Hendrychová

Translated from the Czech by Jitka Kohoutková, MA student at the Department of Gender Studies, Central European University, Budapest.

SOURCES

(A) *Archiv Národního muzea* (Archive of the National Muzeum, Prague), Fond Františka Plamínková (1875-1942).

(A) Author's private archive.

(B) International Information Center and Archives for the Women's Movement (IIAV). *Congress Reports* of the IWSA/IAWSEC/IAW (1908-1946).

(B) *1e Conférence de la Petite Entente des Femmes. Discours prononcés aux séances publiques des 3 et 4 novembre 1923* (First congress of the LEW. Statements from the public sessions of 3-4 November 1923). Bucharest: Tipografia "Dorneanu," 1923.

(B) *La deuxičme conférence de la Petite Entente des Femmes ŕ Belgrade. Discours et rapports de 1-4 novembre 1924* (Second congress of the LEW in Belgrade. Proceedings and reports of 1-4 November 1924). Bucharest: L'imprimerie des livres religieux, 1925.

(B) La lutte de la femme. "La deuxième conférence de la Petite Entente des Femmes à Belgrade" (Second congress of the LEW in Belgrade). *Jus Suffragii* (February 1925): 76.

(B) Theodoropoulou, Avra. "The Third Conference of the Women's Little Entente." *Jus Suffragii* 20, no. 5 (February 1926): 69.

(C) Plamínková, Františka. *The Economic and Social Position of Women in the Czechoslovak Republic*. Prague, 1920.

(C) Plamínková, Františka. *Občanská rovnoprávnost žen* (The civil equality of women). Prague: Státní školní knihosklad, 1920.

(D) Honzáková, A., ed. *Kniha života. Vzpomínky spolupracovnic a přátel k 60. narozeninám F. F. Plamínkové* (Book of life. Memories of the colleagues and friends on the occasion of F. F. Plamínková's sixtieth birthday). Prague: Women's National Council, 1935.

(D) Maxová, Antonie. *Čím nám byla. Projev předsedkyně Společnosti F. F. Plamínkové na pietní schůzi v budově Senátu Československého v listopadu 1945*. (What she meant to us. Speech by the head of F. F. Plamínková's association at the pious meeting in the Senate of the Czechoslovak Republic, November 1945).

(D) Reinfeld, Barbara. "Františka Plamínková (1875-1942), Czech Feminist and Patriot." *Nationalities Papers* 25, no. 1 (March 1997).

(D) Hendrychová, Soňa. "Františka Plamínková." In Alena Wagner, ed. *Prager Frauen. Neun Lebensbilder* (Women of Prague. Nine biographies). Prague and Furth im Wald: Vitalis, 2000.

(D) Musilová, D. "Vztah Františky Plamínkové k rodině Masarykových" (The relation of Františka Plamínková to Masaryk's family). In *Charlotta G. Masaryková. Sborník příspěvků z konference ke 150. výročí jejího narození* Prague, 2001, 45-52.

(E) *Women in a Changing World. The Dynamic Story of the International Council of Women since 1888*. London: Routledge & Kegan Paul, 1966.

(E) Burešová, J. *Proměny společenského postavení českých žen v první polovině 20. Století* (The changes in the social position of Czech women in the first half of the twentieth century). Olomouc, 2001.

(E) Masaryk, T. G. *Otázka sociální* (The social question). Prague: Masarykův ústav AVČR, sixth edition, 2000.

(E) Zimmermann, Susan. "The Challenge of Multinational Empire for the International Women's Movement: The Habsburg Monarchy and the Development of Feminist Inter/National Politics." *Journal of Women's History* 17, no. 2 (Summer 2005): 87-117.

PLAVEVA, Rosa (born Varnalieva) (1878–1970)

Member of the first generation of socialist women in late nineteenth- and early twentieth-century Macedonia; campaigner for women's equality; influential public figure.

Rosa Varnalieva was born in 1878 in Veles, to parents Agna (her mother, who lived to be 103) and Atanas Varnaliev. The Orthodox Christian Varnaliev family had four children: Rosa, Kata, Petar and Ilija, all of whom became active in the town's socialist movement. The Varnalievs were well-off merchants, one of the wealthiest families in Veles, and owned a big estate. The young Rosa finished a (then prestigious) vocational school, the *Radničhka Škola* (in Veles), and became a seamstress.

In 1900, Rosa Varnalieva joined the *Socijalistička organizacija* (Socialist Organization), founded in 1894 by Vasil Glavinov (1869–1929). Socialism attracted her because it incorporated the emancipation of women into its political program, which she felt particularly strongly about, having been raised in a liberal family in harmony with her brothers. Around 1903, Rosa married Ilija Plavev (born Veles 1871–died Belgrade 1940), with whom she had two children: a son and a daughter, Nada (born 1908). As an adult, Nada would support her mother's campaigns for the emancipation of women.

Rosa Plaveva had many Turkish friends (Macedonia being a multi-ethnic country) and tried to draw them into the *Socijalistička organizacija*, especially after the *Mladoturska revolucija* (Young Turk Revolution) of 1908, which made demands for civil rights in the Ottoman Empire. In 1909, Plaveva organized meetings at her home, attended by approximately twenty women, most of them Turkish and sympathizers of the *Mladoturska partija "Edinstvo i napredok"* (Unity and Progress Party). The women discussed causes of women's discrimination and possible campaigns for women's rights. They also criticized the veiling of Islamic women, but because the *Mladoturska revolucija* had changed its civil rights agenda, adopting conservative Koranic codes, this particular campaign was without success. With the establishment of the Democratic Republic of Macedonia on 12 January 1951, a statute was passed—"Zakon za zabrana na nosenje zar i feredze" (against the use of the veil)—that outlawed the practice.

Alongside her great interest in progressive social movements, Plaveva keenly followed developments in the international socialist women's movement. (According to the Rosa Plaveva Fund at the Institute of National History's Documentation Unit, one of her contacts was Rosa Luxemburg.) She was also strongly influenced by the Macedonian revolutionary tradition–a participant in the 1903 *Ilinden* Uprising against Ottoman rule–and her profile as an activist was profoundly shaped by the spiritual values of 'national revival.'

From 1909, Rosa and her husband, Ilija Plavev, began making plans for a new Social Democratic Organization in Skopje. It was founded on 1 May 1909 and used the 1891 Erfurt Program of the German Social Democrats as its platform. Rosa Plaveva, together with Nakie Bajram (1889–1962), took on the task of rallying support for the new organization from women in Skopje. Bajram was a teacher of Turkish nationality, married to Ferid Bajram (1881–1950), a socialist journalist. In 1917, a committee was founded in Skopje for the liberation of Rosa Luxemburg and Karl Liebknecht (in prison in Berlin). On behalf of this committee, Plaveva organized the collection of approximately one hundred women's signatures in support of a petition; this was a significant number considering the conditions in which the signatures had been obtained (World War I and Bulgarian occupation).

The end of World War I brought about a new territorial division of Macedonia among the three neighboring countries: Serbia, Greece and Bulgaria. After the Versailles Treaty from 1919, the territory of modern day Macedonia was incorporated into the newly founded (Balkan) Kingdom of Serbs, Croats, and Slovenes (known from 1929 as the Kingdom of Yugoslavia). Women did not gain any political rights in the new state and in Macedonia, the old Serbian Civil Code (1844) came into force, paragraph 920 of which made adult women legally incompetent, along with minors and the mentally disabled.

Despite the fact that the patriarchal norms in the larger Macedonian towns loosened slightly after World War I, many women and men regarded patriarchal family structures as normative and strongly resisted emancipation movements on behalf of women. Yet this did not deter the indefatigable Plaveva who, along with others, founded the *Organizacija na ženite socijalistki* (Organization of Socialist Women) in Skopje, a branch of the Yugoslav Organization of Socialist Women. Many women attended the Founding Assembly of the Organization, held on 29 February 1920 in Skopje's Workers' Hall. Rosa Plaveva, Sofija Mladenovic, Caja Tasic, Nakie Bajram, Persida Trifunova, Vaska Georgieva, Rosa Jordanova and Stojna Georgieva were some of the appointed members of the Organization's Local Secretariat [listed in the newspaper *Socijalistička zora* (Socialist dawn) and Rosa Plaveva's (unpublished) memoirs]. The Socialist Women's Local Secretariat in Skopje launched a comprehensive campaign against the inequality and discrimination inscribed in and reproduced by the harsh laws of the Serbian Civil Code, as well as urging Macedonian women to resist conservative social and patriarchal norms. Like German Social Democrat women such as Klara Zetkin, Plaveva and her colleagues focused on economic and political discrimination against women: the *Organizacija na ženite socijalistki* demanded equal wages and the abolition of capitalist exploitation and during local and parliamentary elections in the 1920s, it fought bitterly for both active and passive voting rights for women. Women from Skopje, along with the *Organizacija* and Plaveva–whose nicknames included 'Deli Rosa' (heroic or brave Rosa) and later 'the Macedonian Rosa Luxemburg'–established an Agitation Committee for the election years. In the long struggle for women's emancipation, the Skopje socialist women continued to demand women's political independence from men and their entitlement to full civil rights. Women in Macedonia got the right to vote (preliminarily) in 1942 and (legislatively) on 2 August 1944.

Not much is known about Rosa Plaveva's later life. After moving to Belgrade, she joined the Yugoslavian women's movement, remaining devoutly committed to women's emancipation. Rosa Plaveva died in Belgrade in 1970 at the age of ninety. Today she is remembered as an important figure in both national and women's movements.

Prof. Dr. Vera Vesković-Vangeli
Senior Scientific Researcher,
Institute of National History, Skopje

Translated from the Macedonian by Nevenka Grceva, MA student, Department of Gender Studies, Central European University, Budapest.

SOURCES

(A) Institute of National History (Skopje), Documentation Unit, Rosa Plaveva Fund.

(A) State Archives of the Republic of Macedonia, Skopje. Collection: Steering Committee of the *Antifasisticki front na ženite na Makedonija* (Antifascist Front of the Women of Macedonia), 1940–1945, File 1.

(B) "Poziv na zbor!" (Let's unite!). *Socijalistička zora* (Socialist dawn) (Skopje, 16 August 1920).

(B) "Zbor žena" (Women's gathering). *Socijalistička zora* (Socialist dawn). (Skopje, 20 August 1920).

(B) "Akcija za pravo glasa žena" (Action for women's suffrage). *Zena danas* (Woman today) (Belgrade, October 1939; January–February 1940).

(E) Vesković-Vangeli, Vera. *Ženata vo osloboditelnite borbi na Makedonija (1893–1945*) (Woman in the Macedonian liberation wars, 1893–1945). Skopje: Kultura, 1990.

(E) Vesković-Vangeli, Vera. *Ženata vo vitelot na antagonizmot na tradicijata* (Woman in the whirl of antagonistic tradition). Veles: Društvo za nauka i umetnost, 1999.

PODJAVORINSKÁ, Ľudmila (pseudonym), born Ľudmila Riznerová (1872–1951)

Slovak poet, writer of prose, translator, founder of modern Slovak children's literature and distinguished (after 1945) with the title of Honorable National Artist. Versatile figure in late nineteenth- and early twentieth-century cultural life and an active member of the women's organization *Živena*, the first women's organization in Slovakia (founded in 1869). Pseudonyms: 'Božena,' 'Damascena,' 'Ľ. Podjavorinská,' 'Ľ. Šeršelínová,' 'Ľ. Špirifangulínová,' 'Ľudka,' 'Ľudmila,' 'Ľudmila Podjavorinská' and many others.

Ľudmila Riznerová was born on 26 April 1872 in a village called Bzince pod Javorinou. Her mother (name unknown) and father (Karol Rizner, a teacher) had ten children, of which Ľudmila was the eighth. Serious illness affecting her eyes and bodily strength contributed to L'udmila's introverted and meditative nature as a child. She continued to suffer from ill health throughout her life.

Ľudmila attended the elementary school where her father was a teacher, at a time when women had few educational opportunities. The only way to acquire further education was through self-education and the cultural influence of one's environment. Podjavorinská was lucky enough to grow up in the intellectual environment of a teacher's family (the five last generations of men in her family had all been teachers) and, as a child surrounded by books from her father's library, she learned to read in Slovak, Czech, Hungarian and German–later studying and translating literary works from Russian as well. However it was not her parents who encouraged Ľudmila Riznerová to publish her first works in newspapers, but her uncle Ľudovít Rizner, a poor village teacher who had established a library. Ľudmila was brought up to respect her parents and social authority in general, but she soon turned against the traditional lot of the Slovak woman, refusing to respect the social rules that would see her confined to household duties.

Ľudmila Riznerová/Podjavorinská was encouraged by three mentors, all of whom were important contemporary female authors and friends of Podjavorinská: the renowned ***Terézia Vansová***, ***Elena Maróthy-Šoltésová*** and Božena Slančíková-Timrava. The cultural, political and literary activities of these women, including Podjavorinská, were concentrated in the women's organization *Živena*. Male nationalists had created this organization in 1869 with the initial purpose of opening schools for girls–a plan that was postponed for a long time due to state repression of the Slovak national movement. The first two secondary schools for girls were finally opened in 1919 in the town of Martin (central Slovakia). By 1927, there were twelve schools for girls in Martin. Despite frequent financial problems during times of economic crisis, *Živena* never abandoned its main aim of supporting female authors, organizing meetings, establishing a foundation for retired female teachers, as well as publishing books and articles. *Živena* also published *Národné almanachy* (National almanac, ?, 1872); *Letopisy Živeny* (Chronicle of Živena, 1895–1907); the magazines *Živena* and *Dennica* (from 1898) and the magazine *Slovenská žena* (Slovak women, 1920–1924).

Such developments were signs of the times in which Ľudmila Riznerová/Podjavorinská lived and worked. Her first poems were published in the *Slovenské noviny* (Slovak newspaper) in Budapest in 1887. The humorous style of writing and the quality of her work led many of her contemporaries to believe that her pieces had been written by the well-known Slovak author Martin Kukučín, giving her an even greater incentive to write. Two important figures in Slovak cultural life influenced her literary and intellectual growth at this time: Svetozár Hurban Vajanský and Jozef Škultéty. Under the pseudonym 'Ľudmila Podjavorinská,' she published her first pieces in their monthly periodical *Slovenské pohľady* (Slovak views). In 1895, her first poetry book appeared under the title *Z vesny života* (From the spring of life). She was the first Slovak woman poet to publish a book of poetry, written while recovering from a love affair (the man she loved married another woman)–an experience that strongly influenced her work. Podjavorinská herself never married, and it was around this time that the sentimentality that had characterized her earlier work was replaced by a more complex understanding of the human soul and social relations.

Her position as a single female writer was not an easy one. In 1910, her parents moved to the nearby town of Nové Mesto nad Váhom, where they had bought a house. Podjavorinská never adjusted to living in a town but she lost contact with village life too. With the outbreak of World War I, she stopped writing for a while. Her parents died and she remained alone, letting her brother and his family take the family house while she moved into a flat. Women writers like Podjavorinská were in a difficult situation after the war, most of them having to give up writing and find other sources of income. Since Podjavorinská's work did not provide the financial means to live, she was forced to find other forms of paid employment. She worked as a Red Cross officer and was also paid for articles that she sent to the Slovak newspaper *Americké noviny* (American newspaper), in this way sustaining a modest but independent lifestyle.

The official politics of the new Czechoslovak Republic, established in 1918, openly supported women's emancipation. The Czechoslovak declaration of independence, the so-called *Washingtonská deklarácia* (Washington declaration) of 18 October 1918 read: "Women will have the same political, social and cultural rights as men." Women's political activity in Slovakia was lower than in the Czech part of the country and Podjavorinská was among those who called upon women to get involved in politics: "Dear sisters, ... we hereby submit a proposal to the Parliament that women be accepted as Members of Parliament. The historic establishment of the Czechoslovak Republic has brought each individual a new set of duties ... those few men we have are not able to manage even the most urgent problems ... [C]hoose those women who would represent you and who would be willing to work ... Put your heart and soul into working for your national patrimony" [Letter by Ľudmila Podjavorinská published in *Živena* (15 November 1918)]. Such appeals were not very successful; Podjavorinská was alone among well-educated women in seeing a need for women's involvement in Slovak politics and most Slovak women seemed to be awaiting a signal to act from their Czech countrywomen.

Podjavorinská's ballads from the 1930s, which represent her last period of creativity, are considered her best work. She also wrote books for children that were dedicated to helping the development of children's individual personalities. Her first poems for children were published in the magazines *Noviny malých* (Newspaper for children), *Zornička* (Daystar), *Včielka* (Bee), *Priateľ dietok* (Friend of children) and *Slniečko* (Sun). Other ballads and pieces for children by Podjavorinská played no central role in contemporary literature, their value coming to be recognized only later. Nevertheless, they formed the basis of a modern Slovak children's literary canon. Another mark of originality in Podjavorinská's work was the positive representation of the female protagonist in her novel *Žena* (Woman, 1910), in which her literary style resembled that of realist writers such as Timrava and Tajovský. Podjavorinská died in Nové Mesto nad Váhom on 3 March 1951 and was buried in her native village. Under the socialist regime, she was known as an author of children's books without mention of her political and social work on behalf of women. The influence of male authorities on her writing became far better known than the fact that she also cooperated with, and was influenced by female contemporaries.

Andrea Šalingová, Ph.D.
Univerzita Konštantína Filozova, Nitra, Slovakia

SOURCES

(C) Podjavorinská, Ľudmila. "Postavy a figúrky" (Figure and figurine). In *Živena: Vydavateľské družstvo*. Turčiansky sv. Martin, 1942, 249.

(D) Klátik, Zlatko. *Album Ľudmily Podjavorinskej* (An album of Ľudmila Podjavorinska). Bratislava: Mladé letá, *sine anno*.

(E) Tkadlečková-Vantuchová, Jarmila. *Živena–spolok slovenských žien* (Živena–Association of Slovak Women). Bratislava: Epocha, 1969.

(E) Bokníková, Andrea. *Štyri skupinové portréty žien v premenách času–tvorba slovenských poetiek 20. storočia* (Four portraits of women in changing times–the creation of Slovak poets). Dissertation. Bratislava: Univerzita Komenského, 2001.

POPP, Adelheid (1869–1939)

Leader of the Austrian social democratic women's movement and the first Chairperson of its *Frauenreichskomitee* (women's section).

Adelheid Popp (*nee* Dworschak) was born on 11 February 1869, into a poor Viennese working-class family. She was the youngest of five children to survive out of fifteen. Her father (data unknown) was an impoverished weaver and a physically abusive alcoholic. Violence and poverty were an integral part of Adelheid's early childhood. Her father died when she was six years old, leaving the family in even greater poverty. After only three years of formal education, Adelheid had to leave school at the age of ten in order to support her family. Following short engagements as a domestic worker and seamstress' apprentice, she became a factory worker. Her interest in politics began to develop in the mid-1880s. Through a friend of her brother's, she learned of the demands being made by working class social movements and came into contact with social democratic newspapers and literature. While reading reports on the living conditions of working class families, she came to understand the misery of her own life; that her suffering was not individual, but the product of an unjust society. When, in 1889, Adelheid Dworschak went to her first public meeting, accompanied by her brother, she was the only woman at the meeting hall. In 1891, she joined the *Arbeiterinnenbildungsverein* (Working Women's Educational Association), founded by female relatives of social democratic functionaries just one year earlier. Its main goal was to teach women political skills in rhetoric and agitation. She gave her first speech at one of the meetings of the Association. When she heard the speaker describing women's working conditions, she spontaneously reported on her own experiences and pleaded for women's education. The audience, mostly men, applauded and asked her to produce a written version of that speech. From the very moment she entered public life, Adelheid Dworschak became an energetic agitator on behalf of women. Using her own childhood and working experiences to fuel political agitation by generating class solidarity through identification, she encouraged working women to join social democratic associations and unions.

In 1894, the young agitator married Julius Popp (1849–1902), a high ranking official with the *Sozialdemokratische Arbeiterpartei* (Social Democratic Workers' Party) and a man twenty years her senior. In her autobiography, she wrote that she had known that he was the man she wanted to marry long before he spoke any word of love to her. Julius Popp was involved in negotiating and organizing the first Party congress in 1889, an event now regarded as the official foundation of the *Sozialdemokratische Arbeiterpartei Österreichs* (Austrian Social Democratic Workers' Party). As the administrator and editor of the *Arbeiterzeitung* (Workers' newspaper), and later appointed Party treasurer, Julius Popp did not prevent his wife from agitation; on the contrary, he encouraged her to continue recruiting women workers even after the births of their two sons in 1897 and 1901. Adelheid Popp was left a widow in 1902, after eight years of marriage. She lost both children at an early age too: the eldest never came back from World War I; the younger son died of influenza at the age of 24.

The inauguration of the *Arbeiterinnenzeitung* (Working women's newspaper) in 1892 marked the beginnings of the Austrian social democratic women's movement. Adelheid Popp was chosen to be editor of the newspaper. However, dominant attitudes to politics as a set of activities independent of 'the domestic sphere' (where women were seen to belong) inhibited women from seeking political prominence and men from welcoming women's activism. As the Party's first woman official, Popp had to struggle against male chauvinism on the one hand and female political indifference on the other. Politics, conventionally defined, was regarded as an 'unnatural' activity for women. A Marxist focus on class consciousness over gender issues, as well as antifeminist attitudes among the proletariat, caused the social democratic leadership to hold back from promoting women in politics with any enthusiasm. Disillusioned with this state of affairs, women's movement leaders founded a *Frauenreichskomitee* (women's section) without asking Party officials. Adelheid Popp was its first Chairperson. In 1907, when an increase in the proportion of women recruits had still not led to adequate representation of women within the Party leadership, Popp initiated a campaign to introduce the mandatory delegation of women's representatives to Party conferences.

In 1909, the first edition of Adelheid Popp's life story was published. In this work, she set out to demonstrate how gender and class had shaped her life and how she had come to understand these categories. Drawing on the narrative technique of using the personal to illustrate the political, Popp's *Jugend einer Arbeiterin* (The youth of a working woman) became a bestseller, celebrated by her social democratic contemporaries as a paradigm of class-conscious writing. In addition to her autobiographical work, Popp published on the conditions of working women; her study on domestic servants, *Haussklavinnen* (Domestic slaves), was published in 1912. She contributed to the history of the Austrian social democratic women's movement, editing the *Gedenkbuch* (A book of commemoration, 1912) and writing a short work entitled *Der Weg zur Höhe* (The upward path), which came out for the first time in 1929.

Adelheid Popp participated in almost all discussions of the international social democratic women's movement and campaigned for the demands of the movement at a national level: e.g. the eight-hour-working day; prohibition of women's night work and maternity leave. She led the way in re-building the international socialist women's movement after World War I and was elected a women's representative to the executive of the Socialist International (1923–1934).

Adelheid Popp spent the final years of her professional life as a Member of Parliament, devoting herself to social legislation and women's issues. She proposed bills for the reform of family law, directed against men's unlimited powers as heads of households, and demanded legalized abortion and equal pay. Most of her parliamentary proposals were voted down by opposition parties holding a majority. In the early 1930s, Popp resigned. She died after suffering a stroke on 7 March 1939 in Vienna.

Popp was described as a conciliatory person, a mediator between various factions within the Social Democratic Party's women section, as well as between women and the male-dominated Party leadership. Women in the Austrian social democratic movement regarded Adelheid Popp as an inspirational leader.

Regina Köpl
Vienna University

SOURCES

(C) Popp, Adelheid, ed. *Gedenkbuch: 20 Jahre österreichische Arbeiterinnenbewegung* (A book of commemoration: twenty years of the Austrian women-workers' movement). Vienna, 1912.

(C) Popp, Adelheid. *Der Weg zur Höhe. Die sozialdemokratische Frauenbewegung Österreichs* (The upward path. The social democratic women's movement in Austria). Vienna, 1929.

(C) Popp, Adelheid. "Die Jugendgeschichte einer Arbeiterin" (The story of a working woman's youth). In Hans J. Schütz, ed. *Adelheid Popp: Jugend einer Arbeiterin* (The youth of a working woman). Fourth reprint of the 1922 edition. Bonn/Bad Godesberg, 1983, 17–105.

(C) Popp, Adelheid. "Erinnerungen. Aus meinen Kindheits- und Mädchenjahren" (Memoirs of my childhood and girlhood). In Hans J. Schütz, ed. *Adelheid Popp: Jugend einer Arbeiterin* (The youth of a working woman). First reprint of the 1915 edition. Bonn/Bad Godesberg, 1983, 109–219.

POSKA-GRÜNTHAL, Vera (Veera) (1898–1986)

Leader of the Estonian feminist movement; journalist and lawyer; activist in the international women's movement.

Vera Poska was born in Tallinn on 25 March 1898, into the family of Jaan Poska (1866–1920) and Constance Poska, born Ekström (1876–1922). Her father was a lawyer, Mayor of Tallinn (1917–1920), Estonian Prime Minister (1918), Minister of Foreign Affairs (1919) and Minister of Justice (1920). The Poskas belonged to the Orthodox Church and had six daughters and two sons [in order of seniority: Jüri, Niina, Jaan, Anna, Helena, Xenia (Ksenia), Tatjana and Vera]. Xenia studied medicine (1915–1918) at the St Petersburg Women's Medical Institute, and at the Universities of Paris (1919–1921) and Tartu (1921–1923). Her sister Tatjana (m. Arder, Laamann) studied at the Sorbonne in 1920 and 1926.

Vera Poska finished the Tallinna Girls' Gymnasium (high school) in 1915 and was admitted in the same year to the Faculty of Law at the famous *Bestuzhev* Higher Courses for Women in St Petersburg. In 1918, she studied at Voronezh University and in 1919, married Timotheus (Timoteus) Grünthal (1893–1955) in St Petersburg. Timotheus had begun his studies at the Faculty of Ancient Languages of St Petersburg University, but soon asked to be transferred to the Faculty of Law.

In September 1919, the Grünthals returned to 'the motherland,' to Timotheus' native town of Kuressaare. Later, in September 1920, the Grünthals moved to Tartu, where Timotheus began working at the municipal court–in the meantime continuing his studies at Tartu University's Faculty of Law.

Vera Poska-Grünthal also decided to continue her studies while bringing up two children: Konstantsia (1920–2005) and Svetlana (1922–1928). She was admitted to Tartu University as an auditor student (since she had no mathematics grade on her gymnasium leaving certificate). After passing additional exams, Poska-Grünthal enrolled in Tartu University, from which she graduated in 1925. She wrote in her diary that it had taken her ten years to achieve a university degree and that, between 1915 and 1925, there had been numerous obstacles namely the war, which had made it difficult to remain at one university. "[M]eanwhile," she continued, "I gave birth to four children, and our place of residence as well as living conditions changed a number of times" (Poska-Grünthal 1975, 58).

Vera Poska-Grünthal worked as a lawyer (1926–1929) at the Bureau of Legal Advice for the City of Tallinn. She was also assistant to a law barrister in Tallinn (1927–1929) and in Tartu (1929–1935), where her clients were wives in need of legal advice regarding domestic quarrels and divorce cases. While working for the Bureau of Legal Advice, she came to realize that the 1864 legal provisions for family law in the Baltic Civil Code were outdated and contradicted the Constitution of the Republic of Estonia (Poska-Grünthal 1975, 68–70). Indeed, laws regulating the family, marriage and the rights of the illegitimate child and mother were lacking altogether. Vera Poska-Grünthal considered it essential that a future commission working on a family law bill include a female lawyer. She turned for support to the *Eesti Naisorganisatsioonide Liit* (Union of Estonian Women's Organizations)–established in 1920, renamed (1930) the *Eesti Naisliit* (Estonian Women's Society)–at whose 1924 Congress she spoke on the topic of family law. Her presentation was severly criticized by some members of the *Eesti Naisorganisatsioonide Liit,* who argued that there was no female lawyer in Estonia competent to argue with experienced male lawyers over the contents of the Civil Code. Subsequently, Vera Poska-Grünthal withdrew from public life for a while and began acquainting herself with the most up-to-date marriage and family laws of the period (those of the Scandinavian countries). She found support in the *Eesti Akadeemiliste Naiste Ühing* (*EANÜ*, Estonian Association of University Women), established in Tartu in 1926, which sought professional female lawyers to serve on the board of an independent commission working on the new Estonian Civil Code.

In 1928, Vera Poska-Grünthal was a delegate representing the *Eesti Naisorganisatsioonide Liit* to the First Congress on Social Work in Paris (organized by the International Association of Women), at which she took part in a discussion on juvenile courts. It was during this congress that she first thought of establishing an international organization to unite female lawyers. She left the following note (in French) on the bulletin board of the congress: "Female lawyers interested in partnership and cooperation are requested to meet at this bulletin board today at 4 pm" (Poska-Grünthal 1975, 91–94). One French woman and several German and Spanish women appeared at the appointed time and the *Fédération Internationale des Femmes de Carrière Juridique* (International Federation of Women Magistrates and Barristers) was born. The following day, a provisional committee of lawyers was set up that included two French women, one German, one Spaniard and one Estonian. The aim of the organization was to maintain contacts between European women lawyers, as well as to mediate research on family law. The first congress of the organization was held in Paris in 1929. The number of members of the *Fédération Internationale des Femmes de Carrière Juridique* increased with new members from Switzerland, Italy, Belgium, Bulgaria, Denmark, Finland, Norway, Portugal, the USA, Romania, Poland, Great Britain, Austria and Czechoslovakia (Poska-Grünthal 1975, 91–93).

Vera Poska-Grünthal continued to work on a draft Estonian family law code. In 1930, together with Olinde Ilus, she translated articles on Swedish and Finnish marriage law into Estonian. In 1934, as a result of joint efforts by several Estonian women lawyers, a bill on family law was finally completed, with chapters written by Vera Poska-Grünthal on the legal status of illegitimate children (Vilma Anderson addressed the relationship between the spouses; Olinde Ilus addressed the relationship between parents and children).

As a recognized Estonian lawyer, Vera Poska-Grünthal was invited to the Seventh Congress of the International Federation of University Women (IFUW) in Cracow in 1936. Thereafter, she took part in the conference of the legal committee of the IFUW in Paris in July 1937 and in the Open Door International Fifth Congress in Cambridge in July 1938.

As a member of the *Tartu Naisselts* (Tartu Women's Society), Vera Poska-Grünthal was also the promoter and first director of the Estonian feminist reading room (library) of the Tartu women's organizations: the *Eesti Akadeemiliste Naiste Ühing* (Estonian Association of University Women); the *Tartu Naisselts* (Tartu Women`s Society); the *Noorte Naiste Kristlik Ühendus* (Estonian Young Women's Christian Association); the *Eesti Naisüliõpilaste Selts* (Society of Estonian Women Students); the *Eesti Naisüliõpilaste Selts Ilmatar* (Ilmatar Society of Estonian Women Students) and the *Eesti Naisüliõpilaste Korporatsioon Filiae Patrie ja Amicitia* (Filiae Patriae and Amicitia Societies of Women Students). She founded the *Tartu Soroptimistide Ühing* (Tartu Soroptimist Society, 1931), the *Ühing Kodu ja Koo* (Society for Home and School) and the *Tartu Emadekaitse Ühing* (Tartu Society for Mothercare, 1939).

Expounding on themes of interest since her university days and drawing upon her long years of experience and professional knowledge, Vera Poska-Grünthal defended her MA thesis, "Labor-legal protection of the young," in 1939. She received a grant and worked at the Sorbonne in Paris from March 1939 through February 1940. The manuscript of the Ph.D. dissertation, "Penal-legal protection of the young" was completed in 1941 but was never defended; the reviewer wrote that the research did not meet the requirements of a Ph.D. dissertation.

In the meantime, her husband Timotheus Grünthal was elected a member of the Estonian Supreme Court and Lord Chief Justice and, from 1935 to 1940, worked as a lecturer at Tartu University. After the new Soviet occupation in the late summer of 1944, the Grünthals emigrated to Sweden where, from 1947, Timotheus Grünthal worked as a state-supported scholar at Stockholm University until his death in 1955, after which Vera Poska-Grünthal left for the USA.

Under Soviet occupation, the *EANÜ* was forced to abandon its activities in Estonia. On 30 October 1940, the association closed its minute book, which remained closed for over fifty years. After World War II, at Vera Poska-Grünthal's suggestion, the Board of the association in exile sought to restore the activities of the *EANÜ* but, due to IFUW objections that there was no longer a Republic of Estonia, this never took place. Later, in 1976, a group of former members of the *EANÜ* resumed activities in Sweden. The *EANÜ* was reestablished in Tartu on 30 November 1991.

While in exile, Vera Poska-Grünthal took up journalism. In 1952, she founded the Estonian journal *Triinu* in Stockholm, of which she was the long-standing editor from 1952 to 1981. In 1954, the editorial board moved to Toronto. *Triinu* was the journal of the *Toronto Eesti Naisselts (eksiilis)* [Estonian Women's Society (in exile) in Toronto]; it ceased appearing after its 1995 winter issue.

Vera and Timotheus Grünthal had five children: Konstantsia, Ivar, Veera, Svetlana and Tomm. Konstantsia (Tanni) Grünthal studied law (1938–1942) at Tartu University. She was a member of the Estonian Sorority, left for Sweden together with her parents in 1944, later moving from Sweden to Canada (1951), where she worked for an insurance company. From 1982 to 1995, she was acting editor of *Triinu* in Toronto.

Vera Poska-Grünthal died in Stockholm on 29 January 1986. To date, her activities have not received due attention.

Sirje Tamul
Tartu University

Translated from the Estonian by Leili Kostabi, Tartu University.

SOURCES

(A) *Eesti Ajalooarhiiv* (Estonian History Archives, hereafter EHA). Stock 3713 Series 1, Dossier 1-105, *Eesti Akadeemiliste Naiste Ühendus, 1926-1940* (Estonian Association of University Women, 1926-1940).

(A) EHA. Stock 2100, Series 1, Dossier 1859, Vera Poska-Grünthal.

(C) Poska-Grünthal, Vera. *Naine ja naisliikumine* (Women and the women's movements). Tartu, 1936.

(C) Poska-Grünthal, Vera. *See oli Eestis 1919-1944* (Memoirs 1919-1944). Stockholm: Kirjastus Välis-Eesti & EMP, 1975.

(C) Poska-Grünthal, Vera. *Elu jätkub välismaal* (Life will be continued abroad). Toronto: Förf, 1985.

(D) Jaan Poska tütar jutustab: mälestusi oma isast ja elust vanemate kodus (Jaan Poska's daughter's stories of home and family). Toronto: Orto, 1969.

(D) Tamul, Sirje. "Eestlannade õpingutest Venemaa kõrgkoolides enne rahvusülikooli avamist" (Estonian female students at Russian high schools and universities). In Sirje Tamul, ed. *Vita academica vita feminea. Artiklite kogumik* (Vita academica vita feminea. Studies in the history of the mentality, as well as the academic and higher education of women in turn-of-the-century Estonia). Tartu: Tartu Ülikooli Kirjastus (Tartu University Press), 1999, 194-197.

The QIRIAZI Sisters, Sevasti (1870–1949) and Parashqevi (1880–1970)

Teachers; pioneers of women's education and founders (1909) of the first Albanian women's association, *Yll'i mëngjezit* (Morning Star).

Sevasti (Dako) Qiriazi was born in February 1870 in Manastir (Monastir in English, a city in southern Albania), one of the ten children of Dhimiter Qiriazi and his wife Maria. Sevasti finished Greek elementary school and later, American high school in Manastir, finally going on to study at the American College of Istanbul in 1888. After graduating with excellent good results in June 1891, she returned to Albania. To combat the high rate of illiteracy among Albanian women (around ninety percent), she opened the first Albanian school for girls in Korçë (October 1891) with the support of her brother Gjerasim Qiriazi (1861–1894), an intellectual and advocate of Albanian education. As a result of her efforts, the number of girls enrolled in the school increased from 27 (in the school year 1891–1892) to eighty (1909–1910), of which twenty lived in dormitories. This development marked a change of mentality–a challenge to the stigma surrounding the education of young women. The structure of the school was much the same as that of most Western European schools: five years of elementary-level, followed by four years of secondary-level classes. In addition to educating young girls, another important function of Sevasti's school was the training of teachers, a newly emerging trend.

Sevasti was a pioneer of campaigns against women's illiteracy in Albania. In 1909, she participated in the Congress of Elbasan, at which a decision was taken to open the first high school in Albania (the school was opened on 1 December 1909). She was also a member of the commission for curriculum development and the evaluation of textbooks founded by the association *Përparimi* (Progress); she published the school textbooks *Gramatikën elementare për shkollat fillore* (Elementary grammar, Manastir 1912) and *Shkrojtoren e gjuhës shqipe* (Written Albanian), and worked on a series of ancient, medieval and modern histories.

Parashqevi Qiriazi, Sevasti's younger sister by ten years, was born on 2 June 1880 in Manastir, the youngest child of the Qiriazi family. She graduated from Uimins Kollixh in Istanbul in 1904, after which she returned to Albania and began working as a teacher in the Albanian school for girls founded by her sister Sevasti and her brother Gjerasim Qiriazi in Korçë. In 1909, she published *Abetare për shkollat e para* (A beginners' textbook for the teaching of literacy in elementary schools) in Manastir, thus becoming the first Albanian woman to write textbooks. In her writings she advocated democratic ideas such as free mandatory elementary schools in rural areas. In 1908, she was a delegate to the Congress of Manastir, where a standardized Albanian alphabet was established.

The beginning of the organized Albanian women's movement dates from 29 January 1909 when, on the initiative of the Qiriazi sisters, the first Albanian women's association, *Yll'i mëngjezit* (Morning Star), was created in the city of Korçë (in south-east Albania). The main goal of *Yll'i mëngjezit* was to engage and mobilize the women and girls of the city through various cultural, educational and professional activities, with a view to their emancipation and self-development. Women's education was a priority of the association. According to the statutes, the association had a director, a bookkeeper and a secretary. The leading body was elected every four years in a secret voting process. The first head of *Yll'i mëngjezit* was Parashqevi Qiriazi. Through the association, teachers from the 1891 school for girls gave special classes for women in written Albanian. The association organized conferences on behalf of the national movement and classes for women in hygiene, child-rearing, physical appearance and moral education. It also put on several plays for the education and entertainment of its members, who were from all social classes and religious groups.

In 1911, as a result of persistent pressure from the Turkish authorities, *Yll'i mëngjezit* ceased its activities. After the formation of the Albanian government in December 1912 (the year Albania gained its independence), the former leaders of *Yll'i mëngjezit* made an official appeal to the government to reopen their association. Permission was granted and the association was reopened in Korçë on 27 February 1913. The one hundred women and girls from Korçë who were present elected Sevasti Qiriazi as President, Androniqi Z.Grameno as Vice-President and Helidhona Ozado, Evridhiqi Kristaqi, Katerina Ciko, Eftali Petro, Eli Janaqi, Fankë Efthimi and Parashqevi Qiriazi as Board Members. Now that Albania was an independent state and Albanian women had fewer obstacles to paid employment, the reinstatement of the association could–

and did–have a powerful impact on the women's movement. It emphasized the necessity of women's participation in the social and economic sphere and of their contribution to the advancement of the nation.

Members of *Yll'i mëngjezit* held a weekly meeting to discuss the program and progress made during the week. The leaders of the association held lessons in Albanian for members three times a week. Encouraged by the Qiriazi sisters, women in other Albanian cities also began working for women's causes and founding associations such as *Shpresa kombëtare* (Nation's Hope) in Vlora, established in 1914 and led by Marigo Pozio.

On 24 July 1910, Sevasti married Kristo Dako, with whom she had one son. Kristo Dako worked for the Albanian national cause, including that of national education. In October 1914, Sevasti, her husband and her younger sister Parashqevi Qiriazi left Korçë for Romania because the Greek army had occupied Korçë. From Romania, the family moved to the USA, where Sevasti Qiriazi wrote to political representatives of the newly emerging Albanian State (including Ismail Qemali, leader of the national independence movement) about problems related to the education of women. This was Parashqevi Qiriazi's second visit to the USA; the first had been in 1912, when she had continued her postgraduate studies in pedagogy at Oberlin College (Oberlin, Ohio), to return to Manastir in October 1913.

The Qiriazi sisters lived in Boston from about 1915 to 1920/21, where they published a magazine called *Ylli i mengjesit*, after the organization in their home country. This political-pedagogal and literary-social magazine had a national character, dedicated as it was to raising awareness among the Albanian people, but it also discussed the educational and moral problems of women. In the first issue, which appeared on 15 January 1917, Parashqevi Qiriazi wrote an article on "The political value of education." The last number of *Ylli i mengjesit* is dated September 1920. It was in this period that Sevasti's sister, Parashqevi, became a Board Member and Sevasti Qiriazi became President of the *Partia kombëtare shqiptare* (National Albanian Party), an organization located in Worcester that fought for Albanian independence from foreign rule. As a representative of the *Partia kombëtare shqiptare*, Parashevi Qiriazi wrote to the Allied Powers to present the Albanian cause and (from March 1919) participated in the Paris Peace Conference as a member of the Albanian delegation–one of the few female delegates.

Parashqevi Qiriazi returned to Albania on 18 September 1920. On 27 December of the same year, she created the first women's association in Tirana, *Gruaja Shqiptare* (The Albanian Woman), the main aim of which was to advance Albanian women's education and raise funds for people in need of food, clothing and education. The association opened classes in handicrafts and four classes in English and French, cooperating with newly emerging women's organizations in other Albanian cities. Parashqevi Qiriazi was the guiding spirit of the organization.

Sevasti returned to Albania in 1922. On 2 October 1922, the Qiriazi sisters set up a private education institute named 'Qiriazi' in the Albanian capital of Tirana, which gave girls from the age of twelve who had finished elementary school the opportunity to study further. The teaching staff at the institute consisted of five teachers, among them an English woman who taught English and music. Fan Noli, a famous Albanian writer, wrote of the school in April 1923: "This institute will be an important tool for the progress and education of Albanian women. The two intelligent and courageous ladies who have opened the school and are now its professional directors should certainly be honored" (*AQSH*. Fund P. Qiriazi, year 1923, file 13).

After being temporarily disbanded due to the political situation in Albania, the organization *Gruaja shqiptare* was reestablished in 1928 under the direction of Sanije Zogu, the sister of the first Albanian king, Ahmet Zogu (1928–1939). Parashqevi Qiriazi had an active role in the revitalized association and became its secretary. The association created branches in other Albanian cities: Korçë, Shkodra, Elbasan, Gjirokastër, Berat, as well as a branch in Bulgaria led by the Albanian Qamile Asllani. *Gruaja shqiptare* held conferences on economic and social issues, one of which was led by Parashqevi Qiriazi. The association also encouraged women's traditional Albanian handicraft work, such as carpet weaving, and published the magazine *Shqiptaria* (Albanian): one of the most prominent women's publications of the time. The magazine's articles were for the most part written by well-known female intellectuals such as Sevasti Qiriazi, Parashqevi Qiriazi, Kaliopi Plasari, Emine Toptani, Ikbale Çikës and Kaliopi Plasari. They discussed the importance of educating Albanian women for the development of the country, the necessity of forming a network of schools all over the country, the position of women in the family, the education of children and the health problems of women and children.

The Qiriazi sisters examplify the way in which national consciousness shaped and changed the aspirations of Albanian women. The two women regarded education and development to be preconditions of women's emancipation and were pioneers of the first organized Albanian women's movement.

Zenepe Dibra
President of the Association
"Intellectual women of Shkodra"

Translated from the Albanian by Aurora Elezi, MA student, Department of Gender Studies, Central European University, Budapest.

SOURCES

(A) *Arkivi Qendror Shteteror* (*AQSH*, State Central Archives) (SCA). Fund *Shoqerite Shqiptare ne Rumani* (Albanian Associations in Romania), file 20.
(A) *AQSH*. Fund S. Qiriazi, year 1910, file 10.
(A) *AQSH*. Fund P. Qiriazi, year 1923, file 13.
(B) Newspaper *Korça* (13 January 1910).

(B) Newspaper *Arbnija* (Albania), no. 126 (16 January 1931).
(B) *Shqiptarja* (The Albanian woman), nos. 4, 8, 9 (1930); no. 8 (1931).
(D) Dishnica, Dhimitër. *Motrat Qiriazi* (The Qiriazi sisters). Tirana: Encyclopaedic, 1997.
(E) Frashëri, Kristo. *Rilindja kombëtare shqipëtare* (The Albanian national renaissance). Tirana, 1962.
(E) Academy of Science R. P. S. of Albania. *Fjalori enciklopedik shqiptar* (Albanian encyclopedic dictionary). Tirana, 1985.
(E) Musaj, Fatmira. *Gruaja në Shqipëri* (The women in Albania, 1912–1939). Tirana: Academy of Science, Institute of History, 2002.

RACIN, Kočo (Konstantin Solev) (1908–1943)

Macedonian poet, fiction writer, historical thinker and revolutionary; one of the first Macedonian autonomous feminist thinkers and a central figure of Macedonian feminism between the two world wars. 'Kočo Racin,' the pen-name that he used from 1928, comes from the name of Rahilka Raca Firfova, for whom he had a great and unrequited love. The poems, written on postcards that he sent her, are considered to mark the beginning of Expressionism in Macedonian literature. In Macedonian history, the name Kočo Racin is widely accepted and used instead of the poet's Christian name.

Konstantin Solev was born on 22 December 1908, into an extremely poor Orthodox Christian family from Veles. His mother Maria was a housewife and his father, Apostol Solev, a pottery-maker. He was their first child. He had three brothers: Aleksandar, Nikola, and a third one whose name is unknown. Konstantin Solev never married and did not have children. He completed four grades of primary school in Veles and one year of what was then high school in the same town. Then, because of the poor financial situation of his family, he left school to join his father in the pottery workshop (in the basement of the family home), where he spent his days both making clay pots and educating himself with diligence and dedication. In spite of his modest formal education, Konstantin Solev is today regarded as the most important Macedonian intellectual between the two World Wars.

In Racin's time, what is now the Republic of Macedonia had been incorporated into the Kingdom of Serbs, Croats and Slovenes, from 1929 known as The Kingdom of Yugoslavia. Solev/Racin was exceptionally active in revolutionary, communist and union movements (from 1924 until his early death). He made an effort to establish a network between workers and peasants and organized seminars and courses on Marxist topics, as well as literary evenings and other events, often followed by demonstrations. In 1928, he was an elected delegate to the Fourth Congress of the Communist Party of Yugoslavia (*KPJ*) in Dresden, where he became acquainted with international activists and their ideas. In 1933, he was sentenced to four years of imprisonment in Sremska Mitrovica (Serbia and Montenegro) for his work editing and publishing *Iskra* (Sparkle), the clandestine newspaper of the Regional Council of the Communist

Party of Yugoslavia. He was released under partial amnesty after two years of imprisonment.

In addition to working zealously for the community as a revolutionary, Kočo Racin possessed a rare talent for poetry and was a successful essayist. In 1939, in Samobor (Croatia), he published a collection of poems entitled *Beli Mugri* (White dawns), one of the most significant Macedonian collections of poetry. As an essayist, Racin took an interest in seemingly diverse topics such as literature, Hegelian philosophy, the Bogomils (members of Europe's first great dualist church that flourished in the Balkans from the tenth to the fifteenth centuries) and feminism. The common denominator of these topics was their potential to provoke criticism of phallocentric structures of power and probe the possibility for the ethnic, class, or gender restructuring of society along more egalitarian lines. Racin's interest in 'the woman question' can be dated to around 1936. Several fragments and pieces of paper, two articles, and one short story on this topic, all from 1936, have been found preserved in his archives. Several people provoked Racin's interest in women's issues, among them ***Rosa Plaveva***, who came from the same town as Racin and was a key figure in the Macedonian socialist women's movement. A group of Macedonians who participated in the international brigades in the Spanish Civil War, including Alekso Demnievski, Kiro Kjamilov, Trajko Miskovski and Ganco Hadji Panzov, also came from Veles. Racin was a close friend of Rumenika Hadji Panzova, Hadji Panzov's sister, who studied German language and literature in Skopje and Belgrade. Through her brother, Hadji Panzova became acquainted with the international women's movement (the implications of which remain as yet unclear) and popularized it in Veles and Skopje. Of importance for Racin's relations with the socialist women's movement was the Macedonian revolutionary Malina Pop Ivanova, alias Elena Galkina, a close friend of Racin whom he met at the above-mentioned Fourth Congress of the Communist Party of Yugoslavia in Dresden (1928). Racin's most important article on feminism was "Ulogata na feminizmot vo opstestvoto i prvite pocetoci na feminističkoto dviženje" (The role of feminism in society and the beginning of the feminist movement). Structured as a chronology of the international women's movement from World War I, the article, consisting of 22 typed pages, was publicly presented on 8 March (International Women's Day) 1936. In this text, Racin defined feminism as a struggle for fundamental human rights. With reference to the social contract theory of the French Enlightenment philosopher Jean-Jacques Rousseau, Racin exposed phallocentric forms of manipulation as "exploitation": namely the appropriation of women's social and mental property along with the suspension, rather than the distribution of their rights (a thesis possessing currency today). In his article, Racin also provided the names of the most important protagonists of the feminist movement in France, England, and Germany, focusing mainly on Olympe de Gouges and her *Declaration of the Rights of Woman and the Citizen* (1791), as well as Mary Wollstonecraft's *A Vindication of the Rights of Woman* (1792). According to Racin, both declarations resulted in forms of women's activism: the first was followed by the formation of women's clubs; the second led to women's struggle for the vote and amendments made to English Electoral Law. He also pointed to the example of Louise Otto-Peters (1819–1895) from Germany, referring to her open letter to the German government demanding economic and political rights for women. For Racin, these examples emphasized the necessity of relating feminist theory and activism. Urging Macedonian women to establish a feminist movement whose main goal would be the vote, he also listed numerous examples of feminist achievements in Sweden and Norway, such as the equality of men and women in Swedish inheritance law, the granting of limited voting rights to women in the communal councils, and the improved status of extramarital communities with children in Norway.

Interestingly, Racin's views cannot by regarded as a regurgitation of socialist cant and Communist Party declarations of equality. On the contrary, they were an autonomous feminist and gender-sensitive analysis of gender issues in Macedonia. In contrast to prevailing communist notions of the worker as the carrier of new ideas, Racin described the gender consciousness of D. I. Pisarev, an aristocrat and intellectual from the past, and a member of a class stigmatized in communist thought. In the short article "Pogledite na D. I. Pisarev za ženata" (D. I. Pisarev's views on woman), Racin explored Pisarev's ideas on womanhood as a cultural construction and passionately presented his own views as well, condemning prejudices against women as inferior human beings, undermining the belief in a 'feminine nature' and supporting the view that women should be free to make choices regarding their own activities and bodies.

It is also important to emphasize that Racin did not use the term 'progressive women's movement' as was common in communist vocabulary. Instead, he adopted the term 'feminist movement,' at that time identified with the 'bourgeois' women's movement–a digression from the communist norm which seems crucial when analyzing Racin's approach to gender issues. He critically compared the aims of Western 'women's rights' movements with declarations of women's equality in communist ideology. Taking into consideration the historical development of the socialist countries–which, far from establishing equality, contained an inherent 'gender pact,' ignored manifestations of women's inequality and tacitly cooperated with the machoization of society–Racin's analyses reveal an extraordinarily reflexive gender consciousness.

According to the recollections of his contemporaries, Kočo Racin was modest and shy, though also a competent and effective debater and dedicated activist. He lived in Veles, Skopje, Belgrade, Zagreb and Sofia. Because of his revolutionary activities in the period between World War I and World War II, he was imprisoned in Dresden (Germany), Maribor (Republic of Slovenia), Split (Republic of Croatia), Sremska Mitrovica (Serbia and Montenegro) and Sofia (Bulgaria).

He died on 13 June 1943, at the age of just 35. Together with a group of partisans,

Racin managed the clandestine printing house Goce Delčev, at the Lopusunik military base, Bistra Mountain, western Macedonia. Here, Kočo Racin was accidentally shot by the guard of the base when he did not heed the guard's warnings (Koco was partially deaf) and, for reasons unknown, did not answer to the previously agreed upon secret code. The circumstances of Racin's death have provoked conspiracy theories, trying to prove that his death was a consequence of his disagreements with the Communist Party, but these have never been proven.

Racin is one of the most important Macedonian poets, fiction writers, historical thinkers and revolutionaries. The annual International Poetry Festival *Racinovi sredbi* (Racin's Meetings) is organized in his honor in his hometown of Veles. Many cultural institutions and streets in Macedonia are named after him. Equally important, though less well known, he was one of the first Macedonian autonomous feminist thinkers.

Jasna Koteska
Faculty of Philology,
University SS Cyril and Method, Skopje

Ivana Velinovska
Student, Faculty of Philology,
University SS Cyril and Method, Skopje

Translated from the Macedonian by Nevenka Grceva, MA student, Department of Gender Studies, Central European University, Budapest.

SOURCES

(C) Racin, Kočo. *Beli mugi* (White dawns). Samobor, 1939.

(C) Tocinovski,Vasil, ed. *Kočo Racin: Proza i publicistika* (Kočo Racin: fiction and essays). Skopje: Nasa kniga, 1987.

(D) Vesković-Vangeli,Vera. "Kočo Racin i ženskoto prašanje" (Kočo Racin and the woman question). In *Zenata vo vitelot na antagonizmot na tradicijata* (Woman in the whirl of antagonistic tradition). Veles: Društvo za nauka i umetnost, 1999.

(E) *Eminentni licnosti od kulturata* (Prominent people in culture). UNESCO, 1986.

(E) Veleva, Marionka and Jadranka Vladova. "Učenite ženi na Makedonija" (The learned women of Macedonia). In *Istražuvanja od oblasta na rodovite studii* (Gender studies research). Vol. 1. Skopje: Evro Balkan Press, 2002.

REUSS IANCULESCU, Eugenia de (1866–1938)

Romanian journalist, novelist and teacher; pioneer suffragist and one of the leaders of the Romanian women's movement; Board member of the International Alliance of Women for Suffrage and Equal Citizenship (1926–1935).

Eugenia de Reuss Ianculescu was born on 11 March 1866 in Igeşti, Bucovina (then part of the Habsburg Empire), on the estate of the Reuss-Mirza family. She was the daughter of Maria Dinotto-Gusti and Alexandru de Reuss-Mirza, the latter descended from the aristocratic Reuss-Mirza family, which had established itself in Moldova in the fifteenth century. Eugenia received her primary education at the Central School in Iaşi (Moldova), where she became a teacher for a while. She was trained in classics and the arts and traveled frequently to France and Italy, where she was a member of the Hellenic and Latin Association and of two societies for the history of archaeology and art. Education and travel informed Reuss Ianculescu's later feminist activism, enabling her to gain access to the kinds of transnational communication that scholars have found so crucial for the development of women's movements.

In 1889, as a teacher in Iaşi, Reuss Ianculescu tried to establish a suffrage association. Following that unsuccessful attempt, she embarked upon an individual campaign to raise public awareness of inequities in civil and political law regarding women and men. In 1906, she held a series of public lectures dedicated to her feminist ideas at the Romanian Athenaeum in Bucharest, the largest and most renowned cultural hall in Romania.

In the first lecture of this series, entitled "Woman's mission and her future role," Reuss Ianculescu argued that "the feminist question [lay] at the heart of all social questions" and that it was "a matter as pressing as economic issues" (Reuss Ianculescu 1906, 5). In the years that followed, she gave speeches in many cities throughout the country, arguing for the political and economic emancipation of women and presenting developments in the international women's movement. During this period Reuss Ianculescu also published several introspective novels: *Voinţă* (Volition, 1902), nominated for a prize awarded by the Romanian Academy; *Spre desrobire* (Towards liberation, 1903) and *Pentr'o idee* (For an ideal, 1904). *Spre desrobire* was dedicated to her daughter, who died when she was a small child, as the reader is told in a short eulogy at the beginning of the book (information about her marriage is not available).

In November 1911, Reuss Ianculescu founded and became President of the *Asociația "Drepturile Femeii"* ("Woman's Rights" Association), the first feminist suffragist association in Romania. Founded in Bucharest, with branches in several cities throughout Moldovia and Wallachia, the *Asociația "Drepturile Femeii"* was a leading voice in the feminist struggle for political, civic and economic rights for women between 1911 and World War II. Eugenia de Reuss Ianculescu was nominated as the association's life-long President in 1923. From 1912 onwards, the Association published the feminist journal *Drepturile femeii* (Woman's rights), a tribune for debate and activism that also followed and reported developments in the international women's movement.

In the winter of 1913, the association was renamed the *Liga Drepturile și Datoriile Femeii* (League for Woman's Rights and Duties) and adopted a new statute, which declared that "the association work[ed] for the moral, social, economic and legal emancipation of women" [*Drepturile femeii*, (June-August 1913): 141]. According to the new statute, the *Liga Drepturile și Datoriile Femeii* aimed to agitate for changes in family and marriage legislation, women's access to the liberal professions, equal pay for equal work, programs for the prevention of child prostitution and equal political rights for men and women. All the demands listed in the statute were also presented to the two chambers of the Romanian Parliament by two male politicians, Theodor Florescu and Constantin Penescu: the first memorandum claiming political and civil rights for women.

Another innovation in the organization of the *Liga Drepturile și Datoriile Femeii* was the election of a male President, Nicolae Minovici, a legal doctor. This change was in line with Reuss Ianculescu's tactic of securing the support of influential male politicians, professors and doctors, who were often invited to the meetings of the association. The mixed-sex approach also reflected Reuss Ianculescu's philosophy that "woman and man [were] two distinct forces whose qualities and faults complement one another" (Reuss Ianculescu 1906, 9), and that both men and women were engaged in a common struggle for the country's social and economic progress.

In June 1913, the new *Liga Drepturile și Datoriile Femeii* became affiliated with the International Woman Suffrage Alliance (IWSA), remaining the only Romanian association affiliated with the IWSA until 1926, when the *Asociația pentru Emanciparea Civilă și Politică a Femeilor Române* (*AECPFR*, Association for the Civil and Political Emancipation of Romanian Women) and the association *Solidaritatea* (Solidarity) also joined.

Reuss Ianculescu maintained a moderate position with regard to political tactics used in the fight for suffrage. She believed that electoral reform, however limited, nevertheless constituted a major step towards achieving genuine universal enfranchisement. In 1914, as proposals for changes in the Constitution of the Romanian Kingdom were being debated, Reuss Ianculescu supported a petition addressed to one Ioan Al. Brătescu-Voineşti (MP), in which Brătescu-Voineşti was asked to present a proposal that women be granted the right to vote in local elections to the Parliament. The petition was signed by a small group of feminists, including ***Adela Xenopol***, ***Elena Meissner*** and Maria Gavrilescu. It was in this context that Reuss Ianculescu tried to cooperate with the *Cercul Feminin Socialist* (Socialist Feminine Circle), an organization founded in 1912 in Bucharest with the dual purpose of supporting the Socialist Party and women's rights. The Socialist Feminine Circle rejected Reuss Ianculescu's proposal because they held that the *Liga Drepturile şi Datoriile Femeii* was concerned only for the right of educated women to vote and thus excluded working-class and peasant women.

Reuss Ianculescu was active in the struggle for the vote through most of the interwar period. Members of the *Liga Drepturile şi Datoriile Femeii* organized suffragist meetings, wrote political memorandums, collected signatures and attended men's political campaigns and electoral gatherings. At the same time, Reuss Ianculescu joined other feminist organizations that later became leading voices in the movement for suffrage in interwar Romania. After Transylvania and the Romanian Kingdom were united (1918), Reuss Ianculescu became Vice-President of the *Uniunea Femeilor Române din România Mare* (Union of Romanian Women from Great Romania), presided over by ***Maria Baiulescu***. In 1921, the *Liga Drepturile şi Datoriile Femeii* became a member of the *Consiliul Naţional al Femeilor Române* (National Council of Romanian Women), a federation of women's organizations in Romania, founded that year and presided over by the feminist writer ***Calypso Botez***. Reuss Ianculescu was elected Vice-President of the new organization, which also became affiliated with the International Council of Women. Reuss Ianculescu was herself a Board member of the International Alliance of Women for Suffrage and Equal Citizenship (1926–1935).

In pursuing her feminist agenda, Reuss Ianculescu encountered two of the major problems of 'first wave feminism': 'loyalty to the nation' versus 'opposition to war' and the class/gender dilemmas. When, in 1915, Aletta Jacobs invited Reuss Ianculescu to participate in the International Congress of Women in The Hague—which aimed to discuss proposals for a peaceful end to the war—Reuss Ianculescu refused on the grounds that she owed loyalty to Romania. But even as she stood resolutely on the side of 'her nation,' her position allowed for nuances regarding the gender/class tension. She remained largely within the perimeters of her class, seeking support for her ideas among mostly educated, upper-class women and distinguishing her goals from those of the socialist movement. Yet she was at the same time preoccupied with improving the education and economic situation of peasant women, as revealed in her speeches and in her support for a free school for young peasant girls. She died on 29 December 1938 at her home in Igeşti.

Raluca Maria Popa
Ph.D. Candidate, Department of Gender Studies,
Central European University, Budapest

SOURCES

(B) International Information Center and Archives for the Women's Movement (Amsterdam), *Congress Reports* IWSA/IAWSEC (1911-1935).

(B) *Drepturile femeii* (Woman's rights) 2 (June-August 1913).

(B) Bogdan, E. *Feminismul* (Feminism). Timişoara: Tip. Huniadi, 1926.

(B) Mihăilescu, Şt. *Din istoria feminismului românesc. Antologie de texte (1838-1929)* [From the history of Romanian feminism. An anthology of texts (1838-1929)]. Iaşi: Polirom, 2002.

(B) Mihăilescu, Şt. *Emanciparea femeii române. Antologie de texte, 1815-1918.* (The emancipation of Romanian women. An anthology of texts, 1815-1918). Bucharest: Editura Ecumenica, 2001.

(C) De Reuss Ianculescu, E. *Menirea femeii şi rolul ei în viitor. Conferinţă ţinută la Ateneul român* (Woman's mission and her future role. Conference held at the Romanian Athenaeum). Bucharest: Minerva, 1906.

(E) Câncea, Paraschiva. *Mişcarea pentru emanciparea femeii în România 1848-1948* (Women's emancipation movements in Romania 1848-1948). Bucharest: Ed. Politică, 1976.

(E) Predescu, L. *Enciclopedia României. Cugetarea.* (Encyclopedia of Romania. The thought). Bucharest: Georgescu Delafras, 1940.

REZLEROVÁ-ŠVARCOVÁ (also written **SCHWARTZOVÁ**), Barbora (1890–1941)

Journalist, author; activist of the left-wing Slovakian women's movement; editor-in-chief (1923–1925) of the Slovak women's communist weekly *Proletárka* (Proletarian woman).

Barbora Švarcová (born Rezlerová; she used both names) was born on 7 July 1890 in Bleibach (Bavaria, Germany). Her father, Josef Rezler, was a textile worker who had come to Bleibach from Bohemia with Barbora's mother, Jozefína Rezlerová (born Horová). Barbora Rezlerová's father was one of the founders of the Social Democratic Party in Bohemia. When he returned to Bohemia from Germany with his wife and five children, the family settled in the town of Košín, near Prague.

Like her parents and siblings, Rezlerová was a textile worker. In all probability, she moved to Prague during World War I, where she worked as a cook. In Prague, she became active in the left-wing women's movement. She was self-taught, as was her father. In Prague, she met her husband, Ladislav Švarc (Schwartz), then an active communist leader (date of marriage unknown). In 1921, Ladislav Švarc became the regional secretary of the Czechoslovak Communist Party in the town of Banská Bystrica. Rezlerová moved to Banská Bystrica to be with her husband and, together with other left-wing activists, they became central figures in the workers' and communist movement.

For her part, Rezlerová was active in the political organization of women workers. From September 1922 to October 1923, she served as the Regional Secretary of the Communist Party organization *Slovenské ženy* (Slovak Women). From 1923, her political activities intensified. An excellent public speaker and openly critical of the government of the Czechoslovak Republic, Rezlerová was often fined, and on occasion imprisoned for her left/communist views, as was her husband. In 1925, the couple felt obliged to move to Prague to avoid further persecution. From Prague, they moved illegally to Germany, and from there to the Soviet Union in 1926.

The Soviet Union had always represented a place of promise and excitement for Rezlerová. Prior to emigrating there in 1926, Rezlerová had gone to the Soviet Union in 1921, giving birth to her son Vladimír there before returning to Slovakia, where she remained from 1921 to 1925. These latter years formed a definitive period in both Rezlerová's life trajectory and in the historical development of the left-wing Slovakian women's movement. From 1923 to 1925, Rezlerová was editor-in-chief of the Slovak women's communist weekly *Proletárka* (Proletarian woman). She was the first woman journalist in Slovakia to write on feminist issues such as reproductive rights, human rights and the political participation of women, as well as on gender asymmetry in the distribution of political power and legal rights. In this way, she helped make *Proletárka* a powerful feminist forum, as well as other periodicals to which she contributed in the period 1921–1925. No other nineteenth-/early twentieth-century Slovak woman activist presented so radical a Marxist feminist position, even if Rezlerová (towing communist party lines) consistently used the word 'feminism' in a negative sense.

Over the years she spent in Banská Bystrica (1921–1925), Barbara Rezlerová-Švarcová wrote articles not only for *Proletárka*, but also for other communist daily newspapers: *Hlas ľudu* (The people's voice); *Pravda chudoby* (The truth of the poor) and *Spartacus* (a journal for communist youth). Rezlerová's most significant articles appeared in *Proletarka*, for which she probably also used the pseudonym Kamila Kmeťová. She was the author of many articles, glosses and weekly columns and had a written style that was both informative and instructional, combining a direct address aimed at women from the working class with intellectual argumentation. Under her editorial leadership, the distribution of *Proletarka* was 1200 weekly copies, later rising to two thousand. All in all however, the publication had only three hundred subscribers and was losing even these. When in 1925, Gizela Kolláriková became editor-in-chief of *Proletarka*, the publication underwent drastic changes, attuning itself more finely to the goals and activities of the Communist Party, rather than to those of the women's movement.

Barbora Rezlerová-Švarcová left with her husband for the Soviet Union in 1926 and was active and successful there until 1938. In 1927, she gave birth to a second son (Il'ja) and, from 1928, began studying journalism at the State Institute of Journalism in Moscow. Later (exact date unknown), she worked for the prestigious newspapers *Rabočaja pravda* (Workers' truth) and *Izvestia* (News), as well as for the radio station of the *Komintern*. Her husband was the director of several textile factories across the Soviet Union but Rezlerová remained based in Moscow. At this time, her marriage began to fall apart but she and her husband remained friends (according to their son Vladimír). Ladislav Švarc married another woman, later divorcing her too.

In 1938, Stalinist reprisals began and foreigners were among those treated with the utmost suspicion. That year, Rezlerová was expelled from the *Komintern* radio station and forced to take up work as a Czech language teacher for tourist guides. In 1938, she was expelled from the Communist Party and her material situation deteriorated further. Almost driven to suicide, her belief in communist ideals remained unshaken by the hardships she was experiencing, and would continue to experience. She was arrested in 1941 and shot on 2 September 1941 (her younger son then only thirteen). Ladislav Švarc had died in prison one year earlier. They were both formally rehabilitated in the 1950s.

Barbora Rezlerová-Švarcová was an excellent journalist and a capable linguist who wrote fluently in Czech, Slovak and Russian. She educated herself by reading extensively and her journalistic pieces, inspired by the ideas of Rosa Luxemburg and Friedrich Engels, reflected on the position of women in the early twentieth century in a manner typical of the Marxian women's emancipation movement. Not much scholarly attention has yet been paid to Barbora Rezlerová-Švarcová's activities in Slovakia in the years 1921 to 1925, partly because during the Communist period the women's movement was dismissed, partly because Barbora Rezlerová-Švarcová was herself a communist. After 1989, this situation was further exacerbated by a lack of interest in Slovakia's communist past.

Jana Juránová
Writer, publicist,
ASPEKT, feminist publishing and educational project
www.aspekt.sk

SOURCES

(B) *Proletárka* (Proletarian woman) (1923–1925).

(C) (Possibly written by) Rezlerová-Švarcová, Barbora. *Ze zivota prukopniku socialni demokracie* (On the life of the pioneers of Social Democracy). Prague, 1920.

(C) (Possibly written by) Rezlerová-Švarcová, Barbora. *Organisacni ukoly delnickach zen* (Organizational tasks of women workers). Prague, 1922.

(C) (Possibly written by) Rezlerová-Švarcová, Barbora. *Slovensko-obet' cesko-kapitalisticke kolonisace* (Slovakia–a victim of Bohemian capitalist colonization). Prague, 1925.

(D) Čobejová, Eva. *Barbora Rezlerová-Švarcová* (Thesis). Bratislava: FFUK, 1987.

(E) *Encyklopédia Slovenska*. Bratislava: V. zväzok. Slovenská akadémia vied, Encyklopedický ústav (Slovak Academy of Science, Encyclopedic Institute), 1981.

RUDNYTSKA, Milena (1892–1979)

Ukrainian political activist and publicist; organizer of the women's movement and participant in the national liberation struggle in western Ukraine (1918–1939); President (1928–1939) of the *Souz Ukrainok* (Union of Ukrainian Women); deputy (1928–1939) to the Polish Parliament.

Milena Rudnytska was born on 15 July 1892 in Zborov, a small town in eastern Galicia (today in Ukraine), at that time part of the Austro-Hungarian Monarchy. At the end of the nineteenth century, the political situation in this eastern and economically backward province of the Habsburg Empire had been determined by a lasting conflict between Poles and Ukrainians. Roman Catholic Poles had traditionally dominated cultural and political life in Galicia and turned favorable conditions under the Austro-Hungarian constitutional monarchy (which guaranteed the cultural rights of minorities) to their own advantage: namely the integration of the Polish nation. Greek Catholic Ukrainian peasants were economically exploited by Polish landlords and the Ukrainian elite was Polonized. Encouraged by the example of the more advanced nations in the Habsburg Empire (such as the Czechs) and stimulated by competition with the Poles, the Ukrainian intelligentsia fought for the political and cultural rights of Ukrainians and for the territorial autonomy of eastern Galicia. The years of Milena Rudnytska's childhood were marked by the struggle of Ukrainians for access to education in their language and in particular for a Ukrainian university in Lviv.

Milena's mother Olga Rudnytska, maiden name Ida (1862?–1950), came from a poor Jewish merchant family. Milena's father, Myhaylo Rudnytsky (1856–1906), was a public official (notary) from a Ukrainian gentry family. They had waited almost ten years before marrying because the parents on both sides had opposed the union. In the end, Milena's mother had converted to Christianity. Milena remembered her parents' marriage as a happy one. The family spoke Polish; later, Milena's mother Olga learned a little Ukrainian from her children. Milena had four brothers and was surrounded by intellectually and politically active young people throughout her childhood. All her brothers became prominent intellectuals and public figures: Myhaylo (1889–1975), a philologist; Volodymyr (1890–1974), a lawyer; Ivan (1896–1995), an essayist and Antin (1902–1975), a composer and musician. Milena's father, with whom she had a close relationship, participated actively in the cultural life of the Ukrainian community. Milena experienced his early and unexpected death in 1906 as an irreplaceable loss.

Milena Rudnytska attended a gymnasium in Lviv (1903–1910) and later studied mathematics and philosophy at Lviv and Vienna universities (1910–1917). Vienna accommodated a Ukrainian community with a vibrant cultural and political life and in this stimulating environment, Rudnytska developed an interest in politics. She received a diploma in pedagogy (1917) and began writing a doctoral dissertation without ever completing it. In Vienna, she met Pavlo Lysiak (1887–1948), a journalist and a lawyer she had come to know through her brothers. She married him in 1919 and gave birth to a son, Ivan, but the marriage was not a success and Rudnytska ended up raising her child alone. She never married again and devoted herself to professional activity and political work.

In 1918, the Habsburg Empire collapsed but the Western Ukrainian People's Republic, proclaimed in Lviv that same year, did not survive. After a short but severe military conflict between Poles and Ukrainians in 1919, eastern Galicia became *de facto* part of the new Polish state. Its oppressive policy towards national minorities stimulated a national mass mobilization of Ukrainians. Rudnytska enthusiastically supported the short-lived Ukrainian government, but was not satisfied with the inferior role assigned to women within the national liberation movement. She focused her activities on organizing women and raising their civic consciousness. She saw feminism as a means of mobilizing women *en masse,* and involving them in practical political work on behalf of the future Ukrainian nation. [Rudnytska rarely used the term 'feminism' and when she did so, it was usually as a synonym for 'the women's movement:' i.e. practical work among women aiming to educate them as active and conscious citizens of the (future) state. She avoided 'feminist' in favor of 'women's' simply because she was seeking to address a mass female audience.] Rational, energetic and well educated, with an independent mind and strong political talents, Rudnytska was destined to become a leader.

After her return to Lviv in 1920, Rudnytska became one of the activists of the *Souz Ukrainok* (Union of Ukrainian Women), the most influential mass women's organization in eastern Galicia. The *Souz Ukrainok* was established in 1920 after the reorganization of the *Ukrainska Zhinocha Hromada* (Ukrainian Women's Hromada), which had been established in 1908. The *Souz Ukrainok* was also active in other regions of western Ukraine and maintained contacts with Ukrainian women in Europe and North America. According to estimates, it had between fifty and one hundred thousand members in Galicia alone. Most of these were peasant women. The leadership of the *Souz Ukrainok* was recruited from the local intelligentsia: teachers, wives of priests, etc. In addressing the needs of the peasants, the *Souz Ukrainok* tried to combine the aims of economic modernization in the villages with that of strengthening the role of women in the local community. Together with other prominent women (Olena Sheparovych, Olena Sichynska and Olena Stepaniv), Rudnytska supported women's groups and cooperatives and helped set up a women's press, organize women's conferences and represent Ukrainian women at the international level (e.g. in the International Council of Women, ICW). [Between 1920 and 1925, the Ukrainian National Council of Women was affiliated to the ICW. At the Washington congress of the ICW in 1925 "the question arose as to whether, in absence of any responsible government in Ukraine, the NCW of the country could remain a member" (*Women in a Changing World*, 1966, 53). Though the ICW was organized on the national principle and Ukraine, as a stateless nation, could no longer be a member, Ukrainian women cooperated with the Council informally and took part in congresses as observers and invited guests.] In 1928, Rudnytska was elected President of the *Souz Ukrainok* and retained this position until 1939. She also became an ideologist of the Ukrainian women's movement in Galicia and regularly contributed to the Ukrainian press. From 1919 onwards, she wrote for the women's socialist magazine *Nasha Meta* (Our goal) and cooperated with the feminist journals *Zhinka* (Woman), banned by the Poles in 1938; *Hromadianka* (Woman-citizen) and *Ukrainka* (Ukrainian woman). She also wrote for the only Ukrainian daily, *Dilo* (Action). From 1935 to 1939, Rudnytska was the editor of *Zhinka*.

Rudnytska's feminism was a product of her practical political activities. In her early writing, she drew attention to the conflict between family duties and professional interests, suggesting that the unequal distribution of household work was the main obstacle to women's participation in social life. She underlined that, until present times, women had been excluded from human history but now they had a chance to transform the state, society and the dominant culture on the basis of new values. Developing her own vision of the political and social role of Ukrainian women, she stressed that once basic civic rights had been won by women, women had important duties towards the community and the nation. The struggle for equality was only the beginning; the new aim was to make women aware of their equal responsibility for the future of the nation. Influenced by wider trends in late nineteenth-century and early twentieth-century European feminisms–which emphasized women's relationalism as mothers, wives, managers of households and educators of families–Rudnytska combined a commitment to women's emancipation with the idea of the specific social responsibility of mothers for the community. Among Ukrainians in eastern Galicia, lacking a state of their own and struggling for national survival, the emphasis was on women's constructive rather than subversive roles within the traditional institutions of family, church and community. Rudnitska sought to modernize these institutions but also tried to build her feminism upon them. Tolerance and democracy versus radicalism and violence, women's common interests versus class and political conflict, these were the tensions shaping her understanding of feminism. Unlike many other activists, she never felt sympathy for socialism and was never attracted to Soviet Ukraine as an alternative to national liberation. This said, under Rudnytska's leadership the *Souz Ukrainok* was open to women of very different political persuasions.

In June 1934, Milena Rudnytska, along with other activists, organized a mass women's congress in Stanislaviv (now Ivano-Frankivsk). Despite harassment from the Polish authorities, more than ten thousand delegates from Galicia, Volhynia, as well as from Europe and North America, demonstrated the unity and strength of the women's movement. At the congress, the *Vsesvitniy Souz Ukrainok* (World Union of Ukrainian Women) was created, which became a powerful international organization representing Ukrainian women worldwide.

Rudnytska's activities were not restricted to the women's movement. From 1925, she was an active member of the *Ukrainske Natsionalno-Demokratychne Obiednannia* (*UNDO*, Ukrainian National Democratic Alliance), the most influential political party of Ukrainians in Galicia. At the same time, never a slave to party discipline, she tried to keep the *Soiuz Ukrainok* out of party disagreements. When in 1935, during the election campaign for the Parliament, *UNDO* attempted to instrumentalize women and tried to impose its candidates on the *Soiuz Ukrainok*, Rudnytska left the party in protest against *UNDO* policy.

In 1928, Rydnytska became an elected member of the Polish Parliament. An excellent and charismatic speaker and a gifted politician, she fought against ethnic and sexual discrimination and worked on commissions for education and international relations. She used her position to fight against the Polonization of education and to defend Ukrainian teachers against political harassment, but she also defended Ukrainian women's organizations against the repressive measures of the Polish government. Her international activities were also focused on the political and economic situation of the Ukrainians. In 1931, Rudnytska was one of three Ukrainian delegates to the League of Nations, where she denounced the Polish 'pacification' campaign against the Ukrainian national minority and condemned Polish offensives to deny Ukrainians access to education in their own language and crush Ukrainian organizations. She was also invited to give a speech in the British House of Commons on the situation of the Ukrainians in Poland. Another focus of Rudnytska's international activities was the Famine in Soviet Ukraine in 1933, silenced by the Soviet leadership. She tried to bring this catastrophe to the attention of the international public and organize help for its victims.

From the late 1920s, the political conflict between Ukrainians and the Polish state radicalized. Ukrainian women's activities were watched closely by the Polish government, which tried on more than one occasion to ban the *Souiz Ukrainok*, even arresting some of its leaders. With the Soviet occupation of western Ukraine in 1939, most women activists had to leave Galicia; in July 1941, the region was occupied by the German army.

Rudnytska moved to Cracow, later to Prague and Berlin, where her son—who became the prominent historian Ivan Lysiak-Rudnytsky (1919–1984)—was a student. In exile, she concentrated on writing and in 1944, published her book *Zakhidna Ukraina pid bolshevykamy* (Western Ukraine under the Bolsheviks) in Prague; a second New York edition followed in 1958 (both editions were in Ukrainian). After the war, Rudnytska tried to restore the *Souiz Ukrainok* in emigration (Galicia being under occupation by the Soviets) and organize support for Ukrainian refugees. But her political and personal disagreements with other Ukrainian women's émigré organizations left her a marginal figure. In 1950, she moved to the USA, returning to Europe after eight years. She continued her studies, developed interests in philosophy and religion, but did not resume her political activities.

Milena Rudnytska died in Munich on 29 March 1979. She was re-buried in Lviv in 1993.

Tatiana Zhurzhenko
Dept. of Philosophy,
V. Karazin Kharkiv National University, Ukraine

SOURCES

(A) Archives of the University of Alberta (Canada), Milena Rudnytska archive.
(A) Central State Historical Archive, Lviv (Ukraine): collection N319, Central Ukrainian Women's Society *Soiuz Ukrainok*; also collections N 358, 359, 344, 205. State Archive of Lviv Oblast: collections N1, 119.
(A) National Library, Warsaw and the Central State Historical Archive, Lviv, Archive of Ukrainian Parliamentary Representation.
(B) *Nasha Meta* (Our goal) (1919).
(B) *Dilo* (Action) (1922-1926, 1931, 1934).
(B) *Zhinka* (Woman) (1935-1937, 1939).
(C) Rudnytska, Milena. *Western Ukraine under the Bolsheviks*. New York, 1958.
(C) Rudnytska, Milena. *Statti, Lysty, Dokumenty* (Essays, letters, documents). Miroslava Diadiuk, ed. Lviv: Central State Historical Archive, 1998.
(E) *Women in a Changing World: The Dynamic Story of the International Council of Women since 1888*. London: Routledge & Kegan Paul, 1966, 46; 53.
(E) Bohachevsky-Chomiak, Martha. *Feminists Despite Themselves: Women in Ukrainian Life, 1884-1939*. Edmonton: CIUS, University of Alberta, 1988.

RUMBO, Urani (1895–1936)

Albanian campaigner for women's emancipation, especially through education. Founder and supporter of various women's associations, including the *Lidhja e gruas* (Woman's Union) (1920).

Urani Rumbo was born in December 1895 in Stegopuli, a southern Albanian village in Gjirokastër. She had two brothers, Kornili and Thanasi, and a sister, Emilia. Her father, Spiro Rumbo, was a teacher and her mother, Athinaja, a housewife. Urani completed six grades of elementary education at the school where her father was a teacher, in the village of Filat (in the region of Çamëri, now in Greece). One of the school's best students, talented in literature and poetry, Urani soon familiarized herself with the works of Albanian folklorists (such as Spiro Dine and Thimi Mitko) and writers (Naum Veqilharxhi and Konstandin Kristoforidhi). She learned written Albanian and Greek fluently and, from the age of fifteen, began teaching Albanian to people around her. Language became one of the most important political issues in a country struggling for independence (from the Ottoman Empire) and resisting the conquering strategies of its neighbors.

From 1910, Urani Rumbo attended a high school in Janine/Ioannina (a city in northwestern Greece), where she studied works by Homer and Sophocles. Albania gained its independence in 1912. The Balkan War (1913) followed by World War I interrupted Rumbo's education, but she continued to teach herself Italian and French, as well as keeping up her study of Greek and Latin. In this period, she worked with female friends from Stegopuli to combat strong patriarchal traditions, arguing for the rights of girls to an education, to personal independence, to choose a husband or meet friends. Rumbo, who had had to fight in her own family to be allowed to attend the high school in Janine, strongly believed that education was the most effective way of improving women's lives and social status. In 1916/17, she began working as a teacher of Albanian in Dhoksat, a small town in southern Albania, where she promoted the use of the Albanian language and generated great enthusiasm among her students.

In 1917–1918, Rumbo taught in Nokovë and Mingul (villages in the Lunxheri region) and in 1918 and 1919, in Gjirokastër, at the De Rada School (named after the famous Albanian writer, Jeronim De Rada). It was at this time that she initiated a campaign against veiling on behalf of Gjirokastër women, and began working to combat female illiteracy and the bourgeois practice of restricting women to specific areas of the household. In 1920, she opened the Koto Hoxhi School [named after the Albanian patriot and teacher, Koto Hoxhi (1824–1895)], a five year primary school for girls established with the help of supporters from both the lower and middle classes. Rumbo was a charismatic woman and she succeeded in getting girls from different parts of Gjirokastër (including the villages) to attend the Koto Hoxhi School. For the first time, people from different religions were being educated together. Rumbo's school was an effort that reflected contemporary historical and social events in Albania, such as the democratic movement of the years 1921–1924. In this period, Rumbo published in the local Gjirokastër newspapers *Demokratia* and *Drita* (Light) on problems faced by Albanian women, particularly their lack of education: "Schooling," she wrote, "is the education of the soul" [*Drita* (Light) (20 May 1921)]. She also developed vocational training in the crafts of embroidery and custom tailoring, as well as in gardening and agriculture.

Another dimension of Urani Rumbo's work was the organization of school theater performances, through which girls might be encouraged to participate in public events and thereby increase their self-confidence. In a patriarchal climate where girls were forbidden from taking part in theater courses and being an actress was considered shameful, Rumbo introduced theater courses in schools and wrote theater plays. She directed performances of *Agamemnon*, *Kuleta e neqezit* (The wallet of the stingy man), *Fiqtë dhe dituria* (Figs and knowledge) and *Nipi i këpucarit* (The nephew of the shoemaker)—plays which dealt with Albanian history and the desire of women for education. She also wrote poems and song lyrics dedicated to the nation, knowledge and labor, and set up music courses for girls, teaching them to play the mandolin. In time, she became the Director of the Koto Hoxhi School. Not abandoning her passion for foreign languages, she also translated many foreign plays.

On 23 November 1920, Urani Rumbo, together with Hasibe Harshova, Naxhije Hoxha, and Xhemile Bilali—all from Gjirokastër—founded the *Lidhja e gruas* (Union of Women). The women published a declaration in *Drita*, protesting discrimination against women. *Lidhja e gruas* was one of the first prominent Albanian women's organizations to fight for equality and women's emancipation. In 1923, the first Lyceum in Gjirokastër was opened and Rumbo began a campaign, followed by informal meetings of women, for the right of girls to attend the Lyceum together with boys. On 25 July 1924, another women's organization, *Përmirësimi* (Improvement), was founded. Urani Rumbo stated (in the statute of *Përmirësimi*) that intellectual women, teachers, parents and students should meet to discuss the particular problems and injustices commonly encountered by women. In January 1926, Rumbo made a public appeal to women via the local newspapers: "Honest people. Support and do not ignore this benevolent organization, created not in self-serving interests, but in order to serve your moral and material well-being" [*Demokratia* (January 1926)].

Përmirësimi organized courses for women in domestic hygiene and written Albanian; in doing so, it effectively functioned as a place of education and (in many cases) life-long learning for women of different social strata. Rumbo encouraged women brought together by the organization to put on plays and to write to local newspapers protesting patriarchal traditions and practices. The Gjirokastër women's movement was strengthening in a climate marked by the claims–of the Orthodox and Islamic religions and the political regime–that women's lower social status was 'unchangeable.' Thus the movement initiated by Rumbo and other women represented a direct (and dangerous) attempt to counter establishment ideology.

On 4 July 1930, Rumbo was accused by the authorities of permitting girl students at the Koto Hoxhi School (of which she was the Director), to go out into the streets in fashionable stockings and encouraging them to perform in theater plays. Rumbo responded with an article in *Demokratia*, appealing to Gjirokastër readers and denouncing the accusations as absurd. Public opinion supported her, yet she was still transferred to another city, Vlorë (in southern Albania), where she again worked in a school for girls and devoted herself to combating illiteracy and promoting women's causes until her early death on 26 March 1936. The Albanian authorities belatedly acknowledged her efforts on 1 March 1961, awarding her the title of "Mësuese e Popullit" (Teacher of the people), a distinguished award during the communist period.

Urani Rumbo, one of the most prominent figures in Albanian education, mobilized Albanian women. She promoted women's participation in education and other public activities as a means of improving their social position.

Zenepe Dibra

President of the Association: "Intellectual women of Shkodra"

Translated by Aurora Elezi, MA student, Department of Gender Studies, Central European University, Budapest.

SOURCES

(A) Arkivi Qendror Shteteror (AQSH) (State Central Archives) (SCA). Fund 294, year 1926, file 4.

(A) Arkivi Qendror Shteteror (AQSH) (State Central Archives) (SCA). Fund 445, year 1926, file 127.

(B) *Demokratia*, no. 115 (13 August 1921).

(B) *Drita* (Light) (23 November 1920).

(B) *Shpresa kombetare Vlore* (National hope, Vlore) (1921).

(D) Mosko, V. *Urani Rumbo*. Tirana: Shtepia botuese "8 Nentori" (Publisher 8 November), 1977.

(E) Frasheri, Kristo. *Rilindja kombetare shqiptare* (The Albanian National Renaissance). Tirana: Album [Collection], 1962.

(E) Academy of Science of the RPS Albania. *Fjalori enciklopedik shqiptar* (Encyclopedia of Albanian vocabulary). Tirana, 1985, 929.

(E) Musaj, Fatmira. *Gruaja ne Shqiperi (1912-1939)* [Women in Albania (1912-1939)]. Tirana: Botim i Akademise Shkencave (edited by the Academy of Science), 2002.

SCHLESINGER, Therese (1863-1940)

Journalist and editor; Vice-President (1894–1897) of the *Allgemeiner Österreichischer Frauenverein* (*AÖFV,* General Austrian Women's Association); leader and ideologist of the Austrian socialist women's movement; member of the *Nationalrat* (Austrian Parliament) (1919–1923) and *Bundesrat* (Federal Council) (1923–1930); member of the board of the Austrian *Sozialdemokratische Arbeiterpartei* (*SDAP,* Social Democratic Workers' Party) (1918–1933).

Therese Schlesinger (center), 1924, at the 'Parteitag der SDAP' in Salzburg

Therese Schlesinger (born Eckstein) was born on 6 June 1863 in Vienna, into an upper middle-class, liberal, factory-owning family of Jewish descent. Her father, Albert Eckstein, was a chemist from Lieben near Prague. Her mother, Amalie Wehle, was born in Prague. They married in 1860 and had six daughters and four sons. Therese was the third child. The couple's house was open to a variety of intellectual personalities and the family defined itself within the 1848 revolutionary tradition. Friedrich, Emma and Gustav Eckstein (Therese's siblings) all became public figures: Emma, a feminist (like Therese), was one of the first patients of Sigmund Freud; Friedrich was a writer and Gustav, a Social Democrat. The education of the Eckstein daughters took the form of private lessons, the result of endeavors by their parents to compensate for the exclusion of women from higher education.

On 24 June 1888, Therese Eckstein married Viktor Schlesinger, a chief cashier at the *Länderbank*, Vienna, and fifteen years her senior. The couple were married in the large *Stadttempel*, in Vienna's *Seitenstettengasse*, in accordance with Jewish custom. A year later a daughter, Anna, was born. Therese Schlesinger became sick during childbirth, thereafter suffering from stiff hip-joints and disability in her right leg, spending several years in a wheelchair as a result. Meanwhile, her husband died of tuberculosis on 23 February 1891.

From 1894 onwards, Schlesinger became involved in the *Allgemeiner Österreichischer Frauenverein* (*AÖFV*, General Austrian Women's Association), the radical wing of the Austrian feminist movement, recommended to Schlesinger by her friend, Marie Lang. In 1896, the *Ethische Gesellschaft* (Ethical Society) organized an *Enquęte zur Lage der Wiener Lohnarbeiterinnen* (Enquéte on the condition of female Viennese wage-workers), in which Schlesinger participated and through which she became personally acquainted not only with leading Social Democrats, but with the terrible living conditions of the lower classes, especially women–leading her to take socialist ideas seriously. Her plan to strengthen the *AÖFV* financially and organizationally by bringing it together with the *Sozialdemokratische Arbeiterpartei* (*SDAP*, Social Democratic Workers' Party) failed and so, at the end of 1897, she left the *AÖFV* and joined the *SDAP*. The *Lese- und Diskutierclub Libertas* ('Libertas' Reading and Discussion Club) elected Schlesinger as a delegate to the first social democratic women's conference held in the Easter of 1898, an attempt to unite and organize the different social democratic women's clubs independently of the party leadership. In the years to follow, Schlesinger appeared at the center of debates over the best way to win women to the cause of Social Democracy. Her position was clear: the demands of trade union organizations did not extend to securing the political education of women and women's voting rights, equally important demands as far as Schlesinger was concerned. Furthermore, if a new kind of solidarity were to be developed between people within the framework of a socialist project, it was first of all necessary to treat cultural questions pertaining to 'everyday' life and consciousness as political concerns.

Schlesinger's position generated misunderstandings within the party at its proletarian base and resulted in feelings of antipathy towards Schlesinger as a 'bourgeois' Jewish woman. Such antipathy was felt, above all, by the social democratic *Freie Gewerkschaften* (Free Trade Unions). Schlesinger's comprehensive understanding of politics took gender questions into consideration and emphasized the necessity of a moral ethic able to address the gendered as well as classed nature of exploitation and oppression. In her publication *Eine Aufgabe der Arbeiter-Baugenossenschaften* (The task of the construction workers' cooperatives, 1912), Schlesinger addressed the practical implications of the abstract social democratic notion of 'public' appropriation of the 'private' or 'reproductive' sphere. She elaborated a vision of social housing equipped with central laundries, kitchens and childcare facilities, offering three main arguments in favor of such a vision: (i) food purchased in greater quantity and at cheaper rates would be qualitatively revalued, since shops would be run as consumer cooperatives not as profit-making enterprises; (ii) family relationships would be enhanced as a result of increased free time and (iii) women would have the opportunity to devote themselves to their own interests.

During World War I in 1916, past the age of fifty, Therese Schlesinger became an anti-war activist and leader of the *Parteischüler-Bildungsverein 'Karl Marx'* ('Karl Marx' Society for Party Scholars and Education), an oppositional center within the Austrian social democratic movement. She also participated in the *Linksradikalen* (Left Radicals), which later joined the Communist Party, and for which she acted as a contact, representing the Austian left-wing opposition at the third *Zimmerwald* (anti-war) Conference in 1917. At the height of the East Austrian *Rätebewegung* (Council movement) in June and July 1919, Schlesinger, along with ***Adelheid Popp***, was a delegate to the second *Reichskonferenz der deutschösterreichischen Arbeiterräte* (National Conference of the German-Austrian Workers' Councils). She was the only woman to speak at this forum.

From 1919 to 1923, Therese Schlesinger became a member of the *Nationalrat* (National Assembly). Later, she joined the *Bundesrat* (Federal Council), which she left due to her age on 5 December 1930. Under the First Republic, Schlesinger began to refine her broad political arguments, focusing in particular on questions of gender justice in theory, law and practice, as well as questions of social psychology: "We can see how difficult it is to show adult men that women of today are really equal and of equal abilities" (Hauch 1995, 13). She wrote on 'the woman question' for the Austrian Marxist party program on the occasion of the party conference (Linz, 1926), a work which was completed in 1928 and published as a brochure, *Die Frau im sozialdemokratischen Parteiprogramm* (Woman in the program of the Social Democratic Workers' Party).

In the 1920s, Therese Schlesinger formed the center of a circle of young Social Democrats in Vienna which, along with 'the party,' provided a substitute for her own family circle. Since 1905, Schlesinger had lived with her daughter, her mother, her feminist sister Emma and her brother Gustav. Schlesinger often felt torn between working for the party, studying theory and spending time with her daughter. Schlesinger's daughter committed suicide in 1920, after falling into a severe bout of depression which no contemporary therapy, including psychoanalysis, could mitigate. This tragic event had a profound effect upon Schlesinger's later life. In 1916, her brother Gustav passed away. Her mother died in 1921 and her sister Emma shortly after that in 1924, after which Schlesinger's empty apartment was used by young Social Democrats as a "refuge," as ***Käthe Leichter*** called it (Leichter 1933, 6f), and as an information center where internal party matters could be freely discussed. Young people were attracted to Schlesinger because, as a woman politician and intellectual, she was open to internal criticism of the party and radical ideas.

At an extraordinary party conference in October 1933, which took place in the midst of political shifts towards the *autoritärer Christlicher Ständesstaat* (authoritarian Christian corporatist state), Schlesinger left the party leadership due to her advanced years. The failure of the *Republikanischer Schutzbund* (Republican Protection Union, an armed social democratic organization) to defend their party and democracy on 12 February 1934, followed by a ban on social democratic organizations, meant the beginning of growing isolation for the 71 year old Schlesinger. Illegal political activities within the *Revolutionäre Sozialisten* (Revolutionary Socialists, the clandestine social democratic organization) were out of the question. Her physical disability, back and stomach problems did not permit her to leave the house often. With the National Socialist takeover in 1938, Schlesinger faced grave danger as a Social Democrat of Jewish origin and so, at the delicate age of 76 and critically ill, she fled to France. Marianne Pollak (one of the young female Social Democrats who had frequented Schlesinger's apartment in the twenties) picked her up at a train station in Paris. Therese Schlesinger spent the last year of her life in a sanatorium in Blois near Paris. She died on 5 June 1940, one day before her 78th birthday and six days before the invasion of Paris by German troops. Her life and work reveal a permanent break in feminist political debate and definitions of gender equality in Austria under the *Christlicher Ständestaat* and under National Socialism. The topics which had preoccupied Therese Schlesinger were next debated again at the beginning of the new women's movement in the 1970s.

Gabriella Hauch
Johannes Kepler University, Linz, Austria

Translated by Melanie Morgan.

SOURCES

(B) *Die Frau* (Woman) (1923–1933).

(B) *Die Arbeits- und Lebensverhältnisse der Wiener Lohnarbeiterinnen. Ergebnisse und stenographisches Protokoll der Enquête über Frauenarbeit, abgehalten in Wien 1. März bis 21. April 1896* (Enquéte on the working and living conditions of Viennese women wage-workers). Vienna: Verlag Wiener Volksbuchhandlung, 1897.

(C) Schlesinger, Therese. "Mein Weg zur Sozialdemokratie" (My way to the Social Democrats). In Adelheid Popp, ed. *Gedenkbuch. Zwanzig Jahre Arbeiterinnenbewegung* (Book of remembrance. Twenty years of the female workers' movement). Vienna: Kommissionsverlag der Wiener Volksbuchhandlung, 1912, 125–139.

(D) Leichter, Käthe. "Therese Schlesinger und die Jungen" (Therese Schlesinger and the youth). *Die Frau*, no. 7 (July 1933): 6f.

(D) Hauch, Gabriella. "Der diskrete Charme des Nebenwiderspruchs. Zur sozialdemokratischen Frauenbewegung vor 1918" (The discrete charm of the incidental contradiction. Towards a social democratic women's movement before 1918). In Wolfgang Maderthaner, ed. *Sozialdemokratie und Habsburgerstaat* (Social Democracy and the Habsburg State). Vienna: Löcker Verlag, 1988, 101-118.

(D) Tichy, Marina. "Ich hatte immer Angst unwissend zu sterben. Therese Schlesinger: Bürgerin und Sozialistin" (I have always been afraid of dying ignorant. Therese Schlesinger: bourgeois and socialist). In Edith Prost, ed. *"Die Partei hat mich nie enttäuscht..." Österreichische Sozialdemokratinnen* ("The party has never disappointed me..." Austrian women socialists). Vienna: Verlag für Gesellschaftskritik, 1989, 135-186.

(D) Hauch, Gabriella. *Vom Frauenstandpunkt aus. Frauen im Parlament 1919-1933* (From the perspective of women. Women in Parliament 1919-1933). Vienna: Verlag für Gesellschaftskritik, 1995.

(D) Hauch, Gabriella. "Schlesinger, Therese geb. Eckstein" (Therese Schlesinger, born Eckstein). Brigitta Keinzel and Ilse Korotin, eds. *Wissenschaftlerinnen in und aus Österreich. Leben–Werk–Wirken* (Women scientists in and from Austria. Their lives and works). Vienna-Köln-Weimar: Böhlau Verlag, 2002, 650-655.

SCHWIMMER, Róza (Bédy-Schwimmer, Bédi-Schwimmer, Rózsa, Rosika) (1877-1948)

Leading figure of the progressive–liberal wing of the Hungarian women's movement with a strong commitment to political and economic equality, suffrage and pacifism; high-ranking international networker until World War I; worked for peace and world government after her exile from Hungary (1920) and life-long relocation to the USA (1921).

Róza Schwimmer, June 1913, giving a suffrage speach at a public meeting of the Constitutional Party in Budapest, Bakáts square

Róza Schwimmer was born on 11 September 1877 in Budapest, into an upper middle-class Jewish family. Her mother, born Bertha Katscher (1856-1927), and her father, agricultural trader Max Schwimmer (born between 1843 and 1845-d.1922), married in 1877. Róza, who had a younger brother Béla (1878-?) and a younger sister Franciska (1880-1955), grew up in Temesvár (today Timisoara, Romania) and Szabadka (today Subotica, Yugoslavia). After her father's business went bankrupt, the whole family moved to Budapest in 1897 but never recovered from financial difficulties. In addition to four years of secondary schooling, Róza received substantial language training (French and German), a musical education, as well as completing, at the age of 21, an evening trade school in Temesvár in 1899. By the mid-1890s, she had worked as an office employee in Temesvár and Szabadka, and later did so in Budapest as well, although no further formal employment of this kind is reported after March 1904. Schwimmer, from that time onwards, supported herself in various ways, particularly from her writing, public speaking, journalism (at home and abroad) and, at least in the prewar period, from her income as an editor. In later life, she received additional and regular material support from her close friend Lola Maverick Lloyd (whom she had met during her first visit to the United States in 1914-1915; see for instance the agreement between them in NYPL

SLC A478), remaining dependent on Lloyd for decades. After Schwimmer's death in New York in 1948, this support was extended by the Lloyd family to Schwimmer's secretary and co-worker Edith Wynner.

In 1904, Róza Schwimmer called herself Rózsa Bédy-Schwimmer for the first time. According to unconfirmed sources, her formal marriage with the journalist Bédy lasted from 1911 to 1913. She had no children. In the interwar period, Schwimmer was recorded by the Hungarian authorities as being without confession, and married or having been married to Sándor Aszódi.

After the turn of the century, Schwimmer became a key figure in the Hungarian women's movement, enlarging and reshaping the political and organizational landscape of that movement. In 1897, she was a member of the newly founded *Nőtisztviselők Országos Egyesülete* (*NOE*, National Association of Women Employees); in 1899, Vice-President and from 1900 or 1901 to 1908, President. Later, Schwimmer remained a member of the *NOE* Board. In 1902–1903, she worked, in close cooperation with social democratic women, on the foundation of a women workers' association, formally established as the *Magyarországi Munkásnők Országos Egyesülete* (National Association of Woman Workers in Hungary) in 1904, with Schwimmer as the first President. From 1901–1902 onwards, Schwimmer's activities in Budapest and Hungary became increasingly intertwined with her unfolding contacts with journals and representatives of the international women's movement (in particular Dutch feminist Aletta Jacobs), and with endeavors by the International Council of Women (ICW) and the nascent International Woman Suffrage Alliance (IWSA) to expand their organizational base into the Habsburg Monarchy. In 1903–1904, Schwimmer worked to found what was to become the *Magyarországi Nőegyesületek Szövetsége* (Alliance of Women's Associations in Hungary), a member of the ICW from 1904. In the summer of 1904, Schwimmer, together with her close co-worker ***Vilma Glücklich***, participated in the gatherings of the ICW and the IWSA in Berlin. At the latter (the founding congress of the IWSA), she was endowed with the status of a delegate without full voting rights. "Man is happy only when in his own element; you were hap(py) ... in Berlin 1904 ... like a fish in water," wrote Schwimmer's uncle Leopold Katscher (who had accompanied her) to his niece (NYPL SLC K2-Katscher to Schwimmer 29.09.1906). Subsequently, Schwimmer and Glücklich initiated the establishment of the *Feministák Egyesülete* (*FE*, Feminist Association), whose constitutive general assembly was held on 18 December 1904. In April 1905, the new organization decided, despite strong internal resistance to the explicit inclusion of suffrage on the agenda of the *FE*, to make women's suffrage part of its program and activities. Schwimmer became the head of the newly established Political Committee, a function she retained until after the end of World War I. In April 1905, it was also decided that the *FE* should join the IWSA, membership being formally confirmed in 1906. Schwimmer played a decisive role in organizing the Seventh International Congress of the IWSA in Budapest in 1913. Apart from the Berlin Congress of 1904, this was the first time that the IWSA had met in a country not located in North-Western Europe. At the 1913 Budapest Congress, Schwimmer was elected Second Corresponding Officer of the IWSA. In early 1914, Schwimmer moved to London, where she soon took up the position of Press Secretary of the IWSA, an appointment made by the Board of Officers in the same year.

The London appointment was the final episode of the most successful period of Schwimmer's life. Before 1914, Schwimmer, substantially developing her understanding of a whole range of key themes in contemporary feminism, had made a great impact on the agendas and policies pursued by the *FE* and the broader Hungarian women's movement. Her radical quest for gender equity in all spheres of life, the *leitmotiv* of her thought and action, was never restricted to a narrowly defined equality agenda, but was closely related to issues of class and democracy. When she opposed special labor protection for women (except for the shortest possible period of maternity leave), as she did for instance in 1908 and 1911, she also requested a substantial extension of labor protection for men and women. When, in the 1910s, she explicitly promoted restricted woman suffrage in Hungary, she followed the basic strategy of the IWSA, focusing on closing the gap between male and female voting rights, while remaining seriously and publicly dedicated to the fundamental goal of extending democratic rights to all classes. The second key issue in Schwimmer's agenda was individual freedom, to be restricted only if in tension or conflict with the interests of other parties–interests to be protected by the state if necessary. This vision led her in 1908 to argue for legal means to prohibit the reproduction of those suffering from hereditary illness.

From the early 1900s onwards, Schwimmer translated her intellectual capacity and political dedication into an impressive performance as a political and professional writer, both in German and Hungarian. She wrote a range of studies which included analyses of key feminist issues such as motherhood and child protection, the sexual question, household reform, education and suffrage–published in Hungary and in foreign journals such as the Viennese *Neues Frauenleben* (New woman's life). Schwimmer also translated Charlotte Perkins Gilman's highly influential book *Women and Economics. A Study of the Economic Relation Between Men and Women* (Boston, 1898) into Hungarian (as her friend Aletta Jacobs did into Dutch). From 1907, she was the editor (later renamed "responsible editor") of *A Nő és a Társadalom* (Woman and society), later *A Nő. Feminista Folyóirat* (Woman. A feminist journal), the journal of the *FE*. She filled this position even in periods of prolonged absence, and it was kept empty for her after her relocation to the USA in the interwar period.

After World War I, Róza Schwimmer would never return to this type of public engagement. The war marked a turning point in her overall biography and career in the international women's movement. Schwimmer's activities, in which peace had earlier played a minor but explicit role, were to focus on pacifist agendas after the outbreak of the war. At this point, Schwimmer found herself an enemy alien in London. She resigned from her position as Press Secretary of the IWSA. In September 1914, she arrived in the USA with the intention of seeking an audience with President Wilson—part of her plan for a mediation conference of neutral nations. Together with British suffragist Emmeline Pethick-Lawrence, she toured the US, lecturing on pacifism and suffrage and, for a short time in early 1915, working for the Woman's Peace Party. In April 1915, Schwimmer participated in the famous International Congress of Women at The Hague, which aimed to advance the cause of peace. It was Schwimmer who proposed sending envoys carrying the messages expressed in the Congress Resolutions to the governments of the belligerent and neutral nations of Europe and to the President of the United States, and it was Schwimmer who was personally appointed to travel to the Scandinavian countries and Russia (although prevented from entering the latter). She also became Vice-President of the International Committee of Women for Permanent Peace, which had been set up at the Hague Congress and later developed into the Women's International League for Peace and Freedom (WILPF). Soon Schwimmer engaged, with growing impatience, in organizing the controversial "Ford Peace Ship" mission. With the initial support of Henry Ford, the much publicized Peace Ship sailed from the US to Europe to bring the peace activists and journalists on board to an unofficial neutral conference to be held in Stockholm in January 1916. Yet the Peace Ship soon was fraught with political and personal intrigues, ridiculed in the press and sabotaged by the warring powers. As Schwimmer worked on organizing the Stockholm conference, developments resulted in serious tensions within the International Committee of Women for Permanent Peace. Eventually, Schwimmer resigned from both the Committee and the "Peace Ship" adventure. The friendship with Aletta Jacobs broke down completely. Retrospectively, it is clear that although Schwimmer initially occupied a position of high standing in international women's organizations and networks, her dedication to radical and immediate feminist action whatever the political circumstances and larger power relations, as well as her unwillingness to conceive of politics in other ways than lobbying, intervening, and dramatizing, led, after 1914, to her status being questioned and considerably weakened. From 1917, the dramatic change in international relations, the political climate in the US (and beyond) after the entry of the US into the war in 1917 and the Russian Revolution were all significant background factors in the political 'unmaking' of this rising star of the international women's movement. Never again would Schwimmer work smoothly with the international women's organizations.

Schwimmer's short-lived appointment representing the first democratic Hungarian government, the Károlyi government, to Switzerland (November 1918 to January 1919) as an "ambassador extraordinary and plenipotentiary minister" or "representative of the Hungarian government in certain international matters" (both terms are used in official documents of 19 and 13 November 1919 respectively) was equally overshadowed by the new international constellation and political conflicts at home. In addition, political attacks on her and her government made much of the fact that

Schwimmer was a woman. This "feminine incursion" (*The New York Times*, 12 December 1918; cited in Pastor 1974, 278) into the art of diplomacy was denounced as an "ultra democratic" and "perfidious act" (French Foreign Minister Stephen Pichon, cited in Pastor 1974, 278–279).

After the firm establishment of the semi-authoritarian, right-wing Horthy regime in Hungary, which persistently regarded her as a 'politically unreliable' individual in later years, Schwimmer escaped to Vienna, subsequently seeking exile in the United States. Upon arrival in the USA in 1921, Schwimmer found herself the target of a negative propaganda campaign, including charges that she was a German spy, a socialist (related allegations by British and US secret services regarding Schwimmer's earlier mission in Switzerland had contributed to this rumour), a Bolshevik agent, a participant in an international Jewish conspiracy, as well as a perpetrator of various other misdeeds related to the "Peace Ship" mission. Over the years, Schwimmer invested a lot of energy in trying to clear her name, demanding correction of misinformation on various levels. In 1929, after years of legal battling, the Supreme Court rejected her application for US-citizenship because of her refusal to affirm, as the oath demanded, that she would bear arms in defense of the country. In the mid-1920s, Schwimmer definitively withdrew from the Women's International League for Peace and Freedom, declaring that the League was "more a farce than a real peace organization" (NYPL-SLC A169, letter to the FE 20.06.1927). Yet later, Schwimmer would again take up activities on behalf of, and with the WILPF.

In the 1930s, Schwimmer, in close association with Edith Wynner and Lola Maverick Lloyd, launched a campaign for World Government and World Citizenship. In 1937, Lloyd, together with other initiating sponsors, among them Selma Lagerlöf, Albert Einstein and ***Eugénia Meller***, organized the presentation to Schwimmer of an unofficial World Peace Prize Award, endorsed by an International Committee of distinguished personalities, including Emily Greene Balch, Charles Drysdale, Michael Hainisch (son of ***Marianne Hainisch*** and the President of Austria from 1920 to 1928), Anna Kéthly (1889–1976, social democratic Member of Parliament in Hungary) and Stefan Zweig. In 1948, Schwimmer was nominated by a number of European parliamentarians for the Nobel Peace Prize. (Nomination is the first stage in the yearly selection process, and there are usually between one hundred and two hundred and fifty nominees for each prize. Schwimmer died in the period between nomination and the decision-making and the prize was not awarded at all that year. A prize proposed for a person alive at the time of nomination may be awarded posthumously, but this did not happen in Schwimmer's case.)

After Schwimmer's death on 3 August 1948, the journal *Huszadik Század* (Twentieth century)–the same journal that had given Schwimmer's first writings space in its columns almost half a century earlier–published an obituary by Marcell Benedek, summarizing (in view of her peace work) the one "tragic error" in all her life work and endeavors as: "[t]he error that it was possible to create peace by appealing to those with a vital interest in war" [*Huszadik Század* (Twentieth century) 36 (1948): 349].

Susan Zimmermann
Department of Gender Studies, Department of History,
Central European University, Budapest

Borbala Major
SUNY, New York, USA

SOURCES

(A) New York Public Library, MSS. & Archives Section, Schwimmer-Lloyd Collection, Various Series. This collection contains most of Schwimmer's papers and some related to the *FE* from the pre-1914 period, and is a treasury for research on the organized international network of women.

(A) *Magyar Országos Levéltár* (Hungarian National Archives). P999: *Feministák Egyesülete* (Feminist Association); P987: *Szirmay Oszkárné* (Mrs Oszkár Szirmay).

(A) *Budapest Főváros Levéltára* (Archives of the Capital City of Budapest). IV 1407b: *Budapest Székesfőváros Tanácsának iratai. Tanácsi Ügyosztályok Központi irattára* (The administration of the capital and residence city of Budapest. Central archive, writings of the administrative sections) (1873-1918).

(B) *A Nő és a Társadalom* (Woman and society) (1907-1913).

(B) *A Nő. Feminista Folyóirat* (Woman. A feminist journal) (1914-1928).

(B) International Women's Committee of Permanent Peace, ed. *International Congress of Women. The Hague, 28th April-May 1st 1915.* Amsterdam: International Women's Committee of Permanent Peace, *sine anno.*

(B) *Yearly Reports and Congress Reports of the IWSA.*

(B) *Reports of the Congresses of the Women's International League for Peace and Freedom.*

(B) *Államrendészeti zsebkönyv. Kiadja a m. kir. Belügyminisztérium közbiztonsági osztálya* (Handbook of public supervision. Published by the Public Security Department of the Hungarian Royal Ministry of the Interior). *Sine loco, sine anno.*

(C) For the sake of brevity, Schwimmer's extensive own writings are not listed here.

(D) Benedek, Marcell. "Schwimmer Rózsa 1877-1948." *Huszadik Század* (Twentieth century) 36 (1948): 347-349.

(D) Pastor, Peter. "The diplomatic fiasco of the modern world's first woman ambassador, Roza Bedy-Schwimmer." *East European Quarterly* 8 (1974): 273-282.

(D) Wenger, Beth S. "Radical politics in a reactionary age: the unmaking of Rosika Schwimmer, 1914-1930." *Journal of Women's History* 2, no. 2 (1990): 66-97.

(D) Zimmermann, Susan. "How they became feminists: the origins of the women's movement in Central Europe at the turn of the century." *Central European University History Department Yearbook* (1997/1998). Budapest, 1999, 195-236.

(D) Glant, Tibor. "Diplomatanők rivaldafényben: Vira Whitehouse és Bédy-Schwimmer Róza svájci küldetése az elso világháború idején" (Woman diplomats in the limelight. The Switzerland mission of Vira Whitehouse and Róza Bédy-Schwimmer during World War I). *Múltunk. Politikatörténeti folyóirat* (Our past. Journal of political history) 48, no. 3 (2003): 159-179.

(E) Trócsányi, Zoltán. "A budapesti német könyvhurcolás" (German book-hauling in Budapest). *Magyar Könyvszemle* (Hungarian book review) 69 (1945): 1-21.

(E) Bussey, Gertrude and Margaret Tims. *The Women's International League for Peace and Freedom 1915-1965. A Record of Fifty Years' Work*. London: Allen & Unwin, 1965.

(E) Rupp, Leila. *Worlds of Women. The Making of an International Women's Movement*. Princeton: Princeton University Press, 1997.

(E) Zimmermann, Susan. *Die bessere Hälfte? Frauenbewegungen und Frauenbestrebungen im Ungarn der Habsburgermonarchie 1848 bis 1918* (The better half? Women's movements and women's aspirations in Hungary in the Habsburg Monarchy, 1848 to 1918). Vienna/Budapest: Promedia Verlag/Napvilág Kiadó, 1999.

(E) Zimmermann, Susan. "Reich, Nation, und Internationalismus. Konflikte und Kooperationen der Frauenbewegungen der Habsburgermonarchie" (Empire, nation and internationalism. Conflict and cooperation among the women's movements of the Habsburg Monarchy). In Waltraud Heindl, Edit Király and Alexandra Millner, eds. *Frauenbilder, feministische Praxis und nationales Bewusstsein in Österreich-Ungarn 1867-1918* (Envisioning women, feminist practice, and national consciousness in Austria-Hungary 1867-1918). Tübingen 2005 (forthcoming).

(E) *American Reformers. An H. W. Wilson Biographical Dictionary*. Alden Whitman, ed. New York: H. W. Wilson Co., 1985.

(E) *Dictionary of American Biography*.

(F) The Nobel Prize Selection Process, http://www.britannica.com/nobel/cap/onobelp011a4.html, 13 December 2004.

SEKULIĆ, Isidora (1877–1958)

Serbian writer who contributed significantly to the cultural development of the country in the twentieth century; literary critic and educator; co-founder of the *Društvo za prosvećivanje žene i zaštitu njenih prava* (Society for Women's Enlightenment and Protection of their Rights).

Isidora Sekulić was born on 16 February 1877 in Mošorin, Vojvodina (then part of Austro-Hungary, today in Serbia). Isidora's mother Ljubica Sekulić, her father Danilo Sekulić, and brother Predrag Sekulić (b. 1874), all died of tuberculosis within seventeen years of one another (in 1883, 1900 and 1881 respectively), leaving young Isidora with no close relatives. She was educated in Novi Sad, Sombor and Pest, completing the College for Ladies in Novi Sad, later the *Srpska Preparandija* (Serbian Academy) in Sombor. In 1894, she traveled to Pest (Hungary) to pursue a diploma in a scientific field of study, which she obtained with distinction three years later. In 1909, she decided to move to Serbia, finally settling in Belgrade in 1912. (Before 1909 she lived in Vojvodina, then part of Austria Hungary, and had acquired Austro-Hungarian citizenship.) Her marriage in 1913 to Emil Stremnicki, a Polish doctor she met while in Norway, ended abruptly after a year or so in December 1913, when Stremnicki died suddenly on the couple's journey back from Norway to Serbia. She never remarried, nor had children. After her husband's death, she continued her education, receiving her doctorate in philosophy in 1922 (in Berlin) and working as a high school teacher until her retirement in 1931. She wasn't particularly close to her students. An exceptional neatness characterized her teaching and any other tasks to which she dedicated herself.

Isidora Sekulić has been labeled 'Serbia's first woman writer,' a phrase which, although slightly clichéd, accurately describes her status within a male-dominated Serbian literary tradition that did not choose to recognize or acknowledge other women writers to the extent that it recognized Sekulić. In this sense, Sekulić was indeed an exceptional figure, her literary and essayist works having been greatly appreciated by her contemporaries. She wrote numerous pieces of prose, as well as commentaries and essays on art. Her first foray into literary criticism was published in 1910, shortly followed by two books: *Saputnici* (Fellow travelers, 1913) and *Pisma iz Norveske*

(Letters from Norway, 1914). Psychological reflection, impressionistic sketches and intellectual character portraits were important features of Isidora Sekulić's *écriture*, praised by prominent figures in Yugoslavian literary circles, including the critics Jovan Skerlić (1877-1914) and Antun Gustav Matoš (1873-1914). Yet for many critics, Sekulić's best work was yet to come, in the form of her collection of stories, *Kronika palanackog groblja* (The chronicles of a small town graveyard, 1940). Mournfully charting individual and family fortunes, many of these stories opened with descriptions of a small town graveyard and its neglected graves, and through Sekulić's strong, female, but not necessarily 'feminine' characters, they raised critical (though not explicitly critical) questions about male-dominated society.

Sekulić 's critical articles and essays treated a wide range of topics, from national to world literature, as well as visual arts, theater, music, language and moral philosophy–see for example her three volume collection of essays, *Analitički trenuci i teme* (Analytical moments and themes, 1940). The writer Jovan Deretić has divided Sekulić's work into essays and critical writing, drawing a line between fiction and literary criticism. Others, such as B. Stojanović-Pantović, have opted for a more post-modern interpretation of Sekulić's work, choosing to see her essays more as 'critical prose' or, in Barthes' sense, as texts that transcend borders between theory, history and traditional literary criticism. Sekulić wrote about Virginia Woolf (1882-1941) and Sarah Bernhardt (1844-1923), but not specifically as women, concentrating instead on their poetics and literary portrait sketches. This was partly motivated by her own experience of male-dominated critique, particularly the refusal of Jovan Skerlić to treat the works of female writers as innovative or intellectually competent. At the same time, Sekulić sometimes discussed male writers in terms of their female characters–see her descriptive and critical analyses of the work of Milan Rakić (1876-1938), Veljko Petrović (1884-1967) and Ivo Andrić (1892-1975)–in articles written between 1892 and 1975.

In the first half of the twentieth century, Isidora Sekulić was active in the *Kolo srpskih sestara* (Circle of Serbian Sisters, 1903-1944), particularly in the early 1920s. She traveled all over Serbia and Europe with colleagues and activists from the Serbian women's movement and gave talks on suffrage rights and women's position in the modern world. She also left her estate and the proceeds from her literary works to the *Kolo srpskih sestara*. In a patriarchal milieu that transcended the borders of Serbian culture, Sekulić's outstanding position as one of the country's best-known women writers was not only contested in national literary circles. As secretary of the Belgrade PEN club (from 1926), she experienced hostility from foreign writers unhappy with the fact that she was a woman. When a founding member of the influential *Odbor srpske književne zadruge* (Board of Serbian Literary Association) resigned in protest at Sekulić's membership, she too resigned from the *Odbor*. In 1950, she was the first woman ever elected to become a member of the Serbian Academy of Sciences–at the age of 72.

Sekulić's commitment to women's issues–in her writing as well as in her social activism–can be positively identified as early feminist. Her critical exploration of the female and the 'feminine' adressed various aspects of 'the woman question,' particularly the social status of single, widowed or unmarried women. If Sekulić's feminism was sometimes ambivalent, her work raised neglected questions of gender, assisted by her status as the first recognized female writer in national literary tradition.

Isidora Sekulić died on 5 April 1958 in Belgrade.

Iva Nenić
Teaching assistant,
Belgrade Open School (BOS)

SOURCES

(D) Forrester, Sibelan. "Isidora Sekulić as an early Serbian feminist." In Nicholas Moravčevich, ed. *Serbian studies*. Chicago: The North American society for Serbian studies, 1980; *Serbian studies* 5, no. 1 (1989): 85–94.

(D) Ribnikar, Vladislava. *Književni pogledi Isidore Sekulić* (The literary perspectives of Isidora Sekulic). Belgrade: Prosveta, 1986.

(D) Pantelić, Ivana. "Prepreke emancipaciji žena u kraljevini Jugoslaviji (1931–1933)" (Obstacles to women's emancipation in the Kingdom of Yugoslavia, 1931–1933). In *Zbornik Beogradske otvorene škole* (A collection of essays from the Belgrade Open School). Belgrade, 2002.

(D) Stojanović-Pantović, Bojana. "Isidorino kritičko pismo–književnost književnosti" (Isidora's critical writing–the literature of literature). In *Iz srpske književnosti (zbornik radova posvećen Miroslavu Egeriću)* (From Serbian literature, a collection of essays dedicated to Miroslav Egerić). Novi Sad: Filozofski Fakultet i ITP "Zmaj," 2003, 156–165.

SERTEL, Sabiha (born Nazmi) (1895-1968)

Turkish feminist, journalist, writer and activist.

Sabiha Sertel was born Sabiha Nazmi (?) in 1895 in Selanik (Thessaloniki). She was the sixth and last child in the family of customs official Nazmi (1851-1920) and housewife Atiye (1872-1945). The city in which she was born and raised had an impact on her intellectual formation by virtue of being a center of social opposition, containing cultural plurality and western lifestyles. Her family is associated with a certain religious community known as *Dönme* (converted). This was a Jewish sect which, having been expelled from Spain, settled in the Ottoman Empire in the fifteenth century and converted to Islam in the seventeenth century. *Dönme* had their own schools, hospitals, clubs and community houses. Sabiha attended *Dönme* elementary and junior high schools (1902-1908). *Terakki Mektebi* (The Progress School), the high school that she attended from 1908 to 1911, was founded on positivist principles, as the name implies. As a result of their education there, female students adopted a positivist–even secularist–view and cast aside their veils. Since women were not entitled to university education, Sabiha and her friends founded the *Tefeyyüz Cemiyeti* (Progressive Society), collecting fees from students to pay university professors to teach them law, philosophy, sociology and economics.

At around the age of sixteen, using the name Sabiha Nazmi, Sabiha published essays in the journals *Genç Kalemler* (Young writers) and *Yeni Felsefe* (New philosophy). In these essays, she focused on education, women's rights and revolution, as well as criticizing hegemonic interprepations of *sharia* law. She and her future husband, Mehmet Zekeriya Sertel (1890-1980), met through reading each other's writings in *Yeni Felsefe*. Sabiha admired Mehmet Zekeriya Sertel's analysis of women's issues and he, after reading her article "Osmanlı Cemiyetinde Kadın" (Woman in Ottoman society, published in *Yeni Felsefe* and recipient of the journal's 'best article of the year' award in 1911), asked Sabiha Nazmi to marry him, although he knew her only through her writing. The proposal–made by one intellectual to another–appealed to Nazmi, who had no desire to be a traditional housewife and who had always resented her father's attitude towards her mother, even as a child. (At the age of seven, Sabiha had declared that she would never be a servant to any husband.) Sabiha Nazmi's family strongly objected to their daughter's marriage to Mehmet Zekeriya Sertel, a Muslim Turk, but following the surrender of Thessaloniki to the Greeks, her family emigrated to Istanbul in 1913 and here, becoming less rigid in their attitudes, they allowed Sabiha Nazmi to marry Mehmet Zekeriya (1915). The marriage of a girl to a man outside the converted community was an event that appeared in the press. In 1917, the couple's first daughter Sevim (1917–2003) was born. (Sevim would spend her later life in the USA working as journalist.) In 1919, Mehmet Zekeriya Sertel established the periodical *Büyük Mecmua* (The great periodical), but was soon imprisoned for his articles condemning the occupation of Istanbul by the Western powers after World War I. Sabiha Sertel took over as editor of *Büyük Mecmua*, which became the journal of the resistance movement against the occupation. She wrote several articles for the journal under the name of Sabiha Zekeriya, arguing for the increased participation of women in public life and equal rights for women, as well as addressing issues of women's education and political representation. This period of her life reveals a liberal equal rights feminism influenced by Enlightenment thought. Her feminism was also dominated by patriotic and nationalist ideas.

In 1919, Sabiha Sertel received a college scholarship and went to New York with her husband and daughter. While studying sociology at Columbia University, she became acquainted with Marxist classics that had a profound impact on her later ideas—particularly August Bebel's *Women and Socialism* (1879). During her years in the United States as a student, she established a Turkish community society, the *Türk Teavün Cemiyeti* (Turkish Mutual Help Association), and collected considerable donations for the 'Turkish Liberation' War. She also worked to inform workers about labor unions. A woman leading a group of men was a novel experience, both for her and for the workers.

On 1 November 1922 (the day the sultanate was abolished in Turkey), the Sertels had a second daughter, Yıldız. They returned to Turkey in July 1923 and went to Ankara to join in the building of the newly-established Turkish Republic. By 1924, the couple had begun publishing a popular intellectual magazine based in Istanbul called *Resimli Ay* (The illustrated month). Under a column headed "Cici Anne" (The sweet mother), Sertel wrote about relationships between men and women and the position of women in society, radically interrogating the institution of the family. Yet for Sertel, 'the woman question' was primarily a social question and she criticized some feminists (in particular female deputies to the national assembly), as well as contemporary magazines, for indulging in abstract discussions. The primary concern of feminism, she argued, was (or should be) the concrete needs of working and poor women.

After the establishment of the Turkish Republic (1923), a secular Civil Code was adopted in 1926 that forbade polygamy and gave women equal rights in inheritance, property acquisition and as witnesses in the courts. Many obstacles prevented the smooth implementation of the new laws and Sabiha Sertel wrote an article–"Ben İnsan Değil Miyim?" (Am I not a person?), published in 1928 in *Resimli Ay*–about the unwillingness of members of the legal profession to accept women as court witnesses. The article provoked great interest in the press and pushed the Ministry of Justice to issue a circular to the courts demanding consistent application of the new Civil Code and acknowledgment in legal practice of the civil equality of women and men. Later in 1930, Sabiha Sertel became the first female journalist to appear in court when an article she had translated from an American magazine, entitled "The Psychology of the Leader," was accused of having insulted Atatürk.

By the end of 1930, the associate partners of *Resimli Ay* had withdrawn from the magazine because of its dissident profile. In 1934, the Sertels began publishing the newspaper *Tan* (Dawn), which came to occupy an important place in the history of Turkish socialism. In Sabiha Sertel's column "Görüşler" (Outlook), she focused on political issues and criticized racist tendencies in Turkey influenced by the rise of fascism in the West. She was ridiculed by certain journals that supported an alliance with Germany, in cartoons depicting her as a "quarrelsome gypsy with tongs in her hand" or a "Bolshevik unbeliever" (Sertel 1978, 220).

Sabiha gave her name "Sabiha Zekeriya Sertel" for the first time in an issue of *Tan* that appeared on 20 May 1937. Both husband and wife, as writers against the established order, had chosen the surname 'Sertel' (meaning 'harsh hand') when a law for obtaining surnames was passed. In 1941, *Tan* was temporarily banned but the ban was revoked on condition that Sabiha Sertel give up writing. She refused to do so, writing a book about World War II. A group of university student supporters of racist-fascist ideology attacked the *Tan* Press House and destroyed everything (1945). Shortly after, Sabiha Sertel was arrested and given a four month prison sentence because of her article criticizing the single-party regime and defending the right to free opposition. In 1950, under pressure from the authorities, the Sertels decided to emigrate and went to Paris. Sabiha Sertel was never to be allowed to return to her homeland. After Paris, the couple lived in Vienna, finally settling in Azerbeijan in 1963. Sabiha Sertel died of lung cancer on 10 March 1968 in Baku. (Her husband was only able to return to Turkey in 1977.)

Sabiha Sertel was one of the most prominent figures in the history of socialism in Turkey. She did not have an organic relationship with the institutionalized women's movement but worked alone, reaching a broad mass of readers with her strong ideas, flowing style and unrelenting opposition to the established order. She never had a desk of her own, let alone a room, but worked on a dining table without ever giving up her passion for writing. Even on her death bed, her last words were said to be: "What a pity, I still had so much to write!" (Yıldız Sertel 2001, 268).

İnci Özkan Kerestecioğlu
University of Istanbul

SOURCES

(B) *Resimli Ay* (The illustrated month) (1924–1930).

(B) *Tan* (Dawn) (1934–1945).

(C) Sertel, Sabiha. "Ben İnsan Değil Miyim?" (Am I not a person?). *Resimli Ay* (The illustrated month) (1928).

(C) Sertel, Sabiha. *Roman Gibi 1919–1950* (Like a novel). Istanbul: Cem Yay, 1978.

(D) Toprak, Zafer. "Sabiha (Zekeriya) Sertel ve Türk Feminizmi" (Sabiha Sertel and Turkish feminism). *Toplumsal Tarih* (Social history) 9, no. 51 (March 1998): 7–14.

(D) Sertel, Yıldız. *Annem, Sabiha Sertel Kimdi, Neler Yazdı?* (My mother, Sabiha Sertel, what did she write?). Istanbul: Belge Yay, 2001 (third edition).

(D) Özman, Aylin and Ayça Bulut. "Sabiha (Zekeriya) Sertel: Kemalizm, Marksizm ve Kadın Meselesi" (Sabiha Sertel: Issue on Kemalism, Marxism and women). *Toplum ve Bilim* (Society and science), no. 96 (Spring 2003): 184–218.

SHABANOVA, Anna (1848–1932)

Russian doctor (pediatrician); founder and Chairwoman of the *Russkoe Zhenskoe Vzaimno-Blagotvoritel'noe Obshchestvo* (Russian Women's Mutual Philanthropic Society); Honorary Vice-President of the International Council of Women (1913–1918).

Anna Nikolaevna Shabanova was born in 1848, to a noble but not particularly wealthy family from the *Smolenskaia guberniia* (*oblast* or region of Smolenskaia). Detailed information on her relatives is lacking, except for the fact that during the reforms of the 1860s, her family was financially ruined [according to the 1897 *Spisok Dvoryanskih Rodov, Vnesennyh v Rodoslovnye Dvoryanskie Knigi Smolenskoi Gubernii* (List of noble genealogies for the region of Smolenskaya), the family had lost all its real estate]. Anna Shabanova thus had to earn her own living from an early age (at fifteen). Having received a good education at home, later attending finishing school, she began working as a governess and translator. It is likely that around this time she decided to enter the medical profession.

In the early 1860s, Shabanova moved to Moscow, where she became acquainted with the socialist radicals of the so-called 'Ishutin circle' (named after the leader of the circle, N. A. Ishutin), which had regicide as its primary objective. Anna Shabanova was very much taken with these revolutionary ideas and joined one of the secret units of the Ishutin circle, operating under the auspices of a women's sewing workshop. Following Dmitry Karakozov's assassination attempt on Tsar Alexander II (April 1866), the 'Ishutin circle' was destroyed by police. Shabanova was arrested and sentenced to solitary imprisonment. Six months later, having collected the payment sum, Shabanova's relatives stood bail for her and she was discharged. It appears that this prison experience contributed greatly to Shabanova's personal development and worldview, since she never returned to radical politics again.

Although Shabanova graduated from a finishing school, she didn't receive a leaving certificate. In order to test her own knowledge, Shabanova sat an examination at Moscow University in 1866 and became the first woman in the history of the university to pass in Latin. After being refused admittance to the Medical Academy of St Petersburg however, her aspirations for higher education remained unsatisfied. Shabanova returned to Smolensk, where she participated actively in the all-Russian campaign for women's higher education, collecting (according to her own texts) over four hundred signatures from women for a petition demanding that women be admitted to Smolensk University. In 1870, thanks to the patronage of eminent writer Mikhail Evgraphovich Saltykov-Shchedrin, Shabanova gained a Literary Fund scholarship to attend Helsingfors University (now Helsinki, Finland). The only woman to apply to the university, Shabanova suffered many hardships during this period: lack of money, starvation, excessive academic expectations and the taunts of male students.

In 1873, Shabanova returned to Russia in order to enroll on the *Vysshie Zhenskie Vrachebnye Kursy* (Higher Women's Medical Courses) in St Petersburg, opened a year earlier. Since she had spent two years at Helsingfors University studying natural sciences, she was admitted to the second-year program of the Courses and graduated in 1878. She became the first woman pediatrician to work in the hospitals of St Petersburg; she also set up health services for children, carried out her own research and taught medicine in women's high schools and in the Smolnyi Institute for young ladies. She translated numerous works on medical subjects and authored over forty academic texts, including her pioneering research treatise on children's metabolism: "Kolichestvo mocheviny, vydeliaemoi v razlichnyh periodah detskogo vozrasta pri normalnyh usloviiah i pri razlichnoi diete" (Amounts of urea excreted at different stages of childhood development under normal circumstances and under different diets, 1879). By the time she spoke at the Third Russian Medical Congress (St Petersburg, 1899), Shabanova was regarded as a respected pediatrician and social activist–widely known as "Doctor Shabanova."

One of the first generation of women medical students, Shabanova came up hard against all the obstacles and biases commonly faced by women doctors and so decided to devote her life to advocating women's rights. As soon as she had graduated from the Women's Medical Courses, Shabanova championed women's right to work and be acknowledged as attending physicians. It was largely due to her efforts that in 1880, Tsar Alexander III granted a special badge with the abbreviation "ZhV" (*Zhenshchina-Vrach*: Woman Doctor) to graduates of the Women's Medical Courses, as a mark of respect to be observed by male colleagues. Shabanova always emphasized the need to strengthen the position of women making their careers in medicine and was deeply upset by Minister of the Interior D. A. Tolstoi's decision to change the name of "woman-doctor" to "qualified midwife" early in 1883. She spearheaded a petition calling for public condemnation of the government's decision as both disparaging and refusing the reality of women doctors. As a result of the petition, women won back their right to be called "women's and children's doctors," regarded by Shabanova as a victory over "the most powerful Russian ministry" (Yukina, 59).

Shabanova's personal experiences made her aware of the central role women's organizations could play in alleviating some of the problems she had encountered. In 1895, she helped found the *Russkoe Zhenskoe Vzaimno-Blagotvoritel'noe Obshchestvo*

(Russian Women's Mutual Philantropic Society) and became its President soon after (following the sudden death of ***Nadezhda Stasova***, the society's first President, that same year). Despite the wishes of its founders, the society adopted an exclusively philanthropic mission, since other kinds of social or political organizations were forbidden. It opened a hostel and refectory for educated women, an employment service and a kindergarten for poor mothers and their children. Thanks to Shabanova's persistent efforts, the society was permitted to establish a library and hold lectures and seminars for its members. Members of the society petitioned ministers and senior bureaucrats for bills on behalf of women's civil, property, economic and, after the 1905 October Manifesto (guaranteeing the formation of the State Duma), political rights.

In 1899, Anna Shabanova had reached the height of her professional and political career. She participated actively in the Third Russian Medical Congress (St Petersburg, 1897), in the International Congress for Children's Rights (Budapest, 1899) and in the foundation of the Russian League of Peace, which organized a huge demonstration in support of the first Hague Peace conference in 1899. Membership of the *Russkoe Zhenskoe Vzaimno-Blagotvoritel'noe Obshchestvo* reached 1,600 in 1899. As a leader of the Russian women's movement, Shabanova insisted on working within the existing political structure and the law. Emphasizing women's particular role in society (she held an essentialist view, according to which women and men played different but equally important social roles predetermined by 'nature'), she argued for a widening of women's social sphere of activity and regarded the women's movement as working not against the rule of men, but against social injustice. She believed that the success of the women's movement in Russia depended greatly on the ability of feminists to unite their efforts and become integrated into the international women's movement. From 1905, she tried to get permission to organize a women's congress that would result in the formation of an All-Russian Council of Women. To the disappointment of Shabanova and her supporters, the first All-Russian Congress of Women took place only in 1908 and did not have the desired effect of unity; instead, it revealed serious disagreements between liberal and socialist feminists. Nevertheless, Shabanova stuck to the idea of creating a national feminist organization in Russia and it was due to her efforts that the statute of the All-Russian Council of Women was finally approved on 15 March 1917.

Anna Shabanova's social and political activity was recognized internationally. In 1912, she was elected Honorary Member of the International Society of Women Doctors and, a year later (after the death of ***Anna Filosofova***), she became Honorary Vice-President of the International Council of Women. Her participation in international women's congresses (Berlin, 1896; Stockholm, 1911; Rome, 1914) convinced her that the Russian women's movement, in order to be successful, had to become an integrated part of the international feminist movement.

After the Bolshevik revolution in Russia there was no more room for feminists:

their groups were dissolved and achievements soon forgotten. Shabanova continued to work as a pediatrician almost right up to her death and would speak of her work as "an escape from the troubles of life" [S(habanova) 1927, 14]. In 1928, she was honored as an eminent pediatrician: at the celebration of her jubilee, she was made a "Heroine of Labor" and the library of a hospital in St Petersburg was named after her. A devoted social activist, Shabanova never married and little is known about her private life. In 1927, she wrote: "At the close of my days, I have come to think that is no great virtue that, being deprived of the joy and obligations of family life, I was able to devote my energy to academic and social work" [S(habanova) 1927, 14]. She died in Leningrad (St Petersburg) on 25 May 1932 at the age of 84. Her death went almost unnoticed. The library of the St Petersburg hospital named after K. A. Raukhfus still bears the name of Anna Shabanova.

Natalia Novikova
Iaroslavl State Pedagogical University

SOURCES

(B) *Spisok dvorianskih rodov, vnesennyh v rodoslovnye dvoryanskie knigi Smolenskoi gubernii* (List of noble genealogies for the region of Smolenskaya). Smolensk, 1897.

(B) "Russkaya Liga Mira" (Russian League of Peace). *Zhenskoe delo* (Women's action) 1, no. 6 (1899): 69–89.

(B) Afanasiev, N. I. *Sovremenniki* (Contemporaries). St Petersburg, 1910, 2: 456–457.

(C) Shabanova, A. "Kolichestvo mocheviny, vydeliaemoi v razlichnyh periodah detskogo vozrasta pri normalnyh usloviyah i pri razlichnoi diete" (Amounts of urea excreted at different stages of childhood development under normal circumstances and under different diets). *Voenno-medizinskii zhurnal* (Military medical journal) CXXXV, no. 8 (1879): 201–229.

(C) Shabanova, A. "Dva goda v Gelsingforsskom universitete: iz vospominanii zhenshinyvracha" (Two years at Helsingfors University: recollections of a woman doctor). *Vestnik Evropy* (European herald) 1, no. 2 (1888): 538–536.

(C) Shabanova, A. "Vospominanie o zhenskom mezhdunarodnom kongresse v Berline" (Recollections of the International Women's Congress in Berlin). *Novoye slovo* (New word) 2 (1896): 82–93.

(C) Shabanova, A. "Mezhdunarodnyi zhenskii congress v Stockholme" (International Women's Congress in Stockholm). *Vestnik Evropy* 2 (1912): 345–357.

(C) Shabanova, A. *Ocherk zhenskogo dvizheniia v Rossii* (An essay on the women's movement in Russia). St Petersburg: tipografiya akzionernogo obshestva "Samoobrazovanie," 1912.

(C) S(habanova), A. "Pervaia zhenshina-vrach. Avtobiografiia" (The first woman medical doctor). *Ogoniok* (Tiny flame) 41 (1927): 14.

(D) Zabludovskaia, E. D. "Odna iz pervych zhenshin vrachei-pediatrov A. N. Shabanova"

(One of the first women medical doctors–pediatricians). *Pediatriia* (Pediatrics) 6 (1957): 71–78.

(D) Yukina, Irina. "Doktor Shabanova." In I. I. Rogozin, ed. *Kharizmaticheskie lichnosti v istorii Rossii* (Charismatic personalities in the history of Russia). St Petersburg: Petrovskaia Academy of Arts and Sciences, 1997, 56–63.

SHAPIR, Ol'ga Andreevna (born Kislaikova) (1850–1916)

Well-known nineteenth-century Russian writer; one of the leaders and theorists of Russian liberal feminism.

Ol'ga Kislaikova was born in Oranienbaum, near St Petersburg, on 10 (22) September 1850, the youngest of nine children. Her father, Andrei Petrovich Kislaikov, was a military official at the command post in Oranienbaum. Her mother, Louisa Abramovna Kislaikova (data unknown), was a gentry woman of German and Swedish origin. In 1865, Ol'ga Kislaikova completed the Alexandrovskaia *gymnasia* (high school) in St Petersburg, receiving a gold medal for her outstanding academic achievements. Like many educated young women in the 1860s and 1870s, Kislaikova became acquainted with writers and journalists and attended public lectures, including the Vladimirskie Courses (these free courses were one of Russia's first educational initiatives on behalf of women). Although her family supported her, Kislaikova wanted to earn her own living. She translated various articles from German and French into Russian and wrote short news bulletins from St Petersburg for the newspapers *Birzhevye Vedomosti* (Stock exchange news) and *Novoe Vremia* (New times).

In 1871, when Ol'ga Kislaikova had turned 21, she announced her independence from her family, having then been put in charge of Aleksandr Cherkesov's Vasileostrovsky Library (Cherkesov was a well-known owner of libraries and bookstores in St Petersburg and Moscow). In 1872, she married Lazar Shapir, a former student of the Medical-Surgical Academy in St Petersburg, who had been exiled to Novgorod for his participation in the *Nechaevskoe Delo* (Nechaev Affair). Sergei Nechaev was the revolutionary leader of the group *Narodnaia Rasprava* (Popular Punishment). When the government took action against the group, Nechaev fled abroad but his followers were tried and convicted. Ol'ga Shapir managed to get permission for her husband to complete his education; in the meantime, she supported her family through her literary work. This was not typical behavior for a woman of her class, but characteristic of Ol'ga Shapir. Throughout her life, she would challenge norms and stereotypes.

After graduating from the Surgical Academy in St Petersburg in 1874, Ol'ga Shapir's husband became a provincial doctor in the Saratov *guberniia* (region). While residing there, Ol'ga Shapir turned her attention to writing fiction. Her first novel, *Na poroge zhizni* (On the threshold of life), was published in 1879. Her themes–relations between men and women, the psychological suppression of women and the aspirations of downtrodden people–resonated with the intelligentsia.

In the 1880s and 1890s, Ol'ga Shapir became a popular and fashionable writer. Everything she wrote was published in magazines and books. After having returned to St Petersburg in 1881 with her only son Nikolai, she immediately became involved in the work of the *Literaturnyi Fond* (Literary Fund) to support other writers (both men and women) and develop women's activities. In 1895, she joined the newly created *Russkoe Zhenskoe Vzaimno-Blagotvoritel'noe Obshchestvo* (Russian Women's Mutual Philanthropic Society). She served at various times as manager of its Commission on Fundraising and of its *Otdel referatov* (Department of Abstracts), as well as serving as a member of the governing Council which, in the early stages of the Society, defined and shaped organizational policy. The Department of Abstracts was the theoretical arm of the *Russkoe Zhenskoe Vzaimno-Blagotvoritel'noe Obshchestvo* and members presented their research on women's issues at sessions convened by the Department. Ol'ga Shapir regarded the *Russkoe Zhenskoe Vzaimno-Blagotvoritel'noe Obshchestvo* as a 'women's club' (in the fashion of the traditional 'men's club'), gathering women with similar views, discussing women's problems and developing strategies for the organization and for the women's movement as a whole. She opposed the *Russkoe Zhenskoe Vzaimno-Blagotvoritel'noe Obshchestvo*'s involvement in charitable works, preferring instead to promote a political agenda.

Rivalry existed between Shapir and ***Anna Shabanova***, one of the women who had established the *Russkoe Zhenskoe Vzaimno-Blagotvoritel'noe Obshchestvo* in 1895, and who had served as the organization's Chair since its inception. Shabanova was an administrative leader, whereas Shapir was a charismatic and respected intellectual leader. After voicing her objections to the philanthropic role undertaken by the *Russkoe Zhenskoe Vzaimno-Blagotvoritel'noe Obshchestvo*, Shapir resigned from the organization's Council but continued to work for its Suffrage Department, which was then making preparations for the First All-Russian Women's Congress.

In 1905, Shapir also joined the *Soiuz Ravnopraviia Zhenshchin* (Women's Equal Rights Union, 1905-1907), a women's political organization dedicated to securing suffrage. Inspired by the first Russian Revolution of 1905, this organization took part in acts of open civil disobedience, together with left-wing political parties and other organizations, including the Social Democrats, the Social Revolutionaries, the Red Cross and others. In December 1905, they set up medical posts and canteens for rebel workers in Moscow during the *Decabr'skoe vooruzhennoe vosstanie* (December armed revolt) and transferred 32,000 rubles to postal and railway trade unions.

Shapir was a good public speaker and enjoyed a following among the Russian *rav-*

nopravki (equal rights feminists). Her articles and speeches, which advocated women's equality, established her as a theorist in a branch of Russian feminism that she herself referred to as "ravenstvo pri razlichii" (feminism of difference). She believed that men and women were different and that women should not aspire to the uniform standards established by men. Women could not and should not be the same as men, but the differences between men and women should not be a cause for inequality. For Shapir, the purpose of the women's movement was to establish equality while taking into consideration these existing gender differences. In her view, this would take more than changing laws to alter women's status, since inequality was deeply embedded in society, its laws, its customs and cultural traditions. She believed that the women's movement had to change both society's political institutions and gender consciousness; she considered gender inequality the central problem of human society and believed that all other public conflicts were derived from the basic inequality and conflict between men and women (Shapir 1909, 896).

At the First All-Russian Women's Congress in 1908, Shapir declared that women had to cherish their female characteristics and resources (Shapir 1909, 898). Her report "Idealy budeshego" (Ideals of the future) maintained that female experiences and perceptions were important for humankind and its development, and were no less significant than men's experiences.

Although Shapir's theoretical works were only known to a narrow circle of Russian feminists, her fiction was read by a much broader audience and it was in her fiction that Shapir tried to change cultural stereotypes of women and counter prevailing notions of female passivity, obedience and self-renunciation. In this respect, she challenged dominant traditions in Russian literature. In her novels *Lubov'* (Love, 1897), *Mirazhi* (Mirages, 1889), *Ne poverili* (They don't believe, 1889), *Drug Detstva* (Friend of childhood, 1903) and others, she contrasted a positive new image of the educated, middle-class Russian woman with traditional representations. She wrote about women who succeeded in public life; her heroines were pragmatic, professional, self-sufficient; she rejected self-sacrifice as a norm for Russian women and defined women's emancipation as the achievement of self-realization and self-respect, condemning the idea that women should subordinate their interests to those of the family and promoting the unconditional right of women to participate in public life (Shapir 1891; Shapir 1916).

After the 1908 Congress, Shapir continued to work in the Suffrage Department of the *Russkoe Zhenskoe Vzaimno-Blagotvoritel'noe Obshchestvo*. The Department drafted legislative and administrative proposals for women's participation in local government and women's civil rights (inheritance rights and the right to a separation from a spouse). Some of these proposals were adopted by the State *Duma* (Parliament) in the bill "On modifications and additions to laws currently in force on the private property rights of women, on the relationship between the spouses and with respect to children" (1914).

Shapir resigned in 1912 due to illness and died in St Petersburg on 13 (26) June 1916. She was buried at the *Literatorskie Mostki* (Footbridge of the literati) in Volkovskii Orthodox Cemetery.

Irina Yukina
Department of Gender Studies,
Nevsky Institute of Language and Culture, St Petersburg

SOURCES

(A) St Petersburg, Russian National Library, Department of Manuscripts. Fund No. 844. Archival collection of O. Shapir, Document No. 186. Shapir, Ol'ga. *Obrashchenie k Chlenu Gosudarstvennoi Dumy L. Petrazhickomu* (Official appeal to Member of Parliament Lev Petrazhitchky). Unpublished document.

(B) Shabanova, A. (Anna Nikolaevna). *Ocherk zhenskogo dvizheniia v Rossii* (Story of the women's movement in Russia). St Petersburg: Tip. Obrazovanie, 1912.

(C) Shapir, Ol'ga. *Vopreki obychau* (In spite of custom). St Petersburg, 1891.

(C) Shapir, Ol'ga. "Idealy budeshchego" (Ideals of the future). *Trudy pervogo vserossiiskogo zhenskogo s'ezda pri Russkom Zhenskom obshchestve v Sankt-Peterburge, 10–16 Dec. 1908* (Works of the First All-Russian Women's Congress of the Russian Women's Mutual Philanthropic Society). St Petersburg, 1909, 895–898.

(C) Shapir, Ol'ga. "Zhenskoe bespravie" (Women's inequality). *Birzhevye Vedomosti* (Exchange sheets) (16 July 1916): 2–3.

(D) Kazakova, Irina. "Ol'ga Andreevna Shapir." Marina Ledkovsky, Charlotte Rosenthal and Mary Zirin, eds. *Dictionary of Russian Women Writers.* Westport, CT: Greenwood Publishing Group, 1994, 577–580.

(D) Yukina, Irina. *Ol'ga Shapir–ideolog rossiiskogo feminizma* (Ol'ga Shapir–a Russian ideologist of feminism). O. R. Demidova, ed. *Iz istorii zhenskogo dvizheniia v Rossii* (From the history of the women's movement in Russia). St Petersburg: Nevsky Institute of Language and Culture, 1998, 116–127.

(D) Yukina, Irina. *Zabytaia feministka Ol'ga Shapir* (Forgotten feminist Ol'ga Shapir). E. I. Trofimova, ed. *Materialy konferentsii provedennoi 30-ogo maia 1996 goda v Moskve "Zhenshina i kul'tura"* (Materials of the conference "Woman and Culture", Moscow, 30 May 1996). Moscow: Information Center of the Independent Women's Forum, 1997, 20–39.

(E) Yukina, Irina. "Doktor Anna Shabanova". I. I. Rogozin, ed. *Kharizmaticheskie Lichnosti v Istorii Rossii* (Charismatic personalities in the history of Russia). St Petersburg: Petrovskaia Academy of Arts and Sciences, 1997, 80–86.

SHCHEPKINA, Ekaterina Nikolaevna (1854–1938)

Russian historian and journalist; teacher at the *Bestuzhev* Higher Women's Courses; co-founder of the *Soiuz Ravnopraviia Zhenshchin* (Women's Equal Rights Union) and activist of the *Liga ravnopraviia zhenshchin* (League for Women's Equal Rights); contributor to the leading feminist journals, *Soiuz Zhenshchin* (Union of women) and *Zhenskii Vestnik* (Women's herald).

Ekaterina Nikolaevna Shchepkina was born in 1854, into an old Moscow gentry family which, in her generation, included many scholars and academics. Among her siblings and cousins were several noted historians and linguists, including her younger brother Evgenii N. Shchepkin (1860–1920), also an historian. Shchepkina attended the Guerrier courses in Moscow and then the *Bestuzhev* Higher Women's Courses in St Petersburg. As a protégé of the Director, the historian K. N. Bestuzhev-Riumin, she met some of the leading male intellectuals of the day, including Fiodor Dostoevskii and Vladimir Solov'ev. Later (1895–1896 and 1898–1899), Shchepkina taught history at the Bestuzhev courses. From 1890, she also gave history classes for workers at the *Imperatorskoe Technicheskoe Obshchestvo* (Imperial Technical Society). A prolific writer, she published two historical monographs, stories from Russian history for Sunday school students, a Russian history textbook and articles on women's history and the current situation of women in Russia for several of the so-called 'thick journals' (in which poets and writers first published their works for review).

Shchepkina was one of the founders in February 1905 of the *Soiuz Ravnopraviia Zhenshchin* (Women's Equal Rights Union). When the St Petersburg section of the *Soiuz* floundered in factional conflict Shchepkina, along with ***Liubov' Gurevich*** and the *Soiuz*'s secretary ***Mariia Chekhova***, kept this branch of the organization afloat. When some members sought to depoliticize the *Soiuz*, Shchepkina vocally supported ongoing political involvement, arguing that the goal of women's equal rights was political to the core. Shchepkina took part in the 1908 *Pervyi Vserossiisskii Zhenskii S'ezd* (All-Russian Women's Congress) session on peasant women, lecturing on the work and health of peasant women and arguing that peasant women endured a double oppression, as both peasants and women.

The *Soiuz Ravnopraviia Zhenshchin* was defunct by the time of the *Pervyi Vserossiisskii Zhenskii S'ezd* in December 1908. Key activists, searching for a vehicle to continue the fight for women's equal rights, found it in the *Liga Ravnopraviia Zhenshchin* (League for Women's Equal Rights). The *Liga*, unlike the *Soiuz*, was legally registered at its founding in March 1907 and thus able to operate publicly in a period of increased police surveillance and repression. Shchepkina became head of the *Liga*'s lecture bureau. Sister activist Mariia Chekhova served as President (1909–1917) of the Moscow branch of the *Liga*, and Liubov' Gurevich, ***Anna Kal'manovich***, Liudmila Ruttsen and ***Ariadna Tyrkova*** were also active.

Shchepkina remained involved in the *Liga* and, in 1917, was one of the ten candidates on the organization's electoral list for the Constituent Assembly. Others on the list included the President of the *Liga* ***Poliksena Shishkina-Iavein***, as well as ***Mariia Chekhova,*** Marxist and feminist ***Ekaterina Kuskova***, historian Alexandra Efimenko and the populist and advocate of 'legal Marxism' Aleksandra Kalmykova.

Like many others, Shchepkina's family was torn apart by the Revolution. In 1919, the Bolsheviks executed her twin brother, the Kadet Nikolai N. Shchepkin, for counter-revolutionary activity. In 1917, her younger brother, Evgenii Shchepkin, a left Kadet deputy in the first Duma, became a leading Bolshevik supporter in Odessa but died in 1920, his health shattered by the privations of the Civil War. In the early 1920s, Shchepkina continued to write for publication. In 1921, at the age of 67, she published her history of the women's movement during the French Revolution, with a critical introduction by leading Bolshevik women's activist ***Alexandra Kollontai.*** Her next project, an article about the Women's Equal Rights Union, was to appear in *Byloe* (The past) but in 1926 this journal ceased publication. Little is known about Shchepkina's life after this. She died in 1938 at the age of 84.

Rochelle Goldberg Ruthchild
The Union Institute and University and the Davis Center
for Russian and Eurasian Studies, Harvard University

SOURCES

(C) Shchepkina, Ekaterina. "Pamiati dvukh zhenshchin-vrachei" (Remembering two woman-doctors). *Obrazovanie* (Education) 5-6, part 1 (1896): 92–137.

(C) Shchepkina, Ekaterina. "Zhenskoe naselenie Peterburga" (The female population of St Petersburg). *Obrazovanie* 5–6 (1897): 218–32.

(C) Shchepkina, Ekaterina. *Kratkii ocherk russkoi istorii s drevnieishikh vremen do nachala XX veka* (A short survey of Russian history from ancient times to the beginning of the twentieth century). St Petersburg: V. I. Iakovenko, 1907.

(C) Shchepkina, Ekaterina. *Iz istorii zhenskoi lichnosti v Rossii* (A history of women individuals in Russia). St Petersburg, 1914.

(C) Shchepkina, Ekaterina. "Vospominaniia i dnevniki russkikh zhenshchin" (Memoirs and diaries of Russian women). *Istoricheskii vestnik* (Historical bulletin) 8 (1914): 536–55.

(C) Shchepkina, Ekaterina. *Zhenskoe dvizhenie v gody Frantsuzskoi revoliutsii; s obrashcheniem k chitateliu A. Kollontai* (The women's movement in the years of the French Revolution, with an address to the reader by A. Kollontai). St. Peterburg: Gosudarstevennoe izdatel'stvo, 1921.

(D) Ruthchild, Rochelle Goldberg. "Shchepkina, Ekaterina Nikolaevna." In Norma Corigliano Noonan and Carol Nechemias, eds. *Encyclopedia of Russian Women's Movements.* Westport, Connecticut: Greenwood Press, 2001, 72–74.

(E) Goldberg, Rochelle (Ruthchild). *The Russian Women's Movement 1859–1917*. Doctoral Dissertation: University of Rochester, 1976.

(E) Grishina, Zoia V. *Zhenskie organizatsii v Rossii (1905g.-fevral'/mart 1917g.)* (Women's organizations in Russia, February 1905–March 1917). Moscow State University, 1978.

(E) Stites, Richard. *The Women's Liberation Movement in Russia: Feminism, Nihilism, and Bolshevism, 1860–1930*. Princeton: Princeton University Press, 1978; 1991.

(E) Grishina, Zoia V. "Zhenskie organizatsii v Rossii, 1905 g.-fevral'/mart 1917g" (Women's organizations in Russia, February 1905–March 1917). *Vestnik Moskovskogo universiteta* (Moscow University bulletin): *Ser. 8 Istoriia* (History) 2 (1982): 33–42.

(E) Edmondson, Linda Harriet. *Feminism in Russia 1900–1917*. Stanford, CA: Stanford University Press, 1984.

SHISHKINA-IAVEIN, Poliksena Nestorovna (1875-1947)

Russian physician, feminist activist and, until 1918, leader of the *Rossiiskaia Liga Ravnopraviia Zhenshchin* (Russian League for Women's Equal Rights) with connections to the international women's movement.

Poliksena Shishkina was born in Nikolaev in April 1875. Her father, Nestor Shishkin, was a musical military conductor and took part in the Russian-Turkish war (1875-1878). Her mother (data unknown) was from a family of Ukrainian gentry. Poliksena had six brothers, all of whom received higher education: Nikolai (an engineer); Sergei; Zakhar; Grigorii; Vasilii (a military officer) and a sixth (name unknown).

In 1900, while studying at the St Petersburg Women's Medical Institute, Poliksena Shishkina married Georgi Iulievich Iavein (1863-1920), a professor at the Medical-Surgical Academy in St Petersburg. They had two children: a daughter Alla (1902) and a son Igor (1903). Poliksena Shishkina was among the first to graduate from the St Petersburg Women's Medical Institute in 1904.

Shishkina-Iavein belonged to the third generation of feminist activists in the Russian women's movement. Members of this generation, born at the end of the 1860s and the early 1870s, were the first women to succeed in politics, in spite of coming from mostly non-noble families. Among them were ***Ariadna Tyrkova***, Sophia Panina, Anna Miliukova, Elena Stasova, ***Aleksandra Kollontai***, ***Nadezhda Krupskaia*** and ***Inessa Armand***. Those among them who were Social Democrats, such as Stasova, Kollontai, Krupskaia and Armand, had the possibility to become government leaders. Those whose political careers had developed along liberal lines were displaced from the political stage with the revolutionary events of 1917.

The achievements and popularity of Poliksena Shishkina-Iavein were connected with the *Liga Ravnopraviia Zhenshchin* (League for Women's Equal Rights). The *Liga* was established in March 1907 on the basis of the *Soiuz Ravnopraviia Zhenshchin* (Women's Equal Rights Union, 1905-1907) to promote political and civil rights for women. Shishkina-Iavein became the *Liga*'s Chair in 1910 at a difficult time for the movement. The popular feminist magazine *Soiuz Zhenshchin* (Union of women)–

printed in St Petersburg from 1907–1909 by former activists of the *Soiuz*–closed down after the *Soiuz* had disbanded in 1907, and after political disagreements (over the primacy of Marxist theory and the need for feminists to ally themselves with the Left) broke out among members of the journal's editorial board. ***Mariia Chekhova***–the former editor and Chair of the *Soiuz* and of the *Liga* (1907–1910)–left St Petersburg for Moscow disappointed and tired. At the same time, the vigorous campaigns of Russian feminists for universal suffrage (for all men and women)–organized by the highly political *Soiuz* and coordinated in part with revolutionary groups–had not achieved the anticipated results. Women's equality was not an agenda supported by the wider population. Like the *Soiuz*, the *Liga* desired political rights for all but when Shishkina-Iavein became Chair of the *Liga* and the issue of feminist participation in a left-wing coalition was raised once again, the general conclusion was that the women's movement needed to become an independent political force, capable of defining its own strategic goals, developing its own theory and elaborating its own methods of struggle. It was at this time (1910), that the *Liga* began to emphasize a more specific goal than that of universal democracy (the principle that had informed the activities of the *Soiuz*) and sought to exclusively represent the political and economic interests of women.

As Chair of the *Liga*, Shishkina-Iavein was directly involved in initiating the change of policy and she made the pursuit of women's suffrage a fundamental goal of the organization. She also encouraged the publishing and educational activities of the *Liga*. Numbers of members grew from 219 (in 1910) to 1,235 (in 1915). New branches were opened in Tomsk and Ekaterinburg. Since Shishkina-Iavein considered legislative activity the only way to achieve social change, the Council of the *Liga* focused on the actions of the State *Duma* (Parliament). All bills submitted to the *Duma* were subjected to scrutiny for gender inequities by the *Liga*, and the organization directed inquiries, protests and other feedback to the State *Duma* when laws looked set to negatively affect women's interests. Most Russian feminists avoided class distinctions, considering themselves to be working on behalf of all women. Thus, in 1910, the *Liga* directed a petition to the *Gosudarstvennyi Sovet* (the Upper Chamber of Parliament) protesting a government bill on land reform that proposed modifications to the 1906 land reforms of Petr Arcadievich Stolypin (1862–1911). The feminists were worried that, if adopted, the new law would violate women's rights, especially those of peasant women, and offered concrete legislative measures to protect peasant women's rights. Although these measures were disregarded by Parliament, the *Liga* managed to become a persistent influence on *Duma* proceedings, bringing issues such as divorce, spousal separation, the right of women to practice law and women's suffrage to the attention of the Third State *Duma* (1907–1912). The bill "On modifications and additions to laws currently in force on the private property rights of women, on the relationship between the spouses and with respect to children" was passed by Third State *Duma* and confirmed by the Fourth State *Duma* in the February of 1914. Shishkina-Iavein, together with a member of the State *Duma*, Aleksandr Ivanovich Shingarev, prepared a government bill in 1913 for the abolition of state-regulated prostitution. (Under this system prostitutes did not hold full citizenship rights: they could not carry internal passports–as required of other citizens–but only special 'yellow tickets.') Departing from its position on universal suffrage for women, the *Liga* also proposed granting both rural and urban women with certain property qualifications the right to elect officials to self-, local and provincial government institutions. Although some activists of the Russian women's movement criticized the *Liga* for favoring special interests, Shishkina-Iavein thought this position appropriate. If the *Liga* could not achieve universal suffrage for women, it could at least advance voting rights for some groups.

The legislative initiatives of the organization were widely publicized at public assemblies, meetings and public debates, attracting women from different social strata, politicians and the mass media. The reports and speeches of these initiatives were printed and distributed in the larger cities and in the provinces. Shishkina-Iavein's speech, "Zhenshchina-glasnyi" (Woman-politician), delivered in St Petersburg in 1917, reflected the passion of *Liga* meetings. The outbreak of World War I turned *Liga* activities away from politics to charitable war-efforts, opening public canteens and running hospitals and shelters for women and children. Shishkina-Iavein co-organized these efforts, as well as teaching medical courses and working as a physician in hospitals for soldiers.

Led by Shishkina-Iavein, the *Liga Ravnopraviia Zhenshchin* became the largest and most powerful women's political organization in Russia. Shishkina herself had international contacts: she corresponded with English and Swedish feminists; wrote for the feminist magazine *Jus Suffragii* (the official journal of the International Woman Suffrage Alliance / International Alliance of Women for Suffrage and Equal Citizenship); visited Swedish women's organizations and received delegations from various countries (research on this international aspect to her work is currently underway). When *Liga* activists found out that the program of the Provisional Government did not include women's suffrage, and after *Liga* appeals (in support of women's suffrage) to the Revolutionary Council of Workers' and Soldiers' Deputies and to the Ministerial Council of the Provisional Government had failed to obtain results, Shishkina-Iavein and others decided to organize protests. About ninety women's organizations and groups–among them the Women's Progressive Party, the Russian Women's Mutual Philanthropic Society and women-workers' groups–joined this initiative. The resolution demanding suffrage for women was officially handed to the Provisional Government on 4 (17) March 1917.

The appeal to the women of St Petersburg to unite in the struggle for political freedom was posted and distributed in the streets, sent to women's organizations, factories and women's educational institutions. Mass meetings were held, at which Shishkina-Iavein was one of the featured speakers. The *Liga* Council organized a demonstration on 19 March (1 April) 1917, in which about 40,000 women participated. Shishkina-

Iavein and the well-known revolutionary Vera Figner rode along in an automobile at the heart of the demonstration.

At the State *Duma* building, Shishkina-Iavein delivered a speech demanding equal human rights for women. That evening, Prince G. Lvov (head of the Provisional Government) acquiesced to the women's demands and on 21 March (3 April) 1917, a delegation of well-known Russian feminists, including Shishkina-Iavein, ***Ariadna Tyrkova***, ***Anna Shabanova***, Mariia Pokrovskaia and Anna Miliukova, met with Prince Lvov. They received assurances that women would receive the right to vote and would be able to participate in the election of the Constituent Assembly in November-December 1917. The election took place on 12–14 November 1917. Although the Bolshevik government later destroyed the election ballots, it is believed that Ariadna Tyrkova was elected (since she was included in the rolls of the *Kadet* party in three provinces). The Constituent Assembly met briefly on 5 January 1918, before being disbanded by the Bolsheviks. In 1918, the Soviet government abolished all rival parties and political organizations. Shishkina-Iavein and her husband went to Estonia (which gained its independence after the revolutions of 1917), but he died soon afterward and she was not permitted to practice medicine there. Eventually, she returned to the USSR and worked as a physician. She lived through the blockade of Leningrad (as St Petersburg was called between 1924 and 1991) and through World War II. She died in March 1947. Poliksena Shishkina-Iavein was buried in the Nikolski Cemetery in Leningrad (St Petersburg).

Irina Yukina
Department of Gender Studies,
Nevsky Institute of Language and Culture, St Petersburg

SOURCES

(B) Zakuta, O. *Kak v revolutsionnoe vremia Vserossiiskaia Liga Ravnopraviia zhenshchin dobivalas' izbiratel'nykh prav dlia russkikh zhenshchin* (How the League for Women's Equality achieved suffrage for Russian women in the revolutionary period). St Petersburg: Izdanie Vserossiiskoi Ligi ravnopravliia zhenshchin, 1917.

(C) Shishkina-Iavein, P. "Zhenshchina-glasnyi" (Woman-politician). St Petersburg: Liga Ravnopraviia zhenshchin, 1917.

(E) Edmundson, Linda Harriet. *Feminism in Russia, 1900–1917*. Stanford, CA: Stanford University Press, 1984.

(E) Aivazova, S. "Gendernye issledovaniia: perechityvaia A. Kollontai" (Gender research: rereading A. Kollontai). In E. V. Mashkova, ed. *Formirovanie gendernoi kul'tury i studentcheskoi molodezhi* (The formation of gender culture among student youth). Naberezhnye Chelny: Femina, 1995, 40–43.

(E) Yukina, Irina. "Doktor Shabanova" (Dr. Shabanova). In I. I. Rogozin, ed. *Kharizmaticheskie lichnosti v istorii Rossii* (Charismatic personalities in the history of Russia). St Petersburg: Petrovskaia Academy of Arts and Sciences, 1997, 80–86.

SKENDEROVA, Staka (1831–1891)

Bosnian Serb teacher, writer and social worker; founder of the first girls' school in Bosnia-Herzegovina and the country's first published woman author.

Staka Skenderova was born in 1831 into a lower middle-class family, of which little is known. The family moved from Prijepolje in Herzegovina to Sarajevo in Bosnia proper. Skenderova's father Pero was a merchant who died early in Staka's childhood. Almost nothing is known of her mother Mara, sister Savka and brother Ilija, except that they died in Sarajevo in 1889, 1888 and 1866 respectively. From the start, Staka was rare among the girls of her generation. She is said to have been raised like a boy; she socialized with men and often dressed like a man. She was also unusually ambitious. She learned to read and write in her native Serbo-Croatian language (possibly with the aid of tutors) at a time when there were no girls' schools in the country and the literacy rate was just three percent. She regularly attended the old Orthodox Church in Sarajevo, sang in the choir and read aloud for parishioners who were surprised to observe this young literate girl. Because of her brother's position as furrier for the Ottoman army, she also learned Turkish, the official language of the Ottoman Empire (Bosnia-Herzegovina had been under Ottoman rule since the fifteenth century). Skenderova later learned Greek and possibly Russian.

Skenderova established Bosnia-Herzegovina's first girls' school in Sarajevo in 1858. The school offered courses in mathematics, drawing, reading, old-church Slavonic and handiwork, producing some of the country's first women intellectuals and cultural leaders. Although Skenderova's pupils were mainly Bosnian Serbs, later Bosnian Jews and Bosnian Muslims attended as well. Skenderova accepted a broad spectrum of girls, ranging from the very poorest to the wealthiest families in the country. Topal Osman, the Pasha (Governor) of Bosnia-Herzegovina, sent his daughters to Skenderova's school. At first, the school offered just three grades; later it introduced a fourth, as well as teacher training. Some women stayed on to teach at the school upon graduation. After years of financial struggle, Skenderova's school closed in 1875. By this time, a second girls' school had been established in Sarajevo (1869) under the tutelage of Miss Adeline Paulina Irby (1833–1911), an English Protestant philanthropist.

In the nearly seventeen years that Skenderova managed and taught at her school, she made both friends and enemies. Because of her family's contacts in the Ottoman administration, mainly through her brother Ilija, several men from the Bosnian Serb merchant class believed (erroneously) that Skenderova was a stooge of the Ottoman administration. Undeterred, she sought financial support elsewhere from generous locals and individuals of the Ottoman administration and Orthodox Church in Sarajevo. She also traveled to solicit support, maintaining ties with eminent personages, including Serbia's Head of State: Prince Michael Obrenović (1823–1868).

In her spare time, Skenderova read literature and recorded the local social and political news, folk poetry and lore. In 1859, just one year after the opening of her school, she managed to publish her collection in an almanac called *Ljetopis Bosne* (The Bosnian chronicle, 1825–1856). In this way, she became Bosnia-Herzegovina's first published woman author, thus paving the way for others. She did so with the aid of the Russian consul, folklorist and historian Alexander F. Gilferding (1831–1872), who was posted to Sarajevo. He had been impressed with the young Skenderova and had her manuscript translated into Russian and published in St Petersburg.

In 1870, Skenderova took a spiritual pilgrimage to Jerusalem, together with an Orthodox nun. In accordance with Bosnian tradition [whereby pilgrims to the Holy Land, whether Catholic, Orthodox or Muslim, added the prefix 'Hadži' (from the root word 'hadj,' meaning 'pilgrimage') to their name], Skenderova also became known as Hadži Staka Skenderova. Soon after her pilgrimage, Bosnia-Herzegovina underwent a major political transformation. In 1875–76, a massive rural uprising in Herzegovina led by Christian peasants against their Muslim landlords led to an international crisis, settled at the Congress of Berlin in 1878. Here, the Great Powers of Germany, England, France, Russia and Austria-Hungary passed the administration of Bosnia-Herzegovina from the Ottoman Empire over to the Austro-Hungarian Empire.

Under the Austro-Hungarian administration, Skenderova continued to work primarily with the young girls of Sarajevo. Although her school had closed three years earlier, her interest in the welfare of the poorest girls in the city remained, leading her to become the country's first social worker. After opening her girls' school in 1858, Skenderova's home had become a kind of daycare center for girls in need, where girls could receive medicine, advice and a place to socialize with other students from Skenderova's school. Skenderova had regularly taken her girls to church, where they sang in the choir as she had done in her youth. She continued to do this under the Austro-Hungarian administration, when she and Miss Irby cared for orphan girls.

Not much is known of Skenderova's work thereafter. The next time she received public attention was following her tragic death on 26 May 1891 when, on her way home from a social event, a startled horse charged into the crowd where Skenderova stood, inflicting fatal injuries upon her.

Staka Skenderova was a significant figure in the social and cultural history of Bosnia-Herzegovina. A trailblazer, her life was marked by a number of 'firsts:' as a pioneer in education, establishing the country's first girls' school in Bosnia-Herzegovina; as the country's first social worker, as well as its first published woman author and as the first in a long line of culturally and socially influential women. These included the co-editor of the first Bosnian Serb literary-cultural journal, ***Stoja Kašiković***; ethnographer and pedagogue, ***Jelica Belović-Bernadzikowska*** and the writer Nafija Sarajlić (c.1893–1970), who wrote about Muslim women in Sarajevo prior to the outbreak of World War I. Skenderova's educational, social and literary work paved the way for the development of Bosnia-Herzegovina's first female cultural and intellectual elite.

Jelica Zdero
Ph.D. Candidate,
The University of Western Ontario, Canada

SOURCES

(B) *Sarajevski list* (The Sarajevo newspaper) (1891).
(B) *Bosanska vila* (The Bosnian nymph) (1891, 1903).
(B) *Narod* (Nation) (1907).
(C) Skenderova, Staka. *Ljetopis Bosne (1825–1856)* [The Bosnian chronicle (1825–1856)]. St Petersburg, 1859. Also published in Vojislav Maksimović and Luka Šekara, eds. *Ljetopisi. Prokopije Čokorilo, Joanikije Pamučina, Staka Skenderova* (Chronicles. Prokopije Čokorilo, Joanikije Pamučina, Staka Skenderova). Sarajevo: Veselin Masleša, 1976.
(D) Papić, Mitar. "Staka Skenderova." *Prilozi za proučavanje istorije Sarajeva* (Contributions to the history of Sarajevo) 2, no. 2 (1966): 119–136.
(E) Hawkesworth, Celia. *Voices in the Shadows: Women and Verbal Art in Serbia and Bosnia.* Budapest: CEU Press, 2000.
(E) Rizvić, Muhzin. *Pregled književnosti naroda BiH* (A survey of the literature of the people of Bosnia-Herzegovina). Sarajevo: Veselin Masleša, 1985.

SKLEVICKY, Lydia (1952–1990)

Research assistant at the former *Institut za suvremenu povijest* (Institute of Contemporary History)—formerly the *Institut za historiju radničkog pokreta Hrvatske* (Institute of the History of the Workers' Movement of Croatia), currently the *Hrvatski institut za povijest* (Croatian Institute of History)—and at the former *Zavod za istraživanje folklora* (Institute of Folklore Research), now the *Institut za etnologiju i folkloristiku* (Institute of Ethnology and Folklore Research); author of the first Croatian feminist studies, academic texts and articles in the disciplines of history, sociology and ethnology; leading feminist theoretician of the 1980s in Yugoslavia; publicist, translator and activist.

Lydia Sklevicky was born on 7 May 1952 in Zagreb, the only child of Lea and Sergej Sklevicky. The Sklevickys were a middle-class family of central European origin, with roots in the nineteenth-century Russian diaspora. Lydia Sklevicky was given a rigorous 'European' education and studied European languages. Upon finishing high school, she enrolled at the *Filozofski fakultet* (Faculty of Philosophy), University of Zagreb, where she graduated in 1976 with a double major in sociology and ethnology. She was subsequently taken on as an assistant at the then *Institut za historiju radničkog pokreta Hrvatske* (Institute for the History of the Workers' Movement in Croatia), affiliated to the Department of History of the Socialist Period.

Although Sklevicky's work was initially concerned with the social status of women in Croatia under socialism, her research interests quickly led her to investigate long-term processes of cultural change, with reference to historical and anthropological discourses. With exceptional professional dedication and creative curiosity, Sklevicky scoured the historical archives in order to present a range of socialist emancipatory processes within the women's organization, *Antifašistička fronta žena* (Antifascist Women's Front). One of her motivations for carrying out this research was to decode the demagogy at work in revolutionary ideology and analyze the gap between the declarative and the real, particularly the proclaimed emancipation of women alongside the maintenance of patriarchal structures in socialist Yugoslavia.

In her Master's thesis, *Žene i moć–povijesna geneza jednog interesa* (Women and power–the historical genesis of one interest), defended in 1984 as part of a postgraduate degree in the sociology of culture (Faculty of Philosophy, Zagreb), Sklevicky outlined a critique of traditional historical research composed of three elements: (i) the challenging of false universalism; (ii) the need for new questions (e.g. concerning the relation of 'the public' to 'the private') and (iii) the importance of power relations and questions of sexuality for the study of cultural categories, including gender as an analytical category of historical research. Sklevicky worked on the assumption that the consistent insertion of gender into historiographical method would result in a profound rethinking, not only of the historical roles of women and men, but also of political movements and historical periodizations, as well as 'history' itself and its unchallenged 'facts.'

Sklevicky's appreciation of contextual complexity, as well as of the importance of interdisciplinarity and methodological innovation, is vividly apparent in her (unfinished) doctoral dissertation, *Emancipacija i organizacija, Uloga Antifašističke fronte žena u postrevolucionarnim mijenama društva (NR Hrvatska 1945–1953)* [Emancipation and organization. The Antifascist Women's Front and post-revolutionary social change. (People's Republic of Croatia 1945–1953)], published posthumously in 1996 in *Konji, žene, ratovi* (Horses, women, wars) and edited by Sklevicky's mentor and friend, professor Dunja Rihtman Auguštin. By carrying out an in-depth analysis of traditional attitudes towards women in times of 'revolutionary socialist' change, Lydia Sklevicky was at the same time furthering the cause of interdisciplinarity in the social sciences, linking historical research to ethnological and anthropological studies—including her own endeavors in these fields at the *Zavod za istraživanje folklora* (Institute of Folklore Research) in 1988. Addressing women's symbolism and symbolic discourse in general customs and political rituals, iconographic 'femininity,' as well as fashion and other aspects of women's lives in the everyday, Sklevicky combined scientific method, social critique and postmodern irony—undermining disciplinary clichés by insisting on both the evaluation of individual research contributions and gender-specific approaches. She discussed these themes throughout the 1980s in short essays published in various scholarly editions and daily newspapers, such as *Etnološka tribina* (Ethnological forum), *Revija za sociologiju* (Sociological review), *Narodna umjetnost* (Croatian journal of ethnology and folklore research), *Žena* (Woman), *Gordogan* and *Časopis za suvremenu povijest* (Journal for contemporary history)—all included in the *Konji, žene, ratovi* anthology (see Starčević Štambuk 1996, 303–312).

With the birth of a daughter, Nana, in 1978 (from a brief common-law relationship), Sklevicky began developing her ideas on 'chronobiology:' the congruity of specific female experiences with changes in their life cycles, recorded in an historical matrix. Nana's birth was an important moment in Sklevicky's own personal 'chronobiology.' Sklevicky's creative life was cut short by a fatal automobile accident near the town of Delnice, Croatia on 21 January 1990.

During her lifetime, Lydia Sklevicky could not be categorized in accordance with any particular social, political or intellectual 'norms' for women. She was atypical: a middle-class woman who was fascinated by anti-fascist women and a 'bourgeois' of elite tastes, who at the same time adopted a position of solidarity with women at all levels. She was radically and publicly outspoken concerning feminist issues, yet enjoyed traditional values and customs such as Christmas and Easter. Possessed of a razor-sharp wit, courageous and defiant, Lydia Sklevicky's life was a testament to the importance of woman's visibility. Taking a sometimes radical, even eccentric stand, Sklevicky's media appearances drew public attention to her feminist activities, such as her coordination of the first feminist gatherings in Zagreb at the end of the 1970s, as well as her establishment (with others) of the group *Žena i društvo* (*Zid*, Women and Society), founded in 1979 under the auspices of the *Sociološko društvo Hrvatske* (Croatian Sociological Society). She was the coordinator of *Žena i društvo* from 1982–1983 and saw her work for the group as part of a professional commitment to the motivation of feminist academics and the creation of a network of feminist theorists. On the other hand, like other feminist intellectuals around her, Sklevicky's volunteer work for the Zagreb based SOS Hotline for abused women and children formed part of a different ethical commitment to feminism, revolving around the connection between theory and praxis. (Established by Croatian feminist activists in March 1988, the Hotline was the first SOS Hotline for abused women in the socialist countries.) In the late 1980s, as an outstanding and prominent columnist of the popular women's magazine *Svijet* (World), Sklevicky created a public forum for insights into gender issues, alongside other, new and provocative debates. In her series of condensed journalistic essays, she wrote on numerous feminist topics including abortion, the female body, witches and 'respectable' feminists–all the while consciously seeking to deconstruct imposed perceptions of women and tasks invariably assigned to them.

As early as the late 1970s–in conjunction with her exceptional engagement on the local academic and feminist scene–Sklevicky also began actively participating in international academic and scholarly events, ranging from meetings and lectures at universities to publishing papers in international publications. She attended the First International Conference on Research and Teaching Related to Women (Montreal, Canada, 1982), the fourth and sixth *Historikerinnentreffen* (Meetings of women-historians) in Germany (respectively in Berlin, 1983 and Bonn, 1985) and the International Conference on Women's History (Amsterdam, 1986).

With each project she managed, through her innovative contributions, to draw attention to the inadequacies of contemporary research on women's socio-cultural roles. Sklevicky saw every invitation to a meeting of historians or ethnologists, whether in Vienna or Montreal, as an academic and professional challenge; not only did they provide opportunities for her to test out her theories of female subjectivity (particularly in times of revolutionary and post-revolutionary change), but they also facilitated the "dialogical character of knowledge" (an expression she used frequently) that Sklevicky held to be an essential and desirable feature of modern scientific development. In 1983, she coordinated the postgraduate course “Women and Work” at the *Interuniverzitetski centar* (InterUniversity Centre), Dubrovnik and, in 1988, co-organized the symposium “Current Issues in the Anthropology of Gender,” held within the framework of the Twelfth International Congress of Anthropological and Ethnological Sciences (ICAES), Zagreb. She was in contact with well-known European and American feminists–including the feminist historians Barbara Jancar, Gisela Bock, Natalie Zemon Davis and Gerda Lerner–and helped make their work known to the Croatian public. For Sklevicky, such collaborations were important affirmations of new directions in historical, ethnological, anthropological and other social scientific research.

Lydia Sklevicky consistently employed critical feminist methods, regardless of the genre or medium in which she worked; throughout her dynamic and fruitful ten-year career, she published over a hundred studies, texts and articles and translated Erica Jong’s poem anthology, *Fruit and Vegetables* (*Voće i povrće*, 1981). She was on the editorial board of the international journal, *Gender and History* and a member of the editorial team of *Časopis za suvremenu povijest* (Journal of Contemporary History). The first Croatian scholar to address the social history of women from a feminist perspective, Sklevicky’s contribution to the disciplines of history, sociology and anthropology was unique–in many respects unrivalled today–as was her contribution to feminism. She truly was (and is), as feminist theoretician Rada Iveković once put it, a Croatian and Yugoslavian “feministička začinjavka” (one who ‘gives birth’ to feminism).

Biljana Kašić
Program Coordinator,
Centre for Women’s Studies Zagreb

Translated from the Croatian by Susan Jakopec.

SOURCES

(C) Sklevicky, Lydia and Žarana Papić, eds. *Antropologija žene* (Anthropology of women–an anthology). Belgrade: Prosveta, 1983.

(C) Sklevicky, Lydia, ed. *Žena i društvo, Kultiviranje dijaloga* (Women and society. Cultivating dialogue). Zagreb: Sociološko društvo Hrvatske, 1987.

(C) Sklevicky, Lydia. *Konji, žene, ratovi* (Horses, women, wars). Selected and prepared by Dunja Rihtman Auguštin. Zagreb: Ženska infoteka, 1996.

(D) Starčević Štambuk, Anamarija. “Bibliografija radova Lydije Sklevicky” (Bibliography of the works of Lydia Sklevicky). In Lydia Sklevicky. *Konji, žene, ratovi*. Zagreb: Ženska infoteka, 1996, 303–312.

(D) Kašić, B., Đ. Knežević and A. Starčević Štambuk, eds. “Lydia Sklevicky - Tematski broj časopisa povodom pete godišnjice smrti Lydije Sklevicky” (On the occasion of the fifth anniversary of the death of Lydia Sklevicky). *Kruh & ruže* (Bread and roses) 3 (1995): 4–41.

SLACHTA, Margit (1884–1974)

Activist of the Hungarian Catholic women's movement; social worker; leading figure of the *Szociális Missziótársulat* (Social Mission Society); first female Member of Parliament in Hungary; founder (1923) and prioress of the *Szociális Testvérek Társasága* (Society of the Sisters of Social Service). Postwar pseudonyms: 'Margit Nemes' and 'Borbála Nemes.'

Margit Slachta (right), 1935 (at the latest), with her mother and sister Borbála in front of her parents' home. After the death of Slachta's parents in 1936, the villa was turned into a boarding-house managed by one of the sisters of the Society of the Sisters of Social Service. In 1944/1945, around ninety Jews were hidden from Nazi occupying forces in the house (Budapest-Hűvösvölgy, Báthory László utca 10). Today the villa is home to the *Generalate* i.e. the international headquarters of the Society.

Margit Slachta was born on 18 September 1884, in the city of Kassa (today Košice, Slovakia), in the 'northern highlands' (*Felvidék*) of Hungary. Her parents–Kálmán Slachta (1857-1936), descendent of a respectable nobleman of Polish origin, and Borbála Saárossy of Sáros (1855-1936), daughter of a landlord–married in 1882. Margit was the second of six girls; her five sisters were: Mária Antónia (1883-1935), Borbála (1886-1887), Irén (1888-1970), Borbála (1891-1961) and Erzsébet (1896-1988). In 1907, her father, a carefree man who spurned religious devotion, became the general manager of the Kassa Savings Bank but his irresponsibility led to bankruptcy. In 1908, with his wife and three younger children, he emigrated to America.

Margit, who remained in Hungary, claimed the only thing she had inherited from her parents was her headstrong nature. She attended the elementary teacher-training college in Kassa (1901-1903), later the *Kalocsai Miasszonyunk Nővérek Tanárképző* (Teacher Training College of the Sisters of Our Lady's Order) in Kalocsa (1903-1906), where she graduated as a lower-level secondary school teacher of German, French and history. Her life-long devotion to women's causes through Christian social work stems from this period. Organized Catholic charity appeared in Hungary around the turn of the century. In the late 1890s, the widow of Count Pál Pálffy (born Countess Geraldine Károlyi, 1836-1915) founded the first organization to follow the activities of the so-called *patronages* already operative in other European countries. By

1906, this organization had developed into the *Országos Katholikus Nővédő Egyesület* (National Catholic League for the Protection of Women), with Edit Farkas (1877–1942) as Vice-President. In 1908, Farkas set up a new organization, the *Szociális Missziótársulat* (*SzMT*, Social Mission Society), a votive sisterhood of social workers and patronesses. The *SzMT* was approved by the Bishop of Székesfehérvár, but also allowed civil activities. In Farkas' view, only co-workers who devoted their entire lives to the cause within the framework of a religious organization could bring about real change. As a student, Slachta was greatly influenced by the work and charismatic personalities of Edit Farkas and Sarolta Korányi (1868–1935)–the latter was the outstanding leader (between 1912 and 1919) of the *Katolikus Munkásnő Egyesület* (Association of Catholic Women Workers, founded in 1912). Slachta began patronage work and, after completing a training course for social work in Berlin (in the *Soziale Frauenschule*, i.e. Social School for Women) in early 1908, gave up teaching entirely to be able to devote all her time to social work. She was one of the pioneers who joined the *SzMT*. The *SzMT* soon began carrying out social activities among delinquent youth and in prisons, allowing Slachta to bring her spiritual beliefs into worldly spheres and concerns. She was soon a leading figure of the Christian patronage movement and publisher of the *Értesítő* (Bulletin, established in 1912) of the *SzMT*, and related Catholic organizations. Slachta developed a systematic training program for female social workers and, from 1915, became the editor of the journal *A Keresztény Nő* (The Christian woman), which succeeded *Értesítő*. From 1918 to 1920, Slachta edited *Magyar Nő* (Hungarian woman).

Slachta's feminism focused on women's vocational training (for professions considered suitably feminine) and, after World War I, on citizenship rights. Her methods were unconventional, her style and tactics modern. She shared Edit Farkas's view that social welfare involved "more than merely aiding the indigent and suffering ... We must be present in every segment of society, ... where our preventive and sacred devotion is needed" (cited in Mona 1997, 49).

When women's (partial) suffrage was granted in Hungary in 1918, the Christian social women's movement, with the (reorganized) *SzMT* as one of its key components, appeared in politics (in October 1918) as the *Keresztény Női Tábor* (*KNT*, Christian Women's League, the women's section of the Christian Democratic Party) with Margit Slachta as its leader. The *KNT* preserved its autonomy from closely related political parties and other women's associations. Edit Farkas permitted Slachta's nomination in the by-election of March 1920 as the official candidate of the then ruling *Keresztény Nemzeti Egyesülés Pártja* (National Christian Union Party). With a safe majority of the votes, Margit Slachta was elected the first female Member of Parliament in Hungary. During her mandate (1920–1922), she delivered 28 addresses focusing on social conditions and women's rights. In one notorious incident, she requested that stick-beating–the legal penalty stipulated by a law to punish speculators making illicit profit from increasing prices (law XV/1920)–be applied to offending women as well as men.

The parliamentary session ended on 16 February 1922. The *SzMT*'s prioress Edit Farkas would not renew her permission for Slachta to be nominated in the following elections, since the views of the two women differed on how to fight for equal rights for women. (The *SzMT* shied away from political activity, especially at the parliamentary level, while Slachta was keen to fight at all levels and to participate in politics.) The ensuing conflicts led to a break never to be repaired. On 5 May 1923, Slachta (who was considered too radical) and other sisters were dismissed from the *SzMT*, their vows annulled. This ended a decisive period in Slachta's life.

A few days later, on 12 May 1923, Margit Slachta founded the *Szociális Testvérek Társasága* (*SzTT*, Society of the Sisters of Social Service), which she directed as prioress until 1963. Between November 1924 and December 1926, she traveled through the USA and Canada and gave lectures on the history and geography of Hungary, a country which she saw as her "dismembered" homeland, torn apart by the Trianon Treaties after World War I. In 1927, following the American example, she set up fifteen "Everyone's Christmas trees" in various parts of Budapest: decorated pines in public places for people who couldn't afford their own Christmas trees. In the 1930s, she resumed training social workers and also re-entered domestic politics, founding the ethical-religious *Szentlélek Szövetség* (Holy Spirit League) (1933) and editing the journals *A Lélek Szava* (The voice of the spirit) (1938–1944) and *A Dolgozó Nő* (Working woman) (1939–1944). The latter, after the German invasion of Hungary in March 1944, was among the first journals to be banned.

After 1938, Slachta became an open critic of Nazism. In March 1943, after Slovakia had declared its intention to 'free' the country from Jews, Slachta (who had traveled there upon hearing of the deportations) left for Rome. After receiving information on the situation of Jews in Slovakia from Slachta, Pope Pius XII instructed the seven Slovakian bishops to submit protests to the President and his ministers and a pastoral letter of protest was duly read out in every single church in Slovakia. Once home, Slachta demonstrated solidarity with labor camp populations and spoke of those Jews serving in special 'labor service' units of the army, who cleared minefields and performed other dangerous tasks (unarmed) and among whom an extremely high death rate prevailed. "Open your heart to someone in a labor camp, excluded from kindred ties by the spirit of our time," wrote Slachta. "Be bold in these grim, deadly times and ... rid your heart of hatred" (Slachta 1943). In 1944, under her leadership, activists of the *Szentlélek Szövetség*–driven by Christian faith and the spirit of humanism–sheltered and hid nearly one thousand Jews both in Budapest and the countryside.

Slachta returned to official politics early in 1945, when she received a parliamentary mandate as an independent candidate on the list of the *Polgári Demokrata Párt* (Civilian Democratic Party). In 1947, she was re-elected as a representative of the *Keresztény Női Tábor*. Margit Slachta defended the cause of doing good in the name of Christianity without concessions. This resulted in a clear anti-Soviet and anti-communist attitude. Her Marxist peers in the House, as well as some of her fellow

MPs, considered her the epitome of an outdated clericalism and interrupted her speeches with scornful, even vulgar remarks. In such a climate, Slachta's political position became increasingly difficult. On 16 June 1948, she delivered her last speech, in which she argued passionately against the nationalization of church schools. When the bill was passed by a majority and the national anthem closed the session, she protested by remaining seated, resulting in her being barred from Parliament for two periods of six months.

From January 1949, fearing arrest, Slachta hid in a Dominican convent. (She had submitted her application for nomination in the elections of 1949 but had been turned down by the authorities.) On election day (15 May 1949), she risked arrest and appeared at the polls. On the night of 22 June, she left the country with two sisters. She arrived in the USA under the name of Etelka Tóth. From 1950, the *SzTT* could no longer legally operate in Hungary.

As an émigré, Slachta worked for *Radio Free Europe* (under the name Borbála Nemes) and ran correspondence to Hungary (under the pseudonym Margit Nemes). She regularly wrote letters to (and received them from) colleagues, relatives and friends, using a pseudonym out of fear of the Hungarian authorities. In 1951, she went to Vienna in the hope that she might eventually return home. On 5 May 1953, she returned to the USA under her own name. On 6 January 1974, Margit Slachta died at the *SzTT* home in Buffalo. Sándor Sík, a poet and member of the Piarist Order said of her: "Margit Slachta is one of the people I consider to be a saint. Not to my taste, but saints are not usually to our tastes; they generally have tastes of their own" (Sík 1993, 390). In 1985, Slachta was posthumously honored by the state of Israel with the title "Righteous Among the Nations" and a tree was planted in her name in the *Yad Vashem* garden. In 1995, Margit Slachta was decorated "for courage" by the Hungarian Republic.

Margit Balogh
Director, Center for Social Studies,
Hungarian Academy of Sciences, Budapest

Ilona Mona
Retired librarian
Béla Bartók Technical School of Musical Arts

SOURCES

(B) Stollenmayer, Pankraz. "Moderne Formen Katholisch-religiöser Frauentätigkeit" (Modern forms of the Catholic women's movement). *Schönere Zukunft* (Brighter future) 6 (1931): 19.

(B) (Palagyi) Natália. "Narrative of 1944." *DOVE Quarterly* (Los Angeles, California, Spring 1946): 7–14.

(C) Slachta, Margit. *Elkapott sugarak* (Glints of sunshine). Budapest: Testvér Szövetség, 1927.

(C) Slachta, Margit. *A puszták rejtekéből az élet centrumába* (From the hideaway of the plains to the center of life). Budapest, 1928.

(C) Slachta, Margit. "Újévi levél" (New Year's Eve letter). *A Lélek Szava* (6 January 1943).

(C) Söjtöry, Ágota, ed. *Sugárzó élet. Válogatás Slachta Margit testvér gondolataiból* (Shining life. The selected ideas of Sister Margit Schlachta). Budapest: Szociális Testvérek Társasága Magyarországi Kerülete, 1993.

(D) *Slachta Margit, az első magyar nőképviselő politikai működése* (The political work of Margit Schlachta, first Hungarian woman MP). Budapest: Keresztény Női Tábor, 1922.

(D) *Zadjeli Slachta Margit, a Szociális Testvérek Társaságának alapítója 1884. szeptember 18. - 1974. január 6.* (Zadjeli Slachta Margit, founder of the Social Sisters Society 18 September 1884-6 January 1974) n. p. [Buffalo?] n. d. [1975?].

(D) Palko, Magda. "Slachta Margit." In Ilona Sánta, ed. *Politikuspályák* (The careers of politicians). Budapest: Kossuth Kiadó, 1984, 146-154.

(D) Majsai, Tamás. "The Deportation of Jews from Csíkszereda and Margit Slachta's Intervention on Their Behalf." In Randolph L. Braham, ed. *Studies on the Holocaust in Hungary*. New York: Columbia University Press, 1990, 113-163.

(D) Mona, Ilona. "Slachta Margit a szlovákiai zsidókért (1942-1943)" (Margit Slachta on behalf of the Slovakian Jews, 1942-1943). In *Magyarok Kelet és Nyugat metszésvonalán* (Hungarians on the border of east and west). Esztergom, 1994, 391-400.

(D) Sheetz, Jessica A. "Margit Slachta's Effort to Rescue Central European Jews, 1939-1945." In Michael Phayer and Eva Fleischer. *Cries in the Night: Women Who Challenged the Holocaust*. Kansas City: Sheed-Ward, 1997, 42-64.

(D) Adrianyi, Gabriel. "Eine Vorkämpferin für die soziale Gerechtigkeit in Ungarn: Sr. Margit Slachta (1884-1974)" (A campaigner for social justice in Hungary). In *Christliche Sozialethik im Dialog, zur Zukunftsfähigkeit von Wirtschaft, Politik und Gesellschaft,* (Christian social ethics in dialogue, towards a future vocation in economy, politics, society). Gratschaft: Vektor Verlag, 2000, 619-636.

(D) Muranyi, Gábor. "Slachta Margit, az első honanya" (Margit Schlachta, the first Hungarian woman MP). *HVG* XXII, no. 12 1087 (25 March 2000): 103-105.

(D) Mona, Ilona. *Slachta Margit*. Budapest: Corvinus Kiadó, 1997. Slovakian translation: Margita Slachtová. Kosice: Karnat-Karol Pástor, 2002.

(E) Majsai, Tamás. *A kőrösmezei zsidódeportálás 1941-ben. Ráday Gyűjtemény Évkönyve IV-V* (The deportation of the Jews of Kőrösmező in 1941. Yearbook of the Ráday Collection). Budapest: Ráday Gyűjtemény, 1986, 59-86; *Remény* (Tel-Aviv, 1987/3): 12-37.

(E) Majsai, Tamás. *Iratok a kőrösmezei zsidódeportálás történetéhez 1941. Ráday Gyűjtemény évkönyve IV-V* (Documents on the deportation of the Jews of Kőrösmező in 1941. Yearbook of the Ráday Collection). Budapest: Ráday Gyűjtemény, 1986, 195-237.

(E) Sík, Sándor. *A százgyökerű szív. Levelek, naplók... Sík Sándor hagyatékából* (The heart with a hundred roots. Letters, diaries ... From the legacy of Sándor Sík). Budapest: Magvető, 1993.

STASOVA, Nadezhda Vasil'evna (1822-1895)

Russian philanthropist; promoter of women's education in Russia; superintendent of the first Higher Education Courses for Women in St Petersburg (known as the *Bestuzhev* Courses, 1878–1889).

Nadezhda Vasil'evna Stasova was born on 12 June 1822, to the famous court architect Vasilii Stasov (1769-1848), a favorite of Tsar Alexander I, and Mariia Abramovna Suchkova (1796-1831), the daughter of a lieutenant of the *Semenovsky* Guard Regiment. Nadezhda was the fifth child of eight. Two of her three younger brothers were well known: one a literary critic (Vladimir, 1824-1906); the other a liberal lawyer (Dmitry, 1828-1918; the father of Communist Party member and friend of Lenin and Boris, Elena Stasova). She also had two elder brothers (Nikolai and Alexander) and an elder sister (Sophia, 1821-1858), to whom she was very close (the remaining sibling died in infancy). Her father spent much of his time working on building projects at royal residences. After her mother died of cholera in 1831, Nadezhda was brought up by the governess Olga Konstantinovna Nikolaeva. She received the usual education for a girl of her social position: lessons in French and German (she also knew English and Italian), polite manners, music, drawing, dancing and so forth. In addition, through the connections and popularity of her father, the family invited well-known professors from the famous Pedagogical Institute (e.g. Ivan Ozerov) to teach her and her siblings literature, art and history. After their governess left them in 1848 (she moved to Ekaterinburg and founded a boarding school for girls), Nadezhda Stasova entered 'high society.' Together with her younger brother Vladimir and her eldest sister Sophia, she borrowed books from their father and they read extensively. It was from French literature, especially George Sand (1804-1876), that Stasova first learned of women's emancipation. But girls of her social class and generation were supposed to read romantic novels and household companions. Elena Gardiner, in her obituary of Stasova, remembers being told how, when Stasova and her sister once "spoke in public about *Dead Souls* [...] they soon found that only men remained in the sitting room because anxious mothers hastily took their daughters away from these improper young ladies who dared praise Gogol" (Gardiner 1895, 239). During this period of her life, Stasova was mostly concerned with family problems: the death of her father and the marriage, later the death from tuberculosis of her sister Sophia (1858), which she took very hard. This was a turning point for Stasova and she began participating in public life and philanthropy. Meeting ***Mariia Trubnikova*** strengthened her ideas about women's emancipation–in particular emancipation through girls' education. Stasova, who never married and did not have children (in his biography of Stasova, her brother Vladimir writes of the young Stasova's broken off engagement to an army officer and the unhappiness it caused her), devoted the rest of her life to the promotion of women's education in Russia.

In 1861, Stasova joined Trubnikova and ***Anna Filosofova*** in organizing the *Obshchestvo Dostavlenniia Deshevykh Kvartir i Drugikh Posobii Nuzhdaiushchimsia Zhiteliam Sankt-Peterburga* (Society for Cheap Lodging and Other Aid to the Residents of St Petersburg) and worked hard to provide basic means of subsistence to poor women and their families. It was with the Society that she first obtained a role she would assume as part of her other undertakings too, that of supervising supplies. She looked after big orders for the Society's sewing workshop, took care of children while their mothers were working and organized a kindergarten. Stasova was also among the founders of *Obshchestvo Organizatsii Zhenskogo Truda* (Society for the Organization of Work for Women) and *Zhenskaia Izdatel'skaia Artel'* (Women's Publishing Artel) in the 1860s. Between 1861 and 1869, Stasova became involved in the activities of the Countess Dondukova-Korsakova, who did charity work for prostitutes. These two women often housed girls and women taken from the streets in Dondukova's apartment, or helped syphilitic girls who had been sent to the *Kalinkin* Hospital for forced medical treatment. Stasova also worked with Countess Lambert in the *Priiut Sviatoi Marii Magdaliny* (Asylum for Magdalens), an institution that aimed to 'save' young women (mainly from the *Kalinkin* Hospital) through 'corrective' methods of work and study–an approach of which Stasova later came to disapprove.

Stasova's real passion was providing women with education. Her first attempt was in 1860, with the launching of the so-called 'Sunday schools.' Together with her sister-in-law Polixena Stasova, she joined the staff of the Girls' Sunday school located in the building of the Galvanic Regiment, where she worked as a teacher, later becoming the representative of the school at the Council of Private Sunday Schools (founded in 1861). When the government closed all Sunday schools in the summer of 1862 (due to the spread of revolutionary ideas within the network), Nadezhda Stasova organized classes at her own home and continued to teach, explaining why she saw the education of women as a necessity: "Organizing the publishing Artel allowed us to meet with outstandingly hard workers and to discover how little most women knew. Yet although most of these women are half-educated and uncultivated, they want to become literate and are ready for any work that might help them become independent ... And in wanting to help them, in looking for jobs for them, we realized that we had first to teach them" (Stasov 1896, 154). Stasova led the way in organizing educational courses for women. In 1861, women were allowed to attend the public lectures of St Petersburg University professors and in 1868, Stasova, ***Filosofova*** and ***Trubnikova*** obtained official permission to open higher education courses for women. In 1869, Stasova managed to find a building to host the courses; she assembled an excellent team of professors and composed a timetable of lectures. The official opening was held in January 1870 at the apartment of the Minister of Education, Count Tolstoi (who did not support the courses but was ordered to accommodate the initiative by the Tsar, over whom Filosofova's husband had some influence). In 1871, the courses moved to another place–the *Vladimirskii* college–and became known as the *Vladimirskii* courses. Stasova was afraid that student numbers for the courses would be low, but they were attended by around two hundred women. Stasova was thrilled and worked very hard to maintain discipline, as well as providing the women with food, organizing lectures and talking to professors. In 1871 however, Stasova had to go abroad (to Germany) to nurse her two sick nieces (Olga and Sophia). She stayed there until 1876 (when the younger of the two nieces died). During these five years of absence, she kept up continuous correspondence with Filosofova, Trubnikova and other women from the courses, taking the news that the courses had been closed (in 1875) very badly.

Upon her return to St Petersburg in 1876, Nadezhda Stasova immediately began organizing a permanent educational institution for women, which opened in 1878. It took its name (the *Bestuzhev* Courses) from its nominal founder (Professor Bestuzhev-Riumin). Stasova became a superintendent of the courses, providing students with material assistance such as food and accommodation. Stasova and ***Filosofova*** also organized the *Obshchestvo dlia Dostavleniia Sredstv Vysshim Zhenskim Kursam* (Society for Raising Funds for Higher Education Courses) which, as the name implied, aimed to raise money to support the courses. She also managed to find a permanent building for the courses, to which they moved in 1883. Stasova supported the education of Jewish women, whom she helped enroll onto the courses. During the wave of political reaction that began after the assassination of Tsar Alexander II, when the slightest suspicion of 'freethinking' could land a person in prison, enrollment on the courses was prohibited (1886). In 1889, Stasova managed to get the Tsar's permission to re-open the courses but the move formed part of intiatives by the Minister of Education (Pobedonostsev) to get rid of autonomy and self-governance in universities and other educational institutions, which meant that Stasova and other members of the courses' self-governing body were ejected from the managing committee and replaced by more compliant government officials. People around Stasova thought this would be the end of her public life but they were wrong.

Although she was upset that she had been forced out of the courses, she continued her work in the sphere of education, organizing her famous Sunday meetings and helping students. In 1893, together with members of the *Detskaia Pomoshch'* (Child Welfare Society), she organized a nursery for working-class children. Stasova continued her work at the *Obshchestvo Dostavlenniia Deshevykh Kvartir i Drugikh Posobii Nuzhdaiushchimsia Zhiteliam Sankt-Peterburga*, administrating women's lodgings in one of the Society's buildings. She also helped organize the *Russkoe Zhenskoe Vzaimno-Blagotvoritel'noe Obshchestvo* (Russian Women's Mutual Philanthropic Society) in 1895, but these activities came to a halt with her sudden death on 27 September that same year.

Nadezhda Stasova represented the first generation of women active in the women's emancipation movement in Russia. Her life work–centered on the promotion of education for women–helped many Russian women to enter public life and become conscious of issues concerning women and feminism.

Marianna Muravyeva
Herzen State Pedagogical University, St Petersburg

SOURCES

(A) Russian Academy of Sciences, Institute of Russian Literature (Pushkinsky Dom), collection no. 294 (Stasov MSS). Contains over 4000 documents from the Stasov family, including Stasova's memoirs, correspondence, papers related to the Higher Education Courses and other organizations for which Stasova worked.

(A) National Library of Russia, collection no. 738 (Vladimir Stasov MSS). Contains the correspondence of Nadezhda Stasova. The memoirs entitled "From Triest to Vienna. My first steps in Vienna" are mistakenly ascribed to Nadezhda Stasova but in fact belong to her brother, Nikolai Stasov; analysis of the handwriting, text structure and language leave no doubt. They had the same initials–the cause of the confusion. See also collection nos. 41, 110, 423, 502, 585, 602, 621, which contain correspondence with various individuals.

(B) Gardiner, E[lena]. "Nadezhda Vasil'evna Stasova." *Mir Bozhyi* (God's world) 11 (1895): 238-242.

(B) Stasov, V[ladimir] V. *Vospominaniia o Moei Sestre* (Memories of my sister). St Petersburg: Knizhky Nedeli, 1896.

(B) *Pamiati Nadezhdy Vasil'evny Stasovoi* (In memory of Nadezhda Vasijevna Stasova). Commemorative volume. St Petersburg: M. M. Stasjulevitch, 1896.

(B) Jasevitch-Borodaevskaja, V. *Nadezhda Vasil'evna Stasova*. St Petersburg: M. M. Stasjulevitch, 1896.

(B) Stasov, V[ladimir] V. *Nadezhda Vasil'evna Stasova. Vospominaniia I Ocherki* (Nadezhda Vasil'evna Stasova. Recollections and essays). St Petersburg: M. M. Stasjulevitch, 1899.

(B) Schtakenschneider, E. *Dnevnik i Zapiski. (1854-1886)* (Diary and memoirs). Moscow: Academia, 1934.

(D) Salita, E. G. *Stasovy v Peterburge* (The Stasovs in St Petersburg). Leningrad: Lenizdat, 1982, 99-122; 151-154; 206-207; 222; 231; 241-245; 252-253.

(E) Pilyavskij, V. I. *Stasov–Arkhitektor* (Stasov–the architect). Leningrad: Gosstrojizdat, 1963.

(E) Lebedev, A. K. and A. V. Solodovnikov. *V. V. Stasov*. Moscow: Iskusstvo, 1982.

ŠTEBI, Alojzija (Lojzka) (1883-1956)

Slovenian teacher, journalist, politician and women's activist; founder (1923) and President (1923–1927) of the *Feministična aliansa kraljevine SHS* (Feminist Alliance of the Kingdom of Serbs, Croats and Slovenes), renamed the *Aliansa ženskih pokretov Jugoslavije* (Women's Movements Alliance of Yugoslavia) in 1926; editor (1926–1938) of the newspaper *Ženski pokret* (Women's movement); participant in many international congresses, including those of the International Women's Suffrage Alliance (IWSA), the International Council of Women (ICW) and the Little Entente of Women (LEW).

Alojzija Štebi was born on 24 March 1883 in Ljubljana. Her father Anton Štebi was a haulier. Nothing is known about her mother Marija (born Kunstel). Alojzija Štebi went to a girls' school and graduated from teacher-training college in Ljubljana in 1903. In that year, she was employed as a supply teacher in Tinje, Carinthia. A year later, she became a regular teacher in Tržič, then in Radovljica, Mavčice and Kokra. Her socialist ideas and activities brought her into constant conflict with the school authorities and on 23 September 1914, she resigned from her teaching position and became the editor of the socialist daily newspaper *Zarja* (Dawn), for which she had been writing since 1912. From 1912 to 1915, Štebi edited the newspaper *Tobačni delavec* (Tobacco worker), the gazette of the Slovene members of the Trade Union of the Tobacco Workers of Austria. From May to November 1915, she also edited and published *Ženski list* (Women's newspaper), the gazette of Slovene women socialists.

Her publishing and editing activities were closely connected to her political work. As a member of the *Jugoslovanska socialdemokratska stranka* (Social Democrat Party of Yugoslavia), she was an elected member of the Carniolan provincial assembly in 1913. She appeared as a speaker at key social democratic meetings in Ljubljana, Trieste, Trbovlje and Jesenice, and often gave lectures to workers' societies. From June to November 1917, she was the editor-in-chief of the social democratic daily *Naprej* (Forward) and from March 1918 to August 1919, the editor-in-chief of the gazette *Demokracija* (Democracy). With a group of young social democratic women she founded the *Slovenska socialna matica* (Slovene Social Society) in 1917 and supported the establishment of the Yugoslav state. She firmly believed that the new state would solve the Slovene national problem and improve the position of women.

The threat of losing even the few rights women had gained in the Habsburg Monarchy spurred Štebi to defend the rights of women and children in the new Yugoslav State. In December 1918, she became superintendent of the Department for Youth Welfare as part of the commission on social welfare of the national government of the Kingdom of Serbs, Croats and Slovenes in Ljubljana. After 1919, Štebi held several government positions in departments dealing with the welfare of young people and children and social policy issues. In 1927, the Ministry of Social Policy pushed successfully for Štebi's retirement for political reasons (namely her radical ideas). She was re-employed in 1933 as an assistant secretary to the Ministry of Social Policy and National Health in Belgrade. Due to illness, she retired again in 1940 and moved to Ljubljana to live with her brother Andrej Štebi, an engineer, and his wife Cirila (born Pleško), a prominent activist in the Slovene women's movement. From 1941, she collaborated with the Slovene partisan movement, as did her brother and sister-in-law. In June 1942, the Nazis took her brother Anton hostage before shooting him. Her sister-in-law Cirila died in October 1942 in Auschwitz.

After World War II, Alojzija Štebi worked for the Department of Education and Improvement of Human Resources at the Ministry of Work of the People's Republic of Slovenia and, in 1947, became head of this department. In October 1948, she was named chief of the administration board for qualified workers at the Ministry of Work. In May 1950, Štebi was transferred to the Department for Vocational Schools at the Ministry of Education, from which position she retired in September 1950. She continued to receive contracted work there until her death on 9 August 1956. A once influential representative of the prewar women's movement, she was not held in favor by the new communist government.

Štebi began writing about 'the woman question' in 1911, while politically active among workers as an advocate of Social Democracy. In 1918, she published her most important treatise, *Demokratizem in ženstvo* (Democracy and womanhood), in which she outlined a program for the Slovene women's movement, spoke out for the improvement of women's education and requested that women be given civil rights. She believed that women could gain the vote only through organized public appearances. She rejected radical feminist demands and defined her position in terms of the more moderate struggle for women's rights advocated by Tomáš G. Masaryk and Ellen Key. She was actively involved in endeavors to create a unanimous public representation of Yugoslav women. After 1919, she became a member of the *Narodna ženska zveza Kraljevine SHS* (National Women's Association of the Kingdom of Serbs, Croats and Slovenes), later renamed the *Jugoslovanska ženska zveza* (Yugoslav Women's Association). In 1923, due to the political ineffectiveness of this organization, Štebi founded the *Feministična aliansa kraljevine SHS* (Feminist Alliance of the Kingdom of Serbs, Croats and Slovenes), renamed the *Aliansa ženskih pokretov Jugoslavije* (Women's

Movements' Alliance of Yugoslavia) in September 1926. She was President of this organization until 1927, when she moved to Belgrade. The goal of the *Aliansa ženskih pokretov Jugoslavije* was to engage women of all social strata and nationalities in the fight for civil rights and social and political equality in Yugoslav society. In the years 1927 to 1938, Štebi edited the gazette of the Alliance, *Ženski pokret* (Women's movement). In 1934, the Slovene section of the *Jugoslovanska ženska zveza* (Yugoslav Women's Association) made her an Honorary Member as "the spiritual leader of the entire women's movement of the State" (Muser 1956, 245).

In the interwar period, Alojzija Štebi took part in many international women's congresses. In 1923 she attended the Congress of the International Woman Suffrage Alliance (IWSA) in Rome and, as a delegate from a Slavic country, joined the Little Entente of Women (LEW). In October 1925, she attended a conference in Belgrade organized by the LEW and presented her report: "Mišljenje javnosti in feminizem v Jugoslaviji" (Public opinion and feminism in Yugoslavia). In 1925, she attended the Seventh Council Meeting of the International Council of Women (ICW) in Washington D.C., where she met the activist and pacifist Jane Addams. She attended another Women's conference in Prague (1926), the Eleventh Congress of the International Alliance of Women's Suffrage and Equal Citizenship (IAWSEC) in Berlin (1929), the Ninth Council Meeting of the ICW in Paris (1934) and its Tenth Council Meeting in Dubrovnik (1936). In two booklets translated to French entitled *Le travail des féministes Yugoslaves* (1931) and *L'activité des sociétés feminines en Yugosloavie* (1936), Štebi presented the Yugoslav women's movement and its fight for equal rights to an international public.

Prior to World War I, Štebi had been in favor of fundamental social and political changes and considered 'the woman question' to be one aspect of a wider social question. After the war, she increasingly favored a thorough rearrangement of social mentalities, of which a crucial part was the fight for women's equal rights. She considered her engagement with the women's movement as a step towards common human progress. Her contemporaries thought her a good orator of simple appearance, kind but determined and independent in her opinions and beliefs. She was a charismatic leader and prudent politician who became one of the most prominent representatives of the Slovene and Yugoslav women's movement in the interwar period.

Marta Verginella
Department of History,
University of Ljubljana

Translated from the Slovenian by Jaka Andrej Vojevec.

SOURCES

(A) Arhiv Slovenije, Collection No. 1510 (Alojzija Štebi).

(C) Štebi, Alojzija. *Demokratizem in ženstvo. Propagandni spis Slovenske Socijalne Matice* (Democracy and women. Propaganda paper of the Slovenian Social Foundation). Ljubljana, 1918.

(C) Štebi, Alojzija. *O saradnji društava. Referat održan na godišnjem skupu Jugoslovenskog narodnog ženskog saveza u Splitu, 8. oktobra 1929 godine* (On the establishment of the association. A report presented at the annual assembly of the National Council of Yugoslavian Women in Split, 8 October 1929). Belgrade: Čolović & Madžarević, 1929.

(D) "Štebi Alojzija." In *Slovenski biografski leksikon* (Slovenian biographical dictionary). Ljubljana, 1960–1971, 3: 677–680.

(D) Muser, Erna. "Lojzka Štebijeva." *Naša žena* (Our woman) 9 (1956): 245.

STERN, Szeréna, Mrs Pollák (1894–1966)

Hungarian elementary school teacher; leading figure in the social democratic women's movement in the interwar period; leading social politician, who focused on child protection and social services for mothers at the municipal level; first female head of department in the city administration (1945).

Mrs Pollák in her function as Department Head in the Budapest municipality with General Zamercev, military governor of the Hungarian capital from 1945 to 1948, on the occasion of the second jubilee of Zamercev's appointment; also on the picture the deputy mayor, the mayor and the attorney general of Budapest.

Szeréna Stern was born on 15 June 1894 in Nagyatád, south-west of Hungary's Lake Balaton, into a very poor Jewish family. Her mother's maiden name was Rózsa Herstein and Szeréna had at least one younger sister, but nothing else is known of her family. Having graduated as an elementary school teacher, Szeréna Stern became a member (very likely from 1917) of the teachers' union (in all probability the *Mária Dorothea Egyesület* [Mária Dorothea Association] for women teachers) and, in 1918, of the *Magyarországi Szociáldemokrata Párt* (*MSzDP*, Social Democratic Party of Hungary; from 1939 the Social Democratic Party). In 1920, she was elected to serve on the *Országos Nőszervező Bizottság* (National Women's Organizing Committee) of her party, in which she remained a leading figure until 1948. In these early years, Szeréna Stern became close friends and spent most of her free time with other representatives of a new generation of (future) leading representatives of Social Democracy, and particularly with the women among them, including Flóra Martos, Mrs Pál Knurr, Mrs Illés Mónus and Anna Kéthly. Through these circles, she also became acquainted with her future husband, Ferenc Pollák (data unavailable). In this period, she often used the Hungarian surname 'Somogyi' as a pseudonym when making public appearances on behalf of the party. She soon became one of the principal organizers, and later, secretary of the *Magyarországi Munkások Gyermekbarát Egyesülete* (Children's Friends Association of the Workers of Hungary), with which she had worked since 1917.

Under the semi-authoritarian Horthy regime of the interwar period, the *MSzDP* was only really able to remain a visible political actor in the municipalities, particularly

Budapest. Mrs Pollák became an elected member of Budapest's Municipal Council in 1925 and kept this position for one and a half decades. Initiality, she was one of the very few women among the 250 elected deputies, and from the 1930s on, remained the only female social democratic representative. Her work within the Municipal Council soon became well known among party members. She also led party seminars for female workers focusing on municipal politics. The Social Democrats called her the "mother of Budapest" (Kenyeres 1967, 429) and articles such as "Asszonyok a városházában" (Women in City Hall), detailing Mrs Pollák's engagement at the municipal level, were even published in other journals of the Hungarian women's movement such as the *Dolgozó Asszonyok Lapja* (Journal of working women, December 1931), a moderate forum for middle-class working women.

In her speeches at party congresses and articles in the social democratic *Nőmunkás* (Woman worker), Mrs Pollák insisted that there was "no systematic social policy in Budapest" [*Dolgozó Asszonyok Lapja* (December 1931): 187] and devoted herself to building an alternative, systematic and preventive system of social provisions and regulations. In her view, the improvement of living conditions and increased investment in social policy would not only help women to combine work and family, but also constitute a direct response to the pronatalist ideology of the Horthy regime. "A society," she wrote, "which cannot ensure basic living conditions for her members has no right to claim more births from women" [*Nőmunkás* (January 1932): 2–4].

As a member of the Budapest Municipal Council, Mrs Pollák was first elected to the Education Commission, later to the Commission for Social Policy and Welfare and, from 1934, to the newly established Commission for Child Protection, which dealt with day-care facilities, summer holiday camps, nutrition for children and so on. In municipal policy, she poured her energies into the improvement of living conditions and welfare institutions for mothers and children in Budapest. Particularly successful and important initiatives included building a network of day-care facilities and a system of summer holiday camps and facilities for school children, as well as developing foster homes for girls and boys of different ages. Other policy measures introduced in Budapest–such as homes for mothers and their children, the establishment of milk deliveries for mothers and babies, and breakfast for schoolchildren–also owed a great deal to Mrs Pollák's organizational work. She organized municipal distribution of free school textbooks to needy children, and fought for better quality textbooks that would not, as she put it, "contaminate" children from a young age by filling them with hate [referring implicitly to nationalist, revisionist and exclusionary prejudices, see *Nőmunkás*, (December 1930): 4]. She also demanded higher wages for all categories of teachers in municipal schools, and the development of a system of school nurses and physicians. In addition, Mrs Pollák translated her long-time involvement with the special concerns of female servants–who formed a considerable percentage of the female urban labor force–into a struggle for the improvement of the legal conditions of this group at the municipal level. In the years of the Economic Depression after 1929, she proposed special policies to the municipal authorities for the alleviation of social misery, at times with the help of large, public assemblies of women.

As the conservative national government attained greater influence over the Budapest Municipal Council due to the introduction of restrictive election laws, the struggle against these measures and laws–curtailing the political autonomy of the capital city and diminishing the democratic character of its political representational bodies–became another field of engagement for Mrs Pollák. In 1929, the Horthy regime tried to abolish the right of women to be elected to the municipal councils. Mrs Pollák angrily protested this proposal in two speeches delivered to congresses of the social democratic women in 1929 and 1930. Like many other activists of the women's movement in interwar Hungary, she saw a direct connection between increasing the number of female deputies and the improvement of social policies in the municipalities.

By 31 December 1940, Mrs Pollák had been deprived of her mandate in the Budapest Municipal Council due to the enforcement of the second so-called Jewish law of 1939, which aimed to curtail the roles Jews played in public and economic life. She did not attend the ceremonial farewell meeting organized by those of her social democratic colleagues still represented in the Municipal Council. Remaining in Budapest, Mrs Pollák survived the war in difficult circumstances. Her husband, Ferenc Pollák, perished after he, as a Jewish man, was (reportedly) taken for forced labor in 1942. The couple had no children.

Mrs Pollák was a leading figure of the social democratic women's movement in the interwar period. She did not follow the example of other leading female comrades such as Kéthly Anna, Anna Kristóf Koltói or Anna Kovács (Mrs Pál Knurr), whose activities focused in part on positions in party commissions, committees, and who were members of the Central Committee of the *MSzDP*. Yet she was a main speaker at all women's congresses and an important orator at party congresses. In addition to her strong position with the *Országos Nőszervező Bizottság* (National Women's Organizing Committee), she became a leading figure of the party's separate women's council for Budapest, founded in 1930.

From 1945, Mrs Pollák became active once again in municipal social policy, first as acting head and, from the end of August 1945, as head of the *Társadalompolitikai Ügyosztály* (Department of Societal Policy)–the first woman to hold this position in Hungary. She worked with sustained energy to realize her systematically-developed and all-inclusive social policy strategy, focusing on immediate measures aimed at overcoming misery caused by the war, and including a longer-term strategy for developing a system of preventive approaches in all spheres of welfare.

In May 1950, when it was clear that municipal self-government in Hungary would effectively be abolished, Mrs Pollák requested exemption "from her duties" (*BFL* XXIII. 104c. 0065/p. 11) and retirement on health grounds; the latter was granted her as of September that same year. Mrs Pollák, who in 1945 had been a member of the provisional National Assembly for a short period of time, had remained faithful to the *MSzDP* until at least early 1949, the year after the party's enforced merger with the Communist Party, now renamed the *Magyar Dolgozók Partja* (*MDP*, Hungarian Workers' Party). She had become a member of the latter by 1 January 1953. In 1954, she (again) became an elected representative of the Budapest Municipal Council and remained a rank and file member of this significant, yet highly dependent political and administrative decision-making body until the end of her life.

Mrs Pollák received the Hungarian Republic's Gold Medal of Merit in 1947 and is also likely to have received the Gold Order of Labor in 1964. When she died on 2 March 1966, at the age of 72, both the Municipal Council and the Eighth District Committee of the *Magyar Szocialista Munkáspárt* (Hungarian Socialist Workers' Party, the successor of the *MDP*) declared her "one of its own deceased" (i.e. one of their own). Mrs Pollák had given her own resumé in an interview a year earlier: "One does not work for thanks to be returned, but because such work is worthwhile. I myself, as I approach the end of life ... say that it has been worthwhile" (PIL 867. f. 1/P, 110 ő.e.).

Claudia Papp, Ph.D.
Director, Municipal Museum and Archive,
Sachsenheim/Baden-Württemberg, Germany

Erika Varsányi
Department of Innovation Studies and History of Technology,
Budapest University of Technology and Economics, Hungary

SOURCES

(A) *Politikatörténeti Intézet Levéltára* (*PIL*, Archive of the Institute of Political History), 658 f., 4 cs., 7 ő.e.; 696 f., 67 ő.e.; 867. f. 1/P, 110 ő.e.; 962 f., 1. *Pollákné* (Mrs Pollák).
(B) *Nőmunkás* (Woman worker) (1920s-1930s).
(B) *Népszava* (People's voice) (1920s-1930s; 1966).
(B) *Dolgozó Asszonyok Lapja* (Journal of working women) (1931).
(B) *Népszabadság* (People's freedom) (1966).
(B) Gárdos, Mariska. *A nő a történelem sodrában* (Women in the stream of history). Budapest, 1942.
(D) Varsányi, Erika. "Egy karrier a budapesti közéletben–Stern Szeréna (Budapest, 1894-1966)" (A career in the Budapest government–Szeréna Stern). In Mária Palasik and Balázs Sípos, eds. *Házastárs, munkatárs, vetélytárs? A női szerepek változása Magyarországon a 20. században* (Partner, colleague, competitor? Women's changing roles in Hungary in the twentieth century). Budapest, 2005, 207-219.
(E) Ágoston, Mrs Péter. *A magyar szocialista nőmozgalom története* (The history of the Hungarian socialist women's movement). Budapest, 1947.

(E) Tiborc, Zsigmond. *A gyermekbarátmozgalom* (The pro-children movement). Budapest, 1947.

(E) Kenyeres, Ágnes. *Magyar Életrajzi Lexikon* (Hungarian biographical dictionary). Budapest, 1967.

(E) *Budapest Lexikon*, 1993 edition.

(E) Makai, Ágnes and Vera Héri. *Kereszt, érem, csillag. Kitüntetések a magyar történelemben* (Cross, medal, star. Decorations in Hungarian history). Budapest, 2002.

(E) Papp, Claudia. *'Die Kraft der weiblichen Seele.' Feminismus in Ungarn 1918-1941* ('The strength of women's soul.' Feminism in Hungary 1918-1941). Münster: Lit-Verlag, 2004.

(E) Oral information provided by Márta Gelléri, 19 November 2003.

STETINA, Ilona (Mrs Gyula Sebestyén) (1855–1932)

Teacher; leading figure in the national movement to improve women's vocational and teacher-training; co-founder (1885) and Vice-President (1889–1932) of the *Mária Dorothea Egyesület* (Mária Dorothea Association) for women teachers; editor (1890–1915) of the influential periodical *Nemzeti Nőnevelés* (National women's education); director (1911–1926) of Budapest's *Állami Nőipariskola* (State Women's Trade School).

Ilona Stetina was born on 27 March 1855 to a well-off Catholic family in the eastern Hungarian town of Großwardein/ Nagyvárad (today Oradea, Romania). Her father, Lipot Stetina (dates of birth and death unknown), was from landed family in western Hungary (Dunántúl). He qualified as an engineer in Vienna and returned to Hungary to serve as an army lieutenant, earning distinction for his military exploits. After the 1848/49 war, Lipot Stetina married Erzsébet Lipniczky (dates of birth and death unknown), who had been brought up by relatives in Transylvania (the Brádys of Hunyad County), and the couple had a daughter, Ilona (data regarding other children unknown). Shortly after Ilona's birth, Lipot Stetina died and his widow moved from Nagyvárad to the smaller town of Kisjenő further south (today Chişineu-Criş). Ilona spent her youth there without receiving any systematic education. In 1868, the *Magyar Gazdaasszonyok Országos Egyesülete* (National Association of Hungarian Farmer Women) invited Ilona's mother to run their orphanage in the as yet nonunified city that would become Budapest. She accepted the offer and moved to the emergent capital with her daughter. After one year of regular schooling, Ilona Stetina was admitted to the *Állami Elemi Tanítónő- és Nevelőnőképző* (State Institute for the Instruction of Women Primary School Teachers) in Buda (hereafter the Buda Institute). By 1874, she had not only become a qualified primary and intermediate school teacher, but had also been given a teaching post at the Buda Institute.

In the mid-1870s, numbers of qualified female teachers were low in Hungary and opportunities presented themselves to Stetina, who seems to have shown initiative early on. She was taken under the wing of Janka Zirzen (1824–1904), the director of the Buda Institute and later of the separate *Állami Polgári Iskolai Tanítónőképzőintézet*

(State Institute for the Instruction of Women Secondary School Teachers) in Pest (hereafter the Pest Institute). The idea that women's trade institutes join forces with teacher-training institutes received state support in 1876 and Stetina organized and gave courses at the Pest Institute to broaden women's vocational skills. She spent a month in Transylvania studying local industries and obtaining teaching materials in the interest of "strengthening national trade" (Zirzen 1885, 18). Together, Stetina and Zirzen carried out surveys of successfully functioning women's trade schools in Vienna, Munich and Stuttgart. Stetina became a member of the Pest Institute's Examination Board and a supervisory committee member of the new *Nőipariskola* (Women's Trade School), established in 1874 by the *Országos Nőiparegylet* (*ONE*, National Women's Trade Association). In 1878, Stetina helped organize the National Exhibition of Women in Trades, held in Székesfehérvár. The aim of these initiatives was to develop domestic industry within the framework of national advancement. Strategies to achieve this were unclear and this was reflected in constant organizational change at the Pest Institute. Stetina described the instability of her working environment as the product of "underdeveloped" ideas concerning women's education and "insufficient resources" (Kiss and Stetina 1896, 72).

In 1881, Ilona Stetina became Mrs Gyula Sebestyén. Her husband had been teaching at the Pest Institute since 1877 and was the editor of *Nemzeti Nőnevelés* (National women's education), a monthly periodical founded by the teaching body of the Pest Institute in 1879. Prior to the emergence of an openly feminist forum in Hungary after the turn of the century, *Nemzeti Nőnevelés* scrutinized the practical and theoretical implications of women's situation in contemporary society and sought to initiate studied debates of the issues. Stetina and her husband had at least one child together, a daughter called Julia (born 8 January 1886 in Budapest), who became a teacher herself and, in 1932, secretary of the *Mária Dorothea Egyesület* (Mária Dorothea Association) for women teachers (see below).

Upon marriage, Stetina gave up her job to concentrate on family life, "after much anxious deliberation" (Katona Lajosné and Thuránszky 1933, 4). Yet within just two years (in 1883), she had resumed teaching at the Pest Institute, a position she would retain for the next 28 years. In 1890, Stetina took over from her husband as the editor of *Nemzeti Nőnevelés*, continuing in this capacity until 1915. Her (co-authored) study of teacher-training initiatives, *A polgári iskolai tanító- és tanítónőképzés* (Secondary school teacher training), was commissioned by the Hungarian Education Ministry and published on the occasion of the National Millenium celebrations in 1896. Articles published by Stetina in *Nemzeti Nőnevelés* emphasized the importance of women's earnings for the material welfare of families and for national economic development. Stetina promoted a vision of girls' education that integrated knowledge of a trade with economic and household management skills, religious instruction and a sense of social and moral responsibility.

In 1883, at a meeting of the *Népnevelők Egyesülete* (National Teachers' Association), Stetina called for a national organization to improve the intellectual skills and qualifications of women teachers. To this end, Janka Zirzen and Ilona Stetina (among others, including ***Sarolta Geőcze***) founded the *Mária Dorothea Egyesület* (*MDE*, Mária Dorothea Association) in 1885. The *MDE* became central to the national campaign for women's university admission. Stetina led the *MDE*'s section for women teachers (formed in 1887) and served as the Vice-President of the organization from 1889 until her death in 1932. In 1895, the *MDE* generated a debate on 'the woman question' in the national press. Contributions to this debate were edited and published by the *MDE* in the same year as a book, *A nőkérdés* (The woman question), in which Stetina suggested that all women learn to sew, embroider and practice horticulture, and that textile factories and horticultural plots of land replace the nation's tobacco factories.

Stetina was involved in the organization of many school curricula and active in many organizations for the advancement of women's education, including the *Országos Nőképző Egyesület* (National Association for Women's Education), the *Országos Katolikus Nőszövetség* (National Union of Catholic Women), the *Művészet és Művelődési Egyesület* (Arts and Education Association), the *Klotild-Egyesület* (Klotild Association–for the promotion and preservation of women's handicrafts) and the *Magyar Nemzeti Szövetség Szociálpolitikai Osztálya* (Social Policy Section of the Hungarian National Union). She also regarded international connections within the women's movement to be of the utmost significance for Hungary as a "small nation" (Berta 1932, 248) and was a long-standing member of the *Magyarországi Nőegyesületek Szövetsége* (*MNSz*, Alliance of Women's Associations in Hungary), founded in 1904 and (from that year) affiliated to the International Council of Women (ICW). In 1906, at a general meeting of the *MNSz*, Stetina opposed the cause of women's suffrage; however, she had openly changed her position on this issue by 1909. She served on the Board of Directors of the *Magyar Egyesület a Leánykereskedés Ellen* (Hungarian Association against the Traffic in Girls) and organized women's education sections for national congresses on university education (1896, 1926–1927). In 1911, the Ministry of Commerce made Ilona Stetina the director of Budapest's *Állami Nőipariskola* (State Women's Trade School), which had grown out of the 1874 *ONE* school. Stetina retained this position until 1926, during which time she travelled to Vienna, Berlin and Potsdam to study women's trade associations.

After World War I, Stetina was awarded a second class *Hadikereszt polgári érdemekért* (War Cross of Civil Merit) for her work organizing clothing provision for soldiers. With the demise of *Nemzeti Nőnevelés* (closed down by the Communists in 1919), Stetina became a member of the right-wing *Magyar Asszonyok Nemzeti Szövetsége* (*MANSz*, Hungarian National Women's Union), founded in 1918. She wrote for *Magyar Asszony* (Hungarian woman)–the official publication of *MANSz*–and organized and presided over the *MANSz* Women's Education Congress (held under the umbrella of the Women's Education Section of the Third National University Congress) in 1924. In 1927/28, the *Gyermekszeretet-Egyesület* (Child Welfare Association) was established under the auspices of *MANSz* with the support of the wife of the Hungarian Head of State, Mrs Miklos Horthy, and with Stetina as President. In 1931, Stetina was made an Honorary Member of the *Magyar Pedagógiai Társaság* (Hungarian Pedagogical Society), an organization she had joined in 1892 and to which she often delivered lectures on girls' education; on one such occasion (1922), she reprimanded mothers for allowing their daughters to indulge in frivolous activities, "exempting them from their household duties and not encouraging them in diligent study at school" [*Magyar Asszony* (June 1922): 16-17]. That particular lecture, published as a book the same year, became recommended reading for *MANSz* members. Other lectures, delivered in the interwar period to organizations such as the *MDE*, spoke of the necessity of national solidarity among women teachers and of the 'external' threat posed to women's industry in postwar Hungary by the "four regions of the world wishing to steal Hungarian women's handicraft work" (Berta 1932, 247).

In 1925, on her seventieth birthday, the Hungarian Head of State Miklos Horthy bestowed upon Stetina the regal title of *Iparoktatási Királyi Főigazgató* (Principal Director of Vocational Education) in recognition of her fifty years of work. In the last years of her life, Ilona Stetina was working on a project that had long been a dream of hers: a Hungarian teacher-training institution for women specializing in handicrafts along the lines of the famous *Lette Verein* in Germany. She died in Budapest on 25 April 1932 and was buried in Kerepesi Street Cemetery in an honorary grave provided by the city of Budapest.

Anna Loutfi
Doctoral Candidate, Department of History,
Central European University, Budapest

SOURCES

(B) Zirzen, Janka. *A budapesti VI. ker. állami tanítónőképző-intézet és a vele kapcsalatos gyakorló-iskola múltja és jelene, 1869-1885* (Budapest's sixth district state institute for the instruction of women teachers and its affiliated teacher-training schools, 1869-1885). Budapest, 1885.

(B) *Nemzeti Nőnevelés* (National women's education) (1890-1919).

(B) (Mrs) Csáky, Albin, ed. *A nőkérdés* (The woman question). Budapest: Mária Dorothea-egylet, 1895.

(B) *A Nő és a Társadalom* (Woman and society) (1909).

(B) *Egyesült Erővel* (With united strength) (1909-1910).

(B) *Magyar Asszony* (Hungarian woman) (1921-1932).

(B) Thuránszky, Irén. *A magyar tanítónők. Mária Dorothea Egyesületének félszázados története, 1885-1935* (Hungarian women teachers. The 50-year history of the Maria Dorothea Association of Hungarian women teachers, 1885-1935). Budapest, 1935.

(B) Deák, Gyula. *Polgári iskolai író-tanárok élete és munkái* (The lives and literary production of lower-level secondary school teachers). Budapest: Az Országos Polgári Iskolai Tanáregyesület, 1942.

(C) Kiss, Áron and Sebestyénné Ilona Stetina. *A polgári iskolai tanító és tanítónő-képzés* (Secondary school teacher training). Budapest, 1896.

(C) Stetina, Ilona. *Zirzen Janka, 1824-1904*. Budapest: Mária Dorothea Egyesülete, 1930.

(D) Szinnyei, József. *Sebestyén Gyuláné* (Mrs Gyula Sebestyén). In *Magyar írók* (Hungarian writers). Budapest, 1909, XII: 822-823.

(D) *Sebestyén Gyuláné* (Mrs Gyula Sebestyén). In Margit Bozzay. *Magyar Asszonyok Lexikona* (Encyclopedia of Hungarian women). Budapest, 1931, 839-840.

(D) Berta, Ilona. "Sebestyénné Stetina Ilona." In *Magyar Asszony* (June 1932): 246-249.

(D) Katona Lajosné and Irén Thuranszky. *Sebestyén Gyuláné Stetina Ilona emlékezete* (In memory of Stetina Ilona). Budapest: Mária Dorothea Egyesülete, 1933.

(E) Fericsán, Kálmán. *Tanítómesterek, mestertanítók* (Schoolmasters, master teachers). Budapest-Pécs, 2000.

SUBURG, Lilli (Caroline) (1841-1923)

Author, journalist, headmistress (of an elementary private girls' school); women's suffrage campaigner during the rise of the Estonian national movement.

Lilli Suburg, 1916, 75th jubilee at the Mari Raamot school of domestic economy in Sahkapuu, near the City of Tartu.

Lilli (Christian name Caroline) Suburg was born on 1 August 1841 in the township of Uue-Vändra, in the parish of Vändra. Her mother was Eva Suburg (born Nuut); her father, Toomas Suburg, was the keeper of the granary at the Rõusa estate. Soon after Lilli's birth, the family moved to the Vana-Vändra estate, where Toomas Suburg began working as an overseer and her mother as a cheese-maker. Lilli's parents earned a decent income and were soon able to lease the entire estate. The German language and way of life accompanied their prosperity.

Lilli's education began with governess tutorials, taken along with the children of the lord of the Rõusa manor. From 1852 to 1859, she continued her studies in the town of Pärnu, at Marie von Ditmar's private school and at the girls' high school in Pärnu.

Lilli suffered from poor health: in Tartu she was diagnosed as having erysipelas, which left ugly scars on her cheek. From then on, she never had her photograph taken without a scarf on her head. In Tartu, in 1869, Lilli passed the exams necessary to obtain a teaching certificate.

Meanwhile, the Suburgs founded the so-called Waldberg dairy-farming estate in Sikana, near Vändra. Lilli Suburg read extensively in those years: German fiction and philosophy (Johan W. Goethe, Friedrich Schiller, Friedrich G. Klopstock, Arthur Schopenhauer), texts by Thomas Carlyle, books addressing social and feminist questions and works on education by Eugenie John (pen-name 'Marlitt'), Jean-Jacques Rousseau and Johann Heinrich Pestalozzi.

The 1860s marked an era of 'national awakening' in Estonia. In the 1870s, the issue of women's education entered the Estonian press through the writing of Carl Robert Jakobson (1841-1882), an Estonian national leader, writer, farmer and pedagogue. He argued that the education of women would prevent them from becoming snobbish 'town misses' with affected Baltic-German manners. Jakobson had come to live at Vändra in 1872 and, from 1873, often visited the Suburg family.

At the instigation of Jakobson, Lilli Suburg wrote her first original (autobiographical) short story "Liina," published in 1877. Reprints of "Liina" were issued in 1884 and 1927 (and in Finnish in 1892). Some Estonian literary critics saw it as a sentimental yet ambitious piece of prose; its descriptions of the inner struggles of an Estonian girl against Baltic-German manners at school seemed an embittered attack on society by a physically scarred, thirty-year-old female writer. The story provoked sharp reactions within Baltic-German literary circles and discussions in Estonian national newspapers. Lilli Suburg became known as the first female author to write in Estonian; public interest in her was further intensified on account of her activities on behalf of women's suffrage. In this period, again at Jakobson's suggestion, Lilli Suburg turned to journalism. In 1878, she was offered the position of editor of the *Perno Postimees* (Pärnu courier, founded in 1857). Over the following year, she tried to bring the conservative paper politically closer to the radical *Sakala* (Viljandi courier).

In 1880, Lilli Suburg adopted a young orphan, Anna Wiegandt. This was a bold move in a society based on traditional family models. It required decisiveness and self-confidence. In Suburg's later writings, one finds references to the impact this decision had upon her life. In 1880, together with her adopted daughter, she moved to Pärnu and earned her living by giving private lessons.

With the help of her sister, Anette, who was working in Russia, Lilli Suburg began plans to set up a private elementary school that would teach Estonian girls in the Estonian language. However, since only religious instruction was permitted in the Estonian language, Lilli Suburg opened her private elementary school for Estonian girls as a German-language school, with subjects taught in German. Even so, in the Baltic-German seaside resort of Pärnu, the school aroused indignation not only among Baltic-Germans, but also among snobbish Estonians. Despite this hostility, Lilli Suburg was an active social figure: to raise funds for the school, of which she was headmistress, she staged plays and organized charity bazaars. In 1885, Lilli Suburg moved her school from Pärnu to the Viljandi. With a building, students and financial security, Lilli Suburg could begin to pay greater attention to the personal development of her students.

Alongside her teaching in Viljandi, Lilli Suburg continued her publicist activity. In keeping with the style of her short story "Liina," she wrote rather sentimental pieces of prose in instructive tones and in noticeably clumsy, archaic Estonian language [see for example her "Maarja ja Eeva: ehk suguluse truuus ja armastus mehe vasta" (Maarja and Eeva: or relation's loyalty and love for man, 1881) and "Leeni" (1887), a sentimental story of a girl married off against her will, whose body and spirit whither through hard labor].

For years, Lilli Suburg attempted to obtain a permit from the Russian authorities to publish a women's magazine. In May 1888, she became publisher and editor of the first Estonian women's magazine, *Linda: Esimene literatuurlik ja ajakohane ajakiri Eesti naisterahvale* (Linda: The first literary periodical for the Estonian woman), founded in October 1887. *Linda* was meant to teach women awareness of their own rights. Leading articles by both Western authors (translated) and Estonians were usually dedicated to feminist issues such as enfranchisement or women's emancipation in general, but the magazine also covered various aspects of social life such as home and school, and was reviewed in the German press. To win more readers, Lilli Suburg included reviews of scientific news and debates (among other educational topics) aimed at a general readership. She edited *Linda* until 1893 and for a short period in 1894.

After 1899, Suburg lived with her adopted daughter Anna Wiegandt (after her marriage Anna Lammas) and her son-in-law in Oomuli (on the farmstead of Eger), where she established a small private school for Estonian children (1900–1906).

Lilli Suburg's last story, "Linda, rahva tütar" (Linda, the people's daughter), appeared in 1900, in a supplement of the *Postimees* (Courier). It described the ideal goals of an educated Estonian woman: to be self-confident, to have the opportunity to study, to enter professional life and have a good family and home. After 1900, Suburg began writing her memoirs.

As an old lady, Suburg could not take part in the first women's congress organized by the *Eesti Naisliit* (Union of Estonian Women's Organizations) in Tartu in 1917, but she sent her greetings to the participants. In 1916, she was made an Honorary Member of the *Tartu Naisselts* (Tartu Women's Society, founded in 1907) and the *Valga Naisselts* (Valga Women's Society). Estonian women's organizations held jubilee festivities in her name and the Lilli Suburg Scholarship Foundation was set up to support poor female students at Tartu University (1923).

Lilli Suburg died in Valga while visiting her sisters on 8 February 1923, and was buried in Vändra cemetery. The Vändra Women's Society cared for her grave and in 1926, on the initiative of the *Eesti Naisorganisatioonide Liit* (Union of Estonian Women's Organizations, founded in 1920), erected a memorial upon it with the text: "Lilli Suburgile–eesti naised" (To Lilli Suburg–from Estonian women).

Sirje Tamul and **Andra Lätt**
Tartu University

Translated from the Estonian by Leili Kostabi, Tartu University.

SOURCES

(A) *Eesti Kirjandusmuuseum. Eesti Kirjanduslooline arhiiv* (The Estonian Cultural History Archives of the Estonian Literary Museum): Stock 122 folio 6:6, Stock 193 folio 45:24, Stock 194 folio 22:33.

(B) *Tartu Ülikooli Raamatukogu* (Tartu University Library): R B- 342, *Eesti Kirjandusmuuseum. Eesti Kirjanduslooline arhiiv* (The Estonian Cultural History Archives of the Estonian Literary Museum): KMAR AjI 253, *Linda*. Annual volume: Lilli Suburg, ed. (Viljandi, 1887-1894); Heinrich Prants, ed. (Pärnu, 1894-1897); Anton Jürgenstein, ed. (Pärnu, 1897-1902); Jaan Tõnisson, ed. (Tartu, 1903-1905).

(C) Suburg, Lilli. *Maarja ja Eeva: ehk suguluse truuus ja armastus mehe vasta* (Maarja and Eeva: or loyalty of relations and love for man). Tartu, 1881; 1927.

(C) Suburg, Lilli. *Linda, rahva tütar* (Linda, the people's daughter). Tartu: Postimees. Lisaleht, 1900.

(C) Suburg, Lilli. *Suburgi perekonna elulugu* (The Suburg family). Tartu: Eesti Kirjandus, 1923-1924.

(C) Suburg, Lilli. *Kogutud kirjatööd* (The complete works of Lilli Suburg). Aino Undla-Põldmäe, ed. Tallinn: Eesti Raamat, 2002.

(E) Raamot, Mari. *Minu mälestused* (Memoirs). Toronto: Kirjastus Kultuur, 1962, 43-57; 289-326.

(E) Kivimäe, Sirje. "Estnische Frauenbildung in der zweiten Hälfte des 19. Jahrhunderts" (On Estonian girls' education in the second half of the nineteenth century). *Zeitschrift für Ostforschung, Länder und Völker im östlichen Mitteleuropa* (Journal for Eastern European history. States and nations in East Central Europe). Lüneburg: Institut Nordostdeutsches Kulturwerk 2 (1992): 281-308.

(E) Puhvel, Madli. *Symbol of Dawn. The life and times of the 19th Century Estonian poet Lydia Koidula*. Tartu: Tartu University Press, 1999.

(E) Kivimaa, Katrin. "Naine rahvusliku mõtte ja tunde kujundina 19. aajandi teise poole eesti kunstis" (Woman as the symbol of national thought and feeling in Estonian art in the second half of the nineteenth century). *Ariadne Lõng. Nais–ja meesuuringute ajakiri* (Ariadne's clew. Estonian joumal of gender studies). Tallinn: Eesti Naisuurimus- ja Teabekeskus (ENUT) 1, no. 2 (2001): 66.

(E) Põldmaa, Pilvi. *Ajakiri Linda aastatel 1900-1905: kujundus, illustratsioonid ja kunstireproduktsioonid* (*Linda* magazine from 1900 to 1905: design, illustrations and reproductions). Bachelorwork, Tartu University, 2002.

SVĚTLÁ, Karolína (pseudonym; born Johanna Rottová) (1830–1899)

Czech novelist and short fiction writer; founder and President (1871–1880) of *the Ženský výrobní spolek český* (Women's Czech Production Society).

Karolína Světlá was born Johanna Rottová on 24 February 1830, into a patrician family that lived in Prague's 'Old Town.' Her father, Eustace Rott, had come to Prague from the central Bohemian town of Český Brod, from a Czech family that, despite its enforced return to Roman Catholicism after 1620, had retained sympathy for Czech Brethren Protestantism, as Světlá's writing would later show. After an apprenticeship in a trading house, Rott opened his own stationery business. Světlá's mother was the daughter of a Rhineland German who had come to Bohemia during the Napoleonic wars, married a Czech woman and settled there.

The influence of late eighteenth-century liberal thinking was also part of Světlá's upbringing, but though her father attended the Sunday sermons of the theologian Bernard Bolzano, he actively discouraged his daughter's love of letters and was not interested in the nascent Czech patriotism then emerging in the linguistic, literary and historical scholarship of the period. Karolina attended a German school, reportedly until a notebook of her early writings (in German) was found and she was removed from school and educated at home. It was there, at the age of fourteen, that she met Petr Mužák (1821–1892), the family music teacher whom she married in 1852 and from whose birthplace (Světlá pod Ještědem, in the hills near Liberec in northern Bohemia) she took her pseudonym: 'Světlá.' Mužák introduced the family to the ideas of the Czech scholar-patriots and, in 1849, introduced Světlá to ***Božena Němcová*** (1820–1862), then making her appearance as the leading Czech woman writer of the period. Němcová, who would profoundly influence Světlá's intellectual development, corresponded with the young Světlá for several years and the two women exchanged ideas on the social and emotional emancipation of women and literature, particularly the works of George Sand. Both Němcová and Sand served as literary models for Světlá and the latter wrote under a portrait of Sand for the length of her literary career.

After the death of her daughter in infancy (1852), Světlá fell into depression and was taken by her husband to convalesce in his home region, where she threw herself into writing as a means of coming to terms with her loss. The region thus came to have a special significance for her and formed the setting of her most important and popular works. Her first short story, "Dvojí probuzení" (A double awakening), was published in 1858 in the first *Máj* (Spring) almanac. The almanac's title, taken from the 1836 poem by Karel Hynek Mácha (1810–1836), suggested the 'rebirth' of Czech literary life after a decade of neo-absolutist repression. *Máj* marked the emergence of a major new generation of Czech writers, including Vítězslav Hálek (1835–74) and Jan Neruda (1834–1891), whose works display a shift away from the nostalgic idealism found in Němcová's fiction, towards the techniques and thematic preoccupations of Realist writing.

Close friends, Světlá and Neruda also became protagonists in one of Czech literature's best-known love stories. Neruda expressed his love for her openly and passionately, but Světlá chose to remain faithful to her husband, though she found him dull and uninspiring. Some critics have seen echoes of their relationship in Světlá's portrayal of lovers kept apart by the strictures of social convention, especially in her artistically most successful novel, *Vesnický román* (A village novel, 1867). Here, the male central character is shaped into an ultimately 'good man' by the three women in his life but, having been married once, is dissuaded by his mother from marrying the woman he loves, both finally devoting themselves selflessly but joylessly to good works. In this context, Světlá's refusal of Neruda may be seen as her own particular internalization of the philosophy of self-discovery through self-denial and altruism, elaborated by Rousseau in *La Nouvelle Héloïse* (1761).

Světlá's critical attitude to prevailing social norms is evident in her early short stories, set amid the Prague burgher and aristocratic society of her own upbringing. In these stories, her heroines trace Světlá's own journey to a greater awareness of self and to a realization of the injustices and inadequacies of social norms, particularly in relation to women. Most significant in this respect is the novel *První Češka* (The first Czech woman, 1861), in which a woman acquires greater knowledge of herself and the world by escaping to the countryside and ultimately marrying a self-educated farmworker. The end of the story depicts her sons on the Prague barricades in 1848.

Světlá continued to explore the recent historical period in other works, yet it is as the "creator of the Czech rural novel" (Neruda) that her literary impact has been most felt, notably in *Vesnický román* and the more widely read, though technically inferior, *Kříž u potoka* (The cross by the stream, 1868). Essentially these works reflect a shift from static, stately images of the rural idyll to dynamic, almost ethnographic descriptions of rural life, moving away from characters as types towards characters (male and female) as individuals, particularly through the description and psychologization of emotion. The flaws in her writing may be attributed to the transition in Czech prose writing that her works reflect: sentimentalism and didacticism clash with irony and ambiguity; realist characterization and plots jar with elements of schematicism. In her fiction, the theme of women's emancipation, though evident in her accounts of the intellectual awakening of female characters and in her more complex portrayal of women, is overshadowed by a broader moral concern for the individual, particularly when compared with the fiction of her less celebrated sister, Sofie Podlipská (1833-1897), who translated Sand into Czech and whose focus on the contemporary situation of women and on female experience is ultimately more exclusive. Světlá however, like ***Němcová*** before her, created her own literary descendants such as ***Teréza Nováková*** (1853-1912).

Světlá's impact on the women's rights movement was most striking in her non-literary activity, notably her close involvement, from 1871, in the founding of the *Ženský výrobní spolek český* (Women's Czech Production Society), of which she was the President until 1880. The original mission of this organization was the elimination of female poverty, which had been exacerbated by the Prussian-Austrian War (1866). In a few years, the society had grown into 42 branches in Bohemia and Moravia, each with a strong focus on giving women greater opportunities to train for careers of their own in a variety of vocational schools and providing them with employment. In the 1860s, Světlá also helped establish cultural organizations that sought to promote Czech patriotism (in competition with German counterparts) while ensuring women's interests were taken into account. These included the women's section of the *Sokol* gymnastics and physical exercise movement, the arts and humanities society *Umělecká beseda* (Czech Society of Artists) and the first Czech women's society, *Americký klub dam* (American Ladies' Club), in which 'American' stood for 'pioneering' and 'modern.'

As a result of an illness in 1875, Světlá went blind and dictated her subsequent works to her niece, Anežka Čermáková-Sluková (1864-1947). Between 1878 and 1897, she published several volumes of memoirs, correspondence and other documentary materials containing ideas on literature, society and the position of women, alongside more intimate accounts of her life and friendships. She lived her last years in total seclusion and died in Prague on 7 September 1899.

Rajenda Chitnis
University of Bristol

SOURCES

(C) Světlá, K. *Sebrané spisy* (Collected works). Prague: L. Mazáč, 1939-1940.

(D) Hrzalová, H. "Karolína Světlá." In R, Havel and Jirí Opelík, eds. *Slovník českých spisovatelů* (A dictionary of Czech writers). Prague: Československý spisovatel, 1964, 474-75.

(D) Špičák, J. *Karolína Světlá*. Prague: Svobodné slovo, 1966.

(D) Janáčková, J. "Karolína Světlá." In Léhar, Jan, et. al. *Česká literature od počátků k dnešku* (Czech literature from its origins until today). Prague: Lidové noviny, 1998, 275–281.

(E) Balajka, B., et. al., *Přehledné dějiny literatury I* (A survey history of literature, vol. 1). Prague: Státní pedagogické nakladatelství, 1970.

(E) Pynsent, R. B., ed. *The Everyman Companion to East European Literature*. London: J. M. Dent, 1993.

(E) Machala, L. and Eduard Petrů, eds. *Panorama české literatury* (A panorama of Czech literature). Olomouc: Rubico, 1994.

SVOLOU, Maria (born Desypri) (1892?-1976)

Greek feminist and socialist leader during the interwar period; inspector for the National Bureau of Employment; elected member of the National Council of the Liberated Greek Territory; Deputy of the *Eniaia Dimokratiki Aristera* (Unified Democratic Left); co-founder of the *Syndesmos gia ta Dikaiomata tis Gynaikas/Ligue Héllénique pour le droit des femmes* (Greek League for Women's Rights); co-founder (1964) of the *Panelladiki Enossi Gynaikon* (Panhellenic Union of Women).

Little is yet known about the life of Maria Svolou. Since no biography of her exists, we are only able to glimpse her career through her writings, her public activities (mentioned in periodicals, newspapers etc.), her parliamentary career, as well as through the life of her husband, of whom she was an admirer but with whose social democratic beliefs she sometimes disagreed. Parts of Svolou's personal archives were lost when her house was plundered during World War II.

Maria Desypri was born in Athens and lived for a couple of years in Piraeus. She was one of four daughters. When she was very young, her family moved to Larissa, where her father Georges Desypros (?-1915) was appointed director of the Greek National Bank's regional branch. The family moved back to Athens after his death.

The only information available concerning Maria's formal education is that she attended the *Arsakeion* School of Larissa (for girls). She obtained her degree around 1907. In June 1916, she obtained a Certificate of French Studies and in 1919, a license to teach French from the Ecclesiastical and Public Education Ministries.

In 1921, Desypri began working as an Inspector of Employment for the Ministry of National Economy, where she met her future husband, the academic jurist and politician Alexandros Svolos (?-1956). They married in 1923 and stayed together throughout their lives. They had no children, in accordance with her wishes.

Maria Svolou's public career seems to have begun with her involvement in the founding committee of the *Syndesmos gia ta Dikaiomata tis Gynaikas/Ligue Héllénique pour le droit des femmes* (Greek League for Women's Rights), a liberal feminist group. The League was affiliated to the International Woman Suffrage Alliance (IWSA). Svolou played an important role as a leading member (General Secretary) of the

League between 1920 and 1932, the latter year being one of internal disagreements within the League, resulting in Svolou's resignation. From that time on, Svolou would become convinced that no real equality between the sexes could exist without intrinsic changes in general social and economic relations, leading to her involvement with the socialist movement.

Up until 1932, Svolou had concentrated on working towards social reforms on behalf of women, especially rural and working class women, although she disagreed with special 'protective legislation' for women only. In 1925, she persuaded the Board of the League to establish an *Esperini Emporiki Scholi Gynaikon Ypallilon* (Evening Commercial School for Women Employees), which offered professional training to women seeking employment in either the public or private sectors. In 1929, she also inaugurated (through the League) the *Papastrateios Scholi Paichnidion kai Diakosmitikis* (Papastrateios School of Children's Toys and Decorative Arts), which sought to help poor young people of both sexes find work by means of learning an applied craft. She continued to work for the *Papastrateios Scholi* until 1936, as its General Director.

Her detailed reports on Greek women's wages (as reported to the National Bureau of Employment) and her memoranda to the International Labor Office constitute valuable sources of historical information concerning the working and living conditions of women in interwar Greece. From 1932 to 1936, she was nominated Associated Member of the International Experts' Committee of the International Labor Organization.

In the period 1920–1932, Maria Svolou wrote a number of articles for publication in the League's periodical, *O Agonas tis Gynaikas* (Woman's struggle) and in certain daily newspapers, such as *Eleftheron Vima* (Free tribune) and *I Vradyni* (The evening). In these articles, she promoted central tenets of the League such as full equality and citizenship rights for Greek women. As General Secretary of the League, she also initiated women's suffrage campaigns; however, the vote proved to be more difficult to attain than she had originally thought. To further the suffrage cause, she represented the League at some of the congresses organized by the International Alliance of Women for Suffrage and Equal Citizenship (IAWSEC), among them the Tenth Congress in Paris (1926), where she was elected to a committee on equal working conditions for men and women.

After her retirement from the *Syndesmos gia ta Dikaiomata tis Gynaikas*, Svolou contributed to the establishment of the *Syndesmos Ergazomenon Gynaikon* (Association of Working Women) as a supporter of the Greek Communist Party. At the same time, during 1934–36, she cooperated with former feminist associates from the League (e.g. ***Avra Theodoropoulou***, among others). With several Greek women's associations, these women organized political actions against fascism and war and created the *Panellinia Epitropi Gynaikon enantia ston Polemo kai to Fasismo* (Panhellenic Committee of Women against War and Fascism), of which Maria Svolou was secretary. It was at this time that Svolou was appointed to the Board of the International Committee against Fascism.

Svolou's political activities were dramatically interrupted by the establishment of a dictatorship under Ioannis Metaxas (4 August 1936), which dissolved all democratic organizations and persecuted socialists and communists. Svolou's husband was forced to leave the university and exiled to the Greek islands. Under such difficult political and personal circumstances, Maria Svolou was obliged to follow her husband into exile, where she tried to improve conditions in the education of local people.

During the first years of the Axis Occupation of Greece, Maria Svolou worked for the *Ethnikos Organismos Christianikis Allilengyiis* (National Organization of Christian Solidarity), which provided food to starving children; in 1941 she was partly responsible for inspecting milk distribution in Athens.

In June 1943, Maria Svolou and her husband decided to move to the *Eleftheri Ellada* (Liberated Greek Territory). This part of Greece had been liberated by Greek resistance troops, organized for the most part by the *Eniaio Antifasistiko Metopo* (Unified Antifascist Front, backed by the Greek Communist Party) and the *Enossi Laïkis Dimokratias* (Union of Popular Democracy), in which Maria Svolou's husband was a leading figure. Alexandros Svolos was later appointed President of the *Politiki Epitropi Ethnikis Apeleftherosis* (*PEEA*, Political Committee of National Liberation). In April 1944, Maria Svolou was elected National Councilor, along with four other female National Councilors, at the elections organized by the *PEEA*.

Even after the liberation of all Greek territories, Svolou continued to offer her services as secretary of the *Ethniki Allilengyii* (National Mutual Aid Association), a multiparty social organization established during the Axis Occupation, aimed at providing relief for those in Greece still in need. In May 1945, she was elected Vice-President of the reorganized *Ethniki Allilengyii Ellados* (National Mutual Aid Association of Greece). Svolou also wrote a number of articles published in the organization's periodical *Ethniki Allilengyii*, on children's social welfare and Greek women's equality with men.

In 1945, Maria Svolou was elected to the Administrative Committee of the *Idryma Perithalpseos Ethnikon Agoniston* (Relief Organization for National Combatants); from January 1946, this organization cooperated with the *Panellinia Enosis Omiron kai Agnooumenon 1940–44* (Panhellenic Union of Hostages and Missing People of 1940–1944), organizing a polyclinic for people with no access to medical treatement. Most members were volunteers.

During the years 1948–49, Svolou was arrested for her involvement in the Greek resistance and her political commitment to the Left. She was illegally detained at the First Athens Police Station for months without being prosecuted and later transported to the *Fylakes Averof* (Averof Prison) in Athens, where she remained for almost a year. During her stay in the Averof Prison, she recorded in writing the narratives of her fellow female prisoners.

Upon being released at the end of the Greek Civil War (1949), Svolou decided to withdraw from activism at the request of her husband, who expressed fears for her well being. He believed that Maria had been imprisoned instead of him since he, as a socialist deputy and a leading socialist figure in the Greek Parliament, had become a target for the anti-democratic policies of the official Greek state. During the Greek Civil War, Alexandros Svolou was courtmartialed for "inciting Greek people to national discord," an accusation annuled only later, in 1951.

After her husband's death in 1956, four years after political rights had been granted to Greek women, Maria Svolou decided to join the *Eniaia Dimokratiki Aristera* (Unified Democratic Left), a party supported mainly by communists and socialists. Svolou was appointed to the party's Administrative Committee and decided to become a parliamentary candidate; she was elected Deputy of Athens' B district at the 11 May 1958 elections and re-elected for the period October 1961-September 1963 (when she retired). During her parliamentary career, she focused on issues of social security, the working conditions of Greek industrial workers (especially women), environmental pollution, gender equality, youth culture and repressive features of the Greek political system. As a deputy, she also had the opportunity to travel to certain Eastern European countries.

In 1964, Svolou helped establish the *Panelladiki Enossi Gynaikon* (Panhellenic Union of Women) and became a member of the Union's Administrative Committee. Articles written by Svolou between 1956 and 1966 were published in the newspaper *I Avghi* (The dawn).

It was around this time that Svolou began suffering from heart disease and was ordered to take medication, adopt a special diet and rest. Soon after the Greek Coup d'état (21 April 1967), police officials of the Colonels' Dictatorial Regime came to arrest her but did not pursue the matter when they were confronted by a sick and elderly woman. Little is known about her death, which occurred on 3 June 1976.

In the ardor of Maria Svolou's speeches and articles lies also a clarity of opinion, revealing the profile of a woman utterly dedicated to the struggle against male privilege, social inequality and capitalism. Although she played an important role in Greek political history, and in spite of her continuous efforts to combine her feminism with her socialist ideas, she continues to be omitted from mainstream Greek historical bibliographies, except in more recent feminist works.

Dimitra Samiou
Historian, Nea Smyrne

SOURCES

(A) *Archeia Synchronis Koinonikis Istorias* (*ASKI*, Archives of Modern Social History), part of Maria Svolou's personal archives.

(A) *ASKI*, unpublished papers of the *Gynaikeia Bod'thitiki Epitropi* (Women's Auxiliary Committee) of the *Eniaia Dimokratiki Aristera* (Unified Democratic Left).
(A) *ASKI*, draft biography of Maria Svolou by Eleni Rigou, part of an unfinished Ph.D. thesis (no date).
(B) The International Alliance of Women for Suffrage and Equal Citizenship. *Report of Tenth Congress. Paris, France, May 30th to June 6th, 1926.* London: The London Caledonian Press, 1926, 191.
(C) Desypri, Maria. *I gynaika kai i koinoniki pronoia* (Woman and welfare). Athens, 1922.
(C) Svolou, Maria. "I thesi tou feminismou stin Ellada" (Situating feminism in Greece). *O Agonas tis Gynaikas* (Woman's struggle), nos. 9-10 (1924): 16-18; no. 11 (1924): 2-4; no. 12 (1924): 2-4.
(C) Svolou, Maria. "To dikio tis tilefonitrias" (The rights of the woman telephone operator). *O Agonas tis Gynaikas* (Woman's struggle), no. 20 (1925): 7.
(C) Svolou, Maria. "Gyro apo tin gynaikeia psifo" (Some ideas related to the female vote). *Eleftheron Vema* (Free tribune) (17 August 1925).
(C) Svolou, Maria. "Gia tin eirini" (For peace). *O Agonas tis Gynaikas* (Woman's struggle), no. 27-28 (December 1925-January 1926): 14-17.
(C) Svolou, Maria. "Georgiki oikokyriki morfosi" (Agricultural domestic education). *O Agonas tis Gynaikas* (Woman's struggle), no. 31 (1926): 3-5.
(C) Svolou, Maria. "Ekloges" (Elections). *O Agonas tis Gynaikas* (Woman's struggle), nos. 35-36 (1926): 1.
(C) Svolou, Maria. "Oi ergatries tapitourgias" (Women carpet factory workers). *O Agonas tis Gynaikas* (Woman's struggle), no. 41 (1927): 1-2.
(C) Svolou, Maria. "To D' synedrio tis Mikris Entent Gynaikon" (The fourth congress of the Little Entente of Women). *O Agonas tis Gynaikas* (Woman's struggle), nos. 46-47 (1927): 1-3.
(C) Svolou, Maria. "To neo elliniko syntagma schetika me ti gynaika" (The new Greek Constitution on women). *O Agonas tis Gynaikas* (Woman's struggle), nos. 48-49 (1927): 3-4.
(C) Svolou, Maria. "To evdomo synedrio gia tin katapolemisi tis somatemporias gynaikon kai paidion" (Seventh congress against the trafficking of women and children). *O Agonas tis Gynaikas* (Woman's struggle), nos. 48-49 (1927): 5-8.
(C) Svolou, Maria. "I gynaika sto dimo kai stin koinotita" (Woman's work in the municipalities). *O Agonas tis Gynaikas* (Woman's struggle), no. 63 (1928): 1-4.
(C) Svolou, Maria. "I episkepsi ton xenon feministrion. Oi dialexeis" (A visit from foreign feminists. Lectures). *O Agonas tis Gynaikas* (Woman's struggle), no. 68 (1928): 2-7.
(C) Svolou, Maria. "I prostasia tis gynaikas stin ergasia" (The protection of women at work). *O Agonas tis Gynaikas* (Woman's struggle), no. 70 (1928): 7.
(C) Svolou, Maria. "Diakosmitiki morfosi" (Decorative education). *O Agonas tis Gynaikas* (Woman's struggle), no. 87 (1929): 1-2.
(C) Svolou, Maria. "Oi ergazomenes se diogmo" (Working women's persecution). *O Agonas tis Gynaikas* (Woman's struggle), no. 95 (1929): 1-2.
(C) Svolou, Maria. "I dimotiki psifos" (The municipal vote). *O Agonas tis Gynaikas* (Woman's struggle), nos. 98-99 (1929): 1.
(C) Svolou, Maria. "I proti niki" (The first victory). *O Agonas tis Gynaikas* (Woman's struggle), no. 107 (1929): 1-2.

(C) Svolou, Maria. "O diogmos exakolouthi" (The persecution continues). *O Agonas tis Gynaikas* (Woman's struggle), no. 116 (1930): 1-2.

(C) Svolou, Maria. "O diogmos tis ypallilou kai oi epangelmatikes organoseis" (The persecution of women employees and professional organizations). *O Agonas tis Gynaikas* (Woman's struggle), no. 117 (1930): 3-4.

(C) Svolou, Maria. "Gia tin katargisi tou kratikou diakanonismou" (For the abolition of the state regulation [of prostitution]). *O Agonas tis Gynaikas* (Woman's struggle), no. 117 (1930): 4-5.

(C) Svolou, Maria. "Dyo metra–dyo stathma" (Two legislative measures–two responses). *O Agonas tis Gynaikas* (Woman's struggle), no. 119 (1930): 1-2.

(C) Svolou, Maria. "To ergazomeno paidi" (The working child). *O Agonas tis Gynaikas* (Woman's struggle), no. 131 (1930): 2-5.

(C) Svolou, Maria. "To psema" (The lie). *O Agonas tis Gynaikas* (Woman's struggle), no. 132 (1931): 2-3.

(C) Svolou, Maria. "I daskala mitera" (The mother teacher), *O Agonas tis Gynaikas* (Woman's struggle), no. 139 (1931): 1-2.

(C) Svolou, Maria. "I somatemporia kai i KTE" (Trafficking and the League of Nations). *O Agonas tis Gynaikas* (Woman's struggle), no. 142 (1931): 6-8.

(C) Svolou, Maria. "Ta politika dikaiomata tis Ellinidas" (Greek woman's political rights). *Nea Ellada. Dekapenthimeri Politiki Epitheorisi tis Kentrikis Epitropis tou EAM* (New Greece. Fortnightly political review of the Central Committee of the National Liberation Front), no. 1 (5 November 1944): 6-7.

(C) Maria Svolou's interpellations in the Greek Parliament (1958-63). In *Vouli ton Ellinon* (The Greek Parliament). *Evretirion Syzitiseon tou Koinovouliou 1946-1967* (Index of the Discussions of Parliament). Athens, 1984.

(E) Tsirimokos, Ilias. *Alexandros Svolos. I diki mas alithia* (Alexandros Svolos. Our own truth). Athens, 1962.

(E) Partsalidou, Avra. *Anamnisis ap' ti zoi tis OKNE* (Reminiscences from the life of the Organization of Greek Communist Youth). Athens, 1976.

(E) Avdela, Efi and Angelika Psarra. *O feminismos stin Ellada tou Mesopolemou. Mia anthologia* (Feminism in interwar Greece. An anthology). Athens: Gnosi, 1985.

(E) Moschou-Sakorrafou, Sasa. *Istoria tou Ellinikou feministikou kinimatos* (A history of the Greek feminist movement). Athens, 1990.

(E) Liakos, Antonis. *Ergasia kai politiki stin Ellada tou Mesopolemou. To Diethnes Grafeio Ergasias kai i anadysi ton koinonikon thesmon* (Labor and politics in interwar Greece: the International Labor Organization and the emergence of social institutions). Athens, 1993.

(E) Psarra, Angelika. "I 8 tou Marti, oi kommounistries kai i politiki: mia mera sta ASKI" (Eighth of March, women communists and politics: one day in the Archives of Modern Social History). *Archeiotaxio (ASKI)*, no. 5 (May 2003): 64-72.

(E) O 'Éos' tis Kyriakis. "I Dido Sotiriou kai to gynaikeio kinima" (Dido Sotiriou and the women's movement). *Kyriakatiki Elephtherotypia* (3 October 2004): 53-55.

(E) Interview with Zoi Svolou by Dimitra Samiou, [p.] 17.

SZELĄGOWSKA, Anna (1880-1962)

Polish feminist; member of several national and international women's organizations; labor and education activist; publicist; member of the Polish Senate (1938–1939).

Anna Szelągowska (*nee* Paradowska) was born in Warsaw on 20 July 1880, into a prosperous family. After graduating from a private school in 1895, she enrolled–against her parents' wishes–in the first private high school to accept women as students: Izabella Smolikowska's Commercial High School, from which she graduated in 1898. A few months later, her father's death forced her to take a job in order to be able to support her mother and brothers. From 1900, she worked as an office clerk while studying philosophy and social sciences at the so-called 'Flying University,' an underground university for women (Russian universities did not then admit women).

She first learned of the women's liberation movement through the *Czytelnia dla kobiet* (Reading Room for Women) led by ***Paulina Kuczalska-Reinschmit***, and soon became Secretary of the *Polskie Stowarzyszenie Równouprawnienia Kobiet* (Polish Women's Rights Association). In addition to her feminist activities, Szelągowska was also involved in the labor movement, as was her first husband Aleksander Hertz (1879-1928), a socialist bank clerk and future founder and Executive Director of the illustrious Polish film production company *Sfinks*. Even though Szelągowska never officially belonged to the *Polska Partia Socjalistyczna* (*PPS*, Polish Socialist Party), she worked for the *PPS* and acquired the nickname 'comrade Nina.' The Hertzs' Warsaw apartment witnessed many *PPS* meetings and in 1905, the couple founded the *Związek Zawodowy Pracowników Prywatnych Instytucji Bankowych Królestwa Polskiego* (Labor Union for Employees of Private Banking Institutions of the Kingdom of Poland), the first trade organization of bank clerks on the Polish territories. A year later, Szelągowska became a member of the Labor Union's Executive Board. She was among the founders of the *Towarzystwo Zawodowego Kształcenia Kobiet* (Women's Professional Education Society) and taught bookkeeping at the society's supplementary classes for shopkeepers. In 1913, she joined the Labor Union of Bookkeepers. In 1915, a year after she had been dismissed from her post as bookkeeper (depression had severely hit the banking sector), she was made an Honorable Member of the Labor Union for Employees of Private Banking Institutions. The title was a token of respect for the first and only woman on the Board.

Szelągowska spent the World War I years in Warsaw. From 1919 to 1920, she was a member of the *Koło Opieki nad Ochotniczą Ligą Kobiet* (Support Society for the Women's Voluntary Legion), the first independent command of women soldiers in the Polish territories. From 1920 to 1926 (i.e. after Poland's independence in 1918), Szelągowska worked for the Bank of the United Polish Territories. In 1927, she became a member of the Executive Board of the Cooperative Bank of Entrepreneurs and Merchants. Up until 1925, she had also belonged to the Scientific Committee of the Labor Union of Accountants; in 1932, she became a member of the Auditing Commission of this Union. Two years later, in 1934, the Ministry of Internal Affairs appointed her to the Auditing Commission of Warsaw City Hall, where she dealt with finances, accounting and the city budget. In 1936, Warsaw City Hall appointed her to the Auditing Commission of the Municipal Savings Bank. In the same year, she became an accounting expert for the Warsaw District Court. For her achievements, she was decorated with the Golden Cross of Merit by the Polish President on 10 November 1931.

In spite of her numerous professional duties, Szelągowska was an active participant in the Polish feminist movement. In 1919, she joined the *Klub Polityczny Kobiet Postępowych* (Progressive Women's Political Club) and during the parliamentary election of 1927, became a member of the *Demokratyczny Komitet Wyborczy Kobiet Polskich* (Executive Council of the Democratic Electoral Committee of Polish Women). In 1928, along with ***Zofia Moraczewska***, she co-founded the *Związek Pracy Obywatelskiej Kobiet* (Women's Association for Civil Labor) and was a long-standing member of the Association's Board of Directors. In 1929, the delegates of all Polish women's organizations elected Szelągowska Chair of the *Komitet Wystawy Pracy Kobiet* (Interunion Committee of the Women's Labor Exhibition) at the Polish National Exhibition in Poznan. Szelągowska also chaired the *Polskie Zjednoczenie Kobiet Pracujących Zawodowo* (Polish Union of Professional Women), was a member of the *Towarzystwo Oświaty Zawodowej* (Society of Professional Education) and cooperated with the *Instytut Oświaty Pracowniczej* (Institute of Labor Education) in Warsaw–the latter two both progressive organizations.

Strongly supporting the idea of international cooperation, Szelągowska became Vice-Chair of the *Rada Narodowa Polek* (National Council of Polish Women, founded in 1922), which became affiliated with the International Council of Women in 1924. In keeping with her pacifist ideas, she joined the *Towarzystwo Przyjaciół Ligi Narodów* (Friends' Society of the League of Nations) and in 1924 became an elected Polish delegate to the Society's Congress, working on the economic commissions of the Congress.

From 1929 to 1934, she chaired the International Affairs Department of the

Związek Pracy Obywatelskiej Kobiet, and was responsible for maintaining the Association's international network and contacts. On her initiative, this progressive, leftist organization, with many members from the socialist intelligentsia, joined the International Alliance of Women for Suffrage and Equal Citizenship (IAWSEC); the application was accepted at the IAWSEC Congress in Berlin in May 1929. Under the auspices of the Department for International Affairs of the *Związek Pracy Obywatelskiej Kobiet* (Women's Association for Civil Labor), led by Szelągowska, the *Polska Unia Zgody Narodów* (Polish Union for the Concord of Nations) and the *Polski Komitet Rozbrojeniowy Organizacji Kobiecych* (Polish Disarmament Committee of Women's Organizations, connected to the Women's Disarmament Committee of International Organizations) were established and Szelągowska became a delegate to the Polish Women's Disarmament Committee. On behalf of the *Związek Pracy Obywatelskiej Kobiet*, she participated in the activities of the *Komisja Współpracy Międzynarodowej Polskich Stowarzyszeń Kobiecych* (Committee of International Cooperation of Polish Women's Organizations), which aimed to provide assistance for organizations seeking international contacts.

In 1929, on behalf of the Peace Society, Szelągowska attended the Athens Peace Congress of the International Peace Bureau. In 1931, on the initiative of the *Związek Pracy Obywatelskiej Kobiet*, Szelągowska joined a Polish Government team at the League of Nations session in Geneva and in 1932, a governmental team for the Disarmament Conference in Geneva. She also participated in the sessions of the Third Commission of the Twelfth League of Nations Congress on disarmament issues. In the same year (1932), she attended the Congress of the Women's International League for Peace and Freedom (WILPF) in Grenoble; later, at the executive proceedings of this organization held in Geneva, she proposed a motion to universalize the minority treaties contained in the Versailles Treaty, which were supposed to ensure the political rights of national minorities. In 1932, at the Slavonic Institute in Geneva, she delivered two lectures on Polish women's social activities. In 1938, she became an Executive Board Secretary of the *Kongres Społeczno-Obywatelskiej Pracy Kobiet* (Congress of Women's Social and Civil Labor), held in Warsaw (1938) and attended by representatives of over ten women's organizations in Poland. The idea was to encourage cooperation between the organizations and to guide the development of the movement. The Congress established an Electoral Committee of Polish Women for the election of 1938. In 1938, Szelągowska became an elected member of the Polish Senate.

During World War II, Szelągowska helped to create means of support for orphaned children. After the war she settled in Wroclaw, where she worked as a bookkeeper until 1950. In 1955, she went to Geneva at the invitation of the International Federation of Business and Professional Women–the Polish branch of which was founded in 1934, and of which Szelągowska had been Chair–and the UN. From 1959, until her death in May 1962, she lived in Geneva.

Little is known about Szelągowska's private life. Sources from the files of public organizations reveal only her public or professional activities and outstanding achievements. Nothing is known of her children (if she had any), nor of her two marriages. Today, the name, life and work of Anna Szelągowska still remain in relative obscurity.

Dr. Joanna Dufrat
University of Wroclaw Institute of History

SOURCES

(A) *Biblioteka Narodowa w Warszawie* (National Library in Warsaw), temporary sign. 98 (editing underway). Contains the archival collection of the *Związek Pracy Obywatelskiej Kobiet* and the personal papers of Moraczewska.

(B) Bujak-Boguska, Sylwia. *Pamiętnik Klubu Politycznego Kobiet Postępowych 1919-1930* (Memoirs of the Progressive Women's Political Club, 1919-1930). Warsaw, 1930.

(B) Walewska, Cecylia. *W walce o równe prawa. Nasze bojownice* (Fighting for equal rights. Our fighters). Warsaw: Kobieta Współczesna, 1930.

(B) "Życiorysy kobiet, które weszły do parlamentu" (Biographies of women who entered the Parliament). *Praca Obywatelska* (Civil work), no. 22 (30 November 1938).

(B) *Kobieta Współczesna* (Modern woman) (1929-1934).

(B) *Praca Obywatelska* (Civil work) (1928-1933).

(C) Szelągowska, Anna. *Miedzynarodowe Organizacje Kobiece* (International women's organizations). Warsaw: Wydawnictwo ZPOK, 1934.

(E) Majchrowski, J. M., ed. *Kto był kim w Drugiej Rzeczypospolitej* (Who was who in the Second Republic of Poland). Warsaw, 1994.

SZELIGA, Maria (pseudonym), also known in France and the USA as Maria Chéliga or Chéliga-Loevy (1854–1927)

Polish novelist, poet and social publicist; socialist and pioneer of the international Polish women's movement. Other pseudonyms: 'B. Saryusz,' 'Bolesław Saryusz,' 'Cioteczka' (meaning 'Auntie'), 'Marynia,' 'Jerzy Horwat,' 'Matylda Mahon' and 'Vox.'

Maria Szeliga (*nee* Mirecka, first married name Czarnowska; second married name Loevy) was born in 1854 into a prosperous land-owning family in Jasieniec Solecki, in the Kingdom of Poland (a partially autonomous state, later taken by Russia, established after the 1815 Vienna Congress and including areas originally annexed by Prussia and Austria). After the premature death of her father, Maria grew up in the care of her mother and received a broad education at home. At the age of sixteen, she left home for Warsaw and began working on poems and novellas which would be published by the leading socio-literary periodicals of the time: *Opiekun Domowy* (Family carer); *Kłosy* (Ears of corn); *Biblioteka Romansów i Powieści* (Romance and novel library); *Przegląd Tygodniowy* (Weekly review) and *Przyjaciel dzieci* (Children's friend). In 1873, she published in book form her two novels, *Dla ideału* (For an ideal) and *W przeddzień* (The day before), as well as a collection of poems entitled *Pieśni i piosenki* (Songs and lyrics). Influenced by ideas of women's emancipation, Szeliga made the internal conflicts of single women, striving for independence and struggling against the double moral standards of their immediate community, a *leitmotif* of her texts. In part, her own life experiences inspired her when constructing the fate of her heroines.

In 1875, she traveled across Europe, visiting Prague, Munich, Verona, Padua, Rome and Naples. She published reports from this journey in one of the first Polish magazines for women, *Tygodnik Mód i Powieści* (Fashion and novels weekly). Upon her return to Poland in 1876, she and her mother took up permanent residence in Warsaw. In September of that year, she married the publisher of her poems, Stanisław Jan Czarnowski, but the couple decided to separate only a few weeks later and divorce proceedings began. Szeliga stayed in Warsaw for four more years (1876–1880). She wrote plays that were celebrated for their humorous, animated and sophisticated plots, and eagerly performed by open-air theaters in Warsaw, Cracow, Lviv and Poznan. [See, for example, her *Iwan Podkowa* (Ivan Horseshoe, 1876) and *Córka elegantki* (Daughter of a lady of fashion, 1878); her play *Szczęście Walusia* (Good luck little Waluś) received an award in 1878 in the Aleksander Fredro Competition, Lviv.]

After 1876, Szeliga became increasingly involved in socialist educational and cultural activities. She taught Polish history and literature (subjects forbidden in the Kingdom of Poland) and held discussions at meetings of mixed–but in all probability male dominated–workers' groups. When the tsarist authorities uncovered one such group in 1880, Szeliga left for France in order to avoid arrest and deportation to Siberia. She remained in Paris and there married a Polish painter, Edward Loevy. The Loevy residence became a center of Polish émigré life in France and Szeliga continued her literary and journalistic work. She published in Polish periodicals (mainly correspondence, theatrical reviews, recent French literature reviews and translations), as well as articles on women's movements and 'the woman question' in French periodicals such as *Le Figaro*, *La Parole Libre* (The free word), *Monde Moderne* (The modern world) and *Journal des Débats* (Journal of debates). In 1889, she published a novel in Cracow entitled *Na przebój* (Force one's way), dedicated to the question of women's access to higher education. The book was soon translated into French, German, Swedish and Spanish. Her theatrical plays gained recognition in France and were performed on French stages (for example, her *L'Ornière*, *Les Déblaueurs* and *Les Nihilistes*). They were never, however, presented to Polish audiences under Russian partition. The Russian authorities would never have consented to performances of Szeliga's plays, nor to her return to Russia because of the public accusations she had made against the tsarist government. In an 1889 lecture to the International Pedagogical Congress in Paris, Szeliga gave a detailed account of the Russian administration's repressive educational policies in the Polish territories, aimed at the Russification of Polish schoolchildren. In 1901, Szeliga again publicly denounced 'denationalization' policies in both the Russian and Prussian partitions. A letter she had written, protesting the use of corporal punishment at a school in Września (in the Polish territories annexed to the German state) to discipline Polish schoolchildren for speaking Polish, was signed by activists of women's and pacifist movements from all over the world. The letter was subsequently displayed in the museum at Rapperswil. (In 1927 the Rapperswil museum collection was moved to Warsaw, where it was destroyed by a fire in World War II).

While living abroad, Maria Szeliga participated in attempts to unify the Polish socialist movement. In November 1892, she attended the Polish Socialists' Convention in Paris at which the Polish Socialist Party was founded. She also co-edited the Polish socialist magazine *Pobudka* (Reveil) and was active in the French and international socialist movements. In September 1900, as a member of a Parisian association of socialist journalists, Szeliga was a delegate to the International Conference of socialist journalists in Paris, organized on the occasion of the Fifth International Socialist Congress in Paris. However, Szeliga's open declaration of her Polish origin and public presentations combining socialist banners with appeals to restore the Polish state, made cooperation between her and the French journalist community difficult.

While still living in Warsaw (i.e. before 1880), Szeliga also became involved in the international women's movement. Like ***Paulina Kuczalska-Reinschmit***, she established contacts with French, English and American activists (though it is not known whether the two women cooperated in this respect). Szeliga's emigration to France, though imposed, made it easier for her to work in international women's organizations, since in the Kingdom of Poland any legal activity as part of an association remained impossible until the 1905 Revolution. In Paris, Szeliga attempted to strengthen the divided French feminist movement. She worked with (among others) Marie Deraismes, Marie Pognon and Léon Richer [who in 1882 formed *La Ligue française du droit des femmes* (The French League for Women's Rights), regarded as the oldest feminist organization in France]. Her opinions and feminist activity were highly regarded by Victor Hugo, Alexandre Dumas (junior) and Cécile Brunschvicg (French suffrage leader). In the French press, Szeliga supported a suggestion by American activist Susan B. Anthony that an organization be formed to internationally coordinate national women's organizations from different countries; the International Council of Women (ICW) was established in Washington D.C. in 1888.

Szeliga attended the International Women's Congress in Paris, held as part of an international exposition on the occasion of the Centennial of the French Revolution (25–29 June 1889) and organized by Marie Deraismes and Léon Richer. Because the women objected to passing management of the Congress over to men, they had to hold private discussions off the premises of the exposition, in a room belonging to the Geographical Society. Paulina Kuczalska-Reinschmit was elected as one of the Vice-Presidents on the Board of the Congress, alongside other women representing a range of different nationalities. The Polish speeches at the Congress were delivered by three women: Paulina Kuczalska-Reinschmit (on the development of the women's emancipation movement in the Polish territories); Stefania Feinkind (on the economic situation of Polish women) and Maria Szeliga, whose two lectures addressed the right of women to freely choose a husband and women's legal status in the Polish territories and in Russia.

Maria Szeliga and Paulina Kuczalska-Reinschmit were elected onto a committee of six women who prepared the statutes of the *Union universelle des Femmes* (Universal Union of Women). This Union encouraged women's organizations in Europe to unify in order to create national federations (a necessary condition of membership to the International Council of Women). In 1901, the *Union universelle des femmes* was recognized by the ICW as an official representative of French women's organizations. From January 1890 to October 1891, Maria Szeliga was Secretary-General of the *Union universelle des femmes* and editor of its *Bulletin de l'Union universelle des femmes*. In

1895, she became the editor of *Revue Féministe* (Feminist review, 1895–1897) and in 1900, the author of the first edition of *Les Femmes et les féministes* (Women and feminists), which presented outstanding personalities from the international women's movement. She managed and directed theater performances about women and gave lectures at numerous congresses devoted to women's equal rights issues. In 1909, on the initiative of Szeliga and M. Orka-Rajchmanowa, the *Międzynarodowy Kongres Nieustający Spraw Kobiecych* (International Continuous Congress on Women's Questions; French name unknown) was established in Paris, with Szeliga as its President (until 1915). Szeliga was also active in the peace movement, participating in 1896 in the founding of the *Ligue des Femmes pour le Désarmement International* (Women's League for International Disarmament), of which she became Vice-President. Several years later, she led the *Alliance universelle des femmes pour la Paix par l'éducation* (Universal Alliance of Women for Peace through Education).

Organizing the women's pacifist movement in France, Szeliga established contacts with activists from England, Austria, Germany, Sweden, Norway, the USA, Turkey, Persia, Egypt, Algeria and other parts of the world. In Paris, she orchestrated a campaign to promote pacifist ideas among working-class youth. In 1914, Szeliga abandoned the pacifist movement, believing that the war would bring independence to Poland. During World War I, she devoted herself to charity work and continued to do so to the end of her life, establishing an organization to provide care for the old and infirm, the *Croix Violette* (Violet Cross). For those of her compatriots in exile who found themselves in difficult living conditions, she organized legal, medical and financial assistance and supplied them with Polish books. In 1922, she founded a socio-literary weekly, *Ognisko* (Hearth and home), dedicated to the everyday concerns of Polish émigré-workers. Her intense involvement in social work in France, along with her deteriorating health, made it impossible for her to return to Poland. She died on 2 January 1927 at Chaville near Paris, after several years of suffering from heart disease. She was buried in Montmorency Cemetery.

Agnieszka Janiak-Jasińska, Ph.D.
Institute of History, Warsaw University

SOURCES

(B) Wojnarowska, C. W. "Francusko-międzynarodowy kongres kobiecy" (The French-international women's congress). *Głos* (Voice), no. 29 (1889): 365–367.

(B) Kuczalska-Reinschmit, P. "Międzynarodowe Kongresy Kobiece w Paryżu" (The international women's congress in Paris). *Przegląd Tygodniowy* (Weekly review), no. 44 (literary supplement) (1889).

(B) Walewska, C. *Ruch kobiecy w Polsce* (The women's movement in Poland). Warsaw: Wydawnictwo Jubileuszowe E. Orzeszkowej, 1909.

(B) Kuczalska-Reinschmit, P. "Zjazd Ligi wyborczych praw kobiet w Budapeszcie" (Congress of the International Woman Suffrage Alliance in Budapest). *Ster* (Helm), nos. 13-14 (1913): 77-87.

(B) *Księga pamiątkowa PPS* (Commemorative volume on the Polish Socialist Party). Warsaw: Robotnik, 1923.

(B) Walewska, Cecylia. *W walce o równe prawa. Nasze bojownice* (Fighting for equal rights. Our fighters). Warsaw: Kobieta Współczesna, 1930.

(D) Orka, J. "Maria Szeliga." *Tygodnik Mód i Powieści* (Fashion and novels weekly), no. 11 (1909): 5.

(D) Krawczyńska, J. "Wspomnienie o redaktorce 'Ogniska'" (In remembrance of editor 'Ognisko'). *Bluszcz* (Ivy), no. 4 (1927): 13-14.

(D) Moszczyński, S. "Śp. Maria Szeliga" (Maria Szeliga, deceased). *Ognisko* (Focus), no. 256 (1927): 2.

(E) Wawrzykowska-Wierciochowa, D. "O udziale Polek w międzynarodowym ruchu kobiecym" (On the participation of Polish women in the international women's movement). [w:] Pamiętnikarstwo polskie [in:] *Polish Memoirs*, nos. 1-4 (1976): 59-72.

(E) Offen, Karen. *European Feminisms 1700-1950*. Stanford: Stanford University Press, 2000.

SZNARKIEWICZ, Nadzeja (born Kaladzianka) (1897–1974)

Belarussian social and cultural activist, teacher and ethnographer. Co-founder (1931) of the *Ab'jadnanne belaruskih zhanchyn imya Alaizy Pashkievich* (Alaiza Pashkevich Belarussian Women's Organization); co-founder and editor-in-chief of the short-lived magazine *Zhanotskaya sprava* (Women's cause).

Nadzeja Kaladzianka was born on 30 September (12 October) 1897 in Brest. Her father died when she was seven years old, after which her mother moved with her to the village of Wostrawa near Kobryn, and then to Pruhzany. In 1914, Nadzeja graduated from Pruzhany women's gymnasium and, in 1919, after completing courses in pedagogy (the only post-secondary education course available to women in the Russian Empire), she qualified as a teacher. She had already been working as a teacher of boys and girls in Pruzhany County, in the years 1914 to 1915. By the summer of 1915, the ravages of World War I had left Nadzeja a refugee on the Russian Volga. In 1921, after she had returned home (in 1919), western Belarus was incorporated into Poland (in accordance with the Treaty of Riga) and the Belarussians, whose language had earlier been outlawed in the Russian Empire, became an ethnic minority in Poland. They were urged to switch to the Polish language under political (and often police) pressure and issues of national language and education grew increasingly politicized as they were directly related to the issue of the legitimacy of the Belarussian people. From 1925, Nadzeja Kaladzianka lived and worked in Wilno (now Vilnius, the capital of Lithuania) as the head of a dormitory run by the Wilno Belarussian Gymnasium, actively participating in the cultural, educational and social initiatives of the Belarussian School Association (a civic organization for the promotion of the Belarussian language). In 1926, she married Yazep Sznarkiewicz (1888–1974), a political and cultural activist in western Belarus and also a teacher.

In 1931, Nadzeja Sznarkiewicz co-founded the *Ab'jadnanne belaruskih zhanchyn imya Alaizy Pashkievich* (Alaiza Pashkevich Belarussian Women's Organization), named after ***Alaiza Pashkevich*** (***Tsiotka***), a famous Belarussian poet (died 1916). The organization, though short-lived, aimed to "socially and nationally unite conscious Belarussian women" [*Zhanotskaya sprava* (Women's cause) 1931, no. 1]. Sznarkiewicz was one of the founders and the editor-in-chief of *Zhanotskaya sprava*, the first independent women's magazine in the Belarussian language. The intellectual women who had set up the magazine saw their task as one of raising the national consciousness of Belarussian peasant women and uniting them through socially meaningful activities (civic activism). In addition to pieces on national culture, the magazine advised its female readers in matters concerning social life, the upbringing of children and housekeeping. It addressed itself primarily to rural women, since historically most Belarussians lived in villages (the towns of the region were multi-ethnic), and hoped to stimulate broad cultural and educational outreach work through publications in the national language, lecturing and club or association activities.

The first issue of *Zhanotskaya sprava* opened with a manifesto: "To the Belarussian Women." Outlining some of the issues that Sznarkiewicz considered important for women as 'national' wives and mothers, it read (in part):

> Even today in the countryside, mothers often see their daughters' schooling as a useless waste of time: "they are going to get married anyway, so what is the use of this education?"–they say. Yet it is precisely because women run everything in the family that a woman's education is so important. She is the mother, the teacher of her children, and they [children] are the future of our people. Their whole lives often depend on what a mother has put into their heads when they were young. And isn't it clear to everyone that joy and agreement rule in the household of a clever woman and permanent disarray where the mistress is ignorant, undeveloped and unable to establish order in her household. One should not tolerate these superstitions of ancient peasant ignorance, and we, Belarussian women, will fight them and unite to make better lives for ourselves, to make this life more bearable and joyful.

Zhanotskaya sprava was published once a month in Wilno from March to November 1931, when it stopped due to lack of funding. Nadzeja Sznarkiewicz continued to teach. In 1939, western Belarus was incorporated into the Belarussian Soviet Socialist Republic.

For the last 25 years of her life, Nadzeja Sznarkiewicz was crippled by paralysis but remained socially active all the same. She edited her husband's memoirs of the Kletsk and Nyaswizh gymnasiums (unpublished), compiled albums of photos on the history of Belarussian schools and gymnasiums in western Belarus and organized joint projects with the Hudzievičy ethnographic museum in the Hrodna region. Mainly remembered as the wife of Jazep Sznarkiewicz, she died on 21 May 1974.

Aleh Hardzienka
Editor *Nasha niva* (Weekly)

Translated from the Belarussian by Elena Gapova.

SOURCES

(B) *Zhanotskaya sprava* (Women's cause) (1931).

THEODOROPOULOU, Avra (born Drakopoulou) (1880-1963)

Leading figure of the Greek feminist movement; founder (1920) and President (1921–1936 and 1944–1958) of the *Syndesmos gia ta Dikaiomata tis Gynaikas* (League for Woman's Rights), affiliated to the International Woman Suffrage Alliance (IWSA); board member (1923–1926; 1926–1935) of the IWSA and of its successor, the International Alliance of Women for Suffrage and Equal Citizenship (IAWSEC); leading figure of the Little Entente of Women (LEW) (1923–1929) and LEW President (1925–1927); President of the *Panelladiki Omospondia Gynaikon,* (*POG,* Panhellenic Women's Federation) (1946–1947); musicologist and music critic; feminist writer; author of stage plays and short stories.

Avra Drakopoulou was born on 3 November 1880 into a family with strong political and intellectual traditions. Her grandfather, Carolos Drakopoulos, was a well-known fighter in the 1821 Independence Revolution and her father, Aristomenis Drakopoulos, served as Consul General of Greece in Adrianople. No data exists regarding her mother, Eleni. Her sister, Theoni Drakopoulou (1881-1973), was a well-known poet who took the pen name of 'Myrtiotissa' (from 'myrtle'). Her nephew was the famous actor George Papas.

Avra Drakopoulou finished high school and learned French, English and German. In 1900, she graduated from the Athens Conservatoire. For her achievements as a pianist she was awarded the Andreas and Iphigeneia Syngros Silver Medal (1910) and appointed to teach pianoforte and music history at the Conservatoire. She remained there until 1919, going on to teach at the Hellenic Conservatoire (1919-1936) and completing her professional career at the National Conservatoire (1936-1957). She was a member of the *Enosis Ellinon Theatrikon kai Mousikon Kritikon* (Union of Greek Theater and Music Critics).

In 1900, she met Spyros Theodoropoulos (1875-1961), a lawyer, politician, writer, member of the Venizelos governments, rapporteur on labor legislation and one-time President of the *Etaireia Ellinon Logotechnon* (*EEL*, Society of Greek Authors). They married in 1906, had no children and lived together until his death on 20 April 1961.

In her letters written to Spyros Theodoropoulos during a difficult period of courtship, Avra Drakopoulou expressed anger at the authoritarian attitudes of her father and his opposition to her relationship with Theodoropoulos, which she felt indicated the extent of Greek women's oppression. This anger surfaces again in her first play, *Tychin i thelisin* (Chance or will), which was never staged, probably–as her correspondence suggests–because of the objections of her future husband: he believed that the work was too "personal," "real" and "true" to be staged, defying the border line between the private and the public [*Elliniko Logotechniko kai Istoriko Archeio* (Greek Literary and Historical Archives), File I: Correspondence between Avra and Spyros, 1900-1906, Wednesday 15 August 1901]. Several years later, Avra Theodoropoulou wrote another play, *Spithes pou svynoun* (Sparks dying out), which was staged by the famous actress Marika Kotopouli in 1912. Theodoropoulou's participation in theatrical life, cultivated by her family environment and reinforced by her marriage to Spyros Theodoropoulos and their literary milieu, was bound up with her ideas on female emancipation, particularly with her attempts to seek new modes of expression and socio-political intervention.

Avra Theodoropoulou's first socio-political public activity was during the Greek-Turkish War of 1897, when she volunteered her services as a nurse. In the climate of political euphoria which marked the first Venizelos administration (1910-1920)–during which period Spyros Theodoropoulos helped found (in 1911) the *Ergatiko Kentro Athinas* (Athens Workers' Center)–Avra Theodoropoulou and other women were entrusted with setting up the *Kyriako Scholeio Ergatrion* (*KSE*, Sunday School for Working Women) in Athens (October 1911). What distinguished this school from similar institutions organized by the women's movement was that it marked an unclear yet visible transition from education provided on a philanthropic basis, to education demanded as a right. The *KSE* ceased its operations in 1922.

While active in the *KSE*, Theodoropoulou volunteered as a nurse in the Balkan Wars of 1912 and 1913 and was decorated with the following four medals: of the Hellenic Red Cross, of Queen Olga, of the Balkan War and of the Greek-Bulgarian War. Theodoropoulou's activities in this period can be seen in the context of a general spirit of nationalism which had, since the late decades of the nineteenth century, directly linked the social position and vocation of women to the fulfillment of national destiny. Such activities form an important part of the history of women's struggle, redefining the traditional distinction between the sexes as a feature of the nation.

From 1918 to her death, Theodoropoulou consciously struggled for the equality of the sexes. In 1918, she was among the founders of the association *Adelfi tou Stratioti* (Sister of the Soldier), which sought to mitigate social problems created by war. The association's members also desired to carve a public niche for themselves and to be recognized as active members of society. Recognition, they hoped, would help them gain rights, particularly the right to vote–a demand which contrasted with earlier forms of women's activism characterized by the campaigns of upper middle-class women for the right to education and paid work.

In June 1920, Avra Theodoropoulou established, together with Ms Negropontes and other women, the *Syndesmos gia ta Dikaiomata tis Gynaikas* (League for Woman's Rights). The organization aimed to become affiliated with the International Woman Suffrage Alliance (IWSA). Seeking, through radical reforms, to establish sexual equality "from a political, civil and social point of view" (Theodoropoulou 1920, 25), the League became the most dynamic component of interwar Greek feminism. Theodoropoulou was the League's President from 1921 to 1958, with the exception of the period 1936–1944. In 1936, the dictatorship of Ioannis Metaxas forced the organization to cease its activities (which were not resumed until after the Axis Occupation).

From the very first year of the *Syndesmos gia ta Dikaiomata tis Gynaikas* Theodoropoulou sought to lay the foundations for a united women's policy, an aim which she pursued tirelessly. Without contesting an essentializing view of women's 'roles' (identified with maternity as a 'natural' destiny and with a desire for peace), she confined the demands of the *Syndesmos gia ta Dikaiomata tis Gynaikas* chiefly to matters of institutional equality. In order to achieve those demands she worked with women whose ideological positions differed from her own, not hesitating to dissociate herself when she realized that their aims also differed. In 1921, for example, she kept her distance from the more conservative *Ethniko Symvoulio ton Ellinidon* (National Council of Greek Women), established in 1908 and reconstituted in August 1919 as the Greek section of the International Council of Women (ICW). For strategic reasons, the *Syndesmos gia ta Dikaiomata tis Gynaikas* also worked with men who supported its demands and with governments, though its members stated that they did not belong to any political party.

The foundation of the *Syndesmos gia ta Dikaiomata tis Gynaikas* in June 1920 was the occasion for Theodoropoulou and other Greek women to attend the Eighth Congress of the IWSA in Geneva. Joining the IWSA allowed her to transcend national horizons and expand her network into the international field. As the President of the *Syndesmos gia ta Dikaiomata tis Gynaikas* (after 1921), she attended almost all the congresses of the IWSA (IAWSEC from 1926). In 1923, with the end of the Greek–Turkish War, large numbers of refugees flowed into Greece from Turkey, causing the *Syndesmos gia ta Dikaiomata tis Gynaikas* to turn its activities towards caring for women refugees. The *Syndesmos gia ta Dikaiomata tis Gynaikas* organized, among other things, a Supervision Service, consisting of female volunteers posted at fifty settlements for refugees, as well as the orphanage *Ethniki Stegi* (National Shelter), which accommodated 85 orphan girls from six to fifteen years of age. For Theodoropoulou it was a year packed with action: she brought out the League's periodical *O Agonas tis Gynaikas* (Woman's struggle) and took part in the Ninth Congress of the IWSA in Rome (1923). At this latter congress, she became a Board member of the IWSA and served there until its Istanbul congress (1935). The consequences of war, peace and the role of women in such affairs remained the center of her focus. With international communication allowing her to seek new means of intervention, Theodoropoulou helped establish (in 1923) the *Mikri Entent Gynaikon* (Little Entente of

Women, LEW), which included representatives from Yugoslavia, Greece, Poland, Czechoslovakia and Romania. She co-organized and participated in almost all the annual congresses of this organization: in Bucharest (1923); Belgrade, where she was decorated with the Medal of King Alexander of Yugoslavia for her work for peace (1924); Athens (1925); Prague (1927) and Warsaw (1929). Between 1924 and 1929, Theodoropoulou was President of the Greek section of the LEW and for two years (1925–1927) she was also President of the LEW. In the following years, she took part in many other congresses, including the 27th *Conférence de la paix et du désarmement* (Conference of Peace and Disarmament) in Athens (October 1929), the first *Congrčs Féministe Oriental* (Oriental Feminist Congress) in Damascus (1930) and the first *Conférence Balkanique* (Balkan Conference) in Athens (October 1930). She also attended the First Balkan Women's Conference for Peace in Belgrade (May 1931) and the fourth *Conférence Balkanique* (Balkan Conference) in Thessaloniki (November 1933).

During the interwar years, Theodoropoulou's activities represented a progressive force; particularly in the period 1928–1932, when feminists of every persuasion collaborated in the struggle for the franchise. What they gained, in February 1930, was the limited right to elect local authorities based on supplementary restrictions of age and education (which in practical terms meant that no more than ten percent of women could use this right).

From early 1934, the women's movement gathered strength and women's action on the left became more intense because of the part they had played in the Metaxas dictatorship, as well as in the occupation and resistance movements. This climate led to a gradual convergence of radical feminist approaches (such as those of the League) with the anti-fascist policies of collaboration inaugurated by the *Koumounistiko Komma Elladas* (Communist Party of Greece), which called upon all 'progressive women' to play an active role in anti-fascist, anti-war activities.

In November 1944, the *Syndesmos gia ta Dikaiomata tis Gynaikas* was revived but decided to limit its activities to protests due to the political state of affairs created by the Civil War. One such protest was staged in 1945 against the persecution of the Southern Epirus Greeks by the Albanians, and against the deportation of women and children by the guerrillas. This climate tested Theodoropoulou's strategy of allying herself with associations of the left: i.e. those belonging to the *Panelladiki Omospondia Gynaikon* (*POG*, Panhellenic Women's Federation). In early 1946, the *POG*, which was founded on November 1945, offered Avra Theodoropoulou its presidency. Theodoropoulou accepted and took part in the First Panhellenic Women's Congress in Athens (May 1946). She proposed equal citizenship as a basic aim of the *POG* but majorities decided in favor of the protection of motherhood and of children; the political, social and economic equality of women; resistance to fascism and the development of solid foundations for peace. After the Congress, ideological differences reached a head. Theodoropoulou, who still represented the *Syndesmos gia ta Dikaiomata tis Gynaikas* in the International Alliance of Women (IAW, as the IWSA/IAWSEC was called from 1946), submitted her resignation from the *POG* on 17 February 1947, after the IAW was critized by the left-wing *Diethnous Dimokratikis Omospondias Gynekon* (Women's International Democratic Federation, established in December 1945), to which some of the associations of the Pan Hellenic Federation had acceded. Because of her role in the *POG* and her collaboration with communists a year later (1948), she was required by the General Security Police to write a statement of national loyalty.

In the following decade, in spite of her advanced age and the disillusionment she felt regarding the women's movement, Theodoropoulou continued to participate in the congresses of the International Alliance of Women: in Amsterdam (1949); Stockholm (1951); Naples (1952); Colombo (1955); Copenhagen (1956) and Athens (1958).

After her husband's death (1961), she organized his archives, catalogued her and her husband's library and arranged her own personal archives for transferal (as stipulated in her will) to the *Etaireia Ellinon Logotechnon* (Society of Greek Authors), of which her husband had been President for many years and of which she herself was a member. She died in Athens on 20 January 1963 in the Hellenic Red Cross Hospital, of "heart failure and an acute inflammation of the lungs" [Death Certificate of 21 January 1963 (Archives of George A. Mylonas, File Sp. Theodoropoulos family, no. 9)].

Aleka Boutzouvi
University of Athens

SOURCES

(A) *Etaireia Ellinon Logotechnon* (*EEL*, Society of Greek Authors). Archives of Avra and Spyros Theodoropoulos, nine files on different topics (1900–1957).

(A) *Elliniko Logotechniko kai Istoriko Archeio* (*ELIA*, Greek Literary and Historical Archives). Two files containing correspondence between Avra and Spyros Theodoropoulos (1900–1906) and "ideological manuscripts."

(A) Archives of the *Ypourgeion Dimosias Taxis, Diefthinsi Genikis Asfalias/Ypiresia Pliroforion* (Ministry of Public Order, General Security Directorate/ Information Service, 1948).

(A) Archives of the lawyer George A. Mylonas (1961–1963). File: Sp. Theodoropoulos family (44 documents for the period 1961–1963).

(B) *O Agonas tis Gynaikas* (Woman's struggle) (1923–1936; 1964–1967).

(C) Theodoropoulou, Avra. "Spithes pou svynoun" (Sparks dying out). Unpublished three-act play. Archives of Avra Theodoropoulou, 1912.

(C) Theodoropoulou, Avra. *To Kyriako Scholeio Ergatrion* (The Sunday School for Working Women). Athens: Printing Press of the Royal Court of A. Raftanis, 1916.

(C) Theodoropoulou, Avra. *To diethnes Gynaikeion Synedrion tis Genevis* (The International Women's Congress in Geneva). Printed by A. Frantzeskakis and P. A. Kad'tatzis. Athens: 'Syndesmos gia ta Dikaiomata tis Gynaikas' (League for Woman's Rights), 1920.

(C) Theodoropoulou, Avra. *O Agonas tis Gynaikas* (Woman's struggle). Speech in the hall of the Hellenic Conservatory on 19 April 1922. Athens: "Feministiki Vivliothiki" (Feminist Library), 1923.

(C) Theodoropoulou, Avra. "To feministiko kinima–Gyro apo to gynaikeio Synedrio tou Parisiou" (The feminist movement–on the Women's Congress in Paris). *Anagennisi* (Renaissance) I, no. 4 (1926): 210-221.

(C) Theodoropoulou, Avra S. "O feminismos stin Ellada" (Feminism in Greece). *Nea Estia* (New focus) I, nos. 16-17 (1927): 867-869.

(D) Unsigned. "Epifaneis Eptanisiakai Fysiognomiai. Avra Theodoropoulou" (Notable personalities of the Ionian Islands. Avra Theodoropoulou). *Icho* (Echo) 89 (1939): 8-9.

(D) Unsigned. "Theodoropoulou, Avra." In *Megali Elliniki Egkyklopaideia* (Great Greek encyclopedia), date unknown, 12: 510.

(D) Boutzouvi, Aleka. "Avra Theodoropoulou: drastiriotites, ideologia kai stratigikes tis cheirafetisis 1910-1922" (Avra Theodoropoulou: activities, ideology and strategies of emancipation 1910-1922). Doctoral thesis. Athens: University of Athens, Department of History and Archaeology, 2003.

(E) Avdela, Efi and Angelika Psarra. *O feminismos stin Ellada tou Mesopolemou. Mia anthologia* (Feminism in interwar Greece. An anthology). Athens: Gnosi, 1985.

(E) Psarra, Angelika. "Feministries, sosialistries, kommounistries: Gynaikes kai politiki sto Mesopolemo" (Feminists, socialists, communists: women and politics in the interwar years). In G. T. Mavrogordatos and C. Hatziïosiph, eds. *Venizelismos kai astikos eksynchronismos* (Venizelism and bourgeois modernization). Irakleio: Panepistimiakes Ekdoseis Kritis (Crete University Press), 1988, 67-82.

(E) Sklaveniti, Kostoula. "Ta gynaikeia entypa 1908-1918" (Women's periodicals). *Diavazo* (Reading) 198 (14 September 1988; issue devoted to "Greek feminist publications"): 13-22.

(E) Samiou, Dimitra. "I diekdikisi tis isotitas: ta feministika entypa to Mesopolemo (1920-1940)" [The demand for equality: feminist publications in the interwar years (1920-1940)]. *Diavazo* 198 (14 September 1988): 23-28.

(E) Samiou, Dimitra. "Ta politika dikaiomata ton Ellinidon (1864-1952)" [Greek women's political rights (1864-1952)]. *Mnemon* (Remembrance) 12 (1989): 161-172.

(E) Varikas, Eleni. "Gender and national identity in fin-de-siècle Greece." *Gender and History* 5, no. 2 (1993): 269-283.

(E) Varikas, Eleni. *I exegersi ton kyrion. I genesi mias feministikis syneidisis stin Ellada (1833-1907)* [The ladies' revolt. The creation of a feminist consciousness in Greece (1833-1907)]. Athens: Idrima Erevnas kai Paideias Emporikis Trapezas tis Ellados (Foundation for Research and Culture of the Commercial Bank of Greece), 1987. Second edition, Athens: Katarti, 1996.

(E) Avdela, Efi. "Between Duties and Rights: Gender and Citizenship in Greece, 1864-1952." In Faruk Birtek and Thalia Dragonas, eds. *Citizenship and the Nation State: Greece and Turkey* (forthcoming).

(F) Theodoropoulou's numerous feminist articles in *O Agonas tis Gynaikas* (Woman's struggle) can be found (in Greek) in the digitalized form of the periodical at www/genderpanteion.gr.

TOMŠIČ, Vida (born Bernot) (1913–1998)

Slovenian lawyer, member of the Communist Party and the National Liberation Movement; socialist politician and drafter of state policies on women and gender relations.

Born on 26 June 1913 in Ljubljana, a Slovenian town situated between the Alps and the Adriatic sea, Vida Tomšič lived a long and turbulent life, reflecting the history of the area in which she lived. Born in the Austro-Hungarian Monarchy, the territory of her birth became part of the Kingdom of Yugoslavia only a few years after World War I. Her father, Ivan Bernot, was a teacher and her mother Franja, born Rozman, a housewife. Vida had three brothers and one sister. She attended primary and grammar school in Ljubljana. In 1933, she began a course of study in history and geography at the Faculty of Arts, University of Ljubljana, switching to law in 1935 and graduating from the Faculty of Law in 1941.

Vida Bernot's childhood was not a particularly hard one, but she could not overlook the existence of vast social differences and the particular injustices suffered by women. Her early attempts to find like-minded persons within the Catholic Church to support her efforts for the social rights of women and the lower classes were unsuccessful, later bringing her to left-wing student societies such as *Triglav* (the name of a mountain) and *Jadran* (the name of a sea), and women's organizations such as the *Zveza delavskih žena in deklet* (Union of Working Women and Girls) and the *Jugoslovanska ženska zveza* (Union of Yugoslav Women), of which she was not a member but with which she worked from time to time. In 1934, Bernot became a member of the illegal *Komunistična partija Jugoslavije* (Yugoslav Communist Party) and, in 1935, was sentenced to nine months imprisonment. In 1937, she married Tone Tomšič (1910–1942), a law student and leading Slovene communist. In 1940, Vida Tomšič became a member of the Slovene and Yugoslav Communist Party leadership, and at the Fifth Yugoslav National Party Conference held the same year, presented a paper entitled "Naloge Komunistične partije Jugoslavije pri delu med ženskami" (The work of the Communist Party of Yugoslavia among women), in which she outlined the official program of the Communist Party. The party linked the emancipation of women to the social transformation of society, and the liberation of humanity from all forms of exploitation. Within this framework, women's political activity was to be channeled solely into the revolutionary movement of the Communist Party. In the name of the party, Vida Tomšič promised Yugoslav women maternity leave, kindergartens, protection from harmful labor, public services providing medical care for women and children, the legal equality of legitimate and illegitimate children, equality in education and in professional life, equal pay for equal work, passive and active voting rights and the right to abortion for social reasons.

Tomšič joined the National Liberation Movement in the spring of 1941, early on in the occupation of Slovenia and Yugoslavia by German, Italian and Hungarian forces. In August 1941, she gave birth to her son Mihael, but returned to underground activity several months later. In December 1941, Italian and German secret police agents arrested her, along with her husband. Both were severely tortured in Italian and German prisons and the following year, the Italian Military Tribunal sentenced Vida Tomšič to 25 years of prison and her husband to death. He was executed and she was sent to prison in Italy. When Italy surrendered in October 1943, Tomšič returned to Yugoslavia and took up a leading position in the Yugoslav armed struggle against the German army.

After the war, Tomšič gained political prominence in the Socialist Federal Republic of Yugoslavia, which consisted of six republics: Serbia, Croatia, Slovenia, Bosnia and Herzegovina, Montenegro and Macedonia. In May 1945, she became the Minister of Social Policy in the first Slovenian national government (until 1946). She remarried in 1946, to Franc Novak (1908–1999), a former partisan doctor and internationally recognized gynaecologist. They had two children, Živa (b. 1948) and Branko (b. 1947). In the postwar period, Vida Tomšič (who retained this surname until her death) held many important positions in Slovene and Yugoslav governmental and parliamentary bodies and political organizations: she was a member (1940–1982) of the Central Committee of the League of Communists of Slovenia and Yugoslavia; President (1948–1952) of the *Antifašistična fronta žensk Jugoslavije* (*AFŽ*, Antifascist Women's Front, Yugoslavia); President (1971–1978) of the Federal Council for Family Planning; a deputy of the Slovene (1945–1953, 1958–1967) and Yugoslav (1945–1965, 1967–1969) Assemblies; President of the Assembly of Slovenia (1962–1963); President of the House of Nations of the Assembly of Yugoslavia (1967–1968) and member of the Presidency of SR Slovenia (1974–1984). She took part in Yugoslav governmental and parliamentary delegations to many foreign countries and to several United Nations (UN) conferences. She participated in the sessions of the General Assembly of the UN (1954, 1970) and working groups organized by the UN on social development, women's rights, childcare and family planning. She attended the World Population Conference in Bucharest (1974), was the leader of the Yugoslav delegation at the UN World Conference of International Women's Year in Mexico (1975) and attended the UN Women's conferences in Copenhagen (1980) and Nairobi (1985).

Vida Tomšič was also a member of the Board of International Research and Training Institute for the Advancement of Women (INSTRAW) in Santo Domingo (1979–1985). She was the Yugoslav representative on the Social Development Commission of the Economic and Social Council (ECOSOC) (1960–1963; 1971–1974, chairing the Commission in 1963). As a member of several UN working groups (Women and Development, Social Aspects of Family Planning etc.) she wrote papers for international conferences and commissions, among them "The Role of Yugoslav Women in Economic and Social Development" (1971) and "Social Aspects of Family Planning in Yugoslavia" (1973). She also participated actively in numerous international non-governmental meetings on human rights, especially on the status of women. She took part in the International Convocation *Pacem in Terris* in New York (1965) and participated in the Twentieth Triennial Plenary Conference of the International Council of Women (ICW) in Vienna (1973), with a paper entitled "Partners in Development." She also took part in the Tenth International Seminar of the Federal Conference of the Socialist Alliance of the Working People of Yugoslavia, entitled "Woman and Development" in Bled, Slovenia (1977) and in the International conference (Socialism and Developing Countries" in Cavtat, Montenegro (1978), with a paper entitled "On the Global, International Significance of the Struggle for the Equality of Women." At all these forums, she represented the 'official' Yugoslav position, but as a leading political figure she had often been wholly or partly responsible for the formal party line on women's and gender issues. She contributed a great deal to the new legislation issued during the socialist period of 1945 to 1990 as a specialist on gender questions, and it seems reasonable to suppose that the policies she advocated combined both official ideology and Tomšič's own ideas.

Vida Tomšič published many studies, articles and books on the subjects of women's status, political systems, family planning, peace and development, as well as international relations. As a Marxist and communist, she truly believed that if existing private property systems could be dismantled and if the position of every citizen was determined by his or her own labor, then the roots of patriarchal relations would begin to wither and die. She expected women under communism to participate fully in the economic and political life of the country, and hoped that maternity and childcare would cease to be 'social problems' as they were shouldered by the whole society, collectively. But these expectations fell short. As members of a party based on the ideas of Marx, Engels, Bebel and Lenin, male communist leaders may have promoted gender equality in public life, but in their family lives, many preferred to maintain older gender divisions of labor. Tomšič often had problems persuading her party comrades to accept her ideas on issues such as family planning.

Tomšič saw freedom of reproductive choice as a basic human right and demographic trends as part of economic and social relations. In her view, family planning had to be made with respect to women's equal rights, the protection of women's health, the right of both parents to decide when to have children, and how many, as well as the right of the child to a secure, stable and loving family. Freedom did not exclusively mean abortion rights, but also acceptance of contraception as a viable method of family planning. The Communist Party leadership adopted these views and legal abortion was gradually liberalized, while at the same time, efforts were made to promote contraception. Tomšič was one of the main initiators (assisted by her gynaecologist husband, Franc Novak) of a successful campaign across Yugoslavia to put the focus of family planning on prevention. In due course (between the 1960s and the 1980s), contraception was incorporated into the health service and Tomšič was one of the authors of the Federal Constitution of 1974 that gave women and men the right to freely decide in matters concerning childbirth (to be restricted only in the interest of health protection). Yet for Tomšič, it was not enough for the state to establish women's legal equality; women themselves had to fight for their rights. She would say that Yugoslav women had not done enough, that they had to find time to participate in the wider political struggle for a new (socialist) economic and sociopolitical world order—against neocolonialism, racism and imperialism. When discussing women's problems, she referred to political theories that belonged specifically to a 'Yugoslav' context—namely Yugoslav socialist ideas of selfmanagement—in order to emphasize the importance of women's participation in political, social and economic life. In 1975, a selection of her articles and speeches on women's issues was published in English under the title *The Status of Women and Family Planning in Yugoslavia*. Selected articles and speeches were further published under the title *Ženska, delo, družina, družba* (Woman, work, family, society, 1976; republished in 1978). In 1980, her book *Ženska v razvoju socialistične samoupravne Jugoslavije* (Woman in the development of socialist self-managing Yugoslavia) was published in Slovenian, English, French and Serbo-Croat.

Vida Tomšič was a professor of family law at the Faculty of Law, University of Ljubljana; during the late 1970s, she also was made a "Doctor Honoris Causa." She received the highest national awards for bravery and professional achievement (e.g. "National Hero of Yugoslavia") and a number of foreign decorations (e.g. Mexican, Italian, French, Austrian and Polish). She retired in July 1984 but remained politically and professionally active. Soon afterwards, Yugoslavia disintegrated as a result of insurmountable internal tensions. The socialist order proved unsuccessful all over Europe. In 1990, Slovenia became an independent, market-oriented parliamentary democracy. Though some still thought highly of Vida Tomšič, her former political opponents were now being given the floor as well.

The delusions and problems of socialist Yugoslavia have been well documented, but what did the period that Vida Tomšič helped shape accomplish for women? Feminism had been declared an unnecessary, even harmful, 'bourgeois' phenomenon and all women's civil organizations from 'pre-communist' times—the *Jugoslovanska ženska zveza* (Yugoslav Women's Union), the *Splošno slovensko žensko društvo* (General Slovene Women's Association) and the *Krščanska ženska zveza* (Christian Women's Union)–had been abolished. Vida Tomšič shared the opinion that the struggle for women's rights should be part of the common struggle of the working class for full human rights. After World War II, the status of women in Yugoslavia improved substantially.

Vida Tomšič died on 10 December 1998 in Ljubljana. She remained interested in women's issues right up until the end of her life and noted that numbers of women in political life had decreased, that it had become increasingly more difficult for mothers to enter employment and that childcare was more expensive. But she was known to assert that Slovenian women would never let anybody take away the rights they had gained.

Mateja Jeraj
Ministry of Culture,
Archive of the Republic of Slovenia

Translated by Maja Urek.

SOURCES

(A) Archive of the Republic of Slovenia, Vida Tomšič (AS 1413). The personal archive of Vida Tomšič contains hundreds of boxes of personal and official documents, articles, speeches, lectures and correspondence with contacts at home and abroad.

(C) Tomšič, Vida. *Woman, Work, Family and Society*. Ljubljana: Komunist, 1978.

(C) Tomšič, Vida. *Woman in the Development of Socialist Self-Managing Yugoslavia*. Belgrade: Jugoslovenska stvarnost, 1980.

(E) Nedog, Alenka. *Tone Tomšič*. Ljubljana: Zavod Borec, 1969.

(E) Interview with Vida Tomšič conducted by Mateja Jeraj and kept in her personal archive. Ljubljana, 1998.

TOYEN (born Marie Čermínová) (1902–1980)

Czech painter, illustrator; leading member of the Czech interwar avant-garde and Surrealist movements; innovator in painting techniques; pioneer woman artist who broke many taboos in the artistic representation of female sexuality.

Toyen was born Marie Čermínová in Prague on 21 September 1902. Although little is known of her family background, it may be assumed that the relationship between her and her parents was influenced by divergent political views. Toyen sympathized with anarchism and left the family at the age of sixteen. In 1919, she was accepted to the School of Applied Arts in Prague, where she studied at the painting studio led by Emanuel Dítě, graduating in 1922. In the summer of that year, she met a young painter and writer, Jindřich Štyrský (1899–1942), on the island of Korčula in Yugoslavia. Toyen and Štyrský immediately formed an inseparable artistic couple, collaborating on a large number of exhibitions in Czechoslovakia and abroad until the death of Štyrský in 1942. In 1923, they joined the most radical of the Czech avant-garde groups, *Devětsil*. Emphasizing both formal experiments and political engagement, *Devětsil* had a transformative impact on contemporary artistic paradigms. Toyen was the first woman artist to break into the bastion of male-dominated art in newly formed Czechoslovakia after 1918, when roles for women in Czech culture and society began to change perceptibly. In that year, suffrage and equal education rights were introduced under the first Czechoslovak President, T. G. Masaryk (1850–1937), whose life and thought were inextricably linked with the long, well-established trajectory of nineteenth-century Czech feminism.

Early on in her career, Toyen's work was influenced by Cubism and Purism but she soon discovered the poetics of naďve and primitive art. Her canvas series of exotic and circus motifs, painted in the mid-1920s, were stylistically reminiscent of Henry Rousseau (whom she admired) and approached the 'proletarian art' celebrated by *Devětsil*. The biggest 'career break' for Toyen arrived in 1925, when she began working on book-cover designs with Štyrský. Most of these were for Odeon, one of the most innovative Czech publishing houses of the time. From the mid-1920s on, Toyen and Štyrský designed covers for some of the most prominent Czech writers and critics, including

Jaroslav Seifert (1901-1986), Vítězslav Nezval (1900-1958), Jindřich Honzl (1894-1953) and Karel Schulz (1899-1943). Their designs combined photomontage, abstract planes and text, resulting in playful yet formally disciplined compositions. In the autumn of 1925, Toyen and Štyrský traveled to Paris, where they developed and formulated a unique artistic genre: Artificialism. In the manifesto issued in conjunction with the 1927 exhibition of their work in Paris and Prague, they described Artificialism as "an abstract consciousness of reality... defined by poetic perceptions of memories." Marked by innovative painting techniques, such as dripping or spray painting through grids, stencils and various objects, or layering thick and tactile structures, Toyen's Artificialist style emphasized the material properties of paint and radicalized dominant conventions in abstract painting. For a short period of time (1929-1930), Toyen and Štyrský also attempted experiments with Artificialism in the sphere of applied arts. They established a fashion studio where they employed abstract techniques–mainly spraying–to decorate various kinds of textiles (scarves, lingerie, ties etc.). Although regarded as a less significant period in Toyen's career, her intertwining of painting and textile can be seen as part of attempts she made to undermine traditional gender-based, and gender-biased hierarchies such as the opposition between 'high' (masculine) and 'low' or 'decorative' (feminine) art.

In the early 1930s, Toyen's work again began to metamorphose. Small interventions by various, mostly natural objects or their fragments (shells, eggs, stones, crystals etc.) interrupted the abstractions of Artificialism, anticipating the arrival of Surrealism. In time, Toyen became internationally recognized. She participated in important international group shows, her work was written about by prominent figures in the modern art world (André Breton, among others) and she was even included in a prestigious 1928 survey of women artists in the history of Western civilization, entitled *Die Frau als Künstlerin* (Woman as artist) and published by German art historian Hans Hildebrandt.

In 1934, Toyen signed a declaration marking the foundation of the Czechoslovak Surrealist Group, a definitive turning point in her creative life. The poetics and politics of Surrealism preoccupied the artist until the end of her days; she was fascinated and inspired by the use of Surrealist symbolism to unveil hidden or suppressed libidinal and sexual desires. Her paintings and drawings from the 1930s are full of specters, phantoms and dream objects, with strong erotic accents.

Toyen's participation in the international Surrealist movement was more than an artistic gesture. Like most other members, she understood Surrealism as a motor for both the imagination and social and political progress. A lot of her paintings from the second half of the 1930s–prior to Hitler's annexation of Czechoslovakia–had strong political overtones and her anti-war engagement culminated in several cycles of drawings: *Přízraky pouště* (Desert specters, 1937); *Střelnice* (The shooting gallery, 1940) and *Schovej se, válko*! (Hide, war!, 1944). In these works, she evoked the apocalyptic horrors of World War II, projecting them onto innocent worlds of children's games or onto devastated worlds full of abandoned objects and the fragments of human bodies. Despite her life-long commitment to communist ideas, Toyen left Czechoslovakia before the 1948 communist *coup d'état* and settled down in her beloved Paris. Possessing a respected artistic reputation and surrounded by many intellectuals from Surrealist circles (such as André and Elise Breton and Benjamin Péret), Toyen found a welcoming and friendly audience in postwar Paris. From the 1950s until the end of her life, she further developed techniques in magic realism, which she applied to her paintings, drawings, collages and illustrations. She continued to participate in international exhibitions of Surrealist art, including the prestigious New York exhibition: "Surrealist Intrusion in the Enchanters' Domain" (1968). In 1953, Toyen's first monograph was published by Editions Sokolova (Paris) and she launched a solo exhibition at the *Galerie a l'étoile scellé*. Other solo exhibitions in Paris were held in 1947, 1955, 1958, 1960 and 1962. The year 1953 also saw the publication of a French edition of *Přízraky pouště*.

After Toyen left Czechoslovakia, she appeared on the 'black list' of the communist *aparatchiks*; her work challenged the official cultural policy of socialist realism promoted across the Soviet Bloc, and she was considered to belong to the 'imperialist' enemy. (It should be noted that a number of former members of the Czech interwar avant-garde were executed, discredited or exiled, while others opportunistically joined the new regime.) During the 1960s, as Czechoslovak society opened up gradually to alternative ideas, Toyen began to attract renewed interest. For the first time since World War II, her work was exhibited in her home country as part of the 1964 exhibition: "Imaginative Painting, 1930–1950," held in the *Aleš* South Bohemian Gallery in Hluboká nad Vltavou (Czech Republic). In the era of so-called 'normalization' that followed the Soviet invasion of Czechoslovakia (1968–1989), Toyen was again shown, albeit sporadically, by galleries that had managed to purchase her work for their collections. Toyen died on 9 November 1980 in Paris. The largest retrospective of Toyen (curator: Karel Srp) was organized by the City Gallery of Prague in the House of the Stone Bell (2000).

The history of the Czech avant-garde is largely a story written by men about men. While a number of remarkable women artists worked in the decorative arts, the field of so-called 'high' art, including painting and sculpture, remained almost exclusively a male domain. Toyen was the only fully respected member of prewar Czech art. Appropriating the gender-neutral pseudonym "Toyen" and referring to herself as 'he,' the artist often wore men's suits. More provocatively still, the works she produced—pervaded by bold, erotic motifs—represented strictly taboo images, including lesbian desire. Toyen never openly expressed her sympathy to, or support of feminism, nor did she ever speak openly about her sexual orientation. For most avant-garde artists, feminism was seen as a relic of the nineteenth-century bourgeois women's movement that had flourished in the salons of the privileged. By contrast, Toyen's milieu believed in collective creativity and the struggle for an ideal (and also idealized), classless society based on the involvement of the masses, a society in which gender would be largely irrelevant. And yet the life and work of Toyen has greatly contributed to feminist art history and art criticism. She is regarded by many as a pioneer of women's art: a 'role model' who penetrated a modernist male preserve; an artist who represented and challenged women's sexuality, desire and identity (both erotic and homoerotic, symbolic and explicit, even pornographic). But she also introduced a radically new perspective on how women see, reflect and understand themselves in the modern world. Her art has been admired not only by male Surrealists such as André Breton, but also by a host of feminist scholars and thinkers, including Whithey Chadwick, Renée Riese Hubert, Rita Bischof, Mary Ann Caws and Silvia Eiblmayr.

Martina Pachmanová
Academy of Arts,
Architecture and Design in Prague

SOURCES

(D) Nezval, Vítězslav and Karel Teige. *Štyrský a Toyen* (Štyrský and Toyen). Prague: F. Borový, 1938.
(D) Bischof, Rita. *Toyen. Das malerische Werk.* (Toyen. Her creative work). Frankfurt a. M: Verlag Neue Kritik, 1987.
(D) Srp, Karel. *Toyen*. Prague: Argo, 2000.
(D) Pachmanová, Martina. "Reconstructing Toyen." *Art in America* (April 2001): 130–131.
(E) Breton, André. *Surrealism and Painting*. New York: Harper & Row, 1972.
(E) Eiblmayr, Silvia. *Die Frau als Bild* (Woman as image). Berlin: Dietrich Reimer Verlag, 1993.
(E) Hubert, Renée Riese. *Magnifying Mirrors: Women, surrealism and partnership*. Lincoln and London: University of Nebraska Press, 1994.

TRUBNIKOVA, Mariia (1835–1897)

Leader of the Russian women's movement in the 1860s and 1870s; co-founder (1861) and Chairwoman of the philanthropic *Obshchestvo Dostavlenniia Deshevykh Kvartir i Drugikh Posobii Nuzhdaiushchimsia Zhiteliam S-Peterburga* (Society for Cheap Lodging and Other Aid to the Residents of St Petersburg); translator and publisher.

Mariia Vasil'evna Trubnikova, the daughter of a political exile, was born on 6 January 1835 in the eastern Siberian settlement of Petrovskii zavod (Petrov's mill). Her father, military officer Vasilii Petrovich Ivashev (1797–1840), was from a wealthy noble family from the Simbirsk guberniia (now the *oblast* or province of Ulianovskaya). In 1819, Ivashev joined the secret masonic society, the *Soiuz Blagodenstviia* (Prosperity Union). Although he did not take part in the rebellion against the tsarist regime of 14 December 1825 (after which all members of the secret societies were named 'Decembrists'), his name was betrayed during the subsequent inquiry and he was arrested and sentenced to exile in Siberia. Maria's mother, Camille Ledantu (1808–1839), was the daughter of a French Viscountess who had escaped to Russia during the French Revolution, and a French merchant. Camille followed Ivashev to Siberia, where they married (1832) and had four children: Alexander, Mariia, Peter and Vera (Alexander died at the age of two). In 1839, Camille died in childbirth (as did the baby, Elizabeth) and Vasilii's sudden death followed a year later. The children were brought up in the family of Vasilii Ivashev's sister, Princess Ekaterine Khovanskaia, with the family name of Vasiliev. Only in 1856, when amnesty had been proclaimed, could Mariia, Peter and Vera claim back their father's name and title. Mariia's brother, Peter Ivashev (1837–1896), became an artillery officer; her sister, Vera Ivasheva (1838–?), married A. A. Tcherkesov and became one of the leaders of the Russian women's movement.

Mariia Trubnikova was raised in an atmosphere of pious reverence for Decembrist ideals. Since the large and harmonious family of her aunt had always traditionally engaged in charity work, she too became involved in philanthropy from her early youth. She received a good education from highly qualified tutors in European languages, history, literature and music. In 1854, she married Konstantin Vasil'evich

Trubnikov (1829–1904), then a government official, and the young couple settled down in St Petersburg. They had four daughters [one of them, Olga (1858–1953), left memoirs]. With Mariia Trubnikova's dowry, her husband was able to found a banking house and *Zhurnal Dlia Akzionerov* (The stockholder magazine). Mariia Trubnikova's salon in St Petersburg was a meeting place for liberals and radicals.

Mariia Trubnikova made a good impression on people: she was candid, considerate, a convincing speaker and "a born social worker"–as one contemporary, Vladimir Stasov (the brother of ***Nadezhda Stasova***), described her (Stasov 1899, 43–46). In the spring of 1859, with the help of ***Anna Filosofova***, Nadezhda Stasova and other members of her salon, Trubnikova made plans for a new organization, the *Obshchestvo Dostavlenniia Deshevykh Kvartir i Drugikh Posobii Nuzhdaiuchimsia Zhiteliam S-Peterburga* (Society for Cheap Lodging and Other Aid to the Residents of St Petersburg). Its purpose was to provide poor families and unassisted women with decent and inexpensive places to live. By 1861, when the statute of the society was adopted, it boasted several hundred members and Mariia Trubnikova was unanimously elected Chairwoman.

Due to delicate health, Trubnikova spent the winter and summer of 1861 in the south of France, where she received treatment for health problems. During this period she read, and was deeply impressed by Jenny d'Héricourt's *La femme affranchie: réponse à M. M. Michelet, Proudhon, E. de Girardin, A. Comte et aux autres novateurs modernes* (The emancipated woman: a reply to Monsieurs Michelet, Proudhon, etc. and other modern innovators, 1860). She resolved to translate it into Russian (though she never did) and entered into correspondence with the author. Through d'Héricourt, she was put into contact with Josephine Butler, a famous activist of the British women's movement, and Marie Goegg, the founder and Chairwoman of the International Association of Women (founded in 1868). In 1869, Trubnikova's poor health took her abroad once again. She met Josephine Butler and Marie Goegg in Switzerland and maintained friendly relations with them both. According to leaders of Russian women's groups (Anna Filosofova, V. Tcherkesova and others), Trubnikova was regarded by many European feminists as a leading figure of the Russian women's movement. In this capacity, she gave regular updates to Butler on developments regarding the women's cause and feminist initiatives in Russia.

In the early 1860s, Trubnikova's circumstances drastically changed. The banking house of her husband failed and *Zhurnal Dlia Akzionerov* (The stockholder magazine) was transformed into a daily paper, *Birzhevye Vedomosti* (The stock exchange news). In an effort to improve her financial situation, Trubnikova found work with this paper and some other periodicals as a translator. Her relations with Konstantin Trubnikov became increasingly tense and in the late 1870s the couple separated altogether. From then on, Trubnikova had to earn a living to provide for herself and her daughters.

In spite of these family troubles and the threat of destitution, Trubnikova continued her public activities. She resigned from her post as Chairwoman of the *Obshchestvo*

Dostavleniia Deshevykh Kvartir i Drugikh Posobii Nuzhdaiushimsia Zhiteliam S-Peterburga but remained an active member. While working at the newspaper office, Trubnikova helped many people find employment. In 1862, she was among those who attempted to establish the *Obshchestvo Zhenskogo Truda* (Society for Women's Work), which had broad and ambitious aims. The idea underpinning the project–to provide educated women with employment corresponding to their intellectual abilities–crystallized into the *Zhenskoi Izdatelskoi Arteli Perevodchits* (Women Translators' Publishing Cooperative) in 1863. It was expected that the cooperative would not only offer women ways of earning, but would also raise their awareness. The cooperative, also known as the Women Translators' Circle, successfully published many popular works, including the fairy tales of Hans Christian Andersen and Charles Darwin's *On the Origin of Species* (1859; published by the Women Translators' Circle under the Russian title of *O Proiskhozhdenii Vidov*, 1864). By the beginning of the 1870s, after key figures Maria Trubnikova and ***Nadezhda Stasova*** had gone abroad, the activities of the cooperative came to an end.

Mariia Trubnikova was also deeply involved in the campaign for women's higher education that began in the late 1860s. Trubnikova, ***Stasova*** and ***Filosofova***, the so-called "women's triumvirate," initiated petitions for women's courses and even provoked heated public debates. Trubnikova received letters from J. S. Mill and the French feminist André Leo expressing admiration for Russian women's efforts. In her replies, Trubnikova declared close international cooperation to be essential to the women's cause. The campaign for women's higher education resulted in the opening of the *Vysshih Zhenskikh Bestuzhevskikh Kursov* (Higher *Bestuzhev* Courses for Women) in St Petersburg in 1878.

Early in 1881, Maria Trubnikova suffered a nervous breakdown due to overwork and mental stress. From 1882 on, she lived in the provinces with her daughters, visiting St Petersburg only twice (in 1888 and 1890) to meet friends and colleagues. Yet she remained active; she continued to translate and, in 1892 (when many people were dying of famine), she raised money and opened communal kitchens for the starving of the Tambovskaya *guberniia* (province). In the winter of 1893-1894, Trubnikova contracted a severe flu which led to pneumonia and recurrent psychosis. She spent two years in the Tambov asylum and was then moved to the asylum in St Petersburg, where she died on 28 April 1897 in the arms of her youngest daughter. She was buried in the *Novodevichii* Convent Cemetery in St Petersburg, alongside her brother. After her death, prominent leaders of the Russian women's movement paid tribute to Maria Trubnikova as the heart and soul of feminist projects in Russia during the 1860s and 1870s.

Natalia Novikova
Yaroslavl State Pedagogical University

SOURCES

(B) Stasov, Vladimir V. *Nadezhda Vasil'evna Stasova*. St Petersburg, 1899.

(B) *Sbornik pamiati Anny Pavlovny Filosofovoi (1837-1912)* (In memory of Anna Pavlovna Filosofova). Vols. 1-2. Petrograd: Tovarishestvo R. Golike i E. A. Vilborg, 1915.

(B) Bulanova, O. "Dekabrist Ivashev i ego sem'ia" (Decembrist Ivashev and his family). *Byloe* (Recollections), no. 19 (1922): 30-60.

(D) Tcherkesova, Vera. "Mariia Vasil'evna Trubnikova." *Zhenskoe Delo* (Women's cause) XII (1899): 15-37.

(D) Stasova, Poliksena. "Pamiati M. V. Trubnikovoi" (To the memory of M. V. Trubnikova). *Zhenskoe Delo* XII (1899): 43-46.

(D) Bulanova-Trubnikova, O. K. *Tri pokoleniia* (Three generations). Moscow, Leningrad: Gosudarstvennoe izdatelstvo, tipografiya Pechatnii Dvor, 1928.

(E) *Dekabristy. Biograficheskii spravochnik* (The Decembrists. A biographical dictionary). Moscow: "Nauka," 1988.

TYRKOVA-WILLIAMS, Ariadna (1869–1962)

Prominent Russian journalist, writer, public activist, member of the Central Committee of the *Kadet* (Constitutional-Democratic) Party and the *Liga Ravnopraviia Zhenshchin* (League for Women's Equal Rights). Pen-name: Vergezhsky.

Ariadna Tyrkova was born on 26 November 1869 into a noble Russian gentry family of simple means. Her mother, Sophia Karlovna Tyrkova (born Gaily, 1837), came from a modest Protestant family of Baltic Germans. Her father, the lawyer Vladimir Aleksandrovich Tyrkov (born 1835), was from a noble Russian Orthodox family of rich landowners in the province of Novgorod. The social differences between the two families seemed at first to pose an obstacle to their marriage, but, as Ariadna later wrote, her father "could not have given up such a beauty" (Tyrkova 1998, 18) and insisted on marrying Ariadna's mother. Their marriage, which lasted more than fifty years, was very happy and Ariadna always described her parents' home as warm. They had four sons and three daughters: Victor, Maria, Arkadii (1860–1924), Ariadna, Sergei, Alexei and Sophia. Ariadna was the fourth child. Together with her sisters and brothers, she spent a happy childhood at their beautiful family estate: Vergezha, in northern Russia (near the river Volkhov), which Vladimir Tyrkov had inherited from his father. It was difficult to find the money to pay for the education of so many children, but Sophia Tyrkova did her best and did not differentiate between the education of her sons and daughters. Ariadna Tyrkova was sent to the prestigious girls' high school run by Princess Obolenskaia in St Petersburg.

When Ariadna was still young, anti-tsarist ideas had begun to spread through all classes of society and the Tyrkov family was no exception. Ariadna's cousin, Sophia Leshern von Gertsfeld, took part in the *narodnik* (populist) movement and her eldest brother Arkady was a member of the *Narodnaia Volia* (People's Will). In 1883, he was exiled to Siberia for his participation in the terrorist organization responsible for the assassination of Tsar Alexander II. At the age of fifteen, Ariadna Tyrkova was expelled from high school for her radical opinions, although she was allowed to take the final examinations. She had dreamed of being a doctor, but Russian universities did not admit women and the government, in the period of political reaction, closed women's higher education establishments, including medical courses. So Tyrkova chose the department of mathematics at the re-opened *Vysshie Zhenskie Kursy* (Higher Women's Courses). Not taking to mathematics, she studied there for only a year and in 1890, married the engineer Alfred Nikolaevitch Borman (data unknown). The marriage was unhappy and despite the birth of two children–a son Arkadii (b. 1891) and a daughter Sophia (b. 1895)–the spouses soon parted. In her memoirs she neglects to mention her first marriage, after which she reverted to using her maiden name.

After the divorce, Tyrkova had custody of the children and had to support her family. She began to earn money as a journalist (taking the pen-name Vergezhsky) and soon became a popular author. Her personal collection in the Russian State Historical Archive contains a lot of drafts and press-cuttings of her sketches, stories and reports devoted to different social problems. Through her writing, she became acquainted with many prominent Russian radicals and in 1903, began working as a courier for the illegal *Souiz Osvobozhdeniia* (Union for Freedom). Nevertheless, in spite of her revolutionary relatives and her anti-government activities, she adopted liberal, not Marxist, ideas. But since neither were tolerated by the tsarist government, Tyrkova, after several arrests, had to emigrate from Russia, spending eighteen months in France, Switzerland and Germany–together with her children. In 1904 in Stuttgart (Germany), she made the acquaintance of Harold Williams (1876-1928), a special correspondent for *The Times*, who later became Tyrkova's second husband (they probably married early in 1906). He was seven years her junior but their marriage was happy and lasted until Williams' death in 1928. As a widow, Tyrkova wrote a book about Williams in English entitled *The Cheerful Giver* (1935).

The Russian revolution of 1905 gave Tyrkova the opportunity to return home. The first meeting she attended in St Petersburg was, by chance, a meeting of the *Soiuz Ravnopraviia Zhenshchin* (Women's Equal Rights Union). Tyrkova did not join the Union: partly because she was regarded as too moderate by its leftist leaders; partly because she did not think that there was a real problem regarding women's equality. Later, she wrote: "at that moment I was so sure that I was equal to men, I could not imagine the need to prove it" (Tyrkova 1998, 363). But she soon understood that women in Russia did have to prove their right to equal treatment, and became an ardent supporter of women's rights. Her first speech on women's political equality was delivered at the first congress of the *Kadet* Party in January 1906. Together with Anna Miliukova and the lawyer Lev Petratsitski, she insisted on including a statement about equal political rights for men and women in the party program. She was soon elected to the Central Committee of the *Kadet* Party, occupying that position until the end of 1917. She also led the press department of the *Kadets*. She was so influential that opponents of the party sometimes joked that she was the only man in the Central Committee of the *Kadet* Party. Richard Stites is certainly right to point out that it was largely thanks to Tyrkova and Miliukova's activities that the *Kadet* Party became the main supporter of women's political equality in the State Duma (Stites 1991, 287).

Between 1906 and 1917, Tyrkova was an active parliamentary correspondent, delivering articles to several liberal newspapers–mostly to *Slovo* (Word). She was among the organizers of (and participated in) the *Pervyi Vserossiiskii Zhenskii S'ezd* (First All-Russian Women's Congress) held in 1908. At the Congress, she defended the position of liberal feminists. In 1910, she joined the *Liga Ravnopraviia Zhenshchin* (League for Women's Equal Rights), in which she was a prominent figure, writing and lecturing in support of women's rights. The famous women's demonstration in St Petersburg on 20 March 1917, organized by the *Liga*, began with speeches by Tyrkova, ***Shishkina-Iavein*** and Figner in the City Duma. The demonstration managed to extract a promise from the Provisional Government to grant political rights to women.

After the October Revolution, Tyrkova had once again to emigrate from Russia and, together with her husband, settled in London. There, she organized a society to help Russian refugees, which she led for twenty years. She also devoted herself to editorial and writing activity, editing the journal *Russian Life* (1921) and authoring books and novels: *From Freedom to Brest-Litovsk. The First Year of Russian Revolution* (1919) and *Hosts of Darkness* (1921), written together with Harold Williams (both books originally published in English). During the thirty years from 1918 to 1948, Tyrkova worked on a biography of Pushkin; the weighty two volumes of research that she carried out on this subject have recently been published in Russian as *Zhizn' Pushkina* (Puskin's life, 1998). After the death of Harold Williams, Tyrkova moved to France and lived there with her son's family. She survived the German occupation and was interned as a British citizen. In 1951, again with her son's family, she moved to the USA, living first in New York, then in Washington. In spite of her advanced years, she took part in the creation of a Russian political committee in New York and became its Vice-President, continuing to work on her memoirs and delivering lectures and speeches. Those who knew her at that time remembered that she stayed beautiful, clever and strong-willed. The only thing she regretted was not being able to return to her beloved Vergezha, the estate on which she grew up. She died in her son's house on 12 January 1962.

While Tyrkova's feminist period, in the context of her long life, may seem rather short, it is nevertheless significant that she participated in the Russian women's movement during its most intense and interesting period, when the fight for women's political equality was closely connected with the fight for a democratic society. Ariadna Tyrkova managed to make a significant contribution to both, as a feminist and as a democrat.

Olga Shnyrova
Ivanovo State University

SOURCES

(A) *Russian State Historical Archive*. Collection no. 629 (Ariadna Vladimirovna Tyrkova).

(C) Tyrkova, A. V. *Vospominaniia. To, chego bol'she ne budet* (Recollections. That which will not happen again). Moscow: Slovo, 1998.

(E) Stites, Richard. *The Women's Liberation Movement in Russia: Feminism, Nihilism, and Bolshevism, 1860-1930*. Princeton: Princeton University Press, 1991 (first edition, 1978).

UKRAINKA, Lesia (real name Larysa Petrivna Kosach) (1871-1913)

Ukrainian woman-poet, writer, dramatist, literary critic and public activist.

Lesia Ukrianka (left) with Olha Kobylianska, 1901

Lesia Ukrainka (a pseudonym of Larysa Petrivna Kosach) was born on 25 February 1871 in Novohrad-Volynsky, the second child of six. Not wanting her children to grow up in an environment dominated by the Russian language, her mother (***Olena Pchilka***) did not send her children to school. Instead, she provided them all (including Lesia) with a solid home education that consisted of piano lessons, private classes with professors from the Kiev gymnasium for boys (e.g. in Greek and Latin) and tuition in French and German. Later in life, Lesia also mastered English and some Slavic languages and proved to be an able translator. Nevertheless, she always suffered from what she perceived to be her lack of systematic education.

In 1881, Lesia caught a cold that developed into a severe illness, turning her life into a continuous struggle against pain. At first, rheumatism was diagnosed; later, in 1883, bone tuberculosis was suspected and Lesia underwent surgery on the infected bones in her left hand. The operation was unsuccessful and she continued to suffer from diseased bones, joints and later, lungs. Her condition meant that for long periods of time she was removed from her family and others she loved, receiving treatment in Odesa, the Crimea (in southern Ukraine), Berlin, Zurich, Venice and Georgia (then part of the Russian Empire), where she died on 8 August 1913.

Her obvious talent was noticed early on: Lesia was nine when she wrote her first poem, "Nadia" (Hope), and thirteen when her poems "Safo" (Sappho) and "Konvalia" (Lily of the Valley) appeared in the Lviv journal *Zoria* (Star). In 1886, she assisted her mother in putting together the anthology *Pershy Vinok* (First wreath), in which her poems "Rusalka" (Water nymph), "Na Zelenomu Horbochku" (On a green hill) and others were published in 1887. From 1888 onwards, she regularly published in various Ukrainian periodicals and her first poetic collection, *Na Krylakh Pisen* (On the wings of songs), was published in 1893 (in Lviv since the Ukrainian language was then forbidden in the Russian Empire).

Lesia Ukrainka took part in the activities of various public and political (mostly social democratic) organizations. For such activities she was (like her mother) subjected to secret police surveillance. Although she took a strong position on women's issues in her literary criticism and her dramatic writing, as well as in her private life, her poetry was different and was therefore highly praised in her own, and in Soviet times because it absorbed the aesthetics of populist nationalism and reflected dominant political (populist) lines; so much so that Ivan Franko (1856–1916), one of the key proponents of the aesthetic and cultural values of populism, called Lesia "the only man in all of modern Ukraine" (Franko 1981, 269). By contrast, her literary criticism introduced Western European intellectual traditions and new tendencies in European literature into Ukrainian cultural life, providing Ukrainian literary criticism with a new set of theoretical frameworks—see for example her "Dva napravlenia v noveishei ital'yanskoi literature: Ada Negri i d'Annuntsio" (Two directions in contemporary Italian literature: Ada Negri and d'Annuncio, 1899). She was one of the first to address women's representation in modern literature, presenting and later publishing a paper in *Zhyzn* (Life) entitled "Novye perspektivy i staryye teni: 'Novaya zhenshchina' zapadno-evropeiskoi belletristiki" (New perspectives and old shadows: 'The new woman' in Western European fiction, 1900). Similarly, her plays reflected the attempts of a female intellectual to transcend the boundaries set by Ukrainian literary tradition; to reshape dramatic and theatrical traditions and introduce new themes and genres. Through the silent and obedient shadows of Ukrainka's female protagonists, her plays laid bare the social, cultural and religious constraints on women's lives in the everyday. Her first play, *Blakytna Troyanda* (The blue rose; written in 1895/96 and first staged in Kiev in 1899), was harshly criticized by reviewers because it did not conform to populist ideology (as her much lauded poetry did).

Ukrainka's private life in some ways successfully resisted the patriarchal order, but it was a life filled with difficulties. She seems to have been a constant source of anxiety to her family because of her poor health, and she also behaved in ways unthinkable for a woman of her social standing. She engaged in two passionate friendships: one with Nestor Gambarashvili (1871–1966), a student from Georgia who lodged with the Kosaches in 1895 in Kiev; another with Serhy Merzhynsky (1870–1901), a Social Democrat and activist whom she met in 1898, visited in Minsk (Belarus) in 1900, accommodated in her home several times and cared for as he was dying in 1901. For a long time, Ukrainka rejected the marriage proposals of Klyment Vasyliovych Kvitka (1880–1953), a folklorist, ethnographer and musicologist whom she met in 1898 and with whom she lived for a while in a common-law relationship. In 1906, Ukrainka relented and her marriage was registered in 1907 upon her mother's wishes (Ukrainka herself saw marriage and its traditional religious ceremonies as oppressive social practices).

Lesia Ukrainka was buried in Kiev Baikhove cemetery, alongside her father and brother Mykhailo. It is only in recent times, thanks to the research of ***Solomea Pavlychko*** and Vira Ageeva, that Ukrainka's dramatic works have at last begun to attract proper academic interest as powerful feminist manifestos.

Natalia V. Monakhova
Ph.D. Candidate (Comparative Literature),
National University "Kyiv-Mohyla Academy"

SOURCES

(C) Ukrainka, Lesia. *Zibrannia tvoriv u 12 tomakh* (Collected works in twelve volumes). Kiev: Naukova Dumka, 1979.

(D) Zborovska, Nila. *Moya Lesia Ukrainka* (My Lesia Ukrainka). Ternopil: Dzhura, 2002.

(D) Karmazina, Maria. *Lesia Ukrainka*. Kiev: Alternatyvy, 2003.

(E) Franko, Ivan. *Tvory: u 50 t.* (Works in fifty volumes). Kiev: Naukova Dumka, 1981, 31: 269.

(E) Pavlychko, Solomea. "Modernism vs. Populism in *Fin de Siècle* Ukrainian Literature." In P. Chester and S. Forrester, eds. *Engendering Slavic Literatures*. Bloomington IN: Indiana University Press, 1996, 81-103.

(E) Bohachevsky-Chomiak, Martha. *Bilym po bilomu: Zhinky v hromadskomy zhytti Ukrayny* (White on white: women in Ukrainian public life). Kiev: Lybid, 1999.

(E) Smoliar. L. O., ed. *Zhinochi studii v Ukraini: Zhinka v istorii i siohodni* (Women's studies in Ukraine: woman in history and today). Odesa: AstroPrint, 1999.

(E) Ageeva, Vira. *Zhinochy prostir: Feministychnyi dyskurs ukrainskoho modernyzmu* (Women's space: the feminist discourse of Ukrainian modernism). Kiev: Fakt, 2003.

VANSOVÁ, Terézia (1857-1942)

Writer, author of the first Slovak novel for women; women's activist, promoter of women's education, active in the Slovak women's association *Živena* (founded in 1869 and named after an old Slavonic Goddess of life); editor of the first Slovak women's magazine *Dennica* (Morning star) (1898). Pseudonym(s): 'Johanka Georgiadesová,' 'Milka Žartovnická' and 'Nemophila.'

Terézia Vansová, born Medvecká, was one of twins (a boy and a girl) born in Zvolenská Slatina (Upper Hungary, Austria-Hungary; Slovakia) on 18 April 1857. Both twins were rather weak but their parents Terézia (born Langeová) and the almost thirty years older Samuel Medvecký paid little attention to the girl twin, Terézia, their seventh child. After graduating from elementary school, twelve-year-old Terézia attended the private school of K. Orfanides in Banská Bystrica and later, the private institute of T. Fábryová in Rimavská Sobota, where she obtained the fragmentary and sketchy knowledge typical for women's education in that period, as well as language skills in German and Hungarian. She was particularly fond of the German language, which became a source of literary inspiration and the medium of her early literary attempts. Like other socially aware women writers of the period, she later taught herself in order to supplement her non-systematic and insufficient education. Early on, her father had accepted the entreaty of Terézia's teachers to "let the girl learn," but her mother was worried that learning would "make [Terézia] unwomanly. Such learned women are an object of ridicule for the world and so they get married with great difficulty. Who would marry such an eccentric?" (cited in Václavíková-Matulayová 1937, 30). Later, Terézia's husband would also trivialize her literary ambitions, at least initially; he only started to support her after she began editing the journal *Dennica* (Morning star). All these significant turns in life certainly contributed to the resigned and sober attitude of Terézia Vansová to women's emancipation as an ideal directly related to the question of women's education. In a letter to editor J. Škultéty, she wrote: "I would have to be silly not to know that the field for the so-called woman question is infertile in this area [i.e. of education]" (cited in Mráz 1937, 36). She advocated women's education mainly in the Slovak women's association *Živena*, together with ***Elena Maróthy-Šoltésová***, and in her wide-ranging public activities as the wife of a pastor.

Her later steps in life were equally sober and pragmatic. In 1875, she married Ján Vansa (1846–1922), a Lutheran pastor with whom she lived in Lomnička, later in Rimavská Píla and, from 1911 onwards, in Banská Bystrica. Their only child, a son, died in early childhood. As a young mother and pastor's wife living in the German language environment of Lomnička, she wrote in German on children's education and expressed her grief for her son's loss in poems also written in German. It took her a long time to recover from the loss of her child and only her work in the movement for national revival kept her going. Moving to the Slovak region of Rimavská Píla also helped her recover. Vansová and her husband adopted a daughter, Oľga, in addition to which Vansová was involved in many social activities.

In 1889, she published the sentimental novel *Sirota Podhradských* (The orphan of the Podhradský family) in the manner of the German *Familienroman*. The prominent Slovak writer and national activist Svetozár Hurban Vajanský welcomed it as the first Slovak women's novel and praised Vansová's ability to reach a broad female audience. While the use of the Slovak language as a literary language was provocative, Vansová, unlike many of her contemporaries, did not choose to write a story with an explicit national revival motif; instead, she focused on a young woman's moral strength in the face of misfortune.

While Vansová's fiction was dominated by the sentimental style of trivial women's literature, a realistic technique prevailed in her memoir writing, as in the book *Môj muž* (My husband), published serially in a magazine between 1924 and 1926, and as a book under the title of *Ján Vansa* in 1938. In this work, she depicted her everyday coexistence and collaboration with her husband (who helped her edit *Dennica*), their material problems and Vansová's role in caring for her husband, who suffered from mental illness. She also wrote a biography of her mother, *Terézia Medvecká, rod. Lange* (Terézia Medvecká, born Lange, 1900) and, although her mother was not publicly active, included her in her private 'Slavín žien slovanských' (Hall of fame of Slav women), a category created by Vansová to celebrate women. Vansová probably intended to write biographies of several other women as well. In her mother's biography, she spoke of the great importance of a mother's work within the family. Unique in Vansová's oeuvre is the book of travels *Pani Georgiadesová na cestách* (Mrs Georgiades on her travels, 1896), a self-ironic avowal of realism through Vansová's collected travel experiences and reflections on the ethnographic exhibition in Prague (1895).

The Slovak women's movement, founded by the first significant Slovak women writers of that time, was strongly embedded in the national revival movement. This resulted in the framing of women's activities in traditional Christian values and led to specific demands regarding the roles of women and men. The first Slovak women writers, Maróthy-Šoltésová and Vansová, became prominent figures in the national revival movement, paradoxically as a result of political restrictions on the Slovak nation and under the intense pressures imposed by *Magyarization*. In this complicated situation, with most Slovak cultural institutions banned by the state, the women's association *Živena*, presumed to be politically 'harmless,' could play a 'nation-preserving' role. A public sphere of national life was thus opened up for Slovak women because of closure from outside.

In this context, Terézia Vansová became active in the association *Živena* (from 1895 as Vice-President) and co-edited the *Živena* almanacs, which appeared on an irregular basis and included fiction and poetry as well as cultural and political essays. Vansová felt the need for a women's magazine and promoted the Czech *Ženský svět* (Women's world) in Slovakia. In 1898, she accepted an offer made by the Czech public activist Karol Kálal to edit the first women's magazine in Slovakia, thus becoming the founder and editor-in-chief of *Dennica* (Morning star), published in the years 1898 to 1908 and 1910 to 1914. (During the latter period, Vansová was no longer the editor of *Dennica*, which ceased as a women's publication and became a forum for Slovak literary modernists.) Vansová's friend and collaborator ***Elena Maróthy-Šoltésová,*** in her essay "Načo sú tie ženské časopisy" [What good are these women's magazines, 1898; reprinted in *Aspekt,* no. 2 (1994)], defended *Dennica* against critics and analyzed the historical roots of women's illiteracy in Slovakia, although she did not doubt or challenge women's status as 'helpers' of men and of the nation. The friends Vansová and Maróthy-Šoltésová, in compliance with their personal histories and location in the national/ist context of that time, viewed religious education as a primary means of national advancement and within this framework accepted women's roles based on a traditional gender division of labor. *Dennica* was composed from this perspective; it included tips for household and kitchen and articles on child education and social life, but it also contained essays on women writers, historical figures and pieces of fiction. Working in difficult conditions, without payment, the volunteers at *Dennica* managed to achieve an incredible print run of three thousand issues.

After the formation of the Czechoslovak Republic in 1918, the magazine *Slovenská žena* (Slovak woman) was established with Vansová as editor from 1920 to 1923. But it was not "my *Dennica*; it was not the magazine into which I had put my modest thoughts, through which I had spoken to my, in some ways even more modest Slovak sisters, many of whom I had taught to think and read in their mother tongue" (cited in Mráz 1937, 42).

Even in the last years of her life, Vansová remained productive in the field of literature, producing new writing as well as preparing new editions of her existing work. Lonely after the suicide of her husband in 1922, she devoted herself to helping others (her primary ethos), remaining active and lively in her old age. She died on 10 October 1942, at the age of 85. Nowadays, Terézia Vansová is remembered mostly as the author of novels for girls that, while not read much today, were popular until just a few decades ago. She is also remembered for her activities in the Slovak national movement, though less for her activities in the women's movement, due to the fact that the history of the women's movement is still not well known in Slovakia.

Jana Cviková
ASPEKT, feminist publishing and educational project
www.aspekt.sk

SOURCES

(B) *Dennica* (Morning star) (1899).
(C) Vansová, Terézia. *Ján Vansa* (Ján Vansa). Liptovský Mikuláš: Tranoscius, 1941.
(C) Vansová, Terézia. *Danko a Janko* (Danko and Janko). Bratislava: Mladé letá, 1958.
(C) Vansová, Terézia. *Pani Georgiadesová na cestách* (Mrs Georgiadesová on her travels). Bratislava: Tatran, 1977.
(C) Vansová, Terézia. *Sirota Podhradských* (The orphan of the Podhradský family). Bratislava: Ikar, 2002.
(D) Mráz, Andrej. *Literárne dielo Terézie Vansovej* (The literary work of Terézia Vansová). Martin: Živena, 1937.
(D) Václavíková-Matulayová, Margita. *Život Terézie Vansovej* (The life of Terézia Vansová). Bratislava: Nakladateľstvo Slovenskej ligy, 1937.
(E) Pišút, Milan, et. al. *Dejiny slovenskej literatúry* (The history of Slovak literature). Bratislava: Obzor, 1984.
(E) Rudinsky, Norma. *Incipient Feminists: Women Writers in the Slovak National Revival* (With an "Appendix of Slovak Women Poets 1798-1875" by Marianna Prídavková-Mináriková). Columbus/Ohio: Slavica Publishers, Inc., 1991.
(E) *Lexikón slovenských žien* (Lexicon of Slovak women). Martin: Slovenská národná knižnica and Národný biografický ústav, 2003.
(E) Cviková, Jana. "Po boku muža a národa" (Alongside man and nation). *Aspekt–feminist cultural magazine*, no. 1 (2003-2004): 71-78.
(E) Mikulová, Marcela. "Ženy a národ na prelome 19. a 20. storočia" (Women and the nation at the turn of the nineteenth and twentieth centuries). *Aspekt–feminist cultural magazine*, no. 1 (2003-2004): 72-74.
(E) Cviková, Jana. 'Sinnlose' und 'sinnvolle' Emanzipation: Über die Entstehung des feministischen Bewusstseins in der Slowakei ('Senseless' and 'meaningful' emancipation. On the rise of feminist consciousness in Slovakia). Thesis. Vienna: Rosa Mayreder College, May 2004.

VIKOVÁ-KUNĚTICKÁ, Božena (1862–1934)

Czech author and playwright with a keen interest in women's and other social issues; journalist and politician; first woman to be elected to the National Assembly (1912).

Božena Viková born Novotná was born on 30 July 1862 to an innkeeper and grain trader; there is no information about her mother. She studied acting under the guidance of the distinguished Czech actress Otýlie Sklenářová-Malá, giving up on this career after the National Theater burned down in 1881. In that year, she married Josef Vika, a clerk from a sugar factory, and the couple moved first to Uhříněves, later to Český Brod (towns near Prague). They had two children. In the early 1880s, Viková began publishing short stories in the journals *Zábavné listy* (Funny papers) and *Divadelní listy* (Theatrical letters). She signed her prose 'Kunětická,' after the nationally symbolic Kunětická Mount (in eastern Bohemia), and her poems 'Julia Ignota' (Julia Unknown), 'X. Ignota' and 'Ignota.'

Božena Viková-Kunětická published her early short stories and essays in the journals *Lumír* (Lumír) and *Květy* (Flowers), later compiling them for the collections *Čtyři povídky* (Four short stories, 1890), *Staří mládenci a jiné povídky* (Bachelors and other stories, 1901) and *Macecha a jiné črty* (Stepmother and other essays, 1902). Like her later novels, her stories depicted provincial towns or rural environments, employing irony as well as sentiment. Marriage is treated as a life-changing event and comical conflicts characterize family life, but Viková-Kunětická did not avoid tragic themes, often making causal links between the death of a child or an animal and the social conditions in which human ignorance escalates into ruthless cruelty–as in her collection of short stories ironically entitled *Idylky* (Small idylls, 1894).

Viková-Kunětická's irony and crude realism brought her close to the modernist poet Josef Svatopluk Machar. He himself was interested in women's issues, particularly in the situation of middle-class women at the end of the nineteenth century, to whom he dedicated a book of poems, *Zde by měly kvést růže...* (Here, where the roses should flower..., 1894) and a novel in verses, *Magdalena* (Magdalene, 1894). He encouraged Viková-Kunětická to write candidly from 'a woman's point of view,' and to ignore the negative critique of her work that would (and did) follow. Viková-Kunětická's devotion to women's causes gradually radicalized. She was strongly influenced, not only by European realism (Henrik Ibsen, Leo N. Tolstoi, Ivan. S. Turgenev), but by the psycho-physiological and sociological theories developed by Richard von Kraft-Ebing and Max Nordau, which she turned to ironic use in her short story "Staří mládenci" (Bachelors)–about three affluent old brothers and their fetish for female underwear as a substitute for women.

In her longer novels, Viková-Kunětická began exploring what she saw as radical changes in the psyche of middle-class women towards the turn of the century. Her texts became sharply polemical, criticizing traditional notions of female dependency on men and celebrating independent motherhood, as in her novels *Minulost I* (Past I, 1895) and the trilogy *K světlu* (Towards the light, 1910), consisting of *Medřická* (Medřická, 1897), *Vzpoura* (The revolt, 1901) and *Pán* (The master, 1905). She passionately believed in women's emancipation and praised the mother who chose freedom over hypocritical relationships. These critical novels purposely avoided conventional character constructions and her protagonists revealed a latent crisis of manhood in modern patriarchal society, provoking public debates about women's liberty, the essence of true motherhood and its political role in society.

Viková-Kunětická's feminist dramas were also well-received by the general public. Inspired by the Nordic dramatists Henrik Ibsen, Bjornstjerne Bjornson and August Strindberg, her play *V jařmu* (Yoked, 1897) analyzed marital inequality and *Co bylo* (What was, 1902) depicted a tense family atmosphere resulting in the disclosure of a husband's infidelity. The plays *Přítěž* (Burden, 1901) and *Dospělé děti* (Adult children, 1909) are ironic send ups of feminist sloganism, which appears shallow against a backdrop of exaggerated middle-class individualism. Some of her plays about marital relationships–*Sběratelka starožitností* (Collector of antiques, 1890), *Reprezentantka domu* (Representative of the house, 1911) and *Cop* (Braid, 1904)–were performed at theaters in Vienna, Dresden, Zagreb, Ljubljana, Moscow and Paris.

As a modernist female author who sought to discover a specifically woman's view of the world and of literature, Viková-Kunětická also came to play an increasingly important role in political life at the beginning of the twentieth century. In April 1905, she attacked "the American" ***Charlotta Garrigue Masaryková*** in the *Národní listy* (National newspaper). She claimed that lectures delivered by Garrigue Masaryková to the liberal *Ženský klub český* (Czech Women's Club) had so shocked Czech feminist Humpal-Zemanová, that the latter had died of a heart attack, and accused Garrigue Masaryková of "thrusting" her "Protestant coldness" into the "warm Slavonic soul" (*Národní listy*, 16 April 1905). Viková-Kunětická's article on Zemanová's death stirred debate over the political direction of women's associations in Czechoslovakia and deepened misapprehension among the leading representatives of women's movements in Bohemia and Moravia.

In the early twentieth century, Viková-Kunětická published her early political views in a book, *Věřím* (I Believe, 1908), as well as contributing to the liberal newspaper *Národní listy* and the journal *Ženský obzor* (Women's horizon). In an article entitled "Žena a politika" (Woman and politics), published in *Národní listy* in 1907, Viková-Kunětická issued the following provocative statements:

> "Our women's organizations, our gatherings, our associations all seem smothered by an overcoat of false modesty and innocuous entertainment. Nobody is concerned with what women are writing about, their aspirations or what they are fighting for ... A woman can sympathize with any party so strongly that she trembles for its existence, but the party does not care; it does not consider a woman's sympathies in either practical or political terms. And so the middle-class woman stands before today's political events, a spectator of a shadow play performed on a sheet stretched in a doorframe. She can only observe the shadow games of those who are doing politics" (Viková-Kunětická 1919, 53, 79, 82).

In 1907, Viková-Kunětická became a member of the *Národní strana svobodomyslná* (National Free-Thinking Party), also known as the *Mladočeši* (Young Czechs), and established a women's political club within the framework of the party. The *Mladočeši* nominated her as a candidate for the electoral county of Nymburk/Mladá Boleslav (both towns close to Prague) in the 1912 elections to the *zemský sněm* (National Assembly or Bohemian Diet). Viková-Kunětická was elected but František Thun-Hohenstein, Vice Regent of the Austrian Emperor, was opposed to her carrying out the mandate. Despite various protest actions (by women at home as well as abroad), and despite the fact that her election had been presented as evidence of Czech 'progressiveness,' Viková-Kunětická did not finally take up the position. Although Viková-Kunětická aligned her mandate with the party of the *Národní strana svobodomyslná* and more generally with the efforts of the Czech nation as a whole, her success was to a large extent the result of the efforts of women's organizations such as the *Výbor pro volební právo žen* (Committee for Women's Suffrage, headed by ***Františka Plamínková***), campaigns run by social and political women's journals such as the *Ženské listy* (Women's gazette), *Ženský obzor* (Women's horizon), *Ženské snahy* (Women's efforts) and *Právo žen* (Women's rights), and individual women politicians such as Social Democrat Karla Máchová and Plamínková.

In addition to women's emancipation, Viková-Kunětická's political activities included campaigns against the oppression of Czech national minorities living in the (mostly German populated) northern parts of the Sudeten; in this capacity, she was actively involved in the nationalist *Národní jednota severočeská* (Northern-Bohemian National Unity Association), as well as the North-Bohemian branch of *Sokol* (Falcon), the Czech national civic organization for physical education. After the foundation of the Czechoslovak Republic in 1918, Viková-Kunětická's devotion to issues of the Czech minority inside German populated Sudentenland in Bohemia and

Moravia was followed by her political shift (even further) to the right. In her journal articles of that time, as well as in the texts that she published a year later in *Vyznání. Řeči a studie* (Confession. Speeches and studies, 1919), she emerges as a fairly chauvinistic politician and her chauvinistic nationalism against Germans and Poles, as well as her anti-Semitism and anti-Bolshevism (which made her unpopular among the left cultural elite) helped diminish her reputation in the new Republic. Nonetheless, she became a member of the revolutionary *Národní Shromáždění* (National Assembly) and, in 1920, was elected to the Senate as a candidate of the *Národně-demokratická strana* (National-Democratic Party).

Viková-Kunětická was the first woman representative to be elected to the National Assembly. Her controversial ideas on motherhood inspired much debate. She died in Libočany u Žatce on 18 March 1934.

Irena Kreitlová
Academy of Sciences, Czech Republic

Libuše Heczková
Charles University of Prague

Translated from the Czech by Alice Szczepanikova, Ph.D. student at the Department of Gender Studies, Central European University, Budapest.

SOURCES

(A) *Literární Archiv Památníku Národního písemnictví, Pozůstalost Božena Viková Kunětická* (Literary archive of the Memorial of National Literature. Legacy of Božena Viková Kunětická). Compiled by J. Wagner. Prague: Literární pozůstalost B. V. K. (Literary heritage B. V. K.), 1959.

(A) *Státní ústřední archiv, PM 1911-1920–karton (4869) dokumenty místodržitele Fr. Thona* (The State Central Archive, PM 1911-1920–cardboard (4869) documents of the Vice Regent Fr. Thon).

(B) *Národní listy* (National newspaper) (Prague, 1906-1934).

(B) *Ženské snahy* (Women's efforts) (Prague, 1908-1914).

(C) Viková-Kunětická, Božena. *Vyznání. Řeči a studie (1906-1918)* (Confession. Speeches and studies, 1906-1918). Prague: Grafická unie, 1919.

(D) Voborník, Jan. *Božena Viková Kunětická*. Prague: Stránka: 6 Česká akademie věd a umění, 1934.

(E) Wolchik, Sharon L. and Alfred G. Meyer, eds. *Women, State and Party in Eastern Europe*. Durham: Duke University Press, 1985.

(E) David, Katherine. "Czech Feminists and Nationalism in the Late Habsburg Monarchy: 'The First in Austria.'" *Journal of Women's History* 3, no. 2 (Fall 1991): 26-45.

(E) *Sb. Žena v dějinách Prahy* (Collection. Woman in the history of Prague). Prague: Scriptorium, 1996.

(E) Pynsent, Robert B., ed. *The Literature of Nationalism: Essays on East European Identity*. London: Macmillan, 1996.

(E) Hayes, Katleen. "Introduction: Concepts of Woman and the 'Woman Question' at the Fin de Siècle." In Katleen Hayes. *A World Apart and Other Stories. Czech Women Writers at the Fin de Siècle*. Prague: Karolinum, 2001.

(E) Novak, Arne. *Czech Literature*. Michigan: Ann Arbor, 1976; 1986.

VODE, Angela (1892–1985)

Slovenian feminist activist, teacher, member of the antifascist movement, politician and author of the first feminist essays on women's history in Slovenia.

Her name has been virtually unknown in Slovenia for the last fifty years. Yet one could say that her work and her life-story (or "destiny" as she put it) not only form a significant narrative in the history of Slovenia, with its political transformations (including developments and breaks within women's movements and organizations), they also form a part of the wider history of feminism itself.

Born on 5 January 1892, Angela Vode was the third daughter of five children raised in a poor working-class family. Her father Anton was a railwayman (died 1904). Of her mother, Frančiška, it is only known that she died in 1919. Angela was very close to her older sister Ivana Špindler (1888–1975), who, right up until her death, was Angela Vode's roommate, her protector and companion.

The highest level of education Slovenian girls could receive in the nineteenth century was secondary education at a so-called girls' *lyceum*. It was only from the late nineteenth century on that girls were allowed to take final exams (*Matura*) at secondary schools under the same conditions as boys, and they could only take exams at grammar schools as 'private persons' (*Privatistinnen*), which meant that they sat for the exams but did not attend school. Later, they could attend as 'occasional students' (*Hospitantinnen*). Prior to 1919, only twelve Slovene women had completed university studies (in Vienna, St Petersburg, and other universities abroad). Angela Vode worked as a teacher in several primary schools near Ljubljana (from 1911 to 1917), when she lost her job after a political disagreement with the local Catholic authorities. In addition to this, she was known as a 'red feminist' who publicly expressed her opinions regarding political autonomy for Slovene people–an autonomy which she did not believe could ever be realized within the Catholic Austro-Hungarian Monarchy. She was accused of having an irreligious attitude and lacking the patriotic fervor necessary to be a teacher.

Between 1917 and 1921, Vode worked for a bank (*Jadranska banka*), later for a foundry factory as an administrative assistant and after that as a secretary for the

Jugoslovanska socialdemokratska stranka (*JSDS*, Yugoslav Social Democratic Party). In accordance with the educational system of the time, she took private lessons and began to study teaching methods for children with special needs in Prague, Berlin and Vienna. She passed the relevant teaching exams in Ljubljana in 1921 and began teaching at the Special School for the Disabled (also in Ljubljana), where she worked until 1944.

In 1919, she became a member and secretary of the *Socialdemokratska stranka Slovenije* (*SDSS*, Social Democratic Party), thus launching her political career. She was among the founding members of the *Slovenska Komunistična partija* (*SKP*, Slovenian Communist Party), established in April 1920, and remained a member until 1939, when she was expelled because she could not and did not accept Stalin's pact with Hitler. After the outbreak of World War II, she organized humanitarian aid for refugees and their families until February 1944, when she was imprisoned by German fascists for being a communist and sent to the Ravensbrück concentration camp. After six months she was released due to a lucky turn of fate (the exact details are not known; the most likely explanation is that, because her sister in Ljubljana had cared for the ill wife of the German Major Oton Biella, who helped other Slovenes too, Biella interceded for Angela Vode). Given the rarity of surviving such an experience, Vode was treated with suspicion by both enemies and friends thereafter, almost right up until her death. Three years later, she was imprisoned again, this time by the victorious communists in Yugoslavia. She had criticized the first 'democratic' elections after World War II, as well as the new governmental and educational system. At a Stalinist-styled trial, she was accused of treason, condemned to twenty years of forced labor in prison and deprived of her civic rights for five years. She was held in prison for almost six years (from 25 May 1947 to 1 January 1953): first in Begunje, later transfered to the *KPD* (penal and reform institute) at Rajhenburg/Brestanica (a medieval castle, formerly a women's prison and today a museum).

After 'becoming free' in 1953, Vode was not allowed to work or write publicly. Her books disappeared from libraries and her feminist friends (e.g. leading Communist Party woman ***Vida Tomšič*** and Lidija Šentjurc) did not want to, or were not allowed to mention her name. When she was finally released from prison on her 61st birthday (her sister had appealed for this event earlier with no success), she was very ill. Politically isolated because she refused to comply with the regime, she lived with her sister in one room with the economic help of a few friends.

Angela Vode died on 5 May 1985 in Ljubljana. Her name, writings and work were rediscovered in the late 1980s and the 1990s, when a new surge of feminist interest in the history of women's movements took place. Her literary estate, which includes articles, essays and memoirs, was found at the Slovenian School Museum and thereafter published.

Angela Vode's feminist activities prior to World War II were extensive. She was a member of various women's organizations and associations such as the *Splošno Slov-*

ensko žensko društvo (General Slovene Women's Association) and the *Društvo učiteljic* (Association of Woman Teachers), and she was also President of the *Zveza delavskih žena in deklet* (Union of Working Women and Girls). During the so-called 6 January Dictatorship under King Alexander (from 6 January 1929 to 9 October 1934), whenever the government outlawed an association, members registered it under a different name. Subsequently, women like Vode appear in retrospect to have been associated with a vast number of organizations during the interwar period. She was a member of the Slovenian *Ženski pokret* (Women's Movement) from 1926 (the year of its foundation) to 1937, as well as secretary and later President from 1927 to 1937. Vode participated in the congresses of the Little Entente of Women (LEW) in Prague in 1927; of the *Mednarodne ženske alijanse za žensko volilno pravico* (International Alliance of Women for Suffrage and Equal Citizenship, IAWSEC) in Berlin in 1929; and of the *Mednarodne ženske zveze* (International Council of Women) in Dubrovnik in 1936, when the National Council of Women in Yugoslavia acted as host of the Triennial Assembly of the ICW. She was involved in the activities of the *Splošno žensko društvo* (General Women's Association), as well as a member of the *Jugoslovanska ženska zveza* (Yugoslav Women's Union) from 1934 and Commissioner for work and employment for the whole Yugoslav State. In March 1939, the *Narodno obrambni svet* (National Security Council) was established on Vode's initiative, uniting 67 women's and 185 other associations; its members worked on propaganda to combat fascism. Vode was active in the *Učiteljska organizacija* (Teachers Union) and the *Društvo učiteljic* (Association of Women Teachers), and was President of the latter from 1930 to 1931, when the Association received a new name, the *Zadruga 'Dom učiteljic'* (Cooperative 'Home for Women Teachers'), which lasted under her presidency until 1934.

Vode's public activities included teaching, lecturing, organizing (seminars, lectures, various political actions, gatherings, meetings) and writing. As the leader of the *Ženski pokret* Vode, together with other women, attempted to change legislation on women's voting rights and family policy (e.g. the right to abortion on social as well as medical grounds). She was among the organizers of a meeting by women demanding the right to vote, held in Belgrade in December 1939, and the author of the newspaper article "Our Women for Voting Rights," published in *Jutro* (The morning) on 1 December 1939. She campaigned for equal working conditions and equal pay for men and women's work. In spite of the imposition of a political dictatorship in Yugoslavia in 1929, Vode began campaigning in the early 1930s against the ideological implications and dangers of fascism.

In her first essay, "Žena v sedanji družbi" (Woman in contemporary society, 1934), Vode described the general social position of women from a Marxist and socialist point of view, while at the same time appealing to a more layered understanding of social developments, urging women not to be deceived by (as she often put it) "fascist prophets" in the face of the world economic crisis, but instead to struggle against official economic and social policies. She wrote about the disastrous consequences of policies which prevented women from receiving equal pay for equal work, kept women at home with their children and used women's/human needs and struggles for ideological (i.e. fascist) purposes: 'blut und boden ideologie.'

In the late 1930s, Vode published her second and last book: *Spol in usoda* [Gender and destiny, vol. 1 (1938); vol. 2 (1939)], in which she described differences in human destinies arising from gender and exacerbated by social conditions, family environments, education and the upbringing of children, etc. The book encouraged women to act and raise their children in a spirit of equality between the sexes, in the name of a more just society for all. In particular, the book analyzes marriage and the double standards of Slovene Catholic society regarding women, unwanted pregnancies, abortion and prostitution. Such themes provoked a great deal of devastating criticism from the right and Vode finally turned to the courts, where she lost a lawsuit against the author of a particularly malicious and personally offensive article entitled "Kaj pravite?" (What do you think?). This text appeared in various newspapers [*Straža v viharju* (The guard in the storm), *Slovenski delavec* (The Slovenian worker) and *Slovenec* (The Slovene)] and accused both Vode and her books of being "old and ugly," of wanting "free love without law" like the Marxists in Russia and Spain, and of being morally corrupt and dangerous to the spiritual progress of society.

Upon returning from Ravensbrück, Vode wrote her *Spomini na suženjske dni* (Memoirs of days of slavery) and, after having been released from prison, her *Spomini* (Memoirs) and the anthology *Aktivnost slovenskih učiteljic* (The activities of Slovene teachers). These works were only published posthumously as part of her collected works in the years 1998–2000. The collected works include a comprehensive list of sources regarding her life and work.

Karmen Klavžar
The National Education Institute, Slovenia

SOURCES

(A) The Slovenian School Museum, collection No. 296 (f. 296: Angela Vode). Angela Vode's personal archival collection at the Slovenian School Museum contains various materials: her books (published) and texts (non-published), official documents, personal correspondence, newspaper cuttings, etc.

(C) Vode, Angela. *Spol in upor. Zbrana dela Angele Vode, 1. knjiga* (The collected works of Angela Vode, 1. Gender and rebellion). Ljubljana: Krtina, 1998.

(C) Vode, Angela. *Značaj in usoda. Zbrana dela Angele Vode, 2. knjiga* (The collected works of Angela Vode, 2. Personality and destiny). Ljubljana: Krtina, 1999.

(C) Vode, Angela. *Spomin in pozaba. Zbrana dela Angele Vode, 3. knjiga* (The collected works of Angela Vode, 3. Memory and oblivion). Ljubljana: Krtina, 2000.

VOINESCU, Alice Steriadi (1885–1961)

Romanian intellectual; significantly contributed to efforts to rethink women's status in interwar Romania; known primarily for her published *Jurnal* (Diary).

A remarkable intellectual, Alice Steriadi Voinescu came to the attention of the Romanian reading public with the publication of her private diary in 1997, in a post-1989 climate of heightened interest in personal testimonies. Covering the years from 1929 through 1961 (the year of her death), Voinescu's diary attracted attention primarily for its documentation of the communist takeover and the subsequent destruction of the interwar intellectual elite. Her critical attitude towards the communist regime ensured that Voinescu enjoyed a certain standing as a valuable and credible witness of these events. Given this focus, Alice Voinescu's commitment to the amelioration of women's intellectual, social and economic status in interwar Romania has been neglected, even though it was central to her life and work. This makes it all the more important to draw attention to her sustained concerns with young women's access to education, the desirability of women's engagement in public life, work opportunities for women as a means of securing economic independence, women's status in the family and the moral and social dimensions of prostitution.

Alice Voinescu (born Steriadi) was born on 10 February 1885 in Turnu-Severin, to an upper middle-class family. She had two sisters, Valérie and Marietta. In the tradition of the nineteenth-century Romanian educated elite, Alice received an essentially Western European education from her parents: Massinca Poenaru (the granddaughter of a famous Romanian educational reformer, Petrache Poenaru) and Sterie Steriadi (a lawyer with a doctorate in Law from Paris). Having graduated from the Faculty of Letters and Philosophy in Bucharest in 1908, Alice Steriadi continued her studies in Marburg, where she audited Hermann Cohen's courses in the spring of 1911. Later in 1913, upon defending her thesis, *L'Interprétation de la doctrine de Kant par l'Ecole de Marburg - Etude sur l'idéalisme crique* (The interpretation of Kant's doctrine by the Marburg school. A study in critical idealism), she was awarded a *magna cum laude* Ph.D. degree in philosophy at the Sorbonne.

France, and Paris in particular, never ceased to epitomize intellectual life and spirituality for Voinescu. From 1928 through 1939, she traveled yearly to France to participate in a series of meetings at the Pontigny Abbey, organized by Paul Desjardins with the express aim of bringing together an international community of intellectuals concerned over the future of Europe in the wake of World War I. There, she met personalities such as André Malraux, Roger Martin du Gard, Paul Langevin, François Mauriac, Charles du Bos, Jaques Rivière and André Gide, whom she considered an inspiring intellectual model.

Her marriage to Stelian Voinescu in 1915 lasted until his death in 1940 and was a recurrent source of reflection in her diary. The tensions in her marriage–stemming primarily from her husband's infidelities, her efforts at accommodating prevailing understandings of femininity and intellectuality and regrets over their childlessness–moved Voinescu to reflect at length on male self-centeredness and self-importance, as well as 'womanly virtues' such as selflessness in marriage. She came to lay great importance upon mutual understanding and loyalty in relationships between men and women, often assuming that, in marriage, men and women had complementary roles consistent with their gender-specific psychology and biology. At the same time, her and other women's experiences of marriage exposed the relative autonomy of men from family life and women's dependence on it as their primary source of identity as wives and mothers.

Since there was no precedent for aspiring women professors at the University of Bucharest, especially not in philosophy, Alice Voinescu's desire to serve her country had to follow a different route. In 1922, she became a professor of drama history at the *Conservatorul Regal de Muzică şi Arta Dramatică* (Royal College of Music and Dramatic Arts) in Bucharest, where she taught until 1948, the year of her forced retirement by the communist regime. During this period, she published a series of works: *Montaigne, omul şi opera* (Montaigne, life and work, 1936); *Aspecte din teatrul contemporan* (Aspects of contemporary theater, 1941) and a monograph on *Eschil* (Aeschylus, 1946). She also taught at the *Şcoala superioară de asistență socială* (School of Social Work), reflecting on her experience in a brochure entitled *Contribution dans la Psychologie dans l'Assistance Sociale en Roumanie* (Contributions to the psychology of social work in Romania, 1938), delivering lectures at the *Institutul Francez* (French Institute) and the *Universitatea Liberă* (Free University) in Bucharest. In her diverse writings, particularly the collection of essays *Scrisori către fiul şi fiica mea* (Letters to my son and daughter), Voinescu described education of the young as a form of "spiritual motherhood" (in Murnu, ed. 1994, 11–93; 104). Intimate passages from her diary testify to her sense of lack and guilt at not having children and encourage a reading of Voinescu's vocation for education as something which she saw as both an extension and sublimation of women's 'domestic role.' "No matter how drastic changes in social life are, and no matter what woman's role in the future will be, her basic function will never cease to be Motherhood/Maternity, biological as well as spiritual. By this I mean the ability to give life, to animate either the body or an individual or collective consciousness. That is why a normal woman cannot achieve self-fulfillment if she shrinks selfishly around her own physical or psychic self. She can only achieve self-fulfillment when she thrives beyond her selfish ego with the human beings she brings to life from her body and spirit" (in Murnu, ed. 1994, 104).

Voinescu's reflections emerged as much from her teaching experience as from her social work as a member of the *Asociația Creștină a Femeilor* (*ACF*, Christian Association of Women), founded in 1919 by Queen Mary of Romania, an inspiring female role model during her reign (1893–1927). Alice Voinescu's public activism was attuned to the philanthropic milieu in which interwar women's organizations were founded. These organizations functioned as public forums for upper- and middle-class Romanian women and encouraged women to subscribe to cultural constructions of femininity based on selfless devotion and moral care along traditional Christian Orthodox lines, as well as to national demands imposed on Romanian women to act as moral guardians of the national community. Through the *ACF*, Voinescu attended an international conference on prostitution: the First Congress for Social Morality, organized by the International Abolitionist Federation (Budapest, 1934).

In other public appearances, Alice Voinescu emphasized the social importance of women's independence and autonomy and argued that these did not counter specifically 'feminine' roles. In a series of radio speeches—"Din psihologia tineretului de azi" (The psychology of today's youth), "Orientări în educația femeii" (Directions in women's education), "Din psihologia femeii de azi. Femeia și munca" (The psychology of today's working woman) and "Sentimentul pudoarei" (On the sense of decency)—delivered in 1935 and later published (in Murnu, ed. 1994), Voinescu argued that intellect could only be considered a danger to femininity by those who saw women as essentially childish and ignorant. At the same time, she encouraged women to reach beyond "self-sufficient male rationality towards understanding and empathic love" (in Murnu, ed. 1994, 103–107). This approach was consistent with her belief that education or intellect could strengthen women's 'natural' potential for empathy and love: "There is still a prejudice among the staunchest defenders of femininity that education, that is intellect, endangers femininity. As if truth were not healthy for the curiosity of Eve; as if 'knowing' weakens the powers of her heart. 'To learn' means 'to understand' and to understand means 'to love' more deeply" (in Murnu, ed. 1994, 103–107). Furthermore, in Voinescu's view, intellectual women were better equipped to educate and defend social and moral norms, to function as agents of moral care through philanthropic activities, and as potential agents of social change and renewal. Although this line of argument can be said to reinforce traditional constructions of femininity, it also raises a problem addressed by contemporary feminist scholars of 'sexual difference' such as Luce Irigaray and Rosi Braidotti. [These thinkers have revisited notions of "feminine culture" (Irigaray's term)—i.e attributes and values traditionally associated with women and devalued in Western societies]. Alice Voinescu explored gender identity and the potential of "feminine culture" (she speaks of "the feminine profile/face of humanity" in Murnu, ed. 1994, 129) to articulate a relational sense of self as an alternative to the self-sufficient masculine model of identity, and to encourage social compassion as well as a sense of duty and responsibility in political life.

Committed to the amelioration of women's status along these lines, Voinescu was ambivalent towards feminist organizations in Romania. On the one hand, she considered them the outcome of a genuine and welcome desire for emancipation in women. On the other hand, she felt they were shallow imitations of fashionable 'Western models,' incapable of making positive changes to the situation of Romanian women. Several of her radio speeches warned against the danger of homogenization, of the erasure of gender difference that the modern "masculinized woman" represented: the product of indiscriminate claims for equality and imitations of an essentially masculine model of identity (in Murnu, ed. 1994, 104–105). These views suggest an ambivalent attitude towards feminism on the part of Voinescu, an Eastern European woman intellectual committed to changing women's status, as well as a resolute 'Westernizer,' uncertain of the extent to which Romania should follow in the political and cultural path of the so-called 'civilized countries' (i.e. Western Europe).

During the communist regime, Voinescu continued to speak on matters of public importance in the spirit of her public engagement during the interwar years. Following her protest against the forced abdication of the King by the communists in December 1947, she was discharged from her position as professor at the *Conservatorul de Artă Dramatică*. These developments led to her arrest in 1951, her imprisonment for a year and seven months and subsequent exile (for one year) to a village in the north of the country. Consequently, post-1989 public interest in her diary has focused on its testimonial value regarding the destruction of the interwar intellectual elite.

We owe the publication of Alice Voinescu's diary, correspondence and radio speeches to her former student and life-long friend, Maria Ana Murnu. The published diary–along with (auto)biographical pieces written by former friends such as Alexandru Paleologu, Maria Ana Murnu, Virginia Şerbănescu and Aurora Nasta–constitute important sources for reconstructing her life trajectory and documenting her public activism. In view of these sources, one can argue that Alice Voinescu's philanthropic work, teaching activity and public lectures were motivated by her belief in the potentially reinvigorating role of women in the social and political realms, and made a significant contribution to the broader effort of rethinking women's status in interwar Romania. Alice Voinescu died on 4 June 1961 in Bucharest.

Diana Georgescu
Ph.D. Candidate, Department of Gender Studies,
Central European University, Budapest

SOURCES

(C) Voinescu, Alice. *Montaigne, omul şi opera* (Montaigne, life and work). Bucharest: Fundaţia pentru Literatură şi Artă "Regele Carol II," 1936.

(C) Voinescu, Alice. *Aspecte din teatrul contemporan* (Aspects of contemporary theater). Bucharest: Fundaţia Regală pentru Literatură şi Artă, 1941.

(C) Voinescu, Alice. *Eschil* (Aeschylus). Bucharest: Fundaţia Regală pentru Literatură si Artă, 1946.

(C) Voinescu, Alice. *Scrisori către fiul şi fiica mea* (Letters to my son and daughter). Maria Ana Murnu, ed. Cluj-Napoca: Editura Dacia, 1994.

(C) Voinescu, Alice. "Amintiri despre abatia de la Pontigny" (Memories of the Pontigny Abbey). Radio speeches and lecture delivered at the French Institute. In Maria Ana Murnu, ed. *Scrisori către fiul şi fiica mea* (Letters to my son and daughter). Cluj-Napoca: Editura Dacia, 1994, 95–157.

(C) Voinescu, Alice. *Scrisori din Costeşti* (Letters from Costeşti). Constandina Brezu, ed. Bucharest: Editura Albatros, 2001.

(C/D) Voinescu, Alice. *Jurnal* (Diary). Maria Ana Murnu, ed. Includes a preface by Alexandru Paleologu: "Alice Voinescu şi lumea ei" (Alice Voinescu and her world) and an introduction by Maria Ana Murnu: "Alice Voinescu–călăuză şi prietena" (Alice Voinescu–mentor and friend). Bucharest: Editura Albatros, 2002.

(D) Şerbanescu, Virginia. "De vorbă cu André Gide" (Talking to André Gide). *Manuscriptum*, no. 4 (1973): 140–147.

(D) Murnu, Maria Ana. "André Gide şi Roger Martin du Gard în dialog cu Alice Voinescu" (André Gide and Roger Martin du Gard in dialogue with Alice Voinescu). *Manuscriptum*, no. 1 (1974): 162–167.

(D) Şerban Cioculescu, Aurora Nasta, Nestor Ignat, Ion Biberi, Alexandru Paleologu, Mircea Septilici and Dinu Ianculescu. "Evocare Alice Voinescu" (Evoking Alice Voinescu). *Manuscriptum*, no. 3 (1979): 136–154.

XENOPOL, Adela (1861-1939)

Romanian writer, publicist and liberal feminist.

Adela Xenopol was born in 1861 in Iaşi (exact date of birth unknown) into a prominent intellectual family. Her older brother, Alexandru D. (1847-1920) was the first significant modern Romanian historian and a member of the 'Junimea circle,' whose leader, Titu Maiorescu, attacked women's intellectual abilities during a conference held at the Atheneum in Bucharest in May 1882, and was in turn severely lambasted in the feminist press by ***Sofia Nădejde***. Another older brother, Nicolae, was also a publicist, lawyer and member of the National Liberal Party. Adela was strongly supported by her family in her intellectual ambitions. Like her brothers, she received her higher education abroad and was one of the first women auditors at the Sorbonne. After her return to Iaşi, she began an intensive career in publishing, much of it dedicated to discussions of women's issues in the spirit of liberal feminism.

She made her journalistic debut in January 1879 in *Femeia Română* (The Romanian woman) with an article entitled "Chestiunea femeilor" (The woman question). With recourse to orientalist imagery, the article praised *Femeia Română* (edited by Maria Flechtenmacher) for its contribution to "the elimination of ... ideas befitting Asian despots that aim to subordinate women legally and morally, against natural laws and rights" (Xenopol 1879). Xenopol adopted a firm stance in favor of liberal feminism and called for women to join the feminist movement.

From 1896 to 1898, Xenopol edited the monthly *Dochia*: the first Romanian journal to dedicate itself fully to defending, supporting and researching women's rights. The name of the journal was Adela Xenopol's pen-name: the legendary 'Dochia' had supposedly proven her extreme loyalty to the 'ancestors of the Romanian people,' the Dacian tribes, by choosing to kill herself lest the Roman Emperor Traian, who had fallen in love with her, should take her to Rome. In a manifesto published in the first issue of *Dochia*, Xenopol emphasized the economic emancipation of women as the necessary precondition for the improvement of women's social status in the spheres of intellectual, political and legal life. Through the journal, Xenopol provoked public debate and drew prominent cultural figures into discussions on feminism by inviting them to write for the journal, lending visibility and an air of legitimacy to these debates. Among these figures were the famous writers and publicists Vasile A. Urechia, Cincinat Pavelescu, Elena Sevastos, Smara (Smaranda Andronescu-Gheorghiu), Cornelia Kernbach and Maria Cunţan.

Xenopol spoke out fervently against the many prominent politicians who claimed that women, even those with university diplomas, were unable to deal effectively with the pressures of professional life–as men were–and were therefore not entitled to equal education or political rights. Xenopol criticized this patriarchal attitude as being 'out of step' with modern times and linked women's emancipation to a broader liberal agenda: the modernization of state institutions and the economy. In her many publications and talks, Xenopol encouraged women's organizations to adopt broad democratic goals such as land reform, universal voting rights and educational reform.

In the spring of 1914, as broad constitutional reform was being discussed, Xenopol, together with other feminists, approached Ioan Al. Brătescu-Voineşti (a prominent writer and Member of Parliament) with a petition requesting women's enfranchisement, at least for local elections. The petition, along with other liberal-democratic proposals for land reform, was not taken seriously–in part due to the outbreak of World War I.

During the war, Xenopol continued to publish on feminism in the journal *Viitorul româncelor* (The future of Romanian women). She spoke against conquest through war and in favor of democratic republicanism and equal rights for all citizens, which in her view were the only means of achieving peace. Yet, like many other liberal feminists, she also supported Romanian participation in the war to "free their [Romanian] brethren from oppression," a reference to Romanians in the Habsburg Empire (Xenopol 1914). In spite of her nationalism however, Xenopol maintained a critical feminist position throughout the war, opposing the Romanian government's unwillingness to enfranchise women.

In 1925, Xenopol founded the *Societatea Scriitoarelor Române* (Society of Romanian Women Writers) as a way of encouraging more female writers to publish their work. The society published the *Revista scriitoarei* (The woman writer's magazine), dedicated to "cultural-artistic events that aim to showcase Romanian women's talent or genius" (*Revista scriitoarei*, 9). The journal achieved its goal, for it became an important springboard for a number of prominent women writers such as Hortensia Papadat-Bengescu, Izabela Sadoveanu, Constanţa Hodoş, Margareta Miller-Verghy, Aida Vrioni, Natalia Poni, ***Sofia Nădejde*** and Ana Conta-Kernbach. The journal also featured portraits of famous Romanian feminists such as ***Maria Baiulescu***, Elena Văcărescu, ***Alexandrina Cantacuzino***, Lucrezzia Kar and Ana Conta-Kernbach. The prestigious reputation of this publication was evident from the willingness of some of the most prominent male literary figures of the period–Tudor Arghezi, Ion Pillat, I. Teodorescu, Lucian Blaga and Camil Petrescu–to have their work published in its pages.

Adela Xenopol died on 10 May 1939. With her passing, the feminist and democratic movements in Romania lost one of their most important figures.

Ştefania Mihăilescu
Lecturer in Women's History
National School for Political Studies and Public Administration, Bucharest

Translated from the Romanian by Maria Bucur.

SOURCES

(B) *Dochia* (Dochia) (1896-1898).
(B) *Femeia română* (The Romanian woman) (1879).
(B) *Viitorul româncelor* (The future of Romanian women) (1914).
(B) *Revista scriitoarei* (The woman writer's magazine) 2, no. 1 (November 1927).
(B) Bogdan, E. *Feminismul* (Feminism). Timişoara: Tip. Huniadi, 1926.
(C) Xenopol, Adela. "Chestiunea femeilor" (The woman question). *Femeia română* 2, no. 91 (11 January 1879).
(C) Xenopol, Adela. "Zile mari" (Great days). *Viitorul româncelor* (1914).
(D) Predescu, L. *Enciclopedia României. Cugetarea* (The encyclopedia of Romania. The thought). Bucharest: Ed. Saeculum I. O., 1999.
(E) Mihăilescu, Şt. *Din istoria feminismului românesc. Antologie de texte (1838-1929)* [A history of Romanian feminism. An anthology of works (1838-1929)]. Iaşi: Polirom, 2002.

ŻELEŃSKI, Tadeusz Kamil Marcjan (Boy) (1874-1941)

Polish physician, social worker, member of the Polish Literary Academy, poet, writer, critic and translator. An activist doctor with a strong social conscience, Żeleński campaigned in the 1920s and 1930s for the reform of marriage legislation and the introduction of sex education and birth control. Author of *Piekło kobiet* (Women's hell, 1930), a collection of articles about abortion; first editor of the famous novel *Poganka* (The pagan, 1846) by ***Narcyza Żmichowska*** and author of a monograph on Żmichowska entitled *Ludzie żywi* (Living people, 1929).

Boy-Żeleński's father, Władysław Żeleński (1837-1921), was a composer from a noble family dating back to the fifteenth century. In 1873, Władysław Żeleński married Wanda Grabowska (1841-1904), who was from a middle-class family. Both families cultivated patriotic Polish traditions. In the eighteenth century, Grabowska's family had converted from Judaism while the Żeleński family had been traditionally Calvinist (Marcjan Żeleński, Tadeusz Boy-Żeleński's grandfather, converted to Catholicism in 1828). Although Wanda Grabowska had received an outstanding education, the Żeleński family considered the marriage a *mésalliance*. Prior to her marriage, Grabowska had been a student and friend of ***Narcyza Żmichowska***. In 1870, Grabowska made her writing debut in the *Tygodnik Ilustrowany* (Illustrated weekly) with a piece on Żmichowska. Years later her son, Boy-Żeleński, became the first editor of Żmichowska's work in Poland and his edition of her famous novel *Poganka* (The pagan woman, 1846) was followed by an excellent biographical study of Żmichowska in 1929, probably the first Polish text (explicitly) about lesbianism.

Tadeusz Boy-Żeleński was born on 21 December 1874 in Warsaw (under Russian partition), the second of three brothers [the other two were Stanisław (1873) and Edward (1877)]. The family moved to Cracow (under Austrian partition) in 1881. Between 1892 and 1900, Boy-Żeleński studied medicine at the *Uniwersytet Jagielloński* (Jagiellonian University), but after making his debute as a poet (1895) in the conservative Cracovian newspaper *Czas* (Time) he became increasingly interested in literature. In 1904, he married Zofia Pareńska (1885-1956), the daughter of medical professor Stanisław Pareński and his wife Eliza Pareńska (known for her patronage of artists and for encouraging her husband's doctor friends to buy the work of Polish painters). Boy and Zofia were happily married (until his departure to Lviv in 1939), although they both had extra-marital affairs. In 1905, their only son Stanisław Żeleński was born. From 1905 onwards, Boy-Żeleński was an active member of the *Kabaret Zielony Balonik* (Green Balloon Cabaret) and became well known as a humorist, while at the same time working as a pediatrician and publishing numerous medical studies.

In 1905, Boy-Żeleński founded an association called *Kropla mleka* (Drop of milk), which aimed to supply poor children with healthy nutrition and provide mothers with free advice. During the first year of its existence, *Kropla mleka* distributed 20,000 liters of milk. Boy-Żeleński also published articles in the medical and popular press about the importance of proper nutrition for the development of children. In 1906, he opened the the *Biuro Porady dla Matek i Dzieci* (Office of Advice for Mothers and Children), where he personally advised mothers on childcare issues. During World War I, while a doctor in the Austrian army, he translated French authors into Polish. In 1921, the *Uniwersytet Poznański* (University of Poznan) offered him the position of Chair of French Literature, which he rejected to become Literary Director of the *Teatr Polski* (Polish Theatre) in Warsaw from 1922. He was the only person ever to translate the complete works of Molière. For his outstanding contribution to the promotion of French culture, he received the French *Légion d' honneur* and the French Academy awarded him the title of *l'Officier d'Instruction Publique* (both in 1922).

Poland became independent in 1918 and one of the most important tasks for the newborn country was to create new laws. In 1920, the work of the Commission of Codification was begun in order to break with the legal traditions of the Partitions and create new Polish laws. There were two phases in Boy-Żeleński's activism related to the abortion issue. In the first phase, his activities were aimed at influencing the Codification Commission (1920–1932). He advocated the decriminalization of abortion, alimony for single mothers and civil marriage (civil marriages had been possible under the laws of the Partitions, but no uniform civil marriage law for Poland existed even after 1918, a situation which the Codification Commission sought to address). Boy-Żeleński also criticized the growing intervention of the Polish Catholic Church in politics. In 1928, his articles advocating the liberalization and secularization of marriage legislation provoked public debate. In 1929, six articles advocating civil marriage and divorce, previously published in the *Kurier Poranny* (Morning courier), were printed in the volume *Dziewice Konsystorskie* (Consistorial virgins).

Irena Krzywicka (1899–1994), a writer with whom he had an affair (from 1927 until 1939), strengthened Boy-Żeleński's interest in women's emancipation and the promotion of contraceptive methods. In the years 1929 and 1930, Boy-Żeleński published a series of articles advocating freedom of abortion in the *Kurier Poranny* newspaper; they were later collected under the title *Piekło kobiet* (Women's hell) and form one of the best known Polish texts on reproductive issues, even today.

The second phase of Boy-Żeleński's activism related to the abortion issue began with the promulgation of a new Penal Code (1932), according to which abortion was punishable by five years imprisonment for the woman and fifteen years, in the event of her death, for the doctor who had performed the operation. Boy-Żeleński aimed to influence society and provoke public discussions about sexual life and its legal regulation, which he did in a speech entitled "Jak skończyć z piekłem kobiet?" (How can we end women's hell?), delivered at a meeting organized by the *Polska Partia Socjalistyczna* (Polish Socialist Party) on 31 May 1931 at the *Robotnicze Towarzystwo Służby Społecznej* (Workers Social Service Association) and anticipating the later foundation of the *Sekcja Regulacji Urodzin* (Section for Birth Regulation). On 27 October 1931, the first *Poradnia Świadomego Macierzyństwa* (Clinic for Informed Maternity) was opened in Warsaw. The aim of the clinic was to advise women on birth regulation and contraception. The director of the clinic was Dr ***Justyna Budzińska-Tylicka***. Soon after, similar institutions were opened in Lodz, Cracow, Przemyśl and Gorlice. In the spring of 1932, Boy started a regular column in the influential weekly *Wiadomości Literackie* (Literary news) called "Świadome Życie. Dodatek o Reformie Obyczajowej" (The conscious life. Sexual reform supplement). Boy argued that only contraception could diminish "the plague of artificial abortions" (Boy-Żeleński 1930, 15) and that birth control would reduce child mortality and infanticide, as well as suicide among pregnant girls. He stressed that the regulation of fertility would give women more freedom to choose between motherhood and professional life. He was strongly concerned about the situation of the poor, calling his action "a crusade against misery" (Boy-Żeleński 1930, 23).

In April 1934, the *Liga Reformy Obyczajów* (League for the Reform of Morals) was created under Boy-Żeleński's leadership. Other activists of the *Liga* included the writers Irena Krzywicka, Zofia Nałkowska and Wanda Melcer, as well as the physicians Justyna Budzińska-Tylicka, Henryk Kluszyński and Herman Rubinraut. The *Liga* organized numerous protests against the New Penal Code, as well as lectures on women's health, contraception and childcare.

During the 1930s, Boy-Żeleński's attempts to decriminalize abortion and introduce divorce met with hostile criticism and brought him into severe conflict with the Catholic hierarchy. His articles critiquing the position of the Catholic Church were published in 1932, in the volume *Nasi okupanci* (Our occupying regime). After this volume, Boy-Żeleński pursued journalism only sporadically (advocating humanitarian treatment of prostitutes and tolerance towards homosexuals) and turned increasingly to literary projects. He stopped publishing articles dealing explicitly with issues of sexuality and reproduction (though many of his texts addressed sexual minority issues, for example his fifteen essays in *Proust i jego świat* [Proust and his world] 1936–39).

After the outbreak of World War II on 1 September 1939, Boy moved to Lviv, where he became Chairman of French Literature in the *Uniwersytet Jana Kazimierza* (Jan Kazimierz University) and contributed to the cultural life of the town. Upon entering the city on 4 July 1941, the German army arrested and shot Boy-Żeleński along with eighty other Polish intellectuals as part of Nazi-German attempts to eliminate the Polish intelligentsia.

The influence of Boy-Żeleński's work on the present day feminist movement in Poland remains strong and positive: the *Federacja na Rzecz Kobiet i Rozwoju Rodziny* (Federation for Women and Family Planning) advocates continuing his work on reproductive rights in its statute. In 2003, when a collection of testimonies of women who suffered under the Polish anti-abortion law was published, it was entitled *Piekło kobiet. Historie Współczesne* (Women's hell. Contemporary stories). Boy-Żeleński is both accepted and appreciated by Polish feminists, and well known as a women's reproductive rights advocate by mainstream readers.

Katarzyna Pabijanek
MA Student, Department of Gender Studies,
Central European University, Budapest

SOURCES

(C) Boy-Żeleński, Tadeusz. *Dziewice konsystorskie* (Consistorial virgins). Warsaw, 1929.
(C) Boy-Żeleński, Tadeusz. *Ludzie żywi* (Living people). Warsaw, 1929.
(C) Boy-Żeleński, Tadeusz. *Piekło kobiet* (Women's hell). Warsaw, 1930; Warsaw: PIW, 1960.
(C) Boy-Żeleński, Tadeusz. *Nasi okupanci* (Our occupying regime). Warsaw, 1932.
(D) Winklowa, Barbara. *Tadeusz Żeleński (Boy)-Twórczość i życie* [Tadeusz Żeleński (Boy). His life and work]. Warsaw, 1967.
(D) Natanson, Wojciech. *Boy-Żeleński. Opowieść biograficzna* (Boy-Żeleński. A biographical story). Warsaw: Ludowa Spółdzielnia Wydawnicza, 1977.
(D) Sterkowicz, Stanisław. *Po prostu Boy. Kronika życia i twórczości Tadeusza Boya-Żeleńskiego* (Simply Boy. A chronicle of the life and work of Tadeusz Boy-Żeleński). Toruń: Wydawnictwo Adam Marszałek, 1994.
(D) Markiewicz, Henryk. *Boy-Żeleński*. Wrocław: Wydawnictwo Dolnośląskie, 2001.

ZLATAREVA, Vera (1905–1977)

Board member (Secretary) of the lawyers' branch of the *Druzhestvo na bulgarkite s visshe obrazovanie* (Bulgarian Association of University Women). First Bulgarian woman permitted to work as a defense lawyer (1945).

Vera Zlatareva (right), 8 April 1940, after a meeting where government officials promised to resolve the question of women lawyers' rights.

Vera Zlatareva was born on 3 December 1905, in the small village of Goliamo Belovo, 100 kilometers east of the Bulgarian capital, Sofia. Her mother Maria (b. 1880) and her father Dimitar Zlatarevi (b. 1876) were both teachers. After finishing the local village school, Vera graduated from the middle and high schools in Plovdiv, the second largest city in the country. In 1929, she graduated from the Law Department of Sofia University where, in 1931, she would also be granted a Doctorate. In 1936, Vera Zlatareva married Mihail Genovski (1903–1996): lawyer, journalist, ideologue for the *Bulgarski Zemedelski Naroden Sujuz* (Bulgarian Agrarian People's Union) during the interwar period, politician (Cabinet Minister and MP) and, from 1944, professor at Sofia University. The couple had two children: a daughter and a son. Vera Zlatareva never took her husband's name. In a brochure published in 1945, she wrote that the change of name signified "the property relation that a man has towards his wife" (Zlatareva 1945, 12). In the years 1931–1936, Zlatareva worked in the service of the state; from 1931–1932, she assisted the legal adviser to the Ministry of Agriculture and State Property. She represented the Ministry of Agriculture and State Property at the High Administrative Court and participated in governmental commissions, drafting laws on the Bulgarian peasantry. From 1932–1934, she chaired a special section within the Police Department set up to combat "Social vice," in other words prostitution. During this time, she carried out and published research on prostitution in Bulgaria. From July 1934 to July 1936, Zlatareva worked for the town council of Plovdiv, chairing the Social Support Division.

Upon marrying, Vera Zlatareva returned to Sofia, where she lived until the end of her life. From June 1937, she worked at her husband's legal office and began campaigning for the right of women with law degrees to practice as defense lawyers and judges. She was subjected to police harassment because of her leading role in the so-called "women's constitutional commission" (1937), an informal group of women lawyers who worked in close association with the communists. The commission's main goal was to fight for the restoration of the Constitution (suspended after the military coup in 1934) and for the full civil and political rights of women. To this end it sent "An open letter" to the Bulgarian government. As a result of her liberal ideas and democratic activities, and under pressure from the authoritarian, bureaucratic and right-wing government in 1939, Vera Zlatareva was expelled from the *Druzhestvo na bulgarkite s visshe obrazovanie* (Bulgarian Association of University Women) and from the *Sujuz na bulgarskite pissatelki* (Union of Bulgarian Women Writers).

Vera Zlatareva struggled continuously against the exclusion of Bulgarian women lawyers from the bar and won some concessions to her cause. In 1938, the Council of Defense Lawyers in Sofia allowed Zlatareva to work as a defense lawyer for a probationary period. But the district attorney in Sofia contested the decision and it was subsequently annulled by the Supreme Council of Defense Lawyers. In 1942 (after Bulgaria had annexed Macedonia in 1941), the Council of Defense Lawyers in Skopie allowed Zlatareva and a colleague of hers to practice in Skopie. But it was once again the Supreme Council of Defense Lawyers in Sofia which put a stop to this. The protests of women lawyers across Bulgaria were, as Zlatareva's life story shows, reflections of these women's personal struggles with the male legal profession and a direct articulation of their experiences as they persistently came up against obstacles to their professional development. Hence the passion and anger that fueled Zlatareva's actions as secretary to the women lawyers' section of the Bulgarian Association of University Women (affiliated to the International Federation of University Women in 1925). Women lawyers would only be allowed to practice in Bulgaria after the introduction of communist legislation in October 1944, granting women equal rights with men. Vera Zlatareva was the first woman lawyer to exercise this right.

Vera Zlatareva was a prolific researcher into various social issues. She published extensively on prostitution in Bulgaria, as well as on the status of illegitimate children and juridical factors affecting Bulgarian women's status, including labor, property and family relations, alcoholism and gambling. She published in scholarly and popular journals such as *Filosofski pregled* (Philosophical review), *Pravna misul* (Juridical thought), *Zemia I trud* (Land and labor), *Far na vuzdarzhanieto* (Lighthouse of temperance) and *Trezvenost* (Sobriety), as well as in newspapers such as *Literaturen glas* (Literary voice), *Vestnik za zhenata* (A newspaper for women), *Zhenski glas* (Women's voice) and *Advokatski pregled* (Defense lawyers' review). Zlatareva and her husband were both active members of the Bulgarian Agrarian People's Union (the peasant party in Bulgaria) and together they edited the agricultural journal *Zemia I trud.* For many years, Zlatareva was President of the *Bulgarski neutralen vuzdurzhatelen suiuz* (Bulgarian Independent Temperance Union). She was an active member of the previously mentioned Association of University Women in her capacity as secretary to the

Association's section of lawyers and a member of various women's associations affiliated to the *Bulgarski Zhenski Sujuz* (Bulgarian Women's Union).

In the second half of the 1930s, Vera Zlatareva became active in anti-prostitution campaigns. She was an official Bulgarian delegate to the First International Congress on Social Morality held in Budapest, October 1934, and from January 1935, maintained contacts with the *Internationaler Bund der Freundinnen Junger Mädchen* (International Union of Friends of Young Girls) based in Neuchâtel, Switzerland. In May 1937, Zlatareva attended the International Congress of Abolitionists in Paris, presenting a paper on prostitution in Bulgaria. In this, as in all her research on prostitution, she paid special attention to social, economic, psychological, moral and juridical factors, and spoke out against prejudiced 'explanations' of prostitution as a product of 'women's nature.' She was well informed regarding contemporary debates on prostitution and the history of abolitionist campaigns in Western Europe, especially regarding the prominent role of abolitionist Josephine Butler (1828–1906).

Well-known publications by Vera Zlatareva include her Ph.D. dissertation, *Nakazanie I osiguritelni merki* (Punishment and social security, 1931), *Psihologia I sotsiologia na bulgarskata prostitutka* (The psychology and sociology of the Bulgarian prostitute, 1935), *Prostitutsiata I borbata protiv neia* (Prostitution and the fight against it, 1936), *Obshtestveni grizhi* (Social care, 1940), *Iznasilvane* (Rape, 1940), *Imushtestveni otnoshenia mezhdu supruzite* (Conjugal property relations, 1941), *Pravnata zashtita na zhenata* (The legal protection of women, 1945), *Polozhenieto na zhenata po proekta za konstitutsia na Narodna republika Bulgaria* (The situation of woman according to the Constitutional Project of the People's Republic of Bulgaria, 1947), *Seljankata i novoto vreme* (The peasant woman and the New Age, 1947) and *Pravnata zashtita na braka I semeistvoto v Narodna Republika Bulgaria* (The legal protection of marriage and family in the People's Republic of Bulgaria, 1958).

After the communist takeover in September 1944, Vera Zlatareva remained a public figure, working as a lawyer and Member of Parliament for the peasant party. In the late 1940s, she participated in various parliamentary commissions on drafts of socialist law; she was particularly committed to laws granting men and women equal rights and, from 1947, to the socialist Turnovo Constitution project. She insisted that equality between women and men be clearly stated in statute, in order to prevent the discriminatory interpretations of law that she had personally experienced under the 'old regime.' Vera Zlatareva died on 19 August 1977.

Krassimira Daskalova
St. Kliment Ohridski, University of Sofia

SOURCES

(A) *Durzhaven Istoricheski Archiv* (State Historical Archive), Sofia, f. 1752k (Vera Zlatareva).

(A) *Durzhaven Istoricheski Archiv* (State Historical Archive), Sofia, f. 1117k (Maria and Dimitar Zlatarevi).

(A) *Durzhaven Istoricheski Archiv* (State Historical Archive), Sofia, f. 264, op. 6, a. e. 1-47 (Druzhestvo na bulgarkite s visshe obrazovanie, DBVO).

(C) Zlatareva, Vera. *Prostitutsiata i borbata protiv neia* (Prostitution and the fight against it). Sofia: Kooperatsia "Zemia I kultura," 1936.

(C) Zlatareva, Vera. *Pravnata zashtita na zhenata* (Legal protection of woman). Sofia: Bulgarski Naroden Zhenski Sujuz, 1945.

ZLATOUSTOVA, Ekaterina Hristova (1881–1952)

Founder (1924) and long-time President (1926–1937) of the *Druzhestvo na Bulgarkite s Visshe Obrazovanie* (*DBVO*, Association of Bulgarian Women with Higher Education); high-ranking civil servant, teacher and translator.

Energetic, strong-minded, resourceful, practical and persevering–that was how Ekaterina Zlatoustova was once described by her uncle Ivan Batsarov, surgeon, head doctor of the Bulgarian army and for sixty years the most trusted friend of his niece (in private correspondence, 1902–1910). Born in Varna on 22 September 1881, Ekaterina (Katya) Zlatoustova was the first of the four children of Krustina Batsarova (1860–1942) and Hristo Zlatoustov (1858–1900), a professional officer and later (after his participation in the 1886 *coup d'état* against Prince Alexander von Battenberg), an entrepreneur. His early death encouraged Katya, who had adored him and was heartbroken, to follow his predilections for public life, writing and Russophile and Slavophile ideas, but it also left her subject to the controlling authority of her mother (who put an end to Katya's first romantic relationship and ordered her to come back from Russia, where she was studying). Katya had to take up a parental role with regard to her siblings (two sisters and a brother) and financially support her family, casting aside entertainment, a personal life and her natural aptitude for scientific research. From then on, Katya would be influenced most by her mother, Krustina Batsarova, and her large family. Her grandmother, grandfather and one of her aunts were teachers who had helped develop contemporary Bulgarian education; her uncle Ivan Batsarov, an army doctor, was her most trusted friend and her mother, one of the few highly educated female teachers in Bulgaria, encouraged Katya to study music and foreign languages (Russian, German and French). Katya quite naturally saw her mother as a role model. She was a teacher, translator and Chair of the *Burgasko zhensko druzhestvo "Milosardie"* (Bourgas [a town] Women's Society), a charity organization for the education of girls. Katya was also influenced by her cousin Stefan Yonchev (1881–1904), with whom she fell in love. He idealized 'the new woman' as a fighter for women's and national advancement (in accordance with Russian populist ideas).

While Katya was a student at the elite Sofia girls' secondary school (1892–1898), she became interested in women's issues. Problems relating to the secondary and higher education of girls and to the status of female teachers were widely discussed in the school by teachers such as ***Ekaterina Karavelova*** and Elena Radeva-Petrova, as well as in intellectual circles. The period of secondary schooling was shorter for girls than for boys, Sofia University did not admit women (until 1901) and female teachers were paid less than men and lost their positions upon marriage. At secondary school, Katya made friendships that would last her entire life; later she would always contact her classmates when she needed qualified and dedicated women, either for her translation projects or for the *DBVO* (see below).

Following graduation from Sofia girls' secondary school, Ekaterina Zlatoustova went to St Petersburg, where she attended the *Bestuzhev* Higher Women's Courses from 1902 to 1905. This period witnessed the intensive development of her feminist ideas; the milieu in which she moved was full of women influenced by Russian populist ideology. Although she studied history and dreamed of taking up scientific work, this proved to be untenable and she decided, somewhat pragmatically, to undertake a teaching career that would not only provide her with an income and social standing, but also with independence and time for her own scholarly research. For ten years she taught history, geography, Bulgarian and Russian in Shoumen (1905–1907) and at her old secondary school in Sofia (1908–1911; 1911–1918). Her contacts with fellow feminists and with students–some of whom became teachers at the University (including ***Elissaveta Karamichailova***)–date from then. It was obvious that teaching was a vocation for Zlatoustova, who considered that upbringing, education, duty and patriotism were all interrelated.

Following World War I, Ekaterina Zlatoustova was among the first and few women who were immediately promoted to a responsible position in the administration. From 1918 to 1931, she worked in almost all the divisions of the Ministry of Education and, as Head of Department for cultural institutions and funds, she was responsible for state cultural policy. At this time, she also became acquainted with the activities of organizations created under the auspices of the League of Nations after World War I, which inspired her to create a Bulgarian branch of the International Federation of University Women (IFUW, founded in 1919). The name of this branch was the *Druzhestvo na Bulgarkite s Visshe Obrazovanie* (*DBVO*, Association of Bulgarian Women with Higher Education, 1924). Zlatoustova was the *DBVO*'s Vice-President (1924–1926), President (1926–1937, succeeding Elena Radeva-Petrova, Ekaterina's teacher in her Sofia high school and the first Chair of the association) and Honorable President (1937–1950). Under Zlatoustova's leadership, the *DBVO* had a significant impact on Bulgarian society while at the same time building up its reputation abroad, participating in most international forums of the IFUW. Many members of the *Druzhestvo na Bulgarkite s Visshe Obrazovanie* were Zlatoustova's former classmates, colleagues and students, but the *DBVO* united women with higher education from all over the country.

For a quarter of a century, the *DBVO* worked for the professional advancement of women lawyers, artists, writers and teachers. As Chair, Zlatoustova distributed propaganda and advertized the activities of the *DBVO* at annual meetings and open lectures, as well as through publications in the *Uchilishten pregled* (Educational review), published by the Ministry of Education. The *DBVO* was Zlatoustova's greatest accomplishment and even under the Stalinist regime of 1947–1951, she managed to preserve its identity as an informal (and illegal) intellectual circle and restore its international contacts.

Zlatoustova's work at the Ministry of Education was useful to her in other ways too. During half a year of specialization at the French Ministry of Education in Paris (1925), she became personally acquainted with professor Ellen Gleditsch, the President of the IFUW, with whom she kept up a thriving correspondence from 1925 until 1951, just before Zlatoustova's death. It was also in Paris that she met professor Leon Beaulieux, a lecturer at the *Ecole des langues orientales vivantes* (the Sorbonne) who invited her to become his assistant there eight years later. Lecturing to Bulgarian language students at the Sorbonne and proofreading Beaulieux's book on Bulgarian grammar for French speakers, she rediscovered her old passion for scientific research. Later, when finding herself in difficult financial circumstances, she would use the experience gained in Paris to write reviews of grammar textbooks. This was a pleasure for her because she was a polyglot, translating with ease from Russian, French and Polish. After the Communist take-over in 1944, she took up writing professional historical studies, researching the life of her grandfather–Nikola Batsarov (1818–1892), a teacher and prominent leader of the national movement–as well as women's education in nineteenth-century Bulgaria. Some of her historical research was discussed at the meetings of the second women's organization Zlatoustova joined: the *Slavianska zhenska grupa* (Slavonic Women's Group). In existence from 1935 to 1943, the *Slavianska zhenska grupa* was founded in Sofia as a branch of the Slavonic Women's Association in Prague and several feminist organizations, including the *Bulgarski Zhenski Sujuz* (Bulgarian Women's Union), took part in its activities. Its goals were pacifism, revision of the Versailles Treaty system and the advancement of cultural contacts between the Slavonic states (especially Yugoslavia, Czechoslovakia and Poland).

When, in 1947, publishers rejected a book Ekaterina Zlatoustova had written about her cousin (the socialist writer, publicist and reviewer Stefan Yonchev), she resumed her work on the biography of her grandfather. She published fragments of this research over the course of her life, but the manuscript was never published in full and its author remained excluded from the *Saiuz na nauchnite rabotnitsi* (Union of Scientific Workers), of which membership was obligatory for university staff and museum curators after 1947. New directions in Bulgarian historiography dismissed church leaders and pioneers of education (such as Zlatoustova's grandfather Batsarov), as well as scientists without positions in universities or other institutes, such as Zlatoustova. In spite of this marginalization, which affected her deeply, Zlatoustova refused to compromise her text in accordance with political demands. After a period spent quietly with her family–mother, sister, nieces and nephews–she died in Sofia in 1952.

A member of the first generation of Bulgarian women intellectuals who rose to prominence immediately after the creation of the independent Bulgarian State, Ekaterina Zlatoustova was founder and Chair of a feminist organization, a public speaker, teacher, lecturer, high-ranking civil servant, publicist, translator, linguist, critic and historian. Yet even today, her name remains forgotten by Bulgarian historiography.

Georgeta Nazarska
Higher School of Library Studies and Information Technologies, Sofia

SOURCES

A) National Library "St. Cyril and Method"–Bulgarian Historical Archive, f. 612 (Ekaterina Zlatoustova) and f. 328 (Nikola Batsarov).

(A) State Historical Archive, f. 177k (Ministry of Public Education) and f. 264 (Ministry of the Interior).

(B) *Uchilishten pregled* (Educational review) (1922–1948).

(B) *Mir* (Peace) (1916, 1926, 1943).

(B) *Godishnik na Druzhestvoto na balgarkite s visshe obrazovanie* (Yearbooks of the Association of Bulgarian Women with Higher Education) (1930–1932).

ŻMICHOWSKA, Narcyza (1819-1876)

Polish writer, publicist, educationalist; initiated and led the women's group *Entuzjastki* (The Enthusiasts, 1842–1849). Pseudonym: 'Gabryella.'

Narcyza (real name Kazimiera Narcyza Józefa) Żmichowska was the tenth child of Wiktoria born Kiedrzyńska (d. 1819) and Jan Żmichowski (d. 1838), a clerical worker for a salt mine at Nowe Miasto on the Pilica River (central Poland). Narcyza was born in Warsaw on 3 March 1819. Orphaned by her mother, who died on the fourth day after the childbirth, and rejected by her father, who subconsciously blamed her for the death of his beloved wife, she was brought up by her uncle and his wife, Józef Żmichowski and Tekla born Raczyńska. Her three brothers (Hiacynt, Erazm, Janusz) and five sisters (Wiktoria, married name Lewińska; Kornelia, married name Gloger; Hortensja, first married name Keller, second Dunin; Lilia, married name Zaleska and Wanda, married name Redel) all went their separate ways but never lost touch with one another. While their father was alive, the children would gather at Nowe Miasto on the Pilica River; after his death, the homes of the (married) sisters became the center of family life. Thus in childhood, Żmichowska suffered from a lack of parental care while at the same time receiving strength, support and love from her other family members. These contrasting experiences help explain Żmichowska's acute awareness of the role of the family in the development of certain personality traits; in her later pedagogical writings, she would emphasize the importance of relations between mother and child and within the family for providing a natural environment of maturation.

Żmichowska graduated from the well-known Zuzanna Wilczyńska's girls' boarding school in Warsaw and, in the first half of the 1830s, entered the so-called Institute of Governesses. A certificate from this establishment authorized one to open a private boarding school, but Żmichowska did not have adequate financial resources. After graduating from the Institute, she returned to her aunt and uncle Kiedrzyński in the provinces (Mężenin), where she spent several years. In this period, she complained of boredom and criticized the intellectual shallowness of the local nobility. In a letter to her friend Bibianna Moraczewska, she wrote that there was nothing to be heard but “debates about crops, vodka, poultry [and] waxing floors” (Żmichowska 1957-1967, 2: 6). In 1838, on Zuzanna Wilczyńska’s recommendation, Żmichowska was offered the post of governess at the house of Prince Konstanty Zamoyski and his wife Aniela, and she left for France with them. However, she was unable to retain the ‘modest’ and ‘obedient’ role required of her as a tutor. The Zamoyskis disapproved both of Żmichowska’s contact with her brother Erazm, a political emigrant settled in Reims, and Żmichowska’s intellectual aspirations, which took her frequently to the *Bibliothèque Nationale* to pore over the works of (among others) Leibniz, Fichte, the Schlegel brothers and Kant. In September 1839, Żmichowska returned to Poland. On the way, she stayed in Poznan (a town in the western part of Poland under Prussian rule) in the house of her friends, the siblings Bibianna and Jędrzej Moraczewski. There she met eminent liberal politicians and philosophers.

From 1841 to 1843, Żmichowska worked as a governess at the home of Mr and Mrs Kisielnicki, located somewhere near Łomża. The Kisielnickis’ daughter Anna became a friend of Żmichowska and in later letters to Anna, as well as to Bibianna Moraczewska, Żmichowska formulated educational and philosophical ideas, emphasizing what she saw as a need to “sanctify presence,” to show appreciation for everyday existence (Żmichowska 1957-1967, 2: 87). The following years she spent in Warsaw, where, together with a group of eminent women that included Anna Skimborowicz, Tekla Dobrzyńska, Emilia Gosselin and Wincenta Zabłocka, Żmichowska formed the group *Entuzjastki* (The Enthusiasts), which existed between 1842 and 1849. The group was neither literary nor conspiratorial (i.e. plotting military action against the partition of Poland), but a small, loosely-connected and informal group, linked by ties of friendship and sympathy and built upon existing social and family structures. The Enthusiasts did not adhere to any defined ideology, but directed their activity in two directions simultaneously: active participation in public life and personal self-realization, understood in its broadest sense. The Enthusiasts founded and taught in schools, carried out charity work, wrote and edited works for publication, corresponded, distributed literature (including illegal literature), debated issues of public interest, established contacts with leading figures in political and intellectual life and tried to live their lives in accordance with a variety of individual strategies, defending their self-sufficiency and independence both within family life and outside it.

In 1844-1845, Żmichowska again worked as a governess at her friends’ house near Poznan. She kept up acquaintances with liberal politicians and philosophers who were thinking about a new uprising and the possibility of a liberal Poland, among them Karol Libelt and Edward Dembowski. Yet she maintained her own opinions on the question of Poland’s independence; she was opposed to military and conspiratorial activities that in her opinion were both unprofitable and harmful.

It was around this time that Żmichowska’s writing began to mature significantly. In 1841, Żmichowska published the poem “Szczęście poety” (Poet’s luck) in *Pierwiosnek* (Primula), a women’s magazine. The piece was very well received and throughout the early 1840s, Żmichowska published highly original poetic novels and short stories—reprinted in a collective volume published in Poznan under the title of *Wolne chwile Gabryelli* (Gabryella's spare time, 1845). In her private correspondence she took a stand against conspiracy, suggesting in her poem "Capriccio" that to be a poet did not necessarily mean cherishing special ethical values, and that art itself was morally ambiguous. In this way, she questioned the principles of Polish romanticism, the effectiveness of the military struggle against the partitioners, and the cult of the artist. A year later, Żmichowska's most famous novel *Poganka* (The pagan woman) was published. Here, in veiled tones, the author refers to her tempestuous and abruptly-ended friendship with the beautiful, well-educated and fascinating young woman, Paulina Zbyszewska; at the same time, *Poganka* is a treatise on the family: on relationships between parents and children and on tensions between family life and love powerful enough to change individual characters and the human psyche. In 1847, another novel appeared, *Książka pamiątek* (Book of memories), and was published in the *Przegląd Naukowy* (Scientific review). *Książka pamiątek* was based on Żmichowska's experiences working with a circle of Warsaw craftsmen who were interested in holding educational and political meetings and making contacts.

Refused permission by the Prussian authorities to remain in the province of Poznan, Żmichowska returned to Warsaw in 1845. For a time she stayed with her family at Rzeczyca, where she occupied herself teaching her sisters' children. In Warsaw, she socialized widely and maintained contacts with people involved in conspiracy against the Russian authorities. Documents from the political trials and Żmichowska's letters indicate that, despite her negative attitude to conspiracy, she became an emissary and assumed certain other obligations. On 24 October 1849, she was arrested and put in a Carmelite Nunnery in Lublin (in the eastern part of Poland, under Russian rule), from which she was released in 1852, but kept under police surveillance. She was only able to endure this with the support of her sister Hortensja Dunin, at whose home in Lublin she stayed until she was granted permission to return to Warsaw in 1855.

While the period following her release from prison is generally considered to be the most difficult in Żmichowska's life, this is only partially true. Initially, it was indeed hard; she lived in an uncomfortable flat and had no employment. In 1858, however, she moved to Miodowa Street, to the tenement house of her friends, the Grabowskis. Here, in a peaceful and affectionate atmosphere, she taught a group of girls from the private pension of her friend, Julia Baranowska (maiden name Bąkowska), and continued to write. In 1861, four volumes were published under the title of *Pisma Gabryelli* (The writings of Gabryella); the last volume included recent works dedicated to the subtlety of human relations and relations between women in particular, their friendships, solidarity and mutual fascination for one another [see, for example, her "Biała róża" (White rose), which first appeared in the *Gazeta Warszawska* (Warsaw gazette) in 1858].

Żmichowska spent the years between 1863 and 1874 outside Warsaw. She could accept neither the atmosphere following the crushing defeat by the Russians of the '1863 Uprising,' nor the idea of another Polish uprising. For the last two years of her life, she stayed in different places in the city's central district. She prepared an introduction to the collected works of Klementyna z Tańskich Hoffmanowa (1798-1845, a famous writer a generation older than Zmichowska) and a book, *Czy to powieść*? (Is this a novel?), which she never completed. Chronic illness–pain in the muscles and bones–made it increasingly difficult for her to walk. Żmichowska died in a Warsaw flat on 24 December (Christmas Eve) 1876, surrounded by family and friends.

Narcyza Żmichowska was an original writer and thinker. She considered love and friendship to be the foundations of civilization and addressed the influence of family, primarily the influence of the mother, on a child's psychological and personal development. She did not establish an organization for women's emancipation, but she was an early Polish feminist–some might argue the first Polish feminist. She defended her personal freedom, rejected several proposals of marriage (as we know from her correspondence and from the diary of her friend, Julia Baranowska), admired the miracle of living, established friendships with other women, showed an indefatigable capacity for self-education and wrote ephemeral non-fiction prose, free of the constraints imposed by literary convention.

Grażyna Borkowska
Professor, Institute for Literary Research,
Polish Academy of Sciences

SOURCES

(C) Żmichowska. *Wolne chwile Gabryelli* (Gabryella's spare time). Poznan, 1845.
(C) Żmichowska. *Poganka* (The pagan woman). First edition published in *Przegląd Naukowy* (Scientific review) (1846).
(C) Żmichowska. *Książka pamiątek* (Book of memories). *Przegląd Naukowy* (1847).
(C) Żmichowska. *Pisma Gabryelli* (The writings of Gabryella). Vols. I-IV. Warsaw, 1861.
(C) Żmichowska. *Pisma* (The writings). Vols. I-IV, 1885; vol. V, 1886. P. Chmielowski, ed. Warsaw, 1885-1886.
(C) Żmichowska. *Wybór powieści* (Selected novels). Vols. I-II. Maria Olszaniecka, ed. Warsaw, 1953.
(C) Żmichowska. *Listy* (Letters). Vols. 1-3. M. Romankówna, ed. Wrocław, 1957-1967.
(D) Stępień, M. *Narcyza Żmichowska*. Warsaw: Państwowy Instytut Wydawniczy, 1968.
(D) Woźniakiewicz-Dziadosz, M. "Narcyza Żmichowska." In M. Janion, M. Dernałowicz and M. Maciejewski, eds. *Literatura krajowa w okresie romantyzmu 1831-1863* (National literature during romanticism 1831-1863). Vol. 2. Cracow: Wydawnictwo Literackie, 1988.
(D) Winklowa, B. *Narcyza Żmichowska i Wanda Żeleńska* (Narcyza Żmichowska and Wanda Żeleńska). Cracow: Wydawnictwo Literackie, 2004.

(E) Żmichowska, Julia Baranowska. *Ścieżki przez życie* (Paths through life). M. Romankówna, ed. Introduction by Z. Kossak. Wrocław: Ossolineum, 1961.
(E) Borkowska, Cudzoziemki G. *Studia o polskiej prozie kobiecej* (Alienated women. A study of Polish women's writing). Warsaw: Wydawnictwo Instytutu Badań Literackich PAN, 1996 (English version 2001).

Picture credits

p. 21. Istanbul Municipal Library, documents of Fatma Aliye's Hanım Catalogue.

p. 25. From Count Albert Apponyi. *The Memoirs of Count Apponyi*. London, Toronto: Wilhelm Heinemann, 1935.

p. 33. From the magazine *Kommunistka* nos. 8-9 (January-February 1921).

p. 37. From Saulcerīte Viese. *Gājēji uz Mēnessdārzu*. Rīga: Liesma, 1990.

p. 41. From http://www.awin.org.yu/srp/archiva/ulice2.htm

p. 44. Ingeborg Bachmann, 1957. Picture Archive of the Austrian National Library, Vienna.

p. 48. From Elena Bogdan. *Feminismul*. Timişoara: Tip. Huniadi, 1926.

p. 51. Jelica Belović-Bernadzikowska, 1898. Picture cut out by Jelica Belović-Bernadzikowska herself, probably from the journal *Skola*, and glued to the front of her personal memoirs. Historical Archive of Sarajevo.

p. 54. Metropolitan Ervin Szabó Library, Budapest, Budapest Collection. B Small Prints, inventory no. 50289.

p. 58. Hungarian Jewish Archive, Budapest.

p. 62. Vela Blagoeva, Shoumen, 1887. Bulgarian Historical Archive, National Library SS Cyril and Method, Sofia.

p. 70. Lithuanian National Library, Manuscript Department, F. 68, b. 474.

p. 76. From Elena Bogdan. *Feminismul*. Timişoara: Tip. Huniadi, 1926.

p. 80. From Cecylia Walewska. *W Walce o równe prawa. Nasze bojownice*. Warsaw, 1930, 40.

p. 85. Kazimiera Bujwidowa, 1880s. Museum of Odon Bujwid, Cracow.

p. 89. From Elena Bogdan. *Feminismul*. Timişoara: Tip. Huniadi, 1926.

p. 95. From P. Arrian, ed. *Pervyi zhensky kalendar*, St Petersburg, 1898-1917/1908.

p. 99. Private collection. Photograph by the Foto Marubi Studio, Shkodra.

p. 102. From Stefan Dziewulski. *Działaność naukowa i społęczna Prof. Dr. Zofii Daszyńskiej-Golińskiej*. Reprint from *Ekonomista* (Warsaw 1927): 2.

p. 106. From Gordana Stojakovic. *Znamenite zene Novog Sada*. Novi Sad, 2001.

p. 109. Personal archive of Serpil Çakir.

p. 114. From the cover of Gordana Bosanac, ed. *Izabrana djela Blaženke Despot*. Zagreb: Institut za društvena istraživanja-Ženska infoteka, 2004.

p. 118. From Elena Bogdan. *Feminismul*. Timişoara: Tip. Huniadi, 1926.

p. 120. Archive of the publishing house Ileticim.

p. 124. From the cover of E. Mazovetskay. *Anna Engelgardt. Saint-Petersburg in the second half of the XIXth century*. St Petersburg, 2001.

p. 127. Regina Ezera, probably late 1970s. From Regina Ezera. *Dzivot uz savas zemes*. Riga: Liesma, 1984.

p. 131. Auguste Fickert, 1890s. Picture Archive of the Austrian National Library, Vienna.

p. 135. Anna Filosofova, 1860s. From Ariadna V. Tyrkova. "Anna Filosofova i eie vremia." In *Sbornik pamiati, A. P. Filosofovoi*. Petrograd: P. Golike i A. Vil'borg, 1915, 1: opposite 188.

p. 140. From Zvi Gitelman. *A Century of Ambivalence: the Jews of Russia and the Soviet Union, 1881 to the Present*. New York: Schocken Books, c1988, 48.

p. 144. Kaunas State Archive.

p. 148. Archive of the Institute of Political History, 940. f., 26. őe., sheet no. 55; published in *Nők lapja* 17, no. 51 (18 December 1965).

p. 153. From Géza Dvihally, ed. *Rerum novarum. XIII. Leo pápa szociális és társadalomujító szózatának hatása Szent István magyar birodalmában 1891-1941*. A Rerum Novarum Emlékbizottság, s. l., s. a. [1941].

p. 158. From *Fjalori enciklopedik shqiptar*. Tirana: Akademia e shkencave te RPS te Shqiperise, 1985.

p. 162. Schwimmer-Lloyd Collection, Manuscripts and Archives Division, The New York Public Library, Astor, Lenox and Tilden Foundations.

p. 166. Archive of Literature and Art, Slovak National Library (SNK), Martin.

p. 169. From the article by Liubov' Gurevich's daughter, E. N. (Elena Nikolaevna) Gurevich. "L. Ia. Gurevich-Teatral'nyi kritik. " In *Bestuzhevki v riadakh stroitelei sotsializma*. Moscow: "Mysl'," 1969, 188.

p. 173. Picture Archive of the Austrian National Library, Vienna.

p. 178. From Wilma A. Iggers. *Women of Prague. Ethnic Diversity and Social Change from the Eighteenth Century to the Present*. Providence and Oxford: Berghahn Books, 1995, 290. Courtesy of Wilma Iggers.

p. 182. Dimitrana Ivanova, around 1916. Bulgarian Historical Archive, National Library SS Cyril and Method, Sofia.

p. 185. Drawing made by Stjepan Kovacevic.

p. 189. Milena Jesenská, early 1920s, Prague. From a postcard published by Verlag Neue Kritik, Frankfurt.

p. 195. From Dunja Detoni Dujmic. *Ljepsa polovica knjizevnosti*. Zagreb: Matica hrvatska, 1998, 15.

p. 200. Elise Käer-Kingisepp, 1960. From the private collection of Aime Reet Kingisepp, Tartu.

p. 204. Ivande Kaija, 1936. From Paula Jeger-Freimane. *Atzinu celi: teatris, literatura, dzive*. Riga, 1936.

p. 213. Reproduction in *Literatura* III, no. 12 (1928): 446. Copyright: Metropolitan Ervin Szabó Library, Budapest, Budapest Collection.

p. 217. Teréz Karacs, late 1850s - early 1860s. Lithography by unknown artist. *Magyar Nők Évkönyve* III (1863): title page. Copyright: Metropolitan Ervin Szabó Library, Budapest, Budapest Collection.

p. 222. Elissaveta Karamichailova, early twentieth century, Sofia. Bulgarian Historical Archive, National Library SS Cyril and Method, Sofia.

p. 226. Lyuben Karavelov, 1870s. Bulgarian Historical Archive, National Library SS Cyril and Method, Sofia.

p. 230. Ekaterina Karavelova, 1930s. Bulgarian Historical Archive, National Library SS Cyril and Method, Sofia.
p. 235. State Historical Archive, Sofia.
p. 248. Olha Kobylianska, 1908 in Chernivtsi (then part of the Habsburg Empire). From Hannah Polowy and Mitch Sago. *Adam's Sons* (Ukrainian Canadian newspaper), 1969.
p. 253. From Z. Šejnis. *Put' k veršine. Stranicy žizni A. M. Kollontaj.*
p. 262. Eliška Krásnohorská. From *České album. Spisovatelé I.* Prague, 1924.
p. 267. From Vita Zelce. *Latvijas sievietes 19. Gadsimta otraja puse.* Riga, 2002.
p. 269. Nadezhda Krupskaia, 1898.
p. 270. From a postcard published by "Planeta," Moscow, 1983.
p. 274. From Cecylia Walewska. *W walce o równe prawa. Nasze bojownice,* "Redakcja Kobiety Wspóůczesnej". Warsaw, 1930, 15.
p. 278. Ekaterina Kuskova. From Harold Shukman, ed. *The Blackwell Encyclopedia of the Russian Revolution.* Oxford: Blackwell Reference, 1988, 336. Courtesy of Barbara Norton.
p. 282. Zofka Kveder, after World War I. National and University Library, Ljubljana, legacy of Erna Muser, ms 1432.
p. 286. Documentation archive of the Austrian Resistance, picture department, 158/1.
p. 290. From Neda Bozinovic. *Zensko pitanje u Srbiji u XIX I XX veku.* Beograd, 1996.
p. 293. National Library SS Cyril and Method, Sofia.
p. 296. Veselinka Malinska, winter 1949 in Skopje. Private collection.
p. 301. From Mical Kocák. *Elena Maróthy-Šoltésová 1855–1939.* Súbor 29 pohľadníc, photo collection, Martin: Matica slovenská, 1985.
p. 306. From *Nase hlavy, Podobizny nasich Vynikajicich lidi* IX. sesit, Statni nakladatelstvi v Praze, 1937.
p. 311. Ona Masiotiene, probably 1933. From *Moteris ir Pasaulis* no. 1 (March 1937).
p. 316. Group photo with Vera Matejczuk, 1916. Achive of the Museum of Literature and Art of Belarus.
p. 319. Austrian National Library, Sign: NB 514428-B.
p. 324. From C. Walewska. *W walce o równe prawa. Nasze bojownice.* Warsaw, 1930, 32.
p. 328. From Elena Bogdan. *Feminismul.* Timişoara: Tip. Huniadi, 1926.
p. 331. Eugénia Meller, 1913. From *A Nők Választójogi Világszövetségének VII. Kongresszusa Budapest 1913. évi junius hó 15.-20.*
p. 336. The Women's Library and Information Center, Istanbul. Courtesy of Mevlan Civelek's family.
p. 340. From Dunja Detoni Dujmic. *Ljepsa polovica knjizevnosti.* Zagreb: Matica hrvatska, 1998, 196.
p. 344. From P. Arrian, ed. *Pervyi zhenskii kalendar',* St Petersburg, 1898–1917/1912.
p. 348. From Zofia Moraczewska. *Praca Obywatelska,* no 5-6, 25 III 1938: 7.
p. 356. Nezihe Muhittin, 1934. Archive of *Cumhuriyet* (daily newspaper).
p. 360. From Ştefania Mihăilescu. *Emanciparea femeii române: Antologie de texte.* Vol. 1. Bucharest: Editura Ecumenica, 2001.
p. 363. Ella Negruzzi. From Elena Bogdan. *Feminismul.* Timişoara: Tip. Huniadi, 1926.
p. 366. Božena Němcová, 1845. Painting by Josef Hellich.
p. 370. Milica Ninković (right) with her sister Anka. From Neda Bozinovic. *Zensko pitanje u Srbiji u XIX I XX veku.* Beograd, 1996.
p. 372. From *Česká žena v dějinách národa.* Prague, 1940.

p. 376. From the English edition of Eliza Orzeszkowa's novel Argonauci, *The Modern Argonauts*. London, 1901. Translated by S. C. Soisson.

p. 381. Museum of Macedonia.

p. 385. Family archive of Beyza Bürkev, Öztunalı's daughter.

p. 389. From Janko Šlebinger. *Album slovenskih književnikov, Tiskarska zadruga.* Ljubljana, 1928.

p. 392. Serafima Panteleeva in the 1860s. From Longin Panteleev. *Vospominaniia*. Moscow: Izdatel'stvo Khudozhestvennoi literatury, 1958, 657. Original photograph in the Museum of the Institute of Russian Literature-Pushkinskii Dom, Russian Academy of Sciences, St Petersburg.

p. 397. From *Žarana Papić In Memoriam*. Beograd: Zenske studije i komunikacija-Centar za zenske studije, 2002. Goranka Matic (photographer).

p. 408. Alaiza Pashkevicz, some time before 1914. Archive of the Museum of Literature and Art of Belarus.

p. 411. From the dust jacket of Pavlychko's *Letters from Kiev*. University of Alberta: CIUS Press, 1992. Courtesy of Tania D'Avignon (photographer) and CIUS Press.

p. 416. Olena Pchilka, 1882. From L. Kosach-Kvitka. Lesia Ukrainka. Biohrafichni materialy. Spohady. Ikonohrafia. New York/Kiev: Fakt, 2004, 387.

p. 420. From Marija Soljan Bakaric, ed. *Kata Pejnovic*. Zagreb, 1977, cover.

p. 421. From Marija Soljan Bakaric, ed. *Kata Pejnovic*. Zagreb, 1977, xlviii.

p. 424. Picture Department of the Austrian National Library, Vienna.

p. 427. Lithuanian Institute of Literature and Folklore, f. 30.

p. 428. Lithuanian Institute of Literature and Folklore, f. 30.

p. 432. From P. Kroders, ed. *Latvijas darbinieku galerija*. Riga: "Gramatu draugs," 1929.

p. 436. Františka Plaminková, 1920s. International Information Centre and Archives for the Women's Movement (IIAV), Amsterdam, no. 100014703 and 100014704.

p. 441. Rosa Plaveva, 1920s. Museum of the City of Skopje.

p. 447. Picture Archive of the Austrian National Library, Vienna.

p. 450. Vera Poska-Grünthal, 1928. From Vera Poska-Grünthal. *See oli Eestis 1919-1944*. Stockholm, 1975, 50.

p. 454. Sevasti Qiriazi. From *Fjalori enciklopedik shqiptar*. Tirane: Akademia e shkencave te RPS te Shqiperise, 1985.

p. 455. Parashqevi Qiriazi. From *Fjalori enciklopedik shqiptar*. Tirane: Akademia e shkencave te RPS te Shqiperise, 1985.

p. 459. Kočo Racin, probably 1930s. Museum of Macedonia.

p. 463. From Elena Bogdan. *Feminismul.* Timisoara: Tip. Huniadi, 1926.

p. 470. From M. Bohachevsky-Chomiak. *Feminists Despite Themselves. Women in Ukrainian Community Life: 1884-1939*. University of Alberta: CIUS Press, 1988.

p. 475. Urani Rumbo. From *Fjalori enciklopedik shqiptar*. Tirane: Akademia e shkencave te RPS te Shqiperise, 1985.

p. 479. Association for the History of the Labor Movement, Vienna, Sacharchive, L 19, M 56.

p. 484. Hungarian National Museum, Collection of Historical Photographs, inventory no. 50289.

p. 491. From Radovan Popovic. *Isidorina brojanica.* Belgrade: Rad i Vuk Karadzic, 1979, appendix.

p. 494. Sabiha Sertel, 1925. Personal archive of Sabiha Sertel. Courtesy of her daughter.

p. 498. Anna Shabanova, between 1900 and 1910. From the journal *Vrachebnoe delo* no. 1 (1928): 73.

p. 503. From *Sbornik na pomoshch uchashchimsja zhenshchinam*. Moscow, 1901.

p. 510. Courtesy of her granddaughter Nonna Roshina-Iavein.

p. 517. Courtesy of Nana Sklevicky Tadic.

p. 521. Archives of the Society of the Sisters of Social Service, Budapest. Contact via the editors.

p. 526. From V. V. Stasov. *Nadezhda Vasil'evna Stasova: vospominaniia i ocherki*. St Petersburg: Tip. M. Merkusheva, 1899.

p. 534. Archive of the Institute of Political History 686. f., 475. őe., sheet no. 77.

p. 539. Ilona Stetina, circa 1900. From an obituary in the journal *Magyar Asszony* (1932).

p. 544. From Mari Raamot. *Minu mälestused*. Vols. I-II. Kirjastus Kultuur Industrie-Druck GmbH-Geislingen/Stge, 1962, 146. Translations and copyright by Mari Raamot.

p. 548. Karolina Svetlá, 1862. From J. Lehar, et al. *Ceska literatura od pocatku k dnesku*. Prague: Lidove noviny, 1998.

p. 558. From Cecylia Walewska. *W trosce o rowne prawa. Nasze bojownice*. Warsaw, 1930, 79.

p. 562. From Cecylia Walewska. *W Walce o równe prawa. Nasze bojownice*. Warsaw, 1930, 182.

p. 569. Avra Theodoropoulou, probably taken in Athens in 1906. Archives of the Society of Greek Authors.

p. 575. Archive of the Republic of Slovenia.

p. 580. Marie Toyen, around 1920. Reproduced in Karel Srp. *Toyen*. Prague: Argo, 2000. Photographer unknown.

p. 584. Mariia Trubnikova, late 1860s or early 1870s. From the journal *Zhenskoe delo* I, no. XII (December 1889). Original photo in the Russian Women's Mutual Philanthropic Society.

p. 588. From Tyrkova-Williams's memoirs *To chego bol'she ne budet*. Moscow: Slovo, 1998.

p. 592. From F. Pohrebennyk. *Ol'ha Kobylianska: slova zvorushenoho sertsia*. Kiev: Dnipro, 1982, 221.

p. 595. From Michal Kocák. *Vansová - Timrava - Podjavorinská*. Súbor 51 pohľadníc, photo collection, Martin: Matica slovenská, 187.

p. 599. From *České album. Spisovatelé I*. Prague, 1924.

p. 604. Angela Vode, between 1934–1940. From the private collection of Mojca Prinčič, Vode's inheritor and close friend.

p. 608. From Serban Cioculescu, Aurora Nasta, Nestor Ignat, Ion Biberi, Alexandru Paleologu, Mircea Septilici and Dinu Ianculescu. "Evocare Alice Voinescu." Manuscriptum, no. 3 (1979): 136–154.

p. 613. From Elena Bogdan. *Feminismul*. Timisoara: Tip. Huniadi, 1926.

p. 616. Tadeusz Żeleński (Boy), 1930s. Archives of Audio-Visual Records, Photographic Section, Warsaw. Copyright: Polish Press Agency.

p. 620. State Historical Archive, Sofia.

p. 624. Ekaterina Zlatoustova, 1930s. Bulgarian Historical Archive, National Library SS Cyril and Method, Sofia.

p. 628. Jagiellonski University Library, Krakow.

Index of Persons, Organizations and Geographical Names